THE
GLENN GOULD
READER

THE

GLENN GOULD

READER

*Edited and with an
introduction by
Tim Page*

Alfred A. Knopf
New York   1989

THIS IS A BORZOI BOOK
PUBLISHED BY ALFRED A. KNOPF, INC.

Because this page cannot legibly accommodate all acknowledgments, they appear on pages 475–6.

Library of Congress Cataloging in Publication Data

Gould, Glenn. The Glenn Gould reader

1. Music—Addresses, essays, lectures.
I. Page, Tim. II. Title.
ML60.G68   1984   780   84-47819
ISBN 0-394-54067-0

Manufactured in the United States of America
Published December 10, 1984
Reprinted Once
Third Printing, January 1989

CONTENTS

PART FOUR: Miscellany

ACKNOWLEDGMENTS

I owe debts of gratitude to many people—first and foremost to James Oestreich and Elizabeth Thaxton Page, my assistant editors, who helped me shuffle slowly through an immense pile of manuscripts and prepare working copies of Gould's articles; to J. Stephen Posen, Gould's executor, who believed in this book from its inception; to Ruth Pincoe, who catalogued both written and recorded material for Gould's estate; to Ray Roberts, Gould's assistant during the last years of his life, for many services great and small; to Raymond Bongiovanni, my literary agent; and to Robert Gottlieb and Eva Resnikova, my editors at Knopf, for their patience and suggestions; to Patrick Dillon, for his thorough reading and many questions; and to Geoffrey Payzant, whose *Glenn Gould: Music and Mind* must be considered the seminal volume in Gould scholarship.

I must also thank Tina Clarke, Brooke Wentz, Charles Passy, and Bob Silverman for their assistance in the completion of this project; Paul Alexander, whose enthusiasm helped kindle my own interest in Gould; and Susan Koscis, Director of Public Information for CBS Masterworks, who arranged my initial contact with Gould and whose friendship was a spiritual comfort during the difficult days after his death.

I am grateful to Russell and Vera Gould, Glenn's father and stepmother, who entertained me in their Toronto home, and who provided valuable insights into the pianist's early years. Jesse Greig, Gould's cousin and closest friend, was also helpful, supplying some wonderful anecdotes.

Finally, all love and gratitude to my wife, Vanessa Weeks Page, for her devotion and invaluable assistance during this undertaking. She read all the material, served as editor of the music examples, and generally helped to shape the finished book.

INTRODUCTION

Glenn Gould and I often discussed putting together a compilation of his writings. Although enthusiastic, he held back, explaining that it was not yet the time for a summing up. It is impossible to know what he would have eventually included in an anthology of this sort; therefore, the responsibility for the selection and arrangement of the articles in the present volume is entirely mine.

Gould was a supreme perfectionist, and having attained an international reputation before the age of twenty-five, he was in a position to publish anything he wanted. For these reasons, after reading through two overstuffed cartons of manuscripts, I have concluded that most of the unpublished material should remain that way. I have also attempted to avoid duplication of themes and ideas, although some was inevitable. Gould wrote prolifically about his favorite subjects—his writings about Arnold Schoenberg alone would fill a small volume—and was not above recycling a paragraph or two.

Similarly, there exists a quantity of radio plays, television scripts, and the like. Many are wonderful but resist a successful translation into print: Gould understood the crucial distinction between writing to be read and writing to be heard. I hope that his works for those media will eventually reach a wider audience, but this is not their proper platform. Therefore, most of this material is taken from published articles and record liner notes.

These liner notes will come as a particular surprise to those who are unaware of Gould's verbal felicity. He generally provided program notes for music that challenged him and evoked strong personal feelings, whether favorable or unfavorable. Few may agree with Gould's negative comments about the later Mozart, or with his withering assessment of Beethoven's "Appassionata" Sonata, but his opinions are stated with vigor and humor. In fact, his essays are sometimes better than the recordings they accompany: he received a special Grammy award in 1974 for his terse, funny written exegesis of Hindemith's overextended and rather dour piano sonatas.

A born teacher, Gould used the media as his classroom. His didacticism, combined with the unorthodoxy of his thinking, irritated many critics. No doubt B. H. Haggin spoke for a good percentage of the musical public when he complained that Gould preferred "talking nonsense on anything anywhere to playing the piano marvelously in the concert hall." Readers of this volume may conclude, as do I, that there is a supremely logical consistency to Gould's philosophies. But any judgment of such a controversial artist should be an informed one, so let us take a look at Gould's singular career.

Glenn Herbert Gould was born on September 25, 1932, the son of a Toronto furrier and a piano teacher. He began his keyboard studies at the age of three and entered the Royal Conservatory of Music seven years later. By fourteen he had graduated with an associate degree, and he made his first public appearance as a pianist in May 1946. He quickly achieved national fame; by the time Gould was twenty, he had given concerts throughout Canada, including performances with the Toronto Symphony and over the Canadian Broadcasting Corporation.

Gould made his American debut at the Phillips Gallery in Washington, D.C., on January 2, 1955. Paul Hume, the *Washington Post*'s august music critic, heard the concert and waxed ecstatic: "Few pianists play the piano so beautifully, so lovingly, so musicianly in manner, and with such regard for its real nature and its enormous literature. . . . Glenn Gould is a pianist with rare gifts for the world. It must not long delay hearing and according him the honor and audience he deserves. We know of no pianist anything like him of any age." The following week, Gould made his New York debut at Town Hall. David Oppenheim, the director of Columbia Masterworks, was in attendance; he signed Gould to a recording contract the next morning, marking the first time Columbia had ever contracted an unknown artist strictly on the basis of a single concert.

After his initial Columbia album—a fleet, joyous, highly original rendition of Bach's "Goldberg" Variations—was released in early 1956, Gould was suddenly thrown into a maelstrom of professional activity. He toured Europe and the United States, and became the first Canadian artist to perform in the Soviet Union. Gould became famous not only for his extraordinary virtuosity and distinctive musical conceptions but for his temperament, his personal eccentricities, and his tendency to cancel engagements at the last minute.

In 1964, after nine years of superstardom on the concert stage, Gould abruptly announced that he was withdrawing from live performances and would henceforth only make recordings. No famous musician had ever done anything like it. This was heresy: Gould, who had been awarded the highest possible praise—laudatory reviews and sold-out concerts worldwide—was simply walking away from it all.

In fact, the young pianist, then thirty-one years old, had ready explanations for his decision to quit the stage. Briefly, he was tired of what he called the "non-take-two-ness" of the concert experience—the inability of a performer to correct finger slips and other minor mistakes. He pointed out that most creative artists are able to tinker and to perfect, but that the live performer must re-create his work from scratch every time he steps onto a stage. In addition, Gould believed that a "tremendous conservatism" overtakes any artist forced to perform the same music again and again, until it becomes difficult, if not impossible, to move on. "Concert pianists are really afraid to try out the Beethoven Fourth Piano Concerto if the Third happens to be their specialty," Gould observed. "That's the piece they had such success with on Long Island, by George, and it will surely bring them success in Connecticut."

But abandoning the concert hall did not mean a renunciation of music. "Technology has the capability to create a climate of anonymity and to allow the artist the time and the freedom to prepare his conception of a work to the best of his ability," Gould said. "It has the capability of replacing those awful and degrading and humanly damaging uncertainties which the concert brings with it." Gould had hated live performances from the beginning. Now, with his sudden success, he had also discovered that he hated touring, flying, and the extramusical hysteria that accompanied him wherever he went. He finally decided that the whole business of being a concert artist had got in the way of making music. "At concerts I feel demeaned," he complained, "like a vaudevillian."

And, indeed, the public had come to expect a circus act of sorts from Gould. His highly original approach to the piano made him excellent copy for journalists. He favored a very low seating and inevitably brought along his own traveling folding chair to concerts, which set him at about eye level with the keyboard. He wore coats onstage even during the summer—"I have an absolute horror of catching cold," he explained—and would sometimes perform in fingerless gloves. In addition, he liked to sing along—loudly—while he played. Gould apologized for this quirk: "I don't know how anyone puts up with my singing, but I do know that I play less well without it." Those who misunderstood what the writer Lawrence Shames has called Gould's "genuine and profound strangeness" often dismissed him as a crank or as a publicity hound seeking easy celebrity. While there was undeniably a streak of intellectual mischief to Gould's psychological makeup, there was also, almost without exception, a serious angle to everything he said or did.

Any writer in search of concrete events after Gould's seemingly abrupt, but in fact long-considered, retreat from the stage will find little to work with. There is the testament of more than eighty recordings: brilliant, iconoclastic, occasionally disastrous, but always interesting. In addition, Gould left a sizable quantity of works for radio and television. He was especially intrigued by what he called "contrapuntal radio"—sound documentaries that featured up to four voices speaking at once, a celebration of the fugal possibilities of language. In a 1975 article for the *New York Times*, Robert Hurwitz described listening to one of Gould's works in this genre as "comparable to sitting on the IRT during rush hour, reading a newspaper while picking up snatches of two or three conversations as a portable radio blasts in the back-ground and the train rattles down the track." Gould did a series of radio pro-grams about two of his favorite composers, Schoenberg and Richard Strauss, and he also produced a trilogy of one-hour "docudramas" about solitude for the CBC, which show a fascination with the musical qualities of speech.

In the last months of his life, Gould had begun to venture into conduct-ing, working with a pickup orchestra he had assembled in Toronto. The first project was a recording of Wagner's *Siegfried Idyll;* Gould had long loved the piece and had even transcribed it for solo piano and recorded it in the early 1970s. The orchestral recording was in final mix at the time of Gould's death. Surely the slowest *Siegfried Idyll* ever, it is of melting and surpassing tenderness: once heard, it makes most traditional interpretations seem curso-ry. One hopes that this precious taste of what might have been will eventually find its way onto commercial disc.

Gould's writings can stand as a worthy complement to his legacy of record-ings—indeed, much of the most valuable material in this volume is specifi-cally concerned with the recording medium. Like his piano interpretations, Gould's articles are lucid, unconventional, and occasionally outrageous; they range from the brash early "Dodecacophonist's Dilemma," written when he was twenty-three, through the masterful "Prospects of Recording" (proba-bly his magnum opus), to the variety of shorter articles written for *Piano Quarterly* in the last decade of his life. His prose style is uneven. At its worst, it is self-indulgent, puckish, and overly allusive. But at his not-infrequent best, as in the Stokowski profile and several of the liner notes, Gould displays a perception and a vitality largely absent in music criticism since the halcyon days of Huneker, Henderson, and Thomson. Like all important critics, Gould was not afraid of owning up to an unorthodox opinion, and he was never content blithely to reiterate the musicological dogma of his time. Un-abashedly in love with ideas, Gould felt that some thoughts were better real-ized at the keyboard of a typewriter than at that of a piano.

Gould's writings on media and recording have provoked the most con-troversy. As one of the first artists to treat the recording medium as an end in itself, his declaration that the concert was a dying institution provoked a good deal of heated rebuttal. However, on one level, at least, Gould was absolutely right. After all, more people have now experienced Beethoven's symphonies, Mozart's piano sonatas, and Bach's concertos in their homes than will ever set foot in a recital hall. Particularly for those who have grown up in the era of the long-playing disc, records have indeed largely replaced the live concert as the most feasible and economical medium through which to encounter either a composer's work or a performer's re-creation. Whether or not this is the best of all possible worlds, it is the one we live in, and it seems pointless to blame Gould for being the messenger bearing bad news.

Of course, to Gould this was not bad news at all. Rather than bemoaning the passing of the concert hall, he envisioned a brave new world in which technology would free both performer and listener to experience music in hitherto unimagined intimacy. Gould had unshakable faith in the benefits of technology. It matters not that his attitude came out of a distaste for live performances; necessity remains not only the mother of invention but closely related to deduction as well.

Gould died of a stroke on October 4, 1982, only ten days after his fiftieth birthday, a line of demarcation after which, he had always claimed—with what turned out to be bitterly ironic accuracy—he would cease playing the piano. The loss felt by his many friends cannot be overstated. This was a man entirely without malice, a supportive and spiritual presence in our lives. Gould's public image is misleading; he is too often portrayed as a misanthrope, music's answer to Howard Hughes. Nothing could be further from the truth, for Gould cared deeply about people—albeit from a certain distance—and took immense joy in life.

Gould's biographer Geoffrey Payzant once called Gould "an exceedingly superior person, friendly and considerate. He is not really an eccentric, nor is he egocentric. Glenn Gould is a person who has found out how he wants to live his life and is doing precisely that." Gould's tabula rasa manner of living was not for everyone, but he had come to terms with his genius and the particular needs that went hand in hand with his gifts. He worked best in solitude, living the life of a McLuhan-age monk, keeping in touch with the world almost exclusively by telephone, sleeping by day and working through the night. "I live by long distance," he said, laughing, and it was, for the most part, true. Gould felt that personal encounters were by and large distracting and unnecessary, and claimed that he could better comprehend a person's essence over the phone. Gould had some friends whom he never met, except via the telephone; his monthly bill regularly ran to four figures. By telephonic proxy, he would involve his friends in whatever project was currently occupying his thoughts. Gould usually called around midnight, as he sipped an omnipresent cup of tea and prepared to begin his nocturnal workday. Even now, whenever I receive a person-to-person call, especially if it is late at night, I automatically anticipate Gould's cheery voice coming over the line.

The critic Edward Rothstein once observed that Gould "treated himself with a mixture of irony and seriousness, seeming at times both a musical showman and a priest devoted to his art." Gould abounded in paradox: he was a man whose personal life was happily chaotic but whose artistry was refined to an extraordinary degree; he was a hermit of sorts who was the most spontaneous and joyous telephone companion imaginable; he was a deeply conservative recluse who fancied himself a socialist; he was a man who attended no church but spent his long nights reading theology and philosophy.

My most lasting memory of Gould will always be one from our final meeting, on a chilly August evening in Toronto a little more than a month before he died. At 3:00 a.m. we drove to a deserted midtown recording studio, where, clad in his usual indoor summer wear—two sweaters, wool shirt, scarf, slouch hat—he relaxed at the keyboard of a Yamaha baby grand and played through his own piano arrangements of Richard Strauss operas. The Yamaha suddenly became a six-foot-square orchestra: dense contrapuntal lines, translucently clear and perfectly contoured, echoed through the empty room. Far from the eyes and ears of the curious world, the hungry fans and disapproving critics, the lucrative contracts and percentage deals, Gould played through the night, lost in the sheer joy of creating something beautiful.

Tim Page

PROLOGUE

Advice to a Graduation

I know that in accepting the role of advice giver to a graduation, I am acceding to a venerable tradition. However, it's a role that rather frightens me, partly because it's new to me, and partly because I'm firmly persuaded that much more harm than good accrues to gratuitous advice. I know that on these occasions it is customary for the advice giver to tell you something of the world that you will face—based, of course, upon his experience—one that necessarily could not duplicate that which may be your own. I know also that it is customary to recommend to you the solutions that have proved themselves valid within the speaker's experience, sometimes to dish them up anecdotally in the "When I was your age"—or, even more mischievously, in the "If I were your age"—tradition. But I have had to reject this approach, because I am compelled to realize that the separateness of our experience limits the usefulness of any practical advice that I could offer you. Indeed, if I could find one phrase that would sum up my wishes for you on this occasion, I think it would be devoted to convincing you of the futility of living too much by the advice of others.

What can I say to you that will not contravene this conviction? There is, perhaps, one thing which does not contradict my feeling about the futility of advice in such a circumstance as this, because it is not based upon calling to your observation something demonstrable—that is to say, something that need be demonstrated and hence will most likely be rejected—but is simply a suggestion about the perspective in which you view those facts that you possess already and those which you shall subsequently choose to acquire.

It is this: that you should never cease to be aware that all aspects of the learning you have acquired, and will acquire, are possible because of their relationship with negation—with that which is not, or which appears not to be. The most impressive thing about man, perhaps the one thing that excuses him of all his idiocy and brutality, is the fact that he has invented the concept of that which does not exist. "Invented" is perhaps not quite the right word—perhaps "acquired" or "assumed" would be more acceptable—but "invented," to return to it, somehow expresses more forcefully, if not quite accurately, the achievement that is involved in providing for an explanation for mankind, an antithesis involved with that which mankind is not. The ability to portray ourselves in terms of those things which are antithetical to our own experience is what allows us not just a mathematical

Delivered at the Royal Conservatory of Music, University of Toronto, November 1964.

measure of the world in which we live (though without the negative we would not go far in mathematics) but also a philosophical measure of ourselves; it allows us a frame within which to define those things which we regard as positive acts. That frame can represent many things. It can represent restraint. It can represent a shelter from all of those antithetical directions pursued by the world outside ourselves—directions which may have consistency and validity elsewhere but from which our experience seeks protection. That frame can represent a most arbitrary tariff against those purely artificial but totally necessary systems which we construct in order to govern ourselves—our social selves, our moral selves, our artistic selves, if you will. The implication of the negative in our lives reduces by comparison every other concept that man has toyed with in the history of thought. It is the concept which seeks to make us better—to provide us with structures within which our thought can function—while at the same time it concedes our frailty, the need that we have for this barricade behind which the uncertainty, the fragility, the tentativeness of our systems can look for logic.

You are about to enter—as they say on these fearsome occasions—the world of music. And music, as you know, is a most unscientific science, a most unsubstantial substance. No one has ever really fully explained to us many of the primevally obvious things about music. No one has really explained to us why we call high "high" and low "low." Anyone can manage to explain to us what we call high and what we call low; but to articulate the reasons why this most unscientific, unsubstantial thing that we call music moves us as it does, and affects us as deeply as it can, is something that no one has ever achieved. And the more one thinks about the perfectly astonishing phenomenon that music is, the more one realizes how much of its operation is the product of the purely artificial construction of systematic thought. Don't misunderstand me: when I say "artificial" I don't mean something that is bad. I mean simply something that is not necessarily natural, and "necessarily" takes care of the provision that in infinity it might turn out to have been natural after all. But so far as we can know, the artificiality of system is the only thing that provides for music a measure of our reaction to it.

Is it possible, then, that this reaction is also simulated? Perhaps it, too, is artificial. Perhaps this is what the whole complicated lexicon of music education is meant to do—just to cultivate reaction to a certain set of symbolic events in sound. And not real events producing real reactions, but simulated events and simulated reactions. Perhaps, like Pavlov's dogs, we get chills when we recognize a suspended thirteenth, we grow cozy with the resolving dominant seventh, precisely because we know that's what is expected of us, precisely because we've been educated to these reactions. Perhaps it's because we've grown impressed with our own ability to react. Perhaps there's nothing more to it than that we've found favor with ourselves—that the whole exercise of music is a demonstration of reflex operation.

The problem begins when one forgets the artificiality of it all, when one neglects to pay homage to those designations that to our minds—to our reflex senses, perhaps—make of music an analyzable commodity. The trouble begins when we start to be so impressed by the strategies of our systematized thought that we forget that it does relate to an obverse, that it is hewn from negation, that it is but very small security against the void of negation which surrounds it. And when that happens, when we forget these things, all sorts of mechanical failures begin to disrupt the function of human personality. When people who practice an art like music become captives of those positive assumptions of system, when they forget to credit that happening against negation which system is, and when they become disrespectful of the immensity of negation compared to system—then they put themselves out of reach of that replenishment of invention upon which creative ideas depend, because invention is, in fact, a cautious dipping into the negation that lies outside system from a position firmly ensconced in system.

Most of you at some time or other will engage in teaching some aspect of music, I should imagine, and it is in that role that you are most liable, I think, to what I might call the dangers of positive thinking.

I am, perhaps, in no position to talk about teaching. It is something that I have never done and do not imagine that I shall ever have the courage to do. It strikes me as involving a most awesome responsibility which I should prefer to avoid. Nevertheless, most of you will probably face that responsibility at some time; and from the sidelines, then, it would seem to me that your success as teachers would very much depend upon the degree to which the singularity, the uniqueness, of the confrontation between yourselves and each one of your students is permitted to determine your approach to them. The moment that boredom, or fatigue, the ennui of the passing years, overcomes the specific ingenuity with which you apply yourself to every problem, then you will be menaced by that overreliance upon the susceptibly positive attributes of system.

You may remember the introduction that George Bernard Shaw supplied to his collected writings as music critic, and in which he describes an early ambition to develop the native resonance of his baritone and grace the stages of the world's opera houses. He was encouraged in this, apparently, by a lively charlatan, one of those walking fossils of music theory, who already had ensnared Shaw's mother as student and who proclaimed himself in possession of something called "the Method." It seems that after several months' exposure to the Method, Bernard Shaw took to his typewriter and was never able to carry a tune again.

I do not, for one moment, suggest that you minimize the importance of dogmatic theory. I do not suggest, either, that you extend your investigative powers to such purpose that you compromise your own comforting faith in the systems by which you have been taught and to which you remain responsive. But I do suggest that you take care to recall often that the systems by which we organize our thinking, and in which we attempt to pass on that thinking to the generations that follow, represent what you might think of as a foreground of activity—of positive, convinced, self-reliant action—and that this foreground can have validity only insofar as it attempts to impose credibility on that vast background acreage of human possibility that has not yet been organized.

Those of you who will become performers and composers will not perhaps be quite so vulnerable, if only because the market in which you will have to operate is insatiably demanding of new ideas, or, at any rate, of new variations upon old ideas. Furthermore, as performer or composer you will in all likelihood exist—or, at any rate, should try to exist—more for yourself and of yourself than is possible for your colleagues in musical pedagogy. You will not be as constantly exposed to the sort of questions which tempt ready answers from you. You will not have quite so great an opportunity to allow your concepts of music to become inflexible. But this solitude that you can acquire and should cultivate, this opportunity for contemplation of which you should take advantage, will be useful to you only insofar as you can substitute for those questions posed by the student for the teacher, questions posed by yourself for yourself. You must try to discover how high your tolerance is for the questions you ask of yourself. You must try to recognize that point beyond which the creative exploration—questions that extend your vision of your world—extends beyond the point of tolerance and paralyzes the imagination by confronting it with too much possibility, too much speculative opportunity. To keep the practical issues of systematized thought and the speculative opportunities of the creative instinct in balance will be the most difficult and most important undertaking of your lives in music.

Somehow, I cannot help thinking of something that happened to me when I was thirteen or fourteen. I haven't forgotten that I prohibited myself anecdotes for tonight. But this one does seem to me to bear on what we've been discussing, and since I have always felt it to have been a determining moment in my own reaction to music, and since anyway I am growing old and nostalgic, you will have to hear me out. I happened to be practicing at the piano one day—I clearly recall, not that it matters, that it was a fugue by Mozart, K. 394, for those of you who play it too—and suddenly a vacuum cleaner started up just beside the instrument. Well, the result was that in the louder passages, this luminously diatonic music in which Mozart deliberately imitates the technique of Sebastian Bach became surrounded with a halo of vibrato, rather the effect that you might get if you sang in the bathtub with both ears full of water and shook your head from side to side all at once. And in the softer passages I couldn't hear any sound that I was making at all. I could feel, of course—I could sense the tactile relation with the keyboard, which is replete with its own kind of acoustical associations, and I could imagine what I was doing, but I couldn't actually hear it. But the strange thing was that all of it suddenly sounded better than it had without the vacuum cleaner, and those parts which I couldn't actually hear sounded best of all. Well, for years thereafter, and still today, if I am in a great hurry to acquire an imprint of some new score on my mind, I simulate the effect of the vacuum cleaner by placing some totally contrary noises as close to the instrument as I can. It doesn't matter what noise, really—TV Westerns, Beatles records; anything loud will suffice—because what I managed to learn through the accidental coming together of Mozart and the vacuum cleaner was that the inner ear of the imagination is very much more powerful a stimulant than is any amount of outward observation.

You don't have to duplicate the eccentricity of my experiment to prove this true. You will find it to be true, I think, so long as you remain deeply involved with the processes of your own imagination—not as alternative to what seems to be the reality of outward observation, not even as supplement to positive action and acquisition, because that's not the way in which the imagination can serve you best. What it can do is to serve as a sort of no man's land between that foreground of system and dogma, of positive action, for which you have been trained, and that vast background of immense possibility, of negation, which you must constantly examine, and to which you must never forget to pay homage as the source from which all creative ideas come.

PART ONE

Music

WILLIAM BYRD AND
ORLANDO GIBBONS

Three bars into the ninth and last variation of "Sellinger's Round" (William Byrd's final contribution to this disc), a solitary B-flat—the only note of its persuasion to grace this 182-bar opus—at once proclaims the end of this work and the beginning of that new key-oriented chord system to which within a few years most music would subscribe. The note, of course, is by no means without precedent; elsewhere in this album, Byrd situates others of its kind, or modal equivalents at similar cadential crossroads; and all accidentals, for that matter, assume in Tudor music a point and poignancy that they were rarely to attain again until the time of Wagner. But the distinguishing feature of this particular B-flat is that it occurs, first of all, as the denouement of a work in which a C-major-like diatonicism has been rigorously applied (though not, needless to say, in the interests of C major as we know it) and in the context of variations that, while prodigiously inventive in terms of melody and rhythm, propose only the most modest of chord changes in support of the jocular theme at their disposal.

To our ears, inevitably, such a note comes burdened with the baggage of history—of that subdominant bridge building by which Bach, spanning the last strettos of a fugue, comes to ground upon a closing V–I cadence, for instance, or by which Beethoven telegraphs the final paragraphs of a sonata, string quartet, or symphony. Yet, to Elizabethan ears, perhaps, it would represent little more than an instance of enharmonic contradiction—that pawn-takes-pawn technique of modal voice leading so suavely dealt with by the celebrated figures of their era. And, certainly, there are many far more striking moments of chromatic cross-relation in this music; Gibbons's celebrated "Salisbury" Pavan offers one excruciatingly expressive instance of an alto G-natural at odds with a G-sharp in the tenor—while, on the other hand, the same composer's "Italian Ground," for instance, could better illustrate the new notions of triadic compatibility that gave rise to the baroque.

So the truth about this note must lie somewhere in between. Clearly, the two beats allotted to it can sustain no profound analytical conceit; the subtler implications of that harmonic polarity-reversal—the DEW line sys-

Liner notes from Columbia M 30825, 1973.

tem set up by baroque and classical composers to alert us to a code—will
have to wait for a century or two. And yet, because of that splendid isolation
it enjoys within its context, I can call to mind few moments that comment
more perceptively upon that transition between linguistic methods with
which all music of the late Renaissance was occupied to some degree.

That transition, after all, was not toward a more complex or more subtle
language but, rather, toward a language that, in its initial manifestations at
least, consisted of an almost rudimentary chordal syntax. And, as purveyed
in the early seventeenth century by such celebrated masters of Southern Europe as Monteverdi, for instance, and as compared with the sophisticated Renaissance tapestries it succeeds, that language very often seems gauche, artless, and predictable.

Monteverdi, of course, accepted the new language as a fait accompli.
His brash, triadic pronouncements are rendered with the evangelical fervor
of the frontiersman and, by a trick of fortune, have been credited with an
influence out of all proportion to their indigenous value as music. Monteverdi simply dismissed the reasoned appeals of Renaissance technique and
struck out into a type of music that no one had ever tried before. Well, almost
no one, anyway: there is something inherently, and perhaps inevitably, ama-
teurish about the "progressive" music of Monteverdi's later years; and, I suppose, even before his time there must have been a few really awful lay composers who couldn't make the Renaissance scene and who probably wrote
something like it once or twice.

In such cases, however, their executors would likely see to its suppression; in Monteverdi's case, as things turned out, it made him famous. In part,
perhaps, this came to pass because he was the first nonamateur to break the
rules and get away with it; but also, I suspect, it owed something to the fact
that he broke them in the pursuit of a new kind of musical endeavor—opera.
And that, in turn, may well be why, to this day, we, in the instru-
ment-oriented northern countries, sometimes think of opera—especially Italian opera—as being rather less than music and, uncharitably and quite inac-
curately, of opera stars as something other than musicians.

Monteverdi's broken rules found their apologia not only in the service
of music drama but in the development of a new, soon-to-be-codified harmonic practice called tonality. He was not, of course, alone in trying to write
tonal music, but he made more of a splash with it than most of his contemporaries—much more, certainly, than those whose art and outlook were tempered by the relative sobriety of life in northern climes.

The two northern masters represented by this disc, though united by
an imperishable, distinctively English brand of conservatism, are not, all puns
intended, byrds of a feather. They share an idiom but not an attitude; Gib-

bons plays the introspective Gustav Mahler to Byrd's more flamboyant Richard Strauss. For this reason, perhaps, Gibbons, though a virtuoso of repute among his fellows, never shows to best advantage in instrumental music. Byrd, on the other hand, though the creator of incomparable music for the voice, is also the patron saint of keyboard writing. He is, indeed, one of the "naturals"—in his music, like that of Scarlatti, Chopin, and Scriabin, no unfelicitous phrases need apply—and all of his prolific output for the keyboard is distinguished by a remarkable insight into the ways in which the human hand can most productively be employed upon it. Certainly, as the seventh division of "Sellinger's Round" attests, either he or some associate had mastered scales in thirds to a fare-thee-well!

He was not, however, a composer for whom the roulade was permitted to stand in the way of invention. Among the items in this album, indeed, the "Voluntary (for My Ladye Nevelle)" is a dour, stretto-ridden exercise in counterpoint that might well do credit to Jan Sweelinck. Even in this work, however, Byrd's uncanny exploitation of instrumental register is everywhere in evidence—his most ambitious stratagems are inevitably worked out in those areas of the keyboard that realize them best—while in the deceptively relaxed, pre-eminently melodic atmosphere of the Sixth Pavan and Galliard, supporting voices supply solid hymnlike backdrops and simultaneously squirrel away canonic imitations of the theme.

For Orlando Gibbons, on the other hand, vocal music was the prime outlet, and, despite the requisite quota of scales and shakes in such halfhearted virtuoso vehicles as the "Salisbury" Galliard, one is never quite able to counter the impression of a music of supreme beauty that somehow lacks its ideal means of reproduction. Like Beethoven in the last quartets, or Webern at almost any time, Gibbons is an artist of such intractable commitment that, in the keyboard field at least, his works work better in one's memory, or on paper, than they ever can through the intercession of a sounding board.

By the first decade of the seventeenth century, nonetheless, Orlando Gibbons was creating hymns and anthems with cadences as direct and emphatic as anything that Bach would ever set down to celebrate the faith of Luther—music that possessed an amazing insight into the psychology of the tonal system. But Gibbons, like all good Englishmen, shunned the path of the adventurer; although perfectly adept at a usage of the new techniques, a life lived dangerously à la Monteverdi was foreign to his nature. And so, once in a while, when the spirit moved him and the context seemed appropriate, he would engender some weird, ambivalent conflict between the voices, some last-minute detour around all that was most precise and compact and "progressive" in the texture. He would set upon it the mark of his and its past and, in that way, fulfill the implications of Mr. Byrd's B-flat.

DOMENICO SCARLATTI

Domenico Scarlatti's keyboard works were not, of course, conceived as piano music; yet few composers have ever written with such conspicuous flair for the keyboard—indeed, Liszt and Prokofiev are perhaps Scarlatti's only close rivals in the "maximum effect for minimum effort" department. And Scarlatti's shrewd tactile appreciation helps his six-hundred-odd sonatas transfer to contemporary instruments without the least disadvantage to their harpsichord-derived methodology, and to thrive while subjected to the least style-conscious of pianistic tricks. Yet it's not mute testimony to a latent *Augenmusik* potential—the sort of "write it really well and even a quartet of tubas can't do it harm" strategy that works for Bach, let's say—but a tribute, rather, to an extraordinarily farsighted deployment of the keyboard resource.

This is all the more remarkable because, despite their many offbeat gimmicks, Scarlatti's sonatas are far from formula-proof. Most of them are in one full-speed-ahead movement, observe the inevitable binary key change, and with but few exceptions foster their somewhat breathless virtuosity by a gabby two-part texture, which, notwithstanding octave doublings and triad fill-ins, enables Scarlatti to get about the keyboard with a dexterity and manual eccentricity matched by none of his contemporaries. Scarlatti does not develop ideas in that extensive, discursive way which was proper to his generation; he seems almost embarrassed when caught with a fugato on his hands or when embroiled with any but the briefest stretto imitation. Most of the contrapuntal devices which helped to formulate the imposing pronouncements of Bach and Handel are just baroque impediments to Scarlatti. He is at his happiest, and best, glibly scampering from one scintillating sequence to the next, one octave to its neighbor, employing the now current avant-garde trick of using marginal extremes in quick succession, and as a result his music possesses a higher quirk quotient than that of any comparable figure. There is a predictable discontinuity about Scarlatti, and, if his work is not memorable in the conventional sense, if his fantastic fund of melody doesn't easily impress itself upon the listener's memory, the irrepressible vivacity and goodwill of this music ensure that just about any suite of pieces culled from those six hundred sonatas will be one of the surefire delights of music.

Program notes for a CBC broadcast, February 1968.

ART OF THE FUGUE

Bach was forever writing fugues. No pursuit was better fitted to his temperament, and there is none by which the development of his art can be so precisely evaluated.

He has always been judged by his fugues. In his last years, still writing them at a time when the avant-garde of his day was occupied with more melody-oriented endeavors, he was dismissed as a relic of an earlier, less enlightened age. And when that great grass-roots Bach movement began in the early nineteenth century, his partisans were well-intentioned romantics who saw in those massive, glaciated choruses from the St. Matthew Passion or the B-Minor Mass insoluble, if not indeed unperformable, enigmas, worthy of devotion primarily because of the faith they so triumphantly exuded. Like archaeologists, excavating the substratum of a forgotten culture, they were impressed with what they found, but pleased primarily by their own initiative in finding it. To the nineteenth-century ear those modulatorily ambivalent choruses can scarcely have fulfilled any classical-romantic concept of tonal strategy.

And even today we who feel we understand the implications of Bach's work and the diversity of his creative impulse recognize in the fugue the prime forum for all of his musical activity. There is a constant proximity of fugue in Bach's technique. Every texture that he exploited seems ultimately destined for a fugue. The most unpretentious dance tune or the most solemn choral theme seems to beg an answer, appears eager for that flight of counterpoint which finds in fugal technique its most complete realization. Every sonority that he sampled, every vocal-instrumental combination, seems carved out in such a way as to admit a multitude of answers and to lack completeness unless those answers are forthcoming. One feels that just beneath the surface, even in those most gemütlich moments when we find him vending coffee in a cantata or jotting airs for Anna Magdalena, lies a potential fugal situation. And we can sense his almost visible (or audible) discomfort when he must repress the fugal habit and endeavor, from time to time, to join that simplistic search for thematic control and modulatory conformity with which his generation was primarily concerned.

The fugue, however, did not go into eclipse with Bach's death. It con-

---

Introduction to book 1 of Bach's *The Well-Tempered Clavier*, published by Amsco Music Company, 1972.

tinued to be a challenge for most of the younger generation who were growing up, though they didn't know it yet, in his shadow. But it was being
phased out—employed, when at all, as a blockbusting finish to large-scale
choral works, or as pedagogic therapy for budding melodists whose Alberti
basses required enlivening. It was no longer the focal point of musical thinking, and an overdose of fugue could cost a young composer of the day dearly
in terms of public favor. In an age of reason the fugue seemed essentially
unreasonable.

The technique of fugue may have come more easily to Bach than to others, but it is nonetheless a discipline which no one picks up overnight. And
we have as witness to that fact Bach's early efforts at fugue, among them
those ungainly toccata fugues written around his twentieth year. Interminably repetitious, rudimentarily sequential, desperately in need of an editor's
red pencil, they frequently succumb to that harmonic turgidity against which
the young Bach had to struggle. The mere presence of subject and answer
seemed sufficient to satisfy his then unself-critical demands. The first of the
two fugues contained within the Toccata in D minor for harpsichord reiterates its basic thematic proposition on no less than *fifteen* occasions in the
home key alone.

In such works, the inventive aspects of fugue were necessarily subservient
to an examination of the modulatory function of tonality; and despite the
prevailing contrapuntal inclination of that generation, it was a rare fugue
indeed that established a form relevant to its material demands.

This, in fact, is the fugue's historic problem—that it is not a form as
such, in the sense that the sonata (or, at any rate, the first movement of the
classical sonata) is a form, but rather an invitation to invent a form relevant
to the idiosyncratic demands of the composition. Success in fugue writing
depends upon the degree to which a composer can relinquish formulae in
the interests of creating form, and for that reason fugue can be the most routine or the most challenging of tonal enterprises.

A full half-century separates those awkward teen-age attempts at fugue
from the most determinedly anachronistic of the later ones—*The Art of the
Fugue.* Bach died before the completion of this latter work, but not before
having indulged a degree of fugal gigantism which, by the clock at least,
stood unchallenged until the neobaroque exhibitionism of Ferruccio Busoni.
Despite its monumental proportions, an aura of withdrawal pervades the en-

tire work. Bach was, in fact, withdrawing from the pragmatic concerns of music making into an idealized world of uncompromised invention. One facet of this withdrawal is the return to an almost modal concept of modulation; there are but few occasions in this work which Bach invests with that infallible tonal homing instinct that informed his less vigorously didactic compositions. The harmonic style employed in *The Art of the Fugue,* though rampantly chromatic, is actually less contemporary than that of his early fugal essays, and often, in its nomadic meandering about the tonal map, it proclaims a spiritual descent from the ambivalent chromaticism of Cipriano de Rore or Don Carlo Gesualdo.

Most of the basic key relationships are exploited for structural relief and continuity—there is even the occasional full close on the dominant as Bach terminates a major segment within one of the multitheme fugues—but only rarely is this fluid and modulatorily shifty opus endowed with that purposeful harmonic determinism for which Bach's middle-period fugue writing was notable.

Between the immature efforts of his Weimar days and the intense, self-entrenched concentration of *The Art of the Fugue* Bach wrote literally hundreds of fugues, whether designated as such or not, of all instrumental combinations, which reveal in its most fluent form his well-nigh impeccable contrapuntal technique. For all of these, and for all subsequent efforts in the form, the yardstick is the two volumes of his 48 Preludes and Fugues—*The Well-Tempered Clavier.* These astonishingly variegated works attain that rapport between linear continuity and harmonic security which totally eluded the composer in his earlier years and which, because of its anachronistic bias, plays but a minor role in *The Art of the Fugue.* The tonal flair which Bach exhibits in these works seems inexorably wedded to his material and possessed of a modulatory scope that enables him to underline the motivic quirks of his themes and counterthemes. In realizing this conceptual homogeneity

Bach not only is stylistically uninhibited but indeed manages to determine his harmonic vocabulary on an almost piece-by-piece basis.

The very first fugue of volume 1, for example, tolerates only the most modest of modulations and in its stretto-ridden way resourcefully characterizes the fugue subject itself—a bland, diatonic model of academic primness.

Other fugues, like that in E major from volume 2, exhibit much the same sort of modulatory disinclination; and here so tenacious is Bach's loyalty to his six-note theme, and so diffident the modulatory program through which he reveals it to us, one has the impression that the intense and fervently anti-chromatic ghost of Heinrich Schütz rides again.

There are other fugues with longer, more elaborate themes in which the unraveling of the motivic mystery is inseparable from a modulatory master plan, and the B-flat-minor fugue from volume 2 is a good example. Here an energetically spiraling subject of four bars' duration

is put through the customary expository paces, and as the three remaining voices enter in turn, Bach minimizes his accompanimental dilemma by retaining as a countertheme a sequence of alternately ascending and descending semitones.

Later on, the unassuming compliance of this subsidiary strand pays hand-some dividends, for what Bach has in mind is a very different order of fugue from that represented by the C-major or E-major fugues discussed ~bove. He sets forth his material in many different harmonic guises and ____ its some structural phenomena latent within it at each of the major modulatory turning points. Thus, when he dissolves into the mediant and establishes his theme for the first time in a major key (D-flat), a canonic duet ensues between the theme itself, now ensconced in the soprano part, and, one beat delayed and two octaves plus one note lowered, an imitation in the bass. For this episode the chromatic countertheme temporarily va-cates the scene, and in its stead subsidiary voices append their own quasi-canonic comments.

No sonata or concerto of a later generation ever prepared its secondary the-matic area through a more judiciously rationed series of events. But for Bach this is not, in any rococo sense, a secondary area—merely one more way sta-tion on his continuing quest for the relationship between motive and modula-tion.

His return to the home tonality is signaled by the first of several inverted presentations of the theme

and eventually elaborated to include original and inverted statements simultaneously.

These in turn sponsor a suave, chromatic, inner-voice dialogue with which Bach embarks upon an almost promiscuous modulatory sequence. But, in due course, tonal rectitude prevails, and in the closing moments the composer emphatically renounces all foreign entanglements, remains solidly encamped within the original B-flat-minor tonality, and—lest there be any doubt that the harmonic adventures of this piece were inseparable from his superbly paced revelations of its primary motive—takes his exit cue with both an original and an inverted statement of the themes set forth in an unabashedly virtuosic exhibition of double thirds.

In many cases within the "48," there is, as between the fugues and their anticipatory preludes, a true communion of interest and of spirit. Sometimes the preludes are just prosaically prefatory—the C-major and C-minor from volume 1 perhaps falling within that etudish category. But one could not ask a more complete identification with the melancholic rumination of the five-voice C-sharp-minor fugue (volume 1) than is provided by its languorous and wistful prelude. Upon occasion, the preludes are themselves fugally oriented—that in E-flat major from volume 1, for instance, offering, for all its unacademic neglect of expository proprieties, entanglements of fugal texture which quite overshadow the rather glib and conventional proper fugue which it precedes. Bach also upon occasion uses the preludes as probes with which to examine those neatly formulated niceties of binary balance and thematic alternation which were becoming the primary preoccupation of most of his colleagues. (The F-minor prelude from volume 2 calls to mind one of Signor Scarlatti's less indulgently tactile creations.)

Like *The Art of the Fugue*, *The Well-Tempered Clavier*, or excerpts therefrom, has been performed on the harpsichord and on the piano, by wind and string ensembles, by jazz combos, and by at least one scat-scanning vocal group as well as upon the instrument whose name it bears. And this magnificent indifference to specific sonority is not least among those attractions which emphasize the universality of Bach.

There is nonetheless a real tactile awareness about most of the forty-eight preludes and fugues, and in the absence of any accurate poll, one can safely say that the great majority of performances are given on the modern piano. One cannot, therefore, entirely sidestep considerations pertaining to the manner in which that instrument should be employed in its behalf.

Throughout the twentieth century there has been a continuing debate about the extent to which the piano should accommodate the interests of this score. There are those who contend that "if Bach had had it, he would have used it"; the other side of this argument is buttressed by the notion that since Bach did not make allowances for future technology, he wrote, by and large, within the limits of those sounds with which he was familiar.

Bach's compositional method, of course, was distinguished by his disinclination to compose at any specific keyboard instrument. And it is indeed extremely doubtful that his sense of contemporaneity would have appreciably altered had his catalogue of household instruments been supplemented by the very latest of Mr. Steinway's "accelerated action" claviers. It is at the same time very much to the credit of the modern keyboard instrument that the potential of its sonority—that smug, silken, legato-spinning resource— can be curtailed as well as exploited, used as well as abused. And there is really nothing, apart from archival consistency, to prevent the contemporary piano from faithfully representing the architectural implications of the baroque style in general, and Bach's in particular.

Such an approach, of course, necessitates a discriminating attitude toward those questions of articulation and registration which are inextricably bound up with Bach's composing method. It demands, at the very least, the realization that an overindulgence of pedal will almost inevitably bring the good ship *Contrapuntal Ambition* to grief upon the rhetorical rocks of romantic legato. It also necessitates, I think, some attempt to simulate the registrational conventions of the harpsichord, if only because the technique which informs all of Bach's attitudes toward theme and phrase design is based upon an appreciation of dynamic dialogue. If one could express it in cinematic terms, Bach was a director who thought in terms of cuts rather than dissolves.

There are, to be sure, occasions when the linear continuity of his works is of such tenacity that clearly articulated cadence points are simply not to be found, which consequently allows no convincing opportunity for that alternation of tactile effect which is the piano's answer to the harpsichord's lute-stop or coupler-shift maneuvers. Such situations exist very frequently in *The Art of the Fugue,* scarcely ever in the toccata fugues, and in the "48" to degrees dependent upon the harmonic premises employed from one work to the next. (In a fugue like that in C major from volume 1 the continual stretto overlap makes such pivot points rather more difficult to ascertain than is the case, for instance, with volume 2's B-flat-minor fugue.)

Issues of this kind pose undeniable problems of adaptation when one performs the masterworks of the baroque on a contemporary instrument. They are foremost on any list of practical considerations which, however idiosyncratically, a conscientious executant must seek to resolve. Ideally, however, such problems should serve as a catalyst for that exuberant and expansive effort of re-creation which is the ultimate joy that all analytical considerations and argumentative conclusions must serve.

THE "GOLDBERG" VARIATIONS

The "Goldberg" Variations, one of the monuments of keyboard literature, were published in 1742 while Bach held the title of Polish Royal and Saxon electoral court composer. That his apparent apathy toward the variation form (he produced only one other work of that cast—an unpretentious set

---

Liner notes from Columbia ML 5060, 1956: Gould's first recording of the "Goldbergs."

in the "Italian manner") did not prevent his indulgence in an edifice of previously unequaled magnitude, provokes considerable curiosity as to the origin of this composition. Such curiosity, however, must remain unsatisfied, for any data extant in Bach's time has long since been obscured by his romantic biographers, who succumbed to the allure of a legend which, despite its extravagant caprice, is difficult to disprove. Briefly, for those who may not be acquainted with this lore, the story concerns a commission which was tendered to Bach by a Count Kaiserling, the Russian ambassador to the Saxon court, who had as his musician-in-service Johann Gottlieb Goldberg, one of the master's most accomplished pupils. Kaiserling, it seems, was frequently troubled with insomnia and requested Bach to write some reposeful keyboard pieces which Goldberg could perform as a soporific. If the treatment was a success, we are left with some doubt as to the authenticity of Master Goldberg's rendition of this incisive and piquant score. And though we harbor no illusion as to Bach's workmanlike indifference to the restrictions imposed upon his artist's prerogative, it is difficult to imagine that even Kaiserling's forty louis d'or could induce his interest in an otherwise distasteful form.

The most casual acquaintance with this work—a first hearing or a brief glance at the score—will manifest the baffling incongruity between the imposing dimensions of the variations and the unassuming sarabandes which conceived them. Indeed, one hears so frequently of the bewilderment which the formal outline of this piece engenders among the uninitiated who become entangled in the luxuriant vegetation of the aria's family tree that it might be expedient to examine more closely the generative root in order to determine, with all delicacy, of course, its aptitude for parental responsibility.

We are accustomed to consider at least one of two prerequisites indispensable to an air for variations—a theme with a melodic curve which veritably entreats ornamentation, or a harmonic basis, stripped to its fundamentals, pregnant with promise and capacity for exhaustive exploitation. Though there are abundant examples of the former procedure from the Renaissance to the present day, it flourishes through the theme-and-elaborative-variation concept of the rococo. The latter method, which, by stimulating linear inventiveness, suggests a certain analogy with the passacaglia style of reiterated bass progression, is strikingly portrayed by Beethoven's thirty-two variations in C minor.

However, the vast majority of significant contributions to this form cannot be accurately allotted to either of these general classifications, which, to be sure, rather describe the extremities of the working premise of the variation idea, wherein the coalescence of these qualities constitutes the real challenge to the composer's inventive power. A definitive textbook example

could be found in Beethoven's "Eroica" Variations, where each of these for-
mulative elements is treated separately, their ultimate merger being consum-
mated in a fugue in which the melodic motive acts as countersubject to the
tema del basso of the variations.

The present work utilizes the sarabande from "The Little Notebook for
Anna Magdalena Bach" as a passacaglia—

that is, only its bass progression is duplicated in the variations, where indeed
it is treated with sufficient rhythmic flexibility to meet the harmonic contingencies of such diverse contrapuntal structures as a canon upon every degree
of the diatonic scale, two fughettas, and even a quodlibet (the superposition
of street songs popular in Bach's time). Such alterations as are necessary do
not in any way impair the gravitational compulsion which this masterfully
proportioned ground exerts upon the wealth of melodic figurations which
subsequently adorn it. Indeed, this noble bass binds each variation with
the inexorable assurance of its own inevitability. This structure possesses
in its own right a completeness, a solidarity, which largely by virtue of
the repetitive cadential motive make it unsatisfactory for the role of
a chaconne ground. It suggests nothing of the urgent longing for fulfillment which is implicit in the traditionally terse entry of a chaconne statement; rather, it volubly covers so much harmonic territory that, with the
exception of the three minor-key variations (15, 21, 25), where it is made
subservient to the chromatic wont of the minor tonality, there is no necessity for its offspring to explore, to realize and intensify its constructive
elements.

One might justifiably expect that in view of the constancy of the harmonic foundation the principal pursuit of the variations would be the illumi-
nation of the motivic facets within the melodic complex of the aria theme.
However, such is not the case, for the thematic substance, a docile but richly
embellished soprano line, possesses an intrinsic homogeneity which be-

queathes nothing to posterity and which, so far as motivic representation is concerned, is totally forgotten during the thirty variations. In short, it is a singularly self-sufficient little air which seems to shun the patriarchal demeanor, to exhibit a bland unconcern about its issue, to remain totally uninquisitive as to its raison d'être.

Nothing could better demonstrate the aloof carriage of the aria than the precipitous outburst of variation 1, which abruptly curtails the preceding tranquility. Such aggression is scarcely the attitude we associate with prefatory variations, which customarily embark with unfledged dependence upon the theme, simulating the pose of their precursor, and functioning with a modest opinion of their present capacity but a thorough optimism for future prospects. With variation 2 we have the first instance of the confluence of these juxtaposed qualities—that curious hybrid of clement composure and cogent command which typifies the virile ego of the "Goldbergs."

I suspect I may have unwittingly engaged in a dangerous game, ascribing to musical composition attributes which reflect only the analytical approach of the performer. This is an especially vulnerable practice in the music of Bach, which concedes neither tempo nor dynamic intention, and I caution myself to restrain the enthusiasm of an interpretative conviction from identifying itself with the unalterable absolute of the composer's will. Besides, as Bernard Shaw so aptly remarked, parsing is not the business of criticism.

With variation 3 begin the canons which subsequently occupy every third segment of the work. Ralph Kirkpatrick has imaginatively represented the variations by an architectural analogy. "Framed as if between two terminal pylons, one formed by the aria and the first two variations, the other by the two penultimate variations and the quodlibet, the variations are grouped like the members of an elaborate colonnade. The groups are composed of a canon and an elaborate two-manual arabesque, enclosing in each case another variation of independent character."

In the canons, the literal imitation is confined to the two upper voices, while the accompanying part, which is present in all but the final canon at the ninth, is left free to convert the tema del basso, in most cases at least, to a suitably acquiescent complement. At times this leads to a deliberate duality of motivic emphasis, the extreme example being variation 18, where the canonic voices are called upon to sustain the passacaglia role, which is capriciously abandoned by the bass. Less extraneous counterpoint is the resolve of the two G-minor canons (15 and 21). In these the third voice partakes of the thematic complex of the canon, figuratively reproducing its segment in a dialogue of surpassing beauty.

Variation 15

Variation 15

Variation 21

Nor is such intense contrapuntal preoccupation solely the property of the canonic variations. Many of those numbers of "independent character" expand minute thematic cells into an elaborate linear texture. One thinks especially of the fugal conclusion to the French overture (16), the alla breve (22), and of variation 4, in which a blunt rusticity disguises an urbane maze of stretti. Indeed, this husbandly exploitation of intentionally limited means is Bach's substitute for thematic identification among the variations. Since the aria melody, as aforementioned, evades intercourse with the rest of the work, the individual variation voraciously consumes the potential of a motivic germ peculiar to it, thus exercising an entirely subjective aspect of the variation concept. As a consequence of this integration there exists, with the dubious exceptions of variations 28 and 29, not one instance of motivic collaboration or extension between successive variations.

In the two-part texture of the "arabesques" the emphasis on virtuosic display restricts the contrapuntal endeavor to less ingenious pursuits such as that of inverting the consequent rejoinder.

Variation 14

Variation 14

Variation 11

Variation 11

The third G-minor variation occupies a strategic locale. Having already been regaled with a kaleidoscopic tableau consisting of twenty-four vignettes depicting, in meticulously calibrated degrees, the irrepressible elasticity of what was termed "the Goldberg ego," we are now granted dispensation to collect and crystallize the accumulative experience of depth, delicacy, and display, while musing upon the languorous atmosphere of an almost Chopinesque mood piece. The appearance of this wistful, weary cantilena is a masterstroke of psychology.

With renewed vigor, variations 26 to 29 break upon us and are followed by that boisterous exhibition of *deutsche Freundlichkeit*—the quodlibet. Then, as though it could no longer suppress a smug smile at the progress of its progeny, the original sarabande, anything but a dutiful parent, returns to us to bask in the reflected glory of an aria da capo.

It is no accident that the great cycle should conclude thus. Nor does the aria's return simply constitute a gesture of benign benediction. Rather, its suggestion of perpetuity is indicative of the essential incorporeality of the "Goldbergs," symbolic of their rejection of embryonic inducement. And it is precisely by recognizing its disdain of the organic relevance of the part to the whole that we first suspect the real nature of this unique alliance.

We have observed, by means of technical dissection, that the aria is incompatible with its offspring, that the crucial bass by its very perfection of outline and harmonic implication stunts its own growth and prohibits the accustomed passacaglia evolution toward a culminant point. We have observed, also by analysis, that the aria's thematic content reveals an equally exclusive disposition, that the motivic elaboration in each variation is law unto itself, and that, by consequence, there are no plateaus of successive variations utilizing similar principles of design such as lend architectural coherence to the variations of Beethoven and Brahms. Yet without analysis we have sensed that there exists a fundamental coordinating intelligence which we labeled "ego." Thus we are forced to revise our criteria, which were scarcely designed to arbitrate that union of music and metaphysics—the realm of technical transcendence.

I do not think it fanciful to speculate upon supramusical considerations, even though we are dealing with possibly the most brilliant substantiation of a ground bass in history, for in my opinion the fundamental variative ambition of this work is not to be found in organic fabrication but in a community of sentiment. Therein the theme is not terminal but radial, the variations circumferential, not rectilinear, while the recurrent passacaille supplies the concentric focus for the orbit.

It is, in short, music which observes neither end nor beginning, music with neither real climax nor real resolution, music which, like Baudelaire's lovers, "rests lightly on the wings of the unchecked wind." It has, then, unity through intuitive perception, unity born of craft and scrutiny, mellowed by mastery achieved, and revealed to us here, as so rarely in art, in the vision of subconscious design exulting upon a pinnacle of potency.

BODKY ON BACH

The Interpretation of Bach's Keyboard Works by Erwin Bodky is a curious work. It could easily bear the signature of two authors of diametrically opposed temperaments: one, the musicological child of our time—analytic, statistic-minded, intellectually aware of the clarity and definition our age has

Review of *The Interpretation of Bach's Keyboard Works* by Erwin Bodky (Cambridge: Harvard University Press, 1960); from *Saturday Review,* November 26, 1960.

learned to appreciate in the art of the baroque; the other, a typical turn-of-the-century academician, approaching Bach through the misty portals of symbolism and numerology and the fatuous sounds of transcribed approximations. It hardly seems possible that the same man who urges the Bach student to develop his interpretation through analysis of the internal evidence of a composition can, a few chapters later, seriously discuss the integral connection between the fourteen-note subject of the C-major fugue from volume I of *The Well-Tempered Clavier* and the fact that the alphabet positions of the letters in the name of Bach total the number 14, and further that by adding the initials J. S. we can produce the inverted number 41 (my own addition stubbornly yields 43).*

Fortunately, Professor Bodky applies himself in the main body of his work to more substantial inquiry, and the central chapters of the work deal with the demonstrable fields of tempos, dynamics, ornamentation, and articulation. The problems inherent in all of these fields relate to the "scarcity of material on performance practice in musical treatises of this period," to the widely held conviction "that there existed a kind of unwritten code which had been transferred from generation to generation as an oral tradition"—in short, that the composer of Bach's day did not always write what he really meant. Thus, between the composer and the performer there existed such a special bond that the composer was disinclined to spend unnecessary effort in the detailed marking of a score and thereby insult the intelligence of the temperamental musicians with whom he had to associate. Professor Bodky therefore believes that only by the most careful scrutiny of the situations in which Bach did (and did not) see fit to apply supplemental instruction can we realize the true intentions of the master.

Professor Bodky's search for the unwritten laws of Bach literature is on the whole a shrewd job of detection. Especially noteworthy are his detailed comparisons of motives common to both instrumental and vocal literature and his astute observations of the varying treatments which Bach accords similar motives. He is well aware that the origin of a tradition may have simply been the inability of some long-dead performer to give a literal reading. Thus his comments on rhythmic complications, particularly instances of cross-rhythmic relation, are generously dipped in the charity of personal experience.

The instinctive side of Professor Bodky's approach, is, as I have suggested, a highly romantic one; and, like all romantics, he becomes motive conscious. He believes that in many cases the ornamentation accompanying a particular motive should adopt and consistently preserve the nature of the

---

*The error is Gould's; see Geoffrey Payzant's *Glenn Gould: Music and Mind* (New York: Van Nostrand Reinhold, 1978), p. 143, for a discussion of the matter.—T.P.

motive itself. For example, in dealing with the so-called sigh motive in the F-minor prelude of volume 2 of *The Well-Tempered Clavier* or the toccata of the E-minor Partita, he believes that the ornamentation of this motive, in defiance of accepted procedure, should begin on the principal note. His reasons are typical of the contradictions that mark the book. Rationally, he points out that to do otherwise will, in certain cases, produce parallel fifths, the careful contrapuntist's horror, but it is clear that his real concern is the preservation at all costs of the distinct pathos of this motive.

This Schweitzer-induced motivic emphasis is significant, for it points to the real weakness in Professor Bodky's book. This work, like so many others that deal with baroque literature, is almost exclusively theme concentrated. To the author, the "interpretation" of Bach means the solution of those problems that govern the flow of melodic line—the distribution of the trill, the abbreviation of a dotted rhythm, the inherent tempo of a motive. These are all problems which have concerned and continue to concern the Bach student, and seldom have they been handled with greater skill and historical perception than here. But none of these problems can be seen in proper perspective when viewed in the single dimension of its linear aspect. And even if the contrapuntal movement of four voices could be cleansed part by part of all manner of stylistic ills, this would not in itself suffice for a complete realization of Bach's intentions. For Bach's counterpoint is harmonically centered counterpoint, and there is no aspect of Bach's style which is not ultimately mediated by harmonic considerations. The registration of his dynamic terraces, the dissonant twang of his ornamentation, the articulation of contrasting rhythmic figures—all are controlled by the steady pulse of harmonic movement. And, on a larger scale, it is Bach's modulations from key to key that determine the formal posture of a work, that make cohesive the relation of episode to episode.

In dealing with the music of a generation after Bach, no writer would neglect the relation of the individual phrase to the harmonic landscape in which it appears. No one would attempt to define the profile of a theme in Christian Bach or in Haydn without some reference to its place in the sonata structure, or whatever the architectural plan might be—so familiar to our ear is the psychology of theme relation to modulation in the music of the generation after Bach. But when we deal with the more ambulatory shape of the concerto grosso, no such landmarks are provided. Each instance must be examined individually to find the correspondence of thematic repetition to the modulatory plan of the work. Instead of one modulation to the dominant and then the presentation of a new theme, as in the classical sonata, there may be many modulations to the dominant and many reiterations of the same old theme. But it is the overall harmonic architecture of the work, in regard to both the terraces of modulation and the more minute movements within the phrase structure, that determines the character and attitude of the composition. And this analytic approach must be held to stand equally for the more circumscribed shape of the dance movement or the muscular sinews of fugal texture. In fairness, I must add that Professor Bodky frequently warns the student that "an intensive study of the inner architecture of Bach's most formidable harpsichord pieces cannot and should not be spared to them." That he himself grasps the structure of Bach's works in all their dimensions one can have no doubt. His descriptions have the tantalizing familiarity of one who hears more than that of which he chooses to write. Nevertheless, in toto, it is as though someone described in minute detail the stucco ornaments of a baroque edifice but scarcely mentioned the pillars that they enrich.

The opening section of the book is devoted to an explanation of Professor Bodky's preference of harpsichord or clavichord rendition for a representative selection of works and the practical means that encourage or prohibit the choice. This is supplemented by an excellent appendix in which suggestions are offered for the registration, tempo, and articulation of all of Bach's major keyboard compositions. While I find most of Professor Bodky's instrumental preferences eminently suitable, I regret to say that he takes a most jaundiced view of the modern piano. He is understandably shy of public performance of Bach on a contemporary instrument, but the alternative he proposes is to perform on not one but two instruments. Two-piano teams, he believes, can, by the simple expedient of adding octaves in every direction, approximate four-foot and sixteen-foot registration. This is a tacit admission that to the author registration is the only spice that gives this most *instrumentally* indifferent of all music its savor. Further, Professor Bodky supplies us with two bars of the E-flat-major organ prelude as he conceives it on the piano—complete with upbeat bass octaves. If this is a sample of what the future holds, I feel that I cannot but rise to the defense of my livelihood when it is so irresponsibly jeopardized.

Besides, inspired by Professor Bodky, I have recently been delving into the numerological significance of my own family and Christian names and I am delighted to report that the respective totals are 52 and 59, of which, as everyone can see, the numbers 7 and 14 are the horizontal sums. Moreover, I would point out that they jointly tally 111—a figure that renders all further comment superfluous.

OF MOZART AND RELATED MATTERS:
GLENN GOULD IN CONVERSATION
WITH BRUNO MONSAINGEON

BRUNO MONSAINGEON: Glenn, I can't feeling that we've a quite extraordinary paradox here. You've recorded all of the Mozart sonatas in the past few years, so we now have on hand, so to speak, your views on a major portion of Mozart's piano writing. Yet you continue to give interviews in which you make very unsympathetic comments about Mozart as a composer; you continue to insist, for example, that he "died too late rather than too soon." I know that's a comment on his last works rather than on his premature death, but I put it to you: Is it not inconsistent, given those feelings, to record the last sonatas or, when you get around to the concertos, K. 595, for example?

GLENN GOULD: Yes, it certainly is, Bruno, although I don't intend to get around to the concertos, so at least we can set that part of the question aside.

B.M.: You don't intend to record *any* Mozart concertos?

G.G.: No. From the standpoint of my bias, or whatever it is, and as distinct from the sonatas, they're unfixable.

B.M.: But you did record the C-minor concerto some years ago, I think.

G.G.: Yes, in 1961. That was sort of an experiment, really. But, in any case, I've now done my worst by Mozart, and I've no intention of going on to more of the concertos or to the variations, or whatever.

B.M.: But you didn't resent having to record the sonatas?

G.G.: On the contrary. As a matter of fact, when I first announced that I wanted to do the project, the most surprised person in town was my producer, Andy Kazdin, who had assumed that my bias would prevail. But I did want to very much indeed, and, looking back, the experience has been really quite exhilarating.

B.M.: Well, before I try to understand what it is that made it possible for you to record the sonatas but not the concertos, let me try to find out how this all began. Were you always out of sympathy with Mozart, even in your student days?

From *Piano Quarterly*, Fall 1976. Bruno Monsaingeon is a French musician and film-maker whose portrait of Gould was awarded a first prize at the 1975 Prague Film Festival.

G.G.: As far back as I can remember.

B.M.: But, as a student, you must have had to learn and play these works, surely.

G.G.: So far as I can remember, I began to study the Paris sonatas about a year before that—K. 332 was the first, I think.

B.M.: And you always disliked them?

G.G.: What I felt at that time, I think, was dismay. I simply couldn't understand how my teachers, and other presumably sane adults of my acquaintance, could count these pieces among the great musical treasures of Western man. The actual process of playing them, on the other hand, was always very enjoyable. I had a lot of fun running my fingers up and down the keys, exploiting all those scales and arpeggios. After all, they offer the same sort of tactile pleasure as—Saint-Saëns, let's say.

B.M.: I think I should ignore that.

G.G.: Oh, please don't. I admire Saint-Saëns, especially when he's not writing for the piano.

B.M.: But did you not hear any great pianists in your youth who inspired you with their Mozart playing?

G.G.: Well, "inspire" is not a word that I can relate to Mozart, Bruno, but if you substitute "impress" I can think immediately of Casadesus and some of the beautiful 78-r.p.m. concerto records he made—with the Paris Conservatoire Orchestra, wasn't it?

B.M.: I believe so, yes.

G.G.: Also—and this may surprise you—Eileen Joyce.

B.M.: I don't know her playing at all.

G.G.: Well, she played Mozart with real devotion. Even I could recognize that, though I couldn't figure out whence it came. It's funny, too, because I heard her very old recording—late thirties or early forties—of K. 576 just a few weeks ago on the radio, for the first time in perhaps twenty years, and it made me think once again what an extraordinary pianist she really was.

B.M.: What about pianists today?

G.G.: I think Alfred Brendel plays the concertos as well as anyone I've ever heard. I really can't imagine a better blend of zest and affection than that.

B.M.: And conductors?

G.G.: Hmm. Well, offhand, no one jumps to mind. But you were talking about inspirational experiences a moment ago, and I just thought of something in that category. I remember once visiting with Josef Krips when he came to Toronto for a concert. By that time we had played all the Beethoven concertos together; Krips wanted to do some Mozart, and I was running out of excuses—after all, you just don't tell a Viennese that Mozart is mediocre. Anyway, Krips loved to sing through whole symphonies or concertos while having tea—he had total recall of the whole Austro-German classical repertoire—and when I mentioned to him that I had just recorded K. 491, he insisted on going through it from first note to last. (I was the bassoon and/or celli, and Krips sang or gesticulated on behalf of everybody else.) He was a remarkable conductor, you know, the most underrated of his generation in my opinion. He was also the only man who to my ear has ever made Bruckner really work, and that teatime was as close as I ever came to loving Mozart.

B.M.: But there was no particular incident in your student years that kept you from Mozart? For example, no teacher ever suggested that you didn't play it with feeling or understanding or something of that sort?

G.G.: I don't recall anything like that. Mind you, I don't recall that any of my teachers were ever very thrilled about what I did to Mozart, either. But if their enthusiasm had been the relevant criterion, I would have ended up disliking Bach, first and foremost—my Bach renditions of those days were considered outrageously avant-garde, mainly because I avoided all contact with the pedal. But the only thing remotely like a Mozart "incident" that I can recall for you related to my first encounter with K. 333. . . .

B.M.: This was in your early teens?

G.G.: Or just before. Anyway, I was showing off, I suppose—behaving like the obnoxious child I undoubtedly was—and I mentioned to a teacher that I couldn't understand why Mozart would ignore so many obvious canonic opportunities for the left hand.

B.M.: You disapproved of Alberti basses, in other words.

G.G.: Instinctively. And, as a consequence, I was treated to some reminiscences of my teacher's own childhood in general, and Mozart's role in it in particular. The only one that has stayed with me involved an account of how he—my teacher—as a child, had first succumbed to the charms of music by virtue of staying awake nights while his elders practiced four-hand arrangements of the Fortieth Symphony at the parlor piano.

B.M.: Did you know the G-minor Symphony at the time?

G.G.: Yes. I'd already heard it and hated it. I remember thinking that it was an unlikely conversion vehicle, although I certainly had no idea at the time that it was an object of universal veneration. And the story has stayed with me because the G-minor Symphony best represents those qualities in Mozart that I find inexplicable.

B.M.: You can't expect me just to nod sympathetically when you say something like that!

G.G.: I don't expect that, Bruno. I'd be flabbergasted if you did. The loss is mine, I'm sure of it. But, for me, the G-minor Symphony consists of eight remarkable measures—the series of unaccompanied falling sixths immediately after the double bar in the finale, the spot where Mozart reaches out to greet the spirit of Anton Webern—surrounded by a half-hour of banality. I'm perfectly serious when I say that I can find more enjoyment from K. 16.*

B.M.: The First Symphony?

G.G.: Yes, and the only Mozart piece I ever conducted, believe it or not.

B.M.: Well, Glenn, right away two comments come to mind—the fact that you would rather hear a work that may not even be by Mozart (and, if it is, belongs to his seventh year) than one of the greatest of his mature symphonies, and the fact that when you do pause to admire a particular moment, as in the G-minor Symphony, it's because it reminds you of Webern or, at any rate, someone other than Mozart. In other words, its virtue for you is that, for that moment, Mozart takes on another persona altogether.

G.G.: That's absolutely true. But so far as the early works are concerned—and I'm thinking now not of K. 16, obviously, but of the pieces from the 1770s, say—they seem to me to have a purity of voice leading and a calculation of register that are never equaled in the later works.

B.M.: But precisely—those are baroque virtues.

G.G.: Of course they are, and, for me, the first half-dozen piano sonatas, which have those baroque virtues, are the best of the lot. And even though "shorter is better" represents my attitude in regard to Mozart generally, I'd have to say that K. 284, which is probably the longest of the sonatas, is my favorite.

B.M.: Let's come back to baroque virtues for a moment. It occurs to me that many of the qualities that make your Mozart playing an unusual experience come from your interest in baroque conventions. For example, the way in which you minimize dynamic changes or ignore them altogether, or the way in which you sometimes refuse to acknowledge very clear tempo markings.

G.G.: Sure. They belong to an era which I often wish would just go away.

B.M.: So what you really want, I suspect, is to add an improvisatory element to all eighteenth-century music.

G.G.: Well, I think that's legitimate, Bruno.

B.M.: I think so too, up to a point. But I do think that the presence of that

---

*Some scholars attribute this work to Leopold Mozart, Wolfgang's father.—T.P.

element shouldn't be allowed to overrule the relatively more specific notation of Mozart's time—for example, the sforzandos, which you usually
eliminate or reduce in intensity.

G.G.: Guilty. I've always shied away from sforzandos.

B.M.: And I imagine you do because they intrude upon your prerogatives
as an improviser.

G.G.: No, I would have to go much further than that, Bruno. I think they
represent an element of theatricality to which my puritan soul strenuously objects—just one of many such elements, to be sure.

B.M.: Well, that may be, but on the technical level surely they also represent
a disruption of counterpoint, and that brings me to the other subject
that I wanted to raise—the fact that the search for counterpoint compels
you to change or to "correct" voice leading many, many times.

G.G.: Shall I add one more category to your catalogue of complaints?

B.M.: They're just observations.

G.G.: Whatever. As you know, I very often arpeggiate chords which are written conventionally—

B.M.: Indeed.

G.G.: —and I read quite often that the gentlemen of the press assume this is
some sort of parlor-music mannerism. In fact, it's quite the opposite.
It may or may not be justified, but the habit originates in a desire to
keep the contrapuntal spirit alive, to emphasize every possible connection between linear events, and also, and I think most important, to control the flow of information more accurately.

B.M.: Can you elaborate on that a bit?

G.G.: Sure. The nature of the contrapuntal experience is that every note has
to have a past and a future on the horizontal plane. And when large
chord units are inserted into any predominantly linear texture—in the
Bach toccatas, let's say—it's a very unsettling experience. When he
wrote the toccatas, Bach had not yet learned to interrelate his vertical
and horizontal intentions, and the best example of that is the interminable sequencing that goes on in all of them.

B.M.: But isn't that sequential style in reality a kind of harmonic exploration?

G.G.: Well, yes, because Bach was really feeling out the possibilities of a new
extended tonality; in that sense, the toccatas are more "modern" than
most of what he wrote later on. But my point is that, because at that
time he didn't have the technical facility to cope with the purely harmonic consequences of what he was doing, there's a breakdown of communication between the vertical and horizontal dimensions, and one
simply never finds *that* in the suites or *The Well-Tempered Clavier* or
whatever. Now, in the case of Mozart or even, to some extent, Beethoven, it's the same story only in reverse. The Beethoven Op. 2's, for exam-

ple, have great dramatic flair, but they also have an incredibly pure, quartetlike concept of voice leading which you never find in the later sonatas, except perhaps for isolated moments like the first movement of Op. 101 or the second movement of 109.

B.M.: But that's because Beethoven, as also Mozart, I'm sure, wanted to realize intentions, to create effects, that are simply not related to the kind of academic counterpoint you're talking about.

G.G.: Well, Bruno, I'm sure you're right. As you very well know, I have a century-long blind spot approximately demarcated by *The Art of the Fugue* on one side and *Tristan* on the other—everything in between is at best an occasion for admiration rather than love. (No, come to think of it, there's one exception to that—Mendelssohn; I guess I'm the only person I know who would rather listen to *St. Paul* than the Missa Solemnis.)

B.M.: I'm speechless.

G.G.: Well, I also like early Glinka, so there! But, to be serious—not that I wasn't being serious about *St. Paul*—I do find it very difficult to understand why the whole sonata-allegro concept ever caught on as it did. I mean, if one looks at the phenomenon historically, one can see that some such attempt at simplification had to emerge out of the baroque, but I keep asking myself why *that* one, or, more accurately, why *only* that one.

B.M.: Because it isn't just a process of simplification, it's a process of dramatic organization.

G.G.: Well, I admit that without the sonata-allegro, Thomas Mann would never have written *Tonio Kröger*, just as Richard Strauss would not have done *Till Eulenspiegel* without borrowing from the classical rondo.

B.M.: I hope you can find other virtues in the sonata than those.

G.G.: Oh, of course I can. You're making me recklessly defensive.

B.M.: But what you've just said, whether in jest or not, has helped me to understand why you perform sonatas, and especially the first movements of sonatas, as you do—why, for example, you very rarely relax the tempo even a little when you come to a second theme. If you really don't find in the sonata-allegro anything other than a "simplification" of baroque architecture, that kind of dramatic impulse obviously won't occur to you. And I can also understand, in that context, why, as you've said many times, the question of tempo choice is of little importance to you. It's obvious that if you bring baroque harmonic principles to your analysis of the sonata-allegro, you're not going to want to give up the other options that go with those principles.

G.G.: Should I defend myself now?

B.M.: By all means.

G.G.: Well, I can only argue on behalf of what you might call the theory of modulatory distance. Let me put it this way: If you encounter for the nine-hundred-and-ninety-ninth time a sonata in the key of C major which happens to have a second theme in G major, that's not per se a great event, especially if that theme has been arrived at via the customary harmonic routine—dominant of the dominant and all of that. And if it's not a great event (and I don't mean over the long haul of history only; I mean even from the presumed vantage point of the composer of Mozart's era—a composer who is likely to have been short on historical perspective but long on experience, to have heard, perhaps, four hundred and forty-four such thematic setups at court already and to have written two hundred and twenty-two of them himself), then I really don't see why one should attempt to inflect it, to characterize it, as though it were. Now, if, on the other hand, it really does come through hell and high water to get where it's going, if some genuine, untoward event intervenes to keep the sonata-allegro from its appointed rounds, then I'm all for the creation of a tempo shift appropriate to the magnitude of that event. For example, let's take the first movement of Op. 10, No. 2, where Beethoven introduces the recapitulatory material in the key of the submediant. That *is* a magical moment, and it deserves, in my view, a very special kind of tempo adjustment—something that will allow the main theme to regroup, during the D-major–D-minor sequence, and then gradually come back to life as the F-major tonic returns. Now, nothing of that sort is indicated in the score, but that kind of harmonic drama is something that no one can ignore, surely.

B.M.: Is this also the reason that you ignore Mozart's instruction to maintain the tempo intact at the end of the rondo in K. 333?

G.G.: Absolutely. For me, that one page is worth the price of admission. It *is* a cadenza, no matter what Mozart says, and I simply can't imagine how he could possibly expect anyone to charge through the tonic minor and its submediant without going into low gear.

B.M.: But it's always the harmonic climate that seems to influence your thinking, never the aspect of thematic contrast itself.

G.G.: Well, as I said before, Bruno, the basic format of sonata style doesn't interest me all that much—the question of vigorous, masculine tonic themes and gentle, feminine dominant themes seems awfully cliché ridden to me and, in any case, more an excuse for touch variation than for tempo change. Besides, you know, it often works the other way round—aggressive, masculine second themes and so forth. And that's especially true where the thematic contours are identical, as in Haydn so often, or perhaps contain some sort of linear paraphrase. Since you mentioned K. 333 a moment ago, think about the integration of line between the first and second themes of its first movement, which, as far as I can see, could be played in reverse order and still provide a perfectly satisfying contrast.

B.M.: But doesn't this suggest a certain rigidity in terms of tempo? After all, if you play the piano, especially as a soloist, you don't have to be bound by orchestral concepts of tempo.

G.G.: You don't *have* to be, but, in my view, and certainly in this repertoire, you ought to be. You know, I have a sort of motto to the effect that if you can't conduct it, it's wrong—"it" being any piece of piano repertoire penned before 1900, and I'm not sure even that time limit is appropriate. One has to assume, of course, that the listener has a gift for subdivided beats, but I do find it upsetting, to put it mildly, to hear eighteenth- or nineteenth-century music played on the piano with the kind of motoric license that has nothing at all to do with rubato.

B.M.: But surely this is a generational phenomenon? After all, some of the great virtuoso conductors from earlier in the century were very liberal tempo manipulators.

G.G.: That's quite true, but not quite what I'm talking about. Let's take Willem Mengelberg, for example. I'm sure you'd agree that Mengelberg was one of the most formidable of orchestral technicians.

B.M.: Absolutely.

G.G.: Personally, I think that, along with Stokowski, he was the greatest conductor I've ever heard on records—yet he certainly employed some very strange, arbitrary, and, if I can use my yardstick of "modulatory distance" once again, unnecessary tempo changes. (One doesn't have to go further than his recording of the Beethoven First Symphony, first movement, second thematic group, to encounter a really gratuitous molto ritard.) Nevertheless, one *can* conduct it, obviously—otherwise, the Concertgebouw couldn't have played it so gloriously for him. Now, that kind of thing may well be misguided, and it certainly represents a generational gap in approach, as you suggested, but it's essentially structural and analytical in motivation. And in that respect it stands in complete contrast to the diffused and generalized rhythmic attitude toward the piano, which seems to derive from the idea that almost any instability of tempo can be justified simply because the piano will not stand up and refuse to cooperate—as orchestral sidemen almost surely would.

B.M.: So you're recommending that one should play the piano without using all those special qualities of rubato control?

G.G.: No, what I'm really saying—to quote an old string player's saw—is that "just because you paid for the whole bow, you don't have to use it"; to me, that kind of indulgence represents the opposite of control. The tradition is actually harpsichordal in origin: that sort of stop-and-go motion is a substitute for dynamic fluctuation, as it relates to the shaping of phrases, and even the greatest harpsichordists indulge in it. But there is no comparable excuse for it on the piano. I'm not even convinced that one should exploit the instrument that way in late romantic music. I'm not saying that one shouldn't be free to employ subtle tempo gradations—in fact, my modulatory slide rule dictates that in that repertoire they're almost inevitable—but this other thing, which to my ear is a combination of structural negligence and a certain lack of control instrumentally, is something else altogether. I find it disturbing even in Scriabin, say; but in Mozart it's simply grotesque.

B.M.: How does all this relate to your performance of the A-major Mozart sonata, which I think is perhaps the most interesting of your Mozart records, but which certainly does contain a lot of very odd tempos?

G.G.: Yes, it does. And I suppose the exceeding slowness of the Rondo alla turca is the most obvious.

B.M.: That's the least of it, surely. I was thinking primarily of the first movement, in which every variation is set at a different tempo—

G.G.: And also at a faster one than the variation preceding, as I recall.

B.M.: —and notwithstanding Mozart's specific instructions to the contrary in variation 5, which he describes as an adagio and which you perform as an allegro.

G.G.: Well, of course, as the penultimate variation, it's second in velocity only to the finale of the movement, according to the scheme I employed.

B.M.: And I must say it works!

G.G.: I'm really glad to hear you say that, Bruno. Well, the idea behind that performance was that, since the first movement is a nocturne-cum-minuet rather than a slow movement, and since the package is rounded off by that curious bit of seragliolike exotica, one is dealing with an unusual structure, and virtually all of the sonata-allegro conventions can be set aside.

B.M.: Including the convention of tempo continuity?

G.G.: Precisely. I admit that my realization of the first movement is somewhat idiosyncratic.

B.M.: It certainly is. It almost seems as though you employed some sort of inverse variation of your modulation theory in planning the articulation of the opening theme. Did you assume that the melody was so well known that it did not need to be heard again?

G.G.: Something like that, yes. I wanted—if I can invoke the name of Webern once more—to subject it to a Webern-like scrutiny in which its basic elements would be isolated from each other and the continuity of the theme deliberately undermined. The idea was that each successive variation would contribute to the restoration of that continuity and, in the absorption of that task, would be less visible as an ornamental, decorative element. But to get back to your comment about the missing adagio, it seemed to me that once one had launched into that concept, that continuous forward propulsion, there simply could be no turning back; I thought that the nocturne-minuet would supply all the relaxation necessary. I can't say that I'm entirely convinced about the tempo choice for the *Alla turca*. At the time, it seemed important to establish a solid, maybe even stolid, tempo, partly to balance the tempo curve of the first movement—and, I admit frankly, partly because, to my knowledge, anyway, nobody had played it like that before, at least not on records.

B.M.: If every Mozart sonata contained a similar set of unconventional movements, would your task have been easier?

G.G.: I don't think it would have been easier. It might have required a "greater quantity of thinking," to misquote one of the funeral orations about John Donne, but it probably would have been more fun.

B.M.: You were going to talk about the concerto versus sonata repertoire—about the fact that you don't want to record any of the Mozart concertos.

G.G.: Well, you see, Bruno, I don't really enjoy playing *any* concertos very much. What bothers me most is the competitive, comparative ambience in which the concerto operates. I happen to believe that competition rather than money is the root of all evil, and in the concerto we have a perfect musical analogy of the competitive spirit. Obviously, I'd exclude the concerto grosso from what I've just said.

B.M.: And I'm reasonably confident that Webern's Op. 24 qualifies for an exemption.

G.G.: So does Chausson's Op. 30. But, to be serious, everything in between, with the exception of the parodistic concerto-commentaries—the Dohnányi Variations, or the Strauss *Burleske,* which I find irresistible—is, from my particular ideological standpoint, suspect. Probably, the key to my disenchantment has something to do with what we could call double dichotomy—that sounds like the title for a TV game show, doesn't it—in which the purely mechanical division of labor in the concerto of the classical period compounds the already predictable dichotomy of the first theme–second theme relationship of the sonata.

B.M.: Do you mind if I say that that sort of sociopolitical criticism strikes me as awfully old-fashioned?

G.G.: Sorry about that. My primary concern is certainly with the musical product, but, old-fashioned or not, the extramusical perspectives are the only means I have of trying to find a moral basis for our discussion.

B.M.: Does it really come down to a question of morality, then?

G.G.: I think, ultimately, that's exactly what it comes to, yes.

B.M.: Because, you see, I think this whole quasisociological complaint of yours is, if I may say so, about as sophisticated as the Mozart perspectives of nineteenth-century pedagogues—the views in which Mozart was seen as eternally youthful, and cheerful, and gracious, and so on.

G.G.: Well, those views may have been formed in the image of an aesthetic you don't approve of, Bruno, but they're not necessarily invalid for that reason. I think the adjectives you just used are accurate so far as they go. I don't find them derogatory per se, but I don't find them inapplicable to Mozart, either.

B.M.: Well, I do, because I find the decorative aspect in Mozart something akin to an inevitable force in music. I think if music were always reduced to its skeleton, as it were, very, very little could be written—which is why I don't find your Webern analogies appropriate. You know, I dislike *all* generalizations about Mozart. I think I told you once that I don't care for Mozart when he's sad in a minor key, that I much prefer him to be sad in the major mode. And what I was rejecting was not the G-minor Symphony, obviously, but the neoromantic views that cling to it.

G.G.: Well, I reject them, too.

B.M.: I'm not sure that you do. You reject the work, and that's not the same thing.

G.G.: No, I reject the bilateral approach to Mozart. I don't think that his occasional flirtations with gravity warrant a split-screen analysis of output.

B.M.: That's not quite the way I would have put it.

G.G.: But that doesn't automatically augur that profundity resides with the major mode, either.

B.M.: Well, look here, I recently saw Bergman's film of *The Magic Flute*, which I imagine is not one of your favorite works, and, in spite of what I thought was a very bad soundtrack, I was simply moved all over again by the sound of the music itself, which may very well seem to be a sensuous response—but I don't think so. I think it's something purely spiritual. But it would be awfully difficult to find an adjective for that feeling, and I certainly don't think that any of the stereotyped adjectives about Mozart could ever describe it.

G.G.: But, you see, I think we can protest too much, Bruno. I think that when generations of listeners—laymen particularly, because their views usually have an intuitive edge over musicians'—have found it appropriate to attribute terms like "lightness," "ease," "frivolity," "gallantry," "spontaneity" to Mozart, it behooves us to at least think about the reasons for these attributions—which are not necessarily borne of a lack of appreciation or of charity. I think that to a lot of people—and I include myself among them—the words imply not a criticism of what Mozart offers us but a hint of what he doesn't offer. I always think of an extraordinary concept in an essay on Mozart by the theologian Jean Le Moyne, who also happens to be a most perceptive musical layman. In the essay Le Moyne tried to come to grips with just what it was that alienated him from Mozart. And he discovered that in his youth he had mistrusted any art that had, as he put it, "pretensions to self-sufficiency," but that later, having come to realize that genius is somehow related to an ability to understand the world, he nevertheless continued to require of every artist what he called "the polarization, the haste, and the progress" that he observed in the lives of the mystics.

B.M.: I presume he didn't come to terms with Mozart.

G.G.: No. As a matter of fact, he likened Mozart to Don Giovanni, who he claimed was really Cherubino returned from military service. He said that—and I wrote this down for our conversation because I didn't want to misquote him—"despite his easy grace and virtuosity, Don Giovanni doesn't possess himself sufficiently to belong definitely to the absolute and to march unwaveringly towards the silence of being."

B.M.: Well, I admire the poetry, but that's as far as I can go.

G.G.: It's also as far as I can go, because, for me, that says it all about Mozart, or at least as much as can be said for now. So shall we try again next year?

B.M.: With pleasure.

GLENN GOULD INTERVIEWS
HIMSELF ABOUT BEETHOVEN

GLENN GOULD: Mr. Gould, when did you first become aware of your growing doubts about Beethoven?

GLENN GOULD: I don't believe I have any doubts about Beethoven—a few minor reservations, perhaps. Beethoven has played a very important part in my life, and I feel that while the warm glow of his bicentennial celebration remains, "doubts" is a singularly inappropriate word.

G.G.: You must allow me to be the judge of that, if you will, sir. But perhaps you'd care to define some of those "reservations" for us.

From *Piano Quarterly*, Fall 1972.

G.G.: Certainly. Well, there are moments in Beethoven when I'm a bit perplexed, I confess. For instance, I've never been able really to "draw a bead," so to speak, on the finale of the Ninth.

g.g.: That's a fairly common reservation.

G.G.: Exactly, and it certainly doesn't qualify as a "doubt," in my opinion.

g.g.: I see. In your view, then, it's simply an aversion to isolated moments in his music, is it?

G.G.: Well, of course, I don't mind admitting that I have a built-in bias in regard to *Wellington's Victory,* or even the *King Stephen* Overture, for that matter, more or less from first note to last.

g.g.: But among what we may safely call the "mainstream" works, you have no such objection, is that it?

G.G.: No, not exactly. I can't claim to be equally enamored of all the most familiar compositions, certainly.

g.g.: Well, then, which of these works fail to meet with your approval?

G.G.: It has nothing whatever to do with my approval, and I wish you'd stop using words like that. But I suppose, perhaps, I'm less fond of the Fifth Symphony, the "Appassionata" Sonata, or the Violin Concerto.

g.g.: I see. All those works are from what we might think of as Beethoven's "middle" years, aren't they?

G.G.: Yes, that's true.

g.g.: And very significant, too. I suppose, however, like most professional musicians, you have a pronounced penchant for the late quartets and piano sonatas.

G.G.: I listen to them a lot, yes.

g.g.: That's not really what I was asking you, Mr. Gould.

G.G.: Well, those are very problematic works, you see, and I—

g.g.: Please, Mr. Gould, with all due respect, we don't need you to tell us that. If I'm not mistaken, even one of Huxley's characters—what was his name?—

G.G.: Spandrell or something, wasn't it?

g.g.: Yes, thank you—even he committed suicide more or less to the accompaniment of Op. 132, didn't he?

G.G.: That's right. Well, I apologize for the clichés, but those works really are very elusive, you know—very enigmatic, very—

g.g.: How about "ambivalent"?

G.G.: Don't be hostile.

g.g.: Well, then, don't you be evasive. What I'm asking, obviously, is not whether you share the worldwide bafflement in regard to the form of the C-sharp-minor Quartet—I'm asking whether you genuinely enjoy listening to the piece.

G.G.: No.

g.g.: That's more like it. There's no need to be embarrassed here. I suppose, then, it's the early works to which you're particularly attracted?

G.G.: I'm fond of the Op. 18 Quartets, certainly, and the Second Symphony is one of my two favorite works in that genre, as a matter of fact.

g.g.: Very typical. This, of course, is the well-known odd-number-symphony syndrome.

G.G.: No, I assure you, it isn't. I can't bear the Fourth, and I'm not particularly fond of the *Pastorale*, though I will admit the Eighth Symphony is my favorite among all his works in that form.

g.g.: Hmm.

G.G.: You see, I know you'd like to confirm a cut-and-dried diagnosis, but I really don't think it's quite that simple. You're also trying to establish a chronological bias, obviously, and I don't think that's fair, either.

g.g.: Well, Mr. Gould, I admit that our tests are far from conclusive at this stage, but since you've already confessed your admiration for the Second and Eighth Symphonies, perhaps you'd care to enumerate some other Beethoven compositions for which you have special affection.

G.G.: Certainly. There is the Piano Sonata Op. 81a, the String Quartet Op. 95. Then there are each of the Op. 31 Piano Sonatas and, believe it or not, the "Moonlight," for that matter. So you see, I just can't be typecast as readily as you might wish.

g.g.: On the contrary, my dear sir, I think, in relation to the Beethovenian canon at least, you've managed to typecast yourself, and with remarkable consistency. Do you realize that every work you've singled out has belonged to what we might call a transition phase—or, rather, one of two transition phases, to be exact—within Beethoven's development?

G.G.: Forgive me, but that's just hogwash. First of all, I can't buy this notion of the Beethovenian plateau. You'd probably like to convince me that every work he wrote is either "early," "middle," or "late" in spirit, and I think that sort of categorizing is every bit as unprofitable as it is unoriginal, if you don't mind my saying so.

g.g.: I don't mind your saying so, and I've noted your defensive reaction to the suggestion. But since you yourself alluded to this yardstick—this subdivision of Beethoven's creative life into periods—I simply suggest to you that there is perhaps something significant in the fact that all the works you've mentioned, by that very yardstick to which you've alluded, found him at the time of their composition in a state of, for want of a better word, flux.

G.G.: Every artist is in a state of flux or he wouldn't be an artist.

g.g.: Please, Mr. Gould, don't be tedious—in a state of flux, as I say, if not between the early and middle years, then between the middle and late ones.

G.G.: That's nonsense.

g.g.: Are you sure? Do you realize that all the later pieces you've mentioned were written within a period of three years—1809 to 1812?

G.G.: So was the *King Stephen* Overture.

g.g.: There are always exceptions. And all the early ones you've singled out, for that matter, were written between 1799 and 1802. So, that out of a creative life which I assume you will concede to involve—what—perhaps thirty-five years, you've given your stamp of approval to the produce of approximately six of those years.

G.G.: My stamp of approval isn't of the least consequence to Beethoven.

g.g.: No, it isn't, but your enjoyment index is of importance, to yourself at least, and if I'm to be of any help to you, you'll have to let me plot it in my own way.

G.G.: Go ahead, then.

g.g.: Well, of course, we've found that the normal contingency presupposes an enjoyment index which emphasizes the Fifth Symphony, the Violin Concerto, the "Appassionata"—all works which show Beethoven in supreme command of his symphonic powers—

G.G.: Or, at any rate, his sonata-allegro powers.

g.g.: Precisely.—and all works which are conspicuously absent from your own Beethovenian hit parade. They're all large-scale works, as you know, they're all rather heroic in attitude, and they're all triumphantly tonal in terms of key conviction, aren't they?

G.G.: I suppose so.

g.g.: You, on the other hand, have opted for works which, if I may say so, Mr. Gould, are minor league by comparison. They're all relatively brief, of course—

G.G.: Economical.

g.g.: Yes. Notably unheroic.

G.G.: Balanced.

g.g.: Perhaps. Even tonally ambivalent on occasion—you did mention Op. 81a, didn't you? They're all charming, of course, even touching, and certainly well wrought, but they're none of them works with which Beethoven is customarily identified, wouldn't you agree, and they're certainly not among those pieces which have helped him to his pre-eminent place at the very center of the Western musical tradition, are they? So, when, to come back to my question, Mr. Gould, did you start having doubts about Beethoven?

G.G.: About a decade ago.

g.g.: I see. In other words, more or less at that period of your life when you became disenchanted with the concert experience.

G.G.: That's right.

g.g.: Of course, you played a great deal of Beethoven in your concerts, didn't you?

G.G.: Yes.

g.g.: Does this suggest, then, that you found his music, by and large, more fun to play than to listen to?

G.G.: Certainly not. I've already told you that I listen with great pleasure to—

g.g.: —to the Eighth Symphony and the Op. 95 String Quartet, I know. But in your concert-giving days you did play, let's say, the "Emperor" Concerto fairly frequently, after all, yet I haven't noticed it on your list of all-time favorites. So does this suggest, perhaps, that such performances simply provided you with tactile rather than intellectual stimulation?

G.G.: I think that's really uncalled for, you know. I tried very, very hard to develop a convincing rationale for the "Emperor" Concerto.

g.g.: Yes, I've heard some of your attempts at rationalizing it, as a matter of fact, but it's interesting that you say "tried." I assume this means that you found it difficult to realize a spontaneous musical experience in relation to such performances.

G.G.: Well, if by "spontaneous" you mean an occasion when every note fell into place as though programmed by an automaton, obviously not.

g.g.: No, don't misunderstand me. I'm not speaking of technical felicities or anything as mundane as that. I simply suggest that if you were to play a work by—who's your favorite composer?

G.G.: Orlando Gibbons.

g.g.: Thank you.—by Orlando Gibbons, that every note would seem to belong organically without any necessity for you as its interpreter to differentiate between tactile and intellectual considerations at all.

G.G.: I don't think I've been guilty of any such differentiation.

g.g.: Ah, but you have, however inadvertently. You see, this armchair analysis of yours compels you to keep trying to like Op. 132, or whatever, but you don't feel obliged to undertake any similar probe in behalf of Mr. Gibbons's "Salisbury" Pavan, do you? And similarly, the elaborate rationale you concoct in behalf of the Fifth Piano Concerto—whether if you do it very slowly or very quickly it might suddenly and miraculously hang together successfully—isn't matched by any similar apologia when you play Gibbons, is it? Now, I'm sure you'll agree that it's not because Gibbons is less intellectually demanding—

G.G.: Indeed, he's not.

g.g.: —and indeed, given the passage of time from his day to ours, he might even be said to pose the greater re-creative challenge.

G.G.: That's true.

g.g.: But despite that fact, you see, I'm fairly certain that if you sit down to your piano, late at night, let's say—for your own amusement, in any case—it's Orlando Gibbons, or some other composer in regard to whom you evidence no such schizophrenic tendencies, that you'll play, and not Beethoven. Am I right?

g.g.: I don't really see what that proves, and I think—

g.g.: Am I right?

g.g.: But surely I'm entitled to—

g.g.: Am I right?

g.g.: Yes. Can you help me?

g.g.: Do you want to be helped?

g.g.: Not if it involves giving up Orlando Gibbons.

g.g.: That shouldn't be necessary. You see, Mr. Gould, your problem—and it's a much more common one than you realize, I assure you—relates to a fundamental misunderstanding of the means by which post-Renaissance art achieved its communicative power. Beethoven, as I'm sure you'll agree, was central to that achievement, if only chronologically, in that his creative life virtually bisects the three and a half centuries since the demise of your Mr. Gibbons—

g.g.: True.

g.g.: —and it's precisely during that period of three and a half centuries, and specifically at the Beethovenian heart of it, that the creative idea and the communicative ideal began to grant each other mutual concessions.

g.g.: You've lost me.

g.g.: Well, look at it this way. All the works that you've enumerated on your private hate list—

g.g.: It's not that at all.

g.g.: Don't interrupt, please. All those works have in common the idea that their ideology, so to speak, can be wrapped up in one or more memorable moments.

g.g.: You mean motives.

g.g.: I mean tunes. I mean, quite simply, that you, as a professional musician, have clearly developed a resentment pattern in relation to those tunes—forgive me—which represent and which characterize the spirit of their respective compositions.

g.g.: Well, there's nothing very special about the tunes, if you want to call them that, in the "Emperor" Concerto, since you're challenging me on that ground in particular.

g.g.: There's nothing special at all. There is, however, something readily identifiable about them which, by definition, threatens to undermine your interpretative prerogative, don't you see? You resent the fact that, in a work like the "Emperor" Concerto, the elaborate extenuations relevant to those motives have indeed been left in your hands, literally and figuratively, but the raison d'être of those extenuations inevitably devolved upon the kind of motivic fragment that automatically came equipped with certain built-in interpretive biases by virtue of which they can be sung, whistled, or toe-tapped by anyone—any layman.

G.G.: That's nonsense. Mendelssohn's tunes are every bit as good as, and far more continuous than, Beethoven's, and I have no objection to Mendelssohn whatever.

g.g.: Ah, precisely. Mendelssohn's are far more continuous because they relate to a motivic substance which is at once more extended, more complex, and—don't get me wrong, now—more professional.

G.G.: You think so too, then?

g.g.: Everyone does, my dear fellow. It's precisely that impossible mixture of naiveté and sophistication that makes Beethoven the imponderable he is, and it's precisely that dimension of his music—that mixture of the professional's developmental skills and the amateur's motivic bluntness—that is at the heart of your problem.

G.G.: Do you think so?

g.g.: There's no doubt of it. And it's not at all a bad thing, really—a bit anarchistic, perhaps, but, in a way, it's even rather creative—because when you reject Beethoven—

G.G.: But I'm not rejecting him!

g.g.: Please! When you reject Beethoven, as I say, you're rejecting the logical conclusion of the Western musical tradition.

G.G.: But he isn't the conclusion of it.

g.g.: Well, of course, chronologically he isn't. As I've said, he's really the center of it in that sense, and it's precisely those works which are in the center of his own chronology that disturb you most. It's precisely those works in which an elaborate exposé with which only a professional can cope is related to material with which anyone can identify.

G.G.: Hmm . . .

g.g.: And that disturbs you, Mr. Gould, because it represents, first of all, a comment upon the role playing, the stratified professionalism, of the Western musical tradition that you, and not without reason, question. No, it's no accident that you prefer those works in which Beethoven was less emphatically his logical-extremist self—the works written on the way to, or in retreat from, that position—the works in which the predictability quotient is lower, the works in which the composer is less concerned with making the mystery of his art explicit.

G.G.: But on the way to, or in retreat from, that position, as you put it, you encounter a much more professional kind of art—Wagner's professionalism, or Bach's, depending on which way you go—and you have to move a long way back, or forward, as the case may be, to encounter a purely amateur tradition.

g.g.: Precisely. On either side of Beethoven, there's a much more thorough-going professionalism, and that's precisely why those composers appeal to you.

G.G.: Hmm. Well, do you mean, then, that if I do reject Beethoven, I'm on my way to being an environmentalist or something like that? I mean, I think John Cage has said that if *he's* right, Beethoven must be wrong, or something of the sort. Do you think I'm harboring a sort of suicide wish on behalf of the profession of music?

g.g.: My dear fellow, I don't think you should be concerned about it, really. Besides, you're quite a moderate, you know—you didn't choose Op. 132, after all, just 81a and 95. You're vacillating. You're not quite sure whether in making that mystery explicit, in exploiting the dichotomy between layman and professional, we do our fellow man a service or a disservice. You're not quite sure whether in opting for an environmental course, which, after all, puts an end to professionalism as we know it, we're getting at some truth about ourselves more immediate than any professional can achieve, or whether, in doing that, we're simply reining in our own development as human beings. And you shouldn't be embarrassed, because Beethoven himself wasn't sure. After all, he didn't write many "Emperor" Concertos, did he? He vacillated, to a degree at least, and I don't see why you can't. It's just that in celebrating Beethoven, you're acknowledging one terminal point which makes your vacillation practicable, and now you have to find another one.

G.G.: Well, I feel consoled by that, actually. But there's one thing I don't understand: How did you know I had these doubts?

g.g.: Mr. Gould, it was perfectly obvious—you wouldn't have requested this interview otherwise. You'd have authored the piece as you were asked to do.

G.G.: I see. Well, thank you very much—is there anything else?

g.g.: No, I don't think so. Oh, yes—if you don't mind, on your way out, turn down the PA, will you? If I hear another bar of the *Eroica*, I'll scream.

BEETHOVEN'S *PATHÉTIQUE,*
"MOONLIGHT," AND
"APPASSIONATA" SONATAS

Of Beethoven's thirty-two piano sonatas, it is fair to say that, at most, a half-dozen have achieved that special public favor that is afforded by instant recognition. These, without exception, are the tagged sonatas—the *Pathétique,* the "Moonlight," the "Appassionata," and, less fervently acclaimed, the "Pastoral," the "Waldstein," and *Les Adieux.* Yet, with the exception of the "Moonlight" (a daring experiment in organizational balance) and of "Les Adieux" (perhaps the most resourceful of those studies in motivic compression that effected the transition to his later style), none of these celebrated sonatas provided landmarks in Beethoven's creative evolution, and two of the three contained in this album, the *Pathétique* and the "Appassionata," are more notable for the way in which they exemplify the attitudes held by Beethoven at the time of their composition than for their espousal of any particularly adventurous architectural ideas.

Among Beethoven's early piano works, the *Pathétique,* Op. 13, is perhaps the most symphonically inclined. Its first movement is prefaced by an imposing Grave statement of the sort that Beethoven employed as introduction to his First, Second, Fourth, and Seventh Symphonies; and although it is somewhat tangentially related to the primary thematic issues of the subsequent Allegro, the Grave statement is indissolubly linked to the Allegro through the opulent texture of its euphonically balanced triads and the somewhat stage-struck character of its doom-foretelling double-dotted rhythm. In the Allegro portion of the movement, Beethoven derives both dynamic and rhythmic propulsion from the persistent timpani-style tremolandos with which the left hand rigorously chaperones that ill-advised flirtation with rubato that is the constant temptation of the right hand.

This quasiorchestral approach to the keyboard reappeared in Beethoven's piano works from time to time, especially in those rather blustery essays of his middle period. But most of Beethoven's subsequent sonatas explored more intimate and indigenously pianistic sonorities. Indeed, the last two movements of the *Pathétique* already anticipate this aspect of his mature keyboard style. The second movement is a tranquil, modestly embellished Ada-

Liner notes from Columbia MS 7413, 1970.

gio, while the third movement, Rondo, with its angular, two-part counter-point, has always seemed to me to belong in some other work. It would pro-vide a fitting finale to Beethoven's earlier C-minor sonata, Op. 10, No. 1; but in relation to that autocratic first movement, this altogether amiable Rondo scarcely pulls its own weight.

By comparison, the Sonata Op. 27, No. 2 (the so-called "Moonlight" So-nata), although comprising three superficially disparate movements, is a mas-terpiece of intuitive organization. As opposed to the *Pathétique*, which re-cedes emotionally from the belligerence of its opening Allegro to the more modest claims of its concluding Rondo, the "Moonlight" Sonata escalates from first note to last. Beginning with the diffident charm of what is unques-tionably Beethoven's best-loved and most abused melody, the ternary grace of the opening Adagio resolves into the tantalizingly ambivalent whiff of D-flat major that constitutes the second movement. This fragile and autum-nal Allegretto, in turn, disappears within the flash flood that is the concluding Presto. Indeed, the Presto movement of this work seems to crystallize the sentiments of the other two and confirm an emotional relationship at once flexible and assured. Written in the form of a sonata-allegro, such as Beetho-ven would normally employ as a first movement, it is one of the most imagi-natively structured and temperamentally versatile of all his finales. But be-cause of its cumulative zeal, the "Moonlight" Sonata is deservedly high on the all-time eighteenth-century hit parade.

Like the *Pathétique* and "Moonlight" Sonatas, the so-called "Appas-sionata" Sonata, Op. 57, is usually ranked with the most popular of Beetho-ven's keyboard works. But I confess the reasons for its popularity elude me: it is not, surely, one of the formative works in Beethoven's canon, nor is it one of those tense, argumentative middle-period essays that, like the Violin Concerto, get by through a combination of guts and one good tune.

The "Appassionata," in common with most of the works that Beethoven wrote in the first decade of the nineteenth century, is a study in thematic tenacity. His conceit at this period was to create mammoth structures from material that in lesser hands would scarcely have afforded a good sixteen-bar intro. The themes as such are usually of minimal interest but often of such primal urgency that one wonders why it took a Beethoven to think them up. And the elaboration of these motives is not contrapuntally continuous in the baroque manner or decorous in the rococo style. It is, on the contrary, as determined, combative, and resistant to concession as early eigh-teenth-century music is placative, supportive, and amenable to conciliation.

No one had ever before composed with so belligerent an attitude; in some respects, no one has done so since. When it works—when Beethoven's furious onslaughts find their mark—one feels that music's rhetorical de-mands have been transcended by an affirmation at once personal and universal. But when they do not succeed, these compositions of his middle years are victimized by that same relentless motivic pursuit. And I think that in the "Appassionata" Sonata his method does not work.

In the first movement, Allegro, the relation of first and second themes, both of them spawned by an arpeggiated triad figure, is somehow out of focus, with the subsidiary motives in the relative major key following hard upon the opening F-minor statement and without benefit of that inexorable tonal strategy that guides Beethoven's more carefully considered expositions. The development segment is similarly disorganized, offering sequential stereotypes in place of a grand, central fury—that unique amalgam of order and chaos that provides the raison d'être for Beethoven's successful developmental installations.

The second movement, Andante, is a set of four variations that derive from, but fail to expand, a somber confluence of primary chords in the key of D-flat major. The finale, like the last movement of the "Moonlight" Sonata, is essentially a sonata-allegro and, by virtue of the persistent use of a toccatalike accompanying motive, almost but not quite gets its pointillistically conceived horn calls and plucked contrabass effects off the printed page. At the conclusion of the recapitulated statements, and prior to whipping up a frenzied stretto for the coda, Beethoven interpolates a curious eighteen-bar galop that, with its souped-up tempo and simplistic rhythmic format, provides the compositional equivalent of those heroic gestures by which the experienced virtuoso gathers—even for the most ill-conceived interpretation—frenzied approval from the balcony.

For at this period of his life Beethoven was not only preoccupied with motivic frugality; he was also preoccupied with being Beethoven. And there is about the "Appassionata" an egoistic pomposity, a defiant "let's just see if I can't get away with using that once more" attitude, that on my own private Beethoven poll places this sonata somewhere between the *King Stephen* Overture and the *Wellington's Victory* Symphony.

BEETHOVEN'S LAST
THREE PIANO SONATAS

One of the joys of musical anthropology seems to involve consigning to composers' careers, especially the careers of composers comfortably deceased, rather arbitrary chronological landmarks. These are designed to partition the output of even the most unremitting creator into several clearly defined innings known to all students of "music appreciation" as "periods."

This subdivision of the creative estate is usually prompted by fanciful misconceptions regarding the influence of the artist's private life upon his musical consciousness. In order that a "period" may be successfully launched, one need only proclaim the importance of such terminal events as, say, a respite from productivity, transference of interest from one form to another (lieder to symphony, for instance), or, best of all, a change of geographical situation. Regardless of the distinction of personal temper, few men with a will to wander have ever escaped identification with the terminus of their journeys. Indeed, even the most forthright of itinerant chapel-masters, in the course of his climb from Köthen to Weimar to Leipzig, unwittingly hewed with each migration a trail down which, two centuries hence, casual tourists review the carefully calibrated columns of his accomplishment.

But with a nomadic organist like Bach, there might be some defense for such rule-of-thumb designation, since the products of a particular sojourn must reflect to some extent the available musical manpower. How much greater a mischief it is to exploit not an external physical circumstance but an entirely subjective state of mind—to interpret a work of art through philosophical connotation and then to accept this paraphrase as valid depiction of the author's intellectual attitude. And it must be admitted that the ranks of those who have perpetrated these vivid pictorials include not only romantic biographers and lay psychologists but also many skilled historians and analysts who, when faced with the more arduous and less colorful task of assessing the gradual unfolding of an artist's technical concepts, suddenly appear as oracles in the nebulous field of extramusical perception.

It is doubtful whether any compositions by any master have been more seriously maligned after this fashion than have the works of Beethoven's later years. Late works, the efforts of a "final period," hold an especial fascination for musical seers, since one may more readily expect to read into them the

Liner notes from Columbia ML 5130, 1956.

message of a last will and testament. Then, too, Beethoven's creative life comes equipped with several of the criteria mentioned above—the impediment to his hearing which forced him to seek solace in self-contemplation, or the period of relative infertility succeeding the halcyon days of the *Eroica,* the "Appassionata," and the "Rasumovskys." Consequently, the products of his later life have been interpreted as the improbable miscalculations of a deaf man, as *Augenmusik* written by a solitary for the pleasure of his own perusal, or as the joyous restoration of creative powers which transcend all previous achievement, which, indeed, transcend the very function and nature of music.

The wealth of critical writing on the last sonatas and quartets reveals a greater preponderance of nonsense, not to mention contradiction, than any comparable literature. Beethoven's earliest biographers have a tendency to bypass these works with only a comment or two about their unsatisfactory realization in performance. Strangely enough, this attitude appears from time to time up to the present, especially in regard to those works notable for contrapuntal endeavor. Typical is the comment of Joseph de Marliave, who in his work on the quartets recommends the exclusion from performance of both the "Grosse Fuge," Op. 133, and the fugue finale to the "Hammerklavier" Sonata, Op. 106. "On hearing it," he remarks of the "Grosse Fuge," "one also realizes that this time the Master has missed altogether the intimate and contemplative appeal to the ear found to perfection in his last work. . . . Abandoning himself with an almost demoniacal pleasure to his mighty genius, Beethoven heaps one discordant effect upon another, and the general impression of tiresome waste of sound cannot be dispelled by the marvel of its technical construction."

Marliave's mention of "the intimate and contemplative appeal to the ear" illustrates an approach to these works based upon philosophical conjecture rather than musical analysis. Beethoven, according to this hypothesis, has spiritually soared beyond the earth's orbit and, being delivered of earthly dimension, reveals to us a vision of paradisiacal enchantment. A more recent and more alarming view shows Beethoven not as an indomitable spirit which has o'erleapt the world but as a man bowed and broken by the tyrannous constraint of life on earth, yet meeting all tribulation with a noble resignation to the inevitable. Thus Beethoven, mystic visionary, becomes Beethoven, realist, and these last works are shown as calcified, impersonal constructions of a soul impervious to the desires and torments of existence. The giddy heights to which these absurdities can wing have been realized by several contemporary novelists, notable offenders being Thomas Mann and Aldous Huxley.

Those who choose to substantiate these views with musical examples usually have recourse to analogy with the formal outline of the later works.

Conspicuous, of course, is the overall rhapsodic impression created by the unconventional juxtaposition of certain movements. Although this improvisatory quality is more in evidence in works like the C-sharp-minor Quartet, the sonatas Op. 109, 110, and 111 nevertheless reveal, both individually and as a trilogy, an extreme diversity of formal enterprise. The final movements, especially, reveal little of that sense of consummate urgency or dynamic impact associated with the classical finale. Yet each seems to be propelled by an instinctive comprehension of the needs of what has gone before and fulfills its obligation to the total conception while preserving an effect of complete spontaneity. Yet—and here lies the paradox—seldom have movements been constructed more compactly, been developed with greater economy, or, within themselves, permitted to disclose a more rigorous digest of the properties of the classical sonata.

To take but one example: the first movement of Op. 109, a veritable précis of a sonata-allegro, omits the presentation of a subsidiary thematic group, substituting an arpeggio sequence of secondary dominants. This sequence, though entirely without motivic connection with the preceding sentence, relieves the harmonic anxiety of the precipitous opening bars by confirming the impression of a dominant modulation. However, when the corresponding moment in the recapitulation arrives, this episode is not satisfied with a literal transposition of itself, not content to assuage the ardor of the principal theme, but breaks away to build an artful variation upon itself, a variation which, for the first and only time in the movement, aspires beyond the diatonic circuit of E major. And precisely at this climactic moment there occurs a most subtle stroke of Beethoven's musical imagination. The harmonic root progression in these bars, 62–63, becomes the exact inversion of the equivalent instance, bars 12–13. Notwithstanding the many examples of canon and cancrizan to be seen in the melodic figurations of these late works, I would guess this occasion, with its defiance of the automatic semitone adjustment necessary to preserve the sphere of one tonality, to be unique in Beethoven's work.

It would be a mistake to infer that such a device as that discussed above is a contrived mathematical equation. On the contrary, I have cited this example because it is indicative of that consort of unguarded spontaneity and objective discipline which is the hallmark of his later work.

But these are not qualities which were suddenly made manifest in 1820. They were the quest of a lifetime and, more particularly, an attribute of the contrapuntal activation which swept his art in the transitional years 1812 to 1818. They were heralded by the motivic compression of the Seventh Symphony, the Sonata Op. 101, by the harmonic bluntness of the Eighth Symphony, the muscular angularity of the Sonata Op. 81a; and the three last sonatas are in turn harbingers of the more intense quartet music to follow. Yet who can deny that the lush, Handelian—one might almost say, anachronistically, Mendelssohnian—counterpoint of the fugue to Op. 110 is as much a part of the late Beethoven style as are the taut sinews of the "Grosse Fuge"? Beethoven, it seems, will not be confined, not even by those who would retroactively chart his course.

These sonatas are a brief but an idyllic stopover in the itinerary of an intrepid *voyageur.* Perhaps they do not yield the apocalyptic disclosures that have been so graphically ascribed to them. Music is a malleable art, acquiescent and philosophically flexible, and it is no great task to mold it to one's want—but when, as in the works before us now, it transports us to a realm of such beatific felicity, it is the happier diversion not to try.

BEETHOVEN'S FIFTH SYMPHONY ON THE PIANO: FOUR IMAGINARY REVIEWS

REPRINTED FROM THE ENGLISH MAGAZINE
THE PHONOGRAPH

Letter from America   *Sir Humphrey Price-Davies*
Among recent developments of note in the American gramophone industry a certain pre-occupation with rather obscure keyboard repertoire from the nineteenth century takes precedence. One hears of plans in progress for an integral edition of the works of C. V. Alkan, than whom, as my colleague R.Y.P. remarked in the February 1962 issue of this journal, "no one deserves obscurity more richly." The recently founded Astro-disc label has already formulated plans for a recording of the 'Chant of the Caribbean' *(Chant des Caraïbes)* by Louis Moreau Gottschalk (AS-1—£2/10/6), utilising what the company's publicists describe as the 'lush' acoustics afforded by the pub facilities on board the riverboat *Tawanhee* currently moored at Segratoria, Mississippi. And in the releases for the current month, that colossus of American industry, CBS, includes one offering it rather immodestly describes as 'a keyboard first'—Franz Liszt's transcription of the Beethoven Fifth Symphony as rendered by that extravagantly eccentric Canadian pianist, Glenn Gould.

Unusual interpretations of the Beethoven Fifth are, of course, no nov-

---

Liner notes from Columbia MS 7095, 1968.

elty to the British collector. One calls to mind that elegiac statement Sir Joshua committed to the gramophone in his last years as well as that splendidly spirited rendition transcribed under actual concert conditions by the Newcastle-on-Tyne Light Orchestra upon the occasion of the inadvertent air-alarm of 27 August 1939. But no keyboard version of this work has previously been available in our shops and I fancy that the current issue will find little favour in this country. The entire undertaking smacks of that incorrigible American pre-occupation with exuberant gesture and is quite lacking in those qualities of autumnal repose which a carefully judged interpretation of this work should offer.

Mr. Gould has been absent from British platforms these past few years, and if this new CBS release is indicative of his current musical predilections, perhaps it is just as well.

REPRINTED FROM *MÜNCH'NER MUSIKOLOGISCHE GESELLSCHAFT*

Prof. Dr. Karlheinz Heinkel

Is it not notable that in his poetic cycle "Resonance-on-Rhine" *(Resonanz-am-Rhein)* Klopweisser's second stanza concludes the thought:

> With this oft-strident note let man now pause,
> That who shall hear it, sounding thus, shall see,
> That euphony's the one, sure, sacred cause,
> And taking leave of octave doublings, flee
> To that secured and effortless repose
> Upon that tintinnabulating* key,
> And with that quiet confidence which knows
> Here was a note, here was a middle C.

> *The Collected Klopweisser*
> (Dent and Dent)

Ringen, klingen.

This attitude is brought immediately to the mind since a new record on CBS poses very serious problems as to the resonating capacity of the average middle C. The record comprises a transcription of the Fifth Symphony from Beethoven. The transcription is from Liszt and we can leave the decision as to whether it fulfills the moral obligations pertaining to a transcription of German music to our colleagues in anthropological musikology. The purpose of this present paper is to draw attention to bars 197 and 201 of the first movement of this work, in both of which a middle C is missing. A study of the Liszt Archiv reveals that these notes are absent from the score of the transcription and are not, as one might be tempted to assume, an arbitrary dismissal of two critical notes by the performing artist.

If, then, these notes are dismissed by this Hungarian transcriber we must ask why has this been done? Is it that this transcriber thought to be helping Beethoven? Does he dare to instruct us with our own musik? Does he presume to a private knowledge of Beethoven's notes?

It would be appropriate to remind the reader that these notes form in this work a very significant dissonance, which dissonance, as Professor Kimmerle has pointed, is characteristic of this composer. They are, in fact, C's played by the trumpet *(Trompete)* and take their place in a chord in which the bassoon *(Fagott)* is given to D-flat *(des)*. Without this contradiction, we have a typical, weak diminished chord such as any Hungarian composer could write. With it, we have a master stroke—a truly ugly moment.

Why, then, has Franz Liszt removed this ugliness? Does he presume to lecture to us on the nature of resonance in the Klavier? Does he, in his intolerable conceit, fear to be thought to play a wrong note?

Translated by Mathilde Heinkel
(the former Mattie Green)

REPRINTED FROM *INSIGHT,* DIGEST OF THE NORTH
DAKOTA PSYCHIATRISTS ASSOCIATION

S. F. Lemming, M.D.

Paul D. Hicks, in his recent much-reviewed study "The Unconscious and Career Motivation," notes that most of us in middle life suppress occupational stimuli that, if indulged, would necessitate redirecting ambition-patterns. Among the upper-income stratum in American life, Hicks points out, this tendency is sometimes menopausally motivated, but more frequently, and especially among those active in the professions, it involves the reaffirmation of traumatic associations deriving from childhood resentment pertaining to the intrusion of school discipline upon the parental security pattern. As J. H. Tidy pointed out in his review (March *Insight*) of Hicks's work, much more study will be required before any consensus can be attained.

Nevertheless, with the kind cooperation of Columbia Records' medical staff, your correspondent was able to attend last January several recording sessions in New York City which have provided source material for the present analysis. The musical artist involved was Canadian (Hicks recognized no latitudinal differentiation), mid-thirties (the apex of career contradiction, Hicks points out, is attained prior to the fortieth year), male (Hicks commented that, in the female, disorientation is less pronounced and is in many cases a by-product of resentment associated with incipient grandmother status), and appeared to be possessed of average energy quotients (the sessions usually consisted of two three-hour segments separated by a one-hour dinner break and the work being performed appeared to be of average difficulty).

As recording ensued, however, it became evident that career-disorientation was a major factor. The work selected by the artist was, in fact, intended for symphony orchestra and the artist's choice clearly reflected a desire to assume the authoritarian role of conductor. The ego gratification of this role being denied by a lack of orchestral personnel, the artist delegated the record's producer and engineers as surrogates and, in the course of the session, attempted to demonstrate approval or disapproval of various musical niceties by gesticulating vigorously and in a conductorlike manner. He developed increasingly laconic speech patterns as the sessions progressed (Hicks points out that mutism is frequently, though not invariably, a concomitant) and endeavored to telegraph his desires to the control room by the employment of broad, cue like gestures.

The most impressive evidence deriving from these sessions, however, pertained to the escalatory aspects of Hicks's theory. While leaving the studio upon the conclusion of his assignment the artist was overheard singing various melodies from a composition identified by the producer as having been written by an Austrian composer, Malherr, and which evidently necessitates substantial choral as well as instrumental forces.

REPRINTED FROM *RHAPSODYA,* JOURNAL OF THE
ALL-UNION MUSICAL WORKERS OF BUDAPEST

New York Report   *Zoltán Mostányi*

The winter sun relinquished its halfhearted grasp on Thirtieth and Third. A trace of newly fallen snow endeavored to obscure the heartless granite of the office fronts, to relax the hard, grim profiles of those artless monuments to greed. Released till morning from their bonds of toil, the ill-clad workers, lashed by the dry winds of Manhattan, set off, despairing, into the fast-falling night. Columns of limousines, the bars and telephones within their decadent interiors conspicuously flaunted by seductive purplish parking lights, lined the curbside awaiting the pleasure and emergence of their privileged commanders.

From within a building near this fabled corner, curious sounds wafted upon the evening air. Sounds deceptively familiar—sounds of Beethoven, the democrat, of Liszt, hero of the people. Sounds of Beethoven as understood by Liszt and as prepared by him that he might share some rare, uplifting joy of music with the toiling masses. Sounds perverted and distorted now, sounds turned against the people. Sounds now full of avarice and lust for gain. Within that glib and merciless façade a solitary pianist was forced to do the work of eighty men.

What would you think, beloved Franz, were you to know that your most noble and most charitable enterprise, the product of your love and faith in man, that zealous undertaking through which you sought to bring acquaintance of the master's work to those poor blighted souls, depressed, restricted, by the ducal overlords for whom they labored and whom you, too, so heartily despised, who had no private orchestra to play for them, who had no means by which they might encounter princely pastimes, who had no way of knowing that from Bonn had come a prophet of rebellion—a man of music born to bear the burdens of the masses, to issue proclamations with his harmonies and labor on at themes which served as harbinger of that relentless day of wrath to come—what would you say, if you could know that this, your work, your enterprise, distorted, serves only to enrich the few, impoverish the many.

You played for them, good Franz. You did it all yourself because you had to. No glory did you seek, nor profit either. But eighty men denied the right to work, dear Franz. Eighty men whose cold and sickly children will be colder still tonight. And all because one timid, spineless pianist sold his soul to the enslaving dollar, and in his lustful quest exploited yours.

And as I thought upon these things, I chanced to see a lone musician, weary and dejected, frustrated and disconsolate, emerge into that night. A violinist, vainly seeking work, with instrument in battered case clutched in his hand. Moved to pity, I approached him. "Come, my friend," I said, "let's drink together." Touched, and newly hopeful, he agreed. "Salut," I said, when we'd attained the shelter of a bar found at that night-cloaked corner, "my name's Mostányi, and I understand." "Thank you," he said, "I'm grateful that you do, and mine is Stern."

SOME BEETHOVEN AND BACH CONCERTOS

The B-flat-major Concerto is without doubt the most unjustly maligned of Beethoven's orchestral compositions. Until very recently it has been reserved

Liner notes from Columbia ML 5211 and ML 5298, 1957 and 1958.

for occasional appearance as a curiosity piece, and it is still greeted more often than not with critical reserve.

It is, of course, his first major orchestral composition (it antedates the C-major Concerto, Op. 15, by several years), and it was written at a time when Beethoven's prowess as a solo pianist might well have prompted him to mold a showpiece for his own exhibition. Yet his concern for this work seems to have long outlived his personal need for it, for he not only set about revising it in 1800, at a time when the concertos in C major and C minor were extant, but provided a cadenza for the first movement (much the finest cadenza he ever wrote, too) in an idiom of such rugged motivic sculpture that it can scarcely have been written before 1815.

Yet, though this cadenza is no more an idiomatic extension of the rest of the concerto than *Rosenkavalier* of *Figaro,* it does nevertheless reiterate and further expand the most imposing aspect of Beethoven's structural conception of the first movement—the close interdependence and consistent development of the motivic figures in the very first phrase.

Within this opening phrase the dual thematic character of the classical concerto allegro is summed up. The martial reveille of figure 1 (an inverted Mannheim skyrocket) makes an appropriate gesture of symphonic pomposity, is subtly modified by figure 1A and balanced by the lyric attitude of the consequent motive. At once is depicted that play of aggression and reluctance, of power and of pleading, which is the concerto idea. Now, it can be argued that the alternation of two such motives, of triad intervals followed by a slice of the diatonic scale on a contrasted dynamic plane, is the most familiar and the most obvious method of opening a classical symphonic work. But these motives are not long left in the neat package of the opening sentence. They are tried and fitted with each other and with successive motives, assuming a rhythmical guise consistent with the particular episode and often, especially in the development, remaining recognizable only through this rhythmic adherence.

The opening orchestral tutti omits the advance presentation of the secondary theme (or dominant group), making this the only piano concerto in which it is not presented verbatim (although the G-major Concerto reproduces only part of the subsidiary group). This makes for a tighter, Mozartian exposition and also introduces the one moment of really exotic color. At the point (bar 40) when a half-close on octave C leads one to anticipate the F-major second theme, a truly magical inspiration persuades Beethoven to present a sequence of figure 2 (see above) exalted by the austere relationship of the minor mediant. (He tries the same trick with somewhat less effect in the development section.)

The concluding Rondo, seeming thoroughly earthbound after the magnificent, glowing Adagio, nevertheless exhibits in a much less pretentious way the same interest in motivic compression as does the opening movement. It is notable among the concerto rondos for having as its central episode (G minor) a firm organic continuation of the principal theme. Following the superbly turned cello line in bar 116, the G-minor episode seems the only logical extension.

All in all, a work which does not need the consideration of historical precedence to deserve the epithet "remarkable."

However individual a Beethoven concerto may be in its subjective treatment of the thematic material or the solo-tutti antithesis, there remains from the analyst's point of view the comforting thought that in describing its overall design, one may apply certain analytical yardsticks with confidence. So familiar have we become with the propriety of the classical sonata-allegro that we tend to analyze the work as a series of departures from a harmonic norm which can almost be taken for granted. Thus the D-flat-major (minor mediant) episode in the tutti described above can, by its challenge of the expected, be portrayed almost as a literary idea.

But such blind faith in the inviolability of a harmonic cast is not rewarded in analysis of the baroque concerto. Here one can treat of the melodic delineation of the subject matter or of its application to a fugal exposition, of its rhythmic mating with a countertheme—in short, with every aspect of the baroque style which pertains to melodic principle or to harmonic progression within one particular episode. What does not come so easily is the discovery of a unifying principle of key order which would provide a means of reference through which to define the harmonic adventure of baroque literature or even the work of any one composer. There is much less difference in the thematic key regions habitated by the concertos of Mozart and Rachmaninoff than between any two of the Brandenburg Concertos.

Some historians see the baroque sonata style as a century-long testing ground. They recognize that the modulatory capacity of the tonal orbit gradually evolved while each member of the diatonic solar system found for itself the most favorable relationship with the tonic. In this view the virtual equality of modulation characteristic of the early baroque gradually gives way to fields of greater or lesser gravitational force and eventually merges with the rococo sonata, in which the dominant-tonic altercation has assumed primary importance.

This view has the virtue of historical continuity, and it can cite the fact that the very nature of the long-limbed subject motives so favored in the baroque—especially the Italian baroque—do obviate the necessity of subordinate thematic groups and do encourage the stretto entrance, the fugal exposition, the long retreat in falling sequence from an untenable harmonic position—all devices which must be used sparingly if the climactic impetus of classical tonality is to be preserved. But this view does rather overstate the fact that the baroque is a period of harmonic transition, and in its desire to salute the dawn of the classical era it does deny something of the grandeur which is so obviously lacking when one compares the concertos of Haydn or of Paisiello with the models of Bach or of Pergolesi.

If, on the other hand, one approaches the baroque concerto as a harmonically stable institution, one must attempt to prove each individual movement the product of a forceful and entirely controlled idea. No examples could be more rewarding for that task than the allegro movements of the Bach D-minor Concerto.

The first movement is divided into four main sections, each of which commences with the main theme:

They begin, respectively, (1) in the tonic, D minor, bar 1; (2) in the dominant, A minor, bar 56; (3) in the subdominant, G minor, bar 104; (4) in the tonic, D minor, bar 172. Each of the first three sections (the fourth is a coda which remains in D minor through the end) is in turn subdivided into three sections. Considering their respective tonics as those of the above-mentioned bars 1, 56, and 104, these can be designated as (1) in the tonic, (2) in the dominant (i.e., A minor, E minor, and D minor), and (3) in the mediant (F major, C major, and B-flat major). Each of these sections presents an adaptation of the theme of this first theme. The dominant groups (with the exception of the central episode in E minor, which makes striking use of a neutral figure in the viola) present the motive in sequences of falling fifths passing two and one half times around the diatonic sphere and coming to rest upon the mediant groups, where the theme is given its greatest range of dynamic expression and its most ingeniously disconnected profile.

It should be noted also that the character of the dominant episodes within the first and third groups (i.e., the episodes in A minor, bar 22, and D minor, bar 116) do not anticipate or usurp the function of the principal divisions beginning in those keys, bars 56 and 172. In other words, despite the authentic modulations which precede both types of episode, one might say that they illustrate Sir Donald Tovey's distinction between being *in* the dominant and being *on* it.

If space permitted, the final movement would be shown to follow the same structural procedure. It consists of three divisions, the first two (tonic and subdominant) being subdivided in the same manner as the first movement and followed by an extended coda. Unlike the first movement, however, the three sections are linked by transitions which fancifully elaborate the main theme.

Whether or not the ear can recognize in this type of development the psychological strategy which it appreciates in the classical sonata form, the fact must remain that as an individual instance these movements are as tightly interwoven in the harmonic relationships of the various sections and as scrupulously organized as any sonata structure thereafter. Whether there is a common denominator which one could apply to the baroque concerto and concerto-grosso literature, or whether each work must prove to have been designed with a special harmonic framework erected to house its unique thematic attributes, remains an open question. Perhaps if one made a really systematic excavation in the early Italian baroque one might discover the real foundation on which the monuments of baroque culture have settled. To my knowledge, it is a study which has never adequately been undertaken but one which could reap handsome rewards.

Bach's F-minor Concerto appeared as a keyboard work at Leipzig around 1730 but is almost certainly a transcription of an earlier violin concerto. If the original is by Bach (a matter of considerable dispute), it is likely to have been composed at Köthen a decade earlier.

Bach made little effort to rework the material in a manner suitable for solo keyboard. In the first movement the player's right hand reproduces eminently violinistic figures throughout the solo passages while the left hand is filling the role of the continuo which the original possessed: that is to say, it consistently doubles the cello line of the orchestra without attempting to embellish it in the solo passages. Only during the pedal point C (bars 96–101) does the left hand undertake to remind us of the central rhythmic motive of the movement:

By comparison, the transcription for clavier in G minor of the A-minor Violin Concerto is an embarrassment of fancy.

The second movement gives the solo instrument its due with a bewitching cantilena which lies so well beneath the fingers and is so generously ornamented that it is hard to conceive of its belonging to any but a keyboard instrument.

The Presto finale with its brilliantly woven tutti theme

and the perfect rejoinder of the principal solo theme

is the happiest and most adventurous of the three movements. It is also the most representative of the baroque concerto style, which reached its zenith with Bach and Pergolesi.

It is easy for us to misinterpret the intentions of the baroque concerto. We are unable to analyze its formal outline by searching for comparisons with the classical sonata style. By this measure it seems devoid of harmonic direction, to lack the points of culmination, the areas of resolution, which the sonata-style movements provide. Again, by comparison with the bravura concertos of the nineteenth century, it would seem as though the concertos of Bach were, from the soloistic standpoint, simply the first tentative concessions to the emerging ego of the virtuoso.

The baroque concerto subscribed to harmonic principles as scrupulously organized as, but of entirely different intentions from, the classical concerto. Formally the outer movements are closely allied to the cantata-aria style. The element of contrast of dynamic range—the heart of the concerto idea—is just as much in evidence but is achieved by direct rather than devious means. Instead of the subtle gradations of modulation in classical tonality we have the straightforward opposition of texture and dynamic level. The above excerpts illustrate the contrast of solid block harmony (tutti) and finely woven strands of stretto counterpoint (solo). The ingredient of modulation, of contrasting tonal regions, is altogether absent. When Bach modulates, it is to present again the majority of his material in the new key—or keys, since frequently his modulation is of a compound sort in which several closely related areas form one larger digression. It follows that since the baroque concerto does not equate change of key and change of theme, the formal principle involved will utilize a more restricted thematic vocabulary. The essential thing in Bach's bithematic relationships is not their individuality but their interdependence.

Even during Bach's lifetime the word "concerto" came to represent a very different sort of structure. With Bach's sons the ternary principle developed into the more expansive sonata-allegro, which subsequently came to dominate all symphonic form. Essentially, so far as the concerto repertoire was concerned, this change was concentrated on the relationship between tutti and solo. With Johann Christian Bach the opening tutti became a modulatory structure. It adopted a triangular shape, passing to the dominant (frequently without firmly establishing it) and returning before the entrance of the soloist. Thus the element of expectancy was added.

But the tutti had become much more than a fanfare. It had added a new dimension to first-movement structure. With Haydn the modulatory aim of the tutti expanded. The dominant became more than the apex of the triangle. It served to exhibit the principal theme in the new key in a manner which closely resembled the format of the main exposition with the soloist. The orchestral exposition having established the precedence of thematic order, the soloist was free to treat the material ornamentally and discursively.

The great problem which remained was a psychological one—that of trying the listeners' patience by a double exposition. The structural implications of this problem were clearly grasped by Mozart. In his later concertos the orchestral exposition is enlarged to unprecedented size. He not infrequently includes material which is left untouched by the main exposition with the solo instrument but which suddenly reappears in the recapitulation. Thus the mature concertos of Mozart achieve structural unity of the opening orchestral tutti and the principal exposition. This is accomplished by maintaining the tutti in the tonic key, most frequently by omitting reference to the principal secondary theme, reserving its first presentation for the solo instrument, and by a complex orchestral unfoldment of the main thematic group of the movement.

The most awkward area for Mozart is that of the piano entrance through the transition to the secondary key. Obviously the soloist is reluctant to plunge in with the same material which has been so thoroughly developed by the orchestra. If the piano entrance is to make the impression which several minutes of tutti warrant, either it must use new material which is at once arresting and eloquent but which sets no further problems of development, or it must surmount the theme of the tutti in a noble but neutral manner. The latter method is illustrated by the solo entrance in Mozart's Concerto K. 467, with its long shake over the principal motive, but the former method, that of an entirely new theme, is the more frequent occurrence in Mozart.

With Beethoven the orchestra-solo relationship reached the peak of its development. It was with the Fourth Concerto, in G major, that the ultimate of condensation, of unity with the solo exposition, of imagination, and of discipline was attained. The first three concertos, those in B-flat major, C major, and C minor, each attack the problem of the tutti from a different angle and with varying degrees of success. Though it was the earliest of the three, the Concerto in B-flat major, Op. 19, has by far the best-constructed exposition. Here Beethoven adopts the Mozartian trait of omitting the second theme, presenting instead an intriguing variant of a portion from the opening motive. This fragment appears in the tutti cast in the subdued light of D-flat major, which with its close relation to the tonic minor is, in effect, a compromise for modulation.

The Concerto in C minor, while of undeniable breadth and vigor, is as a piece of construction much the weakest of the lot. Here the tutti virtually duplicates the principal exposition. The secondary theme is represented in the relative key, thus disenchanting the later solo statement, and the keyboard entrance is a doubling of the opening measures of the tutti.

The tutti of the present concerto is built more on Mozartian lines. The second theme is present but is introduced in the key of E-flat major, which stands in similar relationship to the tonic as does the D-flat-major episode in the B-flat major Concerto. Indeed, the treatment of it here is not so very different. The E-flat-major statement launches a sequential episode which reaches its climax on the dominant of C minor, and thus the quality of intensive movement within strict harmonic bounds is preserved.

This concerto does present a rather troubled aspect with the initial entrance of the solo instrument. This is the only Beethoven concerto in which the opening piano statement does not again appear after the orchestral transition to the development section, which is, in a way, rather fortunate, since the neutrality of content which was discussed in relation to Mozart's opening themes is here an obsequity of manner quite uncharacteristic of Beethoven. Having dispensed a dutiful twelve bars of nothing, the movement continues on conventional lines. The second movement is a rather lethargic nocturne with an overly repetitive main theme possessed of the typically nocturnal habit of pleading the case once too often.

Of all Beethoven concerto movements, the final rondo owes most to Haydn. It has the characteristically Haydnesque lucidity, economy (not excepting the thematically unrelated central episode in A minor, which in its nonconformity is Haydnesque also), and infectious charm.

A word about the cadenzas.

I can scarcely hope to conceal the fact that my cadenzas to the first and last movements of the Beethoven Concerto in C are hardly in pure Beethoven style. In recent years it has become the commendable practice of musicians to contribute cadenzas which observe an idiomatic identification with the concerto subject. It should also be remarked that the more discreet and tasteful among us have reserved their contributions for those concertos which have no cadenza by the author. That these historical qualms were not always prevalent is amply demonstrated by the great many nineteenth-century writers (including Brahms) who undertook to produce cadenzas for various older works without forgoing their customary vocabulary. In writing these cadenzas I had in mind a contrapuntal potpourri of motives which was possible only in an idiom considerably more chromatic than that of early Beethoven. Thus the cadenza to the first movement turned out to be a rather Regerian fugue, while that to the last movement became a rhapsody built to span the gap between the fermata six-four and the subdued re-entrance of the orchestra in B major. Both, in other words, effect an organic balance with the work, thereby of course denying the original purpose of cadenza writing as a virtuosic display. At any event I have not yet requested the orchestra to file to the balcony while for three glorious minutes the piano is hung decorously from the chandelier.

N'AIMEZ-VOUS PAS BRAHMS?

In a recent, widely discussed testimonial, Mr. Leonard Bernstein drew attention to what he considered certain departures from the interpretative norm in my conception of the Brahms D-minor Concerto. Prior to a performance with the New York Philharmonic, he suggested that it was the most leisurely, in some ways the most intractable, interpretation he had ever heard. As descriptive comment, both of these remarks were quite justified—it was (is) a remarkably leisurely performance, and it held tenaciously to the leisure of its pace (and hence became intractable) throughout. However, the gentlemen of the New York press, who are always eager to have their reviews written for them, were quick to translate leisure as turgidity, tenacity as pigheadedness, and to suggest that undoubtedly one of the classic conductor-soloist feuds was under way. In point of fact, nothing of the kind was taking place. Mr. Bernstein, while totally disagreeing with my view of the work, generously adventured to support my interpretation, and so what resulted, while it may have been arbitrary, was not, at least, a performance in which the components were at odds. We were not by any means engaged in one of those celebrated duels of "anything you can do I can do slower." In fact, the only aspect of Mr. Bernstein's substantially misinterpreted remarks which troubles me somewhat is the conclusion that the oddities of this performance were perhaps calculated per se, were used as attention-getting devices without relation to the musical requirements of the score.

If this had been true, it would have stood in direct contradiction to my views of the nineteenth-century concerto, because I believe that as a genre the concerto has long been a vastly overindulged form. It is no accident that the really successful concertos—successful in both a public and even in some instances an acoustical sense—were written by second-rate composers: Grieg and Liszt, for instance, composers singularly lacking in a grasp of real symphonic architecture. On the other hand, the monumental figures like Beethoven and Brahms almost always come off second best as concerto writers, perhaps because their native sensibilities balk at pampering the absurd conventions of the concerto structure: the orchestral pre-exposition setup, to titillate the listener's expectation of a grand dramatic entrance for the soloist; the tiresomely repetitive thematic structure, arranged to let the soloist prove that he really can turn that phrase to a more rakish tilt than the fellow on first clarinet who just announced it, and above all the outdated aristocracy

Previously unpublished; written c. 1962.

of cadenza writing—the posturing trills and arpeggios, all twitteringly super-fluous to the fundamental thematic proposition. All these have helped to build a concerto tradition which has provided some of the most embarrassing musical examples of the primeval human need for showing off. All these have helped to substantiate the outrageous ego of the soloist. The peculiarities, then, of my interpretation largely concern themselves with an attempt to sub-ordinate the soloist's role, not to aggrandize it—to integrate rather than to isolate.

This is an odd work. It has always been something of a problem child. Its earlier incarnations as sonata for two pianos and as symphonic fragment suggest that even to Brahms, to whom symphonic sculpture never came easi-ly, this one was a special nuisance. And the final result, the concerto, is one of those works that one feels do not quite come off, are not entirely in balance architecturally. Nevertheless, no quibbles about its skeletal stamina can com-promise an admiration for the incredible imagination which Brahms brought to bear upon this work. With all its architectural deficiencies it is the most intriguing of Brahms's orchestral scores. And so one wants to do it—one wants to find a way over its difficult moments and luxuriate in its incompara-ble strokes; and one hundred years of performance have added layers of inter-pretative gesture which have gradually clouded, it seems to me, some of the real strengths, and weaknesses, of this score.

Its strength and its weakness are bound together. One cannot separate architecturally the astonishing nonconformity of its opening measures—the triadic expostulation of B-flat major as the opening of a D-minor work and the confirmation of its chromatic stubbornness by that mysterious A-flat in the third measure—one cannot disassociate all this from the exigencies of formal symphonic behavior to which it ultimately does conform: the poker-faced, absolutely verbatim recapitulation of the secondary the-matic group, for instance. In fact, it is this very struggle of the imag-ination—imperfect, protruding, slapping life into the work—against the demands of the classical exercise, the academic situation to which Brahms ultimately surrendered, that makes this piece so peculiar and enigmatic.

Now, obviously one can deal with such a work in two quite different ways. One can stress its drama, its contrasts, its angularities, and can treat the opposition of thematic tonal relations as a coalition of inequalities. This is the fashionable way to interpret romantic music these days. This way reads into it a plot full of surprises, a moral position full of contradictions. It ap-proaches the perfunctory conventions of the classical sonata structure and its inherent and largely stereotyped plan with a naiveté which accepts the masculine-feminine contrast of theme as an end in itself. Alternatively, one can read the future into Brahms. One can see it as Schoenberg would have seen it: a sophisticated interweaving of a fundamental motivic strand; one can read into it the analytical standpoints of our own day.

And this, essentially, is what I have done. I have valued this structure for its similarities; I have chosen to minimize its contrasts. I have deliberately ignored the masculine-feminine contrasts of theme which have become the cornerstone of sentiment in the classical concerto tradition, because I believe that they have been vastly overstated. As a consequence, I have in the last movement, for instance, adopted a tempo which holds rather relentlessly to its starting pace—at least until at the end Brahms indicates first a brief meno mosso (slightly slower) and then più mosso (slightly faster). I have not attempted to expand the second statement, which is a convenient piano solo, into a dramatic posturing of the soloist's importance. And, similarly, in the first movement I have attempted to shift gears between the main thematic strands as unobtrusively as possible. In the process, certain traditional accents have been avoided; certain dynamic proclamations have been understated; certain opportunities for the soloist to take the reins firmly in hand have been bypassed. And the result, perhaps, is a singularly unspectacular approach to this work. It is not a conciliatory approach, but I do not by any means propose that this is the only way to do Brahms—or to do this piece. Yet I feel that it is an approach which takes cognizance of the nature of the piece and that, within its own necessary limits, it works.

SHOULD WE DIG UP THE RARE ROMANTICS? . . . NO, THEY'RE ONLY A FAD

When the new Juilliard School of Music was officially declared open for tutorial business, courtesy of a network TV commitment a few weeks back, the program selected for the occasion—and entrusted to three of that academy's more celebrated alumni, Van Cliburn, Shirley Verrett, and Itzhak Perlman—at once offered a determined italicization of the "Performing Arts" clause in the charter of Juilliard's host organization, Lincoln Center; a pertinent reminder that academic sponsorship is in itself no guarantee of repertorial integrity; and a worthy contender for the title of "All-Time Awful

First published in the *New York Times*, November 23, 1969.

Inaugural," which I had previously awarded to Montreal's Crystal Palace Association for a concert on the occasion of Canada's Confederation in 1867, which offered Verdi's *Nabucco* Overture followed by a flute soliloquy from *Lucia di Lammermoor*, Beethoven's First Symphony, a violin solo entitled "Souvenirs de Bellini," a song called "The Day Is Done" by Balfe, Mendelssohn's G-minor Piano Concerto, and, since this was not yet the half of it, intermission.

For the Juilliard's opening exercises the bill of fare was perhaps a bit less ambitious and, relatively, a good deal less contemporary, consisting of the first movement from Paganini's Violin Concerto in D, Mozart's "Alleluia" (the tuneful part of his cantata "Exsultate, jubilate"), a roulade-ridden air from Donizetti's *Anna Bolena*, and Franz Liszt's perennially fascinating, if perpetually unsatisfying, First Piano Concerto. There was, to be sure, one item which would have provided a welcome talking-point for any such dedicatory occasion one hundred and twenty years or so ago, and would have been indicative indeed of the more progressive notions of music theatre abroad at the time—Wagner's first- and third-act preludes to *Lohengrin*. But this offering was tailored to the talents of a distinguished guest maestro, Leopold Stokowski, admittedly not a Juilliard grad, and hence perhaps not as yet privy to the latest innovations in program planning.

For, indeed, the most depressing fact about the Juilliard extravaganza was that, while it may well have come to pass through no greater absence of mind than can be attributed to the traditional pedagogic disdain for programmatic cohesion and been intended, in view of the TV exposure, as a prime-time commercial for the American academic knowhow which makes for better living through sharper double-stopping, it managed, however inadvertently, to ally itself with the most recent of those fads which have been pressed into service in a last-ditch attempt to revitalize the concert experience: the romantic, virtuoso-cult revival.

This current renaissance began innocently enough. A few years back, it was the occasional practice of institutions to commission in honor of a state celebration or the like a simulation, or indeed a verbatim reproduction, of the sort of mixed-means grab bag which I uncovered in the Crystal Palace files. The air on such occasions would be thick with nostalgia, the costumes (it was the beginning of that uneasy merger of concert music and theatre) as authentic as a rummage through the available attics of a Ladies Committee could make them. No one, least of all the artists involved, took the matter seriously. A sense of perspective was everywhere in evidence, and the performers were praised as generously for the acquisition of those comic gifts required to keep a straight face—while dashing off cascades of octaves in which one note in six might celebrate some thematic permutation—as for their technical accomplishments and archival initiative.

Then, in no time at all, someone observed that, in an age when comedy is serious business, these diversions were not being given due respect. The attitude at once gained support from that venerable academic assumption that it's a privilege to suffer, in the interests of historical exactitude, those things which could never be borne as entertainment, and from the rather more fashionable premise that, in an era for which the archetypal musical product is the stylistic potpourri, the proper pursuit of eclecticism augurs the abandonment of those highly stratified criteria traditionally employed to define the work of art. All sound sources, Mr. McLuhan has assured us, are music at heart; and to require from them that dramatic cohesion which in less enlightened times—say, a generation back—was presumed to demarcate the romantic symphony, string quartet, or sonata, is as snobbish and unrealistic as it is bad for business. Even the veneer of the romantic showpiece should be welcome in this Malrauvian museum, since, in its total innocence of any contrapuntal involvement, it provides an object lesson upon the folly of subsurface expectations. The cunning thing, of course, is the way in which these arguments, normally employed by the proponents of avant-garde music theatre, have been enlisted in order, simultaneously, to neutralize the one group which might otherwise have stood in opposition and to convey the notion that interest in romantic music, prior to the intervention of its present sponsors, was on the wane (it wasn't) and that this handful of mercifully neglected musical exhibitionists currently on view genuinely represent the spirit of their age (they don't).

It's no accident, of course, that the initial beneficiary in this return to candelabra music should be the one form which made the transition from classicism to romanticism with most fuss and least grace—the concerto. The recent Schwann notes a release of Scharwenka's B-flat-minor horror of 1877 from RCA; CBS has retaliated with a production of von Henselt's F-minor exercise in narcissism; and it's only a matter of time until someone looks into Moszkowski's E-major. Unlike its companion forms—sonatas, string quartets, and symphonies—the concerto offered a surfeit of these redundant gestures and contrived dichotomies which were beloved by nineteenth-century concertgoers, it's true, but which, as the product of the clash of values induced by the merger of that century's mechanistic preoccupations with the formal controls of the eighteenth, were, in fact, simply classical conventions adapted to a romantic environment. Most of the polarities we regard as indigenous to the romantic concerto—the double exposition, the once-straight-for-them, once-inflected-for-me thematic layouts, for instance—became, well before the midpoint of the nineteenth century, tactical embarrassments which only the most skilled strategists could deploy; and the concerto—at least those more grotesque hybrids favored in the current lists—no more represents the true spirit of the romantic age than the first autumnal nudge of a polar high-pressure system applied to a maritime-tropic encampment on the central plains represents winter.

Of course, for that great silent majority (as Mr. Nixon might define it) composed of those of us without any doctrinal axes to grind, romantic music never has, in fact, suffered an eclipse. Most students in my conservatory days found it expedient to contribute vague rumblings of discontent about the "formlessness" of Berlioz, the "bombast" of Elgar, or the "loquacity" of Reger; but proclamations of that kind were simply a hedge against peer-group pressure—the neoclassic and neobaroque revivals of those decades provided the main bones of contention with one's elders, after all, and the generation gap had to be kept open somehow. Most of us, in fact, were devoted secret sippers, and once we'd ascertained that the family was securely bedded down for the night, we would spirit Klemperer's "Resurrection" Symphony or Mengelberg's *Heldenleben* off the shelves and wonder what the world might have become if the distractions of keeping "in" and keeping "up" had never been allowed to cloud the issue.

It is, in fact, rather difficult to maintain a blind spot about any hundred years, and well nigh impossible to nurture a myopic condition of that magnitude when the century in question has been enriched by talents of such opulence as Wagner, such elegance as Mendelssohn, such futuristic perception as Scriabin. Individual blind spots, of course, must be encouraged, since they have the happy faculty of providing incentives for theses and platforms for critics. *The New Yorker*'s Winthrop Sargeant, for instance, has devoted many columns through the years to his belief in the present vindication and ultimate victory of Anton Bruckner; and if, in relation to the domestic market, he's proved right on that one and you're looking for a hot tip for the later 1970s, try Franz Schmidt. But campaigns such as Mr. Sargeant's were more modestly conducted, and there was usually an aura of "isn't it a pity that the rest of you don't understand" about the propaganda that ensued which was sufficiently earnest and affecting to make us at least want to try. Behind the foursquare rhythms of Anton Bruckner, of course, there may well be concealed a foursquare mentality, but Mr. Sargeant's entreaties in Bruckner's behalf are sensibly confined to those points which substantiate the idea of an enigmatic presence.

Right or not as to Bruckner, this approach is faithful to the prime tenets of romanticism—which have to do, after all, with an extension of resource through ambiguity and with the idea that every observable phenomenon has its concealed, psychological shadow. Just as that four-tone harmonic unit worked to death by most romantics—the diminished seventh chord—had as its surface manifestation an apparent reluctance to resolve which could be ruthlessly exploited for its physical presence alone (as Franz Liszt proved in his less lucid moments), it also possessed a multitonic orientation which could serve not only as a phrase pivot but also as a nucleus for the paragraphic structure on which whole works were based (as Bruckner demonstrated so subtly in the tritonic modulation plan of his Eighth Symphony's first movement). Much romantic music makes a similar distinction between an objective phenomenon and the psychological response which it presupposes. At its best, it's not the sort of repertoire that fads can flatter, and with its penchant for concealment it's not even, necessarily, a happy hunting ground for virtuosos. But it does, at that best, represent the last stand of a world determined to circumvent what it conceived of as the limits of quantification, and in view of the many hours of low-fi listening that folks of my generation put in to maintain our midnight indulgences of that conception, it would be a great shame at this late date to let the Juilliard and their ilk persuade us otherwise.

PIANO MUSIC BY GRIEG AND BIZET, WITH A CONFIDENTIAL CAUTION TO CRITICS

Edvard Grieg's Piano Sonata was written in 1865; Bizet's Nocturne and Variations chromatiques, three years later. For those who subscribe to the theory that recording is an inherently archival, as opposed to miscellany-gathering, activity, our text on this occasion will be drawn from century 19, decade 7, part 3.

Unfortunately for the undersigned, the text, as opposed to the theory above-mentioned or, indeed, the music at hand, is uncongenial. If I were to deal with it explicitly, invoking appropriate parallels, stressing pertinent contradictions—acknowledging, in effect, the "compare and contrast" commandment of academia—I should be required to emphasize that both composers operated within a milieu that, according to all subsequent wisdom, was dominated by the very fact of that most upheaval-inducing phenomenon of the "romantic" age—*Tristan und Isolde*.

Now, as it happens, I love *Tristan*. I was fifteen when I heard it first, and wept. These days, needless to say, the tear ducts are out of practice—the

Liner notes from Columbia M 32040, 1973.

psychologically meddlesome, and medically unsound, prohibitions respecting approved emotive patterns for the Occidental male have seen to that. Yet, given a hard day, a late night, and a sequence or two from the "Liebestod," the spine tingles and the throat is seized by a catch that no other music, this side of Orlando Gibbons's anthems, can elicit with equivalent intensity and predictability.

The trouble is: to acknowledge *Tristan* without qualification—to ascribe to it more than subjective impressions—tacitly suggests that one acknowledges as well what I should like to call the "Plateau, Peak, and Precipice" concept of history. Oh, no one else calls it that; but, however unwittingly, most folk offer it accreditation, and *Tristan*, for this century at least, has served the concept as linchpin.

Another servant of the concept and, by no coincidence whatever, worshiper of *Tristan*, was one Arnold Schoenberg—a gentleman persuaded that his own evolution was possessed of Darwinian inexorability (which it may well have been), that *Tristan* provided the incentive for that climate of ambiguity which eventually led to his personal rejection of tonal orientation (which is quite probably the case), and that, by inference, his relationship to Wagner, and any other elder masters you'd care to weigh into the bargain, was one of mantle-ee to mantle-or. Most devout Schoenbergians reasoned similarly, and the list of linchpins grew accordingly—Monteverdi's *Orfeo*, Bach's *The Art of the Fugue*, or any half-dozen Stamitz symphonies (select one only or move directly to jail; do not pass Go and do not collect 200 florins). The converted patriarch Igor Stravinsky nominated Beethoven's "Grosse Fuge," and, in perhaps the most memorable of all linchpin pronouncements, Ernst Krenek avowed that Gesualdo's chromaticism might, but for the inconsiderate intervention of three centuries, have led directly to Wagner. This latter statement, to be fair, and if judged according to the lights of its own zeitgeistlich standards (it was issued, after all, some thirty years ago, when Gesualdo's crimes and times were less exposed to public scrutiny), contained a real measure of insight. It did, however, like all such proclamations, impose long-range linear goals as ultimate criteria and, however inadvertently, convey the impression that God is on the side of enharmonic relationships.

Needless to say, such relationships abound in each of the works included in this album, with Bizet's self-advertising Variations understandably taking a commanding lead in the "accidentals" sweepstakes. None of these works, however, achieves—or, more to the point, strives for—that state of ecstatic prolongation which is the true legacy of *Tristan*, and to judge any of them according to such criteria would be akin to the demand that Sibelius's Fifth Symphony (1914) abandon its suave, romantically cultivated syntax in favor of the motoric punctuation of *Le Sacre* (1913), or that *Le Bourgeois Gentil-*

homme (1918) relinquish its amiable evocation of the rococo past in order to sample the expressionist "present" of *Pierrot Lunaire* (1912). The calendar, after all, is a tyrant; submission to its relentless linearity, a compromise with creativity; the artist's prime responsibility, a quest for that spirit of detachment and anonymity which neutralizes and transcends the competitive intimidation of chronology.

In any event, whatever the expectations, the facts are as follows: Grieg's Op. 7 is a secure, smoothly articulated, postgraduate exercise in which chromatic embellishments enliven an occasionally complacent paragraphic symmetry. The composer's confidence with large-scale forms—in later years, always the effective miniaturist, he became estranged from the sonata concept per se—peaked early in his career, and, indeed, the celebrated Piano Concerto (1868) was a product of his twenty-fifth year. Like the latter work, the E-minor Sonata best conveys its author's geographic distinction—i.e., independence from Austro-German symphonic tradition—by frequent, though entirely nonviolent, resistance to the proclivities of the leading tone and appropriate amendments to the motivic conceits involved. Whatever the mood prevailing in these early works, the innovatory content—the quirk quotient, to recoin one of my own pet phrases—is introduced, much as in the case of Dvořák, with beguilingly unassertive good humor.

Bizet's Variations chromatiques is, in my opinion, one of the very few masterpieces for solo piano to emerge from the third quarter of the nineteenth century; its almost total neglect is a phenomenon for which I can offer no reasonable explanation. Like every opus by this extraordinary composer, from that posthumously discovered teen-age gem, the Symphony in C, onward, the Variations chromatiques is a work that, harmonically, never puts a wrong foot forward. And the harmonic path chosen (one suspects primarily as an experiment, since Bizet could utilize, with equal effect, idioms of relatively unencumbered diatonicism) is a trail strewn with chromatic detours, and on which the possibility of landslide is an ever-present threat. That all such roadblocks are deftly circumvented is a tribute not only to the composer's supremely efficient technique but also to the imaginative, and picturesque, route that he charts and follows throughout.

Even when divorced from the music it maps out, this route is a logician's delight. The "theme"—in essence, a chaconne motive—is simplicity itself: Two chromatic scales—one upward-bound, the other inverted—are punctuated cadentially by open octaves delineating the tonic triad of C minor. The first seven variations—there are fourteen in all—uphold the minor mode, and, in a gesture befitting the even-handed disposition of the theme, the remaining seven adhere to the major. A coda ensues, apparently intent upon lending support to the C-major set; then, almost absentmindedly at first, but, subsequently, with increasing emphasis and conviction, E-flats and A-flats are added to the texture; in due course, D-flats and G-flats tip the balance unequivocally, moody remnants of the "theme" reappear, and the work has come full circle to C minor. The D-major Nocturne, though a less adventuresome concoction, is no less sophisticated. Chiefly concerned with frustrating the cadential inclinations of a melody of Methodistic primness, and coyly telegraphing this intention by an introductory four bars' worth of arpeggiated diminished sevenths, it achieves its aim—one can't say with exemplary directness, since exemplary directness is the very quality Bizet seeks to deny the work—with, let's try it on its own terms, exemplary indecisiveness.

A CONFIDENTIAL CAUTION TO CRITICS

Gentlemen:
For many of you, this disc may well constitute a first exposure to the piano works of Bizet; it did for me, and I share with you the joy of discovery. This repertoire, however, lacks representation in the Schwann catalogue and—although I do not attend recitals—turns up, I should guess, infrequently, if at all, on concert programs. You may, consequently, be at a loss for a yardstick with which to evaluate the performances contained herein.

For those of you who greet the release with enthusiasm, therefore, I should like to propose a phrase such as ". . . vividly and forcefully, as only a first reading can, it partakes of that freshness, innocence, and freedom from tradition that, as the late Artur Schnabel so deftly remarked, is but a 'collection of bad habits.' " On the other hand, for those in doubt as to the validity of the interpretations involved, I venture to recommend a conceit such as ". . . regrettably, a performance that has not as yet jelled; an interpretation that is still in search of an architectural overview." And, of course, for those who prefer to remain, so to speak, on the fence, a structure along the lines of ". . . though, regrettably, a performance that has not as yet jelled, this is, nonetheless, an interpretation that partakes of that freshness, innocence, and freedom from tradition of which the late Artur Schnabel so deftly . . . etc.," should serve.

The burden of this memorandum, however, is to direct your attention to one aspect of the relatively more familiar music contained on side 1 that may well have escaped your notice and that could, potentially, lead to an embarrassing incident: Edvard Grieg was a cousin of my maternal great-grandfather. My mother, née Florence Greig, maintained, as did all the Scotch branch of the clan, the "ei" configuration, while Grieg's great-grandfather, one John Greig, crossed the North Sea in the 1740s, settled in Bergen, and inverted the vowels so as to afford a more appropriately Nordic ring to the family name. As will be readily apparent, any intemperate critical discussion of the performance at hand, therefore—especially along the lines adopted by the Bizet disparagement (see phrase sample 2 above)—would be tantamount to a suggestion that Clara Schumann was misinformed about the inner workings of the worthy Robert's A-minor Concerto.

The sonata, of course, though hardly a repertoire staple, is played and recorded from time to time, and some of you may well feel that my response to it is at almost perverse pains to underline those dour, curiously dispassionate qualities of Ibsenesque gloom that I feel to be on predominant display in even the earliest works of cousin Edvard. Consequently, for those who would espouse a more uptempo, quasi-Lisztian rendition of the work, such epithets as "presumably authentic" or "nonetheless, unquestionably authoritative" will suffice; and, needless to say, in the comments of those inclined to a genuinely enthusiastic response, I look forward to such encomiums as "the very stuff of history," "a truly legendary encounter," or, perhaps, "never, in the annals of recording, has the generation gap been bridged with such unquestionable authority, such incontrovertible authenticity."

Well, I can dream, can't I? Happy to be of help.

Yours respectfully,
Glenn Gould

DATA BANK ON THE
UPWARD-SCUTTLING MAHLER

"Mahler: His Time Has Come!" bannered the September 1967 cover of the record trade mag *High Fidelity*. The proclamation heralded the issue's lead article—a three-thousand-word coming-out party thrown by the soon-to-retire Kapellmeister of the New York Philharmonic, Leonard Bernstein, which jointly celebrated the merits of the Austrian composer and Bernstein's own execution of the first integral recorded edition of Mahler's nine (completed) symphonies.

Nor was Bernstein laboring in isolation in Mahler's behalf at the time—Georg Solti and Rafael Kubelik, with the enthusiastic connivance of their respective labels, had similar integral editions on the drawing boards,

Review of *Mahler*, Volume One, by Henry-Louis de La Grange (New York: Doubleday, 1973); from *Piano Quarterly*, Spring 1974.

and each of their component discs, when separately released, could be counted on to vie with other phono fads of the sixties—Satie, Nielsen, Walter Carlos on the Moog—atop the *Billboard* charts. Less comprehensively, but not necessarily less authoritatively, other Mahler platters were forthcoming from the old guard (Klemperer, Horenstein), the middle generation (Leinsdorf, Abravanel), and the young Turks (Haitink, Maazel), while perhaps the record that best measured the magnitude of the Mahler bandwagon in the sixties was Eugene Ormandy's reading of the Symphony No. 10—a projected five-movement work, only two-fifths complete at the time of the composer's death, and which, through a feat of ciphering that rivaled the Pentagon's breakthrough with the Japanese naval code in 1941, was completed, according to indications hieroglyphically implicit in the composer's sketches, by the English Mahlerologist, Deryck Cooke.

As the seventies dawned, Pierre Boulez, Bernstein's successor at the Philharmonic and, as a doctrinaire serialist, a man who had previously managed to contain his enthusiasm for the post romantic repertoire, made his contribution to the Mahler archives with a recording of the early—and, in Boulez's view, unjustly neglected—cantata *Das klagende Lied.* The composer Luciano Berio, in the course of a work titled Sinfonia, supered a surrealistic gloss upon the third movement of the "Resurrection" Symphony—a movement which Mahler himself had based upon his charming, but not notably symphonic, *Des Knaben Wunderhorn* song "St. Anthony's Sermon to the Fishes." And, to round out a straw poll of Mahler activists among the "avant-garde," it might not go amiss to point out that the author of this massive biography, Henry-Louis de La Grange, garnered a foreword from the guru of the sufi set, Karlheinz Stockhausen. In his introductory notes, Stockhausen, who with each passing pronouncement sounds more and more like a character invented by Hermann Hesse, assures us that "Mahler is a myth—Mahler is this book. Mahler was only transitorily a human being.—Readers of this book will be magically transformed into Mahler." Well, we'll have to wait and see about that!

Mahler, of course, never lacked for advocates: Bruno Walter was a tireless champion for more than half a century; Leopold Stokowski was quick to spot the DeMille-like aspects of the Eighth (the "Symphony of a Thousand") and offered Philadelphia the American premiere in 1916; and, to a man, the Amsterdam Concertgebouw, encouraged by the missionary work of Willem Mengelberg, custodially preserved the Mahlerian collection until, with the Netherlands under Nazi occupation, the composer's non-Aryan background rendered his output symphonia non grata.

But the advocacy of such self-proclaimed radicals as Boulez, Berio, and Stockhausen could not have been predicted by even the most optimistic Mahler booster as recently as twenty years ago, and the change in attitude reveals at least as much about the temper of our times as about the long-range prospects for the Mahlerian canon. One might venture a guess that to Boulez, the attraction would be Mahler's pointillistic handling of the orchestra; to Stockhausen, his attempt to synopsize and transcend all experience through art ("Waves, rainbows, polyphonic composition, must all be approached in the same way," Mahler wrote in 1900); while to Berio, Mahler's mania for montage, his delight in mingling the ridiculous with the sublime, would be a key.

But Mahler has also had his detractors; and if his reputation—unlike that of his contemporaries Hans Pfitzner and Franz Schmidt—was never an exclusively Central European phenomenon and, it is profoundly to be hoped, will not now become a passing fancy of the tweeter testers, his works do impose unusual musical and psychological demands upon the auditor. For his proponents, Mahler's symphonies may count among music's rarest joys— earth-shaking, world-defying, heaven-scaling pronouncements. But for others, they remain bombastic, indulgent, contrapuntally undisciplined ego trips, and his songs—particularly the *Knaben Wunderhorn* set, the material of which is inextricably bound up with the symphonies—naive evocations of a medieval mythscape that seems curiously at odds with the real world inhabited by the sophisticated bureaucrat and ruthlessly ambitious virtuoso conductor who authored them.

For both camps, however, de La Grange's biography is a godsend. The author, though obviously a committed Mahlerian—he devoted almost two decades to the task—has deliberately eschewed any attempt at interpretation. He simply gives us the facts of Mahler's first forty years—volume 2 will cover the hectic decade which led to Mahler's premature death in 1911—and draws to a close as the composer is about to commit the major blunder of his life: his marriage to the twenty-three-year-old concert-hall courtesan Alma Schindler.

But most readers, I suspect, will be hard-pressed to match the author's impeccable objectivity. However disillusioning the revelation, the mass of data de La Grange has subpoenaed suggests that, notwithstanding his celebration of the joys of rusticity, his Tolkienesque attachment to a poetry peopled by nymphs and gnomes, Gustav Mahler was a very nasty man—relentlessly opportunistic, blithely indifferent to the fragility of any ego other than his own. Mahler's first forty years document an appalling case history of upward mobility, Central European style. From Laibach, to Kassel, to Prague, to Leipzig, to Budapest, to Hamburg, we follow Mahler on the make until, with his appointment to Europe's most prestigious podium—the directorship of the Vienna Opera—his continental career attains its apex. Throughout this period (and despite the number of appointments involved, Mahler's track time for the Laibach-Vienna run was a mere fifteen years) his letters, postcards, and transcribed café comments bear witness to Mahler's nonstop manipulation of his colleagues in the interest of his own career.

Not that all was smooth scuttling. In Budapest, two infuriated opera stars sent their seconds to call; in Hamburg, police protection was required to see him safely home from rehearsal; and while in Leipzig, the author notes, "Mahler was not displeased to learn that the task of Karl Muck, his replacement in Prague, was no easier than his own had been and that Muck had already received 'many battle wounds.' " Indeed, Mahler tried desperately to renege on his Leipzig contract, since at the time of his appointment the chief conductor at the Leipzig Opera was the legendary Artur Nikisch. "I cannot resign myself to being no more than a pale moon revolving around the sun of Nikisch—Everyone tells me: 'Patience! You will win in the end' but—patience has never been my strong point!" Patience, as things turned out, was not required; Nikisch fell ill in mid-season, and, as de La Grange observes, "never did a colleague's sudden illness suit Mahler better than that of Nikisch." Mahler himself notes that "thanks to the turn of events, I am on the same level with Nikisch in every way, and now I can fight peacefully [sic] for the hegemony that ought to come to me, if only because of my physical superiority. I don't think Nikisch will keep up the struggle very long."

But enough—the man was a monster! Indeed, de La Grange mentions that in 1900, Mahler became "depressed and irritable" after reading Tolstoy's metaphorically autobiographical study of guilt and self-deception, *Resurrection.* In the volume's most revealing quote, our hero declares that "I'm quite unable to reconcile the meaning of my own life with the truth as revealed by this book." Evidently, the Vienna Opera was as burdensome as Yasnaya Polyana.

Speaking of Tolstoy, de La Grange's biography supports a cast list approximately equal to the dramatis personae of *War and Peace* squared. In addition to awarding walk-on parts to virtually all the luminaries of the day—Brahms, Bruckner, Hugo Wolf, Cosima Wagner, and, of course, Mahler's most celebrated contemporary, Richard Strauss (who, by the way, managed to parry Mahler's paranoid thrusts with notable success and emerged from each of their encounters with honor intact)—de La Grange also gives us battalions of extras, and on their behalf I do wish the author and Doubleday had splurged on one final editorial check. On innumerable occasions, material presumably cut adrift from a previous draft turns up to duplicate, without elaboration and in many cases word for word, information already on record. Thus, both the end of chapter 4 and the beginning of chapter 5 reveal that in the autumn of 1878, and under mysterious circumstances, Mahler left the University of Vienna, only to reappear on campus in 1880. On pages 55 and 68 we're offered identical details of a piano recital he undertook in Iglau (his hometown) on April 24, 1879, while on page 136 we discover (parenthetically) that a vocalist named Betty Frank, who has not previously crossed our path, was the first public performer of his songs. On the following page, this time without benefit of parentheses, the information is recapitulated, though on this occasion we learn, en passant, that the young lady has entered the lists of Mahler's enamoratae, which surely rated top billing on 136. A minor cavil, however, and one that later editions can presumably rectify.

The final three hundred pages, in addition to more conventional appendices, contain detailed analyses of all Mahler's works composed during the seven hundred pages preceding. As in the biography per se, the approach is relentlessly objective. Necessarily, one misses the adjectival excitement, the descriptive fancy that, for example, makes Norman Del Mar's work on Strauss—in which the analysis of a tone poem or an operatic scene becomes the very stuff of drama—a masterpiece of subjective reporting. But a subjective report was not de La Grange's intention. His aim was to retrieve all relevant information before parties competent to speak of and for Gustav Mahler had vanished from the scene. This he has done with care, precision, and, I suspect, genuine affection for his subject. It seems safe to predict that this work and, in all likelihood, its successor volume will become the indispensable data bank for all further research into the life and times of one of the most enigmatic figures of the postromantic era.

AN ARGUMENT FOR RICHARD STRAUSS

A friend of mine once remarked that there was probably a moment in every budding musician's teen-age years when *Ein Heldenleben* might suddenly appear the work most likely to incorporate all of the doubts, and stresses, and the hoped-for triumphs of youth. He was only half-serious, I suppose, but I think he was also half-right; and, although he didn't intend it disparagingly, his remark did suggest the assumption that if one could grow naturally into a sympathy with the flamboyant extroversion of the young Richard Strauss, so one could be expected, with maturity, to grow just as naturally out of it. My own *Heldenleben* period began, courtesy of Willem Mengelberg, when I was seventeen, but—although I have now patiently waited twelve years—I

From *High Fidelity*, March 1962.

have never grown out of it. And though it may well be a damning commentary on the waywardness of my own maturing, I rather doubt now if I ever shall!

So it is not easy for me to write objectively about Richard Strauss, although I intend to try to do so, however, because I write from a position of high prejudice: I believe, quite simply, that Strauss was the greatest musical figure who has lived in this century. This is not a very welcome view today, because, although Strauss does not really need anyone to extol his merits to the world, his reputation has perhaps suffered more unjustly with the passing years than that of any other musician of our time. At first glance, this may appear a rather surprising statement, since Strauss has never been more frequently or devotedly favored in performance than at present, but I am referring now not to those Teutonic lions of the podium who nightly soar from our midst to be with Zarathustra on his mountaintop, nor do I speak of those artful tigresses of the operatic stage for whom no greater challenge nor surer success exists than that which Chrysothemis or the Marschallin assures. I refer, rather, to those cunning currents of fancy which, as they sweep to command the tide of musical taste, make haste to consign old Strauss to the graveyard for romantics, pronouncing him a great nineteenth-century character who had the audacity to live fifty years into the twentieth.

The longevity of Strauss's creative life is pretty staggering, of course—at least sixty-nine years if one reckons his adolescent works as the astonishing creations they really are, or in other words a span equal to the total lifetimes of two Mozarts (if you have a head for that sort of thing). Now, obviously, the length of Strauss's creative life is not important of itself—many composers plan to live to one hundred and six, while I myself aim to withdraw into a graceful autumnal senility at thirty. Yet the longevity of a creative life is a justifiable yardstick within the extent that it measures, and can be measured by, the development of the composer as a human being.

It is the view shaped by the tastemakers of the musical profession that Strauss's evolution as a musician was not consistent with the length of his years. They seem to feel that his development was arrested somewhere within the first decade of this century. They do not always deny him the achievement of his early works: some of them can even whistle a few tunes from the tone poems, and many will admit the dramatic values of his first great operatic successes—the charm and gallantry of *Rosenkavalier,* the strangling impact of *Elektra.* But most of them seem to think that having made himself for twenty-five years or so a bulwark of the avant-garde, Strauss in his mid-forties lapsed into a drought of inspiration which was terminated only by death.

Is it a curious accident, I wonder, that the point in Strauss's career at which, with the precision of hindsight, he is presumed to have gone astray is more or less concurrent with the beginning of the most significant musical revolution (or if you prefer, reformation) of modern times, the development of the musical language without tonality? Or is it just coincidence that even well-informed opinion sees Strauss as having reached the climax of his career just prior to those years in which other composers first broke through the sonic barriers of tonal harmony, and that when he appeared to reject the new aesthetic, the tastemakers and the pacesetters would see him only as a man wistfully attempting to recapitulate the achievements of his youth?

The generation, or rather the generations, that have grown up since the early years of this century have considered the most serious of Strauss's errors to be his failure to share actively in the technical advances of his time. They hold that having once evolved a uniquely identifiable means of expression, and having expressed himself within it at first with all the joys of high adventure, he had thereafter, from the technical point of view, appeared to remain stationary—simply saying again and again that which in the energetic days of his youth he had said with so much greater strength and clarity. For these critics it is inconceivable that a man of such gifts would not wish to participate in the expansion of the musical language, that a man who had the good fortune to be writing masterpieces in the days of Brahms and Bruckner and the luck to live beyond Webern into the age of Boulez and Stockhausen should not want to search out his own place in the great adventure of musical evolution. What must one do to convince such folk that art is not technology, that the difference between a Richard Strauss and a Karlheinz Stockhausen is not comparable to the difference between a humble office adding machine and an IBM computer?

Richard Strauss, then, seems to me to be more than the greatest man of music of our time. He is in my opinion a central figure in today's most crucial dilemma of aesthetic morality—the hopeless confusion that arises when we attempt to contain the inscrutable pressures of self-guiding artistic destiny within the neat, historical summation of collective chronology. He is much more than a convenient rallying point for conservative opinion. In him we have one of those rare, intense figures in whom the whole process of historical evolution is defied.

Throughout those seven working decades the most striking common feature of Strauss's work is the extraordinary consistency of his vocabulary. One can compare, to take virtually the extreme instance, his Symphony, Op. 12, written when he was eighteen, and the *Metamorphosen* for string orchestra, written at the age of eighty-one, and one will have to admit that neither contains any harmonic progression which would have been necessarily unavailable to the other. Basically, both use a harmonic language available to Brahms, or to Hugo Wolf, or, minus his sequences, to Bruckner; both use a contrapuntal style which, although more in evidence in the later work, is still primarily founded upon the belief that, however many contrarieties it may provoke, its fundamental duty is to substantiate the harmonic motion and not to contradict it. And yet for all these similarities the *Metamorphosen* conveys the impression of an altogether different harmonic and contrapuntal scope than the Symphony, and both suggest a unique identity which could not possibly be confused with any earlier master. While there are pages in the teen-age works of Strauss (the First Horn Concerto, for instance) which, at a diagrammatic harmonic level, could easily have been written by Mendelssohn, or even, surprisingly, by Weber, one needs only a few seconds to realize that here, for all of the influence of the early romantic masters, is a wholly original technique.

Although he reached adolescence at a time when Wagner had anticipated the dissolution of the tonal language and had stretched the cognizance of harmonic psychology to a point that some regarded as the very limit of human endurance, Strauss perhaps was more concerned than any other composer of his generation with utilizing the fullest riches of late romantic tonality *within* the firmest possible formal disciplines. With Strauss it was not simply a question of compensating for the overrich harmonic ambiguities of his era (as was the case with the intense motivic concentration of the young Arnold Schoenberg); rather, his interest was primarily the preservation of the *total* function of tonality—not simply in a work's fundamental outline but even in its most specific minutiae of design. Consequently, when one compares any of Strauss's early orchestral scores with, say, a tone poem by Liszt, one is immediately struck with the fact that while Strauss's works demonstrate infinitely greater daring in terms of sheer extravagance of harmonic imagination, they are nevertheless painstakingly explicit at every level of their architectural concept and thus present an impression of a harmonic language at once more varied and more lucid. With this immense harmonic resource laboring within what is frequently an almost rococo sense of line and ornamentation, Strauss is able to produce by the simplest and almost deceptively familiar means an overpowering emotional effect. Who else is able to make the bland orthodoxies of a cadential six-four seem a wholly delectable extravagance?

Rarely among the German romantics is there writing that matches the glorious harmonic infallibility of the young Strauss. Among his predecessors only Mendelssohn and Brahms in their best pages were as conscious of the need to strengthen the vagrant structures of romantic tonality through the emphatic control and direction of the harmonic bass. One would almost suspect that Strauss conceived of the cellos and basses with his feet (as an organist might do), for at every moment—regardless of the breadth of the score, regardless of its metric complexities, regardless of the kaleidoscopic cross-reference of chromatic tonality—the bass line remains as firm, as secure, a counterpoise as in the works of Bach or of Palestrina.

It must not be supposed that striving in this way for the ultimate accentuation of linear clarity led Strauss into the contrapuntist's concern for a linear texture which accords to each voice its own independent existence. Strauss was by no means a composer who practiced counterpoint per se. In his music the absolute contrapuntal forms—the fugue, the canon, etc.—appear primarily in the operas (and even there infrequently) and are almost without exception the occasion for a self-conscious underlining of the libretto. Such occasions are, from a purely academic point of view, quite beyond criticism, but one always has the feeling that Strauss is saying, "Look, see, I can do it, too!" and that he regards such diversions simply as a means to enliven an otherwise static situation on the stage; and yet, although in the vast body of Strauss's work there are few examples of the sort of contrapuntal devices which most other twentieth-century composers, in their search for motivic interrelation, have used constantly, it cannot be overemphasized that Strauss, on his own terms, was among the most contrapuntal minded of composers.

The fundamental strength of Strauss's counterpoint does not lie in his ability to provide an autonomous existence for each voice within the symmetric structure—his whole symphonic orientation is too thoroughly nineteenth-century to make this either possible or, to his mind, I suppose, desirable. Rather, it lies in his ability to create a sense of poetic relation between the soaring, dexterous soprano melodies, the firm, reflective, always cadential-minded basses, and, most important of all, the superbly filigreed texture of his inner voices. There are many more contradictory stresses in the linear designs of Strauss than in Wagner, for instance, whose accumulations of density tend to have perhaps more singlemindedness, more uniformity of stress and relaxation, than do those of Strauss; but by the very mixture of this finely chiseled contrapuntal style and this vastly complex harmonic language, Strauss's climaxes, his moments of tension and of repose, are—if less overwhelming than those of Wagner—infinitely more indicative of the complex realities of art.

When he came under Wagner's influence, Strauss inherited the problem of translating the dramatic possibilities of the former's harmonic freedom into the realm of symphonic music; for Strauss not only began his career as a symphonist (indeed, at first, a symphonist of a particularly straitlaced order) but was, with all his sovereign mastery of the stage, a man who always thought primarily in symphonic terms. The problem of developing a musical architecture that would relate somehow to the extravagance of a richly chromatic tonality and would make use of all the ambiguities contained therein

was, of course, the primary problem for all the composers of Strauss's generation. It was simply unsatisfactory to shape symphonic creations within the
mold of the classical sonata structures with all the implied tonal plateaus
which tradition begged if one wanted to use material chosen less for its thematic profile than for its genetical probabilities. (The problem was certainly
less serious for Strauss than it was for Schoenberg, who seems always to have
had a more relentless determination to exhaust all motivic permutations.)

The young Strauss sought a solution in the symphonic poem, in which
the logic of the musical contours would stand in supposed relation to a predetermined plot exposition that could suggest the texture, the duration, and
the tonal plateaus of each episode. It was at best a halfway logic, for most
listeners are almost certainly little aware of the legal embarrassments of Till
Eulenspiegel or the philosophic posings of Zarathustra and likely care even
less. Probably they recognize, or try to, those correspondences with the
purely symphonic structures which Strauss sought to supplant. What is more
to the point about the tone-poem logic is that in Strauss's mind it provided
a sense of architectural cohesion which might not need to be externally observed. Thus an entirely musical logic, which was always present, was simply
reinforced at conception by a pseudodramatic one that, having fulfilled its
role, could easily be abandoned at birth. The entangling of musical events
with dramatic ones is a risky business; and although Strauss took great pride
in his ability to describe extramusical circumstances musically (a talent which
was later to make him the greatest operatic composer of his time), the essence
of the tone poem structure did not depend on the circumstance that a series
of dramatic occurrences appear in a recognizable paraphrase. Rather, it lay
in the fact that the harmony of dramatic events could be used as a focus for
musical form. (Fascinating that Thomas Mann was always talking about the
reverse procedure—building the novelette like a sonata-allegro.)

As Strauss grew older, his desire to overwhelm us with the musical
equivalent of an epic novelist's entangled plot line abated; and as the tone
poem period came to an end, he began to enjoy what was, at first, a coy flirtation with the *style galant* and then to visit with increasing ardor the spirit
of tonal rebirth and re-emphasis which dominated the preclassic generations.
It has always seemed to me that the pivotal work in Strauss's career is one
of the less spectacular, and certainly in North America least well known,
of his works—*Ariadne auf Naxos. Ariadne* is neither the most brilliant, the
most effective, nor the most likable of Strauss's operas, and yet from its conception date those qualities which can now be numbered as the outstanding
traits of the mature composer. (There may be some amusement in the fact
that this statement, however open to challenge, should be made of a work
written in the same year as Stravinsky's *Sacre du printemps* and Schoenberg's
Pierrot Lunaire—1912.) *Ariadne* finally confirms what must surely have been

suspected of Strauss long before—that at heart his instinct, if not neoclassic, is essentially that of a highly intellectualized romantic.

From *Ariadne* onward his textures will on the whole become ever more transparent, and the buoyancy and stability of his harmonic style will be even more magnificently served. Strauss always fancied himself as a kind of twentieth-century Mozart, and this is not an altogether insupportable conceit: indeed, in many of the operas of the middle-late years from *Ariadne* to *Die schweigsame Frau* we find again and again the delicious transparency which makes these works, in my view, the most valid outlet for the neoclassic instinct. And so, once again, Strauss's concern for the total preservation of tonality finds not only a sanctuary but a point of departure.

I do not want to suggest that Strauss's creative life did not at some time actually undergo that terrifying evaporation of inspiration which plagues the subconscience of all creative people. It has always seemed to me there was some justification for the concern expressed about his artistic future during the period immediately following the First World War. Certainly, the decade following the Great War was the least productive decade of Strauss's life, and his work at that time, while possessed as always of an enormous technical competence, cannot by any stretch of the imagination be regarded as equaling his earlier achievements. Strauss himself, of course (utilizing the composer's and the parent's privilege of making a special pet of the unwanted child), swore to his dying day that *Die Frau ohne Schatten* was the greatest of his operas and besieged major opera houses with requests for its production. He even insisted that, although his health could not possibly permit him to endure the rigors of conducting *Rosenkavalier* (because of its length), he would nonetheless be most happy to conduct *Frau ohne Schatten* (which is slightly longer). The middle operas like *Frau ohne Schatten* are certainly not without admirable qualities; we no longer feel, however, quite that same wondrous stroke of inevitability which in the earlier works—and, indeed, the later ones—bound the first note with the last and made all the ingenious technical diversions not the aim but simply, and rightly, the means.

And so we come to that incredible rejuvenation of Strauss the artist—the fluent, warm, infinitely moving works of his late years. Here, surely, is one of the most fascinating revitalizations of the creative spirit to which we could ever be witness. One could, I suppose, attempt a parallel with the last works of Beethoven by pointing to the fact that they too follow upon a dreary desert of inactivity, from which Beethoven emerged to find not only the assured step of his youth but, indeed, a means to express the mature deliberation of his later years. It is my view that the late works of Strauss afford much the same opportunity to contemplate the mating of a philosophic stance and a technical accomplishment indivisible from it. I feel that in virtually all of his late works Strauss's youthful tendency to celebrate through the techniques of art the human conquest of material order, to applaud the existential character who flings himself unquestioningly against the world—in other words, to be the hero of *Ein Heldenleben*—is now sublimated, indeed, wholly vanquished, by a technical mastery which no longer needs to prove itself, to flaunt its virility—but which has become inseparable from those qualities of sublime resignation that are the ultimate achievements of great age and great wisdom.

Indeed, short of the last quartets of Beethoven, I can think of no music which more perfectly conveys that transfiguring light of ultimate philosophic repose than does *Metamorphosen* or *Capriccio*—both written when their composer was past seventy-five. In these late works the vast harmonic imagination always characteristic of Strauss remains; but whereas in the earlier years it had the positive, convinced, untroubled assurance of metric simplicity, now it is sometimes tentative, sometimes wayward, sometimes deliberately asymmetric, and thus conveys a vivid sense of one who has experienced great doubt and still finds affirmation, of one who has questioned the very act of creativity and found it good, of one who has recognized the many sides of truth.

And yet I wonder how vivid the comparison with Beethoven really is. Beethoven, after all, in the last quartets did virtually bridge the entire romantic era and afford a link with the taut motivic complexities of the Schoenbergian generation. On the other hand, at least from our present point of view, Strauss, in the late years, can hardly be supposed to have suggested any such stylistic o'erleaping of future generations. He has, if my view of him is substantial, simply brought to an inevitable and poignant conclusion his own existence as a creative man; he has promised nothing whatever for the future. And this, I submit, is where the estimation of my generation has passed Strauss by.

I do not for one minute suggest that, with all of my admiration for Richard Strauss, I could possibly imagine that the future of music will somehow be influenced in any actual, stylistic sense by his works. But then what is it that really provides the influence of one generation upon another? Is it simply the retention of stylistic similarities within an ever-moving historical front? Or can it not also be the inspiration to be drawn from a life which contains a total achievement of art? Certainly Richard Strauss had very little to do with the twentieth century as we know it. No more perhaps did he belong in the Age of the Atom than Sebastian Bach in the Age of Reason or Gesualdo in the High Renaissance.

By all the aesthetic and philosophic yardsticks that we must apply, he was not a man of our time. Can we really conceive of *Frau ohne Schatten*

being launched in the inflation-ridden, ragtime-infested Roaring Twenties?*
Is it really possible that *Capriccio,* that autumnal salute to a world of gallant
poise and quiet literacy, could really have been born while the flames of war
swept our world of 1941?

The great thing about the music of Richard Strauss is that it presents
and substantiates an argument which transcends all the dogmatisms of
art—all questions of style and taste and idiom—all the frivolous, effete preoccupations of the chronologist. It presents to us an example of the man who
makes richer his own time by not being of it; who speaks for all generations
by being of none. It is an ultimate argument of individuality—an argument
that man can create his own synthesis of time without being bound by the
conformities that time imposes.

STRAUSS AND THE
ELECTRONIC FUTURE

One of the certain effects of the electronic age is that it will forever change
the values that we attach to art. In fact, the vocabulary of aesthetic criteria
that has been developed since the Renaissance is mostly concerned with
terms that are proving to have little validity for the examination of electronic
culture. I refer to such terms as "imitation," "invention," and, above all,
"originality," which in recent times have implicitly conveyed varying degrees of approval or censure, in accordance with the peculiarly distorted
sense of historical progression that our age has accepted, but which are no
longer capable of conveying the precise analytical concepts that they once
represented.

Electronic transmission has already inspired a new concept of multi-
ple-authorship responsibility in which the specific functions of the composer,
the performer, and, indeed, the consumer overlap. We need only think for
a moment of the manner in which the formerly separate roles of composer
and performer are now automatically combined in electronic tape construction or, to give an example more topical than potential, the way in which
the home listener is now able to exercise limited technical and, for that matter, critical judgments, courtesy of the modestly resourceful controls of his

---

Die Frau was actually composed in the teens and premiered in 1919.—T.P.
From *Saturday Review*, May 30, 1964.

hi-fi. It will not, it seems to me, be very much longer before a more self-assertive streak is detected in the listener's participation, before, to give but one example, "do-it-yourself" tape editing is the prerogative of every reasonably conscientious consumer of recorded music (the *Hausmusik* activity of the future, perhaps!). And I would be most surprised if the consumer involvement were to terminate at that level. In fact, implicit in electronic culture is an acceptance of the idea of multilevel participation in the creative process.

If we think for a moment about the way in which our concept of history has influenced our use of such words as "originality," some conventional judgments about artistic figures are placed in a very curious light indeed. For instance, we are forever being told that although Bach was a great man, he was decidedly retrogressive in his own musical tastes—the implication being that had he been a little less of a genius, his remoteness from contemporary fashion would have quite done in his inspiration. Mendelssohn, after some violent fluctuations of the approval meter, is pretty much out of favor once again, not due to any lack of musical ability but largely for the reason that he was less innovation-prone than some of his colleagues, that his music is therefore less "original" and, one somehow is left to assume, less valuable. As a matter of fact, Mendelssohn provides a rather interesting case, because the question of identification in our historical concept is quite often left to the observation of what you might call the quirk-quotient, the discovery at reasonably frequent intervals of some telltale response to a particular constructive problem for which a certain composer becomes noted. For instance, César Franck became noted for verbatim sequential transpositions: he thereby becomes easier to identify, and the satisfaction of confirming the identification holds, for the uniquely illogical processes of the Western mind, the implication of unity within the particular work. But Mendelssohn, on the other hand, is inclined to spurn positive identity factors of this kind and to draw instead upon what one could call negative factors. His work is more notable for those situations that he prefers to avoid than for the stylistic gestures that he attempts to indulge, and this is what infects his music with such a moving, puritanical quality. Since, however, the negative considerations of unity are out of fashion at the moment, so, unfortunately, is he.

Most of these ideas about the validity or lack of validity in a particular artistic procedure stem from an idea of history that has encouraged us to conceive of historical action in terms of a series of climaxes and to determine the virtues of artists according to the manner in which they participated in, or, better still, anticipated, the nearest climax. We tend to visualize a greatly exaggerated concept of historical transformation, and, for reasons that seem expedient in helping us make history approachable and teachable (in order to make history captive is perhaps closer to the point), we tend to prefer antithetical descriptions of historical point and denial, and to these we assign descriptions, terms that are consequently infected with all sorts of extraneous notions about progress and retrogression.

The absurdity of these assumptions about progressivism could perhaps be illustrated if I were to suggest the various judgments that might be applied to the same artistic experiment if it happened to be labeled in a variety of ways. Let's assume that someone were to improvise at the piano a sonata in the style of Haydn and to pass it off, at first, as a genuine work of that composer. The value that the unsuspecting listener would assign to this opus (let's assume it was brilliantly done and most admirably Haydnesque) would very much depend upon the degree of chicanery of which the improviser was capable. So long as he was able to convince the audience that this work was indeed that of Haydn, it would be accorded a value commensurate with Haydn's reputation.

But now let us imagine that the improviser decided to inform the listener that this was not a work of Haydn, though it very much resembled Haydn, but was in fact a work by Mendelssohn. The reaction to this bit of news would run something along the lines of "Well, a pleasant trifle—obviously old-fashioned but certainly shows a good command of an earlier style"—in other words, bottom-drawer Mendelssohn.

But one last examination of this hypothetical piece: let us assume that instead of attributing it to Haydn or to any later composer, the improviser were to insist that it was a long-forgotten and newly discovered work of none other than Antonio Vivaldi, a composer who was by seventy-five years Haydn's senior. I venture to say that, with that condition in mind, this work would be greeted as one of the true revelations of musical history—a work that would be accepted as proof of the farsightedness of this great master, who managed in this one incredible leap to bridge the years that separate the Italian baroque from the Austrian rococo, and our poor piece would be deemed worthy of the most august programs. In other words, the determination of most of our aesthetic criteria, despite all our proud claims about the integrity of artistic judgment, derives from nothing remotely like an "art-for-art's-sake" approach. What they really derive from is what we could only call an "art-for-what-its-society-was-once-like" sake.

When you begin to examine terms like "originality" with reference to those constructive situations to which they do in fact analytically apply, the nature of the description that they provide tends to reduce the imitation-invention ratio in a work of art quite properly to a simple matter of statistic. Within this statistic no work of art is ever genuinely "original"—if it were, it would be unrecognizable. All art is really variation upon some other art, and the more we divorce the application of terms like "originality" from those analytical observations to which they can profitably apply, the more uncertain is the ground upon which we erect our evaluations of art.

No artist of recent times has suffered more from the strange presumptions of this artistic-chronological parallel than Richard Strauss. Very few of his critics are honestly able to deny that he was one of the consummate masters of the musical craft, but nevertheless he has become a thoroughly unfashionable and greatly misunderstood artist. The case against Strauss rests usually on the argument that (a) he drew no artistic sustenance from the inspiration of twentieth-century life; (b) his later works were in a somewhat less chromatic and hence less "advanced" style than his early works; and (c) he simply lived too long and, as a composer, "dried up." It is not uncommon to find analyses of his work that even attempt to identify the specific instant beyond which he is supposed to have run counter to the times. In recent years we have often been told that the great and truly inspired works of Strauss were all written prior to the First World War, and that thereafter the pressures of his own eminence, the unchallenged facility with which he wrote, the immediate access to the means of production that were at his disposal all took their toll, and that the post–World War I works are but a pallid reflection of his earlier achievements. One of the most startling verdicts of this kind comes not from a present-day writer aiming to put this doddering reactionary in his place but from a 1920 essay by the American critic Paul Rosenfeld, who published a profile of the composer that states:

> Strauss was never the fine, the perfect artist. Even in the first flair of youth, even at the time when he was the meteoric, dazzling figure flaunting over all the bald pates of the universe the standard of the musical future, it was apparant that there were serious flaws in his spirit. ... In those days Strauss was unmistakably the genius, the original and bitingly expressive musician, and one forgave his shortcomings because of the radiance of his figure, or remained only half-conscious of them. ... Today it is difficult to realize that Richard Strauss ever inspired such high hopes, that there was a time when he made Nietzsche's "mad dream of a modern music" appear realizable and that for a while the nimbus of Dionysus burned around his figure.

Rosenfeld goes on to pinpoint the moment at which Strauss, in his view, deserts the Nietzschean orbit. It happened, he seems to feel, with *Rosenkavalier* and *Ariadne*, of which he says, "He [Strauss] has become increasingly facile and unoriginal, has taken to quoting unblushingly Mendelssohn, Tchaikovsky, Wagner, himself even. ... Something in him has bent and been fouled."

Somewhat later in his portrait of Strauss, Rosenfeld drops the rather significant comment that he finds Strauss at his best when at his most brutal and that he notes a disturbing tendency in all his works (*Elektra* included!) toward a certain "lascivious prettiness." It is here, I think, that, right or wrong, he reveals the bias of his particular argument against Strauss, because this comment is quite representative of that large body of opinion that holds that the early works, *Macbeth* through *Elektra,* let us say, hold quality in direct proportion to their motivic muscularity, to the growth of that intense and angrily declamatory music which particularly marks the transition from the tone poems to the earlier operas. To put it another way, the definitions of history are satisfied by the degree to which Strauss's earlier works progress in complexity, dissonance ratio, and rhythmic sophistication. But when the musical embodiment of that "lascivious prettiness" becomes dominant and the post-*Rosenkavalier* works reveal an increasing preoccupation with the retention of tonal formulae, supplemental as opposed to organic dissonance, and rhythmic sobriety, Strauss is accused of deserting the historical movement in which it was assumed he had long coveted a niche.

The deficiencies of this argument arise from the fact that its proponents simply cannot tolerate the idea that the participation in a certain historical movement does not necessarily impose upon the participant the duty to accept the logical consequences of that movement. One of the irresistibly lovable facts about most human beings is that they are very seldom willing to accept the consequences of their own thinking. The fact that Strauss deserts the general movement of German expressionism (presumably, in Rosenfeld's terms, the embodiment of "Nietzsche's modernism") should not be more disturbing than the fact that the unquestioned innovator Arnold Schoenberg found it extremely difficult in his later years to fulfill the rhythmic extenuations of his own motivic theories. The fact is that above and beyond the questions of age and endurance, art is not created by rational animals and in the long run is better for not being so created.

Through all of Strauss's works there runs one prevalent ambition, the desire to find new ways in which the vocabulary of key-signature tonality can be augmented without at the same time being allowed to deteriorate into a state of chromatic immobility. When you examine the condition of the tonal language at the time when Strauss was a young man and then summon the image of that tonality as it existed in his middle period (*Le Bourgeois Gentilhomme*), let us say, or in his late years (*Capriccio*), the contrast is striking. He inherited, after all, the diffuse improvisatory chromaticism of Wagner, the fascinating but never-quite-workable sequential-variation technique of Bruckner; and yet Strauss's work, while being involved with just as high a ratio of nondiatonic harmonic material as that of Bruckner or Wagner, does not begin to approach that condition of satiety through which their structures more than occasionally become top-heavy. What Strauss did was to provide a method by which the chromatic language of late romantic tonality could be erected upon a more stable keel than that which Bruckner or Wagner had.

The harmonic sense that enabled Strauss to do this was unique within the annals of tonality. From his earliest work, teen-age amusements like the Violin Sonata and the Wind Serenade, it is immediately apparent that whatever else this composer lacks or possesses, no surer ear for the centrifugal implications of the tonal cadence ever existed. The achievement of Strauss's harmonic development becomes really significant when you consider that he assimilated the vocabulary of Wagnerian chromaticism, put it to work within the extraordinary vertical organization that he developed, and made it supplement the particular expressive purposes that belonged to Strauss alone. In doing this, he developed an infallible instinct for the harmonic pace of his structure, for deciding upon those areas that must be affirmatively diatonic in order to compensate those in which the extravagant passions of the chromatic idiom had been indulged. And he learned to build primary cadences of a unique cumulative power and resonance. In part, these derived from his habit of treating the bass lines of his harmony as though they were magnetized to the tonal foundation. In this sense, Strauss is closer than any late romantic composer, and, for that matter, any nineteenth-century composer after Mendelssohn, to the genuinely baroque technique of preserving a structural autonomy in those lines and motives that are the foundation for his vertical structures. There is an almost divisible unity about his bass lines, a kind of independent pride and purpose that is found nowhere else in late romantic music.

Above these privately resonating bass forms the texture may be more or less contrapuntal, depending upon the nature and purpose of the particular work. There will almost certainly exist, whatever the texture, a harmonic language that makes frequent and elaborate use of double entendre, just as does the harmonic idiom of most other composers of the period. The short-term effects of the hints and feints of the harmonic progressions are just as clear, or, more accurately, just as purposefully unclear, as in the vocabulary, let's say, of Mahler's Tenth Symphony or of Schoenberg's First String Quartet—both written in the first decade of this century and both leaning toward that indulgence of chromaticism which was shortly to dissolve the tonal language. But it is in its long-term consequences that this ambiguous harmonic language fulfills a different function in the works of Strauss. In the long term the devices of harmonic ambiguity are not, in Strauss's music, as persistently indulged. To take an easy instance, the kind of sequential variation which sets off some form of nondiatonic or extradiatonic contrast which Bruckner likes to use as a household motto and to develop for its long-range harmonic consequences as well, and which Schoenberg exploits in such music as *Verklärte Nacht,* in which it is already preparing for its role as the variative mechanism of "atonality," was apparently indefensible within Strauss's harmonic ethics.

As one observes Strauss's career as a whole, one finds that this sense of mediation that he possessed between the elaborate introduction of dissonant or dissonantly suggestive factors and the cadential formulae necessary to particularize their diatonic, or, for that matter, their nondiatonic, connection grows almost consistently more subtle and encompassing. *Metamorphosen,* for example, which one need not praise by noting that its composer was then eighty, is a work in which the harmonic consequences of triads that divide between them the twelve-tone capacity of the chromatic scale—the same triad relationship that Schoenberg developed as the basis of the tone row in his, coincidentally, contemporaneous work *Ode to Napoleon Bonaparte*—are mined here not for the significance of their mutually complementary interval relationships (upon which Schoenberg develops his structure) but rather for the comparison of those relationships to the casual but never perfunctory sequences of purely diatonic cadence that they resemble and by which they are, at most pivotal moments in the work, quietly supplanted.

One may say, then, that for all practical purposes, very genuine dramatic ends are served by those inhibitions that Strauss acknowledged in regard to tonality and that caused him always to regard apprehensively the organic application of dissonance per se and to search instead for new ways of employing the ornamental, or the exotic, or, as in the *Ophelia Lieder,* the neurotic qualities of nonfunctional dissonance and of reconciling them within the tonality that he had expanded to accommodate them. The question, then, is not whether he succeeded, because most everyone agrees that his success as this world knows success was dazzling, or even whether he contributed something genuinely new, because by any standard other than the blindest assumptions of chronological conformity what he did was new indeed, but simply whether he did right by the historical progression of which we want to make him a part—whether by denying in his music the condition and vocabulary of that ambiguity which has become the stimulus of most art today he denied himself not a greater but a more pertinent achievement.

It is important to realize that if the demands and situations of the electronic age change the function and relevance of the composer to society, they will also change the categories of judgment by which we determine the matter of artistic responsibility. By far the most important electronic contribution to the arts is the creation of a new and paradoxical condition of privacy. The great paradox about the electronic transmission of musical sound is that as it makes available to the most enormous audience, either simultaneously or in a delayed encounter, the identical musical experience, it encourages that audience to react not as captives and automatons but as individuals capable of an unprecedented spontaneity of judgment. This is because the most public transmission can be encountered in the most private circumstance, and because the auditor, or, if you like, the ultimate composer-performer-critic-consumer hybrid, will be exposed to the most astonishing variety of idiom without necessarily having to encounter it in any specific social situation in which the inevitable compromises of multiple audition and of contemporary circumstance are most strongly felt.

It would be most surprising if the techniques of sound preservation, in addition to influencing the way in which music is composed and performed (which is already taking place), do not also determine the manner in which we respond to it. And there is little doubt that the inherent qualities of illusion in the art of recording—those features that make it a representation not so much of the known exterior world as of the idealized interior world—will eventually undermine that whole area of prejudice that has concerned itself with finding chronological justifications for artistic endeavors and which in the post-Renaissance world has so determinedly argued the case of a chronological originality that it has quite lost touch with the larger purposes of creativity.

Whatever else we would predict about the electronic age, all the symptoms suggest a return to some degree of mythic anonymity within the social-artistic structure. Undoubtedly most of what happens in the future will be concerned with what is being done in the future, but it would also be most surprising if many judgments were not retroactively altered because of the new image of art. If that happens, as I think it must, there will be a number of substantial figures of the past and near past who will undergo major re-evaluation and for whom the verdict will no longer rest upon the narrow and unimaginative concepts of the social-chronological parallel.

There is no figure in recent times of whose reputation these prejudices have taken such a toll as Richard Strauss. Whatever the limitations of his personality, whatever the restrictions upon his artistic imagination, he has been victim of the most violent prejudices and has been measured by a yardstick to which it was never his ambition to conform. It is entirely likely that Strauss, a man who seemed remote from the time in which he lived and totally unconcerned about the future, will, because of the new orientation of that future, gather a greater admiration than he ever knew.

RICHARD STRAUSS'S *ENOCH ARDEN*

Enoch Arden was written in 1890, when its twenty-six-year-old composer was fast becoming the most talked-about young musician in Central Europe. In ten years or so of intense activity he had managed to acquire two respectable conducting appointments (Meiningen and the Munich Opera), to acquire a most formidable mentor in the person of Hans von Bülow, and to turn out a dazzling succession of compositions—each one of which spoke the language of romantic tonality with an ever more singular Bavarian accent—culminating in the three most accomplished symphonic poems of his generation: *Don Juan, Macbeth,* and *Death and Transfiguration.*

It was a stimulating time in which to be a musician—the nineties in Germany. Richard Wagner, though now gone from the scene, still cast a hypnotic twilight glow upon most of the musicians of the younger generation. For those who could resist his sorcery there was the accomplished virtuosity of the masterful academician Johannes Brahms. And for young people of vision there existed the hopeful thought that in the not-too-distant future these two opposing forces might in some mysterious way seem to have mutually participated in the great tradition of German romanticism. It was an age in which sheer size of the musical canvas or of the participating forces could at times be mistaken for grandeur. And yet, curiously, it was also an age in which an acute analytical perception was highly prized. It was an age in which a thrilling future of new musical forms and new sonorities seemed close at hand but also in which the terror of the unknown lurked. It was an age of unparalleled accomplishment of musical technique and yet an age in which the tonal order was irreparably in decay.

Into this age came the dynamic figure of Richard Strauss—cocky, ambitious, politically wily, and supremely talented. Strauss was not one who chose sides in the Brahms-Wagner dispute, for, though he began his career as a symphonist of a particularly straitlaced order, modeling himself after Mendelssohn (he considered even Brahms too radical in his teens), he early revealed a unique appreciation of timbre and tonal eccentricity which prevented his being just another postromantic symphonist. Similarly, his enormous admiration for Wagner in his later twenties was compromised by the fact that he himself was a somewhat bourgeois personality, a man less passionately committed. His own special artistic vision was that of a style which

Liner notes from Columbia MS 6341, 1962.

would have both the exaltation of Wagner and the solidity and security of Brahms. There was a measure of the corrective disciplinarian about Strauss and his music (the currently fashionable view of Strauss as a glutton who reveled in the voluptuous excesses of sound is a good instance of confusion between period and participants). And if one compares almost any of Strauss's early works with those of his contemporaries, one notices that along with the sheer technical wizardry goes a most remarkable concern for the stability of the structure.

With all this, Strauss was not really a deeply intellectual artist, and though his literary comprehension was by no means as limited as Hugo von Hofmannsthal's jibes in later years would indicate, he was on occasion—especially in the choice of subject matter—the victim of too much facility and too little reflection. Certainly, it seems difficult to imagine what could have attracted him to Tennyson's drawing-room epic *Enoch Arden.* To be sure, the melodrama setting was a vogue much admired in those days, and it is possible that the young Strauss, who was never averse to picking up a fast mark, may have seized the opportunity of setting Adolf Strodt-mann's translation of the Tennyson poem in order to provide himself with concert fees from his restricted piano-playing ability. At any rate, the least that can be said of *Enoch* is that the score is nothing if not appropriate, since it certainly contains Strauss's most uncomfortably sentimental music.

Enoch does not really own any specific architectural ambition in the ordinary sense. It is more closely allied with the manner of improvisation than with the developing structure. One of the great things about Strauss's music is that most of it does possess a miraculous sense of the spontaneous and an ability to suggest the extemporaneous while in fact holding tight rein on every facet of the architectural concept. But in *Enoch* Strauss only wishes to extemporize and has no desire to disguise thereby a more intense structure. *Enoch* quite simply was a relaxation—a diversion—for Strauss, however unaccustomed our age may have become to a composer's deliberately setting aside some part of the deliberate calculations of his craft. But if there is not any real attitude of development in *Enoch,* the whole work certainly is based upon the recurrence of identifiable and continually altering leitmotivs.

The piano accompaniment is a demonstration of Strauss's prideful pleasure in his ability to parallel extramusical events musically; thus, the leitmotiv associations are heavily indulged, and the symbols which are constructed for various primary and secondary states of mind provide quite a fascinating revelation of Strauss's concept of the interrelation of motive and key. The chief characters are depicted as follows: Enoch Arden—

Philip Ray—

Annie Lee—

Strauss's tonal preoccupations, like those of many other nine-teenth-century composers, were inextricably bound to a peculiarly absolute concept of the physically relative functions of key signature, and to a large extent his peculiar associations with the individual character of keys remained with him throughout his lifetime. Thus, Enoch—the daring, the determined, the man capable of selfless renunciation—is accorded E-flat major, the hero's key of Strauss's imaginings; Philip Ray—quiet, comfortable, reliable, Enoch's friend and rival—E major; and Annie Lee—"the little wife to both"—G major, a key which seems to have manifested a certain quality of gentle forebearance to many other composers as well.

The most interesting part of Strauss's tonal wanderings are the truncations by modulation and the contrapuntal elisions of the score, even though they exist here at a rather rudimentary level. Thus, the death of Annie's child:

(Annie's motive in E minor); Philip's recognition that Annie remains troubled by Enoch's memory:

and subsequently, with that memory banished, Philip and Annie wed:

On a slightly higher or at any rate more ambiguous level are the disguised interlockings in the original motives accorded Philip and Enoch:

and best of all, at the very opening, the mysterious wave symbol in G minor, through which a disembodied version of Enoch's motive is perceived imprisoned in the murky depths of the sea.

THE PIANO MUSIC OF SIBELIUS

Of the one hundred and nineteen opus numbers that make up the lifework of Jan Sibelius, seventeen are devoted to music for the piano. Many of these digits, moreover, represent "Songs Without Words"—like collections, packages of ten or more independent selections—and by that tally Sibelius's keyboard output numbers well over a hundred compositions. Either way, it's an astonishing total, not least because Sibelius's metier was the postromantic orchestra, and, as the axiom would have it, postromantic symphonists traditionally gave short shrift to the keyboard. It's true, of course, that the bulk of Sibelius's output belongs to the bagatelle genre—programmatic trifles with titles like "The Spruce Pine" or "The Village Church" to define the scope of their parlor-music ambition. But there are in their midst works of substance—among them a sonata and two rondinos, in addition to the repertoire surveyed by the present disc—and these, or so it seems to me, by no means deserve the neglect which has thus far been their fate.

For one thing—and, given the era, it was no small achievement—Sibelius never wrote against the grain of the keyboard. At its best, his style partook of that spare, bleak, motivically stingy counterpoint that nobody south of the Baltic ever seems to write. And at—not its worst—its most conventional, perhaps, his keyboard manner is still a far cry from the generalized, octave-doubling-prone textures espoused by most of his contemporaries.

It should not, of course, come as a surprise that Sibelius was disinclined to provide for virtuoso display; one need only contemplate the austere and dignified violin role in his concerto for *that* instrument, or the superbly inte-

Liner notes from CBS M 34555, 1977.

grated vocal line in his "tone poem" for soprano and orchestra, *Luonnotar*, to form an impression of his attitude toward solo exhibitionism. But Sibelius is not simply reacting against the prevailing modes of postromantic keyboard writing; there's no hint of a nose-thumbing neoclassicism here. Rather, as the Sonatines, Op. 67, demonstrate, he discovered, through the development of Haydnesque textures and preclassical contrapuntal forms, a means by which to extract the best the piano has to offer without placing the instrument in a disadvantageously competitive position vis-à-vis those orchestral sonorities which in his day were deemed to constitute the sonic norm. In Sibelius's piano music, everything works, everything sounds—but on its own terms, not in lieu of other, presumably more sumptuous, musical experiences.

The first movement of the Second Sonatine, for example, is built from diatonically uneventful canons.

In the Third Sonatine, the opening movement is principally occupied with two-part-invention-style textures, harmonically enriched by the occasional figured-bass fill-in.

This sonatine, however, is idée-fixedly concentrated on the motive quoted above, and by the end of its second and last movement it has metamorphosed into a texture that would be right at home among Richard Strauss's early lieder accompaniments.

Its companion pieces, however, eschew intermovement relationships, and the first movements of all three works, in fact, function as compact, development-truncated sonata-allegros, complete with the sort of literal recapitulations that would be blue-penciled by even the most conservative of pedagogues. All three sonatines were written in 1912, during a period when Sibelius was otherwise engaged with his most radical form-as-process experiments in symphonic development (the Fourth Symphony, the first drafts for the Fifth); and by the yardstick employed for those particular works, these are remarkably conventional structures. Viewed from a slightly different perspective, however, the conformity of the architecture frequently serves to emphasize imaginative key relationships.

In the exposition of the first movement from the Sonatine No. 1, for example, the tonic key—F-sharp minor—is nowhere to be found. Through a combination of a capella entries for the right hand and chord support for what, with hindsight, we recognize as the submediant, subdominant, and supertonic relations in the left, Sibelius postpones the moment of reckoning. Eventually, however, the structure comes to rest on—or, to preserve Tovey's distinction, "in"—C-sharp minor; and by appearing to confirm a dominant, Sibelius slyly lets us in on where the tonic really was all along. (Even here, however, just to keep us on our toes, Sibelius's alternate chord of preference—a D-major triad—serves not only as the Neapolitan relation of the secondary key but as a mischievously disorienting reminder of its initial, submediant appearance.)

Again, from this perspective, the sequential non sequiturs of the "development," which appears to rush with unseemly haste toward the recapitulation (the "development" sections in each of the sonatines are treated with

Mozartian dispatch; the central episode from the first movement of the second of these works is but nine bars long), and the de facto dominant=tonic transfers of the recapitulation contribute to the plot in direct relation to the exposition's ambiguity. In fact, as things turn out, only the final twenty-five bars of the movement—"the second thematic group" of the recapitulation plus a brief coda—can be said to locate in the "home key," F-sharp minor. And that statistically improbable situation is but one of the gentle, subtle, let-no-stroke-go-for-naught touches with which Sibelius endows these remarkably restrained but touchingly evocative works.

"Restraint" is not a word that comes to mind when describing *Kyllikki*, Sibelius's Op. 41. On the other hand, it might not be the word that comes to mind when describing the relationship of Lemminkainen and his abductee-wife, as depicted in the eleventh runo of the *Kalevala*, either. As realized in W. F. Kirby's metrically unyielding translation:

> Thither came the ruddy scoundrel,
> There drove lively Lemminkainen,
> With the best among his horses,
> With the horse that he had chosen,
> Right into the green arena,
> Where the beauteous maids were dancing.
> Kyllikki he seized and lifted,
> Then into the sledge he pushed her,
> And upon the bare skin sat her,
> That upon the sledge was lying.
> With his whip he lashed the stallion,
> And he cracked the lash above him,
> And he started on his journey,
> And he cried while driving onward:
> "O ye maidens, may ye never
> In your lives betray the secret,
> Speak of how I drove among you,
> And have carried off the maiden."

It's difficult to see just how the finale of this work—a slightly giddy mix of Chopin and Chabrier—relates to the unhappy outcome of their liaison; but the rather blustery first movement, with its diminished-seventh cascades and silent-movie tremolandos, does come reasonably close to the mood of the first Lemminkainen-Kyllikki encounter. (This movement also contains the most elaborately redundant cycle of falling fifths this side of the Arietta from the Beethoven Op. 111. Unlike Beethoven's shameless pad, however, Sibelius's episode stops well short of being a literal sequence—the harmonic root-rhythm is decidedly irregular, and the whole episode is concealed within a whirlwind of activity. It's not one of Sibelius's more ingratiating moments, but if you enjoy musical detective work, perhaps I should just tell you that the root cycle goes from B to B and wish you happy sleuthing.)

In any event, the middle movement of *Kyllikki*—a brooding, ternary-shaped nocturne—needs no extramusical props. It provides striking testimony that even within the more traditional constraints of his earlier, quasi-virtuoso style, Sibelius was able to make a substantial contribution to the all-too-limited piano repertoire from the postromantic era.

ARNOLD SCHOENBERG— A PERSPECTIVE

In the half-century of his incredible career, Schoenberg typified the dilemma of the contemporary musical situation in a very special way. Within the fifty years of his creative life he produced a remarkable series of works which initially accepted and fed upon the traditional musical premise of his time, then challenged it and came perilously close to anarchical reaction, and then, confronted by the terror of anarchy, became almost overorganized, overlegislated by superimposed rules, and finally ended by attempting to coordinate the systems of legislation which he had developed with aspects of the tradition which he had, many years before, abandoned. And so, in this cycle of acceptance, rejection, and reconciliation, we have not only a spectacular chronological development but also the basic pattern for much of what has taken place in the first half of the twentieth century.

It will be necessary for me to speak of Schoenberg's chronology at some length, but it would be a mistake to infer that the chronological relation of events in his work is necessarily typical of every aspect of important contemporary music. It is not, and even if it were, it is very dangerous to put too much reliance upon the rather shaky theory of the relation between the evolution of style and the passing of a given number of years. Not all great art moves in what is analytically a direction of emancipation. On the contrary, it seems to me that even artists who are considered dangerously reactionary by their contemporaries can be credited with great works. One need only call to mind Richard Strauss, who is, after all, one of the true giants of the

Monograph published by the University of Cincinnati, 1964.

twentieth century and whose stylistic growth, far from being concerned with the race against the passing years which preoccupied Schoenberg, takes a direction which can only be described historically as retrograde.

If you are particularly fond of the last works of Strauss, as I am, it is essential to acquire a more flexible system of values than that which insists upon telling us that novelty equals progress equals great art. I do not believe that because a man like Richard Strauss was hopelessly old-fashioned in the professional verdict, he was, therefore, necessarily a lesser figure than a man like Schoenberg who stood for most of his life in the forefront of the avant-garde. If one adopts that system of values, it brings about the inevitable embarrassment of having to reject, among others, Johann Sebastian Bach as also being hopelessly old-fashioned.

In fact, I think there is a fairly good argument in favor of assuming that the technical competence, at least, of a composer like Strauss, who remains securely within the tradition that he knows, may well be more deft, more secure, more reliable, than that of a man like Schoenberg, who was so much involved with the pursuit of an evolutionary concept that he stood at times upon the brink of technical disaster. So, although I cannot imagine an approach to Schoenberg which does not attempt to examine the fascinating evidence of his chronology, I certainly do not believe that because he had a most remarkably inventive mind—he had, as you might say, more "patents pending" than anyone else in recent times—he should, therefore, automatically be considered the greatest or the most substantial musical figure. The historical fascination with Schoenberg's role is already evident. It will likely remain as long as music exists, so crucial is his position; but the greatness that may be attributed to him will have to stem from other criteria, other methods of judgment.

This is the distinction which is only too easy to make in Schoenberg's case—a distinction between his powers of invention (his forward-looking qualities) and his powers of execution (his actual composing abilities). Only at a time of great transition and confusion, such as our century has witnessed, is a distinction like this likely to be made at all. Many people will accept the qualifications of Schoenberg as a vital historical force but will emphatically reject the man's music itself. And it is certainly much easier to prove that Schoenberg was vital and indispensable to our time than to prove that he was profound and that he was great. The fact that people tend to make this distinction between the theories which Schoenberg tried to substantiate and his actual product as a composer haunted and tortured him throughout most of his life. He regarded himself simply as a composer, and he believed that whatever formulations he developed pertained only to his compositions.

Actually, there existed rather less of the dogmatist in Schoenberg's character than one might imagine. He was not by any means a relentless propagandist who attempted to coerce associates and admirers into accepting all the consequences of the technical manifestations of his work, but he did long for the day when they would believe in the work itself. In fact, shortly before his death in 1951, in a lecture in Los Angeles, he offered a very touching summary of this struggle of composer versus theoretician. He opened that lecture with an extraordinary sentence: "I wonder sometimes who I am." He went on to say that he had noticed some newspaper advertisements for his lecture in which he had been advertised as being a famous "theoretician and controversial musical figure known for the influence he has brought to bear on modern music." And then Schoenberg added, "Up to now, I thought I composed for different reasons."

It may be that Schoenberg was right in fearing that he would be remembered for the technical solutions which he had proposed to the contemporary musical dilemma rather than for the masterpieces which he felt he had written. In fact, we already seem to be entering a period in which, although the name of Arnold Schoenberg is known very widely indeed—is in fact almost as frequent a drawing-room reference as Freud or as Kafka or, if you happen to be in a particularly "one up" drawing room, as Kierkegaard—yet many people remark that apart from a few of his docile and romantic early works, his compositions have so far failed to attract any large share of public response.

What makes it so difficult to know about Schoenberg, to know clearly what the future will hold for him, is the fact that his creative activity has taken place during a moment of transition in the arts, a moment of transition at least as profound and perhaps as inevitable as that which occurred toward the end of the Renaissance. In those days, the fantastic complication of modal composition was being replaced by the relative simplicity of the system which we came to call tonality, the system from which all important Western music of the last three hundred years derives. And the great masters of that day, masters like Sweelinck in the Netherlands, Gibbons in England, Monteverdi in Italy, who also stood astride a profound historical transition, had the responsibility of clarifying into what might be called a public, common language the mysterious alternatives of modal technique.

In the early years of the seventeenth century the flowing, lucid part writing of the Renaissance began to take on an appearance of a sturdier, more rigidly controlled harmonic regime, began to be conceived largely in harmonic, that is to say, in vertical terms, rather than in linear, horizontal terms as had been the case in the Renaissance, began to accept an intentionally more limited vocabulary in which the harmonic events would be connected to each other by an attraction which resembled the force of gravity, which provided a centrifugal urge for this music and which bound its harmony together into a preferential order. And so this new music of the seventeenth century seemed (or, at any rate, seems by comparison) music of great simplicity and forthrightness, of public as opposed to private character.

Well, Schoenberg appeared at a time when the process of this transition to tonality was being reversed, at a time when the incredibly rich, sensual harmony of the late nineteenth century was once again giving way to a linear, horizontal direction. He appeared at a time in which there was a need for more rigid control of the compositional elements—a time in which questions pertaining to the fundamental nature of the theoretical process had to be answered, just as they had been three hundred years before. And, like the music of the composers of the early seventeenth century, which was infinitely less complex than that of the masters of the late Renaissance, Schoenberg's music represents, in my opinion, an enormous simplification of the romantic Wagnerian tradition from which it derived.

Now I know that this seems a very odd statement, because we are so accustomed to the idea that music which is rigidly *legislated*, as Schoenberg's music is popularly supposed to be, is complicated or in some way difficult to understand. But it seems to me that this is not at all the same thing as complication. I do not believe that a language like that of Schoenberg, which tries so hard to be logical, to trumpet its logic with organic proof of a raison d'être, is a language which in the true sense of the word is complicated. In my view, the really complex language is the one in which not only are there certain rules and regulations but there is also an element that is not quite susceptible to proof, not entirely demonstrable, but which to a degree is concealed and subliminal. In other words, I suggest to you that the most complicated endeavors in art are those in which the process of rational decision is closely allied with the instinctive process.

In this sense, the language that Schoenberg inherited, the language of Wagner, Strauss, and Mahler, is an immensely complicated language. It is a language in which one wonders what greater intensities could possibly be drawn from its vocabulary, in which one gasps as each work seeks to overwhelm with an emotional jolt greater than that which preceded. It is a language which was the culmination of three hundred years of musical technique—a constantly evolving technique, to be sure, but a technique which was based upon certain common experiences with this particular gravity of chords which is tonality—a language which as it grew older underwent many practices which clarified or crystallized its usage, but which primarily became more expressive, more aware of its potential, more complicated in the true sense of the word. And as it grew older and more familiar, its practitioners discovered that all that was left to add to this language was the abortive gesture, the deliberate slackening of discipline, the willingness, in fact, to do for an expressive reason the wrong thing.

So Schoenberg came upon the musical scene at a time when such fantastic complication existed (if you accept my definition of complexity) that his primary reaction was to provide a legislation which would attempt to organize, to rationalize, to intellectualize, to make outward, what had, to a degree, been inward. If Schoenberg had done that and only that, one would certainly conclude that Schoenberg was not a very subtle artist, that he was a man determined to make understandable those things which are incapable of being completely understood, to legislate those things which cannot ever be governed.

But what must be remembered about Schoenberg and his historical position is that there was an organic disorder which undermined the health of tonality in his day. It was due, of course, to this fantastic complexity of the vocabulary which he inherited, due to the many ambiguous harmonic relationships which then existed, that that simplicity which was the founding purpose of tonality became distorted and unbalanced by the extension of the tonal vocabulary, that those liberties engendered by tonality in its last stages weakened, with their pursuit of an expressive purpose, the fundamental tenets of the tonal philosophy.

Now I am going to consider Schoenberg chronologically for a few minutes and take a fairly close look at this fantastic transition which he so clearly embodies in his work. As a tonal composer, as a man working within a clearly defined key relation, Schoenberg contributed, in my opinion, some of the most glorious music of the early twentieth century. His work within tonality in that period spans approximately twelve years, beginning with the first little songs which he composed as a student and counting up to the last of the works which are unmistakably tied together by an allegiance to one key center—the String Quartet No. 2, written in 1908. These works include the fairly popular string sextet, *Verklärte Nacht;* one of the greatest symphonic poems ever written, *Pelleas und Melisande;* two symphonies for chamber orchestra;* two string quartets; and the mammoth oratorio *Gurrelieder.*

In several of the works of this period, particularly *Pelleas und Melisande,* Schoenberg seems to fit without any discomfort into the idiomatic concepts of Richard Strauss. In fact, at the turn of the century, both Strauss and Mahler had a good deal of sympathy for the young Schoenberg, and both of them seemed to feel that he was one of the bright young men who were definitely going places. They just weren't sure what places! In works like *Verklärte Nacht* or *Pelleas und Melisande,* we find Schoenberg accepting the premises of the late romatic tonal language without much question; and except for

---

*While the greater part of the Second Symphony was written during this period, the work was not completed until 1939.—G.G.

an unusually lively and well-integrated inner-voice structure and at times a particularly wide-ranging bass line, there is nothing that more than hints at the way things were actually developing for Arnold Schoenberg.

In comparison with these earliest tonal works, the works written only a few years later already betray the intellectual power of Schoenberg weightily intruding upon the more instinctive process, and, in comparison with *Verklärte Nacht* or with the early lieder, the chamber symphonies, for instance, are works of incredible power and drive—works which are controlled by a wonderfully firm hand. Just as *Verklärte Nacht* is rhapsodic and whimsical, languid and sequential, the chamber symphonies are tight and driven, functional and classical.

In many of these works, Schoenberg's use of dissonance becomes surprisingly emancipated. The theory of dissonance within the system of tonality is that it must be derived from and resolve into, in fact be an embellishment of, a fundamental progression; but Schoenberg began to experiment with dissonance which was so protracted in duration that it became more and more difficult to relate it directly to a harmony of preparation and resolution. Mind you, in this music he still does relate chords such as this quartal chord from the beginning of the First Chamber Symphony:

Here we begin to notice that the interval components of the chord are being used to provide melodic or linear consequences as well as for purely vertical sensation; and, moreover, the nature of the quartal chord in this particular progression and of its eventual resolution into the chord of F major is such that, although it is provided with the eventual satisfactions of a resolution, the chord itself could resolve in several other directions with equally satisfactory results. And so Schoenberg is here examining the consequences of relating dissonantly conceived chordal progressions to a basic triad harmony, not simply extracting closely related dissonances from triad harmonic formations. In terms of the evolution of his style and of our twentieth-century musical language, this was an enormous step forward for Schoenberg.

This first period of his work ends with the composition of the String Quartet No. 2, Op. 10 (written in the year 1908), which introduces in its last movement a texture of such wildly leaping ninths and sevenths that it can no longer be said to partake seriously of any responsibility to a coordinated tonal center. There is, however, significantly enough, attached to this last movement a vocal part for soprano solo with the rather significant text by the poet Stefan George: "I feel the breath of other planets blowing."

And so we come to the second period in Schoenberg's life, the period in which he attempted to feel his way into this strange new world without benefit of a clearly defined harmonic system. It has often been pointed out by critics of this new music that the error of such a profound change is that it does not evolve as language does: slowly, functionally, within the common reference of the public. It is perfectly true that various devices of contemporary poetry suggest to some degree the calibration of serial technique, but by and large there has been no fundamental change in the nature of literary materials, and there certainly has been no sense of divorce between the writer and the reading public as there would seem to have been between the musician and his audience.

Of course, the early propagandists for atonality pointed with a good deal of pride to the fact that the movement toward abstract art began at almost exactly the same time as atonality, and there are certain comfortable parallels between the careers of the painter Kandinsky and the composer Schoenberg. But I think it is dangerous to pursue the parallel too closely, for the simple reason that music is always abstract, that it has no allegorical connotations except in the highest metaphysical sense, and that it does not pretend and has not, with very few exceptions, pretended to be other than a means of expressing the mysteries of communication in a form which is equally mysterious.

In other words, I believe that no matter how comforting the parallels which may be drawn between music and the other arts in recent times, the only parallels which really count are those which can be drawn with previous circumstances of musical history, such as I have attempted to draw with the late years of the Renaissance. So if my explanation of the relativity of atonality is correct, it must necessarily exclude many of the comments which have been made about atonality and its derivation, particularly those which point to the significance of its having first appeared in the turbulent years immediately preceding the First World War. I do not believe that the undeniable state of chaos in the world at that time had very much to do with the artistic function of atonality or with abstraction in art, for that matter, if only for the reason that not all human beings are equally moved, or, at any rate, moved in the same direction, by the events and tensions of their own time.

Nor should we overdramatize, I think, the shattering blow that came at that time to the comfortable world of the Edwardians. The world knew what suffering could mean long before the days of Kaiser Wilhelm. And, again, the reaction to pain, to suffering, is such a personal thing—it does not necessarily entail the dissipation of order. It can be depicted by an attempt to invoke an artistic order to compensate distress. And so it seems to me a great mistake to read into the fantastic transition of music in our time a total social significance. Undeniably, there do exist correlations between the development of a social stratum and the art which grows up around it, just as the public manner of early baroque music related to some degree to the prosperity of a merchant class in the sixteenth century; but it is terribly dangerous to advance a complicated social argument for a change which is fundamentally a procedural one within an artistic discipline.

In the music that Schoenberg wrote following the Second String Quartet of 1908 and preceding the First World War, there are still, as one might expect, a good many vestiges of a key relation, but these vestiges now have the nostalgia that we associate with the reminiscence of a bygone and much-loved period. Examine, for instance, this passage from the second of the Piano Pieces, Op. 11, in which you will detect a very distant reminiscence of the key of D minor:

Here, on the other hand, is another brief excerpt which also, coincidentally, suggests D minor. It is from Op. 15, *Das Buch der hängenden Gärten*. Notice how much more subtle are the harmonic implications of this song:

In other words, in this music there still exists to a degree an order of preference, a process of selection, determined by the faint reminiscence of tonal procedures. There does not, in the sense that we now use the word, exist atonality. But examine this brief example from Schoenberg's Op. 19, and in it you will not likely detect any real tonal center:

Only about three or four years separate this little piano piece from the song excerpt, but the latter constitutes almost half of an entire bagatelle—indeed, all six pieces of Op. 19, to which it belongs, require not more than five minutes for performance. Can you imagine the change which had occurred in the world of Arnold Schoenberg—a change that would make the man who wrote the *Gurrelieder* and *Pelleas und Melisande* ten years earlier confine himself now to the activity of writing tiny pieces for the piano? Not that there is anything wrong with writing tiny pieces for the piano, but these small pieces tell us more about the desperation of Schoenberg's position in 1911 or 1912 than any words could do. Here he was committing himself to a language which he did not know—a language which he had no means to govern except through his innate musicality. What a temptation it must have been to return to the solid ground that had supported him only a few years before! What a temptation it must have been to forsake the terror of this unknown world of sound! But, of course, this did not—I suppose could not—happen, for Schoenberg was now possessed by the determination to stand or fall upon the path which he had chosen, even if following that path meant confining the energies of his musical craft to minutiae for the piano. In fact, for almost ten years, Schoenberg, except for dallying with his never-to-be-finished oratorio, *Die Jakobsleiter,* wrote almost nothing at all. These were years in which he wondered if he had come too far. Perhaps no man could encompass within a lifetime such an enormous transition.

The problem which faced Schoenberg was to decide in what way this void of dissonance he had created for himself could be organized—in what way it could be manipulated in a more meaningful manner. There were so many ways in which things could go in this strange new world of dissonance; was one way necessarily more meaningful than the next? Well, Schoenberg deduced that if it was the embarrassing riches of chromatic tonal harmony which had provoked this reaction into atonality, and if it was the elaborate melodic manner of the post-Wagnerians which had associated itself with this chromatic vocabulary, then perhaps in these writhing, elongated melodic lines lay the clue to organizing the language of atonality. Would it not be possible, he thought, to build motives of such length and endurance that they not only would provide the nucleus of other motives whichwould relate to them but would, perhaps, give a clue to the sense of proportionate relation between the structural components, both of melody and of harmony?

Within the aesthetic which Schoenberg employed, the basic sentiment which governed the spirit of his work was an insistence upon regarding a work of art as a totally comprehensible, totally organized object. This is the concept which has caused such great confusion about Schoenberg as an artist and which has subjected his historical theories to very serious challenge indeed, because, of course, the question which governs all art is to what degree is it entirely logical, to what degree can it be entirely worked out before the fact. Schoenberg was well aware, I suppose, that these questions were essentially mysteries which must go lacking a firm answer and which can at best be expected to hold a relative answer for any creative person; but his own persuasion lay in acknowledging a conception before the fact—in which form a certain embryonic cell which represented itself as the governing factor in the creative judgment the work would spring. And, finally, after the many years of silence which Schoenberg endured in this period, his conception of the nature of this embryonic cell crystallized in the formation of what has become known as the twelve-tone technique.

This, of course, was the system which made Schoenberg the favorite target of the critics of contemporary music, for now Schoenberg was not simply asserting his own right to wander in the strange world of atonality: he was suggesting that there was an application of logic of which this world deserved to know—a logic that would justify the use of total dissonance. At first, not only did this system seem perverse and arbitrary, it seemed almost laughably naive, for its basic premise was that this embryonic cell, the tone row or the tone series, would not itself necessarily be part of the work. Though it might appear as a melodic unit on occasion, it would essentially stand aloof from the work and simply be a source of reference to which the composer's invention would apply. But it would not be part of the work the way, let us say, the keel of a ship is part of that ship; it would lie instead like some mysterious, unborn specimen upon the composer's writing table, and from it, by contemplating and pondering it, by inventing certain numbers of variations upon it, the composer would create a work. The principles which govern the manipulation of this system—the relations of the tone row to the work—were in Schoenberg's earliest conception of them so elementary as to give it the appearance of a concoction of childish mathematics. And, as you can imagine, with the formulation of this strange new code,

Schoenberg became the most hated, feared, laughed at, and, very occasionally, respected composer of his generation.

But the odd thing about it was that with this oversimplified, exaggerated system Schoenberg began to compose again; and not only did he begin to compose: he embarked upon a period of about five years which contains some of the most beautiful, colorful, imaginative, fresh, inspired music which he ever wrote. Out of this concoction of childish mathematics and debatable historical perception came an intensity, a joie de vivre, which knows no parallel in Schoenberg's life. How could this be, then? By what strange alchemy was this man compounded that the sources of his inspiration flowed most freely when stemmed and checked by legislation of the most stifling kind? I suppose part of the answer lies in the fact that Schoenberg was always intrigued by numbers and afraid of numbers and attempting to read his destiny in numbers—and, after all, what greater romance of numbers could there be than to govern one's creative life by them? I suppose part of it was due to the fact that after fifteen years awash in a sea of dissonance, Schoenberg felt himself to be on firm ground once again. Still another part of it is certainly that all music must have a system, and that particularly in those moments of rebirth such as Schoenberg had led us into, it is much more necessary to adhere to the system, to accept totally its consequences, than at a later, more mature stage of its existence.

And so, with the first cautious exercises in twelve-tone composition, Schoenberg began the third major period of his creative life. Since the system itself was so new, the formal posture of Schoenberg's compositions at this time acquired, strangely for him in view of his nineteenth-century background, an almost entirely eighteenth-century foundation. The movements of these first twelve-tone works are still rather short ones and take the form of gavottes, musettes, gigues, of simple canons and mock-violent preludes, and of gentle minuets.

I suspect that eventually these earliest twelve-tone works will come to be regarded, perhaps in addition to the tonal works of the early years of the century, as the most entirely happy products of Schoenberg's life. It is true that both periods were times of conciliation and that those approaches which he made toward a liaison between twelve-tone technique and the musical forms of the eighteenth century could not, at best, provide more than a passing shelter. But imagine how thrilling it must have been to discover that there was a way to adapt the motivic scope of atonality and the licentious freedom of its harmonic possibilities within a familiar formal design. It may also be that there was such a mating of conservative and radical in Schoenberg's disposition that these two periods in his life were especially happy, precisely because of that measure of conciliation, of amalgamation between those things which he dared to try and the reminiscence of those things which he dearly loved.

The works of Schoenberg's later years can be said, on the whole, to consolidate his thinking about the use of twelve-tone technique. Considering that Anton Webern was already writing in that curiously "pointillistic" manner of his during Schoenberg's life, it is perhaps significant that Schoenberg's works, as he grew older, tended to grow once again larger in scope, broader in design, than the early twelve-tone compositions. Indeed, it was in this later period that he once again toyed with the idea of writing within a key signature. There are only a few works of this kind, to be sure, of which the most interesting are the *Kol Nidre* for chorus, narrator, and orchestra; the *Ode to Napoleon Bonaparte* for reciter, string quartet, and piano; and the Variations on a Recitative for organ. The prevalence of tonality in these works is rather variable, the organ variations being solidly D minor (which seems to have been rather a favorite key for Schoenberg), while the *Ode to Napoleon* reflects a tonal center only at crucial moments.

The sense of tonality here is altogether grayer, less colorful, than the flamboyant chromaticism of Schoenberg's youth. In fact, this is not in the conventional sense of the word "chromaticism" at all. The harmonic language has a slight resemblance to, let us say, Max Reger in a droll mood, but we soon realize that something rather odd is going on here. The fact is that the prevailing triadic course of this music is not arranged according to the respect of tonal voice leading but is derived out of a twelve-tone principle furnished by using a row which favors division into triadic groups. Thus the harmonization in the example below from the *Ode to Napoleon*—the relation between the chords of B major and B minor, G major and G minor, and E-flat major and E-flat minor—forms part of a harmonic cycle of major and minor chords which with one permutation relates to the twelve-tone spectrum.

No one can really say why Schoenberg began exploring an arbitrary tonal direction so late in his life. It was not in any sense, I am sure, a concession to the commercial spirit of Hollywood, his home. Whatever may have been the reason, Schoenberg's quasitonal works of this period provide one of the most valuable lessons that we learn from him in the use of serialism, because with these works Schoenberg refutes a good deal of the idealism of his early twelve-tone method, and he also provides important examples of the serially derived harmonic focus. That is to say, with these works we discover that serial organization does not necessarily have to operate in a world devoid of preference, and Schoenberg foreshadows a development which is now taking place—of concessions which are designed to provide a focus upon a particular harmonic unit which will recur more emphatically than statistical equality would allow. In short, these works, if not altogether satisfactory in themselves, represent one of the most important aspects of Schoenberg's later twelve-tone thinking.

These quasitonal works were only a very small part of Schoenberg's output in his later years. Among the major works of the American residence were the Violin and Piano Concertos and the String Trio, all written in a more conventional twelve-tone discipline. Each of these works, despite the evident mastery of his craft, exhibits, it seems to me, a rather more aloof and dispirited profile than that which we had come to know from the Schoenberg of the 1920s and early 1930s. There is a certain coldness, an architectural precision, which seems on occasion to have taken precedence over a more fluid invention. There is also once again that curious collaboration between the aims of an earlier period—in this case the nineteenth century (and its architectural devices)—and the exigencies of his own serial situations; and there is, of course, despite the many legitimate reservations about his later works, some of the most beautiful music of recent times.

Well, finally, what about this man Schoenberg? What sort of influence has he wielded upon our world? I think we must admit that a fundamental change has come over the world of music and that Schoenberg's works and ideas have been responsible for a good deal of that change. It is perfectly true that at the present moment there is such fantastic variety of musical idiom simultaneously in use that no one person can be credited or criticized for everything that is happening today. But if it is true that, as Roger Sessions, I believe, once said, "all of us, no matter in what way we compose, compose differently because of Schoenberg," what, then, has really been the effect of this new world of sound introduced by Schoenberg?

I think there can be no doubt that its fundamental effect has been to separate audience and composer. One doesn't like to admit this, but it is true nonetheless. There are many people around who believe that Schoenberg has been responsible for shattering irreparably the compact between audience and composer, of separating their common bond of reference and creating between them a profound antagonism. Such people claim that the language has not become a valid one for the reason that it has no system of emotional reference that is generally accepted by people today.

Certainly concert music of today—that part of it, at any rate, which owes a great deal to the Schoenbergian influence—plays a very small part in the life of many people. It cannot by any means claim to excite the curiosity that was generally aroused by significant new works fifty or sixty years ago. One must remember that at the turn of the century, any new work by a Richard Strauss or a Gustav Mahler or a Rimsky-Korsakov or a Debussy was a major event not only for the cognoscenti but for a very large lay audience as well. This isn't to say that they approved everything they heard, but by and large the current musical production in those days was perhaps the most interesting part of the repertoire to its audience, and the concert programs and operatic events of fifty or sixty years ago were heavily laden with music of that generation. It is perfectly true that the focus of music was very much narrower then than it is today. It extended back in the ordinary course of concertgoing to only about the time of Beethoven, with the occasional work of Mozart or Haydn thrown in, and, for the true antiquarian, the very occasional introduction of one of the more familiar works of Johann Sebastian Bach. By contrast, today we would suffer from malnutrition on a diet like that, which extends only over a hundred years or so. But have we simply transferred our interest to other periods of music because the music of our own time has failed to command our affection and attention?

No matter how little interest there may be in the more significant developments of music in our time, I think that there is little doubt that there are some areas in which the vocabulary of atonality—using this term now in a collective sense—has made quite an unobjectionable contribution to contemporary life. It has done this particularly in media in which music furnishes but a part—operas, to a degree (if you can consider styling Alban Berg's *Wozzeck* a "hit"), but most particularly in that curious specialty of the twentieth century known as background music for cinema or television. If you really stop to listen to the music accompanying most of the grade-B horror movies that are coming out of Hollywood these days, or perhaps a TV show on space travel for children, you will be absolutely amazed at the amount of integration which the various idioms of atonality have undergone in these media.

When this background music creeps up on us subliminally, as it were, we seem to accept the devices of a dissonant vocabulary as being perfectly comprehensible. It is rather frightening, though, to realize that the integration of dissonance, from which all of this new music of our day has emanated, has assumed a character in the minds of many people which is satisfactory only for displaying the fundamental beastliness of the human animal and which tends to be dismissed when it attempts to lead a life of its own, a life which is capable of as wide a variety of emotional impact as that of any other musical style.

However, composers are on the whole an incredibly persuasive lot, and one can be reasonably confident that, in the end, good relations between composer and audience can be restored. It may even be that these various forms of integration in which the references of atonality have so far achieved some success—the horror movie, the science-fiction space-travel epic—may provide to a degree the necessary common bond. Not that I would wish to perpetuate horror movies, and not that space travel may have much to do with serialism, but I suspect that the cliché nature of these devices is the public character of this atonal vocabulary, and that it will, for our own strange, twisted times, provide something of the same sort of public reference that the Lutheran chorale provided in the church services of Northern Europe in the late sixteenth century. There is no question that the Lutheran chorale acquainted many hostile parishioners with the strange new organization which was to become known as tonality, and I have a suspicion that the *Adventures of Captain Stratosphere* and all other such lunacies that hold us, and particularly our young, captive these days will have some significant part in making a rapprochement between a hostile public and the music of our time.

And so, if this happens and the estrangement is ended, then Schoenberg will not, cannot, be regarded as a perpetrator of deviltry. He will come to be regarded as one of the crucial pivot composers in musical history. The only thing that will remain for us to decide about Schoenberg will be the worth of the man's music itself—not the justification of his historical position. A year or so ago, I was asked by the Canadian Broadcasting Corporation to prepare a radio documentary on Schoenberg's life, and in doing so I interviewed a number of people who had known him; but I was careful to choose not only those who had loved him or been in awe of him but also those who had feared him and even hated him. And so I got a fascinating cross-section of opinion when I asked each of them one question: What will happen to Schoenberg in the year 2000?

The opinions ranged from that of a music critic in one of the leading American national magazines, who said that probably nothing very much would be in store for Schoenberg in the year 2000, in fact that his style was already in decline, to that of a celebrated composer who told me that he believed that Schoenberg's musical expression was a very powerful but a very tortured one, and that certain of the works would undoubtedly survive as artistic reminders of the turmoil and instability of our age. There were many other points of view covering every shade of opinion, but none of them quite as absorbing as the absolutely charming quotation which I was able to find in a speech that Schoenberg had written shortly before his death and which he called "My Evolution." In it he began to reminisce about his youth in Vienna and told a marvelous and poignant anecdote about the Emperor Franz Josef. Here it is: "Our Emperor Franz Josef I usually honored openings of important industrial or artistic expositions by his presence. On such occasions, the chairmen of the committees were allowed to present prominent industrialists and artists to the Emperor. On these occasions, the chairman would introduce the guests in this manner—'Your Majesty, may I present Mr. So and So, the great industrialist.' Thereafter, turning to the gentleman, he added, 'His Majesty, the Emperor.' After he had been through this several times, the Emperor said softly, 'By now, I hope the gentlemen will know who I am.' " And then Schoenberg added, "May I hope that in another fifty years they will also know who I am."

We are too close to Schoenberg to really evaluate him. Anything that we may say about him now is the result either of guesswork or of blind faith or of reading into his views on historical evolution an importance which we transfer to his music. But if you want my guess, and if you will accept it as from one who has made a real effort to separate the theorist from the composer and has endeavored not to confuse the less-than-perfect logic which sometimes governed Schoenberg's theories with the value judgment of his work, it is, then, that I would guess that we will someday know indeed "who he was"; we will someday know that he was one of the greatest composers who ever lived.

THE PIANO MUSIC OF ARNOLD SCHOENBERG

For Arnold Schoenberg, the piano was an instrument of convenience. He turned to it as a solo vehicle on five occasions—six, if one counts the Piano Concerto—and used it also in his lieder, as partner to the voice, and in certain of his instrumentally assorted chamber works. To some extent, then, it is possible to trace the development of Schoenberg's stylistic ideas through his writing for piano; and in doing so, one comes to the conclusion that with the appearance of each subsequent work, the piano per se meant less and less to him. Mind you, it would be unfair to imply that Schoenberg was unsympathetic to the mechanics of the instrument. There is not one phrase in all of his music for the piano which is badly conceived in terms of execution on

Liner notes from Columbia M2S 736, 1966.

a keyboard. There is certainly no trace of that excessively arbitrary anti-instrumental bias which increasingly marked Schoenberg's writing for the violin and which came to a remorseless conclusion in the congested figurations and impractical harmonics demanded of that instrument in the Fantasy, Op. 47.

Schoenberg does not write *against* the piano, but neither can he be accused of writing *for* it. There is not one phrase in his keyboard output which reveals the least indebtedness to the percussive sonorities exploited in an overwhelming percentage of contemporary keyboard music. Either Schoenberg recognized that the *moto ritmico barbarico* method was absolutely the dead end it has since been proved (an insight granted to few of his confreres) and that its heyday could endure only so long as the last tendon stayed unstretched, or, as I hold to be the case, he possessed almost from the outset of his career a very different opinion as to how the instrument might serve him best. He asks very little of the piano in terms of instrumental eccentricity. One might cite the pedal harmonics in the first movement of Op. 11 (which almost invariably fail to carry beyond the first row) and the demonic metronome markings of the Piano Concerto (which his courteous foreword suggests be taken with a grain of salt) as indulgences, but there are precious few other instances in which Schoenberg demands of the instrument anything that goes against the grain of its sounding board. Though Schoenberg uses an instrumental equivalent of Sprechgesang in much of his fiddle music, there is no attempt to capitalize upon such extravagances in his writing for piano.

Schoenberg, of course, did not write, or at any rate publish, a composition for solo piano until he was ready to abandon the late-blooming tonal luxuriance of his first style. In his first period, however, he did produce masses of lieder. And in the best of these Op. 1 and Op. 2 lieder, as well as in the songs of Op. 3 and Op. 6, Schoenberg managed to employ an accompanimental style which is, in my opinion, more original and indeed more suited to the instrument than the lieder accompaniments of Brahms or Hugo Wolf, and not less imaginative—which is saying a great deal—than those of Richard Strauss. Indeed, I can think of no song by Strauss which exploits the quasisymphonic resources of the contrapuntally employed piano to better effect than "Warnung" of Schoenberg's Op. 3 or "Verlassen" from his Op. 6. Perhaps one should conclude this brief comment on the pre-atonal keyboard style of Schoenberg with its increasingly complex polyphony by mentioning that the orchestral accompaniments of the Six Songs, Op. 8, were provided with piano reductions by no less an authority than Anton Webern, which for sheer ledger-line unplayability are equaled only by Eduard Steuermann's transcription of the First Chamber Symphony and by my own (mercifully unpublished and after-hours only) reduction of Bruckner's Eighth.

In the Second String Quartet (1907–08) Schoenberg offered his last essay in chromatically extended tonality. (The quasitonal experiments of the late years, whatever their superficial similarity to his early style, have an altogether different harmonic focus, which I discussed in some notes to volume 3 of CBS's "The Music of Arnold Schoenberg."*) And in the final movement of this Quartet, he began, most tentatively, to explore the uncharted cosmos which he was sure existed beyond the gravitational pull of tonality.

It was at this time, about 1908, that Schoenberg began to use the piano as a solo instrument. Perhaps no other composition was as crucial to Schoenberg's future, and if one accepts the eventualities of that future, then also to twentieth-century music, as the Three Piano Pieces, Op. 11. They were not his first atonal works, for besides the last movement of the Second Quartet, many of the songs in his magnificent cycle *Das Buch der hängenden Gärten*, Op. 15, predated Op. 11. But in terms of a sustained structure (the second of the Three Piano Pieces runs to nearly seven minutes), Op. 11 was the first major test of the possibilities of survival in a musical universe no longer dominated by a triadically centered harmonic orbit. And the survival potential was, on the basis of Op. 11, eminently satisfactory.

Op. 11, No. 1, is a masterpiece. Judged by any criteria, this glorious vignette must rank with the very best of Brahms's intermezzos. Op. 11, No. 2, is not nearly so successful. It is a long, somewhat gawky construction that keeps posing sophisticated melodic utterances over a D-F ostinato which, in view of the speculative uncertainty of the harmonic universe into which Schoenberg now projected himself, was perhaps retained for that same degree of consolation and reassurance that Linus in "Peanuts" seeks in his blanket. Op. 11, No. 3, is the first example of those flamboyant studies in sonority with which Schoenberg experimented in these transition years and which he was shortly to employ in the Five Orchestral Pieces, Op. 16. If it is not quite so successful as Op. 11, No. 1, it is still perhaps the most courageous moment in Schoenberg's middle period.

I wonder if any group of pieces of comparable total duration (five and a half minutes, give or take a *Luftpause*) has ever elicited as much analytical scrutiny as Schoenberg's Op. 19. Ironically, these Six Little Piano Pieces, which were once described as having condensed a novel into a sigh, have been subject over the last fifty years to enough critical attention to fill a small encyclopedia. The first reaction to these pieces—the reaction of academics conditioned to think of breadth of outline, developmental sequence within a structure, and coloristic largesse as inevitable concomitants of Occidental musical tradition—was that they either annihilated the mainstream of nineteenth-century romanticism or forever alienated Schoenberg from

---

*See p. 134.

it. Either Schoenberg had indeed discovered a new way in which to order and direct musical progression or he had declared himself emotionally bankrupt.

The truth, I think, lay somewhere in between. These are puzzling, even infuriating little pieces, and the initial reaction to them was not altogether unjustified. It *is* disconcerting to admit that Schoenberg, the creator of the colossal *Gurrelieder,* should be reduced to writing keyboard trifles. Furthermore, one is tempted to read these works in the light of their influence upon Schoenberg's disciples. The phenomenon of their brevity so fascinated the young composers under Schoenberg's tutelage that, with an apostolic fervor equaled in recent years only by the cult of the aleatoric or the curse of the reversible tape, these pieces reappeared almost instantly as Webern's Op. 9 and as Alban Berg's slightly more substantial Op. 5. Suddenly, the art of the miniaturist was prospering; pianissimos proliferated, and rests acquired fermatas. A new day of *Augenmusik* was at hand. It was, of course, an escape hatch, an emergency exit for the uncomfortable stowaways aboard the good ship *Post-Wagnerian Romanticism.*

But Schoenberg was not of this company: his *Verklärte Nacht, Pelleas und Melisande,* the Quartet in D Minor, and the Chamber Symphony in E were never an appendix to the postromantic movement. They were, rather, its intense and resourceful culmination. Schoenberg had earned the right to experiment; however, Op. 19, despite being a stimulus to the pointillistic manner, was not, for Schoenberg, a profitable experiment. Shortly, he was to withdraw into a decade of reflection and meditation. To continue as a miniaturist was not to be his role. Indeed, the very best of his miniatures, the penultimate song from *Das Buch der hängenden Gärten,* Op. 15, makes its effect not only because of pointillistic novelty but also through the contrast implicit in its location within the spacious architecture of that last of the great romantic song cycles.

With Op. 23, composed in 1923, Schoenberg returned to a more conventional scale of duration. These Five Piano Pieces are not unlike Op. 11 in texture, but they are infinitely more elaborate in terms of the motivic involvements. For Schoenberg was on the brink of his still controversial technical breakthrough—the system of composition with rows consisting of twelve tones. The fifth piece of Op. 23 is the first legislated twelve-tone composition—a statistic for the record only, since in all other respects it is dwarfed by the superbly inventive, not quite totally organized composing process which produced Nos. 1 through 4. Schoenberg's method, while verging on the twelve-tone procedure, was an extension of the semisystematized motivic variation which he used to great effect in such works of his atonal period as the monodrama *Erwartung,* Op. 17. It is a method by which a sequence of intervals recurs ad infinitum, the statements being distinguished from one another only by variables of rhythm, transposition, and dynamic projection. For the continuance of these primary motivic groups (there need not, as in the early practice of the twelve-tone system, be only one group), such conceits of classical-romantic organization as first theme, secondary theme, episode, and so forth become meaningless—or, at any rate, change their spots to match the dynamic, rhythmic, and, if I may borrow a useful bit of Princetonian terminology, pitch-class conditions.

Consider this "thematic" passage from Op. 23, No. 2, a ten-tone row in which the last tone is the enharmonic equivalent of the first:

A sequential section that occurs later on in the piece employs tones one through nine:

Finally, the row, minus the first tone, appears inverted in three simultaneous statements, the initial pitches of which—G, B, E-flat—are four semitones apart (B serving to inaugurate the triadic superpositions).

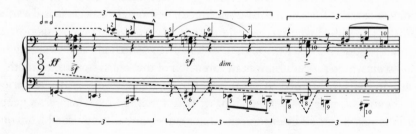

Of Op. 25, composed in 1925, I cannot speak without some prejudice. I can think of no composition for solo piano from the first quarter of this century which can stand as its equal. Nor is my affection for it influenced by Schoenberg's total reliance on twelve-tone procedures. The fact that some of Schoenberg's greatest works were produced in the last half of the 1920s is undoubtedly related to his use of the twelve-tone method. But indirectly! Schoenberg, the prophet who had fallen silent, had found his voice again. From out of an arbitrary rationale of elementary mathematics and debatable historical perception came a rare joie de vivre, a blessed enthusiasm for the making of music. And the Piano Suite, along with the other exuberant neo-rococo essays of this period (Serenade, Op. 24; Wind Quintet, Op. 26, etc.), for all its reliance on binary dance forms and its sly digs at preclassical convention (the French Musette's pedal-ostinato is an insistent tritone) is among the most spontaneous and wickedly inventive of Schoenberg's works.

Actually, limitation is the key to Schoenberg's inventive capacity here. Not only did he follow his twelve-tone method strictly, but he deliberately selected row material that further restricted his intervallic choices. Throughout the Piano Suite, only four basic positions of the row are heard: the original and its inversion, beginning on E, and a transposition of these two forms beginning on B-flat. (Note the G–D-flat tritone common to all four, as well as the perhaps not quite accidental B-A-C-H motive formed in reverse order by tones 9 through 12.)

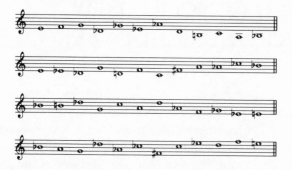

The two pieces of Op. 33 (1929 and 1932) are a bit of a letdown. They make use of the harmonically subdivided row devices with which Schoenberg was increasingly preoccupied during the last two decades of his life. This is the technique that appeared in most of his twelve-tone works from the time of *Von Heute auf Morgen* and *Accompaniment to a Film Scene* (1929 and 1930) on. In somewhat modified form, it was to produce the haunting, quasitonal harmonies found in many of the late works (*Kol Nidre, Ode to Napoleon Bonaparte,* etc.) and also to encourage in the more conventional twelve-tone essays of the last period (Piano Concerto, Violin Fantasy, etc.) an exploitation of invertible hexachords as row material. In Op. 33, however, the vertical aspects of the tone-row technique had not yet been assimilated, and the result is a somewhat pedestrian exposition of three- and four-tone superpositions decorated by what are for Schoenberg rather rigid melodic ideas.

Experiment was the essence of Schoenberg's musical experience, and we can be grateful that in carrying out his experiments he turned on five occasions to the solo piano. Each of these compositions either inaugurates or shares in the inauguration of a new chapter in Schoenberg's development. And given his pragmatic relationship to the instrument, it is not surprising that when in his later years he occupied himself with an experiment of conciliation between the twelve-tone method and harmonic structures reminiscent of his pre-atonal style, the piano, incidental to the symphonic vocabulary which he now recalled, was no longer suited to his purpose. But during the crucial moments of the most significant experiments of his career, during the years when Schoenberg was reworking the contemporary musical language, the piano—inexpensive to write for, instantly able to demonstrate the dangers and the possibilities of a new vocabulary—was his servant. Schoenberg repaid it with some of the great moments in its contemporary literature.

PIANO CONCERTOS BY
MOZART AND SCHOENBERG

This record contains two concertos which represent, virtually, the terminal positions of the literature for piano and orchestra. Possibly greater contrasts and/or historical point could have been obtained had we linked a concerto grosso (Handel, for instance) with a concerto grosso (Hindemith, perhaps); but for the purpose of illustrating the transition into and out of the great concerto manner these two works will do very well indeed. The assumption is, of course, that the concerto *idée* is now more or less an unserviceable mold for the present techniques of musical composition, although in the guessable future composers will undoubtedly find other means to satisfy the primeval human need for showing off.

The one hundred and fifty years between Mozart's K. 491 and Schoenberg's Op. 42 added many resourceful variations to the fundamental areas of dynamic contrast and rhythmic stress which helped the baroque masters

Liner notes from Columbia MS 6339, 1962.

exploit the solo-tutti antithesis. Somewhere along toward the middle of the eighteenth century, the acoustical corollary of the solo-mass idea—the *pian-e-forte* aspect of concerto-grosso style—became fused with the new symphonic adventures in thematic contrast, and the concerto became, in effect, a showpiece adjunct of the classical symphony; and ever since, with a few eccentric exceptions, the evolution of the concerto manner has been inextricably bound up with that of symphonic form.

The one great distinction between concerto technique and that of its symphonic model has always lain in the peculiarly redundant distribution of material which the solo-tutti forces required. The difficulty of supplying to the soloist something to keep him duly occupied that will not, at the same time, wholly disrupt the symphonic flow of events has constituted the concerto problem through the years, and it is a problem which has only rarely been solved. Perhaps for this reason the most popular and successful (though never the best) of concertos have usually come from composers who were somewhat lacking in a grasp of symphonic architecture—Liszt, Grieg, etc. —composers who had in common a confined, periodic concept of symphonic style but who were able to linger without embarrassment upon the glowing melodic moment. Perhaps also for this reason, the great figures of the symphonic repertoire have almost always come off second best in concerto writing, and their relative failures have helped to give credence to the widespread and perfectly defensible notion that concertos are comparatively lightweight stuff. (After all, there is something slightly hilarious when a master of Olympian stature like Beethoven, for instance, from whom we expect the uncompromising pronouncement, qualifies his symphonic "This is my final word" with the concerto-genre equivalent, "This is my final word—but you won't mind if I say it again.")

The most exceptional development of the classical concerto's attempt to "say it again" was the feature of the orchestral pre-exposition. This two-or-three-minute capsule of the basic material from the opening movement allowed the solo instrument, upon its entrance, a greater degree of freedom in treating themes which had previously been heard in some perspective. It also allowed the solo instrument to play throughout the exposition proper more continuously than would otherwise be desirable.

The Mozart Concerto in C minor, perhaps for the very reason that it contains some of the master's most exalted music, is not a very successful concerto. It opens with a magnificently constructed orchestral tutti—the sort of pre-exposition which Sir Donald Tovey was always chiding Beethoven for not having written. It consists, in fact, of two or three of the most skillfully architected minutes in all of Mozart. But with the first entrance of the piano we soon modulate to a much less elevated region. Having successfully avoided the mood and pleasure of the relative major key (E-flat) throughout the orchestral tutti, the piano now leads us there with a vengeance—and gets hopelessly stalled in that key. Once, twice, three times, separated by unimaginative sequences, the soloist caresses E-flat with material wholly unworthy of the magnificence of the introduction. And by the time the tutti material returns in the development, we are left wishing that Mozart had given his tutti and a few clavier lessons to Haydn and let the boundless developmental capacities of that gentleman go to work on it.

The writing for the solo instrument, moreover, is somewhat anachronistic, since the left hand of the soloist is more often than not engaged in doubling the cello and/or bassoon parts. Consequently, the total impression of the soloist's contribution is an annoying confusion of fickle virtuosity in the upper registers and an unrealized continuo in the left hand. (The author has taken a very few liberties in this regard which he believes are wholly within the spirit and substance of the work.)

The second movement contains some subtly contrived woodwind scoring that contrasts strikingly with the complete innocence of the solo instrument's principal theme, which, when it is played on the discouragingly sophisticated instruments of our own day, is almost impossible of realization. It is the last movement which holds the Mozart of our dreams. Here, in a supremely beautiful set of variations, is a structure with a raison d'être, a structure in which the piano shares without intrusion, in which, as variation upon variation passes by, the chromatic fugal manner which Mozart in his philosophic moods longed to espouse is applied to the ephemeral realm of the concerto with brilliant success.

If the Mozart C-minor represents the concerto form as it merged into the virtuoso tradition, the Schoenberg Concerto represents the beginning of the end for that tradition. The solo contribution throughout (cadenzas excepted) is really only that of an enlarged obbligato. This, despite the fact that Schoenberg was at the time of its composition (1942) experiencing a return to large-scale architectural interests and was moreover, upon occasion, experimenting once again with the use of tonality—albeit a somewhat grayer and more stringently controlled tonality than he had used in his early years. It is probably no accident that his Violin and Piano Concertos were written during these years in which he was most conscious of his link with the romantic symphonic tradition, but the Piano Concerto (several notable analysts to the contrary) is not one of the works in this neotonal cycle and is in fact fairly typical of Schoenberg's later twelve-tone writing.

Schoenberg had taken his first, tentative, twelve-tone steps in the neoclassic environment of his middle years—years in which the alarming license of tonal free trade caused him to gravitate toward a rational classicism for which the architectural formulae of the eighteenth century provided scholastic discipline.

As was proper to their eighteenth-century models, his first essays in twelve-tone writing were exercises in straightforward row technique. Such architectural forms as the dance suite, for example, provided a convenient mold into which the first twelve-tone fluid might be poured. Thus the most marked feature of these early twelve-tone efforts is a rather external poise and grace.

Schoenberg had long been aware that before twelve-tone music might be said to have achieved sovereignty, the forms engendered by it would have to own of something specifically related to twelve-tone procedure —something in which the growth of the most minute organism, the embryonic cell of sound, would be reflected. It has been said quite seriously that whatever forms Schoenberg applied to music, the only constant constructive force in his work was the principle of variation. Indeed, the variation concept in its most natural state—that of constant evolution—provides the best synthesis of twelve-tone theory.

Schoenberg, in his early twelve-tone works, frequently presented two transpositions of the row simultaneously, thus making a distinct division between melodic and harmonic participation. In the middle thirties, he began more and more frequently to use one transposition at a time, subdividing it into harmonic groups so that a succession of chords was formed from the row with points of melodic line appearing as uppermost factors of these chords. Thus the harmonic control of the tone row was tightened, while the melodic dimension was somewhat released from bondage. By the later thirties, Schoenberg was attempting to amalgamate both procedures by a simultaneous exposition of two transpositions of the same row—but a row so devised that, should it be reproduced at a specific interval and (usually) inverted, the first six tones of the original become, though in shuffled order, the last six of the inversion, and—if there is anyone who is not now thoroughly confused—vice versa.

The Piano Concerto possesses such a row. Its original form is so arranged that if it is inverted at five semitones above, the following results:

EXAMPLE I

If these two transpositions are combined, it will be seen that the first six tones of the original and the first six tones of the inversion produce one complete twelve-tone spectrum, while utilizing only the interval combinations of half the row. Thus, within the harmonic range of a full tone row, a greater economy of interval structure is achieved.

If the row of the Piano Concerto is subdivided into four chords of three tones each, two positions of the same seventh chord are formed by the superposition of tones 1–3 and 4–6.

EXAMPLE 2

The same procedure applied to the consequent tones, 7–9 and 10–12, makes a combination of fourth chords and whole-tone units, and passages such as the following are derived:

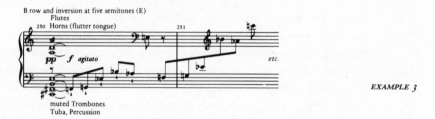

EXAMPLE 3

In somewhat subtler ways the two halves of the row are frequently assigned distinctive rhythmic shapes or perhaps consigned to different clefs.

EXAMPLE 4

The work is in four movements joined without pause—or, perhaps more accurately, with apostrophes—and each of these four movements develops a special aspect of the harmonic treatment of the row. In the first movement, which is a theme and variations, the theme is assigned to the right hand of the piano and consists of the four basic applications of the twelve-tone series—the original form, the inversion, the retrogression, and the retrogressive inversion. The inversion and retrogressive inversion appear in the transposition at five semitones. The accompaniment in the left hand consists of discrete comments derived from the row in use. Therefore, the theme of the first movement effects a pseudotonal solidarity by confining itself to one transposition (if the inversion at five semitones be regarded as indigenous) of the row. Each successive variation (there are three, separated by episodes of rhythmic preparation) increases the number of participating transpositions of the series and hence puts pressure on the harmonic pace and results in a truncation of the main theme itself. In the first eight bars of variation 3 the original theme, or rather the first of its four sentences, is derived by excerpting and accenting individual notes drawn from no fewer than seven transpositions plus their complementary inversions.

The second movement is an energetic scherzo propelled by this rhythmic unit:

EXAMPLE 5

In this movement, Schoenberg, counting on greater aural familiarity with the properties of the three-tone chord units illustrated in examples 2 and 3, begins disconnecting successive tones of the original row and concocting new melodic and harmonic material by leapfrogging tones 1, 3, 3—2, 4, 6; similarly tones 7, 9, 11 and 8, 10, 12. The even numbers of the antecedent (2, 4, 6) and the odd numbers of the consequent (7, 9, 11) form chromatically adjoining fourth chords while the remaining tones (1, 3, 5—8, 10, 12) produce a wry diminutive of tones 10–12 from the original set:

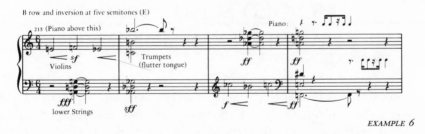

EXAMPLE 6

Utilizing this division of the series and playing it off against the original's consequent segment of whole-tone units in fourth chords, Schoenberg gradually eliminates all other motives and realizes in the final bars of the scherzo an almost total technical immobility.

If the scherzo is the dynamic vortex of the work, the emotional center is surely the superb Adagio—one of the greatest monuments to Schoenberg's technical skill. Here the procedures of both of the preceding movements are elaborated and combined. The divisi melodic leapfrogging of the scherzo creates in the opening tutti of the third movement a new melody of true breadth and grandeur:

EXAMPLE 7

Once again, as Schoenberg assumes a greater psychological comprehension on the part of the listener, a further relaxation of the twelve-tone bondage is permitted. The four harmonic blocks of the original row (examples 2 and 3) are concentrated in a long solo for the piano. Then, with consummate mastery, these two procedures are brought together in an orchestral tutti which is one of the grandest edifices of the mature Schoenberg.

The final movement is a rondo—a pure, classically proportioned rondo—in which the central episode is a series of three variations upon the theme of the third movement (example 7). In this movement Schoenberg returns largely to the straightforward row technique of the first movement, constructing a principal theme of jocose gallantry with admirable limitation of serial means, and the movement proceeds with the sort of virtuosic abandon and incorruptible simplicity that the rondos of Mozart and Beethoven reveal.

ARNOLD SCHOENBERG'S
CHAMBER SYMPHONY NO. 2

Schoenberg completed the Second Chamber Symphony in 1939, six years after coming to America and thirty-three years after first taking up work on this piece. It was originally intended as a companion to the exuberant symphony for fifteen solo instruments (1906) and was begun in the same year as its sister work. Schoenberg usually worked quickly once a concept had gestated, but despite the fact that he attempted on several occasions, notably in 1911 and 1916, to pick up the elusive traces of his original plan, no reconsideration of the material and emotional prospects of this work seems to have encouraged its completion. For three decades it remained, like *Die Jakobsleiter,* a disturbing skeleton in Schoenberg's musical closet. When he did return to it in 1939, the present E-flat-minor epilogue to the second movement

Liner notes from Columbia M2S 709, 1967.

was added (to replace a third movement of independent, maestoso character which Schoenberg had envisioned at one time), and the main body of the second movement—the G-major scherzo—was completed from the earlier sketches and was to some extent harmonically and orchestrally refurbished. The result is one of the most hauntingly beautiful of his "late" scores.

I use the word "late" advisedly, because the Second Chamber Symphony—and not just those parts of it that were added in 1939—has very much to do with the late Schoenberg manner, more so indeed than with the tempestuous, chromatic style of his early years. Even though one can make a distinction between the harmonic style of the first movement and of the E-flat-minor epilogue, which in effect serves as a reprise of it, one finds that the first movement, indisputably a product of the early years, poses certain problematic harmonic situations which await an answer and a solution in the epilogue. I suggest that these were problems of harmonic style for which Schoenberg, in 1906, did not yet have an answer, and that this, rather than any lack of inspiration, was the real obstacle that prevented him from completing this work during those many years.

It has become depressingly easy to encounter analyses in America that divide Schoenberg's work into two opposing columns: one in which we find a list of those pieces that represent the continuation of his European dodecaphonic style, and which includes the Violin and Piano Concertos, the String Trio, the Violin Fantasy, and so on, and the other comprising those of the later works which superficially suggest a return to tonality—the Variations on a Recitative for organ, *Kol Nidre,* the Variations for Band, etc. It is sometimes argued that this curious duality relates to some psychological schism in Schoenberg's character—that the later twelve-tone works represent the evolution of the mainstream of his musical thought and, of course, point directly to the future, while the "opposing" series of neotonal compositions are therefore depicted as a nostalgic recollection of youth, an anachronistic concern with the world that had been. These arguments, necessarily, are based upon the notion that these late works are *conventionally* tonal and upon the idea that any conspicuous return to tonality on the part of the leading radical of modern music, unless excused by an appeal to that charity with which we grant old men the telling of their fondest stories twice, would be a betrayal of the ideals which the younger generation has long since accepted from Schoenberg's example.

I believe that this departmentalizing of Schoenberg's activity is dangerous, because it is based upon a misconception of the nature both of tonality and of serialism, or at any rate of that rather puritan conception of serialism which Schoenberg held. I believe that the late "tonal" works are every bit as essential to Schoenberg's development as are the late dodecaphonic compositions. Moreover, I think that both series of works examine, essentially, the same problems, and that this examination would be just as incomplete if Schoenberg had omitted writing the late "tonal" works as it would have been had he not given us the twelve-tone works of his last period. And I believe, further, that both series of works would have been impossible without the new perceptions and technical assurance that Schoenberg had gained through the composition of that glorious catalogue of early twelve-tone masterpieces which includes the Wind Quintet, the Third String Quartet, and the Variations for Orchestra.

To be sure, the line dividing tonality from the appearance of tonally reminiscent sequences is not always easy to define in Schoenberg's later works, because the arbitrary selection of motivic material upon which he settled as sponsor of his twelve-tone structures tends with the later works to become more dependent upon interval connections which, if not in themselves tonally reminiscent, are at least triadically reminiscent. Schoenberg's fondness for the sort of row that would provide him with a series of triad forms was prompted less by an interest in triads per se than by a concern for finding twelve-tone situations in which the two halves of the row would not only be complementary in terms of their division of the chromatic scale but would also emphasize similar interval combinations within both antecedent and consequent portions. The reasons for this concern with interval duplication can be summarized as a desire to achieve total chromatic equilibrium while concentrating upon stringently controlled motivic resources; in effect, the principle of diversity within unity that governs practically all of Schoenberg's works is here expressed in terms peculiar to twelve-tone organization. Schoenberg found certain solutions to this problem which greatly appealed to his peculiarly pedagogical instincts, and he manufactured one row which he was pleased to call the "miracle set" and which, with minor alterations, served him as the basic set for the *Ode to Napoleon Bonaparte*, Op. 41.

With material such as this, Schoenberg unavoidably created a series of triadic relationships, which, depending upon the qualifications that the accompanying texture imposes, do foster varying impressions of quasitonal substance.

Occasionally, these impressions are deliberate and calculated, and the row material is manipulated accordingly, as in the C-minor "Victory" motive in the *Ode to Napoleon Bonaparte*

"*The earth-quake voice of victory*"

or the closing E-flat-major cadence of the same work. But, generally speaking, these works are much less concerned with providing for us an approachable point of reference with which to comprehend the harmonic aspects of serialism than they are with attempting an idea of harmony *within* serialism that might be more accurately described as a vocabulary of triadic relationship beyond the scope of key-centered tonality. Insofar as the vertical superimpositions of such linear material as Schoenberg's "miracle set" can be forced to exhibit exclusively triadic forms, they are, of course, inescapably replete with tonal association. But the substance of tonality has less to do with triads than with the connecting matter that holds them together and provides a pattern of tension control for the textures of tonality, whereas what is here available to Schoenberg is an interminably balancing, endlessly triadic flow attained through the systematic serialization of triad forms, just as perpetual dissonant suspension was available through the same means. Even though he seldom uses these units in situations in which their triadic aspect is present without some form of contrast or relief, the harmonic texture in the later twelve-tone works relies heavily upon the dualistic, hexachordally contrived balances inherent within this type of invertible and triad-prone sequence. And the degree to which this sort of twelve-tone manipulation is reflected in the neotonal works of the late years is really quite astonishing. They, too, are full of textures that, though perhaps less diligently contrived, are unmistakably related to Schoenberg's twelve-tone experience of that period. Triads abound, of course, but as often as not in formations that suspend the conformation of one tonal center for at least brief periods of time and achieve this, furthermore, not simply by interpolating dissonant forms between the triad properties but also by the very swiftness with which the triads follow each other—triads which neither confirm nor deny the tonal suspicions which they inevitably arouse.

In addition to this vocabulary of revolving triadic forms, which are present in substantially the same degree in both the twelve-tone works and the "neotonal" works, we also find that there is a remarkable similarity in the use of textural support as between both types of Schoenberg's later compositions. The late neotonal works are just as full of those half-contrapuntal figures evolving from the earlier tone-row practices wherein Schoenberg invariably searched the various transpositions of his basic set for interval groups that reflected or amplified their opposite number in some closely related row transposition. The twelve-tone works of the later years tend to be full of this kind of inner-voice writing, in which much of the supporting texture has to do with comparative values between corresponding interval groups from a variety of row transpositions.

Piano Concerto

And by the same token, the neotonal works also depend upon contrapuntal elaborations which behave exactly as though they, too, were conforming to some predetermined motivic sequence and within which the nature of subsidiary motivic discipline involves comparative identifications of short, secondary motives which seem to be reacting against each other within a tightly disciplined interval control.

Chamber Symphony No. 2

There is nothing so futile as the attempt to make a work of art serve a system of analysis for the conformation of which it was not created. And it would be perfectly idiotic for me to suggest that in the Second Chamber Symphony there are not harmonic sequences that would fall conveniently within the glossary of any late romantic composer. Of course there are! But I do suggest that we can use this piece as a key to the harmonic evolution of Schoenberg's style, and that it provides us with most remarkable evidence of the subtle transformation of his technique.

Essentially, Schoenberg's evolution of Wagnerian tonal extension falls into three phases—the last of which, I believe, because of the misguided views that are widely propagated about his later works, has by no means received its proper value. The first phase, of course, has to do with that method of elusiveness, that deliberate encouragement of a condition of ambiguity, which is the special distinction of all the post-Wagnerians. In this phase, the composer takes advantage of the many and varied resolutions that can apply with equal validity to such enharmonic chameleons as the diminished factors of ninth chords, and by such means achieves a harmonic strategy of interminably postponed, or frustrated, resolution. And the earliest works of Schoenberg, the *Gurrelieder,* for instance, respond to precisely that sort of principle. They are still concerned with resolution, but the drama of achieving resolution is heightened by the fact that the structure is made to countenance other equally responsible possibilities which can postpone the primary cadential formations almost indefinitely.

The second phase of chromatic extension with which Schoenberg was involved is that which sponsors most of the so-called atonal works (1908–23), as well as the harmonic condition of the earlier twelve-tone compositions. Its origins, however, are to be found in the later works of the first tonal period, particularly in such conspicuous examples as the Chamber Symphony,

Op. 9. This is the phase in which the nature and quality of the suspending device becomes more important to the composer than the resolution being withheld. It is in the exploitation of the conjunctive factors, such as the fourth-chord progressions in Op. 9—which seem to have just stepped out of the last chapters of Schoenberg's famous textbook, the *Harmonielehre*— that we realize how the variety and quality of material by which the triadic resolution is postponed have, for Schoenberg's method, taken precedence over the reconciliation of dissonant suspension with triadic release. One need only remember in this regard that the emphatic credo of the more diligent twelve-tone devotees in Schoenberg's earlier days was the avoidance at all cost of any duplicative or triadically suggestive factor.

I propose, then, that in addition to these two phases of Schoenberg's harmonic evolution there is a third phase, one which concerns itself with harmonic forms that produce, so to speak, a lower dissonant yield—often with triadic units or variants thereof, and in that sense with certain material prospects not so very different from phase one. But unlike phase one, phase three of Schoenberg's harmonic thinking sees the triadic connection as being, or having the capability of, instantaneous connection. It minimizes the role of the dissonant suspension factor, though it does not necessarily eliminate it, and attempts to express motivic unity within diversity in vertical as well as in horizontal terms. It is, I suggest, this phase with which Schoenberg is occupied in the late neotonal works, and it is during this phase, therefore, that we find him reworking the sketches of his Second Chamber Symphony.

This conjunction of distant triadic forces is, in a sense, not as new as it might seem. For one thing, all of the later symphonic works of Anton Bruckner are related at some level to sequential patterns which concentrate around such harmonic centers as normally, in tonal music, require a good deal of preparation and intercession. It is the mark of Bruckner's "modernism" that he makes a very conscious experiment with the psychological effect of first setting up such distant relationships, complete with their conjunctive factors, and, having set them up in this way, removes the conjunctive harmonies and, with only the reminiscence of that intercession to guide us, exposes the most distantly related polarities to each other. So what Schoenberg does, then, is precisely the same thing, except that he does it in terms of adjacent chord relationships rather than of phrase-by-phrase or sentence-by-sentence comparison.

In addition to the fact that at the most obvious structural levels—the basic key identifications between movements—the E-flat-minor–G-major alternation represents the hexachordal property of the "miracle set," the whole work is filled with relationships between tightly impacted triadic forms to which we must attach new significance, not because of their correspondence with the patterns of the early tonal works but rather because of their correspondence with the harmonic manipulations of the twelve-tone works. In the first movement the texture sometimes suggests a certain tonal ennui—the music is full of a surprising number (for Schoenberg) of harmonic parallelisms, sequences of stepwise, nonadjusting chromatic movement. But although the harmonic textures of this first movement seem rather sluggish in comparison with the glinting contrapuntal virtuosity of the earlier tonal works, this is not because Schoenberg had reduced his concentration upon contextual background or was more concerned with ends than with means. Not at all—I suggest that he was already, though unconsciously perhaps, examining that revolving triadic prism that was to become his dominating harmonic concern many years later. And we see this quite clearly when we compare with the first movement the E-flat-minor epilogue which he added in 1939, for here, in addition to the virtues of a better-focused motivic emphasis and a sharper rhythmic edge, we find the basic motives of the first movement accompanied by those "triadic" forms that connect, without the help of interceding units, the most distant poles of the tonal orbit.

Chamber Symphony No. 2

Schoenberg once said that in his view there remained a great deal of good music yet to be written in the key of C. Disciples of revolutionary figures being what they are, it was widely reported that this comment was merely meant to express the catholicity of his taste and to placate his less venturesome colleagues. But I wonder if that is *all* it was about. I would suggest that Schoenberg was perhaps speaking of a situation much closer to home than was generally realized. I would venture that some specific musical involvement prompted that remark, and I would suggest further that—in its allusion to the possibility of a new consideration and organization of low-yield dissonant forms, and, consequently, a new approach to preferential tonal status—with those conciliatory words Schoenberg was providing a genuinely radical postscript to the articulation of his musical thought.

A HAWK, A DOVE, AND A
RABBIT CALLED FRANZ JOSEF

Arnold Schoenberg is a tough man to biograph. He was, of course, the century's—well, okay, the first half-century's—most controversial composer, and much of the controversy related to the logic, or lack of it, in his convolutedly quirky stylistic evolution. Simply to trace the connections between his early postromantic tonal works, the transformation from gigantism *(Gurrelieder)* to miniaturism (the Six Little Piano Pieces) which marked the beginning of his "atonal" phase, the move from "atonality" to the twelve-tone technique (most listeners can't tell the difference—Schoenberg didn't mean them to; but the implications are immense, nonetheless), and, in his last years, the merger of tonal sounds and twelve-tone principles, is a major musicological task in itself.

But, in addition, he was one of the most complicated, cantankerous, and contradictory characters in recent musical history—a Jew who converted to Catholicism, then re-embraced his original faith, a socialist turned monarchist (he advocated the restoration of the Hapsburgs), the composer of antiwar tracts during and after World War II *(Ode to Napoleon Bonaparte, A Survivor from Warsaw)* and prowar tracts during World War I (a 1916 march called "The Iron Brigade" celebrated Lance-Corporal Schoenberg's first year of service with the Hoch- und Deutschmeister-Regiment).

In many respects, indeed, Schoenberg was the stuff of which Ken Russell screenplays are made. Despite a relatively quiet life on the domestic front (two wives, five children, several dogs, one rabbit), he gave full rein to an ego of Wagnerian proportions. In 1921, when he formulated the twelve-tone technique, he modestly declared that "I have ensured the supremacy of German music for the next hundred years." (Reviewer's note: Would you believe thirty-five?) A compulsive teacher and lawgiver, he became obsessed with the idea that his students would endeavor to usurp his authority and pre-empt his innovatory claims. "Told Webern about short pieces. . . . Webern starts writing shorter and shorter pieces—follows all my develop-

Review of *Schoenberg: His Life, World, and Work* by H. H. Stuckenschmidt, translated by Humphrey Searle (New York: Schirmer Books, 1978); from *Piano Quarterly*, Fall 1978.

ments (exaggerates). . . . Webern seems to have used twelve tones in some of his compositions—*without telling me* [italics Schoenberg's]. . . . Webern committed many acts of infidelity with the intention of making himself the innovator."

Schoenberg confided those dark thoughts to his diary in 1940—approximately a quarter-century after the events in question—but Stuckenschmidt remarks that "if he did not hear from a friend for a long time, he thought that he had been forgotten or neglected," and this tendency clearly grew apace during the years of his American exile—1933 to his death in 1951. In the last years, indeed, such suspicions were no longer confined to European colleagues whose contacts with him were interrupted by World War II but included American nationals and, for good measure, some of his fellow exiles as well. The year before his death, the American Music Center asked him to supply a list of compositions written since 1939, and from Stuckenschmidt's description of his response to this routine request one senses that Schoenberg's egocentricity had merged with senility. He left the inquiry unanswered but made a marginal note on the stationery: "The person who demands a favor of Herr Schoenberg should first present himself with the necessary respect. For he must give a clear explanation whether this favor he demands serves a purpose which is friendly towards Herr Schoenberg. For Herr Schoenberg does not want to help his enemies."

The most celebrated—certainly the most publicized—of Schoenberg's innumerable feuds, rifts, and brouhahas concerned his fellow exile Thomas Mann. In many ways they were remarkably similar characters; among other parallels, Mann, like Schoenberg, was a hawk during World War I ("Reflections of an Unpolitical Man," "Letters to Paul Amann") and a dove in World War II ("Achtung, Deutschland"—his overseas broadcasts for Voice of America), and, not surprisingly, they became good friends during the first years of their mutual residence in Los Angeles. But then came 1947 and the publication of Mann's novel *Doctor Faustus*—the story of a composer who sells his soul to the devil and invents the twelve-tone technique. Schoenberg, who suffered from a serious eye ailment during his later years, never actually read the book; had he done so, he might have realized that it dealt not with his own work or character but, allegorically, with the collapse of post-Wilhelmian German culture. He relied instead upon such master gossips as Alma Mahler-Werfel (the widow of composer Gustav Mahler) and his own wife, Gertrud, and wrote to a friend: "From my wife and also from other quarters, I heard that he had attributed my twelve-note method to his hero, without mentioning my name. I drew his attention to the fact that historians might make use of this in order to do me an injustice. After prolonged reluctance, he declared himself prepared to insert, in all subsequent copies in all languages, a statement concerning my being the originator of the method." Mann did so, in good faith, noting in the second printing that the twelve-tone technique was indeed the invention of Arnold Schoenberg—"a contemporary composer and theoretician." But Schoenberg was not to be placated; he denounced Mann in the *Saturday Review of Literature,* accusing him of stealing his cultural property and of compounding the crime by his prefatory insertion: "In two or three decades," the composer declared, "we will know who was contemporary with whom."

The source of most such Schoenbergian temper tantrums was his ambivalent relationship with the zeitgeist. The world proclaimed him a revolutionary, but Schoenberg was in fact a profoundly conservative man who was preoccupied with maintaining tradition, convinced that his own work represented the logical continuation of the Austro-German romantic school, and tolerated no dissent from those whose views of the historical process led to other conclusions. His own knowledge of musical history, however, was surprisingly limited; essentially an autodidact, he had little interest in music prior to the time of Bach, was suspicious (and possibly a bit envious) of such musicologically erudite disciples as Krenek and Webern, and regarded medieval modes as "a primeval error of the human spirit."

Stuckenschmidt, indeed, makes clear that Schoenberg's use of the word "tradition" invariably implied *German* tradition, but this persuasion did not preclude his occasional enthusiasms for such unlikely figures as Puccini, Milhaud, and George Gershwin. Indeed, some of the most vivid sequences in the book deal with Schoenberg's response to the West Coast life-style, in deference to which he occasionally took on the characteristics of a septuagenarian Sunset boulevardier. He exchanged visits and correspondence with such colleagues as Charlie Chaplin, Groucho Marx, and Oscar Levant, reveled in the tennis prowess of his teen-age son, Ronny, who threatened for a time to become the Jimmy Connors of Brentwood Park, and had his astrological horoscope plotted—he was convinced he would die on the thirteenth of a month, and did.

In short, as noted above, a tough man to biograph, but H. H. Stuckenschmidt brings admirable qualifications to the task. A former student of Schoenberg, he is the author of previous biographies of Ravel and Busoni and is widely regarded as the dean of European music critics—one of the very few critics on any continent, indeed, who are accorded something close to universal respect within the musical profession. Further, although he has clearly had access to virtually all relevant materials (his volume bears a dedication to the composer's daughter and son-in-law, Nuria and Luigi Nono), he offers some startling insights into Schoenberg's immensely complicated character and avoids any hint of an "authorized" biographical imprimatur. And although his volume contains more zany anecdotes per chapter than any comparable study, we are never allowed to lose sight of the fact that, for all his behavioral extravagance, Schoenberg was one of the greatest composers who ever lived.

There are, however, some problems. Stuckenschmidt seems to have been determined to make his study the indispensable reference for all future Schoenberg scholars (he may well have been successful!) and, as a result, tells us more about the day-to-day happenings in the Schoenberg household than I, for one, really wanted to know. (I concede that this ostrichlike reaction may be a purely personal quirk; illusions are important to me vis-à-vis artists I admire, and after a perusal of Stuckenschmidt's study I can no longer maintain mine intact.) Nevertheless, Stuckenschmidt frequently inserts his most insightful comments within paragraphs otherwise devoted to laundry-list trivia and, in the process, imposes upon the reader a heavy burden of editorial selectivity. On page 342, for example, the author offhandedly remarks: "In addition to the Old Testamentary belief in being chosen, Schoenberg also had a pride in suffering of a very Christian kind." Now, if I had said that—and I certainly wish I had—it would, at the very least, have served me as leitmotiv for a chapter on Schoenberg's spiritual development, after which I might well have announced my retirement. Stuckenschmidt, on the other hand, happens upon this stunning insight while commenting on a letter which Schoenberg wrote to his sister-in-law (who had been ill) and, after a brief quotation from *that* document, proceeds, in the following paragraph, to tell us that "the Schoenbergs made plans for travel. They first of all wanted to found a tennis club somewhere with Rudolf Kolisch, his quartet, and Mitzi Seligmann." So much for what Schoenberg liked to call "developing variation"!

Stuckenschmidt's book offers many such revelatory insights, as well as several set-piece chapters, including one on "Schoenberg and Busoni," which deviate from the prevailing diarylike approach and establish themselves as major essays. In the main, however, he follows a relentlessly chronological course—from time to time providing anecdotal material which, precisely because of this approach, appears to need further elucidation. When he gets around to July 1917, for example, Stuckenschmidt mentions that "a mysterious American called Kohler [the author is particularly partial to foreign-intrigue-style bit players with tantalizing one-shot walk-ons] who was sent to Vienna on a commercial and political mission . . . took up the plan of performing the *Gurrelieder* in New York with the composer conducting. There was talk of ten performances and a fee of $5,000. Schoenberg . . . was sceptical." Schoenberg had every reason to be; the United States had entered the war three months earlier.

The author provides an analytic sketch of almost all Schoenberg's compositions, and these interludes frequently find him at his evocative best. Describing Schoenberg's early song "Warnung," for example, he observes that "for the first time we find an aggressive passion which sticks at nothing"—as nimble a description of the modulatory ambiguities and spiritual restlessness of the young Schoenberg as I expect to encounter.

Occasionally, to be sure, he can be arbitrary: In discussing the tone row of the Piano Concerto, Op. 42, for example, he lists its intervals correctly but in a sequence beginning on A-natural; actually, the primary row of this composition begins on E-flat—psychologically, as far from A-natural as it is possible to be in a tonal context. Now, to be sure, the Piano Concerto is not set *in* a conventional tonal context, but it is one of those late Schoenberg works in which formal, intermovement continuity is linked to specific tone-row transpositions, and Stuckenschmidt's unsubstantiated claim that this variant is in fact the original row form is puzzling indeed. In a lighter vein, a comparably arbitrary moment occurs when Stuckenschmidt quotes a letter from a certain Mrs. Lautner—Schoenberg's first pupil in his original American teaching assignment in Boston. "He completely left our little class, and the Malkins were compelled to send us to his teaching in New York by ship—the cheapest way of travelling."

Stuckenschmidt's study was originally released in Europe in 1974, coincident with the Schoenberg centennial celebrations, and is made available to English readers through Humphrey Searle's serviceable, if occasionally Germanicized, translation. ("When the first generation of his pupils were fledged," for example, or "Schoenberg's end of being employed at the bank has been described in various differing ways.") More disturbing is the apparent shortage of blue pencils in the London offices of John Calder—the firm responsible for the English adaptation. The comma appears to be unknown thereabouts ("In spite of his friendship with Dr. David Josef Bach Schoenberg felt himself no longer allied to Austrian social democracy"), typos abound (*Verklärte Nacht* is described as a "strong sextet"), some sentences go begging a conclusion ("When Schoenberg was represented in the first exhibition of the 'Blaue Reiter,' founded about the 'green-eyed water-bread with its astral appearance.' "). My own favorite is a gem from page 320: "More than twenty years later Schoenberg remembered this period in a letter written more than twenty years later."

Notwithstanding all such production flaws, Stuckenschmidt's text survives. I might wish that he had indulged his analytic gifts a little more—given us more essay chapters à la "Schoenberg and Busoni"—and kept a tighter rein on his bent for social trivia; but he manages to touch every facet of Schoenberg's troubled person and has left an indelible impression in the process. I will never again be able to contemplate Schoenberg's last years, or to think of his diasporic wanderings in search of refuge in America, without recalling a story which the author includes in a chapter devoted to the war years. The time is December 1941, Pearl Harbor but a few days in the past, and the Schoenbergs' gardener, Yoshida, and his wife, Mio, who did their cleaning, have just been interned: "One evening . . . the two boys, Ronny and Larry, and the rather older Nuria appeared with a white rabbit. It was a gift from Mio. Schoenberg hesitated to take a Japanese rabbit into the house. After a long palaver with the children, Nuria explained that the animal had been born in America and so was not Japanese and it should stay in the house. It was called Emperor Franz Josef."

HINDEMITH:
WILL HIS TIME COME? AGAIN?

In the 1930s, the options were open. For the "progressives" there was Schoenberg—not one Schoenberg, in fact, but two: the uncompromising twelve-toner of the Third and Fourth Quartets or the Violin Concerto, and the harmonically conciliatory author of *Kol Nidre* or the organ Variations. For the neoclassicists there was Stravinsky, who during the decade turned in the Symphony of Psalms, *Perséphone,* and the Symphony in C. And for those who elected to avoid the more extreme disputes of doctrine and dogma, a generous supply of middle-of-the-road alternatives was available: folkloristic modality (Bartók), folkloristic tonality (Copland), postromantic symphonic pessimism (Pfitzner, Schmidt, Berg—yes, yes, I know, an odd bracket), postromantic symphonic optimism (Prokofiev, Shostakovich, Walton), American eclecticism (Harris, Hanson), English isolationism (Vaughan Williams), Francophilic pragmatism (Roussel, Martin), Francophilic idealism (Messiaen), Germanic pragmatism (Orff, Brecht*), Germanic idealism (Webern), and, lest we forget, the aging and well-nigh uncategorizable legend Richard Strauss, whose best years lay both far behind and, though no one guessed it at the time, just ahead.

Well, I dislike labels and lists, and this one, like most, is full of holes, hunches, and half-truths. (The reader is invited to submit his own; send no labels—all entries judged on neatness, penmanship, and catholicity of outlook.) But despite the fact that in the 1930s Paul Hindemith's reputation reached its zenith and his place among the middle-of-the-roaders enumerated

---

Liner notes from Columbia M 32350, 1973.
*Presumably Weill and Eisler.—T.P.

above seemed secure, I've omitted his name from my list, because I simply have no idea where to place him on it. Germanic pragmatism? Maybe. But a man who devoted a good portion of his last years to a reconstruction of his own early output is surely something more than a pragmatist. Germanic idealism? Hardly. He did, after all, set out to supply each member of the wind choir with its very own sonata, and saw no reason to exempt the tuba. (One can't imagine Webern dabbling in that project!)

In a sense, indeed, Webern provides a yardstick—an example of everything that Hindemith was not.

	WEBERN	HINDEMITH
Output	Minimum productivity	Maximum productivity
Formal Schematics	Material-derived and/or binary preference	Materially indifferent and/or ternary preference
Harmonic Bearing	Nontonal	Quasitonal
Textural Density	Parsimonious pointillism	Value for money
Contrapuntal Bearing	Canons preferred	Fugues preferred
Rhythmic Inclination	Asymmetry	Symmetry
Instrumental Preference	Chamber groups	Plays the field
Profile (Re contemporaries)	Low	High
Subsequent Influence	Incalculable	Negligible

It's the last two categories that, as of this date, make the difference. While alive, Webern was of interest only to colleagues; his posthumous canonization was primarily an acknowledgment of the ideas engendered by his work and only secondarily attributable to the works per se. (N.B. to G.G.: File under "Controversial Pronouncements" and prepare defensive posture.) Hindemith, on the other hand, always had a public—not, perhaps, the sort of public that would turn up presold for the premiere of a Shostakovich symphony, no matter the rebuffs Tovarich Dmitri's last effort might have suffered via *Pravda* and the Presidium, nor the sort that would attend at the Royal Albert while Sir Adrian had a go at RVW's new opus, secure in the knowledge that even if the Fourth did defy good breeding and voice leading as the academy decreed, the chap is one of us and, given that, Nostalgia Waives the Rules. (N.B. to G.G.: File under "Potential Puns" and prepare defensive posture.)

But Hindemith's was not a public motivated by nostalgia, and only indirectly by ideology. Rather, it turned to him, I suspect, with the not unrealistic expectation that, in a musical milieu rife with dogmatic dissent, he would consistently provide—to quote one of his own favorite terms of approbation—a climate of intellectual "repose." And this, over an extraordinarily productive career, he tried to do. In fact, as his career drew to a close, Hindemith drew consistency around him like a Linus blanket.

The free-wheeling dissonance of his work in the 1920s—that abrasive harmonic arrogance that can be sampled at its strident best in such efforts as the Kammermusik for violin and orchestra, Op. 36, No. 3 (1925)—gave way in the 1930s to an almost self-effacing determination to bring dissonance to heel in the interests of structural cohesion. Not that Hindemith was ever to become a diatonicist—a quite singular approach to chromatic resource was the key to both the vertical and horizontal conceits of his style from the mid-1930s on—but he did, nonetheless, meticulously classify chord structures according to their dissonant yield and attribute to each a gravitational intent that discounted the romantic and postromantic concept of the root as a psychologically perceptible, but not necessarily physically demonstrable, presence.

Hindemith's method, which endowed his later works with idiomatic consistency (few musicians provide such instant giveaways for the "Who's the Composer?" version of Twenty Questions!), was fundamentally phenomenological. "I vibrate, therefore I am" might well have been his motto. And as a result, in direct proportion to his progress toward idiomatic confidence and stylistic identity, his work was somehow diminished by the systematic exclusion of all that was ambiguous, ambivalent, or otherwise resistant to analysis. The two versions of his epic song cycle *Das Marienleben* provide pertinent illustration: Draft 1 (1923) is a passionate, if occasionally untidy, masterpiece; Draft 2 (1948) is a sober, indeed impeccable, revision that approaches its subject with healthy respect in lieu of ecstatic devotion.

In any event, once Robert Craft forged the Stravinsky-Schoenberg axis in the 1950s and the eclecticism of the 1960s alleviated the austere serialism of the previous decade, the futures market in Hindemithian repose was struck by panic selling. To be sure, a handful of his works have held their place in the repertoire—the *Symphonic Metamorphoses on a Theme by Weber*, the Concert Music for brass and strings, and, above all, the magnificent triptych drawn from his opera *Mathis der Maler*. But the bulk of his output turns up nowadays on student programs (how many other major figures indulged the aspirations of tuba virtuosi?), organ recitals (the kist-o'-whistles clan is inherently conservative, and Hindemith now seems in contention for the spot previously reserved for Rheinberger and S. Karg-Elert), or on the occasion of archival projects ("Let's see if we can get all of them on one disc!") like this one.

And that's a pity! Because even though some of the clichés offered as comment on his work ("more fun to play than to listen to"; "always competent, rarely inspired") contain a modicum of truth, the works themselves are possessed of a validity that ultimately renders such comment irrelevant. They are well made; they do contain, admittedly amidst chapters with benumbingly anticipatable plot lines, paragraphs, even pages, in which musical characterizations are drawn not only sympathetically and insightfully but with an ascetic commitment to detail that suggests the medieval mating of ritual and ecstasy.

In Hindemith's work, to be sure, ecstasy is a commodity most frequently purveyed by fugal situations—the finale to the Third Piano Sonata being perhaps the most conspicuous example this album provides. On occasion, as in the outer segments of the *marcia funebre* from the First Piano Sonata, Hindemith's slow movements attain a comparable intensity. Even here, however, one can, to adopt the lingo of tape editing, see the splices going through—the central episode of the movement, though it undoubtedly measures up to Hindemith's personal yardstick of chord-group fluctuation, guide-tone orientation, and melodic diversification, behaves rather like the new boy on the block, unsure as to whether one can, or should, make friends with the kids next door. A similar gaffe is evidenced by the otherwise beautifully structured adagio of the Third Sonata, in which, as a secondary episode and for no apparent reason, Hindemith previews, note for note and at approximately half tempo, twenty-four and a half bars of the scintillating third subject from his upcoming triple-fugue finale. It is a lapse that attests not only to his fondness for contrapuntal mischief but to his not infrequent miscalculations in stage management—the miscalculation is not inherently musical but theatrical.

For Hindemith, however, and by his own admission, the ritual of craft preceded the vision of the creative idea. In this regard, it's perhaps instructive to think of Hindemith as the obverse of Scriabin, a composer for whom reason was the by-product of ecstatic experience. And Hindemith, like other composers with similar priorities—Sweelinck, Telemann, Reger, Miaskovsky—will, I suspect, be the subject of many revivals and many attempts at re-evaluation. Whatever the verdicts of future generations, they will have to reckon with a composer of prodigious gifts, a composer who, in many ways, embodied the fin-de-siècle stylistic dilemma of his era, but who, in his anxiety to validate his syntax, to propagate his theorems, sometimes permitted those priorities to divert his attention from the goal he so often acknowledged and which, when properly adduced, is the true amalgam of ecstasy and reason—repose.

A TALE OF TWO *MARIENLEBENS*

Das Marienleben is the pivotal work in Hindemith's development as a composer. Its two realizations—published a quarter-century apart—succinctly define his evolution, both as musician and as thinker, and, in the process, set something very like a historical precedent. Certainly, I can recall no comparable instance in which a great master, taking as his source the most influential and substantial of his youthful essays, re-creates it according to the technical and idiomatic lights of his maturity.

Facile comparisons come to mind, of course: Alban Berg's twelve-tone rewrite of his early song "Schliesse mir die Augen beide," for example. But, all considerations of scale aside, the distinctions between the two *Marienlebens* are far subtler than the simplistic tonal-atonal rivalries of Berg's settings. A more accurate, if inevitably imaginary, approximation of what Hindemith has wrought could perhaps be attained through a comparison with composers whose styles metamorphosed in a similar, relentlessly organic manner—Bach, say, or in more recent times Richard Strauss. As with Hindemith, both masters pursued a superficially uneventful evolution and shielded their listeners from technical innovations of a revolutionary order, but for the sake of our comparison Strauss provides the better example. For Bach, by and large, proceeded from simplicity to complexity; his early, diatonically redundant toccata fugues, for example, rewritten in the convolutedly chromatic manner of *The Art of the Fugue,* would not serve our comparative case at all. But Strauss, like Hindemith, moved in the opposite direction—complexity to simplicity—and via a route which gradually replaced daring gestures with confident routines. If, then, Richard Strauss had rewritten *Till Eulenspiegel* in the style of the Oboe Concerto, one would have a reasonable comparison to stand against Hindemith's undertaking.

For the relationship of the two *Marienlebens* is emphatically not that of first to second draft. Notwithstanding the vast amount of reprocessed material, the reproduction intact of one song ("Stillung Mariä mit dem Auferstandenen") and the inclusion of another ("Pietà") which boasts such minor alterations as make no matter, the two versions proceed from very different compositional concepts. The first *Marienleben* derives from Hindemith's youth, from a time when change was in the air, tonality in the process of an expansion which threatened its disintegration, and when the then twenty-seven-year-old Hindemith spearheaded a contrapuntal revival intended to

Liner notes from CBS MZ 34597, 1978.

buttress the about-to-be-inundated foundations of tonal harmony. It is a work of infectious spontaneity, of divine intuition, in which connections are felt to exist long before an exegesis can confirm their presence. The second *Marienleben* is the summation of Hindemith's lifelong quest for systematic coherence—a product of intense cerebration, thorough calculation, and thoughtful consideration for the vocal and instrumental personnel concerned.

On the occasion of its publication in 1948, the composer appended a supplementary essay in which he expressed his not unexpected preference for the later version. The essay is brilliantly written, tightly argued—indeed, one of the finest of Hindemith's not inconsiderable literary efforts—and, in addition to the inclusion of some shrewd comments on the then current musical scene (they read as though written yesterday!) and a vivid evocation of the compositional climate of the 1920s in which the first *Marienleben* was conceived, offers some remarkable musical and theological insights. More to the point, Hindemith advertises the (to his mind) inherent superiority of the second version by delineating the following major themes: (1) that the cycle in its original form was ungratefully conceived for the voice; (2) that it lacked dramatic coherence; (3) that the new version incorporates motivic and harmonic relationships worthy of its complex theological subject. He does not say in so many words that the original *Marienleben* lacked these latter qualities but suggests, rather, that "although in the *Marienleben* I had given the best that was in me, this best, despite all my good intentions, was not good enough to be laid aside once and for all as successfully completed."

With (1) I cannot disagree—nor, I am sure, would anyone who attempts to sing the original version. The vocal line is conceived with something like Beethovenian indifference, subjected to nonstop, instrumental-style activity, and in the more conspicuously contrapuntal segments the soloist is rarely allowed up for air. And yet it is precisely this chamber-music-like intensity which is, to me, one of the glories of the original version. The soprano part is not relieved by gratuitous piano solos, fortified by doublings, or reassured by entry cues, and as a result the vocalist is enabled to convey an urgency wholly in keeping with the more declamatory segments of the text in particular, and to cultivate a degree of abstraction unparalleled in lieder literature—an approach, in my view, which is singularly appropriate to this particular subject.

The second *Marienleben* risks no such ambiguities. The piano part is not only less interestingly conceived, it is also, curiously, far less idiomatic. (Hindemith acquired some bad piano-texture habits in the 1940s; his 1945 Concerto contains more embarrassingly redundant octave couplings than any comparable work this side of Max Reger's F-minor.) The wiry, stringlike textures of the first version have given way to complacent chord clusters and predictable, cue-oriented interludes.

Original version

Revised version

As regards Hindemith's second major point—that the original version "was essentially a series of songs held together by the text and the story unfolded in it, but otherwise not following any compositional plan of the whole"—the composer points out that the cycle is divided into four "clearly separate groups" (though the original version was as well), that the first of the groups (songs 1–4) deals with the "personal experience" of the Virgin, the second (songs 5–9) contains "the more dramatic songs . . . in which a considerable number of persons, actions, scenes, and circumstances are shown," the third (songs 10–12) offers "Mary as sufferer," and the fourth (songs 13–15) is "an epilogue in which persons and actions no longer play any role."

Hindemith, indeed, supplies a graph detailing the expressive and dramatic intensity levels attained in the various segments, and here, to be sure, there is one major structural change: song 9—"Von der Hochzeit zu Kana"—is now conceived as the culmination of group 2 rather than, as in the original version, the prelude to group 3. Further, Hindemith claims that it is "the dynamic climax of the whole cycle . . . the song which in volume of sonority, in the number of harmonies employed, in variety and power of tonality, and in compelling structural simplicity of form represents the highest degree of physical effort in the presentation of the whole work. . . . The curve of dynamic expenditure rises from the beginning of the cycle to the 'Hochzeit,' and falls from there to the end."

In this emphasis Hindemith is, quite properly, more faithful to Rilke than to conventional interpretations of the Gospel According to St. John; the importance he accords this song in the latter setting, however, puts him firmly in the camp of those exegetes who decode from the Cana story the irruption into history of the Messianic hour of Jesus. Rilke transforms Christ's enigmatic reply "Mine hour is not yet come" into a merger of the symbols of water, wine, and blood, and Hindemith in both versions transforms this Rilkean elaboration into an extended coda that serves to set the stage for the Passion songs of group 3. In the process, "Hochzeit zu Kana" grows from 82 bars in the original version to 166 in the revision and from a compact fugato into a rather cumbersome aria preceded by a 48-bar piano solo.

Original version

Revised version

The second version, however, does offer one surpassingly affecting moment—an anticipation of the opening chords of "Pietà" to underline the words "and the whole sacrifice was decreed, irresistibly. Yes, it was written." In general, however, the dissolve from the bustle of the wedding crowd to Mary's sudden realization of the miracle as prophecy is much more effectively managed within the scale of the original.

Hindemith's points about harmonic structuralism are less easily countered. He offers an elaborate series of tonal symbols—the key of E to represent the person of Christ, B for Mary herself, A to depict divine intervention, C for the concept of infinity, C-sharp or D-flat for inevitability, E-flat for purity, and so on. It should be pointed out, of course, that these concepts of key association bear no relation to such Scriabinesque absolutes as C major = red or D major = yellow, etc.; rather, they represent a system in which all judgments are relative to a given fundamental. If, for example, Hindemith had selected B as the tonal parallel for Christ, then F-sharp, as its dominant, would presumably represent Mary, and E would stand in for states of divine intervention. Hindemith comments that "I do not expect in this tendency to freight musical sound so heavily with ideas that I will encounter any too enthusiastic agreement." He cites the example of fourteenth-century isorhythmic motets and remarks that "here as there what is involved is the overcoming of the mere external sound. In the mere act of listening one can hardly become aware of the intellectualized working principle that was operative in the construction."

While I confess that without benefit of Hindemith's analysis it would never have dawned on me that the key of F, tritonically related as it is to Mary's tonal symbol, B, is therefore "connected with everything that moves us by its mistakenness or shortsightedness to regret and pity," I cannot, in good conscience, feel that my appreciation of "Argwohn Josephs" (No. 5)—an F-oriented song in both versions—is lessened by this oversight. On the contrary, it seems to me that precisely because of Hindemith's tonal-symbolic fixations, the second version is deprived of much of the magic and ambiguity of the original. For *Marienleben*, after all, is a cycle about a mystery, and to establish an a priori network of finite tonal symbols to which the incomprehensible is directed to conform (even when incomprehensibility itself is replete with its own harmonic parallel) seems to me dramatically self-defeating.

In the third poem ("Mariä Verkündigung"), for example, Rilke consigns to a sublime parenthesis the legend of the unicorn. ("Oh, if we knew how pure she was! Did not a hind that, recumbent, once espied her in the wood, so lose itself in looking that in it, quite without pairing, the unicorn begot itself, the creature of light, the pure creature?") Hindemith, in the respective versions, responds as follows:

Original version

Revised version

That the earlier version focuses on C-sharp (the key which Hindemith, in his subsequent deliberations, assigned to fixed and inevitable states) rather than, as in the second instance, E-flat (the symbol of purity), seems to me a small price to pay for the glorious recitative provided by the original. With the neo-Gregorian reiterations of its organumlike accompaniment, with a declamation unimpeded by conventional metrical concerns, this is one of the dramatic highpoints of the first song group. In the later version, Hindemith succumbs to his predilection for sewing-machine rhythms and down-home harmonies and, in the process, relegates Rilke's inspired interior monologue to a casual aside.

In the sixth song ("Verkündigung über den Hirten") the text "You fearless ones, oh! if you knew how upon your gazing vision now the future shines" is set as follows:

Original version

Revised version

The comparison, I think, speaks for itself: the original contrasts the pragmatic concerns of the shepherds with the messenger's feverish determination to communicate the impending radiance to them. It does this via the superb independence of its counterpoint and with an assist from the three-against-two beat divisions; the second version, on the other hand, introduces several of Hindemith's late-period calling cards—the Hanon-like keyboard figurations, the unnecessary doublings, the sacrifice of rhythmic invention at the altar of cadential affirmation. One senses no duality of purpose, no need for an attempt at angelic intervention; these shepherds are a captive audience.

To be sure, there are moments in which Hindemith's preoccupation with architectural clarity makes a contribution to the second *Marienleben*. "Vor der Passion" (No. 10), for example, as realized in the original version, is possibly Hindemith's closest brush with atonality; but the nature of his art was never well suited to a regime divorced from tonal centers, and, although his intention to convey through their absence a state of inexpressible grief is clear enough, he does not in fact manage it all that successfully. Although in the later version this song remains tonally distracted, Hindemith does provide a more careful weighting for the relativity of its dissonance.

In both versions, the longer songs are governed by variationlike concepts. "Die Darstellung Mariä im Tempel" (No. 2) is a passacaglia offering twenty realizations (nineteen in the revision) of a seven-bar bass motive with entirely different intervallic properties in the two versions. The first of the three songs devoted to the death of Mary (No. 13) employs a basso ostinato for the outer segments of its ternary form, while No. 14 ("Vom Tode Mariä II") is a conventional theme with six not-so-conventional variations. One might expect that such structures would benefit, in their second incarnations, from Hindemith's vast accumulation of experience as a contrapuntist. And there are, to be sure, moments in which the control of chromatic relationships, details of voice leading, are more securely in hand in the later presentation. More frequently, however, the superb contrapuntal interplay between voice and piano, which in the first version offers textures to rival the harmonic fluidity of a Bach trio sonata, is replaced in the later set by predictable keyboard figurations and unimaginative vocal writing.

"Die Darstellung Mariä im Tempel"
Original version

"Die Darstellung Mariä im Tempel"
Revised version

Those songs in which Mary herself is in the foreground are invariably confined to triple meter. The entire first group is so organized, with signatures of 3/4 for "Geburt Mariä" and "Die Darstellung Mariä im Tempel," 6/4 for the "Mariä Verkündigung" and 12/8, 9/8 for "Mariä Heimsuchung." In later years such rhythms, particularly in slow tempos, often compromised Hindemith's work; he frequently employed them to convey states of lullaby-like calm and, almost invariably, associated them with a certain motivic and harmonic complacency. Even in the original version, this temptation is not entirely overcome—the lofty Gregorian melodic touches of "Geburt Mariä" are supported by some decidedly pedestrian V–I chording—but Hindemith's harmonic imagination is operating in high gear throughout the cycle and almost always saves the day.

With songs 5 and 6 ("Argwohn Josephs" and "Verkündigung über den Hirten") Hindemith embraces that idiom which throughout his life inspired his finest compositions. Joseph's work-oriented realism (No. 5) and the Shepherd's earthbound reluctance to accept revelation (No. 6) are conveyed by a relentless motoric energy, with baroquish motives firmly ensconced in a rock-solid duple meter.

Song No. 7 ("Geburt Christi")—one of only three in which Hindemith actually troubles to inscribe the prevailing meter in the score—is in fact a metrical elision (3/4, 2/4) and also offers one of the composer's rare attempts at polytonality. Since Hindemith did not provide an analysis of the original version, one can only guess at the meaning of these bitonal, bimetrical relationships—the obvious explanation relating to the concept of God's appearance as Man, of the celestial realized in earthly form. Indeed, the striking ambiguity of this song (superficially, a gentle lullaby) is underscored in the keyboard part immediately following the final words: "He brings joy." The piano's response is an excruciating dissonance—a C-sharp major 6/4 in the right hand supported by C-major tonic and dominant tones in the left. It is as though at the moment of Christ's birth the Virgin contemplates the suffering which the future holds, and we are reminded, once again, that both Rilke and Hindemith are telling their story entirely from Mary's point of view.

For song No. 8 ("Rast auf der Flucht in Ägypten") Hindemith returns to triple meter (but a very uptempo triple meter, be it noted!) and provides one of the most striking minidramas in lieder literature. (Indeed, I can think of only one other song written in this century which attempts to portray so many moods within so short a span—the opening item, "A Wanderer's Song in Autumn," from Ernst Krenek's great cycle *Songs of Later Years*.) "Flucht in Ägypten" touches every relevant mood—the frantic rush of the escape (an impulsive, *lebhaftlich* C minor), Jesus calm versus his parents' concern (a series of recitatives alternating with abortive ravvivandos), and, finally, the "rest" itself (twenty ecstatic elaborations of an A-flat-major ostinato).

Drama of a conventional sort, of course, was never Hindemith's forte—his Brahmsian preoccupation with purely musical relevance precluded any abandonment to overt theatrical effect—but here, in little more than four minutes, he summons a musical parallel for every gesture, every impulse, every inclination of the text. I suspect that the secret of his dazzling success with this uniquely moving song is in the challenge which the recitative ravvivando sequence offers to its motoric bookends. Like many composers for whom rhythmic compulsions were linked to a more generalized formalist preoccupation—Mendelssohn, say, or Bruckner, perhaps —Hindemith was, perversely enough, at his best in moments of transition, moments which actually threatened the motoric continuum. (The tripartite sequential link between the third and fourth movements of Bruckner's String Quintet, for example, is unquestionably the most dramatic moment in that much-misunderstood composer's output.)

Like "Flucht in Ägypten," "Hochzeit zu Kana" (No. 9) is conceived as a dramatic, rhythmic, and dynamic decrescendo and segues to the first of the Passion songs ("Vor der Passion," No. 10). This is succeeded by the two simplest songs in the cycle ("Pietà" and "Stillung Mariä mit dem Auferstandenen")—the two which, as noted earlier, are presented virtually intact in the later version.

As mentioned above, the first two songs on "The Death of Mary" are variatively inclined—"Vom Tode Mariä I" using the basso ostinato of its outer segments to frame a glorious chant-cum-recitative. In "Vom Tode Mariä II" (theme and variations), Hindemith is once again on somewhat precarious polytonal ground. The theme itself, consigned to the piano, merges elements of C minor and C-sharp minor and works through to a not entirely convincing close in D major. The song is highlighted by two superb canonic variations (Nos. 3 and 4), in which the tonality of D assumes primary importance, and a masterful coda (variation 6). This sequence offers an ingenious division of labor: the upper registers of the piano are assigned a canonic ostinato based on the dirgelike left-hand motive which, in the theme, depicted Mary's death; meanwhile, the soprano is assigned the lowest part, suspended beneath the inspired monotony of the keyboard, and provided with a truncated version of the piano's original right-hand motives; these, to borrow from Hindemith's own tonal lexicon, defined the "inexorability" of Mary's "entrance into infinity." With this inspired stroke of role-reversing inverted counterpoint, Hindemith achieves a uniquely persuasive imagery: the perfect musical counterpart for the concept of Resurrection.

The ability to sum up a work of substance was never a strong point with Hindemith. (In this also he shares a tendency with Brahms and Bruckner.) He lacks some ultimate, transformational impulse—the willingness, perhaps, to set aside the burden of motivic development—the very quality through which, as so often in the final measures of a Wagner opera or a Strauss tone poem, the motivic strands themselves are ultimately dematerialized. Any number of Hindemith's finest sonata-style compositions are coda-compromised by this inability to transcend his material, this urge to exhibit ever more concretely the process of its working out. In the piano sonatas, for example, the codas are frequently marred by unnecessary triad fill-outs, chord clusters in inconvenient registers, and a thematic predilection which one can perhaps best define as "when in doubt, augment."

I would dearly like to say that "Vom Tode Mariä III" is the exception that proves the rule. This concluding song, however, sees Hindemith suc-

cumbing once again to his familiar finale temptations. Though its central segment finds him in his nimblest trio-sonata mood, its primary theme transforms the motives of Mary's birth into a vigorous alla breve, octave-doubled
in keyboard registers five octaves apart, and the concluding fourth chord—
open fifths in C and B-flat respectively—is hammered home by a final embarrassing reinforcement in the upper regions of the treble. It's the sort of
windup gesture one might perhaps countenance as a musical postlude to a
meeting of the Loyal Order of Imperial Moose, but it emphatically does not
provide a proper conclusion for a composition that deals with the miracle
of transcendence. As a result, the work ends perfunctorily and without emotional reference to the intense devotional atmosphere which otherwise per-
meates it. And I am saddened to concede this point, because, as the reader
may perhaps have gathered already, I firmly believe that *Das Marienleben*
in its original form is the greatest song cycle ever written.

Footnote: In a diary entry dated January 1949, an unusually distinguished
critic made the following notation:

"The *Marienleben* has been put on anew. Earlier, so P. H. confesses,
it was only a demonstration of power. Something had to be overcome, and
anyone who perhaps believes that this could be the result of inspiration was
completely wrong."

The critic was Arnold Schoenberg, who, according to his biographer
H. H. Stuckenschmidt, had "more sympathy for Hindemith's gifts than the
orthodox Schoenbergians liked" and who "regarded the [*Marienleben*] cor-
rections with displeasure." And so say I.

PIANO SONATAS BY
SCRIABIN AND PROKOFIEV

The development of Russian music in the nineteenth century can be divided
into three distinct phases. Phase one was the important era—the consequence
of all those court-sponsored productions of Italian opera and French farce
that constituted salon culture, Petersburg-style, circa 1800. This phase culmi-
nated in the early works of Mikhail Glinka, those facile compotes of the alle-
gro-furioso galops of middle-period Beethoven, the harmonic method of

Liner notes from Columbia MS 7173, 1969.

Ludwig Spohr, and the better tunes of Fanny Mendelssohn. All that Czar Peter had commended to his people was accomplished—their music, like their architecture, had become a pale but impeccable copy of the best that the West could use no longer.

Glinka provided a bridge to phase two—a brooding identity quest that distinguished the work of his immediate successors, such as Modest Mussorgsky with his singular search for the Russian soul. Mussorgsky's instincts were those of the coffeehouse aesthete, the good-hearted but irrevocably dissolute fellow who, in rare moments of lucidity, would seize some noble idea and, uninhibited by considerations of technique, set it down in one mad burst of creative enthusiasm. For all the unashamed awkwardness of his style, Mussorgsky was Russia's musical coming-of-age.

Then, overlapping Mussorgsky, came phase three—the export generation. The most successful artist of the period and, indeed, the only Russian composer of his time with a universal appeal was Peter Ilich Tchaikovsky. A man of absolutely superior facility, he could adopt or disdain the influence of nationalists like Mussorgsky as occasion demanded, and he remains to this day Russian music's chief tourist attraction. Tchaikovsky's career was a triumphant refutation of the concept of Russian insularity, as was that of the twentieth-century cosmopolite Sergei Prokofiev. Yet even in Tchaikovsky's time the dour ruminations of Russian music had not yet found an end, and in a certain sense the partyline protocol of the postrevolutionary generation is a throwback to, and/or an extension of, the Mussorgskian quest.

But, straddling some fine personal line, a few Russian artists have managed to combine the introspection of Mussorgsky and the extroversion of Tchaikovsky in a style that perhaps can best be described as "mystic." Chief among these is Alexander Scriabin, who was twenty-five when he wrote his Third Piano Sonata in 1897 and who was then on the brink of some of the most fascinating harmonic experiments attempted in modern times. (His later work, including the last half-dozen of his ten piano sonatas, through a curious blend of determination and spontaneity explores an attitude to harmony and its interaction with melodic figuration that supplements, if it doesn't exactly foreshadow, the work of Arnold Schoenberg.)

The Third Sonata, however, is an exercise in more conventional design. A work of only moderate length (its running time is slightly over twenty minutes), the four movements of this sonata offer a profile of imposing gravity without at any time—barring perhaps a few sequences in the finale—managing to confuse busyness with complexity, size with grandeur, or repetition with unity, as the sonatas and symphonies of such more recent composers as Miaskovsky and Shostakovich tend sometimes to do.

According to many analysts, the early work of Scriabin betrays the influence of Chopin—a fondness for languorous cantilenas and noodling alto-tenor figurations. But if it does, then surely Chopin with a difference! The worthy Frédéric scarcely ever kept a large-scale structure going with the impetus Scriabin gives to this sonata, solving the architectural problems posed by interpretive rubato, embroidering with intraparagraph ambiguity the sure, clean key shifts of his primary modulations.

The first movement is typical. It's an expansive and declamatory sonata-allegro in which the bittersweet nostalgia of the secondary thematic group is held in check by the foreboding double-dot interpolations of the primary theme's chief rhythmic component. It's "music to read *Wuthering Heights* by"—a hypnotic, self-centered piece of doom foretelling.

The second movement is a scherzo with an angular barline—defying primary motive in the left hand and with a Vincent d'Indy–like series of harmonic twists in both. In the third movement, Scriabin turns his unerring harmonic sense to the task of undercutting the expected cadential climaxes. Whenever the gelatinous, post-Wagnerian chromatic texture seems to augur some emphatic *Heldenleben*ish climax, Scriabin demurely steps aside, reiterates the just-concluded phrase with elaborations, only to step aside again.

There's a remarkable, almost Pavlovian insight into the psychology of denial in this music. Despite all euphonic resemblance, it's the antithesis of the quasi-improvisatorial method of Richard Strauss—even if on first hearing it does suggest the sound of cocktail-hour piano as played in the better bars on Fifty-ninth Street ("And I said to her, 'Marsha, my dear, the outfit is absolutely stunning.' . . . Waiter, check please!"—"Yeah, well, Harry, as I see it, J.D. is on his way out at Consolidated Cornerstone.") Anyway, there's no talking allowed by Scriabin's finale, an elaborate treatise on the vertical possibilities of a rhythmic continuo.

When Sergei Prokofiev completed his Seventh Piano Sonata in 1942, Soviet music was enjoying unprecedented acclaim in the major musical centers of North America. Those were the days when Wall Street tycoons stumped the country talking up subscriptions for Russian war relief, when Stalin briefly metamorphosed into "Uncle Joe," and when the score of that motoric monstrosity, Shostakovich's Seventh Symphony, was flown to New York so that Stokowski and Toscanini could vie for the honor of its premiere. (Toscanini won!)

Well, the American enthusiasm for such less-distinguished products of that period as the Shostakovich Seventh went out with the era of Joseph McCarthy, and most of those bloated Slavic tone poems with first themes depicting front-line heroism and subsidiary motives doing homage to the gallant sacrifice of maidens garbed in premature widows' weeds have long since disappeared from the standard repertory. But there are exceptions, and like his Fifth Symphony, composed in 1944, Prokofiev's Seventh Sonata is built to last. He began working on it during that uneasy truce bought by the 1939 Nonaggression Pact of Comrade Molotov and Herr von Ribbentrop, and kept at it, off and on, until 1942, when, with Field Marshal von Bock's retreat from the suburbs of Moscow, "Operation Barbarossa" had sustained its first real setback—an omen of the prospects for "Festung" Europa itself.

And the sonata, with its schizophrenic oscillation of mood and its nervous instability of tonality, is certainly a war piece. It is full of that uniquely Prokofievian mixture of bittersweet lamentation, percussive intensity, and "there with the grace of a more judicious foreign policy go we" lyricism.

But for all its heterogeneous extravagance, this is an extraordinary work. Its first movement contains not only some of Prokofiev's best music but, in open defiance of the instant-accessibility credo of Soviet musicology, perhaps the closest thing to an atonal harmonic plan that he ever employed. By comparison, the second movement with its rather cloying main theme helps fulfill the quota of the composer's collective, and the finale, in 7/8 time, is one of those "just as our lines are beginning to crumble comes another column of our impregnable tanks even if they do happen to be Shermans and to have arrived lend-lease at Murmansk last week" toccatas.

The tempo subtitles that Prokofiev provides for these movements are singularly evocative, both of the piece and of its era: Allegro inquieto; Andante caloroso; and, finally, for the toccata, Precipitato.

MUSIC IN THE SOVIET UNION

It is almost impossible to pick up a newspaper or magazine these days without finding some dispatch about the current crisis in the arts in the Soviet Union. To recall just a few of the items that have recently received headline attention: There was the sudden fall from grace of Russia's celebrated young poet Yevgeny Yevtushenko, who just last spring was browsing around Greenwich Village coffeehouses reading his poetry to American beatniks; then came the surprise defection from his homeland of the pianist Vladimir Ashkenazy, which seems to be amicably resolved for the moment, but which calls to mind last year's appeal for political asylum from the dancer Rudolf Nureyev.

Then there was the occasion a few months back when Mr. Khrushchev,

---

From a lecture delivered at the University of Toronto, 1964.

taken for his first view of an exhibit of abstract art, responded as have many other frustrated viewers, East and West, before him, by suggesting that a cow's tail slapped across a canvas could do a better job. This opinion would hardly have been distinguished by the originality of its invective had it not been that within a matter of days the Ministry of Culture chimed in with a reminder that abstraction had never been considered beneficial to the interests of the Soviet people, that it was a decadent tendency of bourgeois society, and that artists who contemplated painting in this style must recall their duty to communicate with the common man and must renounce any esoteric language which their public could not readily understand.

Perhaps the most astonishing incident of this kind was the sudden withdrawal from a Soviet newspaper of the serialized memoirs of Ilya Ehrenburg, an old-line Bolshevik if ever there was one, as well as a writer whose career has tended to serve as a weathervane for the artistic climate in postrevolutionary Russia. It is perhaps no accident that Ehrenburg's most celebrated work was a novel called *The Thaw* which he wrote a few years back and in which he predicted that a more productive climate of artistic freedom would soon be felt throughout the Soviet nation. This work in fact was taken by many observers in the West to indicate that there would be a gradual liberalization of artistic control by the Soviet government and that with Mr. Khrushchev's rise to power the oppressive restrictions of the Stalin era would come to an end. Until recently, this has indeed seemed to be the case.

Well, it is likely that we shall be hearing even more about the tortured situation in the Soviet artistic community, because just a few weeks ago the Central Committee of the Communist party was called into special session to make specific judgments about the course of Soviet art and to establish standards to which that art must conform. No one knows, of course, exactly what the practical results of this meeting will be, but it is a safe guess that, temporarily at least, the hard-won gains of artistic freedom are to be frustrated once more.

This is not, of course, the first time that the Soviet government has seen fit to dabble in the role of impresario and provide members of the artistic professions with legislation which, if they want to preserve their relatively well heeled positions in Soviet society, they are expected to observe. Indeed, the strange relations of the Soviet government to the artistic community have produced a situation which is virtually inconceivable in Western terms and one which seems to follow a cyclical pattern of harmony alternating with disenchantment between the two factions. Within this cyclical pattern there are, it seems to me, certain criteria which lend themselves to charting, as the stock-market analyst might say, the long-term and the short-term outlook for the course of Soviet art. And so, based upon my observations of these cyclical trends, and hoping for better luck than with my own stock-market forecasts, I am going to try to construct a theory which will enable us to hazard certain projections of the future of Soviet art.

First, the short term. This is based upon the pattern of conflict between government and the arts in the years since the revolution. One of the indicators here is that whenever the Soviet economy is enjoying a prosperous rate of growth, there tends to be a more laissez-faire attitude on the part of the political commissars toward the eccentric carryings-on of the artistic community, and there also tends to be an approach to artistic relations with other countries which is much less fervently nationalistic. On the other hand, in those periods in which things are not going at all well, in the field of either external relations or internal economy, there tends to be a much more stringent control of the arts, a demand for conformity, and a preoccupation with nationalism. There tends in fact to be a belief on the part of the political machine that for the good of the nation, the artistic community must be straightaway put under very rigorous surveillance. One thinks immediately of the circumstances surrounding Stalin's purges of 1936 and 1937. These purges were directed at almost all levels of Soviet society and included the imprisonment or outright slaughter of leaders of the military and of industrial management as well as of the Communist party itself. Indeed, in relation to the violent bloodletting of that time, the reprisals against members of the artistic community seem relatively insignificant. Nevertheless, those years produced the most uncompromising bureaucratic judgments applied to art in any modern state.

But let us think for a moment about the external political situation of that day. In 1936, the Soviet government was well into the second of the Five-Year Plans, and although the consolidation of the revolutionary state was unchallenged for the moment, there was a most serious threat presented by the dominance of fascism in Western Europe. It was not only Germany and Italy that were of concern politically. There was also at that time a fairly significant fascist movement in France; and because of all these difficulties, the extent of the Soviet commitment to the Spanish Civil War had to be very cautiously determined, particularly since the Soviet Union was by no means then prepared for a major armed conflict. Stalin's response to this external threat was to suspect everyone at home as well as abroad as a potential enemy of the state. It was against this background that the terrifying purges of those years took place and the limitations of free speech, artistic and otherwise, were imposed.

There are many other parallels of this kind to be drawn between political uncertainty and tension and artistic restriction, although there have been no other artistic purges as spectacular as that one. Nevertheless, there were some stern denunciations of the liberties being taken by Soviet artists in 1949 and 1950, at a time when the tension building over Korea was the paramount international issue of the day, and when the Soviet Union, because it was not then able to achieve nuclear balance with the West, was once again extremely nervous about a major international conflict. At that time Soviet composers were instructed that they should not employ any musical style more advanced than that of the late Sergei Rachmaninoff—a rather unfortunate choice, since Rachmaninoff, though indubitably the conservative model required, had the political disadvantage of dying a resident of the United States.

Bringing the matter up to date, we come to the present series of incidents, most of which were set off—not too coincidentally, I suspect—during Mr. Khrushchev's current political difficulties. It is surely no accident that we began to hear these reports of stern measures imposed upon the artists at a time when Mr. Khrushchev's political fortunes, because of Cuba, because of Laos, and because of the growing rift with Peking, were at a low ebb.

From 1936 onward, the attention of the Soviet Ministry of Culture to the life and work of all musicians in the country—and, more specifically, its prognostications of the future of music in Soviet society—had been based wholly on a totally insupportable historical analysis. Music and all the arts, this theory purports, are always the symbols, the reflections, of their time. Therefore, an era of social progress will be reflected in music of great vitality, and an era of social stagnation will be reflected in music of a decadent, dilettantish nature. Art is believed to possess an absolute value consequent to the value of the society from which it stems. Needless to say, in reviewing the past, allowances are made for an individual artist who may have been well beyond his time and who may possibly, by some mode of behavior—even one totally unconnected with his production as an artist—have defied the society in which he lived. Beethoven is the favorite point of reference for this strange pseudomusicology practiced in the Soviet Union. It is claimed that Beethoven reflects in his music the fundamental character of the French revolutionary period and consequently generates an unmistakable sense of displeasure with the aristocracy of his day. And so, even in the most restrictive famine years of Soviet musical policy, Beethoven was the favorite historical figure, though this enthusiasm did not prevent performances of the Ninth Symphony with a socialist text substituted for Schiller's "Ode to Joy."

Bach, of course, took a bit more explanation. In fact, in the years immediately preceding the Second World War, Bach, while still the subject of academic study and conservatory practice, was considered dangerous to the proletariat because of his pronounced ecclesiastical leanings. I am happy to say that this has now been remedied, as a recent talk at the Moscow Conservatory by Miss Svetlana Vinogradova indicates. Miss Vinogradova has obviously been untiring in her research and in her attempt to restore Bach honorably to the masses. She has pounced upon Friedrich Engels's remark that

"Bach was a gleam of light shining in the darkness of utter degradation," which is certainly all the approval that anyone can use. Miss Vinogradova continued by saying that "some Soviet critics have written that Bach's music is too rigid, too constrained. This is because Bach was repressed by the decaying feudal society in which he lived. Nevertheless, we appreciate him because his melodies are at heart the music of the people. This is the basis of Bach's melodic genius: his closeness to the people."

Odd that she should think so: Bach, with all his burgherish simplicity as a person, is music's supreme example of the genius wholly out of touch with his time, not because in the historical, chronological sense he was ahead of it but because all that was most significant in his music looked backward to an age of polyphonic glory which had long since closed for the world around him. But let's not tell Miss Vinogradova; it would only upset her.

Andrei Olkhovsky, in his perceptive analysis of musical aesthetics in the Soviet Union *(Music Under the Soviets: The Agony of an Art* [New York: Praeger, 1955]), has remarked that "the essence of the Party's methodology of art is reduced to the teaching that art is a superstructure over the economic foundation and, as such, is always a class phenomenon, and that in the sphere of art there are not and cannot be values which are independent, neutral, and nonpolitical." In the jargon of Soviet aesthetics the most damning epithet used to enforce these rigid concepts is a word which has fallen into such disuse in the West that it is now virtually without any precise translation—"formalism." It can be most generously translated as pertaining to that art whose only business and purpose is its own existence: in other words, art for art's sake. But in the Soviet Union it has been used so indiscriminately over the last quarter-century that it has long since lost whatever overtones and critical implications of eclecticism and academic disposition it may originally have possessed. It can and does appear in the most unlikely places and can be applied by the most unlikely persons. As one harassed Czech composer put it, "Formalism applies to what one's colleagues are writing." The underlying suggestion, of course, is that the purpose of art is not to serve its own end, from which each man will derive what he chooses to derive, but rather to serve the end of an omniscient State, which must be conveyed by aesthetic reflection to the attending masses. The "reasoning" of Soviet musicology, if one can dignify it by that term, is of course based upon the belief that art is dependent upon society for its raison d'être and that in return art must be expected to chronicle and complement the metamorphosis of the State. Even within the argument of art's validity as a social force (and there are vast reservations to that), Soviet society rejects the critical faculty of art—the possibility that the artist will disapprove of the State—while acclaiming just such restless virtues in artists of earlier epochs. It rejects similarly the individual direction of an artist's conscience, wherein his vitality may exist only in an expression of contradiction to the aims of society. But, above all, it makes superficial and self-conscious all that is most genuine in the character of the artist—the unconscious, indeterminate subliminal relationship of a man's work to the society from which he comes.

The relation of an artist to a society can hardly be determined by his acquiescence to the supposed best interests of that society; his work may in an appreciative sense produce its effect, its reaction, many generations after his own time, as Bach's did. And, therefore, the assumption that the art of the present is at all necessary to the present health of the community remains debatable. At the very least one must concede that if the good of the community does not necessarily augur the good of art, then those values which in an artistic sense may be most prized cannot be so judged by their contribution to the welfare of the community. In short, art can play its proper role—which is to say in some cases no role at all—only when it is allowed to stand wholly outside the relationships of moral good and evil which are constructed to govern the community; it must remain, as Jacques Maritain expressed it, "disengaged."

The question is, though: What makes the relationship of politics and art so uneasy in the Soviet Union? What makes that nation hold so defiantly to the concept that the aims of art and the aims of government should be the same and that artists must exist, like any other group of workers, to serve the present purpose of the State? It is convenient to be able to say that it is the nature of the Communist state itself—convenient, but not really a satisfactory explanation. It is true that the ethics of communism tend to demand a subservience of personal interest to the needs of society—tend to censor the process of communication when the thought or analysis communicated, regardless of its truth, runs counter to the current interests of the community. But then one remembers that in Poland and East Germany, for instance, most artists are allowed to communicate within any vocabulary they choose, so long as political subjects are dealt with discreetly. There, musicians and painters and (with the above reservation) writers tend to express themselves in more or less the same variety of idiom at present employed by their counterparts in the West. In short, many of the painters in those countries deal in the same abstract idiom that provoked Mr. Khrushchev's wrath last autumn. The composers tend to be exposed to and to employ the significant contemporary techniques, particularly those of the avant-garde—such as the systems of Arnold Schoenberg and his followers, which are both abhorred and banned in the Soviet Union. Since these satellite states are just as determinedly Communist in aspiration (if not yet in realization) as the Soviet Union, a conclusion must be drawn that it is not communism itself that produces this situation.

No, I believe that the cause resides much further back in the history of the Russian people—that the present situation was not created by the Communist state during its relatively brief span but is merely the latest example of a long-standing historical problem. In the arts, and particularly music, Russia has followed a course quite different from that of any Western nation. First of all, there was no music in Russia by any native composer of importance until the second quarter of the nineteenth century. At a time when Beethoven was already dead, when composers as relatively modern as Wagner and Berlioz were young men, Russia still had not been able to produce a single composer of any importance. To enlarge the perspective a little, let us go further back, about one hundred and fifty years, and recall that at the end of the seventeenth century, when such composers as Bach and Handel were already embarking on their careers, no music familiar to the Western ear was even *performed* in Russia. It was not until about the year 1700 that, under the influence of some fairly liberal czars, particularly Peter the Great, the court and aristocracy began to sample, largely out of the compulsion to be fashionable, the diverting products of Western art.

The fact is that until that time, music in Russia was controlled by a much more vigorous authority than the present Communist state: the Orthodox church. Orthodox belief held music to be a very sinful practice, likely to undermine the morale of the nation, and it legislated the appearance of any musical ingredient within its services; only the very strictest chant was permissible. All secular music (except, I suppose, the spontaneous sounds emitted by a Moscow aristocrat singing in whatever served for a bathtub in those days) was forbidden. Consequently, there existed in Russia an absolute distinction between the sacred use of music and its secular application; and the restriction implicit in the church's preoccupation with chant—one musical line sung all by itself, unadorned by any harmony with other musical lines—made it impossible for the musical experience of the Renaissance to be understood in Russia: the nature of Renaissance music, of course, was a concern with musical adornment, a constant enrichment of the musical texture with many voices doing or singing about many things simultaneously.

It would have been unthinkable in the Russian church for a composer like the fifteenth-century Flemish master Josquin des Prés to take themes from troubador love songs and use them as the basis of his music for the sacred service. Similarly, it would have been unthinkable to have a composer like Bach, who in his church music drew to such a large extent upon the texts and themes of Martin Luther and then built them up into towering structures which, even to contemporary ears, are astounding in their complexity. In the Russia of those days, all such indiscriminate juxtapositions of the sacred and secular styles would have been considered impure, sinful, capable of polluting the spiritual life of the Russian people; and, just as surely as any novel or painting of the present that offended Mr. Khrushchev, such art would have been banned.

And so nothing similar to the Western musical experience was known in Russia, nothing of its harmonic development, nothing of the commonplace alliance of sacred and secular techniques, nothing of the Renaissance notion that good and evil, as in life, intermingled in the creation of a work of art. Because Russia had missed the Renaissance, the qualities of stimulation and reformation that have provided the great cultural push of the last five hundred years were meaningless to the Russian mind. Russia had remained a state of medieval consistency. Indeed, the very word "medieval" is inappropriate to Russia, because the legacy of Byzantium which was the foundation of its culture, with all the implications of its Orientalized Hellenic tradition, was in essence a view of a spiritual world that was essentially impregnable and unchanging.

Throughout most of the history of modern Russia, there has been this extraordinary distinction between art which was sacred or which in some way contributed to the highest contemplative occupations and art which was secular and aimed only to be diverting and entertaining. Now, it's perfectly true that one can make such distinctions about art in other Western countries. It's obvious that a Bach cantata is more likely to induce a beneficial state of contemplation than the score for a Broadway musical, but by and large there has not been a basic differentiation in the nature of the techniques involved in creating such works. Bach's so-called "Coffee" Cantata, one of his few vocal works of an outright secular nature, uses the same sort of musical textures and themes that one might find in his most fervent music for the church. And it is this concept of the unity of the artistic impulse that has lent to Western culture the idea that art must exist for art's sake.

Not that it exists in the West without challenge. We are all of us guilty of a certain self-deceit in the matter, for, fond as we are of talking about art for art's sake, fond as we are of using it as our handiest contradistinction to what we observe as the monolithic nature of Soviet culture, we have, because of built-in prejudices, never really practiced this idea in any really conclusive, socially committed way. Nevertheless, we in the West have come to accept the idea (if only as an axiom to be subsequently ignored) that an artist has the right to tell us something that is extremely inconvenient, something that we would much prefer not to hear; and we have learned from experience that the ultimate value of what he is saying may hold no particular relation to just how flatteringly it falls upon our ears.

But such a position of disengagement was scarcely understandable in Russia. The view there was that society was essentially corrupt, that artists were more corrupt than most, and that if they were left to their own devices, their irresponsibility to society would wreak moral havoc upon the social fiber. We can find this great dilemma reproduced generation after generation in the Russian conscience. We also find it confused with notions of communication and of the importance of instantaneous receptivity in art. Ernest Simmons, in his biography of Leo Tolstoy, points out that Tolstoy believed that the majority of the art produced by the upper classes was never understood or valued by the great masses of mankind; this refined art was intended only for the pleasures of the genteel and is incomprehensible as a pleasure to the working man. Tolstoy believed that the feelings that formed the subject matter of the art of the aristocracy were basically three insignificant ones: pride, sexual desire, and a feeling of the weariness of life. He believed that the best and highest art was that which invoked the precepts of Christ, the love of God and one's neighbor, and that when these religious perceptions were consciously acknowledged by all, then the distinction between art for the lower and art for the upper classes would disappear.

Tolstoy, of course, while a profoundly religious man, was viewing this situation in the light of the ethical individualism of his time, and so his views are not exactly an appeal to the Orthodox traditions of his country's past, though they suggest strongly a latent awareness of the medieval rituals of Orthodox purification which played such an important part in the daily life of the Russian laity in early centuries. They also suggest a lingering, if unacknowledged, resentment at the background of the imported nature of aristocratic culture in Russia. It is fascinating to find a man in late-nineteenth-century Russia consolidating, by ingenious argument and magnificent writing, essentially the same precepts that had governed the conscience of the Russian nation for centuries.

Now let us take the question one step further and bring it up to date in a society in which the maternal role of the church has been taken over by the paternal state. We find a situation in which the same argument of art's purpose exists, the same unwillingness to accept the fact that art can produce an effect that is benevolent and ethically propitious without being so directed. And we find a situation in which the State expresses itself in terms of directions to the artist that except for the professed agnosticism of the State read very much like the ethical pronouncements of Tolstoy or the moral and spiritual dictums of the Orthodox church. We find the same preoccupation with an art that communicates easily with the masses, the same insistence upon an overt message to be communicated, the same unwillingness to accept the fact that artists left to their own devices can be other than destructive.

In the history of music in Russia, then, apart from the music of the church, we are dealing with a span of approximately two and a half centuries; and for half that period—from approximately 1700, when Peter the Great began to defy the church by introducing Western art into his palace and the circles of the aristocracy, until 1825—the art was almost entirely a matter of select importation. It was mostly frivolous stuff—Italian comic opera or light French drama. It was very rarely the really significant music or theatre of the day, but it did provide the first real contact between a certain segment of the Russian population and a substantial, if perhaps not too profound, segment of the artistic community of its time. And it meant that when a group of Russian composers capable of addressing themselves creditably to their public began to develop, the music they tended to contribute was a rather flavorless imitation of the imported music that they were told was the latest Western fashion.

We think, in this instance, of composers such as Glinka, who was certainly one of the most dexterous assimilators of Western fashion Russia ever produced. His earliest works show the Italianate influence of Rossini with a bit of the allegro-appassionato manner of early-middle Beethoven, and just a trace of the drawing-room perfumery of Felix Mendelssohn's sister Fanny thrown in for good measure. In his later years the Italian manner wanes as the Germanic technical accomplishment solidifies, and Glinka begins to greet it with certain melodic and rhythmic attributes that are noticeably his own.

In some measure, most of the generation that followed Glinka was greatly stimulated by his later work, and part of that generation formulated a concept of what Russian music ought to be—a concept that viewed any work of art that imitated Western trends as immoral and contrary to the best interests of the Russian nation. And so toward the middle of the nineteenth century a violent conflict was going on between musicians in Russia.

On the one hand, there was a group who looked almost entirely to the West for their inspiration and who felt, perhaps, that since they themselves lacked the tradition upon which the Western nations could draw, the only possible solution was to accept the basic precepts of Western European culture. On the other hand, there was a crop of men who believed that somewhere deep within the soul of the Russian people was a unique creative force, which ought to be allowed to express itself unimpeded by Western conventions. In this group were composers such as Mussorgsky; although they usually lacked the refinement of their more academic colleagues, they tended to have a very rare quality of Slavic gloom about their music which quite sets it apart from any other music of its time.

One of the interesting things about Mussorgsky is that from the technical point of view he is one of the least accomplished composers of his time. His greatest effects are those that are entirely mismanaged from a scholastic point of view. He knew nothing of the Germanic discipline of contrapuntal poise and balance (his bass lines are almost inevitably an awkward duplication of whatever the melodic germ of the upper voices happens to be, and only rarely—largely by accident, one assumes—do they manage to provide any kind of proper counterpoise). He knew little of the French lucidity of form. His structures tend to be disjointed and lacking in any sense of refined architecture.

But somehow Mussorgsky captures, in his own awkward manner, the troubled, mournful presence of Russian belief. His harmonic effects, perhaps because of their mammoth awkwardness, are strangely believable and human; his very lack of formal concentration tends to absent the rhetorical instinct from his music and to give us a curious and almost unique sense of honesty. He is like a person who ceases to talk the moment he has nothing further to say.

Then came the third generation, which tried to effect a compromise between these two standpoints, to balance Mussorgsky's native impetuosity of rhythm and his peculiarly dour qualities of melody within an art that still drew largely upon the technical achievements of Western music. The most successful of these composers—indeed, the only Russian composer of his time who made a really great impact throughout the music world—was Tchaikovsky. He did this by being, first of all, a great technician, a man of absolutely superior facility, and by being also a sufficiently shrewd cosmopolite that he could turn on or shut off the nationalists' influences at will. He was by no means the greatest composer of his day, but his art does have a unique communicative quality. He remains Russian music's most frequently visited tourist attraction.

Basically, everything that can be said of the postrevolutionary situation has been hinted by this capsule summary of the composers of the nineteenth century. Soviet composers still seem uncertain as to the direction of their art—whether it should draw upon the present techniques and idioms of Western music or concentrate entirely upon what is specially indigenous to their culture. And so we have music that purports to deal with the optimistic spirit of the communal worker or which attempts to imitate the sound of the latest dam project on the Dnieper. (A composition entitled *Iron Foundry* by a man named A. Mosolov left me none too eager to investigate whatever else Mr. Mosolov may have written.)

On the other hand, you get the more sophisticated composers, who have a certain breadth of experience with Western music and have somehow, in the manner of Tchaikovsky, managed to fit this experience into something specifically Russian in character. By far the most successful of these—and in my opinion the only really great composer of postrevolutionary Russia—is Sergei Prokofiev. And it is no accident that it is the Prokofievs—the important composers who have achieved real distinction in the international artistic scene—who have been subject to the greatest degree of vilification, while it is the Mosolovs, with their *Iron Foundrys* and so on, who are upheld in the Soviet community as the admirable models of the artisan composer: the breed that is least argumentative, most acquiescent to the dictates of the State.

In general, the present picture of music in the Soviet Union is a rather dismal one. Besides Prokofiev, other men of great talent have made their artistic impact since the revolution; but they have been few, and even those few have tended to undergo a rather bewildering metamorphosis in their music. It is a commonplace to observe that around 1925 one of the most prodigiously gifted young men of music was Dmitri Shostakovich. As everyone who has heard it will bear witness, his First Symphony, which was written at that time, is as lucid, imaginative, and joyously autobiographical as a first symphony ought to be. It is an extraordinary work—one in which this teen-ager sampled without inhibition the cultural reservoir of Western music, dipped cautiously into the expressionistic extravagance of Gustav Mahler, borrowed a bit of the motoric rhythms of the neoclassicists, sampled the double-entendre pivot chords of the early Schoenberg, and whipped all of this up into a confection that chronicles the adolescence of a young man of such prodigious gifts that he might reasonably have been expected to become the great one of the coming generation.

That he did not become so may be counted as one of the genuine tragedies of twentieth-century music. Shostakovich today is occupied with Symphony No. Fourteen or so. He turns out works which no longer speak with the intensity of Mahler because there is no longer anything that he wishes to be intense about. The rhythmic propulsion of the early works has turned into the incessant pulsing of an organism, fatigued and overworked and trapped by a treadmill of historical delusion which shows no sign of relinquishing its incessant demands of productivity. The skillful ambiguities of Schoenbergian double meaning have become frigid and tawdry, stylized clichés embarrassing in their frequency. All that remains is the occasional moment of some strange ecstatic adagio (Shostakovich, like all real symphonists, always had a sense of adagio) to indicate what might have been. Superficially, at any rate, Shostakovich would seem to be a victim of the stultifying conformity that the regime has demanded.

And yet one wonders about this in the case of Shostakovich. To all intents and purposes, the first blow to his pride, the first genuine interference with his creative aims, took place in 1936, when he was denounced for the opera *Lady Macbeth of Mtsensk*, and we have perhaps permitted ourselves to overdramatize the results of that particular denunciation on Shostakovich's future course. I would not, I think, have said that a month or so ago, because I was not yet familiar with the work. But within the last few weeks

I have (with some difficulty) managed to acquire a photostat copy of the original, unexpurgated score of *Lady Macbeth,* and I have to confess that in my judgment those who condemned the work were precisely right: it is a piece of unadulterated trivia. We may still assume that they condemned it for the wrong reasons—that they read into its story of adultery and murder an anti-Party activity. We may even assume that to a man of Shostakovich's inordinately sensitive temperament, such criticism may have had a long-range effect of inhibition and confinement. But the fact remains that whatever went wrong with Shostakovich as a creative artist had already begun by the time he wrote this work.

I should say that Shostakovich suffers less from the nagging persecutions of Party-imposed direction (after all, a man of his ingenuity could surely surmount some of that simply by taking refuge in the spiritual ivory tower of his work) than from an overdose of the Russian guilt complex—that he struggles unsuccessfully against a conscience which encourages the idea that duty has named a certain goal for his talents and that, whatever the cost, he must adapt himself in the manner required to attain it. Dmitri Shostakovich may yet write another great work, but I doubt it. I suspect that the twitching, weak-eyed teen-ager put down in the First Symphony in one grand burst of synoptic power all his love of and fascination with Western culture. When that first fresh, uncomplicated exposure of youth had ended, he became paralyzed by the unshakable conceit of duty and responsibility. He became a prisoner of a society in which this kind of love and admiration was condemned.

When I was in the Soviet Union a few years ago, I had the occasion of meeting at the Leningrad House of Composers a number of the more prominent younger composers of the day. Of course, as in most similar associations in Western countries, the internal machinations are such that one is most likely to meet those figures whose most prominent gift is their political talent, and so I have no way of knowing how typical these younger composers may have been of the present generation. Nevertheless, one thing was very interesting to me. The limitations of idiom superimposed upon the craft of the present generation of Soviet composers is such that those who expect to have their work given public audition must subscribe to fairly rigorous legislation—not quite that of the 1949 dictum urging quasi-Rachmaninoff stylistic pursuit, but even at its most licentious it allows for little more than a paraphrase of the preferential idioms and materials of the early years of this century. About the most daring style that might be contemplated would approximate that of Aaron Copland in his popular ballets, or perhaps the earliest works of Benjamin Britten.

Among the other composers who do not risk even these formal liberties, the best music from a technical point of view is being written by those who do not in fact hanker for liberties—by composers like Dmitri Tolstoy (no relation to Leo, as far as I know) who write in a formidably contrapuntal style someplace between Max Reger and Sergei Taneyev. This music does not seem to me very important, but neither does it seem particularly disturbed, because I think its complacence of stylistic search may be balanced by a particular refinement of academic technique which, temporarily at least, brings the composers considerable satisfaction. Throughout the twentieth century, of course, the academic tradition, though self-conscious, has continued to be a powerful restraining influence upon Russian culture—and in the case of music, perhaps the only thing that, in view of the arbitrary dictates of nonexperimentation, has allowed the profession to give a more or less creditable display.

In terms of striking stylistic concessions, perhaps the man most affected by this regimentation has been Nikolai Miaskovsky. He is known to most of us now largely because he has the dubious distinction of having written more symphonies than anybody else since Haydn. But his distinctions go beyond that. In terms of formal experimentation, he was after Scriabin perhaps the most interesting composer in Russia in the early 1900s. He was not a very well equipped composer technically. Like most of his academic fellows of that generation, he had a confused notion that busyness equated with complexity, that largeness equated with grandeur, and that repetitiveness equated with unity. But there is a certain aura of conviction about Miaskovsky that (again excepting Scriabin) is lacking in every other Russian composer of his generation. There is a subjective quality, a deeply ruminative concept of form.

In Miaskovsky's First Piano Sonata, written in 1907, there is an extraordinary innovation for a work of its background and period. Its first movement has the distinction of being in fugal style—bad fugal style, admittedly, but fugal style nonetheless. Miaskovsky has the same love for the linear that marks his colleague Sergei Taneyev. He has that same concept of the mystery of the single voice being joined in some processional harmony through the imitation of its fellows, and in a piano sonata out of the virtuoso tradition of the turn of the century, that is absolutely astonishing.

Miaskovsky builds each of the movements of this sonata out of the same fugal material, though he drops the outright fugal style after the first movement. And because of the not-so-casual imitation of late Beethoven, because of the fundamental richness of the idea, and because of the subjectivism which seems to stem directly out of the plaintive questing for identity of Mussorgsky's generation, this work is perhaps one of the most remarkable pieces of its time.

For another decade or so, Miaskovsky went on writing music of even greater fascination. His idiomatic preferences tended at times to have an astonishing resemblance to those of Charles Ives, with the same willingness to experiment, the same fondness for lavish colors and startling contrasts; and through all of the breadth of sound and texture thrown up by these canvases, there is the same fundamentally honest and likable artistic disposition. But even more than in the case of Shostakovich, something went tragically wrong with Miaskovsky's creative life. At the time of his death in 1950, he was writing music in the form of simple sonatas and children's sonatines, which in their weary and plodding way are their own sad comment on his evolution.

Such indications of this disintegration of temperament and artistic personality make clear that the essential stuff of the Russian character cannot flourish under the present superimposed restrictions of the regime. But there is also the question of whether, and how effectively, it can flourish if exposed to a sudden cold douche from the wake of Western culture. Russians have on many occasions gone abroad to seek their fortune in the world, and the results usually have not been too happy. The most celebrated Russian expatriate abroad in the world today is probably Igor Stravinsky. Stravinsky occupies a very special place in the musical history of the twentieth century, one which makes it very difficult to speak of him as typical of any particular attitude of turn-of-the-century Russia. And yet in a curious way, and without undue contradiction, he is extremely typical indeed. I refer, of course, to the strange sequence of styles that he has adopted throughout his career. He began using the symphonic language and method of Scriabin and Rimsky-Korsakov; within a very few years he had already abandoned the plush, sensual vocabulary of *The Firebird* for the terse, laconic, biting, sarcastic ejaculations of *Le Sacre du printemps;* a few more years and he had succumbed to the international craze of neoclassicism and had reduced it, with the kind of frenzied exaggeration of which he was capable in those days, to an absurd pastiche of neoclassic intent.

Stravinsky wrote scores like *Pulcinella* and the Symphony in C which abused the original intention of neoclassicism simply because they did not attempt to apply the urgency of its reconstructive force to the solution of any continuing technical problem. In other words, neoclassicism in Stravinsky's middle period was not the necessity that the adoption of eighteenth-century forms became for Schoenberg or that the deft, sonatalike constructions were for Hindemith. Stravinsky, unlike these other men, did not see neoclassicism as a refurnishing of the same house. He saw it as a completely new move to a different and altogether tidier district. But it was a district without trees, without sod, without all of the comfortable amenities of life; and only his relentless vitality offers the hope that human energy could surmount such barrenness. We are not really grateful for the restorative influence of neoclassicism in Stravinsky, because there was no continuing tradition waiting there to be restored. We simply tolerate its coming and wonder when it will move on to something else.

And move on it does. In the last decade Stravinsky, in defiance of most of his previously published judgments of twentieth-century music, has become one of the foremost serial composers of our time. He has adopted the refinement of Webern in terms of textural pleasures with just a hint, here and there, of the barbarous rhythmic energy that marked his earlier writing. (I might add that from my own point of view, this last decade of his works contains his most enjoyable music.) He is, however, one of the more conservative composers employing serial means, although, perhaps because of his advanced years, any transformation of this nature is considered so remarkable that he automatically is awarded the leadership of the avant-garde. And it *has* been an incredible transformation, as indeed his entire life has been an event-filled, but incredibly misdirected, journey.

As I look back on this life, one thing seems to me to be of particular importance about Stravinsky, however well disposed one may be toward him and areas of his work: he has never learned to synthesize his experience. Stravinsky has remained a wide-eyed tourist in the world of music, full of curiosity (which is good), willing to sample everything and to participate extensively in many things (which is commendably honest but has certain inherent liabilities), and he has never been able to decide which things are pertinent to his spiritual being and which are superficial. He has accepted and loved and adopted many things in sequence and without discrimination, and he has never been able to find, apart from this constant transition of fleeting identifications, the real personality of Igor Stravinsky. This, of course, is tragic.

But what is this indecision of Stravinsky's relation with the world—what are the adoptions and renouncements of vows from one decade to another—what are the bursts of enthusiasm and then the sudden cooling of ardor for a certain experience of the past—if not in a certain way the quintessence of the Russian spiritual problem? What are they if not the ultimate embarrassment of the man who recognizes that his enormous capacity and technique and perception are not enough, who recognizes that he is not made to play the part of one of the great men of history? And so he turns his life into a pathetic search for the identity and conviction and repose that he knows exist in the great world but which he knows too that he shall never find. I cannot imagine a man of Stravinsky's talents having lived such a life had he been born a German or an Italian or even an Englishman. He might, given that degree of talent, have put it to even less concrete use, but surely he would not reveal the unhappy spectacle of an unfulfilled life which we now see in its last years.

Stravinsky is the spiritual émigré par excellence. But he represents a kind of acceptance of influence which is rare in the world today and which is a liability only because it is an inquisitive and consecutive adaptation of Western preference and is not poised upon a background of any confirmed Russian tradition. There is a certain kind of artistic temperament that flourishes in a peculiar sort of way: not by assimilating all influences more or less simultaneously but by coming upon one influence at a time, casually, with almost childlike surprise. Not to be patronizing, but at a certain level of creative effort, perhaps—the level that Russia has now attained—it is this kind of childlike delight in the sudden discovery of an influence already absorbed by more sophisticated peoples that can be responsible for a particular kind of stimulation. It is this kind of lovable, childlike wonder that we recognize in Stravinsky, though he may be far too excessive an example to be pertinent to the present time-lag situation between the two cultures. It is perhaps not yet possible for Soviet music to produce an artist of quite so gullible a disposition.

But it would be a great mistake to assume that in the artistic "cold war" it is we in the West who must prevail with some sort of cultural Marshall Plan to resurrect from centuries of silence the musical and artistic life of the Soviet republics. Not only would this be intolerable conceit; it would be, if practiced in precisely that manner, a tampering with one of the most potentially beneficial cultural situations that Western man could experience.

What I mean is that we tend to be rather complacent in our assurance and conviction that all men must share equally from the same cultural reservoir. I grant that dipping into this reservoir is what is responsible for an artist's choice of imitative procedure and ultimately for the sophistication of his technical development, and so there is no denying that the Russian people can benefit to an extent by an approach of assimilation toward Western culture. But it would be extremely shortsighted and even hypocritical to assume that the way to rectify this time-lag situation between the musical and artistic histories of the two cultures is to stuff Russians full of the latest goods of the West, to decorate their lives with the outpourings of current contemporary fashion and fetish. The greatest value of the Russian people at the moment is that which stems directly from this liability of isolation. It is a value inherent in the fact that certain kinds of insulation tend also to stimulate the creative mentality.

We see this at many levels of Russian society. The conductor Walter Susskind, in a conversation I had with him last week, told me that on his recent visit to Czechoslovakia he was astounded to find to what puritanical excess the satellite nations now carry the Russian passion for isolation from current Western fashion in matters of dress and of luxury conveniences of one kind or another—that, at least on a bureaucratic level, they find in the very abstention from fetish a positive virtue. This, of course, has far deeper implications than the supposed Anglo-Saxon puritanism which stresses that to be uncomfortable is worthy. To the Russian, this particular concept allies itself to some degree with an attitude that goes deep into the medieval religious mind of the Russian people and which stresses an unchanging, timeless view of historical participation. (A qualification must be made at this point. There is also in the Russian character an ability to interrupt occasionally this tranquil acceptance of a contemplative tradition with the violent spasm of a volcanic social eruption. But because of the fundamental turgidity of that character, these eruptions are usually reabsorbed into the gradual unfolding of the Russian presence.)

This particular ability to live with an isolated situation may have strange and wonderful repercussions in the future. What is of importance in the Russian experience of isolation is that when certain of the time-lag facets have been compensated for—when, in another century or two, the Russian experience with organized sound is more proportionate to the Western one, and if that experience of isolation has been consistently nurtured, not as a legislative prescription but as an idealistic alternative within the artistic atmosphere—then the damaging lack of experience that the Russian artist displays today will be balanced by his ability to speak confidently from a position not wholly part of the international determinant of Western fashion.

In other words, if we want the full flowering of Russian culture, we have to resolve ourselves at some point along the line to accepting that inherent dilemma which Russia's nineteenth-century artists recognized so very clearly: whether the immediate issue, the present competitive fact, ought to be resolved by rapid assimilation or whether, rather, an attitude should prevail that—not for this generation, nor for the next, but for the eventual future—would nurture a creative ability to render in artistic terms more or less accessible to the West the mysterious, brooding presence of the Russian soul.

I said some time back that I would try to provide a long-term as well as a short-term analysis of this fascinating situation. The short term—the analysis of the cyclical rise and fall of artistic freedom in the postrevolutionary period and of its relation to the diplomatic involvements of the State—is useful only insofar as it may tell us what to expect in the immediate future; and it does seem likely that a period of more rigorous discipline lies immediately ahead for the artistic community—an official tendency to be less cordial to the artistic persuasions of the West and less lenient about the adoption by Soviet artists of Western techniques of expression.

But the long-term graph is something else again. It indicates that the concept of legislation of art by outside control has always been present in Russia to some extent and that the almost pathetic search for a Russian identity in the art of music has tended for generations to produce a constant friction. Yet it also attests to the inordinate musicality of the Russian people, because within a musical history only a fraction as long as that of most Western countries, Russia already has managed not only to produce a few composers of great distinction but in certain instances to give us that marvelous quality of human nobility which we find more consistently, but no more poignantly, in their greatest literature, such as the novels of Dostoevsky. (One need only think of a work such as the Fifth Symphony of Prokofiev to know what enormous power resides in the expressive capacity of these people—what ability to surmount external challenge, war and devastation, terror and bureaucratic intrigue, and still produce art of the most luminous and inspiring order.)

It may be, then, in the long-term projection that the ethical confusion which confounds the Russian mind—the question of whether art is necessarily a communicative experience relating only to the present—and the aesthetic confusion—the question of whether total freedom of artistic conscience would be beneficial or disastrous—are instinctive provisions to harbor and nurture the rather delicate musical culture of Russia. It may be that they are an intuitive tariff that is applied toward the outside world to compensate for the fact that centuries of experience are lacking in the Russian cultural tradition and that Russia cannot, therefore, afford quite the same uninhibited free trade that the Western nations enjoy.

But it seems likely, whatever the immediate peril of political interference, that the creative mentality in Russia will continue to concern itself with this agonizing question; that the cumulative experience of musical language will eventually achieve a point of saturation from which new ideas and idioms of communication must necessarily follow; and that these musical idioms, which may or may not pursue the current corresponding path of Western musical language, will quite likely be espoused by composers who somehow manage to consolidate the spiritual qualities of the Russian people within the larger frame of Western experience.

Indeed, one would like to assume that as the generations pass and musical experience broadens, Russia, without ever recapitulating precisely the Western, Renaissance-orientated culture, will produce its own cultural continuity, in which the spirit of the Russian people is provided with the technical resource and the aesthetic terminology to do it justice. We must profoundly hope that this will come to pass, not only because we can contribute the immeasurable historic resources of our Western culture to Russian artists, but also because they, who possess such a fascinating, frightening, troubling, and deeply moving spiritual heritage, must be given the chance to find a form in which they can transmit this heritage to us.

THE IVES FOURTH

I should confess straight off that I have no proper qualifications as a reviewer of Charles Ives's music. In fact, until a few weeks ago when I took a cram course in CRI records, my total exposure to his works consisted of Balanchine's *Ivesiana* (circa 1954), which as I recall left me much impressed with the relationship between Ives and perhaps the one modern master to whom he has not at some time been compared—Alban Berg; a Bernstein performance of the Second Symphony, a couple of years ago, which left me thoroughly confused about Ives's musical antecedents; and, most indelibly, my own sight reading, when I was a teen-ager, of the "Concord" Sonata, which left me absolutely exhausted. The most that can be said is that I do represent to some degree that larger audience for which any exposure to Ives is still a rather special and, often as not, puzzling experience.

So it was for me with the Fourth Symphony, which was given its world premiere in Carnegie Hall on April 26, 1965, by Leopold Stokowski and the American Symphony Orchestra. The work has a rather complicated chronology, for the elucidation of which I am much indebted to Leonard Marcus's informed and informative program notes (as well as for a most prodigious job of hymn spotting—a pursuit that for the dedicated Ivesian holds promise of that jubilation known to the diligent Arctic ornithologist who catches a red-necked phalarope [*Lobipes lobatus Linnaeus*] napping), and from which I take the liberty of the following excision:

> It has taken half a century for Charles Ives's Fourth Symphony to achieve a complete performance. Eleven years after it was finished, Eugene Goossens . . . assembled an orchestra made up of New York Philharmonic members and . . . conducted the first two movements in a Town Hall concert on January 29, 1927. . . . The third movement of the Fourth Symphony also has been performed previously. In the early 1930s Bernard Herrmann played a slightly reorchestrated version of this fugue several times on CBS radio. . . . [The first movement] was written in 1910–1911. . . . The [second] movement, derived from the second movement ("Hawthorne") of the "Concord" Sonata, was written in 1915–1916 shortly after the Sonata was completed. . . . [The third movement] is actually an orchestral transcription of the first movement of the First

From *Musical America*, July 1965.

String Quartet . . . ("A Revival Meeting") written in 1896. . . . The slow ominous finale composed during 1911–1916 is derived from Ives's Memorial Slow March for organ of 1901. . . . [This movement] existed merely as an uncollated mess of illegible manuscripts scattered throughout the Ives household. . . . [After his death] the pages of the fourth movement were assembled and it was discovered that about one quarter of them were missing. . . . While assorting a trunkload of unidentified pages in Ives's notation, [James Ringo] . . . working at the American Composers' Alliance . . . accumulated one pile that didn't seem at first to belong to anything. They turned out to be the missing pages of the Fourth Symphony. . . . That was over ten years ago. It has taken all this time to decode, edit, renotate, and copy the parts.

There is no doubt that all of this added up to an extraordinarily moving experience, but I am not at all sure that it is appropriate to describe it as, in the ordinary sense, a musical experience. I mean to be neither disrespectful nor persnickety, but simply to suggest that Ives's music does not necessarily yield its secrets to conventional analytical methods.

To be sure, there are more than enough extramusical reasons for feeling well disposed to Ives. To begin with, there is the whole enchanting Ives pastorale—the shrewd and solitary Yankee, dazzlingly successful in business, and exploiting that success to insure himself (no pun intended) a productive autonomy for his art—rather like Borodin, the chemist-composer, in that respect, I should think. And with this goes the nostalgia for the Ives country—forever letting his music call to mind the gentle mixed-farming tracts of southern New England, as surely as Faulkner conjures Mississippi, or Stephen Leacock my old stamping ground of Lake Couchiching, Ontario.

Then there is Ives the innovator or, more accurately, the innovation anticipator, the man whom his partisans so often celebrate as having got in the first licks of polytonality or the first major post-Renaissance ones of polyrhythm, some months or years ahead of Stravinsky or Bartók or whomever. I am not sure that this claim or argument, or whatever it is, really proves anything very much about Ives's genius, any more than Josef Hauer's claims of having beaten Schoenberg to the twelve-tone system could make him automatically a composer of significance. There is no question that Ives had an impressive precognitive ability—an ability to intercept the psychic transmissions of his age and to crystallize in his art something of that turbulent metamorphosis which was taking place just before World War I. But the fact that he did sense it, did manifest certain technical responses to it in advance of others similarly engaged, is proof of invention, not of greatness. Somehow, I cannot help feeling that for many people Ives's superb, untutored instinct is made to serve as an antidote to that self-conscious literature of America in isolation—the America that Henry James's *Ambassadors* evokes, the America that Sinclair Lewis's *Dodsworth* cartooned—an America estranged from and uncomfortable with the supposedly "sophisticated" culture of the old world. For here is Ives, without doubt the most imaginative American artist of his time, managing to spin off all these new devices that the European culturati would soon after argue about and analyze and finally admit to the circles of academe. And Ives all the while just "did" these things and hardly bothered about precedence and consequence and their, or his, historical role. I simply wonder whether, with justifiable defensiveness, it isn't really *this* Ives, the natural artist, the instinctive rather than calculating innovator, that his partisans really celebrate. But if this be so, it follows that there is a problem in dealing with Ives—a problem created by this same absence of argumentative theorizing in his work, this same laconic, pragmatic, and wholly unacademic spontaneity which is Ives's trademark.

Let me give you a for-instance relevant to the Symphony No. 4. Consider the third movement—it's a fugue of the sort that Taneyev might have written had he chanced to recompose Brahms's *Academic Festival Overture*. It's in C major with relatively little tonal straying, and it's full of voice leadings that are not so much awkward as tedious—stepwise basses, hopelessly stuck in sequence, and so on. And it's the sort of fugue matter that, were it presented as a scholastic exercise, one would be inclined to pronounce as the product of an author full of promise and for whom one would want to recommend a bit more work with fourth-species counterpoint.

But now we come to what seems to me the real critical problem with Ives: the problem of the analytical double standard. Is this fugue simply a spot of sluggish counterpoint, or is Ives aiming at a value beyond the composing process itself? Is this, in short, an ill-considered third movement for the symphony or does it, coming between the enormous complexity of the second and fourth movements of the work and representing, Ives said, "an expression of the reaction of life into formalism and ritualism," manage the perfect aural evocation of Mrs. Pennyweather, the organist down at West Gwillimbury Methodist, caught out extenuating the Offertory one Sunday, when the collection plates were late in coming up, the Faux Bourdon '32 was ciphering, the left heel of her "Aunt Marys" coming loose, and the lower pedal octave entirely out of bounds? You see the problem!

Then one comes to the other side of Ives, as represented in this symphony by the second movement and to a degree by the fourth—the Ives of polyrhythm, and polytonality, and vast jungles of strettos. Here is this absolutely impenetrable complex of sound subdividing the orchestra into rhythmic platoons (two assistant conductors were involved in the Fourth Symphony, by the way), and in a sense it is complexity for the sake of complexity. The superimposed strands of thematic material are built up with only one concern, really—a concern for the totality of the sonic complex—and for the most part Ives seems oblivious to interlocking relationships within the material. I somehow recall a story that Schoenberg used to tell about his student days in which he and his colleagues apparently invented a game, the object of which was to search out previously unidentified motives in *Tristan*, and played it with some rule such as "any melodic strand appearing twice is a leitmotiv." And the point is, of course, that in the *Tristan* texture, or in any of the labyrinthine involvements of the German expressionists, the ability to separate and isolate factors and partial textures is what makes the complexity significant.

But in Ives it is just not so. In his music you can find the most incredible complexity; break it into components of sixteen different hymn tunes and march-pasts and into as many different rhythmic complexes as he felt up to, and you will still be hard pressed to decide that any integral relationship exists between the supporting strands of this texture. Ives is extraordinarily short on the organic cell-motive continuations of the Austro-German tradition, and, as I said a while back, in this respect he reminds me, curiously enough, of Alban Berg—that side of Berg, at least, which is concerned with theatre music primarily and which, though at all times more rigidly organized than Ives would ever want to be, often employs something of that same disinterested density. Take any of the head-over-heels passages of later Ives with their pointillistically doodling piano obbligatos, tighten up the basses a little, square off the rhythms a bit, add a saxophone for sex, and you've got the *Lulu* transition music. One must concede, though, that Ives holds these incredible densities together with an altogether professional scansion—with an infallible sense of climax sustained through carefully managed marginal points and, just as in Berg's theatre music, guides them toward brilliantly conceived dissolves.

If the middle movements of this score represent the extremes of Ives's idiomatic cantankerousness, the outer movements seem to my ear more obviously attuned to each other in the conventional symphonic sense. Both have substantial reference to a tonality of D major; there is a certain amount of motivic identification above and beyond the hymn and march quotations, which, of course, abound everywhere; and both movements make modest employment of a small chorus (intoning wordlessly in the final movement, and in the first movement sounding an invocation to worship with "Watchman, Tell Us of the Night").

Leopold Stokowski's performance was a marvel of identification with the score. He is surely made for such music, or it for him, as the case may be, and one can only recall again the debt which we owe to this superb artist, who has so often led us into an encounter with the great and/or problematic works of our age.

The program balanced off the Ives's Fourth with Beethoven's Fifth, preceded it with Sibelius's *Swan of Tuonela* (a happy inspiration to combine Ives and Sibelius, who really do have some character traits in common), and opened with Wagner's *Flying Dutchman* Overture, in which Stokowski skippered a taut and quite astonishingly modern ship—diesel powered, stabilizer equipped, radar in the crow's nest. I could have left my Dramamine at home.

A FESTSCHRIFT FOR "ERNST WHO???"

At Toronto's Royal Conservatory of Music in the summer of '53, the big news was the appearance of Ernst Krenek. And the first reports I heard about the appearance of Krenek had to do with Krenek's *appearance.*

"Would you believe it," a confrere confided, "no socks!"

"Come again?"

"No socks. The guy crossed University Avenue with no socks, and in a pair of sandals, too."

"Incredible," I conceded, mobilizing my backup scarf as a Linus blanket. "But L.A.'s a breeding ground for eccentrics, you know."

Later reports, and firsthand observation, confirmed that Krenek also wore his learning lightly. In town, on that occasion, to conduct a master class, he impressed as a brilliant analyst who nonetheless reckoned with the perils of cerebral exclusivity. I remember once confronting him with the score of Schoenberg's Piano Concerto, for which I'd prepared a tone-row errata—a list of deviations from the operative series. "Could any of these be other than a slip of the pen?" I asked. "I mean, could any of them possibly be [*blush—stammer*—this was '53, after all, and most of us were hard-edged constructivists] the result of [*gulp*] inspiration?"

"I wouldn't want to second-guess Schoenberg," Krenek replied, "but I don't see why not."

Krenek, in short, was, and is, a scholar and a gentleman, or, to cite one of Igor Stravinsky's insufferably patronizing pronouncements (as orchestrated by Robert Craft), "an intellectual and a composer—a difficult combination to manage. He is also," Stravinsky informed his Boswell, "profoundly religious, which goes nicely with the composer side, less easily with the other

Review of *Horizons Circled: Reflections on My Music* by Ernst Krenek, with contributions by Will Ogdon and John Stewart (Berkeley: University of California Press, 1974); from *Piano Quarterly,* Winter 1974–75.

thing." (What a pity Bob and Igor didn't try hanging that on Etienne Gilson.)

Krenek is indeed one of the least understood of contemporary musical figures. The most prolific major composer of our time—the late Darius Milhaud, depending upon how much major-ness you accord him, would be his only serious rival in the numbers game—Krenek is perhaps best known to the public at large as "Ernst who?" Of his output to date—two hundred and twenty-five works and counting—fewer than half a dozen (none of them major items) are represented in the current Schwann catalogue. He fares better in Europe; some of his twenty-odd operas (the cornerstone of his output) are mounted with reasonable frequency, and most of his commissions originate on the Continent. But Krenek remains an enigma to many because that vast output is not idiomatically concentrated in the manner of, say, Hindemith or Britten or Shostakovich—half a dozen works from any of those gentlemen provide a reasonable overview of their aesthetic. Krenek's work, on the other hand, employs a bewildering collection of idioms and a formidable arsenal of techniques. In the twenties, he tilted toward Bauhaus-baroque, then flirted with jazz and an overlay of social comment; in the thirties, he converted to Schoenberg's twelve-tone technique; and in the forties he modified it by a rotational system of his own—somewhat akin to the leapfrog row technique of Alban Berg. In the fifties, he employed a multiparametered serialism. In the sixties he puttered about with tape technology; and in recent years he has come to grips with the postserial dilemma of choice versus chance.

Casually enumerated, it reads like the dabbling of a dilettante, like the overanxious "me too"–ism of the born eclectic. But it isn't. For though Krenek does have an insatiable musical curiosity and is quite capable of an "I'll try anything once" response to external stimuli, he is quite incapable of the argumentative, Stockhausenesque carbon dating which subs for analytic comment in the columns of so many European music journals. ("Sir: In response to your article 'Structural Principles of Inaudibility,' I should like to point out that I, and not my colleague Hans-Heinz Hopflinger, must take credit for the introduction of isorhythmically organized fermatae. I draw your attention to the tacit timpani in my *Permutations IV,* which anticipates by no less than seventeen days Hopflinger's *Asymmetry XVI,* and which was completed August 21, 1955. If further verification is required, I refer you to my former copyist, Felix Daub, who can be contacted c/o Zauberberg Sanatorium, Zurich.")

All of Krenek's mature work, indeed, no matter the idiom, is of a piece—held together by a unique musical temperament. His work tends toward the lyric, the elegiac, the euphonic—qualities which mirror a singularly generous, contemplative, unaggressive personality. He is indeed the antithesis of the artist as egotist—which may well be the basis for his PR problem. It could also explain his correct but rather strained relations with the late Arnold Schoenberg—the very model of a modern major genius. "One always felt that he was testing you," Krenek related recently, "waiting for you to make a mistake; and then he would start a fight, hoping to destroy you."

One does not, needless to say, produce two hundred and twenty-five works while catering to a crisis of confidence, and Krenek is not unaware of the value of his contribution and is by no means uninterested in its effect upon posterity. Indeed, in a cryptic and rather uncharacteristic comment in his 1951 essay "On Writing My Memoirs" he disclosed that arrangements had already been concluded with the Library of Congress for the deposit of private autobiographical papers which will go public fifteen years after his demise. "Why should I expect anybody to trudge to Washington fifteen years after my departure from this world in order to find out what I thought I had been doing while still alive? The main reason for my writing this huge autobiographical book [is] my conviction that someday my musical work will be considered far more significant than it is at this time and that then people will try to discover what made me tick."

There is, however, a pervasive repose at the core of his being, and its musical corollary—a certain lack of tension, an absence of agitation—is responsible for the deceptively bland impression which his works sometimes leave with the uninitiated. On the other hand, it is precisely this quality which makes his *Lamentations of the Prophet Jeremiah* one of the great musical-religious experiences of our time and his *Symphonic Elegy* (on the death of Webern) perhaps the most moving tribute ever paid by one musician to another. I also suspect that this sense of perspective, of detachment, which characterizes so much of Krenek's music, however superficially au courant it may appear to be, is not simply the product of a facile technique (though certainly the poignant note-by-note agonies of an Alban Berg are unknown to Krenek), or even of the dialectical compromise between Marxist activism and Christian forbearance which merge in his character to form an almost Shavian exuberance, but relates rather to the fact that Krenek is one of the very few composers with a sense of history.

By and large, composers shy away from history much as pop stars avoid learning to read scores. Both breeds are spooked by book learning and frequently prefer to treat inspiration as a subterranean flow without geological consequence. For Krenek, however, history is not simply an ordnance depot for a personal crusade (though his extensive research into the fifteenth-century Flemish master Johannes Ockeghem certainly provided ammunition for his theories of twelve-tone evolution) but rather, I would guess, a means by which his own contribution can be seen in relation to a larger good. Still, he *is* a composer and, from time to time, Hamlet-like, gives that old devil ambivalence its due.

In the first of the four lecture reprints which form the centerpiece of *Horizons Circled,* Krenek states,

> I have been criticized because I apparently found it necessary to search for historical prototypes in order to justify modern compositional methods. I feel that such objections are based on a misunderstanding. The fact that the melismata of Gregorian chant displayed inversion and retrogression, or the fact that some medieval composers like Dufay used the cantus firmi as basic melodic patterns from which they derived individual motivic shapes for their polyphonic designs, did not in my opinion justify application of such procedures in the twelve-tone technique. . . . What I was interested in was observing and experiencing the permanency of certain ways of musical thinking. I was also interested in the existence of archetypes that seemed to run through the known history of occidental music and, from time to time, to crystallize in the shape of stylistic entities. . . . Today I am no longer so convinced that this historical orientation is as necessary or useful as I thought under the impact of my own historical study. . . . If we feel that history takes its course according to some inexorable internal necessity, it would not seem to make very much difference whether or not we are aware of its preordained pattern. If we feel that we are *making* history as free agents, we may not pay much attention to precedent, only to be told afterward that our actions were a logical consequence of all that went before. "To be or not to be historically oriented" is a question that cannot be answered any better than the question "To be or not to be," period—or rather, question mark.

The lectures were originally delivered in 1970, when Krenek was appointed Regents Lecturer at the University of California, San Diego, and throughout the set the author deftly mates general observation with personal experience. The historical reflections in the first paper encourage him to ponder his own stylistic development; in the second, which explores the political ramifications of art, Krenek supers a description of his operatic masterpiece, *Karl V,* the work which put him on the Nazi blacklist, upon a backdrop devoted to Anschluss stratagems in his native Austria.

The third lecture is an analysis of the socioeconomic dynamics of art, and the fourth, a dissertation on serialism in general and Krenek's *Sestina* for soprano and ten instruments in particular. This work (even for those of us who remain skeptical about the "logic" of serialism) is a triumph of communication over process, and for the musician Krenek's schematic diagrams are invaluable. Nevertheless, despite Krenek's gently waspish comments about aleatory music, group improvisation, and mixed media ("I share the attitude of the Shah of Persia who, when invited by the Austrian emperor to watch the horse races, replied, 'Thank you very kindly, Your Majesty, but I know that some horses run faster than others, and which ones, I don't care.' "), this latter piece will be rather heavy going for the lay reader, as, indeed, will Will Ogdon's *"Horizons Circled* Observed"—a detailed analysis of the orchestral work which lends its name to the present volume.

On the other hand, the minutes of a conversation in which Ogdon plays Jonathan Cott to Krenek's Stockhausen (I avoid the more obvious Craft-Stravinsky analogy because Krenek has never been in need of a ghost writer) neatly sum up the composer's attitude toward the contemporary scene. The remaining items in what is essentially a Festschrift geared to Krenek's seventy-fifth birthday are an appendix chronologizing his complete musical and literary output and a brilliant essay by John Stewart on Krenek the litterateur. This latter piece is of particular value because Krenek is, to put it mildly, a nifty stylist, and an analysis of his verbal skills is long overdue.

Krenek has served as his own librettist for sixteen of his operas, his own lyricist for innumerable songs and choral pieces—though Rilke, Kafka, John Donne, Gerard Manley Hopkins, St. Paul, and (I'm not making this up) the Santa Fe Railroad timetable have all been given a piece of the action at various times. Through the years, first in German, more recently without benefit of translation, he has contributed meticulously crafted essays on subjects ranging from Johann Strauss to the collected works of Franz Kafka—not to mention his specifically musicological studies.

Last year, in these pages,* I compared Krenek to George Santayana—strictly on stylistic grounds; similarities of character and outlook would be hard to come by. I speculated that the superb sense of cadential rhythm which both authors possessed might relate to the fact that, not having been born to the language, both were therefore free to super its data upon Central European rhythmic conceits. As a musician, I was, of course, primarily preoccupied with matters metrical, but Stewart, as a professor of literature, is more concerned with thematic analogy and claims that

> like many contemporary writers he [Krenek] is concerned with man as a member of a group—with the identity of the individual in terms of traditions that make possible selfhood in communion, with the meaning of a moment of personal experience in the history of a culture much threatened by disorder. His kinship therefore is more with writers like Yeats, Eliot, Mann, and Faulkner. Or, in his attention to the absurd, with writers like John Barth and Beckett.

---

*See p. 221.

But the one he most resembles is Joyce, unlike as they are in temperament. Both are acute observers of the human scene, with a relish for the ridiculous. Both have a strong sense of historical parallels and use the legends of Greece and their native lands to interpret the present. Both are versed in Catholic doctrine and know well the paradox of man's need for support from such ancient dogmas, coupled with his need to assert and maintain his individuality before them. Both have used that paradox in exploring problems of freedom, order, "progress" in the arts, the artist as seer, the relation of the arts to action. Though seeking to speak through their works on some of the great issues of their age, both have been driven by the momentum of their creativity, and by their refusal to compromise, into using idioms that have alienated them from those they wish to reach. Both have enjoyed the admiration of their fellow artists, who, more readily than most, have seen what they were about and could appreciate the effort, integrity and achievement.

Finally, apropos of nothing in particular, a fan's note: On Easter Sunday, 1964, at Orchestra Hall, Chicago, I played my last public concert. It was an event to which I'd looked forward for a decade, and, by way of celebration, I decided to spend three days in training, need it or not, and to choose works which through the years had held a special meaning for me. The program drew upon Bach's *The Art of the Fugue*, Beethoven's Op. 110, and the Third Sonata by Ernst Krenek.

PIANO MUSIC OF BERG, SCHOENBERG, AND KRENEK

In 1908 a young man named Alban Berg produced a piano movement which must surely be considered among the most auspicious Opus Ones ever written. At the time Berg was twenty-three, was completing his studies with the most demonic disciplinarian of the day, Arnold Schoenberg, and his work was in effect a graduate thesis. In consigning his apprenticeship to Schoenberg, Berg had made a wise choice. Schoenberg, for all his growing reputation as a radical, was in reality one of the least anarchic of musical theorists and even at that time was as busily engaged in clarifying the laws of classical tonality as were his works in rupturing them. It was just such a personality

Liner notes from Columbia ML 5336, 1958.

that could wield influence upon the intense, fervently romantic young Berg. From Schoenberg he learned that whenever one honestly defies a tradition, one becomes, in reality, the more responsible to it. He came to see that the molten flow of Wagner's melody was not necessarily irreconcilable with the architectural logic of Brahms.

And so he produced an Op. 1 which was as fine as anything he ever did (I am aware that this remark is open to contradiction) for the reason that here he possessed the perfect idiom both to accentuate his restless genius and to cloak his rather dissolute habits. This is the language of collapse and disbelief, of musical weltschmerz, the last stand of tonality betrayed and inundated by the chromaticism which gave it birth. It permitted Berg his ecstatic tensions, his sorrowful resolutions, his unashamed revelation of himself. It also indulged his weaknesses—the jacked-up sequence, the melodic line supported by chromatically sliding sevenths, the plagiarism of the whole-tone scale.

This sonata is nominally in the key of B minor, to the extent, at least, that it begins and ends within the fold of that signature and that the secondary thematic group pays a token homage in its three appearances by suggestions of A, E, and B major respectively. But in between these points of tonal repose the harmonic texture is shifting continuously, and it is the more astonishing that despite the vaporous quality of the harmonic progressions, despite the fact that phrase after phrase resists root analysis, the work as a whole does convey fulfillment, does give the impression of great peaks and lesser crests, calibrated as carefully and achieved as inevitably as in music of a more orthodox nature. How, then, is this achieved?

First of all, by constructing within the melodic complexes a unity of motivic intension so firm, so interdependent, as to lend a complete coherence of linear flow. The opening three-note motif, for instance, is a central generative cell of the movement

creating such variants as the troubled and searching

and the benign and wistful

In this fashion, the horizontal relationships at least are given a common de-nominator.

But one cannot forever tolerate standing on a precipice, and such was the position of composers like Alban Berg in the early years of the century. The absolute limit of key relationships had been transcended. Chromaticism had so undermined the orbit of triad-governed harmonic progression that the only step remaining (if one was to continue in that direction) was to deny allegiance to the pivotal chord system of tonality—to deny the hereditary claim of the bass line as the embodiment of harmonic good conduct.

Schoenberg's first tentative steps into the world of atonality were taken with his Second String Quartet, Op. 10, and affirmed by the Three Piano Pieces, Op. 11, which appeared in the same year as the Berg Sonata. There is little reason for these pieces to stand together, apart from the fact that each deals with aspects of the problems confronting Schoenberg at the time. The second piece, which was earliest in point of composition, strikingly empha-sizes the transitional effects of tonal reminiscence. The third shows the Schoenberg who played with great thunderbolts of tone clusters, sought pseudoharmonic emphasis with octave doublings, indulged in the most ex-treme dynamic alternations, and tried to punctuate (perhaps to cadentialize?) the rhythmic structure with latent pauses and explosive apostrophes.

The first piece of Op. 11 is a masterpiece—a true successor to the finest of Brahms's intermezzos. Like the Berg Sonata, it is spun from an inner cell of motivic ideas without particular consequence of themselves. This indeed is the fundamental distinction between this sort of compositional technique and that in which the melodic line (no matter how organically conceived) is given importance per se. Here the material is less important for what it is than for what it can become.

The first few bars of Op. 11, No. 1, serve to illustrate:

Regarded motivically, the first phrase breaks down into two easily defin-able motives of three tones each, of which the second is an extension of the first—the A–F in bar 2 being an enlargement of the B–G-sharp in bar 1. This motivic sequence with its subsequent augmentations and diminutions and its vertical representation as in bar 3 (lower voices) dominates much of the movement. Schoenberg, however, was already thinking over rhythmic groups as well as between them. Thus, between tones 2, 3, and 4, and again between 3, 4, and 5, we have two other interval groups which bear mathema-tic correspondence to each other. In both groups the first interval has exactly half the span of the second, while tones 3, 4, and 5 together constitute an augmented inversion of tones 2, 3, and 4. In the lower voices one finds that this interval relationship of half to whole as in tones 2 to 4 and 3 to 5 has also penetrated. In the alto appear two retrogressive versions of tones 2 to 4, the second in inversion, and the bass proclaims an inverted retrogression of tones 3 to 5, while the tenor goes all the way with an augmentation (not an exact one, though) of tones 3 to 5.

The accompanying vertical synchronizations of these motives—bars 2 and 3, second quarter-note, and bar 4, third quarter-note—do not, except for the superposition of tones 1 to 3, indicate any similar motivic penetration. These three chord structures are built on a declining ratio of intensity so that the melodic line is supported by a relaxation of dissonance—the dimin-ished triad in the lower tones of bars 4, 6, and 8 producing an effect analogous to that of an elongated cadence. In discussing the harmonic (i.e., the vertical) aspects of atonality, one is confronted with problems which refute mathemat-ical precision and demand, rather, more speculation than one can comfort-ably allow in analysis. Schoenberg was always aware of the fact that no inter-val system could ever fulfill its function with equal diligence in both dimensions simultaneously, but he devoted much thought to the problems of bringing the harmonic and melodic dimensions into accord—the accord of like relation to a preordered nucleus—and eventually came up with the idea of harmonically conceived interval groups. This was one aspect of his celebrated twelve-tone period which occupied the last quarter-century of his life. If there was one direction in which his experiments with twelve-tone technique followed, it was the clarification of the harmonic responsibility of the row. From the first tone rows of 1924, which were rather like exten-sions of the opening of Op. 11, he gradually developed a technique of har-monic rows which figure more and more frequently in his later works—the Piano Concerto, the Violin Fantasy—and within which he constructed one work in its entirety—the *Ode to Napoleon Bonaparte*.

The tone rows of works such as these were generally contrived to ex-hibit motivic combinations which intentionally limit rather than increase the available material. Most frequently this took the form of rows which neatly divide themselves in two, the second half providing in one way or another a reflection or duplication of the first half. Schoenberg revealed a partiality for rows which when transposed and inverted at a given interval would present as their first six tones the last six of the original row and, consequently, as their last six the first six of the original. Thus, by using both rows simultaneously, it was possible to present the full twelve-tone series within an interval span of only six tones and thereby to suggest the penetration of the horizontal series into the harmonic units of the composition.

No system, however, no matter how thoroughly developed and conscientiously adhered to, can do more than implement the more nebulous qualities of taste and good judgment in its practitioners. Among the hundreds of works strictly adhering to the tenets of twelve-tone faith as understood and practiced by their authors, only a handful give the impression that their form, their idiom, their vitality—indeed, their existence—owe anything at all to the system which they employ. Few composers possess the discipline to express themselves freely and joyously within the confines of twelve-tone writing. It is essential for a composer to treat his serial possibilities with an expansive amiability and not regard them as representing an iron-bound code of honor. Within a framework of devout fidelity, it is the occasional deviation, the spontaneous expansion, the structural tenuto, which is capable of attracting singular attention. It is the intentional infidelity to the provisions of the row which is capable of arresting the fancy, as is the drama of a fugal distortion in Beethoven or the poignancy of a tortured cross-relation in the Elizabethans. With respect to all the ingenuity that can be plotted in advance, the moment of doing still issues its supreme challenge of inspiration.

Ernest Krenek's Third Piano Sonata is possessed of this quality. Concerning his large and varied output for the piano, Mr. Krenek has written:

> Ever since, in 1918, I wrote my Op. 1, a double fugue for piano, I have turned to that instrument time and again, when I was moved to test new stylistic or technical ideas. My early "atonal" style is reflected in Toccata and Chaconne (1922), my "romantic" period in the Second Sonata (1926). In Twelve Variations (1937) I summarized the experience of my first dodecaphonic phase. The principle of serial "rotation" with which I began to experiment in the Third Sonata paved the way to my present style of total serial integration.

The original row of this Third Piano Sonata is composed of four segments of three tones each, of which the first and last are fourth chords, and the second and third are fourth chords with one interval augmented:

Thus, this tone row may be seen to possess that symmetry which characterized Schoenberg's later serial combinations. However, while the potential of this triadic kinship is not overlooked as a means of harmonic reference, and the row's natural division into two complementary six-tone groups underscores what Mr. Krenek has referred to as the principle of serial rotation, the treatment of it is altogether different from the block-harmonic juxtapositions of Schoenberg's later twelve-tone writing.

Mr. Krenek's gentler, more lyric style focuses attention upon the intermediary combinations within the row—those motivic groups centered around the joints of the fourth chord segments; hence, his use of the serial facilities is panoramic rather than static. In his division of the row into antecedent and consequent bodies, the sixth and first and the twelfth and seventh tones are regarded as adjacent, and hence each half of the row is revolved upon this axis.

An example—the opening of the second movement (Theme, Canons, and Variations)—will illustrate. The comments in brackets refer, respectively, to antecedent or consequent segments; the original, inverted, or retrogressive presentation; and the number of the serial tone on which each segment begins; and, lastly, the numerals denote the distance of the transposition from that of the original row.

It will not pass unnoticed that certain suggestions of a centrifugal tonal scheme are present—of the thirteen presentations of the six-tone groups, all but one either begin or end with A-flat, as well as five with D-flat and four with B-flat. The effect is, needless to say, not that of A-flat major, but the result is just as surely a secure, if less definable, polarity. The subtle interrelationships of these groups evidence a rare sensitivity to harmonic balance and order, and the most striking feature lies in the fact that with all the conscious control which is exercised the final effect is one of artless candor.

The sonata consists of four movements, of which the first is a masterly sonata-allegro, the second—as its title indicates—an idyllic theme followed by a sequence of lucid canons and inquisitive variations, the third a frenetic scherzo, and the finale an elegiac and somewhat overdrawn adagio.

Altogether it is one of the proudest claims of the contemporary keyboard repertoire.

KORNGOLD AND THE CRISIS
OF THE PIANO SONATA

In some respects, Korngold's Second Sonata is the archetypal pianistic by-product of the Wilhelmian era. Its essential structural integrity as well as its occasional lapses into bombast, its virtuosic felicities as well as its not infrequent instrumental miscalculations, derive from a climate in which piano music was universally regarded as the poor relation of its orchestral model and counterpart. It was an era in which the grandeur of the post-Wagnerian orchestra constituted the sonic norm, in which most major efforts in the field of chamber music and practically all large-scale compositions for solo instruments were conceived as reproductions of that norm, and in which, consequently, the formal dilemma confronting the symphony itself—the degree to which textural sophistication could reinforce the structurally imperiled sonata-allegro concept without simultaneously adding to that peril its own inevitable corollary of modulatory ambivalence—was automatically transferred to those more intimate media.

The operative adjective, of course, is "Wilhelmian": in the field of cham-

Liner notes from Genesis GS 1055, 1974, a recording of Korngold's piano music played by Antonin Kubalek.

ber music, both Ravel and Debussy deserve exemption from the generalizations above, and among solo efforts the what's-in-a-name later "sonatas" of Alexander Scriabin—arguably the most indigenously pianistic conceits of the twentieth century—were subservient to no symphonic master plan. But the Austro-German school, after all, provided most of the symphonic action; it alone addressed the problem of structural evolution with at least quasiscientific continuity, as opposed to the ad hoc inspirations from west of the Rhine or east of the Oder, and it is therefore significant that none of the Austro-German masters of the period wrote with enthusiasm for the piano.

But let me say straight off that I have no fault to find with the concept of instrumental option-granting, the concept which puts *The Art of the Fugue* up for grabs registrationally, which makes of Carl Ruggles's laissez-faire pronouncements re the forces required for the performance of his music something more than the cantankerous, defensive Yankee quirkism they were originally presumed to represent—in point of fact, a shrewd, insightful comment on the nature of abstraction. The notion to which I do object, and strenuously, is the conventional wisdom that turn-of-the-century pianism represented some sort of summit for performance tradition (it simply isn't true, of course; the hand-is-quicker-than-the-eye tricks which constitute the Liszt pianistic legacy, for example, can be assimilated rather more quickly than the average Bach invention), that the source material supplied for that summit must therefore have been endowed with qualities of surpassing virtuosic ingenuity, and that the giants of yore, consequently, were enabled to simulate the breadth and scope of an orchestral canvas. And that, needless to say, isn't true either!

Exhibit A: Gustav Mahler, patron of pointillism—an artist who single-handedly set the stage for the timbral reformation of the post-Wilhelmian orchestra *a divisi,* who should, theoretically, have been willing to exploit the specific opportunities afforded by the piano with at least as much care as he devoted to the cowbells, and yet who contributed, in his frequently revised, never completed, Piano Quartet (originally drafted while the composer was playing hookey from Anton Bruckner's counterpoint classes at the Vienna Conservatory), a generalized, octave-doubling-prone continuo which totally ignored all indigenous pianistic opportunities.

Exhibit B: Anton Webern, miniaturist par excellence, *Klangfarben* melodist per occasion, Mahler's spiritual descendant—an artist whose mature works, and in particular, of course, his only solo composition, the Variations, Op. 27, are occupied with Mondrian-like geometric concerns which bypass timbral considerations, whose adolescent opus, the one-movement Quintet for Piano and Strings, is only slightly more open to keyboard opportunity than is Mahler's Quartet, and whose make-work transcription tasks for his teacher Arnold Schoenberg (the orchestral lieder, Op. 8; the Chamber Symphony, Op. 9; etc.) adopt an every-note-that-can-be-there-will-be-there stance.

Exhibit C: Arnold Schoenberg, lawgiver or revolutionary, conservative or radical, depending upon your point of view, an artist who did write with considerable care and flair for the instrument but whose five solo works were primarily conceived as tryouts for new formal concepts with which he, or his disciples, would shortly be involved on a larger, usually more symphonic, scale. Thus, the first and last of the Three Pieces, Op. 11, introduced that stream-of-consciousness technique (antitechnique?) which found its mark in the most Joycean of music dramas, *Erwartung,* Op. 17; the Op. 19 miniatures set the stage for the lifework of Anton Webern; and Schoenberg's masterpiece for piano, the Suite, Op. 25, occupies a special niche as the first work embodying a consistent application of twelve-tone technique.

None of these works, however, comes directly to grips with the specific problem of sonata form, though Schoenberg's other master pupil, Alban Berg, did manage an ecstatic farewell to the sonata-allegro, at least, in his one-movement Op. 1, a structure which must be numbered among the most successful twentieth-century works of its kind.

Ironically, it was left to Richard Strauss, with his penchant for rococo evocation, to write, if not extensively, at least accommodatingly, for the keyboard. The piano contribution to his *Ophelia Lieder,* Op. 67, for example, rivals Schoenberg's *George Lieder* as an exercise in accompanimental free will, and the continuo obbligato in his *Bourgeois Gentilhomme* music can be viewed as the harbinger of the Bauhaus-inspired concerto-grosso piano style of Hindemith. But Strauss, alas, did not write extensively for the instrument, and his only major concerted work—the *Burleske*—though far from the ungrateful invention Bülow thought it was, does not represent him pianistically, orchestrally, or structurally at his best.

Most of these works, then, are either sketches for more elaborate drafts to come, as in the case of Schoenberg (one should, I suppose, create a special category for the preorchestral prototypes of Ravel), or—and this is where the problem really lay—reductions, in fact or in spirit, of a prevailing orchestral genre. Which brings us to Erich Wolfgang Korngold and the problems peculiar to his keyboard manner.

Korngold, of course, was a pianistic prodigy, and, inevitably, his Second Sonata contains a good deal of instrumental savvy and no material entirely devoid of tactile sensibility. It does, however, in deference to the conventions of the day, contain much that is texturally redundant and pianistically self-defeating. Those conventions include the doubling of every available strand to simulate Wagnerian brass-support techniques, woodwind-style mezzo-piano bleats to convey an illusion of syncopation (Korngold makes persistent use of this device in the third movement of the sonata), scoop-up bass appoggiaturas in lieu of independent contrabass lines, and, above all, stretto-struck octave canons which frequently founder in the keyboard's mercilessly exposed outer regions. Indeed, immediately prior to the main-thematic-group reprise in the slow movement of the sonata, Korngold treats us to a pair of A-flat octaves, a mere four octaves apart, both of which, the lower via a gratuitous F-sharp *en passant,* are attempting to dock on G and ineffectually tugged toward port by a pathetically underpowered minor third—D and F, a dominant-ninth allusion—in the treble octave.

Needless to say, none of these objections (with the possible exception of the A-flat octave combination, which, however skillfully orchestrated, would give the ghost of J. J. Fux a start) would necessarily be out of bounds in an orchestral environment. It is, in fact, worthy of note that in later years Korngold himself, as evidenced by an eloquent, long-since-deleted recording of the sonata, was in the habit of using the structural data of the slow movement, at least, as a kind of inverse figured bass—adding to it on occasion, to be sure, but more frequently, and more significantly, subtracting from it redundant and/or pianistically ill-conceived permutations.

So the problem, then, as the composer himself clearly recognized, is the distribution of material—too much synchronicity, too little information withheld. Instead of compelling the listener to flesh out, via his imagination, the material supplied on the printed page (the real secret of all successful keyboard writing), Korngold and his colleagues of the Wilhelmian era sought to take us by force of fingers alone and thereby sacrificed the opportunity to build indigenously creative pianistic structures.

This one, to be sure (I refer only to the sonata—the *Fairy Pictures,* as an eclectic circus, is, because of its less ambitious design, relatively more successful instrumentally), suffers the octave-overload fate of almost all post-Brahmsian piano writing. And that's a pity—because with no allowance whatsoever for the tender age at which he wrote it, Korngold has supplied us with the blueprint for what might well have made one of the better symphonic essays of its time.

CANADIAN PIANO MUSIC IN THE TWENTIETH CENTURY

The selection of the three works in this album is merely a token of the author's (highly prejudiced) regard for their composers. These pieces do not by any means constitute a representative cross-section of that embarrassment of idiomatic riches which has been the most notable feature of recent musical developments in Canada.

Until World War II, it was possible to evaluate the Canadian music scene in terms equivalent to that two-nation policy for which, in the present Parliament, Prime Minister Pearson is frequently and sharply rebuked by the Honourable Gentlemen opposite. The patron saints of this English-French musical dichotomy were long since acknowledged to be, respectively, Healey Willan (born 1880*) and Claude Champagne (1891–1965).

But postwar immigration brought the world in microcosm to Canadian shores, and it is perhaps no accident that two of the three composers represented here came from abroad. Although Jacques Hétu was born in Trois Rivières, Québec, in 1938, Oskar Morawetz (born 1917) came from Czechoslovakia in 1940, and Istvan Anhalt (born 1919) arrived from Hungary in 1949.

These and other gifted émigrés helped to internationalize Canada's musical outlook, and even the briefest survey of present composing activity in Canada will turn up loyal adherents for each of the main international fetishes. There are Boulez-bound serialists, of whom perhaps the most persuaded and persuasive is Montreal's Serge Garant. A few aleatoricists, such as the nimble Otto Joachim, also of Montreal, have contrived to grant us options. There are Messiaenic exotics like François Morel, and one or two composers whose work, in its Henze-like eclecticism, defies more precise categorization. John Weinzweig is currently pecking away at modified post-Webernian pointillism, after an adventurous and productive exploration of less fragmented sonorities. Harry Somers has written operas, ballets, symphonies, and sonatas, ranging from moods of expressionist ecstasy (Passacaglia and Fugue, for orchestra, 1954) to late-Schoenbergian chordbursts (the ballet *House of Atreus*, 1964) to the translucent textures of his still more recent settings of twelve (significance, significance!) poems in Japanese haiku form.

Liner notes from CBS 32110046, 1967, featuring music by Oskar Morawetz, Istvan Anhalt, and Jacques Hétu.
*Died 1968—T.P.

In recent years, the neoclassic strictures of the High Priestess of Fontainebleau have been taken with a grain of salt, though despite her pedagogic demagoguery Madame Nadia Boulanger has been the preferred camp counselor for many native-born talents, including the late, greatly gifted Pierre Mercure. Also in decline is the influence of those unto-the-Berkshire-Hills-and-far-away American neoprimitives and idyllicists. Perhaps the only major composer who still manages a persuasive synthesis of Copland, Milhaud, and C-major Stravinsky is Saskatchewan's Murray Adaskin. Electronic composition has been the well-guarded secret of the labs at the University of Toronto and McGill University, Montreal, though the latter city's Expo 67, with its many pavilion commissions, may prove a major encouragement for the local sine-wave set. And, of course, in Canada, as elsewhere, convinced Cage-ites hold forth with pregnant silence at all the better coffeehouses.

This, then, is the scene as Canada moves into its second century of nationhood. As yet, no one figure, awesome and solitary, has arrived or arisen to dominate it. But many important and arresting works are being written, and three of them, I think, are on this record.

Oskar Morawetz's Fantasy (1948) is the first of three compositions for solo piano to bear that name. It was given its first public performance by me in 1951, at which time the entirely logical, if rather unfashionable, parenthesis "(in D minor)" was appended to its title.

Even in 1948, it required a measure of courage for a composer to advertise key relationship in a title. But the music of Morawetz is nothing if not courageous. For a quarter of a century he has compiled, with fervor and facility, an imposing catalogue of compositions that have remained constant in their attachment to the formal prerequisites of an earlier generation.

In the case of the present work, the parenthetic appendage as to its tonality is, in fact, more relevant than the title "Fantasy." For despite its length and its extravagant invention, the work is but a generously expanded sonata-allegro, observing all the definitions of theme and key order thus implied (first theme, D minor; second theme, F major; second theme, recapitulation, D major, etc.).

The fantasylike attributes have to do with a sense of proportion. The development segment within this particular sonata-allegro introduces a substantial body of new material. The coda, though a contrapuntally souped-up version of the opening measures, is itself an appendage to a wistful postlude which terminates the tripartite sonata structure. Even the matter of supplementary key relationship is treated with a Bruckner-like latitude (the tempestuous subgroup of the second theme appears in the exposition, not surprisingly, as an F-minor statement, but then turns up in the recapitulation, emphasizing, in relation to the home key, the tritonic ambiguity of A-flat minor).

The influences behind this work, and Morawetz's style in general, are not difficult to assess. The piano writing, as such, is possessed of a tactile fluency which often recalls Prokofiev; that sense of unhurried motivic stock-taking, generated by the several bridge passages through which fragments of the primary themes flicker fitfully, suggests Franz Schmidt; the pursuit of a tonality, challenged but never imperiled by chromatic elaboration and made to bear the brunt of the work's secure rhetoric, invites comparison with the best of the postromantic contrapuntists, from Max Reger to Paul Hindemith. There is also, and it is perhaps Morawetz's trademark, a certain rhythmic quirkiness which, though it surfaces more prominently in later works, identifies uniquely with Bohemia's meadows, forests, and conservatories.

Istvan Anhalt's Fantasia (1954) provides an excellent example of the work of one of Canada's least prolific but most dependable composers. Like such other products of his pre-electronic phase as the tensely argued Symphony (1958) and the dourly measured Funeral Music (1954), it is a spacious, guarded, somewhat diffident composition. Though in some respects it acknowledges a debt to the later style of Schoenberg, especially in the unselfconscious use of ostinato and the generally expansive attitude toward tone-row motivation, it delivers its timely homilies in an accent that is both arresting and spontaneous.

Perhaps the most impressive quality of Anhalt's music is its total lack of ostentation. While always persuasively projected, his structures never strain to make a point; organized with superb coherence, they never strive to impress us with virtuosity. His music paces itself so judiciously that one cannot be distracted by the ingenuity of its manipulation. Inverted canons come and go; four-tone splinters detach from the row, unravel into lethargic ostinatos, recoil into clusters; climactic paragraphs are delineated by the unmannered persistence of a treble or bass outline, secured with a Berg-like inexorability, uncompromised by any Berg-like exaggeration. And so one remains aware not of the method of operation but only of the singularly purposeful voice which is allowed to speak because of it.

Anhalt's music has not had the recognition it deserves. Perhaps, even to its staunchest partisans, it is something of an acquired taste. If so, it is a taste that, via this Fantasia, I urge you to acquire, because in its doleful, understated way, this is one of the finest piano works of its period.

"Understated" is scarcely a word that one can apply to the music of Jacques Hétu. His Variations (1964) is an ebullient and stagey piece of work. Hétu's flair for the instrument is unmistakable. Everything works and sounds and lies rewardingly beneath the fingers. Yet the impressive thing about these Variations is that despite their unabashedly theatrical inclination, they are held together by a sure sense of the purely musical values inherent in their material.

The material in this case is a tone row with some conspicuously tonal properties. Like many of the rows which Schoenberg employed in his later works, this one can be divided into two groups of six tones, the second of which is an inversion of the first. Both of these divisions contain a four-tone compilation of minor thirds that when sounded together produce that ubiquitous diminished-seventh chord of hallowed nineteenth-century memory, the neo-Lisztian ambiguity of which is not lost upon the composer at several of the more virtuosic moments.

After an introduction which serves in lieu of theme and in which the row material is set out via some accented treble octaves, each of the four variations becomes occupied with an increasingly dense and/or decreasingly literal utilization of the row. The first variation adopts an exclusively canonic presentation, while the second draws harmonic suppositions from the series. Variation 3 is a fughetta in which the somewhat straitlaced semitone countertheme recalls Vincent d'Indy, and variation 4 a headlong toccata which owes something of its propulsive momentum to an enthusiasm for those devices of sequence and strettos which the twelve-tone technique is supposed to obviate.

Throughout the Variations, Hétu accords priority to certain primary transpositions of the row. At most pivotal moments, he settles upon that presentation of it which commences on C-sharp and which was first proclaimed in the introduction. The result—a singularly euphonic approach to twelve-tone material—is like an infinitely expanded tonality of C-sharp. To evolve a vocabulary which necessitates such sophisticated compromise is no easy task. The fact that Hétu does so, with verve and spontaneity, augurs an important career.

THE DODECACOPHONIST'S DILEMMA

One can surely engage in no more disenchanting an occupation than the perusal of a forgotten thesis in which one confidently reinforced an argument with a prediction. This was evidenced for me recently upon rereading the

From *The Canadian Music Journal*, Fall 1956.

manuscript of a commemorative lecture which I delivered at the Royal Conservatory of Music of Toronto in observance of the death of Arnold Schoenberg in 1951. This paper was primarily eulogistic in content and for most of its length apotheosized the deceased despot of dodecacophony. Toward the close, however, I fell victim to that age-old curse of orators—the search for an effective ending. It seemed only fitting to end with a jubilant credo affirming once for all my unshakable faith in the preservation of the Schoenbergian aesthetic universe. This I accomplished (rather cleverly circumventing the subject) by confiding my trust in an unspecified corps of young adherents into whose loyal hands it gave me great pleasure, and a very effective ending, to delegate the future.

The precocity of my pronouncement will be thought the more startling when it is understood that, although appropriately conversant with the work of the founding fathers of atonal enlightenment, I was not at that time familiar with one composition by any young twelve-tone composer. However, during the very semester when I was mollifying Torontonians with my dauntless assurance and buoyant optimism, a less amenable young man, M. Pierre Boulez, was attempting to administer the coup de grâce to the Schoenbergian regime by means of an article with the rather alarming title "Schoenberg est mort." Boulez, who has been depicted by his employer and artistic mentor, the actor Jean-Louis Barrault, as possessing the mercurial disposition of a young tiger, brought forth a bitter denunciation of Schoenberg's retention of certain traditional elements of musical architecture.

And when, in due course, the tremors of this cultural quake reached the musical seismograph of Toronto, it became clear that the camaraderie of the twelve-tone fraternity had undergone its first serious upheaval, which had left a doctrinal schism that forced each of us to declare his allegiance or take his stand against the new order.

For me the decision was especially urgent, for, since I was an ardent Schoenbergian who had just proclaimed the glorious future of musical coexistence, I found myself at the cataclysmic moment with one foot planted on each side of an ever-widening crevasse and perilously exposed to the ideological splits. In order to rectify my precarious balance, as well as to satisfy no mean curiosity, I proposed to acquaint myself with the work of M. Boulez and his associates. Having done so, it seems appropriate in this year 1956, which presumably marks the completion of our young Parisian adventurer's first five-year plan, for me to deliver myself of a few observations gleaned from the contemplation of his aims and strategems.

This does not aspire to be a critical summary of contemporary twelve-tone achievement. Rather, I intend to comment primarily on the one aspect of twelve-tone writing which has too long been borne with critical indulgence—its harmonic relevance. And since I will endeavor to develop a chronological sketch of the harmonic application of twelve-tone principles, Boulez's work will serve as a vantage point from which to survey the musical world which he inherited and rejected.

Boulez, despite his rapid rise to notoriety as the most venturesome of contemporary musicians, is nonetheless a representative, if also personally an intensification, of the musical faith of a postwar generation, much as the emergence of Stravinsky personified the intellectual clime of the Roaring Twenties. No matter how opposed their ambitions, there is a remarkable parallel in the artifices which they invoke to assist them. Both Stravinsky and Boulez are agitators who not only speak against the trends of the immediate past but who find in the vast sea of musical antiquity but a few small islets of content. Both are prone to accept the external qualities of an earlier epoch as proof that the creator of that time surmounted problems analogous to their own. Consequently, the insurgents who rally round them can propagandize a liaison with olden times. And if the neorococo "return to Mozart" of thirty years ago has been replaced by a "back to Josquin" movement today, that merely illustrates the more sophisticated historical orientation of the present generation. To adopt Albert Schweitzer's penetrating observation of eighteenth-century German theological scholarship, "Like every period when human thought has been strong and vigorous, it is wholly unhistorical. What it is looking for is not the past, but itself in the past."

What Boulez is looking for was apparently not to be found in Schoenberg. Despite his indebtedness to the twelve-tone trailblazing of the Viennese master and the tutelage of the very gifted Schoenberg scholar René Leibowitz, Boulez traces his spiritual lineage through Schoenberg's pupil Anton Webern. Until very recently, Webern, in the popular conception, has been allotted a niche in an indissoluble trinity comprising Schoenberg, Berg, and himself. But now Boulez has made us realize that for his faction of the twelve-tone hierarchy, at least, Webern appears not as a disciple but as an initiator, his work not as an appendage to Schoenberg's acquisition but as the provocation for a rejuvenation of the musical language.

In his introductory notes to his Second Piano Sonata, Boulez says: "Tous les contrepoints sont également importants: il n'y a ni parties principales, ni parties secondaires." This astonishing admission (which, incidentally, might be construed as a retaliation against Schoenberg's habit of designating principal and subordinate voices) clarifies Boulez's twelve-tone philosophy. It requires that the listener accept the complete equality of all melodic strands—an equality which can only be realized when the demands of harmonic tension are denied, when contrapuntal texture forsakes its role of polyphonic sidestepping.

Now, in theory, such premises have always been fostered by the idealism of twelve-tone practitioners. Yet in Schoenberg's work they were subordinated to his desire to create a congruent vertical authority through the conjunct subdivisions of his row material. This necessitated breaking the row into three- or four-note groups which, when superimposed as chord units, related to each other either through uniformity of interval structure *(Ode to Napoleon Bonaparte)* or stepwise voice leading (the Piano Concerto). The problem of extracting from a wealth of discursive variation a residuum of harmonic force without, at the same time, harboring the least reminiscence of a former tonality, occupied Schoenberg throughout the last two decades of his life.

While his approach varied with each composition, one can nevertheless draw certain general conclusions. Schoenberg seems to have been growing less interested in the consecutive presentation of the row. The choice of row material becomes increasingly exclusive, in contrast to many an early twelve-tone row, which sought the maximum of motivic freedom by incorporating a variety of interval patterns. Schoenberg seems to have been intrigued by the possibilities of a split row, with both halves corresponding either through interval contour (example 1) or through a specific transposition which causes the transposed antecedent group to portray the harmonic potential of the untransposed consequent, and vice versa (example 2):

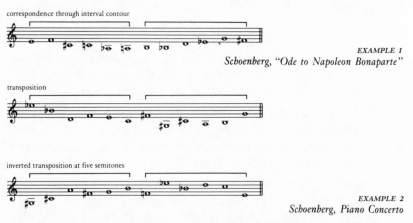

correspondence through interval contour

EXAMPLE 1
Schoenberg, "Ode to Napoleon Bonaparte"

transposition

inverted transposition at five semitones

EXAMPLE 2
Schoenberg, Piano Concerto

This plan, when successfully manipulated, offers the juxtaposition of harmonic regions in a manner not altogether unlike the primordial sequence of tonality: IV, V, I. Whether or not an ear psychologically adjusted to tonal receptivity can avoid reading into such row technique the implications of a chromatically inundated tonality is very doubtful; whether one should attempt to avoid it, still more so. In passages such as this beautiful episode from the Violin Fantasy it is difficult not to apply conventional analytical jargon on describing so sensitive a harmonic treatment of this classical bass line, and equally difficult to restrain the pedagogical urge to find a figured bass in B-flat:

EXAMPLE 3
Schoenberg, Violin Fantasy

Unfortunately, Schoenberg is not always disposed to such subtlety. All too often the subdivision method becomes a convenient way of slipping in the neglected tones of the row, whether or not the musical moment requires them. This is especially noticeable with rows like the *Ode*'s (example 1), which when stacked vertically consists entirely of triads, alternately major 6/3 and minor 6/4. Incidentally, this row carries the craze for consistency still further. It is only transposable one semitone up. Beyond that, every transposition merely reiterates the harmonic units of the original and first transposition. In the *Ode*, Schoenberg indefatigably exploits his unique triad-conscious tone row, leaving the impression of a perpetually undulating tonality. This is particularly marked in the habit of dividing the antecedent and consequent portions of the row between piano and strings. While a legitimate means of contriving the superposition of all twelve tones, it is a rather ungracious manner of trumpeting the emancipation of dissonance:

EXAMPLE 4
Schoenberg, "Ode to Napoleon Bonaparte"

As might be gathered from examples like this, Schoenberg in his later years developed the rather Max Reger–like trait of employing all constituent factors of a chord whenever possible. In those of his works which unashamedly espouse tonality (the organ Variations, for instance) it has the effect of undermining contrapuntally contrived preparation and resolution. The functions of chromatically achieved passing chords are transferred to triad blocks which frequently progress in parallel motion, often supplanting the dominant cadential effect with the sliding uncertainty of a flattened supertonic.

Indeed, the organ Variations and other works of the early forties which exhibit a key signature do not really constitute a second tonal period. They are a lifetime removed from the powerful, romantic creations of his youth, and while they occupy an unmistakable (if slightly swamped) tonality, their harmonic progressions would not completely satisfy the analytical criteria of, say, *Verklärte Nacht*. They are, in fact, but another facet of his tone-row experimentation. In a recent article the English writer Oliver Neighbor pointed out an extraordinary correspondence between certain harmonic progressions in the organ Variations and in the rigidly twelve-tone Fourth String Quartet.

It will be seen, then, that in his later years Schoenberg was seeking a tone-row logic which would permit the establishment of a pseudotonal organization based upon the harmonic relationship of component segments of the row. But what of those whose work served different ends?

Recently I had the good fortune to acquire a manuscript copy of an unpublished student work by Anton Webern, the Quintet for Piano and Strings. Written when Webern was twenty-three years old and under the guidance of Schoenberg, it sheds much light on his future treatment of twelve-tone problems. Despite a nominal tonality (C major) and a surprising Schumannesque melodic sweep, the underlying voices manifest a concentration of motivic detail which is quite beyond the accommodating capacity of a concise tonal framework. The harmonic rhythm becomes so seriously undermined by the overzealous motivic configurations, must so frequently abandon its normal inclination to support the misguided frivolities of the accompaniment, that the instinct of tonal direction so vital to the idiom he chooses is completely frustrated. Yet even though it provokes the uncharitable view that Webern would have benefited by a brief course of keyboard harmony, the Quintet is more than a boyish celebration of Schoenberg's custom of leaving no contrapuntal stone unturned. Clearly each note is calculated to function as an indispensable participant in the constructive idea, however unrealistic this idea in view of the exigencies of the tonal orbit.

In the opening of the Quintet (example 5) one is conscious of the caden-

EXAMPLE 5
Webern, Quintet for Piano and Strings

tial preparation, or rather lack of it, in bars 6 and 14. Bar 6 avoids a conclusive secondary dominant on II, causing the bass E-flat to descend uncomfortably to G. Notice the constant alteration of semitone and minor third in the bass (C-B-G♯—G♯-F-E—E-E♭-G), a characteristic Webern motive.

Webern's only published work which exhibits an unchallenged tonality is the Passacaglia (in D minor) for orchestra, Op. 1. Here, by contrast, is a masterpiece, largely because Webern's motivic excursions are subjected to the watchful scrutiny of the strictest of baroque chaperones—the eight-bar ground. I think the contrast of these two works, the loose-jointed Quintet and the forceful and disciplined Passacaglia, possibly provides a solution for a puzzle which has recently been made of Webern's role of musical miniaturist. From Op. 2 until the formulation of the twelve-tone technique, fifteen years later, Webern's spatial concepts appear to be shrinking until the almost timeless immobility of some fifteen-second numbers for string quartet reveals a complete mistrust of development. In my opinion, the mature Webern, unlike most men of great talent, carries an instinctive awareness of his own deficiencies, and in the transitional years between the dissolution of the tonal dynasty and the adoption of the tone-row technique, he cautiously confines himself to the smallest possible canvas. Yet, strange to say, his most enthusiastic statesmen have long made a positive virtue of this reluctance to reiterate, finding in it the last delight of the epicurean palate, the perfect synthesis of artistic communication. (To my knowledge, no Beethoven fancier has as yet pronounced the Bagatelles, Op. 126, works of more ingenious refinement than the adjoining Ninth Symphony, Op. 125.)

Our description of the early Webern works suggests that the young composer was at his best when the form was regulated by an external pressure, as in the Passacaglia. This not only helped curtail Webern's linear loquacity but also fortified the occasionally flagging harmonic pulse. Throughout his work he relies heavily on arbitrarily imposed mathematical formulae, especially the device of canon. The use of canon in Webern does not call to mind the discreet alteration of an accidental, the fifth's casual adjustment to a tonal answer—in short, the conciliatory disposition which is prerequisite to classical counterpoint. Webern is a literal-minded individual in his application of such devices. The works of the transitional years abound in canon, inversion, and cancrizan—all treated with unswerving fidelity to their interval structure, all resisting compromise with the want of the harmonic dimension.

From 1926 or so onward, Webern was using the twelve-tone technique exclusively. From that date his works, while still governed by classical conciseness, utilize more extended forms, reveal wider dramatic scope, radiate a newfound assurance. For if ever a composer was born to the system and lacked his natural element without it, this is surely he. And despite the fact that Webern adheres to the twelve-tone properties in a very strict fashion, his works, paradoxically, display greater flexibility, especially in regard to the regulation of dissonance, which is the consideration of the present study. This is partly because Webern was now able to calculate in advance the various diversions in which his tone row might participate, to tabulate those forms of the set which, through inversion, retrogression, or transposition, suggest motivic reminiscences of the original, and then to combine them in such a way that their related portions overlap or succeed one another and thus supply a stabilizing force.

I suspect that an attempt to coordinate the harmonic attributes of Schoenberg and of Webern has already been undertaken by several notable composers. René Leibowitz in a work called *The Explanation of Metaphor* evolves a Webern-like perpetual double canon from the row of Schoenberg's *Ode to Napoleon Bonaparte*. Many relatively conservative twelve-toners, Giselher Klebe and Luigi Nono among others, have experimented with the effect of a sustained note or chord common to several row transpositions being held through a maze of polyphonic intrigue. But these attempts are concerned only with reworking superficial aspects of style. Boulez above all others is an individual. For all his rash and irreverent dictums, his talent and imagination are unquestionable. His persuasive manipulation of rhythmic shift, dynamic contrast, and, best of all, intermotivic correspondence are worthy of the scion of Webern. Yet in the consideration which concerns us here—the collaboration of motivic and harmonic detail—he concentrates exclusively on developing that aspect of Webern's technique where the terminal tones of a figuration appear through repetition the focal point of a harmonic implication:

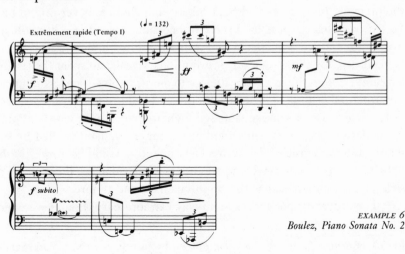

EXAMPLE *6*
Boulez, Piano Sonata No. 2

Boulez, however, is a composer who builds vast structures of extreme contrapuntal complexity, and I do not think that his leaping, vaulting sonorities betray the firm command of relative dissonance which Webern always exhibited in moments of intense contrapuntal endeavor. If Boulez continues to work in large forms, for which he is admirably fitted with a superb grasp of dramatic pace, he must inevitably cross swords with this dilemma which confronts our time.

I like to think that in Pierre Boulez and the other composers of the post-Webern generation we have artists capable of correlating the vertical and horizontal dimensions of twelve-tone activity, but I can no longer conclude with a triumphant proclamation that the brave new world is at hand. There are times when the puritan productions of the aging Schoenberg appear to me as a stern, valedictory pronouncement that music's metamorphosis has come too soon. But perhaps the past five years have simply witnessed the onset of that lifelong calcification of the imagination which brings to all men the languorous ennui that disavows the work of those who follow.

BOULEZ

For many of us in North America, Pierre Boulez's first claim to notoriety was not as a composer or conductor but rather as the author of a singularly nasty little temper tantrum published in the English magazine *The Score.* The year was 1951; the issue was ostensibly designed to commemorate the death, the previous July, of Arnold Schoenberg, but Boulez, never one to be deflected from his purpose by a sense of occasion, turned in a heavy-handed manifesto entitled "Schoenberg est mort." His thesis was predictable: Schoenberg, for all his own once-revolutionary zeal, had spent the last quarter-century of his life in a futile attempt to merge twelve-tone technique with the structural criteria of postromanticism and had become, in a word, irrelevant. (Relevance, or some suitable synonym thereof, is a big word in Boulez's vocabulary.) The torch had passed to a younger generation (led by guess who?), and the music of the future, consequently, would borrow only those of Schoenberg's theories which pertained to pitch, adapting them where possible to such parameters as rhythm, dynamics, and timbre.

The argument per se was in no way extraordinary; Boulez was, and is,

---

Review of *Boulez: Composer, Conductor, Enigma* by Joan Peyser (New York: Schirmer Books, 1976); from *The New Republic,* December 25, 1976.

a persuasive advocate for the musical ideology in which he believes. And serialism, the multiparametered integrational technique mentioned above, became the catchword of the fifties—first in Europe; later, and less pervasively, in America—with Boulez its most vocal proponent and, some would hold, most persuasive exponent. But the fact that this singularly uncharitable diatribe was included among tributes solicited for a memorial occasion—and solicited, moreover, by William (later Sir William) Glock, the adventuresome but solidly proestablishment head of music for the BBC, tells us a great deal about the phenomenal European celebrity which had already attached to the then twenty-six-year-old Boulez. A full decade after the publication of the article, indeed, Schoenberg's widow, Gertrud, still declined to mention Boulez by name. In a radio interview with this reviewer taped in 1962, she commented: "Such things will not harm Schoenberg; they will only help —well, I don't want to discuss personalities."

Despite the international brouhaha which attended the "Schoenberg est mort" incident, it was by no means the first time that Boulez had managed to confuse reasoned exegesis with polemical dispatch. In 1945, on the occasion of the first all-Stravinsky concert in postwar Paris, he directed a brigade of vocal saboteurs from a command post in the Théâtre des Champs-Elysées in order to harass the local neoclassic faction led by Nadia Boulanger. Unfortunately, such occasions were neither isolated incidents nor the idle pranks of a retarded adolescent. Boulez's life, as recounted by Peyser, seems to have consisted thus far of an interminable succession of plots and counterplots, fallings-out and reconciliations. Political advantage and musical conviction constantly intersect; colleagues are tabbed as opponents or accomplices according to the trends exhibited in their latest works; and though it would appear that the composer-conductor has mellowed somewhat during his six years with the New York Philharmonic, this is a depressing, disturbing, even frightening story.

It is also, in one respect at least, a rather confusing one. Peyser incorporates into her narrative texture a paramilitary vocabulary which becomes at times indistinguishable from Boulez's own manner of speech. "Warring camps," for example, "fight," "engage in combat," "destroy," "vanquish," "crush," "annihilate," "demolish," and even "obliterate" each other with astonishing frequency. Such "triumphs" come about, of course, through "confrontations" in which a "hero," a "steel-tempered soul," or possibly even a "king," sees to it that "lines are firmly drawn" and that "rivals," "enemies," or, indeed, even "archenemies," who are "waiting for the kill," are "exterminated." After "the struggle," "the leader," if he hasn't already enjoyed a coronation, will be "crowned" and his opposite number "dethroned." In happier times, a "truce" will be proclaimed, "allies" will be sought, "liaisons" will be formed, though, unhappily, most of these turn out to be "stormy." This, of course, leads inevitably to "abuse," "ridicule," and "contempt," and frequently "guerrilla warfare" will break out and the cycle will begin anew.

Needless to say, linguistic invention of this order cannot be sustained indefinitely, and the occasional chronological lapse is inevitable: a "Mafia" appears from time to time, various unlucky courtiers have "blocks knocked off" or "rugs pulled out" or "knives put in." But then, as Maître Boulez has pointed out, "History is much like the guillotine. If a composer is not moving in the right direction, he will be killed, metaphorically speaking."

Perhaps a few lines from the biographer will serve to convey the flavor of the piece. "In any case, if one wants to get anywhere in France—or, for that matter, in most countries—it helps to have a steel-tempered soul: how better to test the quality of the steel than to engage in combat with the powerful father, be he composer, teacher, or conseiller of arts. To carry the question one step further: how better to test one's ultimate strength than to insult, attack, and repudiate one's country and then move on to bigger and better nations?" The reference to the "powerful father" is central to the author's thesis. Having declared the obligatory indebtedness to Erik Erikson in her introduction, she sets about a psychobiographic portrait and, unfortunately for her subject, produces one. Boulez, we are told, rejected his own father. "In reconstructing the battle today, Boulez speaks with pride of his own and his sister's strength: 'Our parents were strong. But finally we were stronger than they.' " He also discovered at the age of five that a brother, bearing his Christian name, had died in infancy. "At an age when children first become aware of death, Pierre stood at the head of this tiny grave and read on the headstone, *Pierre Boulez.* 'I am a Darwinian,' Boulez explained. 'I believe I survived because I was the stronger. He was the sketch, I the drawing.' "

Peyser pursues her twin of filial rage and fraternal guilt with a vengeance. Boulez, it appears, in earlier years, was required to "kill" all father figures, whether teachers (René Leibowitz, Olivier Messiaen) or elder statesmen (Igor Stravinsky, Arnold Schoenberg), and, in more recent times, to fight a rearguard action against younger "brothers" who threaten his own position (Karlheinz Stockhausen, Henri Pousseur). His accomplice in the first of these pursuits is his sister, Jeanne—the book's dedicatee and most fascinating character. Her brother's only intimate friend, according to the author, Jeanne sees Pierre as a "Jesus-like figure," celebrates the "clear-cut decision against . . . father" in which she served as comrade-at-arms, and is able to match him ploy for ploy because "he is strong. But I am strong, too." Such material, needless to say, encourages Peyser to compose a set of variations on the theme of Thomas Mann's *The Blood of the Walsungs,* which, however, she manages with a modicum of subtlety—something that cannot be said for the repetitive, tasteless, and ultimately unproductive inquiries into

Boulez's sexual proclivities which she undertakes with a little help from her friends.

If, from the relative isolation of the provinces, I may say so, this book is the archetypal product of the American Eastern Seaboard megalopolitan mentality. Peyser, who is married to a psychiatrist, appears irresistibly drawn to analytic jargon and, consequently, manages to muddy the waters for her readers, her subject, and, one would guess, his prospective future biographers as well.

She does, however, write rather well, in a manner that might be described as *New Yorker* profile extended. She has a good eye for detail, though she does not evoke a sense of period with that combination of cinematic precision and personal commitment that marks the work of such *New Yorker* alumni as, say, Renata Adler. Her description of musical life in the 1950s, though, is shrewd and well researched, and in describing Boulez's activities during more recent years, she manages some memorable vignettes, including the hilarious account of a TV chat with a woefully unprepared Dick Cavett. Insofar as one can judge, she also has a good ear (and/or a reliable cassette), though her reconstruction of Boulez's first CBS recording sessions with the New York Philharmonic—a transplant from an earlier *New York Times* Sunday feature—opens with producer Andrew Kazdin announcing "insert 1, take 1." Kazdin, as I can testify from personal experience, is no slouch about the studio, and the odds against his beginning a session with an "insert"—supplemental material designed to repair or extend a basic "take," and which by definition can begin anywhere *but* the beginning of a work—are long indeed.

Perhaps because Peyser regards Boulez's career as a conductor as an escape from composition and hence a fall from grace, she discusses his New York years (which will terminate this season) in considerable detail but with no particular vigor, and at times in a positively giddy manner midway between Charlotte Curtis and Rona Barrett. For example:

> Amy Greene runs the beauty shop at Henri Bendel, one of the most fashionable stores in New York. She is married to Milton Greene, who used to photograph Marilyn Monroe. The Greenes are good friends of the Leonard Bernsteins. One afternoon when I was in her shop, Mrs. Greene told me that . . . she had not been to the Philharmonic since Bernstein left because she heard that "nothing good was going on there." . . . A woman from Long Island was trying eye shadow: "I dropped my subscription," she said, "because my husband is tired at the end of the day and he just wants to listen to music he likes."

In earlier chapters, Peyser describes and characterizes Boulez's major compositions without attempting to analyze them. This is, I think, an appropriate response for a work of this kind, and if the author had let it go at that, her book would have served as a useful introduction to Boulez's music for the lay reader. Unfortunately, she is as consumed by delusions of relevance as is her subject, and though, in her introduction, she proclaims him "a genius," it becomes increasingly apparent, as her thesis unfolds, that she regards him as a composer whose day has come and gone, who was "displaced by Stockhausen" and from whom "the rug was pulled" by John Cage. Translated, this means that Boulez subscribed to a set of principles which for one brief, heady moment—in the late forties, early fifties—made him as au courant as any good avant-gardist could hope to be; but because, with minor modifications, he held fast to these principles—displayed, in effect, ideological inflexibility—he missed the boat on the aleatoric developments of the later fifties and the theatre music of the sixties. (One shudders to think how Peyser would deal with the Indian summer of Richard Strauss or describe the Palestrinian counterpoint of Bruckner's E-minor Mass.) She labors, in fact, under what I have called elsewhere "the curse of the zeitgeist," And the irony of the situation, of course, is that so does her subject. Boulez, never known for collegial charity, is here the victim of something very close to a hatchet job, and Peyser's biography becomes, in effect, a "live by the sword, die by the sword" morality play. But only inadvertently. One cannot for a moment doubt that Peyser sympathizes with the sword rather than its victim.

History, thank God, should not and does not work that way. The process of historical selection is notoriously insensitive to who got where first but deeply involved with who did what with most sensitivity. Peyser would do well to reflect upon a quote from Olivier Messiaen which she features on page 1 of her introduction and, in an edited variant, at the end of chapter 14: "There are people who go unperturbed through change. Like Bach. Like Richard Strauss. . . . But Boulez cannot. This is extremely sad because he is a great composer." If Peyser had seen fit to adopt this quote as a leitmotiv, she might well have produced a more balanced, temperate study. Boulez may not be a "great composer," but he is certainly an interesting one, and despite—or, more accurately, because of—his own self-conscious and self-destructive reading of history, he deserves a biographer whose judgments are not impaired by similar conceits and who is able to offer more objective coverage than the present volume affords.

THE FUTURE AND
"FLAT-FOOT FLOOGIE"

In "Music for Eternity"—an essay published in 1938—composer Ernst Krenek enumerated the contents of a tonal time capsule prepared for entombment during prewar America's last great fling, the New York World's Fair of 1939. According to Krenek, the cultural commissars of that exposition elected to confound prospective ethnomusicologists in the year 6939 (the torpedo-shaped capsule accommodated a five-thousand-year time lock) with a musical mummy case which listed among its contents a miniature score of Sibelius's *Finlandia*, Sousa's "The Stars and Stripes Forever," and a composition entitled "Flat-Foot Floogie" by the celebrated triumvirate of Bob Green, Slim Galliard, and Slam Stewart. Now, as it happens, the same Ernst Krenek is one of thirty advisers to the editor of the present volume and the contributor therein of one of the major thematic think pieces, a deftly balanced, if ever so slightly defensive, apologia for serialism—the eloquence and urbanity of which alone justifies the rather stiff price of admission. (I wonder when someone will trouble to take parenthetic note of the fact that, like George Santayana, Krenek's impeccable English prose owes much to the fact that he was not born to the language and instinctively imposes Middle European rhythmic conceits upon its more mundane metrics.)

This volume, indeed, offers the most scrupulously fair-minded world-view available to the United States Eastern Seaboard musical establishment; twenty-five of those thirty advisors are American by birth, naturalization, or extended residence, and the influence of such luminaries of academia as Milton Babbitt and Roger Sessions is warily and numerically offset by the representation of such aleatoric option grantors as John Cage and Christian Wolff. To be sure, the individual surveys of music abroad are assigned (to all appearances) to responsible nationals. My knowledge of the respective scenes in Chile and Australia is insufficient for a detailed appreciation of the contributions from Juan Pablo Izquierdo and Larry Sitsky, though the latter author's vivid notes on one of his own operatic compositions, *Lenz* (1970), which, he tells us, veers between "ecstatic mysticism and blasphemy," cannot fail to stimulate the imagination. The U.K. entry, on the other hand, assigned

---

Review of *The Dictionary of Contemporary Music*, edited by John Vinton (New York: Dutton, 1974); from *Piano Quarterly*, Fall 1974.

on a pre-1945, post-1945 basis to the team of Geoffrey Sharp and Tim Souster, is a model of restraint and a reminder, courtesy of Mr. Sharp's confession that Elgar's "emotional depths . . . have for this writer no parallel in any other music," that there is nothing new under the setting sun of empire. The Canadian scene, similarly, is described with monochromatic diplomacy by that indefatigable chronicler of our times and climes John Beckwith. In addition, individual composers, particularly those resident abroad, are assigned uniformly sympathetic biographers: Henry-Louis de La Grange, H. H. Stuckenschmidt, and Luciano Berio, for example, all contribute recognizable portraits of their respective subjects—Gustav Mahler, Boris Blacher, and Henri Pousseur.

For the practicing musician, the volume's indispensable contribution is the chronological work list and bibliography appended to the biographical notes on each composer. There are remarkably few shortcuts here—even composers whose works are summarized in a few lines may well be accorded half a page of subsidiary listings, though a notable, and ironic, exception is the aforementioned Mr. Krenek, whose baroque-scale output, however, would give any editor pause.

But the *permanent* value of this dictionary—if, indeed, permanence is the proper pursuit of an encyclopedic enterprise—rests with its function as a photo album for the preferences and prejudices of musical America, circa 1970; and it is precisely at this level—theoretically its source of greatest strength—that I fear for its posterity and even make so bold as to question its current value. As one peruses the portraits of many of the major American figures, it is virtually essential to bring to bear upon them some knowledge of the political machinations involved in their respective careers, and as I read Krenek's superb essay and such notable companion pieces as Kurt Stone's treatise on notation or Barney Childs's sketch of indeterminacy, I kept wishing that I could be around a millennium hence when some enterprising archivist digs up this volume and makes a rush to judgment about the music of our time accordingly.

NOVEMBER 30, 2974 *(Special to Interplanetary News Service)* For the third successive year, Professor Werner von Blau, curator emeritus of Sound Collection at Infinity U. and newly appointed monitor-general of Silence, has been awarded the von Däniken prize for intergalactic studies. Professor von Blau was cited for "the production of evidence pertaining to the existence on the long-vacated planet Earth of a rituallike sound ceremony known as 'frequencizing'—a ceremony which appears to have existed as late as the third quarter of the twentieth century." Of particular importance, according to the awards committee, was Professor von Blau's retrieval from an excavation at the newly authenticated site of the community of Princeton, New Jersey, of a volume of some eight hundred pages, the equivalent of .0064 verbunes, which describes in detail the major frequencizers of the period. With characteristic modesty, Professor von Blau has insisted on sharing the award with his colleague Hans-Heinz Schlessemann. "Without his [Schlessemann's] vigorous spade work at Princeton," Professor von Blau has stated, "it would have been impossible for me to fully evaluate the data made available in this volume."

According to von Blau, Schlessemann has "convincingly demonstrated that the community of Princeton was designed, following Earth War I, as a maximum-security shelter for a celebrated astrologer of the period, Albert Einstein, whose theories of the universe were a cult object in their day and were even credited with a determining influence on the American belligerent capability in Earth War IA itself. Upon the cessation of hostilities, the community, in effect, metamorphosed into a medium-security internment camp and was subsequently utilized to house practitioners of interdisciplinary numero-magic whose presence and, one must presume, wide following were regarded as a threat by their more scientifically motivated colleagues on nearby Manhattan Island."

Like most men of science, Professor von Blau is reluctant to supply a press précis on a work-in-progress (he plans to elaborate his findings in a forthcoming treatise, "The Hexachord and Its Relation to Glacial Stratae"), but he has made available to IPNS the following brief summary of his findings:

> On the basis of print-space allocation in the volume at hand, one may safely assume that the major frequencizer of the third quarter of the twentieth century was an inmate of Princeton, one Milton Byron Babbitt. This much-heralded sound dispenser is credited by his biographer, Benjamin Boretz, with having "extended the musical universe in a multitude of directions and respects and [having] taken it near to the bounds of human conceptual and perceptual capacity while taking it as well to the heights of contemporary intellectual accomplishments," and is understandably awarded the most substantial single entry, five and a half pages (.000044 verbunes), but significant attention is focused as well upon such other prominent frequencizers as John Cage (four pages), Arnold Schoenberg and Igor Stravinsky (three pages each), and Karlheinz Stockhausen (two and a half pages). Babbitt's chief preoccupation appears to have involved sonic mutations of the number twelve, and, as his biographer remarks with enviable lucidity, "just as transposition can be represented as addition of a 'constant,' so inversion can be

represented as complementation or subtraction from a 'constant' (i.e., the octave as a 'quantity' of twelve semitones). And so too can retrogression be represented as order position complementation. . . . Thus emerges a notion of *segmental invariance* as a compositional resource of twelve-tone systematic music. . . . And the special case of nonduplication of pitches over stretches of set counterpoints is generalized as a notion of combinatoriality. . . . Such, and strictly such, is the role of mathematics in Babbitt's musical thought."

It is by no means beyond the pale of speculation, though it is beyond the scope of the present investigation, that Babbitt may well have had contact with the incantatory notions of the fourteenth-century sonarist Landini of Fiesole, whose theories of frequency manipulation, though of a notably more sophisticated order, were essentially similar to those of his American successor.

As mentioned, generous representation is accorded one John Cage, as well as certain of his disciples, notably Christian Wolff, David Tudor, and, in particular, La Monte Young. Each of these frequencizers, all of whom lived in, or close to, New York City, was of a notably scientific bent—a characteristic which contrasts strikingly with the abacuslike experiments of Babbitt; and, according to an unsigned biographer, La Monte Young conceived for his "Theatre of Eternal Music"—a frequencization entitled *The Tortoise, His Dreams and Journeys* which is "very long and comprehensive and unfolds through the performance of sections each day." Frequencizer Young, moreover, hoped to "perpetuate the work through the establishment of Dream Houses designed particularly for its continuous performance." We are further told that in 1966 Young began a section of *The Tortoise* entitled "MAP OF 49's DREAM THE TWO SYSTEMS OF ELEVEN SETS OF GALACTIC INTERVALS ORNAMENTAL LIGHT YEARS TRACERY" and that "the performances consist of continuous frequencies in sound and lights, generally at least a week in duration."

It seems reasonable to deduce that these environmental structures with their touching, if premature, attempts to create "galactic intervals" and "ornamental light-years" were designed as sonic sublimations for the atmospheric pollution which, as we know, engulfed the Eastern Seaboard of the U.S. during the later decades of the American empire, that the reflexive, usually electronically motivated, playback mechanisms which were utilized by many frequencizers of this persuasion were rejected constructs for sonar probes designed to test visibility and radiation levels, and that the primitive electronic equipment of the day could neither adequately satisfy nor interpret the environmental situation. This deduction is substantiated by titles such as that cited above—*The*

Tortoise, His Dreams and Journeys—which was unquestionably linked to the humanoids' ill-prepared suboceanic retreat occasioned by the glacial acceleration of century twenty-one. The tortoise thus appears as a symbol of the amphibious life force, and the "Dream Houses" referred to by the frequencizer Young are clearly modules prepared for suboceanic refuge. It is, however, instructive to note that the widely held theory of frequencization as an exclusively climatic phenomenon—indeed, as a preoccupation of temperate-zone humanoids—can no longer be defended; an entire paragraph is devoted to a Finnish frequencizer, Sibelius, who wrote one symphony, his "Fourth."

Although Professor von Blau conceded that this data will require many years of further research for proper evaluation, he did take particular satisfaction from the news that Schlessemann has recently uncovered a major sonar find at Flushing Meadows, New York, which includes among other memorabilia frequencizations by the aforementioned Sibelius and such celebrated colleagues as Sousa, Greene, Galliard, and Stewart.

"It would appear," Professor von Blau acknowledged,

that the frequencizers represented in this collection, which was providentially encapsulated immediately prior to Earth War IA, derived their impetus neither from the practical and scientific pursuits of the Cage circles nor from the incantatory, musico-astrological traditions of the Babbitt disciples. Preliminary examination has suggested that the only common denominator pertaining to these exhibits was an inclination to foster a concept known as "entertainment"—a concept which played no known role in frequencizing during the years between Earth Wars IA and IB. Given the exigencies of an impending holocaust, these items were obviously code indexed in great haste; and, although my colleagues have not as yet broken the code in question, we feel confident that its eventual deciphering will provide much useful information about the essential nature of the humanoid and his frequencizing proclivities.

The Princeton discovery [Professor von Blau continued], given its clearly demarcated coexistence between rudimentary musico-magico practices, and relatively more sophisticated forays into the field of sonar wave control, is a comparatively accessible body of evidence. The Flushing find, on the other hand, possessed of no discernible impulse toward practicality and guided by no immediately obvious interdisciplinary relationships, may well prove the most elusive and analytically complex of all the Schlessemann retrievals.

"If only," Professor von Blau sighed, "I were a younger man."

TERRY RILEY

[Spoken Over Riley's In C]

And you thought Carl Orff had found an easy way to make a living?
... The formula this time belongs to a young American named Terry Riley,
and it consists of fifty-three separate phrase doodles—average length, ten
notes—which are required reading for each of the eleven instrumentalists
who participate in the piece. There is no conductor, and the participants can
dawdle for as long as they dare over each of the phrases, with only one mutually agreed-upon premise—no fair going back—to guide them. The piece
can be regarded as at an end when the eleventh man gets to home base on
number fifty-three, and that quest, according to the composer's laissez-faire
foreword, can take anywhere from forty to ninety minutes.

The piece is called *In C,* and all fifty-three of those phrases do display
an overwhelming compulsion to support triad clusters in that key; but even
though in its tonal simplicity, and for that matter in its flirtation with boredom, it calls Carl Orff to mind, *In C* would almost surely have been labeled
"cultural Bolshevism" by the same Nazi commissars who gave the stamp of
approval to *Carmina Burana.* For all the superficial resemblance to Orff's exercise in musical hypnotism, it is, in fact, a work which summarizes, better
than most, much of what has been happening in the sixties.

First of all, it is a "funny" piece, I suppose, though perhaps more in
the sense that it provokes wry comment than through any overt humor. For
that was one sign of the times—a soft-pedaling of anecdotal entertainment
and an upswing for the sort of neoslapstick vehicles that derived much of
their inspiration from the medium to which they were attached. Bob New-
hart's delightful but, in Marshall McLuhan's word, "linear" routines were
very big in the early years of the decade, but the hit-and-run pointillism of
the "Laugh-In" method better defined the mood at the end of the sixties.
The distinction lay less with the fact that linear humor tapped sources which
required a modicum of leisure for the telling than that it told of things external to the medium with which it happened to be involved. Most humor in
the later sixties was wrapped up inextricably with the devices which enabled
it to be recounted in the first place.

The second thing about *In C* is that it is, to use the favorite word of
the McLuhanites, "participatory." The stringent serial disciplines of the
1950s fell, if not altogether into disrepute during the past ten years, then cer-

From a CBC radio broadcast, late 1960s.

tainly into disuse, and by the end of the decade were taken, even by their own most ardent advocates, with a grain of salt. Pierre Boulez, who was celebrated in the fifties not only for the serial economies he employed in his compositions but for his ferocious condemnation of all methods which dared to differ from his own, metamorphosed during the decade into one of the better-known baton wielders—the Cleveland Orchestra's principal guest, the BBC Symphony's chief conductor, and if all contractual obligations are fulfilled, incoming director of the New York Philharmonic. It's no slight upon Boulez's directorial capabilities to suggest that somewhere among his credentials in the eyes of the august gentlemen who govern those orchestras is included the fact that ideologically he's a confirmed devotee of the last of the orthodoxies, or, at any rate, the most recent of those compositional ploys which yield to educational supervision. Music like *In C* requires instructions rather than instruction, and that's an altogether more subjective matter.

The third thing of note about *In C* is that it is indeed in C, a key in which, as Arnold Schoenberg once remarked, there is still much music to be written. Schoenberg did not mean it literally, of course; he meant it as an expression of tolerance toward tonal writing in general from the vantage point of his own twelve-tone-induced nostalgia, and he certainly did not have in mind anything as monotonously monochromatic as Mr. Riley's opus. But the irony is that, whatever the disparity between prophecy and fulfillment, his prediction has by and large come true. Schoenberg's inability to foreclose on tonality, at least as practiced by others, has been vindicated in the sixties, while Boulez's preoccupation with music as a mathematically demonstrable commodity has proved to be as much a dead end as his cruel, superficial, and analytically insensitive pronouncement of two decades back —"Schoenberg est mort"—was wishful thinking. A great deal of the liveliest music today, when not in fact at sea, is, more or less, in C.

GOULD'S STRING QUARTET, OP. 1

The Quartet was written between 1953 and 1955, at a time when on all my concert programs and at the drop of a conversational hat I thought of myself as a valiant defender of twelve-tone music and of its leading exponents. Thus, an unexpected and thoroughly reasonable question arises—how, in the midst

---

Liner notes from Columbia MS 6178, 1960, featuring Gould's Quartet as played by the Symphonia Quartet.

of enthusiasm for the avant-garde movements of the day, could one find a work which would have been perfectly presentable at a turn-of-the-century academy, a work that did not advance the challenge to the laws of tonal gravity more boldly than did the works of Wagner, or Bruckner, or Richard Strauss? Was it perhaps that I was simply imitating a language which was extremely familiar to me and to my audience and would pose no special barriers of communication? Or was I presumptuously and unworthily attempting to recapitulate the thoughts of my musical elders?

In any event, the fact was that to find in the mid–twentieth century a work by a young composer that seemed to evoke reminiscence of Viennese romanticism was a rather startling experience. And the first piano read-through of the work astonished and even shocked friends who had expected from me, perhaps, a work of pointillistic precision. How could I, they protested, with all my professed admiration for Schoenberg and Webern, have turned so violently from the cause?

Well, the answer is really quite simple. Unlike many students, my enthusiasms were seldom balanced by antagonisms. My great admiration for the music of Schoenberg, for instance, was not enhanced by any counterirritation for the Viennese romantics of a generation before Schoenberg. Sadly, today it seems almost inevitable that admiration be the parent of snobbery, and one sees on every hand superbly informed and historically oriented young musicians who are only too eager to tell you what is wrong with all music between 1860 and 1920, who seize every opportunity to isolate the development of twelve-tone writing from nineteenth-century tradition. I, for one, have never been willing to admit that any love must be balanced by a concurrent disaffection, that every adoption must cause a rejection, and I preferred to see in Schoenberg and Webern composers who rose swiftly without apology from the romantic twilight of tonality, to see in the twelve-tone technique as it existed in the hands of Schoenberg a logical extension of nineteenth-century motivic treatment. For me, Schoenberg was not a great composer because he used the twelve-tone system, but rather the twelve-tone system was singularly lucky to have been exploited by a man of Schoenberg's genius.

For some time I had had the urge to write a work in which the achievement of Schoenberg in unifying motivic concepts would be applied to an idiom in which the firm harmonic hand of key relationship would be invited, its discipline acknowledged, and the motivic manipulation controlled thereby. Naturally, there would be adjustments to be made—the very nature of the diatonic scale is compromise—but it would be fun, I thought, to see how far one could proceed in extending an absurdly small motive as the nucleus of every thematic strand of the work without at the same time violating the harmonic rhythm of the whole. This was not to be a work in which the contrapuntal intrigues stopped the show. They must fit naturally, even spontaneously, into the total plan, which, while it ought to be modified and augmented by developments of motivic procedures, should remain recognizably formal.

If this sort of theorizing suggests the same grim resolve with which every composer sets about an exercise in style, I must state that whatever may have been my academic motive initially, within a very few measures I was completely in the throes of this new experience. At once I was writing a work within a harmonic language utilized by composers whom I adored, yet I was working in this language with a kind of contrapuntal independence which I had learned from more recent and, indeed, from much older masters. Hence, I felt myself to be saying something original and my artistic conscience was clear. Whatever I had set out to prove pedagogically, it was soon evident that I was not shaping the Quartet—it was shaping me.

The four-note motive to which all major thematic developments relate is first heard played by the second violin over a pedal point of the lower strings:

EXAMPLE 1

During a lengthy introduction it permeates every voice of the Quartet in constantly elaborating patterns:

EXAMPLE 2

The Quartet is, quite simply, an enormously expanded movement taking for its precedent the sonata-allegro or classical first-movement design. The relation of thematic areas to each other is eminently orthodox (that is, the severity of the F-minor tonality is assuaged by secondary thematic groups in A-flat major in the exposition, in F major in the recapitulation), although, needless to say, in a work of this size innumerable plateaus of modulation extend the harmonic orbit considerably.

The principal theme of the exposition proper could be described as "arrived at" rather than "derived from" the formative motive (example 1):

EXAMPLE 3

By the time of its first appearance in the viola, it represents a complex of many motivic and rhythmic shifts prepared in the introduction. The subsidiary A-flat-major group begins with this theme:

EXAMPLE 4

which later expands to join example 3:

EXAMPLE 5

The central development section is in B minor, as far removed as one can be from the home tonality of F, and takes the independent form of a fugue, followed by a series of choralelike statements, working back to F minor:

EXAMPLE 6

In the fugue, example 3 appears as countersubject:

EXAMPLE 7

The recapitulation, which is prefaced by its own fugatolike introduction, is in no sense perfunctory. All of the thematic strands heard previously are present but have grown and mingled contrapuntally:

EXAMPLE 8

The form thus described is preceded by a lengthy introduction of about one hundred measures and followed by a section which, since it consists of some three hundred measures, not even I have the temerity to call Coda. This latter section is certainly the most unusual feature of the work. Within it the instruments review many of the contrapuntal evolutions induced by the four-note motive without literally quoting any of the principal themes identified with the main body of the work:

EXAMPLE 9

This section was conceived on planes of declining dynamic emphasis, and although many subclimaxes are attained, it gradually works back to a harmonization of the imperturbable pedal point of the opening.

The Quartet represents a part of my musical development which I cannot but regard with some sentiment. It is certainly not unusual to find an Op. 1 in which a young composer inadvertently presents a subjective synthesis of all that has most deeply affected his adolescence ("influenced" is perhaps too determinate a word). Sometimes these prodigal summations are the harbingers of the true creative life. Sometimes the brilliance with which they reflect the past manages to excel all that their composer will do thereafter. In any event, though the system must be cleansed of Opus Ones, the therapy of this spiritual catharsis will not remedy a native lack of invention. It's Op. 2 that counts!

SO YOU WANT TO WRITE A FUGUE?

In the pages ahead you will find a recording that is, in effect, a five-minute, fourteen-second singing commercial. An *unsponsored* commercial, let it quickly be noted, and a rather special one in other ways, too, for it light-heartedly recommends a product not ordinarily packaged. What it plugs is one of the most durable creative devices in the history of formal thought and one of the most venerable practices of musical man. The device in question is called fugue, and the process in question is fugue writing, and since these began a century before Columbus sailed west, they are almost as old as the practice of singing rounds, a less sophisticated creative activity than fuguing but one that somewhat resembles it in its earliest days. With its play of words and tunes, the composition recorded here takes the form of a fugue *about* the writing of fugues. Alluding to the joys, satisfactions, hazards, nuisances, and even the terrors long associated with this tough but intriguing kind of contrapuntal acrostic, my fugue becomes a musical conversation among four vocalists, aided and at moments contradicted by the comments of a string quartet. As the announcers used to say of forthcoming soap-opera programs, this chapter Asks The Question "So you want to write a fugue?" The question is proposed initially in the bass, and in textbook terms the tune that proposes it is, of course, the "subject" of the fugue.

Article accompanying a plastic disc bound into the April 1964 issue of *HiFi/Stereo Review*, containing the first issue of Gould's *So You Want to Write a Fugue?*, a seven-minute composition recorded by the Juilliard String Quartet and four vocalists, under the direction of Vladimir Golschmann.

As the other voices "answer" or repeat this tune in a rising sequence (tenor, alto, soprano), a debate is developed concerning certain special qualities required by this peculiar enterprise. The basso begins by suggesting that a certain degree of courage is involved: "You've got the nerve to write a fugue, so go ahead." The tenor is concerned with the utility of the finished product: "So go ahead and write a fugue that we can sing." The contralto, even though her own contrapuntal demeanor is beyond reproach, advocates an audaciously antiacademic method: "Pay no mind to what we've told you, give no heed to what we've told you, just forget all that we've told you and the theory that you've read." To this point of view, the soprano—though equally guiltless, at least at this point, of any offending lapse of fugal discipline—lends her support. These sentiments—"Pay no mind, give no heed," etc.—form countermaterial to the original subject, "So you want to write a fugue?" The latter now appears in a variety of keys identified with this further notion: "For the only way to write one is to plunge right in and write one, just ignore the rules and write one, have a try." The heady intoxication of this radical admonition at last becomes reflected to a modest degree in the musical structure. The vocalists, their parts ever more closely overlapping, plunge into a precarious sequence of imitative strettos. And here, at last, the stern hand of academic justice demands forfeit of their freedom. Even as they render tribute to the patron saint of fugue writing—"The fun of it will get you, and the joy of it will fetch you, you'll decide that John Sebastian must have been a very personable guy"—the bass and tenor surrender their self-respecting autonomy to the hollow ravages of parallel fifths, a contrapuntal debacle that any primer of the art will tell you is perfectly ghastly. As a gesture of tribute (as well as a summons to sobriety), the string quartet now renders a quodlibet of four of Bach's more celebrated themes (you'll note, among them, the second Brandenburg Concerto). Then, appropriately, the quartet turns to the contralto for a brief lecture on the perils of exhibitionism: "But never be clever for the sake of being clever." This, with its attendant warning—"For a canon in inversion is a dangerous diversion and a bit of augmentation is a serious temptation"—creates an entirely new thematic substance. Hereupon the string quartet renders a grandiose if minor-inflected quotation from *Die Meistersinger*—the archetypical example of musical cleverness—after which all concerned engage in a joyous recapitulation. The bass and tenor return to the thematic substance of "So you want to write a fugue?" The contralto and soprano accommodate to it the newly exposed countertheme—"But never be clever for the sake of being clever." And the strings keep up their own incessant dialogue of baroque-ish fragments.

Before I pursue further some of the larger implications of the fugal activity of these performers, a parenthesis is in order here regarding nomenclature.

In these paragraphs I use, without defining them, a number of terms indispensable to the discussion of fugue: "exposition," "development," "recapitulation," "subject," "answer," etc. I do not define them, because they are self-explanatory to anyone even casually interested in musical form. Certain other terms are main entries in college-level dictionaries (in addition to having been in student texts on counterpoint for three centuries).

But as fugue crosses the semantic forests of the twentieth century, it is increasingly subject to verbal analysis of a much more disconcerting sort than was possible with the simple and accessible nouns listed above. You will hear it said, for example, that fugue is not a *thing* but a *process*, and even that it is not a *form* at all but a *texture*. And if you speak of "tunes" or "melodies" in relation to fugue, you will certainly be frowned upon down at the fugal equivalent of City Hall. It is true that such terms can be misleading. In ordinary reference, a tune or melody—"Yankee Doodle," let us say—is explicit, self-sufficient, and complete: it has a beginning, a middle, an end. But fugue does not and cannot use such melodies, because it stops itself dead in its tracks if it does. Fugue must perform its frequently stealthy work with continuously shifting melodic fragments that remain, in the "tune" sense, perpetually unfinished. And to bring up an even more critical current issue, what are we to say of contemporary fugues that arise in that unposted harmonic wilderness where familiar tonality has vanished but is somehow still remembered, even by those who disown it? Such contingencies recommend our caution, and we consequently use more abstract but safer concepts, such as "motivic material" in place of "tunes," and "linear strands" in place of "melodies"—and even "nonoriented tonality" in place of the bald "atonality" that was fashionable just ten years ago. Unless we are very careful, such verbal egg-stepping leads us also to outright jargon, a fancy hermetic language of questionable usefulness even to specialists. But the temper of the intellectual times forces this risk upon us, and so you may be sure that, in just a moment, the word "aleatory" will be upon us with it.

Returning now to our performers, we find that the final result of their labor (except for the irreverent quotes from Bach and Wagner) is a fairly typical example of the academic fugue tradition. In its exposition, in its modulative sequences, in the introduction of its countertheme material, and in the superimposition of these elements in its recapitulation—throughout its course the piece rigorously observes the protocol of fugal tradition. Centuries of contrapuntal legislation make up this tradition, and if you mean to write a fugue you unquestionably yield to it. Even as the text was mischievously snooting the requirements of bookish counterpoint, the music was taking refuge behind the protective cloak of approved academic procedure. This particular wrap is stained and weatherbeaten from exposure to generations of unimaginative abuse, but it still shelters a prodigious variety of musical activity. Even in our own vigorously antiacademic generation, fugues are blasted out by jazz combos and improvised or approximated by aleatory charts. Indeed, fugues are even being attempted within the nonoriented tonality of serial composition. In any of these novel situations, of course, fugues present something of a contradiction in terms, because the unique organizational method of fugue has very much to do with the key-signature tonal system, and that system now appears to be in the process of dissolution. Yet the persistence of fugue is evidence of the degree to which, acoustically and psychologically, certain devices peculiar to its structure—devices of subject and response, of statement and answer—are embedded within the consciousness of modern man. Although it was a tonal preoccupation which lent them balance and gravity and a certain kind of equilibrium, they have survived as part of an effective organizational method even beyond the general collapse of this preoccupation. And perhaps the main reason for this is that they are not devices native to tonality at all. All of the effects of fugue (except that of the vertical gravitation of key and key contrast) were effects formulated in the early years of the Renaissance—in the generations before the tonal grammar of tension and relaxation had been made articulate. And their participation in the poise and balance of centrifugal harmony, the weblike detentions of cadence structure, seem largely the result, at most, of a synchronicity that was voluntary on their part.

Thus the ancient experience of linear antecedents predating tonality has enabled fugue to continue to exist in the uncertain vista of our post-tonal present. And it is the consequent familiarity of these fugal devices with situations which are not (in the post-Renaissance sense) tonally committed that provides for fugue its extraordinary relation to the chronological development of tonality. For the fact is that, to a very large extent, the construction of fugue has managed to defy the harmonic concerns of any particular generation—especially those generations not oriented to a tenaciously contrapuntal point of view. In periods when a concern for the integrity of linear structure was considered outmoded, such fugues as were written tended to resist any easy harmonic confirmation which would reveal them conspicuously as the servant of the times. This explains to some degree why it requires only a very slight lapse of analytical judgment in order to attribute a fugue by Mozart to Brahms, a fugue by Mendelssohn to Miaskovsky—or, as Joseph de Marliave once ungenerously suggested, a fugue by Beethoven to a demon. Even in my little piece, the harmonic allegiance draws upon a surprisingly wide fund of idiomatic reference. Its overall harmonic effect—which is to say, its most frequently observed dissonance-consonance ratio—is determinedly Mendelssohnian; indeed, the piece subscribes to that resonant but supremely polite brand of chromatic endeavor which, emanating from Mendelssohn, went to the opera with Humperdinck and Saint-Saëns, to the choir loft with Sir John Stainer and Sir Arthur Sullivan, and to the concert hall with Anton Rubinstein, becoming for a time the nineteenth century's most widely traveled set of harmonic components. But if one could apply to this fugue the musical equivalent of a stop-frame camera technique, one would find that there also exist within its boundaries several other significant areas of stylistic allusion. Its opening exposition, for instance, is decidedly Bachian with its propulsive bar-line dissonances and its concentration of imitative figuration at such times as the main thematic strands have lapsed into transition or episode. On the other hand, in the last measures prior to the coda all of the vocalists work themselves up into a frenzied motivic conflict supporting the frustration of the soprano (who shrieks, "Write us a fugue that we can sing, come along now"). And these hectic measures could, but for the very un-Hofmannsthalish lyrics, have been lifted from any reasonably flamboyant page of Richard Strauss.

A major difficulty in analyzing the harmonic environment of fugue becomes apparent if we compare it with a radically different creature, the classical symphony. In fugue the preoccupation with form is of an altogether more subjective nature than is the case with symphony. In fugue the disposition of modulating harmonic plateaus is not customarily committed to any one species of developmental criteria or legislation. It is true that the subject matter of fugue can, and indeed must, appear in sequences of sharply contrasted harmonic focus. But these harmonic areas are not likely to be subject to categorical legislation comparable to the tonic-dominant, masculine-feminine polarities of the classical symphony—polarities which tend to telescope the structural concerns of the symphony very conveniently within the ruling harmonic preoccupations of the late eighteenth or early nineteenth century. We note that the preoccupying formality of the classical symphony becomes progressively more involved with what might be called tactics of delay, with an attempt to erect substantial spans linking islands of contrast and temperament—islands which are almost, if not quite, self-sustaining. In contrast to this, fugue writing tends to be deeply involved with relatively confined areas of musical expanse and with an intense subjective concentration upon the concern of the moment—a concern which it seeks to magnify and to project urgently into every fiber of the work. Thus we note that fugue is not involved to any great degree with broad aspects of dramatic altercation, or with elaborate shifts of texture or dynamics, such as render the classical symphonic structure so explicit. Rather, fugue is involved with the adjustment of a certain number of semiautonomous linear patterns which it proposes to maintain at a more or less constant density. Among these patterns, the effect of textural variety is fostered by a sensation of pregnant pause within one or another of the contributing voices—and not, as in the mannerisms of the classical symphony, by a sense of utterly unpredictable contour, by violent theatrical interruption, or by the haunting presence of an unresolved thematic residue.

The idea to which fugue is most conspicuously the servant is a concept of unceasing motion. It is this nonstatic concept which makes fugal structure the perfect vehicle for the adventurous and subjective harmonic traffic of baroque art. And since this concept is carried forward into other eras, it offers us a partial explanation of the extraordinary historical unification of fugal practice. And it is the alliance of this concept of unceasing motion with our previous notion of consistent density that really determines the shape of fugue. For within this forward movement and this consistent density, each phrase, each musical sentence, will inaugurate its own special problem, its own unique cause for anxiety. Each of these will be open to a series of more or less expedient solutions, and each will relate in some cohesive way to the fundamental motivic propositions of the piece. The events involved in these solutions will, of necessity, demonstrate a certain kind of developmental procedure. But here again we note that fugal development is not the kind which is elaborated in the major cyclic forms. It avoids the vivid alternation of a sense of relaxation (as manifested in transitions) with the accumulation of tension (inspired by modulation) that we find, for example, in a Beethoven sonata. Rather, fugal events will be required to provide some specific contribution to the original subjective idea from which the fugal structure sprang. They will furthermore be expected to combine the original motivic proposition with subsidiary thematic notions, and these combinations will not, if the fugue is properly done, recur in precisely the same relationship at any subsequent time. In other words, a sense of constant variation is the ideal of fugue, but variation of a particularly *nomadic* order—variation which leaves the impression that the thematic concepts with which we have to deal in fugue belong to a special, generic store of musical ideas, and that they can, in some ruthlessly self-preoccupied mathematical way, implicate a wide variety of contrapuntal choices.

In the case of *So You Want to Write a Fugue?*, both the opening subject and the main subsidiary material—"But never be clever for the sake of being clever"—were designed as relatively uncomplicated motivic strands. They do not, when examined independently, necessitate any one series of harmonic progressions. Instead, their innocence of any untoward chromatic suggestion makes it possible for them to endure together through a variety of metrical displacements and through a series of pitch transpositions (relative, that is, to the basic distance between them). Before I wrote the piece, it was necessary for me to be aware that the moments of structural emphasis in this work had to be designed in compliance with those forthcoming occasions when

I could first introduce some major variant in the disposition of these themes. Most fugal structure is responsive to subjective considerations of this kind. In Bach's *Well-Tempered Clavier,* a great many of the fugues choose as their moment of highest tension that occasion when, for the first time, the primary subject is heard, or seen, in one of the contrapuntal strands turned upside down. The prerequisite of contrapuntal art, more conspicuous in the work of Bach than in that of any other composer, is an ability to conceive a priori of melodic identities which when transposed, inverted, made retrograde, or transformed rhythmically will yet exhibit, in conjunction with the original subject matter, some entirely new but completely harmonious profile.

It is this fascination with motivic experimentation which links all the practitioners of fugue into an unorganized but very genuine guild of spirit. This guild counts among its members those skeptical natures who are uncomfortable without the shelter of a discipline which is to some degree susceptible of proof. Many of these are composers who feel somewhat ill at ease with the concept of the star-gazing artist waiting upon some hallucinatory seizure of inspiration that will determine the shape and intent of his next work. When they happen to be resident in periods which promote this romantic concept as a fundamental article of the artistic temper (as was to a large extent surely the case at the turn of the last century), then these gentle misfits—among whom one might number composers like Reger and Miaskovsky—find in fugue a welcome shield from the pressures of fashion. In fugue they submit to a discipline in which each successive decision demands that intensive scrutiny which excludes all concerns beyond the burden of the moment. Meanwhile, the fuguing guild also includes those who, while living in an age hostile to the contrapuntal persuasion, become involved with their own personal renaissance of fugue (Beethoven is perhaps the best example), and who weld its concepts firmly into the structural criteria of other forms. And finally, this guild includes those happy figures who are really fuguists to the manner born. All aspects of their thought occur initially in the form of contrapuntal dialogue, and because of their constant preoccupation with the subjective commitment of form, they are able, as was Bach, to mount a glorious defiance to the domination of a historically hostile chronology.

Now that the tonal system and its governing polarities have become the victims of a nonoriented harmonic ideal, it is very difficult to visualize the future permutations of fugue or even the certainty of its survival. Even though major figures like the late Paul Hindemith may devote a lifetime to nourishing the ancient linear values within a daringly altered tonal perspective, it becomes difficult to predict whether this represents something other than simply a facet of the intense baroque revival of the present. But without doubt, the persistence of fugue through the centuries does suggest that it draws upon conceptions as permanent as any that the still-young art of music may be said to own. There is the great fascination that it holds as a form within which a mystique of numbers can unravel its secrets. There is, to the composer, the enormous satisfaction of dealing with a musical form in which the form *itself* becomes the servant of a subjectively manipulated concept of thematic relation. And then, perhaps, beyond even these considerations is the fact that fugue arouses some primeval curiosity which seeks to uncover in the relations of statement and answer, of challenge and response, of call and of echo the secret of those still, desert places which hold the clues to man's destiny but which predate all recollection of his creative imagination.

PART TWO

Performance

LET'S BAN APPLAUSE!

The good citizens of Toronto, my hometown, received last spring their annual visit from the Metropolitan Opera Company. This is an occasion much looked forward to by all of us, and this season was the subject of special attention, since it involved the transfer of that splendid ensemble from the regal expanse of a hockey arena to the more confined proscenium of a new theatre constructed in our behalf through the generosity, civic vision, and tax advantage of a local brewing firm. The Metropolitan, with its accustomed tact and diplomacy, wisely declined to present to us the alcoholic dissipations of Sir John Falstaff or the aphrodisiac delusions of Master Tristan or, indeed, any other tableaus which might compromise the corporate image of its host. But, despite these courtesies, the visit was attended by a most disagreeable correspondence in the local press. This emanated from the displeasure which several writers voiced with the relatively restricted capacity of the new salon and from sympathy with those of our less affluent fellow citizens who found the consequent raise in admission prohibitive.

It was not these modest, though justified, complaints that arrested my attention, however, but the grave alarms raised by several of our more worldly-wise columnists (those who have attended concerts as far afield as Buffalo) that what we had lost with the reduced attendance at the Metropolitan was not money—a concept which all Torontonians could readily grasp—but was, rather, that intangible spirit of theatrical excitement generated by those whose native customs permit the unabashed display of enthusiasm or displeasure. We had, we were told, callously excluded the services of that indispensable component of grand opera—the upper-balcony jeer leader. This view, disseminated in the local press, caused much consternation among my fellow citizens, an effect it would surely not have achieved in any other city. This is, of course, because Toronto is one of the last bastions of puritan influence in North America, and, despite the encroachment of science, Henry Miller, and immigration, we have managed to hold firm those convictions upon which the faith of our fathers was founded.

We do not regard the theatre as an intrinsically wicked institution; we do consider it in need of careful and constant scrutiny.* But once we have satisfied ourselves as to the moral discernment of its productions, we proceed to it with a total humility born of reverence for that which we do not wholly

---

From *Musical America*, February 1962.
*At the time of this article, Gould had not yet retired from public performing.—T.P.

understand. It would never have occurred to us to demand for ourselves the right to proclaim our approbation demonstratively by rudely punctuating a work of musical theatre. Even less would we presume, by forwarding uncomplimentary noises from the stalls, to express our distaste for the message of a composer which we found difficult or the hapless screechings of an ill-advised soprano.

This is not to say that we would withhold a measure of encouragement from an artist whose work and whose private life are beyond reproach. I have seen elderly ladies remove their gloves to render their tribute to the symphonies of Mr. Elgar—after all, he was well received at court, wasn't he?—and certainly our pleasure with Dr. Mendelssohn knows no bounds. And I can attest from personal experience that Torontonians are well able to convey their consternation at the beeps and groans of Mr. Anton Webern by a silence as timeless as those within that gentleman's music itself.

But now we were being told by this racy contingent of high-living newspapermen that we must surrender our right to the genteel response of our cultural tradition and look for leadership to those whose heritage does not consider musical theatre an adjunct of the church (as ours does) but rather as a comfortably upholstered extension of the Roman Colosseum. This has given me occasion to ponder the relationship of applause to musical culture, and I have come to the conclusion, most seriously, that the most efficacious step which could be taken in our culture today would be the gradual but total elimination of audience response.

I am disposed toward this view because I believe that the justification of art is the internal combustion it ignites in the hearts of men and not its shallow, externalized, public manifestations. The purpose of art is not the release of a momentary ejection of adrenaline but is, rather, the gradual, lifelong construction of a state of wonder and serenity. Through the ministrations of radio and the phonograph, we are rapidly and quite properly learning to appreciate the elements of aesthetic narcissism—and I use that word in its best sense—and are awakening to the challenge that each man contemplatively create his own divinity.

The effect of this newly acquired introspection has been salutary upon our culture as a whole. Never before have Ockeghem and Costeley invaded our drawing room in the company of Chopin and Liszt. Never before has Gesualdo competed with Schubert for our attention. Never before has a composer been able to render electronically the exact specifications of his intention without resorting to the self-centered affectations of a performing middleman. If, then, it has been possible to achieve within one generation this degree of conditioned listening, surely the next generation will find it no mighty task to carry this quality of introspection one step further—into the concert hall and theatre themselves.

There are those, of course, who counsel that only in the theatre, only with the direct communion of artist to listener, can we experience the high drama of human communication. The answer to this, it seems to me, is that art on its loftiest mission is scarcely human at all.

"But surely," some may counter, "applauding after a performance is as natural to a listener as sneezing at the sun on a windy day." I reply that one may listen to a recording of a Beethoven symphony alone or in the company of friends and, though deeply moved at its conclusion, experience no more urgent need than a quick trip to the icebox for a soda water. And if we concede, then, that it is the law of the heard that governs the response of an audience to a performer, can this response be further justified?

"Democracy, the rule of Majority," someone argues. "Why should the paying customer be deprived of the right to voice his opinion?" Well, apart from the fact that the other paying customers did not subscribe to hear his opinion, one must take into account the peculiar laws of acoustical psychology, whereby a strategically placed rooter or detractor may, by applying the proper vocal leverage at a judicious moment, enlist the bellowing echo of many hundreds of his fellows.

"But what harmful effect can it have?" someone asks. "Everybody knows that artists are incredibly conceited and quite able to survive the taunts of an impolite laity." Ah, are they indeed? I ask. Or are the absurdly competitive extravaganzas of our operatic colleagues not the product of, or maybe the antidote to, the vulgar artistic hostility of those sun-baked societies who have built an operatic tradition in which their primal instinct for gladiatorial combat has found a more gracious but thinly disguised sublimation?

"All right," our disputant allows, "granted that a few of the less sturdy vocalists must concede in the fray, but what about the composers? Let's not forget that many of our great composers became famous by having more disorderly premieres than their colleagues were able to muster. Let's not forget Stravinsky and the riots at the *Rite* or Schoenberg and the pummelings at *Pierrot.*" True, I retort, they did become famous, and they deserved to become famous, but not because of the riots and not even, I would venture to suggest, because of those particular works. A more just citation, if you will allow me, would be an incident at one of our own Toronto premieres—an incident which deeply shocked all true Torontonians. It happened several years ago, at the first performance of a new concerto by a Canadian composer, a lady of considerable gift, though perhaps of less resilient spirit than a Stravinsky or a Schoenberg. Preceding the performance, an introductory speaker (non-Torontonian) spoke harshly to us on the subject of apathy toward contemporary composition. He urged us, as only a non-Torontonian would, to express our approval of the works we enjoyed, or, if we were so inclined, our disapproval. Now, this adjuration would certainly have gone for naught but for the unlucky chance that in the audience that night there sat another non-Torontonian, a historian by profession and an intelligent chap, but a fellow whose musical sympathies stop somewhere short of Josquin des Prés. Well, as you can imagine, the new concerto did not fall upon receptive ears, and so our friend the historian, having been encouraged to voice his estimation, did so. Regrettably, he was being closely scrutinized at the time by some eager members of his graduate class (non-Torontonians all), who were seated nearby. And so "Hoot," said the professor, and "Hoot, hoot," said the students, while visions of better grades danced in their heads. I wish I could relate that the concerto and its composer became infamous that night, but such was not to be the case, and it has not been rendered since. There is, however, a sequel to the story. The lady composer had another premiere in Toronto quite recently—a new symphony. Our historian was not present, but nonetheless the new work was shown the same intolerance as its elder brother—the only work in our concert season to be so honored. Clearly, the herd is breeding.

"Aha," says the disputant in a final effort to demolish my case, "this fellow Gould speaks with a singular passion. Perhaps he, too, has been put to his heels to escape the wrath of an outraged public!" Yes, I admit candidly, there was such an occasion. It was in Florence, or, as we international men prefer to say, Firenze. I had just concluded a performance of the Schoenberg Suite, Op. 25, which, although it was at the time thirty-five years old, had not yet been admitted to the vocabulary of the Florentines. I arose from the instrument to be greeted by a most disagreeable chant from the upper balcony, which was at once contradicted by feverish encouragements from the lower levels. Although I was new to this experience, I instinctively realized that no harm could come to me so long as I permitted the spectators to vent their fury upon each other. Therefore, I cunningly milked the applause for six curtain calls (an exceptional acclaim for Op. 25), and, thereafter, the exhausted audience sat back in a liverish somnolence to attend the "Goldberg" Variations.

I feel that I have now presented my case with true candor, and so it only remains to suggest ways and means to implement my proposal that the audience of the future should be seen but not heard. To this end, and for the assistance of any concert manager who may care to make use of it, I have drawn up the Gould Plan for the Abolition of Applause and Demonstrations of All Kinds, hereinafter referred to as GPAADAK. Needless to say, GPAADAK in its early stages will require, in addition to an active promotional campaign, a measure of goodwill on the part of artist, audience, and management alike.

The first step in instituting GPAADAK will be the scheduling of applauseless concerts on each Friday, Saturday, and Sunday. These three days, with their inherent liturgical connotations, are best able to evoke a suitably reverent state of mind. Concerts during the balance of the week, Monday to Thursday, could be billed as Family Excursion Events, if I may beg a term from the airlines. Reduced prices would apply, and, of course, applause would be permitted. Children would be encouraged to attend during the week, and the duty to guide them there would provide a convenient excuse for those of the older generation who found the conversion difficult. The performers, naturally, would be strictly second-team. At the prestige week-end concerts, the most serious problem in the early stage of GPAADAK will be the selection of appropriate repertoire—works which will most contribute to the overall solemnity. I would suggest that large-scale oratorios be tried first, followed, perhaps, by a series consisting of music composed by members of royal houses. There is a wide field here, and works such as the Piano Concerto in A by Louis Ferdinand of Prussia or the *Pastorale Cantata for Lady Augusta's Birthday* by Frederick Louis, Prince of Wales (and father, incidentally, of George III), deserve a firm place in our musical life. There might, of course, be certain judicious exclusions. Perhaps a composition by the Maharaja of Porbandar would not be appropriate for a Sunday concert in Karachi.

The next area of repertoire to be included in GPAADAK should be the presentation of ninth symphonies—anybody's Ninth Symphony, really, although Shostakovitch's might be a little flip—but, after exploring the Beethoven-Bruckner-Mahler parallel, it would be wise to conclude with Schubert's Ninth, since, being really his Seventh, it would introduce an appropriate note of secularism into the numerical piety of the series. I think that these few suggestions already indicate that the concert managers of the future will be under pressure to display an unaccustomed initiative in programming. Indeed, under the aegis of GPAADAK, many of these gentlemen may well advance from their present status as bookers and become worthy of the old and noble title of impresario.

In the early stages of GPAADAK, the performers may feel a moment of unaccustomed tension at the conclusion of their selection, when they must withdraw to the wings unescorted by the homage of their auditors. For orchestral players this should provide no hazard: a platoon of cellists smartly goose-stepping offstage is an inspiring sight. For the solo pianist, however, I would suggest a sort of lazy-Susan device which would transport him and his instrument to the wings without his having to rise. This would encourage performance of those sonatas which end on a note of serene reminiscence, and in which the lazy Susan could be set gently in motion some moments before the conclusion. I foresee a heavy run on Op. 109, which could almost be staged, provided there were a clear understanding between the soloist and the commissionaire backstage.

As the founder and chronicler of GPAADAK, I feel that it behooves me to be among the first to put it into practice. Needless to say, I have given this responsibility much consideration. Regrettably, Toronto does not provide the ideal site, since, apart from the fact that it needs GPAADAK less urgently than almost any other center, I personally would be confronted with the age-old civic antagonism for the local boy with a vision. It has occurred to me as a codirector of the Stratford Music Festival that the unique intimacy of our beautiful stage there might be especially appropriate for applauseless concerts, but then, those actors are such a wild, unpredictable bunch. Perhaps my chance will come at Mr. Tom Patterson's recently announced Dawson City Festival of 1962. Here indeed is virgin territory. Here is an audience without prejudice, without preconception. I wonder how Diamond Lil would react to the Maharaja of Porbandar?

WE WHO ARE ABOUT TO BE DISQUALIFIED SALUTE YOU!

Montreal's first International Violin Competition was this year's presentation by the International Institute of Music of Canada—an organization which made its debut last season with the production of that city's first International Piano Competition and which is threatening, in the fullness of time, to sponsor seconds of both. The violin trials were held during the first three weeks of June and taxed the stamina of thirty-seven aspiring superstars from three continents, the methodistic tolerances of nine equally representative adjudicators (three from Western Europe, three from North America, and three from behind the Iron Curtain), and the patience of an audience which, from a mildly curious knot of spectators at the first preliminary events, grew numerically and in the intensity of its attachment until by the final evening's trophy time, it had become a hushed, rapt, committed, partisan, odds-quoting, bookmaking mob.

It also seemed to tax the vocabulary of the local critics. Mr. Eric McLean, the customarily astute music editor of the Montreal *Star*, who summarized the semifinal results with the comment that "other bouts" would

From *High Fidelity*, December 1966.

follow, conceded parenthetically while reviewing the finals that a certain decision seemed "unpopular" with the crowd. The appearance of these chill-
ingly pugilistic turns of phrase was, I suspect, no accident. Certainly, it was
no simple case of thesaurus fatigue—Mr. McLean is a fast man with an adjective. Nor can it have been one of those coy intradepartmental send-ups which
frequently disrupt big-city journalism, for unlike their colleagues on such
papers as the *New York Times,* where the senior fine-arts reviewers are traditionally apprenticed to the sports desk and after a lifetime of faithful service
on the culture beat go to their reward in the stamps and coins, the Montreal
Star's staffers have never been encouraged to indulge the cult of the rotatable
critic. I suspect, rather, that the *malaise McLean* was merely one of the more
detectable symptoms of this particularly virulent outbreak of competitionitis
which, through those weeks, held the city in its feverish grip, its citizens
quarantined by the placards and the three-sheets of a false aesthetic—an in-
fection not only debilitating to performers and audience but detrimental and
antipathetic to the spirit of music.

The festival was a particularly alarming event upon the Canadian musical scene because until recently, such international tournaments have been
virtually unknown in this country. In the English-speaking provinces such
events are discouraged through both a tacit understanding of the futility of
musical jousts and an entirely credible concern with the showing of the home
team. There is, to be sure, a minor-league festival tradition in English Canada—one which is concerned not with the do-or-die fortunes of budding pro-
fessionals but with an annual series of regional adjudications for students presided over by superannuated British academicians. At these events—such is
their aura of charity and good fellowship—a mark of 80 is automatically accorded a contestant merely for showing up (79 is considered a stain upon
the family honor and reserved for platform indiscretions of a most grievous
order, such as sticking out one's tongue at a fellow competitor or playing
one's test piece caution-to-the-winds, and with a most un-British brio).

The adjudicators, moreover, being compelled to deliver their remarks
before the assembled parents, neighbors, and schoolmates of the respective
contestants, develop an altogether endearing strain of report-card euphe-
mism: "I say, that's jolly good, Number 67—smashing spirit and all that.
Have to dock you just a point for getting tangled at the double bars, though.
Four times through the old exposition is a bit much of a good thing, what?"

Unhappily, this commendable emphasis upon amateur music making
has never been accepted among *les québecois* as the respectable limit of competitive exhibitionism. Brooding in provincial splendor upon the isolation
of their culture and their language, *les canadiens* reckon a postgraduate flight
from the North American scene the appropriate reward for an industrious
musical apprenticeship and some form of Prix d'Europe the most likely

means of attaining it. Hence, there has lately developed in *la province* a disconcertingly continental tradition of *musique sportive et combative,* for which, as in this most recent example, the escalation of the competitive pot is one of the inevitable concomitants. The stakes at the Montreal Festival were indeed considerable—the premier award of ten thousand dollars roughly quadrupled the prize Van Cliburn or Jane Marsh captured at Moscow and thus related the Montreal event to the Tchaikovsky Competition as the Carling Cup relates to the British Open—a bit short on prestige, perhaps, but distinctly long on cash.

For the handicappers in the audience, it was no easy task to dope out the likely recipients of the major prizes. Several of the heavier favorites held impressive track records, including some near misses at other recent events on the international festival circuit. But would the jury in its wisdom be swayed by the determined traditionalism of the Soviet contestants, by the suave and fluent fiddling of the French delegation, perhaps, or by the cultivated reserve of the Japanese? To appreciate the actuarial probabilities of such questions, one must first form a clear impression of the particular values represented by any given set of adjudicators. In certain European competitions (the Tchaikovsky and the Queen Elisabeth of Belgium among them) the jury is empaneled from a list of the stellar performers of the day—artists who, because of the security of their own worldly success, are often as not astonishingly liberal in the dispensation of their judgments. In Montreal, however, the ladies and gentlemen of the jury—capable and respected fiddlers all—consisted for the most part of musicians whose own careers have attracted heretofore something less than universal renown. And it is, I am afraid, equally characteristic of musicians thwarted in their aspirations for international acclaim to decry the unaccountable mysteries of personality, to downgrade those virtues of temperamental independence which signal the genuine re-creative fire. Indeed, the syllabus of test pieces for this competition, with its mandatory selections from the output of those sterling artists Niccolò Paganini and Eugène Ysaÿe in addition to Bach and Beethoven, seemed tacitly to confess that pursuit of mechanistic prowess which is not least among the deceptions menacing these events.

There was, let me concede, one enterprising repertoire requirement. The twelve finalists were each asked to master a work especially written for the competition, the manuscript of which was delivered into their respective hands six days prior to a final appearance with orchestra, and the contestants thereupon, according to the society's most tantalizing press release, delivered to a practice cell within a convent or monastery "somewhere in Montreal." The work, observing the best neo-Hellenic tradition of the current avant-garde, was called *Pyknon* (density), by the Canadian André Prevost.

It turned out to be a cogent piece of post-Schoenbergian twelve-tonery, which, though it may have been designed to separate the men from the boys, succeeded primarily in separating the East from the West—since the Soviet bloc contingent, hampered by its hard-and-fast notions about the errors of bourgeois formalist constructivism, found it tough slogging indeed. However, the imposition of *Pyknon* did not materially deter the jury in its quest for violinistic virtue, since they managed to award first prize to the one finalist who became hopelessly ensnared in the ostinato labyrinth which forms the coda of Prevost's piece.

The victor was Vladimir Lancman of the Soviet Union, who offered, in compensation for his debacle with *Pyknon*, a remarkably poised and lyrical account of the Sibelius Concerto. Second place was divided between Hidetaro Suzuki (a Japanese now resident in Canada) and Georgi Badev of Bulgaria. Suzuki provided a magnificent account of the Bartók Second Concerto—a work which, with its mechanistic competence and emotional deprivation, is singularly appropriate competition fare. Badev's concerto choice was the Tchaikovsky, and while he offered a reading with every Auer-like cliché in place, it was with regard to his victory that Mr. McLean recorded the protestations of the audience.

For these ears, the most satisfying, stimulating, and individualistic talent was consigned, not surprisingly, to fourth place. The name, Jean-Jacques Kantorow—and I urge you to keep it in mind. One of two French contestants to attain the finals, Kantorow made a unique experience of the Brahms Concerto—approaching it through an extraordinary amalgam of deliberation and inventive freedom. In the first movement, his tempos were indeed so deliberate that the orchestra's expert and accommodating conductor, Otto Werner-Mueller, was occasionally caught with his subdivided beat showing. But so assured was Kantorow's architectural scheme that he was able to invest even the most funereal moments with the sort of stylistic diversions which seldom endear contestants to jurors. Sometimes he was heard to drop nonchalantly beneath the orchestra as, in much earlier repertoire and on other instruments, a continuo player might do. The first movement's cadenza was delivered as an interior monologue with phrases casually thrown away like asides in a soliloquy—something no self-respecting graduate of the Moscow Conservatory would risk. And he inflected the whole with a daring détaché bowing style which put me much in mind of Johanna Martzy—an artist who has always seemed to me to be, at least in North America, the most underrated of the great violinists of our age.

In the finale, Kantorow isolated the motives of the opening theme, imposing a series of what at least seemed like unpremeditated apostrophes, and produced thereby an effect of such irresistible buoyancy and hasteless momentum that the orchestra, which, to a sideman, had until then appeared determined to unhorse him, found themselves harnessed to the contagious spirit of his reading and joined with him in a devilish stretch-drive for the coda. On the basis of this performance, I would judge Kantorow a spectacular talent, the most prodigiously original violinist I have heard in this generation.

Prodigality may indeed be courted in the competitive quest, but originality must at all costs be discouraged. It is surely one of the considerable ironies of the contemporary musical scene that these gatherings of the best young talent from each continent ignore the ethnographic revelations implicit in their regional distinctiveness in the interest of preserving a consensus of mediocrity—a mean line of temperamental indifference. If the future is kind to Jean-Jacques Kantorow, it will be precisely because of those special qualities which stamped him a loser (or, more accurately, a lesser winner) at Montreal.

It is sometimes argued that without the competitive frenzy consensus engenders, the aspirants would fail in the perception of their own potential. But I suspect that what happens, rather, is that because of consensus the observant contestant—and no other kind turns up a winner—becomes uncomfortably aware of the potential of his fellows, becomes conscious of all the misguided traditions which constitute "style" in musical performance, his initiative blunted by the supreme fallacy that performance is essentially a repetitive act, and this precisely at that time in his life when a muted response to the world outside and sharpest attention to the vibrations of the inner ear could most propitiously shape and characterize his art. Competitions, then, rarely benefit the supreme artist whose career would come to pass regardless. (Let us concede that there can be exceptions, and that the competition-accelerated careers of Van Cliburn and of Leon Fleisher serve to confirm the rule.) Most frequently, however, competitions merely befriend the artist whose vision, though perceptive, falls short of the ecstatic, whose merits, though unexceptionable, fail to attain the transcendental. And if this is their prime function, then I submit they should be so advertised, prescribed like medicines with toxic side-effects for cases on referral, with skull and crossbones on the entry forms and an antidotal formula—six months of singing plainchant, perhaps—appended to the flyleaf of the syllabus. (Not only would that penance serve to mortify the pretension of virtuosity, but in Montreal, at least, it would help to amortize the practice cells.)

It would be foolish to discriminate against a level of competence without which our musical life would be the poorer. But while it is entirely proper to speak of competent electricians and plumbers, and hazardous—if not indeed in contravention of civic maintenance bylaws—to bargain for ecstatic ones, the notion of ecstasy as the only proper quest for the artist assumes competence as an inclusive component. The menace of the competitive idea is that through its emphasis upon consensus, it extracts that mean, indisputable, readily certifiable core of competence and leaves its eager, ill-advised suppliants forever stunted, victims of a spiritual lobotomy.

THE PSYCHOLOGY OF IMPROVISATION

Some years ago a friend of mine, who was then at medical school, had been reading about experiments in action painting and in chance music; and one night, having nothing better to do, he decided to sit down and compose his own chance-action poem. He decided that since this was to be a very contemporary work, it must straddle that fine line between deliberation and chance, and that therefore, however arbitrarily, it must acknowledge a system. The system he decided upon was the selection of every eleventh word from the editorial page of his evening newspaper, and he kept selecting these words until he had enough of them to furnish a fourteen-line sonnet—in matters of form, he was old-fashioned. Now, as it happened, the editorial page that day was heavily weighted with foreign comment, and the poem, as it emerged, took on a quite unique quality of international awareness. When it was finished, the author pruned certain lines where the metrical balance seemed too casual and, with that done, turned to his most important creative responsibility—choosing the title. He was sufficiently au courant to realize that the most influential works of this kind have in common titles which are entirely unrelated to their contents, and he also knew that, even in works with a decidedly aleatoric approach, the title must convey some very solid and concrete idea such as to suggest that despite the radical techniques incorporated in the poem, its author harbors a genuine social concern. Well, at that time, he could not think of any more solid title than the name of the man who was then President of the United States (my friend was an American)—Mr. Harry Truman. So he called the poem simply "Harry Truman," filed it, and forgot it.

But at this point the plot thickens! The class wag heard about this poem, decided to get hold of a copy and mail it to the President along with the author's return address. And so several weeks later the mailman brought a letter on White House stationery, written by the secretary to the President

From a CBC radio braodcast, early 1970s.

and containing some highly complimentary remarks—"The President wishes to extend his thanks for the splendid poem which you forwarded to him and to tell you how very happy it makes him to know that young people, such as yourself, are finally able to appreciate just what he is trying to do."

Well, it seems to me that the moral of this story—which is, I swear to you, absolutely true—touches upon a process central to our ability to form judgments about a work of art. Most of us tend to look for signs of premeditation even when we are dealing with works in which the creative operation has been carried out without any sort of planning aforethought. When we listen to a musical composition for the first time, we try to convince ourselves that we're not simply involved in an errant, sensuous experience. We want to believe that, however formless the work may seem, it is surely the product of a deliberate intelligence—and if formless, then it is so, at least, because the author intended it that way. We cannot bear to think of ourselves as the dupes of an aimless and indiscriminate mind. We need to feel assured that what is being said *has* to be said and that our time in attending it is gainfully employed.

At times it's a question of guiding our perceptions by wishful thinking, of encouraging, if necessary, a false perception in order to achieve an aesthetic kick. If President Truman did, if fact, read that poem, he may have accepted it as a glowing testimonial to his statesmanship, and if so, he was obviously able to convince himself that behind its seemingly elusive rhetoric, a deliberate creative intelligence was, however deviously, at work. In a way, it's the old and quite unanswerable question of whether or not a lumberman, wielding his axe upon a block of wood and carving out by accident the likeness of a man of whose existence he does not know, has created a work of art. Most of us would prefer not to know how casually the blow was struck.

These questions take on a further dimension when we analyze a musical experience, because music has the frustrating habit of proving in the end to have been about nothing in particular—it allows a great latitude for indulgence to its author and to its listener, and we sometimes are tempted to objectify the musical experience in a manner that would never occur to us when dealing, for instance, with the written word. For if, by comparison, we find in the daily paper a story defaced by typographical errors, blurred by ink splotches, and distorted by makeup editors' cuts, we can still manage to piece together a reasonably comprehensive account of the item concerned simply by making connections which our experience with language and with human motivation conveys to us as reasonable. We know that given time, the reporter and his editor would have hoped to make it a coherent account, and it does not upset us unduly if we must allow that their deadline was hard upon them before this could come to pass. It's even possible for us to derive a certain amusement from paragraphs where the syntax is as elusive as used to be the case in the press conferences of—now let me say this—Dwight Eisenhower. And the reason is simple enough: like those Sunday painters who confess to not knowing much about art but to knowing nonetheless what they like, so it is with the written word; we all improvise with it continually, we are all of us on terms with the artist—which, if you think about it, was Nikita Khrushchev's problem in a nutshell.

But it is not easy for the layman to enjoy that camaraderie with the musical profession. For ever since the Renaissance the explosion of instrumental styles in music has obliterated for all practical purposes whatever chant forms and folk modalities once served to cement a relationship between audience and artist, and, consequently, the laity have long been convinced that the making of music is a game regulated by such arcane devices that they couldn't be expected to understand in any event. What they do expect is that the composer must know the score, as a plumber knows sewage systems—must know it not as an intuitive experience but as a thoroughly reasoned argument, even if the probes and cavils of that argument are not apparent to them—and that whatever extemporaneous elements are involved must be subject to the laws of musical rhetoric. It's an attitude that bears special watching today, because this is the age of the debatable motive, of concern with whether and to what degree our thoughts and our works derive from a conscious industry or result from concealed and unacknowledged desires.

CRITICS

"Advise your reviewers to be more circumspect and intelligent," wrote a young German composer to the editor of a Viennese music journal in which he had been criticized, "for many a younger composer, who perhaps might go far, may take fright." The author was Ludwig van Beethoven and he conveyed the views of most artists on the subject of adversary journalism.

The critic as aesthetic arbiter has, I think, no proper social function, no defensible criteria upon which to base his subjective judgments, and, historical precedent to the contrary notwithstanding, no strong case at law with which to defend them. Depending upon the nature of the society in which he serves, one might make a case for the critic as propagandist, borrowing Jacques Ellul's expanded definition of that term.

An easier task would be to redefine the critic's role as consumer advo-

From *The Canadian*, February 26, 1977.

cate. It is possible, certainly, using scientific method, to measure the acuity of Nathan Milstein's intonation, the rhythmic precision of Alexis Weissenberg's scale passages, the frequency of the six-four chord in Richard Strauss. One must remember, of course, that computer-music programmers can and do adjust for imprecision, imbalance, inequality—*superimposing*, in effect, not elements of error but of human discretion—and that, consequently, such categorical statements as one may make about Milstein, Weissenberg, or Richard Strauss do not imply value judgments.

Conceivably, then, the critic could be retrained as a data collector, confined to the production of objective statements, and encouraged to redeem himself in a society for which, as Beethoven suggested almost two centuries ago, he has served as a morally disruptive, and aesthetically destructive, influence.

STOKOWSKI IN SIX SCENES

I am not by nature a stage-door John. Though never reluctant to leap into print with a declaration of enthusiasm—indeed, advocacy journalism is the only critical yardstick I recognize—I have rarely been eager to meet the artists I admire. Sometimes, needless to say, a confrontation has been inevitable—professional circumstances being what they are—and from most such encounters I have managed to escape with my illusions more or less intact. But by and large, and given my druthers, I have all my life avoided the company of musicians.

I have done this not because of any conviction that musicians as a breed are inevitably frivolous, or worldly, or consumed by the need to chatter on about their own most recent triumphs; some are, to be sure, and these one would seek to avoid in any case. And I'm well aware, moreover, that there are, in our profession, colleagues with whom one can talk of theology, or politics, or the psychology of the soap opera, or, alternatively, in whose presence one can dare to be alone with one's own thoughts and share that unembarrassed silence which is the true mark of friendship.

But, generally speaking, musicians tend to talk of music—it is, after all, the obvious conversational icebreaker. They tend to talk about the analytic theories, or the emotional revelations, or the tactile experiments which have accrued by virtue of their recent study of a score, or attendance at a lecture,

From *Piano Quarterly*, Winter 1977–78 through Summer 1978.

or exposure to a colleague's performance. And even if such talk is motivated by infinite charity and fraternal goodwill (and all too often it is not), it virtually necessitates some response, some comment or counterargument, at least in a conversational context. In print, or via the electronic media, the same data have quite a different impact; they can be edited to suit one's mood, to fit one's experience, to protect one's vulnerability. As a last resort, a dial can be twiddled, a set tuned out, a page turned. But in conversation, courtesy demands that the addressee react and, in so doing, relate his own experience to the analytical, emotional, or tactile propositions under discussion.

And it is, in my view, a dangerous exercise. Artists, I think, work best in isolation—in an environment where their knowledge of the world outside is always under editorial control, and never permitted to intrude upon the indivisibility of that unit formed by the artist's idea and its execution.

So I have never been a stage-door John—except in the case of one colleague: Leopold Stokowski. And when we met, one Sunday evening in June 1957, my lack of fan-club expertise was showing.

I

The locale was improbable enough—the railway-station platform at Frankfurt am Main. We had both been on tour in Europe—though neither of us had been working in Frankfurt—and were both waiting for the call to board the sleeper on the Amsterdam–Vienna express. I turned suddenly to check out the whereabouts of the porter and my luggage and sighted, just down the track, the century's most celebrated podium profile. The Maestro appeared to be taking a constitutional, pacing back and forth over a course that at its closest point put him within about eight feet of the post I had staked out just beyond the sleeper's steps. I watched while he measured off the same short, triangular circuit three or four times. On each occasion, he tacked right toward the train, right again toward the station, then started back down the homestretch toward my post. Each time he did this, I worked out a breezy, surefire introductory line: "Good evening, Maestro! Lovely weather, isn't it? By the way, my name is . . ." or "Maestro Stokowski, permit me to introduce myself. I'm one of your greatest admirers, and I . . ." Impossible; you can't hit a moving target with a cliché like that. Besides, he never did close that eight-foot gap, and there was something about his slow, firm tread, with its relentless pursuit of the same patch of concrete—rather like a priest at exercise in the courtyard of a seminary, scriptures in hand—that made any move of mine seem an intolerable intrusion on his person.

On the other hand, I had not relinquished my post, and it was an advantageous one. Sooner or later, the boarding call would come, and then *he* would have to make the approach; *he* would be, however briefly, on *my* territory.

The call came, and so did he. And so did other passengers. And so did porters and luggage racks, and not one of my snappy lines fit the occasion. "Good evening, Maestro, quite a crowded Pullman, isn't it?" "How do you do, sir. These Germans certainly do make the trains run on time, don't they?" I had no more time to think. He was only three steps away—two—one. I did the only thing possible: I dropped my ticket. Right beneath his nose. Accidentally, of course. Casually, almost. He had to stop while I bent to pick it up. "Damn it," I said, in a just barely audible tone which was intended to lend the ploy some credibility. I took my time retrieving the ticket, and as I looked around, ostensibly to apologize to whichever good burgher might have been momentarily inconvenienced by my mishap, I did manage (or at least I like to think I did) a look of genuine incredulity. "Why, it's—it's—it's Maestro Stokowski, isn't it?" I was still in the process of straightening up as I offered this perceptive observation; Stokowski looked down at me and, in a benignly weary voice which had been developed from decades of dealing with pesky press types and dumb questions about what Greta Garbo was really like, replied: "It is, young man."

I straightened up, I introduced myself (I decided on the moment to leave out the part about being a fan), and Stokowski, with that impeccably paced and punctuated delivery, said: "I have read that you were recently in Leningrad." (It was incredible: he knew who I was; he knew what I'd been doing.)

"Yes, indeed, Maestro, just two weeks ago, in fact."

"Perhaps, then, later in the evening, I will visit with you. I would be interested to learn your impressions of Leningrad today, and perhaps you might have some interest in my impressions of Leningrad many years ago." I assured him I would; I would have been interested in his impressions of Mickey Mouse if it had made a visit with him possible.

But he had said "perhaps"—*perhaps* he would come and visit. He wouldn't—I was sure of it; besides, he probably hadn't noticed which compartment I was in. Perhaps, I reasoned, I should ask the porter to let him know where I was. I resolved to wait for an hour and, if he hadn't come by then, to try my luck with the porter.

The knock came within half an hour.

Music per se was discussed only once. By way of opening pleasantries, we checked out itineraries (we were both taking part in the Vienna Festival the following week), and I mentioned that I was en route from Berlin. "What did you play there?" Stokowski inquired politely. "The Beethoven Third," I responded, then added, rather proudly, "with Karajan." "The Beethoven Third," Stokowski mused, as though attempting to recollect a web of motives that, on one or two occasions, he might possibly have encountered under lesser hands than his own. "The Beethoven Third," he said again. "Is that not the lovely concerto in G major?" It was a superb gambit, and my first experience of the harmless games Stokowski liked to play while putting the world, as he would have it, in perspective for his interlocutors. Lovely or otherwise, the Beethoven Third is in the key of C minor, as Stokowski knew all too well; but in one seemingly innocuous, skillfully indirect sentence, he had let me know that he was not in awe of the "Generalmusikdirektor of Europe," that soloists, as a breed, were to be shunned on principle, and that concertos, as a symphonic subspecies, were quite beneath his notice.

Otherwise, as scheduled, we talked of Leningrad—of the city then and now, of the buildings rebuilt on Nevsky Prospekt, of the Bolshoi Hall, of the Philharmonic and Mravinsky, of the tea at the Hotel Europa, of the mood of the city and the mood of the country. (It was the era of "the thaw," of "B. & K.,"* an era when relatively few visits from North America were permitted.) We talked for an hour, or perhaps a little less, and then, in that same deliberate, courtly manner with which he had announced his intention to visit, he took his leave. "We will meet in the Vienna station in the morning," he declared.

I am not, and was not, starstruck—as I have already twice protested—but nonetheless a dream had come true.

II

In the beginning, the dream was more like a nightmare. I was eight when *Fantasia* hit Toronto, and I hated every minute of it. It played at a long-since-demolished theatre called Shea's Hippodrome, where each run of a feature was preceded by a twenty-minute organ concert. These interludes were a showcase for what was referred to on the marquee as the "Mighty Wurlitzer"—an electronic mammoth which was disgorged from beneath the stage and lit so that each manual and row of couplers appeared in a different color. I took a dim view of colors as a child, and in fact I still do. Battleship gray and midnight blue are at the top of my personal color chart; I can neither work productively nor think clearly in a room painted with primaries, and my moods bear an inverse relationship to the degree of sunlight on any given day. ("Behind every silver lining there's a cloud," I tell myself when things threaten to get bright.)

In addition, when I was eight my idea of a movie was something with a plot—preferably a plot with a war theme. My favorites featured shots of German battle cruisers, emerging grim and gray from fog banks in Norwegian fjords, and with cuts to the blacked-out bridge of some hapless British

---

*Bulganin and Krushchev.—T.P.

destroyer, where Clive Brook or John Clements or Jack Hawkins might say something like: "Men, we are about to engage Scharnhorst and Gneisenau. I need not tell you that their range exceeds ours. But the First Lord has ordered us to hold the beasts at bay, and that we shall do at any cost."

In any event, my parents informed me that I was going to see *Fantasia*, that it was in color, all about music, and that I would get to hear one of the world's greatest conductors. At the time, I had only seen one movie in color —*Snow White*—and I hadn't been too thrilled with that; besides, everybody knew that the really good movies—the ones with plots, and enemy agents, and German battle cruisers—were in black and white. The "all about music" part didn't please me, either; I went, though, because I figured that maybe this great conductor would be taking his orchestra to entertain the troops at Dunkirk and that they would all be blown to smithereens by some nice black Stukas that would come out of the clouds all of a sudden and drop their five-hundred-pounders while the Messerschmidt 109s strafed the beach.

I did not, however, figure on pink hippos, or green dinosaurs, or scarlet volcanoes, and it began to seem less and less likely that Jack Hawkins or John Clements or Clive Brook or any other self-respecting destroyer captain would ever agree to turn up in a movie like that. I went home depressed, feeling faintly nauseous, and with the first headache I can remember; the images of the Mighty Wurlitzer and of the Disney creations had all run together in my head. I told my parents I couldn't eat any dinner and went to bed hoping that I could rid my mind of that awful riot of color. I tried to imagine that I'd just closed down the conning-tower hatch on some cool, gray submarine and that I would soon submerge beneath the midnight-blue waters of the North Atlantic.

III

Stokowski was at the height of his fame when *Fantasia* was released, but for a young music student growing up at that time, it was not quite "done" to admire him. In fact, if one frequented conservatory halls and was wary of peer-group pressure, it was best to keep an interest in Stokowski to oneself. He was, or so my colleagues insisted, a "sellout"—a man who had given up a "serious" career in order to cash in on his popularity and profile. No one denied that his tenure in Philadelphia had altered the course of symphonic music in America; no one denied that he had created, in his own image, an orchestra that could stand comparison with the greatest in the world—that by the time he left, it indeed may have been the greatest in the world; no one denied that he had put his reputation and his box office on the line, time and again, in the interests of new music; and, of course, no one denied that, for some mysterious reason, his innumerable recordings tended to *sound* better than those of most of his colleagues—no one denied it, but, at the time, no one was much interested in thinking about why that might be, either.

For he was, after all, a "sellout." He had left Philadelphia, succumbed to the blandishments of Hollywood, and offered what seemed like a lame and fatuous excuse for this heresy. "I go to a higher calling," he was reported to have said to the press conference which was called to announce his departure. (His appearances on the silver screen had been with the likes of Deanna Durbin and Donald Duck; "Some higher calling!" my colleagues might well have snorted in response.)

Besides, there was another conductor as famous as Stokowski who in academic circles was considered more respectable. In the American context, Toscanini related to Stokowski much as Weingartner related to Mengelberg overseas. Toscanini was, or so it was said, a "literalist"; for him, the composer's instructions were gospel. Whichever notes, tempo marks, dynamic indications were set before him in the score were, to the best of his and his orchestra's ability, what you heard. And that orchestra—the NBC Symphony—was a fixture of American broadcasting in the thirties and forties; it could be heard every Saturday at five from Studio 8H, and those weekend music specials were much discussed and much admired by my conservatory confreres. To my ears, it seemed that the sound was edgy and unbalanced, that Toscanini's interpretations did not carry one forward with the visionary sweep of his fellow literalist Weingartner, and that the playing, by and large, born of terror rather than conviction, was sloppy. But the time was right for Toscanini. It was the age of the artist as artisan—of craftsmanship, of *Gebrauchsmusik,* of reaction against the giddy willfulness of the twenties, of preparation for the rigor of compositional choice which the fifties would bring.

Above all, it was an age which paid homage to the spirit of Sebastian Bach. One hundred and fifty years of campaigns waged by such luminaries as Baron van Swieten and Felix Mendelssohn had finally paid off: the name of Bach was now synonymous with musical integrity. Bach, of course, had always been regarded as a technical whiz, but his spirit had never before dominated an era as it did the thirties and forties. Virtually every major musician was determined to follow *his* example, to work as it was deemed *he* had worked—as an artisan, a sober, conscientious craftsman in whom diligence and inspiration were inextricably intertwined. Stravinsky, for example, claimed that his "Dumbarton Oaks" Concerto was written in "the spirit of the Brandenburgs." Heitor Villa-Lobos began his celebrated series of *Bachianas Brasilieras*—Latin tunes ecumenically merged with Lutheran harmonies. Alfredo Casella wrote "Ricercari" on the name B-A-C-H. Schoenberg used the same motive—B-flat, A, C, B-natural—in his first twelve-tone row.

"You play the organ, and you claim to like Bach," said one of my teachers, a Toscanini advocate. "How can you possibly approve of Stokowski?" (We all knew of the transcription travesties for which he'd been responsible in the name of the cantor of Leipzig.)

It was, to be sure, the Achilles' heel in the anatomy of my admiration, for I had already wasted long hours of practice in a futile attempt to make diapason-heavy church organs simulate E. Power Biggs's Sunday-morning sound from the "Germanic Museum" at Harvard. I thought of myself as a purist, and I scoffed at the Stokowski transcriptions; nowadays, strange to say, they hardly bother me at all.

I was not, however, prepared to let my views on Bach determine my reaction to Stokowski's work in general. My first encounter with master-pieces I'd read about and wondered about—Schoenberg's *Gurrelieder*, for example, or Mahler's Eighth—were via his broadcasts and recordings, and after such radio or phonograph exposures I invariably found myself in a state that I can only call exalted. It didn't matter that my colleagues rambled on about Stokowski's eccentricities and deviations from the text and then segued to an account of Toscanini's latest metronome steeplechase; for me, Stokow-ski had already redefined the role of the interpreter.

Stokowski was, for want of a better word, an ecstatic. He was involved with the notes, the tempo marks, the dynamics in a score, to the same extent that a filmmaker is involved with the original book or source which supplies the impetus, the idea, for his film. "Black marks on paper," he would say to me a quarter-century later. "We write black marks on white paper—the mere facts of frequency; but music is a communication much more subtle than mere facts. The best a composer can do when within him he hears a great melody is to put it on paper. We call it music, but that is not music; that is only paper. Some believe that one should merely mechanically repro-duce the marks on the paper, but I do not believe in that. One must go much further than that. We must defend the composer against the mechanical con-ception of life which is becoming more and more strong today."

IV

That quote was featured in a Canadian Broadcasting Corporation radio docu-mentary which I produced in 1970. The subject was Stokowski's life and times, and the program was based upon the last, and most successful, of three interviews which he granted me during the preceding five years. From the first of these—my first "professional" contact with the Maestro, indeed—I learned a valuable lesson: though an easy man to talk to, Stokowski was diffi-cult to interview; never less than courteous and rarely impatient, he was rather frequently bored. Perhaps it was simply that at his age, virtually all the questions that could be asked, had been. To be sure, he still thought, and spoke, paragraphically, but the paragraphs, as time went on, were short, designed primarily for efficiency and dispatch, and their sentences, though superbly manicured—often, indeed, even seemingly rehearsed—functioned on occasion like interchangeable modules.

It was still possible to get a great interview from him—an interview with lines that soared and caught the ear, and ideas that flirted with, then triumphed over, the clichés they sometimes mimicked—but for that, as has been said of an anecdotally celebrated donkey, one had first to get his attention. And on the occasion of our initial interview, in November 1965, this was a trick that I had not yet mastered.

At the time, I was working for *High Fidelity* magazine on an essay called "The Prospects of Recording,"* and, as a counterpoint to my text, the margins were to be given over to corroborative or contradictory testimony from a variety of expert musical witnesses. Everyone agreed that Stokowski's comments were a "must." By the time that first interview took place, he had spent forty-eight years in the recording studio; and there were to be twelve more—twelve incredibly productive years—which would bring forth his finest work since the 1930s. No other musician of our time had given so much thought to the prospects of recording or had better exemplified, through his major career decisions, the practical and philosophical consequences of technology.

At about eight one evening, I arrived with Leonard Marcus (then special-projects editor, later the editor, of *High Fidelity*) at Stokowski's Fifth Avenue apartment. The Maestro met us at the door, invited us to settle in before the fireplace, offered a drink, made a waspish comment in response to my profession of teetotalism, and shuffled off to the kitchen to attend to our orders in person. While he was gone, Leonard checked out the cassette he'd brought along, then drifted over to the window which looked out toward the lights of the Central Park reservoir. I fidgeted with a question outline I'd stowed in my jacket pocket; somehow, that fireplace demanded conversation rather than interrogation. I thought that the use of notes might seem premeditated, even unprofessional, but I was sure I'd forget some of the great lead-ins I'd jotted down before leaving my hotel. In the end, I opted for the impromptu approach, consigned the notes to my pocket, and joined Leonard at the window.

"That is a view," he observed (Leonard tolerates New York but lives in the country). "Right," I responded (I can't tolerate New York with or without the Central Park reservoir). "I mean, if you've got to live in this town, that is the view to have," Leonard insisted. "Sure is," I conceded; I kept hoping that Leonard would keep his admiration under wraps so that

---

*See p. 331.

I could keep at least some of those great lead-in lines in my head until the Maestro returned.

(I knew exactly what I wanted from Stokowski. I wanted him to describe to me, as he would do four years later, how he had begun in the studio —reluctantly, intimidated by the limitations of the recording process and by the necessity for compromise which it imposed.

> I remember—I think it was in the year 1917—that a recording company asked me to make records and I said: "May I listen to some of your records?" and they permitted me to do that. They were so terrible, I said, "No, I cannot distort music; sorry, but no, I will not do it." Then, a little after that, I realized how stupid I had been to refuse. I should try to make the records, and if they were bad, try to discover why they were bad and do something about improving the quality. I thought to myself, "You're a fool; you shouldn't have said no." So I then said to them, "Please forgive me, but may I try?" We did try, and the records were not good.

I wanted him to relate the excitement he experienced with the advent of electronic recording.

> I thought I must try to understand how it could be done electronically, so I asked the Bell Laboratories: "Could I come to you and study electricity as regards recording music?" They permitted it, and soon after that they said, "We would like to create a laboratory underneath the stage of the Academy of Music in Philadelphia." (At that time I was the conductor of the Philadelphia Orchestra.) Bell made a laboratory underneath the stage from which they listened to all our concerts and all our rehearsals and used that as material for the betterment of recording techniques.

I wanted him to establish, as he would in that later interview, that a recording should not attempt to duplicate a concert experience on disc.

> Of course, the concert hall is something we have known from our ancestors. Our grandfathers always heard music from the stage, but I believe the time will come when we shall make records in the open air, where every instrument has its particular pickup and is amplified to the right extent. All those sounds are then brought together into one composite, with the right intensity of amplification for each instrument at each moment, because sometimes the woodwinds should be louder than the strings, or the brass should be louder than everybody, or a certain percussion instrument should be louder than any other instrument. Or it could be done in a large enclosed space, but the point is that I should

like to have one hundred different results from each individual instrument and give them their due intensity or volume of sound according to that moment in the music.

I knew exactly what I wanted but, at that time, did not know how to get it.)

Stokowski rejoined us, handed Leonard his drink, and poured my tea. "Ready?" he asked; I was not, but Leonard turned on the cassette and the interview began regardless.

I asked questions that were reasonable and in other company might even have been appropriate. I asked whether composer-recorded testaments rendered conventional "interpretation" obsolete. Stokowski obviously thought not. I asked whether he modified his studio interpretations to suit the acoustic conditions of living-room playback; indeed he did. I asked whether one might not find something to say in favor of the omnipresence of music in our lives—the much-criticized Muzakian environment. I've always felt one might; Stokowski disagreed.

Today we hear so much musical sound all the time, in trains, in airplanes, in restaurants, that we are becoming deadened to it. Our sensitivity to music is in danger of being lost, as we are becoming insensitive to the stupid brutality we see so much of on television or in the motion pictures. Now, I love the cinema and go to it often. And I think that television is a medium of enormous potential. But we see how modern developments and techniques can be very harmful. Still, we are able to turn off the television, or walk out of the bad motion picture or poor concert. You can't walk out of the airplane.

Such questions might well have been appropriate for a deejay or an A&R man, perhaps, but they did not take advantage of the Stokowskian presence; they were all wrong for this particular interview guest, and I think we both knew it. Nevertheless, he answered each thoughtfully, precisely, and with those perfectly formed sentences which were a tape editor's delight. (Stokowski's rare interview fluffs were invariably deliberate—another aspect of his game strategy. At one point in the later, radio documentary interview, while referring to music education, he said: "We must give it *geschmeidig*—no, *souplesse*—no, that's not good—what's a good English word?—'subtlety'?—we must give it subtlety; we must give it elasticity." "Subtlety" and "elasticity" were, of course, where he was heading all along; *"geschmeidig"* and *"souplesse"* were international calling cards intended to emphasize the universality of the concept he was attempting to articulate as well as the cosmopolitan nature of his own experience. It was a typical Stokowskian touch, and in the radio program I left the "fluff" intact in the master voice track.)

As he neared the end of each answer, Stokowski would signal a cutoff with his right hand. These gestures were usually set six or seven words back into the final sentence and put the interviewer on notice that the answer was about to conclude and that supplementary questions, if any, should follow forthwith. On the occasion of our first interview, I found this mannerism exceedingly unnerving; several times, indeed, I went blank on a follow-up question and had to fight back the impulse to reach for my lead-in sheet. As a consequence, after about thirty minutes of ill-conceived questions, truncated answers, and disconcerting cutoffs, I gave my own signal to Leonard; short of reaching for my notes, I could think of nothing more to ask the Maestro—the interview was over.

Leonard looked disappointed but turned off the cassette, and we both thanked Stokowski for his cooperation. Then, as we prepared to leave, Stokowski suddenly turned to me and said: "May I ask why we have never been invited to make records together?" I was stunned—after all, he hated soloists, he disapproved of concertos, he associated the Beethoven Third with the key of G major!—but I ad-libbed something about thinking he was committed elsewhere contractually. He responded with a brief lecture on the virtues of being a free-lance. ("I am able to record with you for your company," he pointed out, "but you are not able to record with me for mine.") I continued my improvisation by observing that were it not for this misconception, CBS would naturally have sought him out as a concerto collaborator years before. (In truth, there was nothing "natural" about it; Stokowski and the concerto repertoire were deemed mutually exclusive, and no such thought, to the best of my knowledge, had occurred to anyone.) Then, donning an A&R hat which I was by no means entitled to wear, I asked if he would consider recording the "Emperor" Concerto that very season.

This time, there were no key-association games. "With pleasure," he responded. "But I would wish to use my own orchestra—the American Symphony."

"Naturally," I agreed; I had now promoted myself to vice-president in charge of marketing and was not about to be deterred by such trifling matters as Columbia's contractual commitments to the New York Philharmonic. Notwithstanding the bargaining power my new office conferred, I stopped short of discussing royalty splits, album titling, and photo credits, told him I was sure CBS would be in touch within a day or two, thanked him again for the interview, and said good night.

Once in the cab, I told Leonard about the visit on the train and the Maestro's "recollection" of the Beethoven Third; we tried to remember if he had recorded any piano concertos since his association with Rachmaninoff in the thirties. "He was probably just being polite," I said.

"I don't think so," Leonard replied; "I got the impression he meant it."

"But I played several concerts with the Houston Symphony while he was music director there, and he was never around; there were always guest conductors."

"I still think he meant it," Leonard affirmed.

"Well, I'll get on the phone in the morning," I added, "but I'll bet you it will never come off."

And, indeed, as I thought about it that evening, it did seem an improbable piece of casting; on the other hand, eight years before, on the train to Vienna, the knock had come on time.

V

The studio dates with the American Symphony were scheduled for the first week of March 1966. CBS was counting on a late-spring release; postproduction—editing and mixing—had to follow immediately. Five days prior to the recording sessions, I had a piano runthrough with Stokowski, during which I functioned as both soloist and sidemen.

"What is your tempo?" the Maestro inquired, as I settled in at the instrument.

"My tempo is your tempo," I responded in a bad imitation of Rudy Vallee. "I hope, however," I continued, rather cautiously, "that, whatever the tempo, we can make this piece into a symphony with piano obbligato; I really don't think it ought to be a virtuoso vehicle." I did not expect Stokowski to argue against that proposition, but I was not attempting to buy his interpretive vote; rather, I wanted to indicate to him my willingness to accentuate the positive in a musical genre toward which, in general, I have a profoundly negative attitude, and to enlist his aid in an attempt to demythologize the virtuoso traditions which have gathered round this particular work.

Some years earlier, during my concert-giving days, I had developed various strategies designed to sabotage the intrusions of solo exhibitionism upon concerto architecture. On occasion, these amounted to rather obvious metaphors and were confined to matters of platform presentation: I had no difficulty at all, for example, persuading Herbert von Karajan to conduct a performance of Bach's D-minor Concerto from the lip of the stage so that the piano could be surrounded by, and integrated with, the strings of the Philharmonia Orchestra. More frequently, however, they involved tempo ratios which were intended to undercut the you-play-your-theme-then-watch-me-do-it-slower-softer-subtler-than-you-can dichotomy which characterizes the conventional relationship between soloist and tutti force, between heroic individual and subservient mass. Josef Krips had been a willing accomplice in a cycle of Beethoven concerto performances in which we gave short shrift to the competitive absurdities of the form; Leonard Bernstein, on the other hand, was a reluctant collaborator when the same approach was applied to Brahms's D-minor Concerto.

After a preamble in which I outlined my views on these matters, Stokowski asked again, rather warily this time: "May I hear your tempo?" I explained that I had, in fact, two tempos at the ready and demonstrated with a few sentences from the opening movement's tutti and from the beginning of the finale. Exhibits A were uptempo versions—brusque, businesslike, and, I thought, rather lacking in character; Exhibits B were, or so I hoped, possessed of a certain martial melancholy. Neither set, however, was a comfortable, middle-of-the-road tempo choice, and both were designed to encourage continuity rather than pace variation. To my delight, the Maestro expressed his preference for the slow set, and with that decision taken, I turned back to the piano and began at the beginning.

I played the orchestra's opening tonic chord, held it with the pedal, and beat a broad two-three-four with my left hand. I did this without looking at Stokowski—who would, I felt sure, begin his own countdown immediately—because this gesture was intended to prepare him for a measured, metrically unyielding statement of the piano's first introductory cadenza, and it would not have surprised me had he called a halt at that very moment. In earlier years, startled glances were frequently directed my way from the podium while this passage was being rehearsed. Tradition has it that, during the first movement's three prefatory cadenzas, the soloist is entitled to wing forth like a bat out of hell; I preferred to insert a series of relatively earthbound interpolations in order to link the measured beat of those opening orchestral chords to whichever tempo was to govern the movement proper. To be sure, one could not sustain these harmonically static, Czerny-like roulades without the intercession of *some* rubato; but in my view all scales, arpeggios, trills, and other decorative materials, to which so much of the piano's attention is directed in this work, should be treated as supportive elements of the texture—rather like continuo passages in a baroque concerto grosso. In any event, Stokowski made no comment as I introduced him to my reined-in interpretation of the first cadenza, and during the two subsequent orchestral chords I relaxed my left-hand gestures when I noticed, out of the corner of my eye, that his beat appeared firmly in accord; the in-tempo cadenzas, apparently, had passed the test.

Like most of Beethoven's middle-period blockbusters, the "Emperor" Concerto is a rather simpleminded work harmonically. It concentrates on primary chord materials, modulatory subtleties are at a premium, and nowhere this side of the Grand Ole Opry can one encounter more unadorned

II–V–I progressions. A role of some psychological importance, however, is assigned to one rather off-the-beaten-track harmonic region—the major key relation based on the minor sixth degree of the scale. The second movement of this E-flat-major work is set in the key of B major—no precedents are shattered; a similar intermovement relationship, C major to A-flat major, exists in the First Piano Concerto—and in the first movement, the tonic chord of this key, frequently altered enharmonically in deference to its attachment to the nominal minor region and notated with the rather arcane signature of C-flat major, serves as the pivot point of the exposition and the climax of the development.

In the first of these segments, which occurs immediately prior to the orchestra's marchlike second theme, the piano contributes two related sentences: a subdued, quasisyncopated anticipation in B minor, and eight athematic bars' worth of the tonic and dominant chords of C-flat major. And at this point one encounters yet another venerable convention. For since the orchestra is about to annunciate its theme with fortissimo vengeance, metrical persistence, and, predictably, in the dominant key, B-flat major, the soloist is invited to emphasize his own so-close-and-yet-so-far semitone's separation from that secondary key; he's expected to surround the quite conventional outlines of the C-flat-major passage with a halo of pedal, allow the pulse of the movement to relax almost to the point of extinction, and, for twenty seconds or so, wander footloose in a world of unrestrained rubato. Such gestures, of course, are intended to characterize the concerto's dramatis personae: the orchestra, obviously, depicts worldly necessity, hard-nosed practicality, the constraints of the collective; the soloist, infinite refinement, imperturbable self-reliance, the triumph of the individual. That there are no instructions in the score to justify these mood and tempo demarcation points is not, I think, a proper argument to use against them; at any rate, given my own record of textual infidelities, it is not an argument on which I would choose to make a stand. Perhaps, however, there is, in human nature, some intuitive perception of coherent formal patterns which individuality per se cannot bestow, and collectivity per se cannot deny; if so, it renders the hierarchical divisions and competitive impulses of the virtuoso concerto psychologically naive and architecturally destructive.

In any case, I knew that this passage would provide the acid test. I wanted to inflect it primarily through variations of touch rather than of tempo, and I felt that if Stokowski could accept that concept here, there could be few disagreements elsewhere. As I played it, I emphasized the left-hand crotchets, made few concessions in the direction of rubato, re-established tempo primo a bar before the orchestral tutti, then continued with a few bars of the second theme and stopped. "Okay so far?" I ventured.

"Please proceed," Stokowski replied.

"There's one thing about this tempo," I added, getting carried away. "It makes all these themes work within the same perspective."

"Yes, that is true," the Maestro conceded. "But do you not think there are a few moments which should perhaps go a little faster and a few which might go a little slower?" It was, of course, a masterpiece of understatement as well as of tact, and, as so often with Stokowski, I felt that he had read my mind; I made a mental note to broaden the equivalent passage in the recapitulation just a bit.

"Yes, of course, Maestro, I quite agree," I lied. "But I'll tell you another thing about this tempo: given the acoustics of Manhattan Center, it's the only way to go."

Manhattan Center is a late-nineteenth-century complex of meeting rooms, banquet halls, and auditoria located near Thirty-fourth Street and Eighth Avenue in the borough whose name it bears. Its seventh and eighth floors house a shaggily elegant ballroom that appears to have given up on its grooming after the last debutante chose it for a first curtsy to society. It has a high ceiling, a mezzanine which encroaches on three sides, and as a recording studio, only one natural blessing—a generous decay which adds ambient interest to music that is neither contrapuntally complex nor intellectually challenging. For many years this room was CBS Records' prime full-orchestra hall in New York City, smaller ensembles being accommodated in the more refined and specific acoustics of their studio at Thirtieth Street and Third Avenue.

I had worked in Manhattan Center only once before—a session with Leonard Bernstein and the New York Philharmonic—and had found that, despite the undeniable glamour of the sound it afforded, it was almost impossible to keep in ensemble touch with the more distant reaches of the band. One's natural tendency while playing there, I felt, was to surrender to the Center's "wet" sound and settle for a diffused and generalized approximation of ensemble—sometimes referred to in jacket notes as "sweep and grandeur." I had, in fact, vowed never to work there again, and in the weeks preceding the "Emperor" recording I had moved, without success, for a change of venue.

When I arrived some twenty minutes into the first session, Stokowski was busy rehearsing the major tuttis. I took my place unseen at the as yet unpositioned piano and, as the orchestra approached the end of the first movement's central episode, appended, by way of a greeting to the Maestro, the sequence of chromatic scale, trills, and arpeggios which completes the transition from exposition to development. Stokowski's first words to me—"I cannot hear you well"—came as no surprise at all; the stage was set for another battle with the acoustics of Manhattan Center.

Or, rather, it was being set. Producer Andrew Kazdin approached from the booth and guided the stage crew as they maneuvered the piano from a position adjacent to the back desk of the fiddles, where it had been parked, to within hailing distance of the podium. "Do you think that will give you enough eye contact?" he asked.

"I can *see* the Maestro—that's not the problem," I responded. "It's just that I can't hear anything in this bloody place."

Andy shrugged; he has an abiding affection for the Center and, by devising improbable seating plans, has frequently succeeded in wedding its cathedrallike resonance to precise, detailed, even pop-style pickups.

"Come, please, let us try—letter C," Stokowski commanded. The crew dispersed, Andy returned to the booth, and we began to rehearse the interludes which follow the opening tutti.

The "Emperor" poses fewer problems of togetherness than any of Beethoven's other concerted works—it's virtually devoid of the sticky ensemble wickets which are scattered throughout the Third and Fourth Concertos, for example—and I was confident, indeed, that with the approach we'd agreed on at the runthrough, it would all but play itself. I had, of course, managed to overlook the fact that in order to accommodate my continuo-style figurations, which played so large a part in our grand design for this interpretation, the orchestral volume would have to be reduced accordingly, and that in lightly scored sections this would simply compound the acoustic problems of the Center.

We came to grief a few bars after letter D, where solo passages for woodwinds are mated to triadic figurations in the piano part, and Stokowski signaled a halt. "Mr. Kazdin," he called to no mike in particular, "it will be necessary for me to see Mr. Gould's hands." (The Maestro was in the unenviable position of having to coordinate this inarticulate swirl of sound with a solo instrument that had been stationed so as to allow for maximum separation and minimum intertrack leakage.) "I'm coming out," Kazdin responded.

While the piano was repositioned—angled so that Stokowski could practice the digital equivalent of lip reading—I took Kazdin aside. "Andy," I said, "I can't hear the winds at all; you're really going to have to be our ears. There's simply no way for us to tell whether we're covered on anything out here."

The way to tell that is to retreat to the booth for playbacks, but the economics of orchestral recording rarely allow for a perusal of any material other than basic takes—and most of those are encountered while the orchestra members enjoy their obligatory union breaks. The supplemental inserts which provide the indispensable mortar for the construction of any well-edited tape product are, of course, overheard by the producer during the session, but not even the most experienced studio hand can guarantee his artists that every insert will mate successfully in terms of tempo, dynamics, and instrumental balance with the material it's intended to cover. Indeed, Stokowski and I were both so apprehensive about a number of the wind-and-piano dialogues in the first movement that a special listening session was hastily arranged for the following morning.

As it turned out, Andy Kazdin had indeed listened well: we were covered, though in some cases by the skin of our teeth. The Maestro joined me, somewhat to Andy's annoyance, in a denunciation of the ballroom as a recording site, but both of us were convinced that the second and third movements would benefit by this additional listening experience—as indeed they did.

In the meantime, Donald Hunstein, a veteran Columbia photographer, arrived to take cover shots. It was decided that we could not afford to waste time at the Center and should adjourn to Columbia's photo studio, where a pint-size Steinway was being prepped to resemble its concert-grand cousin.

Hunstein wanted a rehearsal-style shot; I was to sit at the piano, apparently poised for action, while Stokowski, standing in the bend of the instrument, was to offer a grandfatherly gaze to me and an appropriately thoughtful right profile to the camera. Each time Hunstein began to shoot, however, Stokowski would turn his head to the right and begin to scrutinize the bass strings; on occasion, by way of variety, he would raise his eyes to the ceiling, as though communing with the ghost of Hans Richter—but at best our glances were intersecting at a 90-degree angle. Stokowski never did explain these curious maneuvers, and though Hunstein repositioned him time and again, the photographer continued to encounter new and ingenious variations on the same strategy. I suddenly realized that I had rarely seen anything but a left profile shot of Leopold Stokowski, and in the end Hunstein had to settle for the right-angle intersect. This was, I thought, a prudent choice, for the only layout which would have satisfied both conductor and photographer would have necessitated a 180-degree turn of the piano with Stokowski, left profile exposed, looking on from the bass end of the keyboard. This, of course, would have involved an unwarranted waste of studio time and—worse—placed the camera to *my* right, a notoriously disadvantageous angle.

The day following the second session was devoted to a definitive splice-point selection; the first movement was reviewed, the second and third surveyed for the first time, and Stokowski worked tirelessly from early afternoon till late in the evening. His concentration was total, focused as much on the piano part as on the orchestral material—although I have been known to look out for my own interests on such occasions—and appeared to render him immune to compliments. During the session the day before, I had found his interpretation of the second movement quite overwhelming, and now that we were able to listen to it at leisure, I was tempted to indulge myself with requests for repeated, and unnecessary, playbacks. In particular, I was unable to let one two-bar orchestral interlude pass by without comment. The Maestro had molded this passage with an intensity which I had never before encountered—introducing an impassioned crescendo to the center of the phrase and a plaintive diminuendo thereafter—and created, in the process, one of those patented Stokowskian moments. To this day—twelve years after the event—it produces an involuntary shudder whenever I hear it, and at the editing session I was simply unable to control myself. Each time this segment passed over the tape heads, I would say something like: "Oh, my God, that's so beautiful—let's hear it again." Stokowski invariably fussed with his score and pretended not to notice—rather like a child embarrassed in the presence of his schoolmates when given too good a grade—but I think he, too, was pleased.

Toward the end of this session, engineer Ed Michalski returned from a coffee break and announced that the pop sounds which had occasionally penetrated our listening space from the booth next door were produced by, for, and in the presence of—Barbra Streisand.

"You mean Streisand's next door?" I said.

"Yeah, they're mixing her new album," Michalski replied.

"Um, Andy—if you don't mind—since we're stopped anyway, I think I'll just wander down the hall for a moment," I announced.

"Fine," Kazdin replied.

I am not, as I believe I have mentioned elsewhere, a stage-door John. I am, however, a confessed Streisand addict, and as I headed for the water cooler, I had occasion to lament the fact that the editing cubicle doors at CBS are atrociously designed. It's one thing to discourage sidewalk superintendents—no windows at all would do that very effectively; it's quite another to inset into each cubicle entrance a piece of glass approximately eight inches by twelve inches, which prompts and at the same time prohibits surveillance.

During the recording session, Stokowski and Kazdin had had a protracted discussion about the penultimate passage of the finale—the duo for timpani and piano. Stokowski had at first insisted that the timpani should be moved closer to the piano for a separate insert on this passage; Kazdin, himself a percussionist, argued that the intensity Stokowski wanted could be better attained by leaving the timpani alone and moving the mikes instead. Next evening, when we had worked our way through to the finale, the Maestro asked Ed Michalski for repeated playbacks of this passage, each time requesting more volume and more intensity from the timpani. Kazdin's miking had indeed produced the sound he was after, and Stokowski, turning to Michalski, said: "How is it that when I ask you to do something, I hear the result immediately? When I ask my orchestra for such a result, I am not always so rewarded." It was a charming, though typically indirect, gesture of concession.

As we were working through this passage, with frequent tape rewinds to satisfy the Maestro's demands, someone commented on what sounded like a light knock at the door. We waited for a moment; it did not recur—no nose appeared at the eight-by-twelve-inch glass, and nobody bothered to do anything about it. Stokowski began to discuss the closing measures. For the six-bar solo-piano scale sequence which follows the timpani passage, I had made one relatively strict take and one considerably more unbuttoned version which was virtually oblivious of bar lines. "I like very much the wildness of that version," Stokowski said. "I think it is necessary to introduce such a mood at this moment."

As we were discussing the pros and cons of this inclusion, the knock came again, rather more firmly this time, and a nose could most definitely be seen in the glass inset. Kazdin went to the door and discovered two visitors.

"Hi," said their spokeswoman. "I just wanted to say hello, because I'm a fan, and since we were leaving, I thought I'd just stop by and tell you that, and I . . ."

Unfortunately, I do not remember most of what followed. I do remember that Andy appeared uncertain as to whether "Won't you come in?" or "How nice of you to drop by" would be the appropriate thing to say. I remember that Elliott Gould was grinning from the right side of the door frame, and I remember that, since none of us did or said anything decisive, the lady was finally reduced to adding, "I'm Barbra Streisand." And I remember, to my eternal embarrassment, contributing the most maladroit moment of that or any other conversation by saying "I know."

Mostly, though, I remember noticing that Leopold Stokowski, sitting beside me, appeared vaguely annoyed about the whole thing—about the interruption of his discourse on the importance of that penultimate moment, about the appearance of this talkative young woman whose name he either did not catch or did not know, and that he drummed his fingers on the arm of his chair—more or less in the rhythm of the timpani solo—to indicate his displeasure. And I remember realizing, as I started to stand up, that this time I had no train ticket to drop. You win some, you lose some.

VI

My last interview with Stokowski took place on a December afternoon in 1969. The scene was once again his New York apartment, but this time, for the benefit of a camera crew, I sat next to the window that looked out toward Central Park and Stokowski sat opposite, across a desk, and with a score of one of Haydn's "Paris" symphonies opened before him. He had been instructed by the director, Peter Moseley, to speak directly to the camera—my questions were to be deleted from both audio tape and film—and to ignore me; once again, our glances intersected at 90 degrees.

The project was initiated earlier that year by John Roberts, then director of music for CBC radio, who had written to ask whether I would be interested in producing a documentary about Stokowski. At that time, and for many months prior, I was at work on a complicated, fourteen-character documentary-drama on the subject of outport life in Newfoundland, and I replied that when the last of our down-easters was securely in the can, I would welcome a rest, a change of pace, and a much simpler assignment. I conceded that something on a musical subject would provide the change of pace, but indicated that I was not at all sure about Stokowski as a "simple assignment." Roberts suggested that the program could be pretty much what I wanted to make of it and that if the Stokowski interview did not pan out too well, we could supplement it with any amount of testimony about his career. I said that a conventional documentary—the sort of program that would rely on the reminiscences of elderly parishioners who could remember him in the organ loft of St. Bartholomew's in 1905—would not interest me at all. I could visualize only a program in which Stokowski, supered upon a non-stop musical montage largely drawn from his own recordings, would serve as subject and narrator. What I had in mind was a sort of seamless soliloquy, and for that, I pointed out, I would need a superb basic interview. I suggested that we contact Stokowski, do the interview at his convenience, and that if we came up with material which could sustain such a concept, I would sign a contract and proceed with the production; if we did not, I would donate my interview services, and the tapes could be donated to CBC Archives.

In the meantime, Curtis Davis, then director of cultural programming for National Educational Television, told me that he had commissioned a film portrait of Stokowski and that, as one of its sequences, he would like to include some footage which dealt with the making of *my* documentary. I replied that I wasn't sure there was going to *be* a documentary, and Curtis countered with the offer of a semicollaborative effort: NET would be allowed to film my interview in its entirety, use one on-camera sequence in their production, and have access to my audio "outs" for voice-over material; in exchange, if my interview did not meet expectations and if I still intended to proceed with the project, a substantial Stokowski archive would be at my disposal. This, of course, would necessitate quite a different sort of production from what I had in mind, but it shortened the odds somewhat, and as I sat drinking tea with Stokowski while the NET crew checked out their equipment, I told myself that if this did not become a masterpiece, it would at least be a solidly professional piece of work.

For in the meantime, during the years since our chat for *High Fidelity,*

I had become a pro. In addition to Newfoundland outporters, I had logged radio interviews with politicians, academics, theologians, artists, psychiatrists, bureaucrats; I had interviewed a Northern Service nurse and Canada's thirteenth Prime Minister; I had learned to cope with reticent interview guests (filmmaker Norman McLaren, Mrs. Arnold Schoenberg) and garrulous ones (the Right Honorable John Diefenbaker, composer Milton Babbitt); I had encountered some, like Marshall McLuhan, who were reticent and garrulous by turn. No, I said to myself, his cutoffs are not going to throw me this time.

I even felt that as a pro, I could afford to appear unprofessional; I took several pages of notes from my jacket pocket and set them on the desk in front of me. This gesture was not lost on Stokowski, who looked up from the Haydn to ask: "May I know your questions?"

"Certainly, Maestro," I replied. "Let's see, now—"I began to study the notes as though I couldn't quite remember them myself. "—Oh, yes, I'd like to ask you about the music of all the late romantic composers, but particularly Mahler and Schoenberg [the so-called romantic revival was in full swing at the time]; also, I'd like to have your views on Charles Ives [I had attended, and reviewed,* the world premiere of Ives's Fourth Symphony, which Stokowski conducted in 1965]; and then I thought we might talk about the meaning of 'tradition' in music and of 'fidelity' to the score—of the composer-performer relationship, generally; and, of course, I want to ask you for your recollections of early experiences in the recording studio and for your predictions about future contacts between music and technology."

Stokowski nodded and appeared satisfied. I put the sheets back on the desk. "Of course," I smiled, "I really shouldn't tell you my questions in advance—I should try to surprise you." (I could afford to smile—I still intended to surprise him.)

"I think we're finally ready to go," Peter Moseley said. "Right," I responded. "I'll just check on *our* equipment." I walked across the living room and spoke to Del McKenzie, then CBC's New York office manager, who was subbing as a technician. "We've already wasted an awful lot of time while they set up," I said. "I want to ask a very important question right at the top of the interview—and I won't be able to ask it twice—so if you're having any problems, this is the time to say so."

"I'm miking him as tightly as I can," Del replied, "but it's not going to be as clean as an audio product should be unless we can keep the camera crew quiet. Maybe you could speak to Moseley." I did so and then returned to my seat by the window.

---

*See p. 185.

Stokowski was now becoming impatient and had begun to tap on the desk with the pencil he'd been using to mark the Haydn score. "Speed," the NET audio man called out. "Whenever you're ready," Peter Moseley whispered.

I waited for eight to ten seconds by way of dramatic pause, squirmed in my seat as though I'd forgotten what I'd come for, and then took the biggest gamble of my career as an interviewer.

"Maestro," I said, "I have this recurring dream. In it, I appear to be on some other planet, perhaps in some other solar system, and, at first, it seems as though I am the only Earthman there. And I have a tremendous sense of exhilaration because I seem to believe, in the dream, that I have been given the opportunity—and the authority—to impart my value systems to whatever form of life there might be on that planet; I have the feeling that I can create a whole planetary value system in my own image."

Stokowski, anticipating a short question, had been looking at the camera, as instructed, but he was now looking directly at me, and with a look that seemed to say: "Whose interview is this, anyway?" I could sense that Peter Moseley and the crew were stirring uneasily, as though wondering whether they should save film until my preamble had come to an end. But I was now well past the point of no return and plunged on.

"In any event," I continued, "my dream always ends badly. I usually sight some other Earthman on this planet and realize that I am not alone and will not have the opportunity to proceed, uncontradicted, with my project. But now let us suppose that, by some technological miracle, we could transport you to such a planet and give you the power that I do not have in my dream; and let us suppose also that, on this planet, there is a race of highly developed beings who, to all appearances, have achieved a state of peaceful coexistence—a state of civilization higher than our own—and have done this, moreover, without reference to the notion we call 'art.' Firstly, would you want them to know about the 'artistic' manifestations of our world? And, secondly, if you did, how much would you want them to know?"

Stokowski continued to stare at me, moving his lips without uttering a word, and for some moments I thought that he was not going to answer at all. Then, very slowly, he returned his gaze to the camera and began to speak.

"Think of our solar system, its colossal size. I have the impression that there are many solar systems, that ours is a very big one, but that there are others which are much larger. And that their distance from other solid bodies floating in the atmosphere, this distance is enormous. I have also the impression that not only is there endless space and the endless mass of the solar systems that are in that space, but there is endless time and endless mental power, that there are great masses of mind of which ours, in this little Earth that we live on, is only a small part. We all live on this same planet. We breathe the same air and we are under the power of the light which the sun gives. No sunlight, no existence on this Earth. We are all under the same conditions, and it is our privilege to make the best of those conditions—of the air we breathe, of the light we receive from the sun, that life-giving light."

It was perfect, it was poetry, it was exactly what I'd come for; if he could keep it up, I had a program.

"At present, all over the world is war—so much destruction and so little, compared with that destruction, that is creative. Many minds who are in what we call 'war'—those minds might have enormous creative power. But they are killed, smashed by the destruction. If one studies history, one sees a series of wars. One sees clearly that nobody wins any of those wars. Everybody loses. They are madness. They are the lowest form of intelligence. The men who control things at the top, they have this low form of intelligence. They create these wars. It is time all humanity understood."

Vietnam was at its height in December 1969; Stokowski had no answers and no pretensions as a historian, but he had that special gift which old age frequently enhances: the ability to state the obvious without embarrassment. And it lent to his conversation, as so often to his music making, two paradoxical qualities: an improvisatory freedom which could absorb and transcend even the most hackneyed cliché, and a sense of the inevitable. An "inevitable" improvisation ought to be a contradiction in terms, but Stokowski, in words and in music, gave it meaning.

"The artist, then, is living under the same conditions, making the best of those conditions, realizing that no matter how much effort he gives to improve his art, no matter how great an effort, there is no limit upward, no limit. No matter how much a great artist improves his art, develops it, there is no limit to further improvement, further reaching upward."

He had now gone nonstop for three minutes and twenty seconds—already the all-time longest Stokowski answer on record. I risked intruding upon the frame of the shot by leaning toward him, nodding supportively in consort with each prospective comma, and gesturing with particular enthusiasm when any cadential period threatened. At all costs, I had to keep him going.

"Art is like the deep roots of a great oak tree, and out of those roots grow many branches, many kinds of art: the dance, architecture, painting, music, the art of words, the art that Shakespeare had. In a marvelous way he understood those things—our faults, our strengths, how we struggle to live. I travel in many countries, and I notice that Shakespeare is translated into the language of that country, is performed in that country, his poetry is read, and he is not merely the artist of one country, but the artist of the world. What a wonderful solution to life! The artist of the world."

He had a film editor's sense of rhythm. His soliloquy, beginning with a shot of the cosmos, had tightened its frame of reference as he contemplated our planet, then dissolved to a close-up of the artist as prototype. In my final mix, this portion of his commentary would be supered upon three musical sequences—excerpts from Schoenberg's *Verklärte Nacht,* Holst's *The Planets,* and Scriabin's *Poem of Ecstasy.*

"I find that every day come new possibilities and new ideas, and they must not be ignored, they must be examined. For example, there are many kinds of sounds. Don't be shocked at what I'm going to say, but I like the sound of street noises. Taxicabs are blowing their horns and all kinds of sounds are going on—they have a rhythm, they have a blending of life in the streets, and it is a kind of music. Some people would say that it is just a horrible noise, and they have a right to their opinion, too. To their ears, it *is* a horrible noise. To my ears, it is interesting, because it is life. Those who think it is nonsense will either not listen at all or they will listen with prejudice, and prejudice is a very dangerous disease. The others will listen and perhaps will receive that mysterious message which is in all music, which words cannot express. Shakespeare used the word for dramatic reasons, but he also used the word for poetic reasons. He selected language which sounds to me like music. The words and the rhythms of the words are just like music to my ears."

(Later, by correspondence, we would play out one last Stokowskian game. I wrote to tell him of the musical process which I intended to use in the documentary—that I planned to employ no fewer than twenty-two musical selections and that the great majority of these would be segued via dissolves—gradual harmonic overlaps—with hard cuts confined to a monaural sequence which illustrated his early studio experiences. He replied: "Dear friend: I have never believed in 'montage.' Do you agree? Are you willing to remix?" I applied to Curtis Davis, the most astute Stokowski watcher I knew, for advice. "When you write him, be sure to define your process as a 'symphonic synthesis.' I think that term will not be lost on him," Curtis replied. It was not; Stokowski could hardly disown *his* symphonic syntheses of Wagner, and I proceeded with my mix as planned; hard cuts might have been appropriate for a radio portrait of Toscanini or George Szell, but they were emphatically not suited to the character, life-style, or musical proclivities of my subject.)

"It is quite possible that the so-called cave man had such ideas too, on his level, in his way, according to his ideas of the best life of that time. There have always been persons on this Earth who love beauty and order. It is so important to know what we really do know definitely, and to realize the immense mass of possibilities there are to life that we do not know. There may be corresponding forms of life on other planets. It is difficult to know what they are feeling and what they are thinking. Their life might be quite different from our human life or our animal life. Also, there would be the question of language, the question of how we communicate. So it would be very difficult. Yet I would think it a great privilege if I could know their ideas of what is orderly and what is beautiful. That would be the first step, I think, to try and understand *their* life, to find out what *they* think and feel and desire."

(In the end, this soliloquy ran to eight minutes, thirty-eight seconds. It would later be divided so as to provide bookends for the one-hour program—the division occurring after the first Shakespeare reference, and the concluding phrase would be regenerated from his first sentence. For, with his film editor's gift, he had already sensed the need for a process-reversal, for a mirror image of his opening thoughts. Beginning with the second Shakespeare reference, he had begun to move inexorably from the particular to the universal.)

"If I did have that possibility, I would do my best to give a clear impression to what other form of life there might be on that planet, of what I think is beautiful and orderly, what I think is creative and what I think is destructive. It would be possible, I hope, to let them see what is happening on this Earth—so much destruction, so little that is creative."

His original answer ended with those words, but I could not bear to take my leave of Stokowski while he mused upon man's capacity for self-destruction. I felt that his mirror image must be completed. I had deleted two words from his first sentence so that something could be held in reserve for the end—and now, in its regenerated repetition, that sentence was restored to its original form. After all, Stokowski himself refused to regard the score, or the material with which he had to work, as Holy Writ; for him, it was rather like a collection of newly discovered parchments for a gospel yet to be transcribed. Besides, it seemed to me that to perfect a structure through creative deception—to cheat with the help of the technological resource in the interest of a more satisfying form—was a particularly Stokowskian thing to do. In his lifetime he had witnessed the triumph, and confirmed the essential humanity, of those technological ideas which had inspired his activity as a musician; for him, technology had indeed become a "higher calling." He had understood that through its mediation one could transcend the frailty of nature and concentrate on a vision of the ideal. His life and work had testified to our ability to remove ourselves from ourselves and achieve a state of ecstasy.

"Think of our solar system, its colossal size, its possibility."

RUBINSTEIN

"You would have canceled the concert, wouldn't you?"

"Ah, well, Maestro, I'm not sure, actually. I suppose that I . . ."

"Of course you would have. . . . I see it in your eyes."

It was not an auspicious introduction, but that's the way I met Arthur Rubinstein. The occasion, in January 1960, was his more or less annual visit to Toronto, my hometown, and a recital devoted to the music of Chopin, a composer with whom, as most everyone knows, Rubinstein shares a mutuality of sentiment that almost singlehandedly justifies the oft-suspect post-Renaissance specialization of performers, but whom I, as self-appointed bearer of the local neoclassic cross, had frequently gone on record as debunking. Indeed, the late Artur Schnabel's celebrated crack about Chopin, "the right-handed genius," ranks as a modest cavil compared with some of the putdowns I'd bandied about in relation to the Polish master, and Rubinstein's Toronto recital, consequently, was an event at which I preferred to have my presence go unnoticed, not only by the public at large and, of course, by the local press but, for altogether different reasons, by Rubinstein himself.

"Are you feeling better, Maestro?"

"Much better, thank you. But why didn't you take a seat out front—surely you can't enjoy the sound back here?"

"On the contrary, Maestro. I always prefer to listen in the wings."

My master plan had been to wait until proceedings were under way (the opening work—the B-flat-minor Scherzo—was by no means at the top of my private hit parade), pull up my parka, make a dash for the stage door (I'd renounced local platforms at that period of my life but had kept up my contacts with the backstage set), and settle in for the duration in a seldom-used broadcast booth I knew about. The booth, as luck would have it, was locked, and the stage doorman, who lacked a key, did possess the information that Rubinstein had arrived in town more or less at the last minute, victim of both a delayed flight and a debilitating flu ("A hundred and one degrees, they say; amazing how a chap can play, stuffed up like that!"), and since in those days my anti-Chopin bias was exceeded only by my hypochondria, I spent the balance of the evening shuffling between a makeshift listening post near the onstage entrance—a bit lacking in high-frequency response, but the essentials always came through—while the concert was in progress,

From *Look*, March 9, 1971.

and a germ-free retreat close to the commissionaire's post some dozen yards away, when it wasn't.

As Rubinstein came down the homestretch—the Andante Spianato and Grande Polonaise was the last work listed—I decided the time for leave-taking had come. I'd calculated that at least three or four encores would follow and that, consequently, I'd have plenty of time for my Scarlet Pimpernel act before the Maestro's admirers could make the pilgrimage backstage. Alas, I'd reckoned without the determination of the Chopin devotee. When I turned toward the stage door, the route was blocked by a regiment of Rubinstein diehards—most of them Poles and fully cognizant of my Chopin deprecations, I reasoned in the panic of the moment—and I beat a retreat to the only possible haven, virus infected though it undoubtedly was: Rubinstein's dressing room.

As he emerged for a refill of Kleenex after encore number two, the cramped dialogue set out above ensued, and once the ranks of glad-handers had thinned, I headed out into the night, making straight for the only pharmacy in town that offered round-the-clock service. We had, however, promised to pick up the threads of that none-too-promising conversation later, and ten years after the fact, in Rubinstein's New York hotel, the promise was kept.

A.R.: I'm taking this suite for the time being—for my stay in the United States. We used to keep an apartment in New York, but I am a born hotelier. I am a hotel man. I married only when I was forty-five, and I have always lived in hotels. I love them.

MRS. RUBINSTEIN [*serving coffee*]: You know something? So do I.

A.R.: You have the possibility of room service, breakfast in bed. In an apartment, you don't have such services, and there is in a hotel a certain ani . . . anim—

MRS. R.: Anonymity.

A.R.: Animon—what's it again?

MRS. R.: Anonymity, my darling, anonymity.

A.R.: That's it. There's certainly that in a hotel.

G.G.: I'm a motel man myself. In my opinion, the motel is one of the great inventions of Western man. The idea of having one's bill to society paid in advance, of having the option to check out whenever you feel so inclined—I think that's a great psychological gift.

I have a couple of motels that I go to twice a year or so along the north shore of Lake Superior—a fantastic route, the most extraordinary scenery in central North America.

A.R.: Lake Superior? The north shore?

G.G.: Yes. There's a town every fifty miles or so. Most of them are lumber towns or mining towns, and they have an extraordinary identity, each of these towns, because they have all grown up around one industry or one plant that has built up the town.

A.R.: A sort of hierarchy, then?

G.G.: Yes, yes indeed. They're run paternalistically, and being there is like taking part in a scene from Kafka. But I go there to a motel and write for a few days, and if I could arrange it, it's really the sort of place in which I would like to spend my life.

A.R.: You see, this is something that I have understood about you from the first moment when we talked. You remember my first question was "Why don't you like to play?" I knew about you a long time before you came out with the "Goldberg" Variations—I was vastly interested. But suddenly you just abandoned the field, so to say, and that was a tremendous astonishment. It was very strange, and I've thought a lot about it because it is a great loss.

G.G.: Records don't count?

A.R.: Of course, of course, they count, and radio and TV, but they all deprive us of that personal impact that I too, after all, need. But I have the feeling you will come back to it, you know.

G.G.: Oh, I'll never go back to giving concerts.

A.R.: I would think so.

G.G.: No, no.

A.R.: Think of my words.

G.G.: I will, I promise. But I also promise that if this is a bet, you will lose it.

A.R.: But was there never a moment when you felt that very special emanation from an audience?

G.G.: There really wasn't. There were moments when I felt I was giving a good performance, but . . .

A.R.: But you never felt that you had the souls of those people?

G.G.: I didn't really want their souls, you know. Well, that's a silly thing to say. Of course, I wanted to have some influence, I suppose, to shape their lives in some way, to do "good," if I can put an old-fashioned word on it, but I didn't want any power over them, you know, and I certainly wasn't stimulated by their presence as such. Matter of fact, I always played less well because of it.

A.R.: There we are, absolute opposites, you know. We are absolute opposites! See, I will tell you something. Don't laugh at me, please, because it is ridiculous, maybe, but I cannot help it. You see, I have a feeling that we have a power in us. You know, there is always a word that nobody has been able to explain, there is no expliqué—nothing—to lead you toward an answer as to what it means, yet all the languages use it so frequently that it has become an everyday word. The word "soul," *"l'âme," "anima"*—what the hell is *"anima"*? Where is it? We know pretty well the anatomy, we know pretty well what we are doing and how it functions and all that. But what the devil is the soul?—you see? Well, this soul appears to be so frightfully necessary, as religion is necessary or seems to be—we must have it—and in all the cultures, as far as we can trace, there was always something there to worship, there were all those totems and God knows what. Well, soul is a kind of power. And the power has been very much exploited, sometimes in a ridiculous way, sometimes in a childish way. Well, now, in my young days—you were also not born to that—there was much activity in, you know, séances—spiritistic, spiritualistic experiments—in which I was very active, very, *very* active. It was a very serious affair. There were great scientists like Sir Oliver Lodge, whom I knew very well personally. On a crossing together once, I talked with him every day. He was persuaded that he was talking to the dead and having communication with them and so on. Well, in any case, you know, at the séances, the tables were actually—without tricks, I assure you—the tables were responding. I know that—no tricks—I had open eyes, and besides, there was enough light. But the fact that we were holding hands and were committing our concentration created a response, you see. But now comes the funny thing. Somehow I was always, at those séances, chosen as the boss, you know, the fellow who talks with the ghost. Well, whenever somebody spoke, it was to Napoleon—one always likes to speak to Napoleon or Chopin or your grandfather or somebody like that of importance—but I always knew who was coming along and what he was going to say. The others would be astonished: "Ah, what emanations!" "Did you hear that?" "He said this and this." But not me. What does it mean, after all? It means simply that I concentrated the powers of the others in me. You see, I believe a fellow like Napoleon or Hitler or Mussolini or, you know, Stalin—certain men with some sort of emanation—had much, much more of that power than other people.

I speak of that because if you would have followed the pianistic career for many years as I have—over sixty-five years, you know —you would have experienced this constant, constant, constant contact with the crowd that you have to, in a way, persuade, or dominate, or get hold of, you know. For instance, the feeling at the beginning when the audiences arrive—they come from a dinner, they think about their business, the women observe the dress of other women, young girls look for good-looking young men, or vice versa—I mean, there is a tremendous disturbance all over, and I feel it, of course. But if you are in a good mood, you have the attention of all of them. You can play one note and hold it out for a minute—they will listen like they are in your hand, in a way, and this emanation cannot be done by a record. There, I am coming to the point. You see, it cannot be done at all by a record.

G.G.: Well, maybe so. Certainly, when you're making a recording you are left alone. You're not surrounded by five hundred, five thousand, fifty thousand people who are in a position to say at that moment, "Aha, that's what he thinks about that work, eh!" But that seems to me a great advantage. Because I think that the ideal way to go about making a performance or a work of art—and I don't think that they should be different, really—is to assume that when you begin, you don't quite know what it is about. You only come to know as you proceed. As you get two thirds of the way through the session, you are two thirds of the way along toward a conception. I very rarely know, when I come to the studio, exactly how I am going to do something. I mean, I'll try it in fifteen different ways, and eight of them may work reasonably well, and there may be a possibility that two or three will sound really convincing. But I don't know at the time of the session what result is finally going to accrue. And it does depend upon listening to a playback and saying, "That doesn't work; it isn't going to go that way; I'll have to change that completely." It makes the performer very like the composer, really, because it gives him editorial afterthought, it gives him that power—it's a different kind of power than you were talking about, certainly, but it's very real nonetheless. Well, obviously, this is something that you cannot do in a concert, if only because you can't stop, as I always wanted to, and say, "Take two."

A.R.: Well, yes, that is plausible. Recording is a different thing—it is a different affair. But do you do what I do? I make a few, you know, whole takes, and it's very rare that I want to pick up anything. Sometimes, something happens with one wrong note, and you fix it like a false tooth—you just chip it off and replace it from the other take, you know, so it sounds right. But I like to play the whole thing once I've started because I cannot bear breaking it up.

G.G.: No, I can bear it because, first of all, I believe in editing. I agree that it's helpful to make one full take per movement, but I see no particular reason why one couldn't do something in one hundred and sixty-two different segments and never, in fact, do it straight through. I don't work that way myself, but I see no reason why one couldn't.

A.R.: I think, simply, it is not persuasive when it is labored, you know. It is not art anymore. In a circus, you see, a man does fantastic things—he jumps, let's say—I don't know, anything fantastic. Well, he likes always to miss one jump with a little sly smile, and that is only to show you how difficult it really is, you know. But he does that because it must be shown as easy thereafter.

G.G.: Exactly. It doesn't follow that because it looks easy or sounds easy, it is easy, in fact. You know, in the last few years, I've spent roughly half my time working on radio and television programs that have nothing at all to do with music. And, consequently, I've had to try to express the totality of an idea without worrying too much about the integrity—if I can use the word that way—of its individual components. Last year, for instance, I produced a radio documentary about Newfoundland—though it was really about the conditions under which one can live in isolation and solitude, and Newfoundland was an excuse for the program, in fact—and spent almost four hundred hours in a studio editing that program. Anyway, we had one character among the fourteen whom we interviewed who was most important to the story. We needed him very badly. He was a delightful man, very articulate and very perceptive, but he had a habit of saying "um" and "uh" and "sort of" and "kind of" constantly—so constantly, in fact, that you got absolutely sick of the repetitions. I mean, every third word was separated by an "um" and an "uh." Not only that, being a very scrupulous man linguistically, he was in the habit of rejecting his own adjectival choices. He would get eight words into a sentence and decide the adjective wouldn't do, and without thinking of our problem, our splicing problem, he would just throw in another adjective, probably at a different dynamic level.

Well, we spent—this is no exaggeration—we spent three long weekends—Saturday, Sunday, and Monday, eight hours per day—doing nothing but removing "um"s and "uh"s, "sort of"s and "kind of"s, and righting the odd syntactical fluff in his material. We figured at one point we were making four edits of some kind in every typewritten line. There were thirty lines of double-spaced page, so that's a hundred and twenty edits per page. And there were fourteen pages of his testimony, so we made a conservative guess that there were sixteen hundred edits in that man's speech alone in order to make him sound lucid and fluid, which he now does. We made a new character out of him. You see, I don't really care how you do it. I don't think it's a moral issue. I don't think that kind of judgment enters into it. If it takes sixteen hundred splices, that's fine. I mean, take your record of the F-minor Brahms Quintet with the Guarneri, for instance—

A.R.: You like it?

G.G.: I'm drunk on it. I've now heard it five times in the last few weeks.

A.R.: For heaven's sake!

G.G.: It's the greatest chamber-music performance with piano that I've heard in my life.

A.R.: Have you heard the three quartets yet?

G.G.: No, not yet, but I'm going to get them.

A.R.: Oh, this is something I must send you. Will you accept a gift?

G.G.: I'd be delighted.

A.R.: Because I have the feeling we did better.

G.G.: Really?

A.R.: Yes, we did better. But the Quintet was pretty good.

G.G.: It was fantastic. It had a flexibility and a range that no one, I am sure, no group of people in a concert could ever improve upon or even approach. It's the most spontaneous performance imaginable, but at the same time it's so organized, so tight, so right, and everything goes. . . .

A.R.: We played it the other night, you know.

G.G.: Really?

A.R.: Yes, we did a concert.

G.G.: Oh!

A.R.: But, you see, as I'm fifty years your senior, I lived in another world, of extreme emotionalism—I don't like the word "romanticism," because that's something that disgusts me, you know. It disgusted even Chopin, did you know that?

G.G.: No, I didn't.

A.R.: Even Chopin, who lived in the Byronic time when people were ashamed not to have a romantic duel or not to faint or something like that, you know. All those things were accepted—that was how one had to live. Well, I inherited a little bit still from that time. Machines came to me as a great surprise—a little frightening at first. The first time I heard a radio, I thought, "What is it speaking of?" Even now, sometimes I get shocked when I get home and suddenly I hear a man's voice in my wife's room and I think "She has a lover" or something, you know. But it is the radio, it is only the radio, and I am not quite used to it. It is all for me still a great surprise, a great novelty.

G.G.: Well, I did a radio program last year about an extraordinary man who lives in Quebec. His name is Jean Le Moyne, and he is a theologian primarily but also a poet and a theorist of technology. He does all those things, but the spirit of theology is still a part of everything he says and does. Anyway, he was asked about technology and what it was doing to people, and he said, "Well, there should be no contradiction between technology and the humanities, in particular theology." I won't attempt to quote him word for word, but he said something to the effect that technology has now given us something like a network—a radio network, a television network, an oil network, a railway network, a communications network of all kinds—and this network has circumscribed the earth in such a way that we can no longer go to nature, we can only go to nature through the network. But when we do that, we realize that technology exercises a great charity on our lives. And he meant, I think, that it's not there to hurt people, to hinder them, to impede them, to get in the way of human contact. It is there to speed it, to make it more direct and more immediate, and to remove people from the very things —the self-conscious things, the competitive things—that are detrimental to society in fact. I believe in that idea. I believe that technology is a charitable enterprise; that when one makes a recording, as you did with the F-minor Brahms, you are influencing not only many more people numerically than you could perhaps in a concert, but influencing them forever—not just for one moment, one evening, which they may or may not recall, but forever. You will have been able to change their lives forever, as my notion of what Brahms represents has been changed by your recording.

A.R.: Well, you begin to persuade me. I was born in another epoch, you see. I trail the old things that hang all around me like—well, like the tin cans they hang on the wedding car, you know. They stay with me. But you were born into another world than myself—therefore, all your own talent is being taken in by that, is absorbed by that, by the circumstances of your entourage. My children look at the world as though it came together with the airplane. Well, there you are, you see. I remember still that I was dreaming of Daedalus and Icarus—I feel so sorry for him that he lost his way. But somewhere, we are going to meet with our ideas, you know. I can't say how that will happen, exactly, but remember my words: somewhere we will meet.

MEMORIES OF MAUDE HARBOUR, OR VARIATIONS ON A THEME OF ARTHUR RUBINSTEIN

I recall an interview with his son, John Rubinstein, the actor, in the *New York Times*. John says his father started him at the piano when he was a small child but only discovered he couldn't read music when he was fourteen. Such can be the life of the touring musician.

From *Piano Quarterly*, Summer 1980.

I mustn't forget to mention Mr. Rubinstein's incredible memory. He describes conversations with waiters, chambermaids, train conductors —miles of trivia are scribed, in detail, going back more than fifty years. And so no one shall have any doubts about his memory, he states in the preface to this volume [*My Many Years* (New York: Knopf, 1980)], "This work was done out of sheer memory without the help of documentation or exterior help." Mr. Rubinstein says he memorized Franck's Symphonic Variations in a matter of hours, on a train. And upon arriving at his destination, he reports, he cabbed to the rehearsal and played the work from memory. Mozart, move over.

So much for the eagerly awaited second and last volume in this remarkable autobiography. Those who choose to tell their own story are usually selective about what they let us know. Here the interest lies not only in what is missing but, particularly, in Mr. Rubinstein's views of life.

If you enjoy reading about food, affairs of the heart, and gossip, then this book is highly recommended. Since I read it while suffering from food poisoning, the reader may detect a certain biliousness in my approach.

I had scarcely begun the first supper show of my gala season at the Maude Harbour Festival when, as was my habit, I glanced toward the boxes. And there, seated on one marked "Live Bait—Do Not Refrigerate," was a vision of such loveliness that it instantly erased from my mind the memory of all four amorous adventures which had befallen me between lunch and five o'clock tea. Delightful as the company of those ladies may have been, I realized at once that my future, my fate, my destiny, belonged to the dazzling enchantress who now, with such demure grace, hid her bubble gum beneath the crate of worms on which she sat and attempted to come to terms with the ardor of my gaze. I resolved to address every note of my performance to her and her alone and to inquire into the county's statutory-rape provisions at intermission.

As I began my Scarlatti group, our eyes locked in an optical embrace of such intensity that the cross-hand passages in Longo 465 were obliged to depart from the urtext. Undoubtedly, to the common herd lounging in the stalls these departures would be mistaken for wrong notes; but to my beloved—who now with such chaste and childlike concentration retrieved her eyelashes from her Pepsi glass—it was clear that these three-octave leaps brought with them the rich promise of exuberant chromatic embellishments which carried *my* Scarlatti far beyond the confining bounds of eighteenth-century diatonicism and made of it an exercise in *Tristan*esque ambiguity. As my readers will be the first to attest, I am the last fellow in the world to belabor the obvious supremacy of my own art, but I do insist that it is my unquenchable love of life and of inaccuracy which has always set *my* Scarlatti apart from the predictable and premeditated re-creations of Landowska and Kirkpatrick. Inevitably, the concert was a triumph, and the audience's insatiable demand for the Webern Variations, as an encore, enabled me to bring down the house.

The official reception was held at the Oddfellows' Hall, and I was much agitated to discover that Reeve Doolittle had absented himself and had delegated in his stead Deputy Reeve Silverman—a fellow so lacking in musical discrimination that, while conspicuously seated in the front row at my concert, he had presumed to tap his toes throughout the Webern Variations and, adding insult to injury, had beaten out the celebrated fermata-ritard in the third movement and thrown me a subdivided cue at the onset of the epilogue. At the reception, moreover, he boasted, before the very cream of Maude Harbour society, that, despite the ingenuity of my rubato, I had been unable to shake him off. (It was, of course, a vile canard; there were at least three occasions on which I had left him and his sandals scrambling to catch up.) Apart from the reeve, however, the reception was attended by everyone who counted in Maude Harbour as well as by several who had not yet learned to; the aforementioned Silverman had had the audacity to invite the members of the local Carl Orff kindergarten—urchins who should long since have been packed off to bed by their parents and who kept up an intolerable din with the cutlery. Though I was showered with compliments, and though all who mattered concurred with my own assessment that I had been at the very peak of my powers, it was nonetheless a sad occasion. For, despite the elegant and fashionable turnout, there was but one face that I longed to behold, one voice from which I longed to hear a confirmation of my own view of my greatness—and that, alas, was denied me; my beloved was nowhere to be seen.

The reception over, I adjourned at twilight to the splendid island retreat of my hostess, the legendary beauty Peggy Muhlheim, who was extremely well connected in Maude Harbour, since her sister's second husband's first cousin had once been engaged to the town's chief sanitary engineer. As we swam, side by side, across the 472-meter inlet which separated the mainland from the rock on which Peggy pitched her tent in summer, she playfully displayed, for my amusement, a reverse Australian crawl in imitation of the stick technique of Carlo Maria Giulini and simultaneously sang, in a somewhat waterlogged fashion but with impeccable intonation nonetheless, the opening measures of Frank Martin's *Le Vin herbé*. (As my readers will surmise, Peggy possessed the quick wit and easy erudition which I have always found irresistible in women.)

Not to be outdone, I immediately adopted a breaststroke which perfectly simulated the conducting style of Herbert von Karajan, but I declined to join her in the Martin opus (though, having once conducted it from the piano on three days' notice, I, of course, knew it by heart), since I quickly realized that she had not hit upon this particular excerpt by accident but had, rather, chosen this subtle retelling of the Tristan legend so as to slyly convey to me her suspicions about my intentions with regard to my beloved. At first, I was mildly amused by this impertinent stratagem, but as I examined her motivation in more detail, I realized that it was, in fact, an intolerable intrusion into my personal life. "Is it possible," I asked myself, "that she fancies she has some sort of claim upon me, just because we've lived together for three years?" I resolved to have it out with her—just as soon as she had fed me.

Whatever her other defects, Peggy laid a sumptuous picnic blanket, and I have never enjoyed my traditional postconcert repast of Arrowroots and Poland Water more. Somewhat placated, I resolved to defer the inevitable explosion until morning, and as we lay back upon the rock to watch Maude Harbour glamorously backlit by the play of the aurora borealis, we reviewed the highlights of my triumph.

Suddenly, from across the bay, but drawing ever closer to the island, we heard the unmistakable whine of an Evinrude 9.7. This was a most unwelcome sound to my ears, since it foretold the arrival of Zoltán Mostányi—a loutish, uncouth fellow from Budapest who summered in Maude Harbour and whom Peggy, in an outburst of misguided philanthropy, had befriended. Mostányi was alleged to be both pianist and musicologist—though I personally saw no evidence of either gift in him. His chief claim to fame was a monograph entitled "Haydn and Serfdom: The Tyranny of the Minuet." Despite Peggy's entreaties, I steadfastly refused to read it, since Mostányi had the discourtesy to decline my generous offer to purchase the original manuscript and the effrontery to lecture me on what he termed the "bourgeois decadence" of the collector's instinct. As to his pianism, it was apparently confined entirely to a large discography which I was disinclined to peruse; I had carefully explained to the fellow, on an earlier occasion, my unshakable conviction with regard to the mystical transcendence of the spontaneously inept moment which public performance permits, and he had petulantly and pointedly absented himself from my concert thereafter.

I was determined to avoid any further encounters with Mostányi and, as his skiff neared the island, made ready to swim back to the mainland alone. But once again, as at all pivotal moments of my life, fate intervened; I perceived, in the front of the skiff, dimly outlined by the glow from the town across the bay, the precious figure upon which I longed to cast my eyes. How or why she had fallen into the unworthy company of this Hungarian scribbler, I could not imagine. I was simply willing to accept the fact that fate, at times, moves in ways more mysterious than even I can comprehend.

Peggy greeted her guests with tolerable warmth, but was clearly put out by my beloved's unexpected arrival. She offered them the crumbs from the Arrowroot box, which I had emptied, and resumed humming *Le Vin herbé,* casting meaningful glances in my direction as she did so. For my part, I was content to feast my eyes upon the face of my beloved (now gently illuminated by the Chinese lantern which Peggy had hung above the rock), and it was clear to me at once that in the few hours since last our glances intertwined, she had undergone a momentous metamorphosis. The coy, girlish ways in which I read such promise of fruition as I scaled the Scarlattian heights were now transformed; the shy, uncertain, awkward adolescent of the afternoon had, in truth, become a woman of the evening. There was, of course, but one explanation, and I was humbled before the mystery it implicitly conveyed. Clearly, the hypnotic spell cast by my concert had worked its wonders and released from its cocoon the magnificent butterfly who now alit upon our rock.

Peggy, meanwhile, had engaged Mostányi in a discussion of theories of the leisure class. Under his baleful influence, she had been rereading Thorstein Veblen and was prepared to harangue all who would attend her on the subject. (As my readers will surmise, Peggy possessed the sort of intellectual intolerance and exhibitionism which I have always found repugnant in a woman.) Sensing my discomfort and maliciously choosing to exploit it, she implied that my beloved would be incapable of understanding her concept without first contesting with her in a game of Monopoly. Mostányi instantly professed himself in agreement, claiming that this absurd pastime served as a metaphor through which to observe the evils of capitalism. Well, by Jove, I was resolved to have none of it; but when my beloved willingly—indeed eagerly—agreed to participate, there was little I could do to dissuade her, and I was compelled to join in this folly.

I have, of course, always been a virtuoso at cards, and in no time I had accumulated all four railroads, Ventnor, Atlantic, and Marvin Gardens, and had secured a foothold on the Boardwalk. Mostányi, the obnoxious lout, made a clean sweep of Kentucky, Indiana, and Illinois and as he began to extend his grasp on the second corner of the board by securing Tennessee and New York, proclaimed that his every purchase struck a death blow against American imperialism and that in his hotels there would be neither color TV nor room service. By contrast, my beloved's behavior in the marketplace was a model of tact and diplomacy. Time and again she went to jail without complaint, passed Go without collecting, and paid luxury tax on an estate which bordered on bankruptcy. It tore my heart to shreds to see her mortgage her hard-won toehold on Mediterranean and Baltic, and I resolved that when my victory was assured, I would redeem her precious properties and make her mistress of the very finest houses.

The struggle raged throughout the night, and victory continued to elude my grasp since Park Place, the key to my conquest of the Boardwalk, had fallen into Peggy's greedy hands. I bid for it with zest, offering her in exchange all railroads, plus Connecticut (which would give her control of the first corner) and a massive infusion of cash, of which, as I was well aware, she was in short supply. She rejected my offer out of hand and, in violation of every rule by which the game was founded, sold the vital property to Mostányi for a single "Get out of jail free" card and, as she put it, "future considerations." Moreover, Miss Muhlheim had the audacity to claim that she was operating in the best interests of the free market system and thereby assuring that the lesson she sought to teach my beloved would not go unobserved.

I was outraged; every moral fiber in my being was affronted, and I demanded satisfaction from Mostányi; as the first light of dawn broke across the bay, I threw the board and all its accoutrements into the water, save only for the deeds to Baltic and Mediterranean, which I resolved to have set by the most fashionable of jewelers and to wear, as a pendant, next to my heart forever.

Mostányi was spared the beating he so richly deserved when we perceived the sleek Chris Craft of Deputy Reeve Silverman approaching. I assured Mostányi he would not escape my wrath unscathed, but for the moment I felt obliged to make my way down the rock and to help Silverman tie his launch to Peggy's sewer outlet. He explained that the motor vessel *Siddhartha*, which regularly plied the waters of the Muskox Lakes—for which Maude Harbour serves as the undisputed artistic and intellectual capital—had grounded on a sandbar overnight, stranding a group of Transylvanian tourists in the process. He begged me to come at once and entertain them in the ship's salon, thereby preventing a riot which would undoubtedly cause the *Siddhartha* to capsize and undermine the local tourist trade for years to come. I agreed, but not before exacting a heavy price from the fellow. He gave assurance that, in future, appropriate publicity would be undertaken in behalf of each of my appearances, with brochures distributed to every stationery store and notion counter in town, that I would henceforth receive complimentary tickets to each of my own concerts at the festival, and that he would never again presume to tap his toes as I unraveled the subtle serialism of Anton Webern.

It broke my heart to leave my beloved stranded on the rock and in the company of such lamentable influences, but, as my readers will attest, I am not one to deprive a needy and clamoring public of my presence. Silverman invited me to take the wheel of his runabout, and under my direction it skillfully skimmed across the glasslike early-morning calm of the bay. As it did so, I mused upon the changes in my life and fortune which a benevolent fate had decreed, and I realized at once that with the breaking of that dawn I had left my youth forever behind.

I could no longer be content to abandon myself to vain and idle pursuits; I could no longer rely upon the surpassing agility and spontaneity of my art and abuse these unquestioned virtues while I followed a life of frolicsome indulgence. Henceforth, the superficial gesture, the hedonistic pursuit, would be forever exiled from my nature. I would dedicate my life and my art to my beloved. I would forsake all others, work my fingers to the bone, and create for myself a place of pride in the great world which I would lay before my consort's feet as a token of my love. I was a new man, and she alone, with the redeeming power of innocence, had brought about this transformation. I resolved that when next we met, I would ask her for her hand and, indeed, for her name, which I had neglected to elicit.

I was hoisted aboard the *Siddhartha*, cheered by the cream of Transylvanian society, and as I began my Scarlatti group, I glanced, as was my habit, toward the boxes; and there, seated on one marked "Depth Finder—Fragile—Handle with Care," I beheld———

YEHUDI MENUHIN

I don't know just how things were in New York City in 1916 when Yehudi Menuhin was born, but I do know—I had it from my grandmother, when I was growing up two decades later—that in the part of rural Canada where she lived all her life, it was considered no asset at all to be an artist. It was, in fact, a way of life from which all dutiful grandmothers warned their brood, not primarily through the simple, mercantile prejudice of what was still an essentially agrarian society—though come to that, a life spent before the bar or even behind the pulpit could promise an incomparably more secure existence than that to which the itinerant minstrel or privately published poet could look forward—but rather because of an idea common to most essentially puritan societies: that to be an artist was to put oneself needlessly in the way of damnation. For it meant, after all, that in addition to keeping company of the most lamentable sort, to seeking (or, at any rate, not refusing) that degree of idolatrous adulation which stands neighbor to blasphemy, one would inevitably be exposed to a plethora of dark and troubled thoughts and be compelled to deal with them in such quantity, to represent them with such facility, and to project them with such vitality that one would almost surely in the end be seduced by them.

From *Musical America*, December 1966.

Now, it has always seemed to me that this puritan view of the artist as a jeopardized being is not only dramatically viable but psychologically accurate. It is the stuff of Faustus, to be sure, but it is the substance of lesser bargains as well. Just as censorship, that ultimate weapon in the puritan missile system, flatters the power of words to infect and inflame in a way that the laissez-faire of the liberal literati never can, this view of the artist as wielder of demonic power, as a being whom ordinary mortals should approach with caution, implicitly conveys a respect for his role far beyond that egalitarian affection with which today's unionized troubadour—weeding the garden at the split-level by day, dispensing fugues and fantasies by night—is casually welcomed within the fold of the community.

But puritan societies were, above all, pragmatic social structures constantly exercised by the need to define their own highest purposes. And for this, they required not just opponents but leaders and, upon occasion, even artists, not as antagonists but as spokesmen. And one of the fascinating things about the puritan tradition was the way in which a rather unique bargain was sometimes struck—an uneasy entente between artist and townsmen. This allowed that, given exceptional circumstances, impeccable character, and always assuming that vigilant attention which alone holds the forces of darkness at bay, the rarest of artists might indeed be capable of a spiritual transfiguration such as could be counted larger than life and attributed directly to the transcendence of his art. This, of course, was the view of art as an instrument of salvation, of the artist as missionary advocate.

It was a notion to which my grandmother wholeheartedly subscribed. If I mistake not, it was embodied for her in an artist such as Paderewski, whose concerts she boasted of having traveled many miles to attend. Even more surely, it revealed itself to her through the manuscripts of those indefatigable anthem composers of the English Victorian tradition, whose works she kept stacked on the console of her reed organ, and to the greater glories of whose Mendelssohnian euphony she would pump furiously at the bellows pedals, convinced that with each scrupulous avoidance of parallel fifths the devil was given his comeuppance, and responding to the inevitable compression of a tonal answer at a cadential stretto as to an article of faith.

So far as I know, Grandmother never heard Yehudi Menuhin play. But I suspect that if she had, she would have found her definition of the artist as spokesman confirmed. She would have sensed the existence of that same unmistakable, if essentially extramusical, mystique.

I don't mean to suggest that Menuhin is in any sense the last of a Victorian breed, nor even that my nostalgic recollections of Grandmother's terminology are necessarily the most appropriate way to define his role. Because the first thing to be said of him is that he is an astonishingly au courant musician, as ready to discuss the latest breakthrough at Baden-Baden or the doldrums at Darmstadt as the possibility of an alternate bowing for the Bach Chaconne. Above all, an omnivorous curiosity seems to propel him—a curiosity in the midst of which he nonetheless never fails to exert his own most individual perceptions. He knows the exhilaration to be had from new ideas and the danger of being awash in them.

"Schoenberg," I once said to him, referring specifically to a passage in the Violin Fantasy, "must surely have been possessed by some stern, Old Testament morality."

"I've never understood," said he, "why minor seconds are so moral this century."

The frequency and gentle audacity of these insights make Menuhin well-nigh unique as a chamber music collaborator—an achievement to which his recordings of Bach, with the splendid harpsichordist George Malcolm, or of Beethoven, with his sister the admirable Hephzibah, bear witness. On the whole, his activity as a conductor has been notable heretofore where it has tended to extend the range of his chamber music sympathies—his recordings of the Bach suites with his own Bath Festival Orchestra are possessed of an ungainsayable conviction which often as not puts the echt-baroque renditions of more specialized ensembles quietly but firmly in the shade. And some of his own most notable realizations of the standard concerto repertoire have been in performances which he either conducted for, or had conducted by, his distinguished colleague David Oistrakh. But this year a sterner test will come, for Menuhin appears in New York this month for the first time as a conductor, leading the American Symphony Orchestra in a Purcell-to-Bartók program which, in addition to a brace of violin concertos, is to include the deceptively straightforward but logistically perilous Fourth Symphony by Robert Schumann. Next summer he returns here with his orchestra from Bath, which he will conduct in both Montreal's Expo '67 and Lincoln Center's Festival '67.

But it is, of course, from his activity as a solo artist that Menuhin's chief fame derives. And here, forsaking all his other diverse interests and promotions, from the recently founded shelter for insufferable prodigies outside London to his West End health-food shop, he devotes a major portion of each year (this, his fiftieth, qualifies notably as a semisabbatical) to checking the trap lines of the international concert circuit. It is a life of incessant travel. He detests flying but screws his courage to the luggage stickers anyway. Depressingly uniform hotel suites become less austerely antiseptic on those occasions when his wife, the incomparably irrepressible Diana, accompanies him and sets out a bureau top of family portraits at each day's wayside stop, as though to lend a sense of permanence to a pilgrimage where change rules all.

It is a life full of the challenges of new faces and new pieces, of dyspeptic conductors and ulcer-ridden managers, of promises to learn a new sonata by next Thursday (Menuhin is the sort of quick study who would give even Padre Martini pause) and then of the frantic search for time and place in which to practice. It is a life which—such is my distaste for the international concert establishment—ordinarily seems to me, and especially so in this day of electronic communication, futile and irrelevant.

And yet, by some alchemy which I plan never to understand, Menuhin is able to minimize its incalculable emotional demands, to ignore the petty sniping of thwarted colleagues, to defy the banal drudgery of its routine, to accept the adrenaline-sapping crises that in this life are routine as well, and surmount all with an equanimity of disposition and a generosity of spirit which are legendary. Not that he achieves this euphoric state unaided. To find him ensconced in his dressing room ten minutes prior to curtain time, only vaguely aware of the repertoire submitted for the evening's program and, while manipulating his fiddle through some quarter-tone exercises that would make Alois Hába nauseous, assuming the serene squat of a fakir newly matriculated from a school for cobra charmers with a high accident rating, is to realize something of the output required. Even I can dismiss my prejudice long enough to concede that this life, with the constancy of its anxiety, the certainty of its frustration, provides an unimprovable mise-en-scène in which the sacrificial aspects of the artist-spokesman's role can be projected. Indeed, it is as if in the contact of the concert Menuhin were searching for the most common denominator of a most uncommon tie.

Menuhin, more conspicuously perhaps than any other performing musician of his generation, is surfeited with an almost universal regard. He is the recipient of a collection of medallions which would force a pawnbroker to expand to the suburbs: the Légion d'Honneur, Ordre de la Couronne, innumerable doctorates, and, just last year, Knight Commander of the British Empire (and that, mark you, for a citizen of the United States).

His is a household name to Americans ("So help me, Theodore, get back to your practicing or you'll never be a Mischa Menuhin!"). In the United Kingdom, he is the protean patron saint of self-effacing soloists and interchangeable chamber players ("I say, Cecilia, my dear, I see by the *Times* that Mr. Menuhin is sitting in with the Amadeus this evening. Does seem a bit odd; string quintets at the Royal Albert?"). He has been rescued by wandering tribesmen in the Sahara who, having helped to dislodge his auto from drifts which had blown free since last they felt the tread of Rommel's Afrika Korps, suddenly exploded with incredulity, "C'est Menuhin, c'est lui!" And if, as I hope, and as I have urged him to, he someday visits the outpost communities of Arctic Canada, I have no doubt that he will return with a trunkful of ethnographic tabulations, the sketch for an improved system of Eskimo shorthand, and the manuscript of a lecture detailing the nutritional deficiencies of the barren-ground caribou.

With the people of India, Menuhin has enjoyed a very special spiritual contact. A tireless propagandist for the culture of the subcontinent, friend and confidant of the late Jawaharlal Nehru, Menuhin is received in that country with a frankness and understanding which make the term "nonaligned nation" seem an irrelevance. A few years ago a visitor from America, waiting upon a Madras sage in the latter's modest quarters, noted as he glanced to the far wall of the room a Krishna with a light burning below, and beside it a photo, also lighted. When the sage entered the room, the visitor asked whether he might perhaps be mistaken in thinking it the portrait of a celebrated musician, to which came the reply: "Indeed, it is Menuhin. That is the way we look upon him in this country."

Humanists, I suppose, respond to Menuhin's disinterest in doctrinaire persuasions, his preference for dealing in aesthetic rather than moral judgments. Puritans approve his endless capacity for work, his clearly focused sense of mission. But such definitions are, in the end, merely matters of taste or points of privilege. For many of us, Yehudi Menuhin, artist extraordinaire, human being nonpareil, seems one of those rare individuals who could in time succeed to that unique place in the affections of mankind left vacant by the death of Albert Schweitzer.

Grandmother, I feel confident, would concur.

THE SEARCH FOR PETULA CLARK

Across the province of Ontario, which I call home, Queen's Highway No. 17 plies for some 1,100 miles through the pre-Cambrian rock of the Canadian Shield. With its east-west course deflected, where it climbs the northeast shore of Lake Superior, it appears in cartographic profile like one of those prehistoric airborne monsters which Hollywood promoted to star status in such late-late-show spine tinglers of the 1950s as *Blood Beast from Outer Space* or *Beak from the Beyond,* and to which the fuselage design of the XB15 paid the tribute of science borrowing from art.

Though its tail feathers tickle the urban outcroppings of Montreal and its beak pecks at the fertile prairie granary of Manitoba, No. 17 defines for

From *High Fidelity,* November 1967.

much of its passage across Ontario the northernmost limit of agrarian settlement. It is endowed with habitation, when at all, by fishing villages, mining camps, and timber towns that straddle the highway every fifty miles or so. Among these, names such as Michipicoten and Batchawana advertise the continuing segregation of the Canadian Indian; Rossport and Jackfish proclaim the no-nonsense mapmaking of the early white settlers; and Marathon and Terrace Bay—"Gem of the North Shore"—betray the postwar influx of American capital. (Terrace is the Brasilia of Kimberley-Clark's Kleenex-Kotex operation in Ontario.)

The layout of these latter towns, set amidst the most beguiling landscape in central North America, rigorously subscribes to that concept of northern town planning which might be defined as 1984 Prefab and, to my mind, provides the source of so compelling an allegory of the human condition as might well have found its way into the fantasy prose of the late Karel Capek.

Marathon, a timber town of some twenty-six hundred souls, clings to the banks of a fjord which indents the coast of Lake Superior. Due to a minor miscalculation by one of the company's engineers as to the probable course of the prevailing winds, the place has been overhung since its inception two decades ago with a pulp-and-paper stench that serves to proclaim the monolithic nature of the town's economy even as it discourages any supplemental income from the tourist trade. Real estate values, consequently, are relative to one's distance from the plant. At the boardwalk level, the company has located a barracks for unmarried and/or itinerant workers; up a block, hotel, cinema, chapel, and general store; at the next plateau, an assortment of prefabs; beyond them, at a further elevation, some split-levels for the junior execs; and, finally, with one more gentle ascent and a hard right turn, a block of paternalistic brick mansions which would be right at home among the more exclusive suburbs of Westchester County, New York. Surely the upward mobility of North American society can scarcely ever have been more persuasively demonstrated. "Gives a man something to shoot at," I was assured by one local luminary, whose political persuasion, it developed, was somewhere to the right of Prince Metternich.

A few hundred yards beyond Presidential Row, a bulldozed trail leads to the smog-free top of the fjord. But from this approach, one is held at bay by a padlocked gate bearing a sign from which, in the manner of those reassuring marquees once used to decorate the boarding ramps of Pan American Airways, one learns that "your company has now had one hundred and sixty-five accident-free work days" and that access to the top is prohibited. Up there, on that crest beyond the stench, one can see the two indispensable features of any thriving timber town—its log-shoot breaking bush back through that trackless terrain and an antenna for the low-power relay system of the Canadian Broadcasting Corporation.

These relay outlets, with their radius of three or four miles, serve only the immediate area of each community. As one drives along No. 17, encountering them every hour or so, they constitute the surest evidence that the "outside" (as we northerners like to call it) is with us still. In the outpost communities, the CBC's culture pitch (Boulez is very big in Batchawana) is supplemented by local programming which, in the imaginative traditions of commercial radio everywhere, leans toward a formula of news on the hour and fifty-five minutes of the pop picks from *Billboard* magazine. This happy ambivalence made my last trip along "17" noteworthy, for at that time, climbing fast on all the charts and featured hard upon the hour by most deejays was an item called "Who Am I?" The singer was Petula Clark; the composer and conductor, Tony Hatch.

I contrived to match my driving speed to the distance between relay outlets, came to hear it most hours and in the end to know it, if not better than the soloist, at least as well, perhaps, as most of the sidemen who were booked for the date. After several hundred miles of this exposure, I checked into the hotel at Marathon and made plans to contemplate Petula.

"Who Am I?" was the fourth in a remarkable series of songs which established the American career of Petula Clark. Released in 1966 and preceded the year before by "Sign of the Times" and "My Love," it laid to rest any uncharitable notion that her success with the ubiquitous "Downtown" of 1964 was a fluke. Moreover, this quartet of hits was designed to convey the idea that, bound as she might be by limitations of timbre and range, she would not accept any corresponding restrictions of theme and sentiment. Each of the four songs details an adjacent plateau of experience—the twenty-three months separating the release dates of "Downtown" and "Who Am I?" being but a modest acceleration of the American teen-ager's precipitous scramble from the parental nest.

And Pet Clark is in many ways the compleat synthesis of this experience. At thirty-four, with two children, with three distinct careers (in the forties she was the British cinema's anticipation of Annette Funicello, and a decade later a subdued chanteuse in Paris niteries), and with a voice, figure, and (at a respectable distance) face that betray few of the ravages of this experiential sequence, she is pop music's most persuasive embodiment of the Gidget syndrome. Her audience is large, constant, and possessed of an enthusiasm which transcends the generations. One recent visitor from the Netherlands, a gentleman in his sixties who had previously assured me that American pop trends were the corrupting inspiration behind last summer's "Provo" riots in that country, became impaled upon his grandchildren's enthusiasm for "My Love." He said it called to mind the spirit of congregational singing in the Dutch Reform church and asked to hear it once again.

Petula minimizes the emotional metamorphosis implicit in these songs, extracting from the text of each the same message of detachment and sexual circumspection. "Downtown," that intoxicated adolescent daydream—

> Things will be great when you're Downtown,
> Don't wait a minute, for Downtown,
> Everything's waiting for you.

is as she tells it, but a step from "My Love," that vigorous essay in self-advertisement—

> My love is warmer than the warmest sunshine,
>   Softer than a sigh;
> My love is deeper than the deepest ocean,
>   Wider than the sky.

and from the reconciliatory concession of "Sign of the Times"—

> I'll never understand the way you treated me,
> But when I hold your hand, I know you couldn't be
>   the way you used to be.

The sequence of events implicit in these songs is sufficiently ambiguous as to allow the audience dipping-in privileges. It's entirely possible to start with "Who Am I?" as I did, and sample "Downtown" later at one's leisure. But a well-ordered career in pop music should be conceived like the dramatis personae of soap opera—dipping in to "The Secret Storm" once every semester should tell you all you really need to know about how things are working out for Amy Ames. And similarly, the title, tempo, and tonal range of a performer's hits should observe a certain bibliographic progression. (You thought Frankie had other reasons for "It's been a very good year"?) I'm inclined to suspect that had the sequence of her songs been reversed, Petula's American reputation might not have gained momentum quite so easily. There's an inevitability about that quartet with its relentless on-pressing to the experiences of adulthood or reasonable facsimile thereof. To a teen-age audience whose social-sexual awareness dovetailed with their release dates, Petula in her well-turned-out Gidgetry would provide gratifying reassurance of postadolescent survival.

To her more mature public, she's a comfort of another kind. Everything about her onstage, on-mike manner belies the aggressive proclamations of the lyrics. Face, figure, discreet gyrations, but, above all, that voice, fiercely loyal to its one great octave, indulging none but the most circumspect slides and filigree, vibrato so tight and fast as to be nonexistent—none of that "here comes the fermata so hold on" tremolando with which her nibs Georgia

Gibbs grated like squeaky chalk upon the exposed nerves of my genera-tion—Petula panders to the wishful thinking of the older set that, style be hanged, modesty prevails. ("Leave the child be, Maw, it's just a touch of prickly heat.")

The gap between the demonstrative attitude of the lyrics and the re-straint with which Petula ministers to their delivery is symptomatic of a more fundamental dichotomy. Each of the songs contrived for her by Tony Hatch emphasizes some aspect of that discrepancy between an adolescent's short-term need to rebel and long-range readiness to conform. In each the score pointedly contradicts that broad streak of self-indulgence which per-meates the lyrics. The harmonic attitude is, at all times, hymnal, upright, and relentlessly diatonic.

Well, come to that, almost all pop music today *is* relentlessly diaton-ic—the Max Reger–Vincent d'Indy chromatic bent which infiltrated big-band arranging in the late thirties and the forties ran its course when Ralph Flanagan got augmented sixths out of his system. But Tony Hatch's diatonicism, relative to Messrs. Lennon, McCartney, et al., is possessed of more than just a difference in kind. For the Beatles, a neotriadic persuasion is (was?) a guerrilla tactic—an instrument of revolution. Annexing such vox populi conventions of English folk harmony as the "Greensleeves" -type nonchalance of old Vaughan Williams's lethargic parallel fifths, the new minstrels turned this lovably bumbling plainspeech into a dispa-raging mimicry of upper-class inflection. They went about sabotaging the seats of tonal power and piety with the same opportunism that, in *Room at the Top,* motivated Laurence Harvey in his seduction of Sir Donald Wolfit'sdaughter.

Tonally, the Beatles have as little regard for the niceties of voice leading as Erik Satie for the anguished cross-relation of the German postromantics. Theirs is a happy, cocky, belligerently resourceless brand of harmonic primi-tivism. Their career has been one long send-up of the equation: sophistication = chromatic extension. The willful, dominant prolongations and false tonic releases to which they subject us, "Michelle" notwithstanding, in the name of foreground elaboration, are merely symptomatic of a cavalier disinclina-tion to observe the psychological properties of tonal background. In the Liv-erpudlian repertoire, the indulgent amateurishness of the musical material, though closely rivaled by the indifference of the performing style, is actually surpassed only by the ineptitude of the studio production method. ("Straw-berry Fields" suggests a chance encounter at a mountain wedding between Claudio Monteverdi and a jug band.)

And yet, for a portion of the musical elite, the Beatles are, for this year at least, incomparably "in." After all, if you make use of sitars, white noise, and Cathy Berberian, you must have something, right? Wrong! The real attraction, concealed by virtue of that same adroit self-deception with which coffeehouse intellectuals talked themselves into Charlie Parker in the forties and Lennie Tristano in the fifties, is the need for the common triad as purgative. After all, the central nervous system can accommodate only so many pages of persistent pianissimos, chord clusters in the marge, and tritones on the vibes. Sooner or later, the diet palls and the patient cries out for a cool draught of C major.

In filling this need, however, the Beatles are entirely incidental. They get the nod at the moment simply through that amateurishness which makes the whole phenomenon of *their* C major seem credible as an accident of overtone displacement, and through that avant-garde article of faith that nothing is more despicable than a professional triad tester. The Beatles' "in" versus Petula's relative "out" can be diagnosed on the same terms and as part of that same syndrome of status quest that renders Tristano's *G minor Complex* arcane, Poulenc's Organ Concerto in the same key banal, the poetry of the Iglulik Eskimos absorbing, Sibelius's *Tapiola* tedious, and that drives those who feel diffident to buy Bentleys.

But for Tony Hatch, tonality is not a worked-out lode. It is a viable and continuing source of productive energy with priorities that demand and get, from him, attention. "Downtown" is the most affirmatively diatonic exhortation in the key of E major since the unlikely team of Felix Mendelssohn and Harriet Beecher Stowe pooled talents for

> Still, still, with Thee, when purple morning
>   breaketh,
> When the bird waketh and the shadows flee. . . .

"Sign of the Times," on the other hand, admits one fairly sophisticated altercation between the tonic with its dominant, and the minor-mediant relation, similarly embroidered, which twice underlines the idea that "Perhaps my lucky star is now beginning to shine"—the harmonic overlay suggests that there is still sufficient alto-stratus cloud cover to hamper visibility. "My Love," though, remains firmly persuaded of its nonmodulating course. Throughout its two minutes and forty-five seconds, the only extradiatonic event which disturbs proceedings is the near-inevitable hookup to the flattened supertonic for a final chorus—two neighborly dominants being the pivots involved. Indeed, only one secondary dominant, which happens to coincide with the line "It shows how wrong we all can be," compromises the virginal propriety of its responsibly confirming Fuxian basses, and none of those stray, flattened leading-tones-as-root implies a moment's lack of resolution. It's all of a piece, a proud, secure Methodist tract—preordained, devoid of doubt, admitting of no compromise. And as legions of Petulas gyrate, ensnared within its righteous euphony, galleries of oval-framed ancestors peer down upon that deft deflation of the lyrics, and approve.

After the prevailing euphoria of the three songs which preceded it, "Who Am I?" reads like a document of despair. It catalogues those symptoms of disenchantment and ennui which inevitably scuttle a trajectory of emotional escalation such as bound that trilogy together. The singer's "Downtown"-based confidence in the therapeutic effect of "noise," "hurry," and "bright lights" has been shattered. Those alluring asphalt canyons, which promised "an escape from that life which is making you lonely," have exacted a high price for their gift of anonymity. For though she has now found a place where "buildings reach up to the sky," where "traffic thunders on the busy street," where "pavement slips beneath my feet," she continues to "walk alone and wonder, Who Am I?"

Clearly, it's a question of identity crisis, vertiginous and claustrophobic, induced through the traumatic experience of a metropolitan environment and, quite possibly, aggravated by sore feet. There is, of course, the inevitable apotheosis, complete with falsetto C, in behalf of the restorative therapy of amour. ("But I have something else entirely free, the love of someone close to me, and to question such good fortune, Who Am I?") Yet the prevailing dysphoria of that existentially questing title is not to be routed by so conventional and halfhearted an appendage.

Motivically, "Who Am I?" plays a similar game of reverse "Downtown"-ism. The principal motivic cell unit of that ebullient lied consisted of the interval of a minor third plus a major second, alternating, upon occasion, with a major third followed by a minor second. In "Downtown," the composite of either of these figures, the perfect fourth, became the title motive and the figures themselves were elongated by reiterated notes ("When/you're/a/lone/and/life/is"), shuffled by commas ("downtown, where") ("to help, I") (["Pret]-ty, how can"), and constantly elaborated by the sort of free-diatonic transpositioning which seems entirely consistent with the improvisatory fantasies of youth.

In "Who Am I?," however, the same motive, though introduced and occasionally relieved by scale-step passages ("The build-ings-reach-up-to-the-sky") is most often locked into a diatonic spiral—the notes F-E-C and C-A-G serving to underline "I walk alone and wonder, Who Am I?" Furthermore, the bass line at this moment is engaged with the notes D-G-E and G-E-A, a vertical synchronization of which would imply a harmonic composite of the title motive. Now, admittedly, such Schoenbergian jargon must be charily applied to the carefree creations of the pop scene. At all costs, one must avoid those more formidable precepts of Princetonian Babbittry such as "pitch class," which, since they have not yet forded the Hudson unchallenged, can scarcely be expected to have plied the Atlantic and to have taken

Walthamstow studio without a fight. Nevertheless, "Downtown" and "Who Am I?" clearly represent two sides of the same much-minted coin. The infectious enthusiasm of the "Downtown" motive encounters its obverse in the somnambulistic systematization of the "Who Am I?" symbol, a unit perfectly adapted to the tenor of mindless confidence and the tone of slurred articulation with which Petula evokes the interminable mid-morning coffee-hour laments of all the secret sippers of suburbia.

Strictly speaking, the idea of suburbia is meaningless within the context of Marathon. From waterfront to Presidential Row is but five blocks, and beyond that elevation one can pick out only two symbols of urban periphery: the Peninsula Golf and Country Club (NO TRESPASSING—KEEP OFF THE GRASS—BEWARE THE DOG) and, as summer alternative, a small pond cared for by a local service club in lieu of the fjord, which was long ago rendered unfit for swimming. Both are well within range of the transmitter, though its power rapidly declines as one passes beyond the country club toward the highway, and consequently, whether via transistor or foyer PA, one remains exposed to the same single-channel news and music menu.

The problem for citizens of Marathon is that, however tacitly, a preoccupation with escalation and a concern with subsequent decline effectively cancel each other out. And the result, despite the conscientious stratification of the town, is a curiously compromised emotional unilaterality.

There are, of course, other ways to plan a town. Terrace Bay was designed two years after Marathon and apparently profited by the miscalculations which plagued its eastern neighbor. Wind direction (predominantly nor'westerly) was carefully plotted and the plant accordingly located to the north and east of the settlement. The town was designed around a shopping plaza and set on level ground two hundred feet above Lake Superior. The executives were encouraged to locate like den mothers, one to each prefab block. "Coddling the men don't work," Prince Metternich assured me. "Just robs them of incentive!" I resolved to have a look and set off at dusk for The Gem of the North Shore.

No. 17, patrolled at night, affords a remarkable auditory experience. The height of land in northern Ontario, a modest two thousand feet, is attained immediately north of Lake Superior. From beyond that point all water flows toward Hudson's Bay and, ultimately, the Arctic Sea. Traversing that promontory, after sundown, one discovers an astounding clarity of AM reception. All the accents of the continent are spread across the band, and, as one twiddles the dial to reap the diversity of that encounter, the day's auditory impressions with their hypnotic insularity recede, then re-emerge as part of a balanced and resilient perspective. . . .

This is London calling in the North American service of the BBC. Here is the news read by ——. And it's forty-six chilly degrees in Grand Bend. Say there, Dad, if it's time for that second car you've been promising the little woman, how's about checking the bargains down at ——? Et maintenant, la symphonie numéro quarante-deux, Kochel sept-cent-vingt de Mozart, jouée par——. Okay, chicka-dees, here's the one you've been asking for and tonight it's specially dedicated to Paul from Doris, to Marianne from a secret admirer, and to all the men in special detention detail out at the Institute from Big Bertha and the gals of H.M.S. Vaga-bond, *riding at anchor just a cozy quarter-mile beyond the international limit—Pet Clark with that question we've all been asking . . . "I walk alone and wonder, Who Am I?"*

STREISAND AS SCHWARZKOPF

I'm a Streisand freak and make no bones about it. With the possible exception of Elisabeth Schwarzkopf, no vocalist has brought me greater pleasure or more insight into the interpreter's art.

Fourteen years ago, an acetate of her first disc, "The Barbra Streisand Album," was being smuggled from cubicle to cubicle at CBS; I caught a pre-view, and laughed. Not at it, certainly—her eager mentor, Martin Erlich-man, was simultaneously doing his own number in an adjacent office, and it wouldn't have been good corporate policy in any case. And not always with it, either—though it was obvious even then that parody would play a vital role in Streisand's work. What happened, rather, was that I broke into a sort of Cheshire-cat grin that seems to strike its own bargain with my facial muscles, deigning to exercise them only when confronted with unique exam-ples of the rite of re-creation.

Sometimes this curious tic is caught off guard by novelty (Walter Car-los's Moog meditations on the Third and Fourth Brandenburgs, for example, or the Swingle Singers scat-scanning of the ninth fugue from *The Art of*). Sometimes it cracks up over repertoire for which I have no real affection. (I always felt that I could live without the Chopin concertos, and managed to—until Alexis Weissenberg dusted the cobwebs from Mme Sand's salon and made those works a contemporary experience.). Sometimes, inappropri-

Review of Barbra Streisand's "Classical Barbra" (Columbia M 33452, 1976); from *High Fidelity*, May 1976.

ately perhaps, it surfaces in the presence of a work for which poker-faced solemnity is considered de rigueur. (Hermann Scherchen's boogie-beat *Messiah* was, for me, one of the great revelations of the early LP era.) Sometimes it conveys my relief upon discovering that a puzzle I had thought insoluble has fallen into place. (Strauss's *Metamorphosen,* for example, is a work I have loved, on paper, as a concept, for nearly thirty years but which I had long since written off as a vehicle for twenty-three wayward strings in search of a six-four chord. All that changed a couple of years ago when I first heard Karajan's magisterial recording. For weeks, night after night, on occasion two or three times per—I'm not exaggerating—I played that disc, passed through the eyes-uplifted-in-wonder stage, went well beyond the catch-in-throat-and-tingle-on-the-spinal-cord phase, and, at last, stood on the threshold of . . . laughter.) I have the same reaction to practically everything conducted by Willem Mengelberg or Leopold Stokowski, and always—well, almost always—to Barbra Streisand.

For me, the Streisand voice is one of the natural wonders of the age, an instrument of infinite diversity and timbral resource. It is not, to be sure, devoid of problem areas—which is an observation at least as perspicacious as the comment that a harpsichord is not a piano or, if you insist, vice versa. Streisand always has had problems with the upper third of the stave—breaking the C-sharp barrier in low gear is chief among them—but space does not permit us to count the ways in which, with ever-increasing ingenuity, she has turned this impediment to advantage. I cannot, however, let the occasion pass without mention of a moment of special glory—the "Nothing, nothing, nothing" motive, securely focused on D-flat and C-natural, from the final seconds of that Puccini-like blockbuster "He Touched Me."

In truth, though, one does not look to Streisand, as one does to Ella Fitzgerald or, as some will have it—I'm not sure that I will, but that's another story—Cleo Laine, for vocal pyrotechnics. The lady can sing up a storm upon demand, but she is not a ballad belter in the straightforward "this is a performance" manner of the admirable Shirley Bassey. With Streisand, who relates to Bassey as Daniel Barenboim to Lorin Maazel, one becomes engaged by process, by a seemingly limitless array of available options. Hers is indeed a manner of much greater intimacy, but an intimacy that (astonishingly, for this repertoire) is never overtly in search of sexual contact. Streisand is consumed by nostalgia; she can make of the torchiest lyric an intimate memoir, and it would never occur to her to employ the "I'll meet you precisely 51 percent of the way" piquancy of, say, Helen Reddy, much less the "I won't bother to speak up 'cause you're already spellbound, aren't you?" routine of Peggy Lee.

My private fantasy about Streisand (about Schwarzkopf, too, for that matter) is that all her greatest cuts result from dressing-room runthroughs in which (presumably to the accompaniment of a prerecorded orchestral mix) Streisand puts on one persona after another, tries out probable throwaway lines, mugs accompanying gestures to her own reflection, samples registrational couplings (super the street-urchin four-foot pipe on the sophisticated-lady sixteen-foot), and, in general, performs for her own amusement in a world of Borgean mirrors (Jorge Luis, not Victor) and word invention.

Like Schwarzkopf, Streisand is one of the great italicizers; no phrase is left solely to its own devices, and the range and diversity of her expressive gift is such that one is simply unable to chart an a priori stylistic course on her behalf. Much of the *Affekt* of intimacy—indeed, the sensation of eavesdropping on a private moment not yet wholly committed to its eventual public profile—is a direct result of our inability to anticipate her intentions. As but one example, Streisand can take a lightweight Satie satire like Dave Grusin's "A Child Is Born," find in it two descending scales (Hypodorian and Lydian, respectively), and wring from that routine cross-relation a moment of heartbreakingly beautiful intensity. Improbable as the comparison may seem, it is, I think, close kin to Schwarzkopf's unforgettable musings upon the closing soliloquy from Strauss's *Capriccio,* and in my opinion the bulk of Streisand's output richly deserves the compliment implied.

Unfortunately, the present disc is one of those "almost always" exceptions. Another that comes to mind is the irritating sing-in for the Now—or, rather, Then—Generation, "What About Today?," produced in 1969. Unlike that latter package, however, "Classical Barbra" is obviously not intended to placate the zeitgeist. Other than as a curio, it can hardly be expected to attract musicology majors; its tight, pop-style pickup (personally, I adore it!) will almost certainly alienate the art song set; and its contents overall will quite probably turn off the casual MOR shopper to boot.

So a measure of courage is involved here; Streisand has obviously risked a good deal in order to cater to the boundless curiosity of her hardcore fans, and, if only out of gratitude, we should make clear that, if this is not really a good album, it is certainly not a bad one, either. It is considerate to a fault of the presumed prerequisites of the repertoire it surveys and, as such, to take the most obvious comparative route, puts to shame the ill-considered renditions of Broadway showstoppers offered by such talk-show groupies from the classical field as Beverly Sills, Roberta Peters, or, occasionally, Maureen Forrester. (One should probably exempt Eileen Farrell, who really did "have a right to sing the blues.")

But it's the presumption of those prerequisites that causes problems. Nothing in this album is insensitive or unmusical—unless it's the gratuitous reverb slopped into the Handel orchestral tracks, which reaches a peak of stylistic defiance at the end of both excerpts, where an engineer's quick pull on the pot only makes us more aware of its excremental presence. Throughout, though, Streisand appears awed by the realization that she is now face to face with The Masters. The entire album is served up at a reverential range of mezzo-piano to mezzo-forte, and none of the cuts could be described as "uptempo." Notwithstanding the fact that the lady is the most adroit patter-song purveyor of our time ("Piano Practice," "Minute Waltz"), this predilection for an unvaried sequence of andante-grazioso intermezzi is not unique to this disc. It turned up as early in her career as "The Third Barbra Streisand Album" but was not then allied, as in the present instance, to an austere dynamic compression.

It is also virtually a one-stop performance; Streisand pulls out her choir-boy-innocent eight-foot and settles in for the duration. This is, to be sure, one of her most effective registrations, and when mated with appropriate repertoire it produces spellbinding results. For Orff's "In Trutina," Streisand, using the fastest vibrato in the West and the most impeccable intonation this side of Maria Stader's prime, provides a reading second to none in terms of vocal security while stripping this rather vapid air of its customary theatrical accoutrements. More to the point, perhaps, she turns in the only current version possessed of exactly the right Book of Hours–like accommodation to the text.

In the Berceuse from Canteloube's *Songs of the Auvergne* Streisand cannot match the suave production of de los Angeles, but on its own folklike terms her performance is quite extraordinarily touching. She does well with Debussy, too, and if Eileen Farrell, who also opened a Columbia collection with "Beau Soir," stakes out her territory as a sophisticated Parisienne, Streisand replies, not ineffectively, as a Marseillian gamine.

It's in the German repertoire that Streisand runs aground. In Schumann's "Mondnacht" she keeps a maddening cool during the final stanza, plodding relentlessly through "Und meine Seele spannte, weit ihre Flügel aus." In Wolf's "Verschwiegene Liebe," she simply sets aside her unique powers of characterization, keeping no secrets and wearing no veils.

About the most that can be said of her "Lascia ch'io pianga" from *Rinaldo* is that it is a model of analytic clarity when set beside the glissando-ridden 1906 production of Mme Ernestine Schumann-Heink. Streisand delivers it according to the approved Royal Academy (1939) method—glissandos were out by then, but ornaments had not yet been invented. (Ironically, it is left to Alfred Deller's superb collaborator Eileen Poulter to turn in the definitively Streisandesque version of this air.)

I do not, however, want to leave the impression that Streisand should give up on "the classics." Indeed, I'm convinced that she has a great "classical" album in her. She simply needs to rethink the question of repertoire and to dispense with the yoke of respectability which burdens the present production.

My own prescription for a Streisand dream album would include Tudor lute songs (she'd be sensational in Dowland), Mussorgsky's *Sunless* cycle, and, as pièce de résistance—providing she'll pick up a handbook or two on baroque ornamentation—Bach's Cantata No. 54. To date, in my experience, the most committed performance of this glorious piece was on a CBC television show in 1962. It featured the remarkable countertenor Russell Oberlin and a squad of strings from the Toronto Symphony. It also involved a harpsichordist/conductor of surpassing modesty, who has requested anonymity; I am, however, assured by his agent that if Ms. Streisand would like to take a crack at "Widerstehe doch der Sünde," and if Columbia would like to take a hint, he's available.

INTERLUDE

*Glenn Gould Interviews
Glenn Gould
About Glenn Gould*

glenn gould: Mr. Gould, I gather that you have a reputation as a—well, forgive me for being blunt, sir—but as a tough nut to crack, interview-wise?

GLENN GOULD: Really. I've never heard that.

g.g.: Well, it's the sort of scuttlebutt that we media types pick up from source to source, but I just want to assure you that I'm quite prepared to strike from the record any question you may feel is out of line.

G.G.: Oh, I can't conceive of any problems of that sort intruding upon our deliberations.

g.g.: Well then, just to clear the air, sir, let me ask straight out: Are there any off-limit areas?

G.G.: I certainly can't think of any—apart from music, of course.

g.g: Mr. Gould, I don't want to go back on my word. I realize that your participation in this interview was never contractually confirmed, but it was sealed with a handshake.

G.G.: Figuratively speaking, of course.

g.g.: Of course. And I had rather assumed that we'd spend the bulk of this interview on musically related matters.

G.G.: Do you think it's essential? I mean, my personal philosophy of interviewing—and I've done quite a bit of it on the air, as you perhaps know—is that the most illuminating disclosures derive from areas only indirectly related to the interviewee's line of work.

g.g.: For example?

G.G.: Well, for example, in the course of preparing radio documentaries, I've interviewed a theologian about technology, a surveyor about William James, an economist about pacifism, and a housewife about acquisitiveness in the art market.

g.g.: But surely you've also interviewed musicians about music?

G.G.: Yes, I have, on occasion, in order to help put them at ease in front of the mike. But it's been far more instructive to talk with Pablo Casals, for example, about the concept of the zeitgeist, which, of course, is not unrelated to music—

g.g.: Yes, I was just going to venture that comment.

G.G.:—or to Leopold Stokowski about the prospect for interplanetary travel,

From *High Fidelity*, February 1974.

which is—I think you'll agree, and Stanley Kubrick notwithstanding—a bit of a digression.

g.g.: This does pose a problem, Mr. Gould, but let me try to frame the question more affirmatively. Is there a subject you'd particularly like to discuss?

G.G.: I hadn't given it much thought, really—but, just off the top, what about
the political situation in Labrador?

g.g.: I'm sure that could produce a stimulating dialogue, Mr. Gould, but I
do feel that we have to keep in mind that *High Fidelity* is edited primarily for a U.S. constituency.

G.G.: Oh, quite. Well, in that case, perhaps aboriginal rights in western Alaska
would make good copy.

g.g.: Yes. Well, I certainly don't want to bypass any headline-grabbing areas
of that sort, Mr. Gould, but since *High Fidelity* is oriented toward a
musically literate readership, we should, I think, at least begin our discussion in the area of the arts.

G.G.: Oh, certainly. Perhaps we could examine the question of aboriginal
rights as reflected in ethnomusicological field studies at Point Barrow.

g.g.: I must confess I had a rather more conventional line of attack, so to
speak, in mind, Mr. Gould. As I'm sure you're aware, the virtually
obligatory question in regard to your career is the concert-versus-media
controversy, and I do feel we must at least touch upon it.

G.G.: I have no objections to fielding a few questions in that area. As far as
I'm concerned, it primarily involves moral rather than musical considerations in any case, so be my guest.

g.g.: That's very good of you. I'll try to make it brief, and then, perhaps,
we can move further afield.

G.G.: Fair enough!

g.g.: Well now, you've been quoted as saying that your involvement with
recording—with media in general, indeed—represents an involvement
with the future.

G.G.: That's correct. I've even said so in the pages of this illustrious journal,
as a matter of fact.

g.g.: Quite so, and you've also said that, conversely, the concert hall, the recital stage, the opera house, or whatever, represent the past—an aspect
of your own past in particular, perhaps, as well as, in more general
terms, music's past.

G.G.: That's true, although I must admit that my only past professional contact with opera was a touch of tracheitis I picked up while playing the
old Festspielhaus in Salzburg. As you know, it was an exceedingly
drafty edifice, and I—

g.g.: Perhaps we could discuss your state of health at a more opportune moment, Mr. Gould, but it does occur to me—and I hope you'll forgive me for saying so—that there is something inherently self-serving about pronouncements of this kind. After all, you elected to abandon all public platforms some—what was it?—ten years ago?

g.g.: Nine years and eleven months as of the date of this issue, actually.

g.g.: And you will admit that most people who opt for radical career departures of any sort sustain themselves with the notion that, however reluctantly, the future is on their side?

g.g.: It's encouraging to think so, of course, but I must take exception to your use of the term "radical." It's certainly true that I did take the plunge out of a conviction that given the state of the art, a total immersion in media represented a logical development—and I remain so convinced. But, quite frankly, however much one likes to formulate past-future equations, the prime sponsors of such convictions, the strongest motivations behind such "departures," to borrow your term, are usually related to no more radical notion than an attempt to resolve the discomfort and inconvenience of the present.

g.g.: I'm not sure I've caught the drift of that, Mr. Gould.

g.g.: Well, for instance, let me suggest to you that the strongest motivation for the invention of a lozenge would be a sore throat. Of course, having patented the lozenge, one would then be free to speculate that the invention represented the future and the sore throat the past, but I doubt that one would be inclined to think in those terms while the irritation was present. Needless to say, in the case of my tracheitis at Salzburg, medication of that sort was—

g.g.: Excuse me, Mr. Gould, I'm sure we will be apprised of your Salzburg misadventures in due course, but I must pursue this point a bit further. Am I to understand that your withdrawal from the concert stage, your subsequent involvement with media, was motivated by the musical equivalent of a—of a sore throat?

g.g.: Do you find that objectionable?

g.g.: Well, to be candid, I find it utterly narcissistic. And to my mind, it's also entirely at odds with your statement that moral objections played a major role in your decision.

g.g.: I don't see the contradiction there—unless, of course, in your view discomfort per se ranks as a positive virtue.

g.g.: My views are not the subject of this interview, Mr. Gould, but I'll answer your question, regardless. Discomfort per se is not the issue; I simply believe that any artist worthy of the name must be prepared to sacrifice personal comfort.

g.g.: To what end?

g.g.: In the interests of preserving the great traditions of the musical-theatrical experience, of maintaining the noble tutorial and curatorial responsibilities of the artist in relation to his audience.

G.G.: You don't feel that a sense of discomfort, of unease, could be the sagest of counselors for both artist and audience?

g.g.: No, I simply feel that you, Mr. Gould, have either never permitted yourself to savor the—

G.G.: —ego gratification?

g.g.: —the privilege, as I was about to say, of communicating with an audience—

G.G.: —from a power-base?

g.g.: —from a proscenium setting in which the naked fact of your humanity is on display, unedited and unadorned.

G.G.: Couldn't I at least be allowed to display the tuxedoed fallacy, perhaps?

g.g.: Mr. Gould, I don't feel we should allow this dialogue to degenerate into idle banter. It's obvious that you've never savored the joys of a one-to-one relationship with a listener.

G.G.: I always thought that, managerially speaking, a twenty-eight-hundred-to-one relationship was the concert-hall ideal.

g.g.: I don't want to split statistics with you. I've tried to pose the question with all candor, and—

G.G.: Well then, I'll try to answer likewise. It seems to me that if we're going to get waylaid by the numbers game, I'll have to plump for a zero-to-one relationship as between audience and artist, and that's where the moral objection comes in.

g.g.: I'm afraid I don't quite grasp that point, Mr. Gould. Do you want to run it through again?

G.G.: I simply feel that the artist should be granted, both for his sake and for that of his public—and let me get on record right now the fact that I'm not at all happy with words like "public" and "artist"; I'm not happy with the hierarchical implications of that kind of terminology—that he should be granted anonymity. He should be permitted to operate in secret, as it were, unconcerned with—or, better still, unaware of—the presumed demands of the marketplace—which demands, given sufficient indifference on the part of a sufficient number of artists, will simply disappear. And given their disappearance, the artist will then abandon his false sense of "public" responsibility, and his "public" will relinquish its role of servile dependency.

g.g.: And never the twain shall meet, I daresay!

G.G.: No, they'll make contact, but on an altogether more meaningful level than that which relates any stage to its apron.

g.g.: Mr. Gould, I'm well aware that this sort of idealistic role swapping offers a satisfying rhetorical flourish, and it may even be that the "creative audience" concept to which you've devoted a lot of interview space elsewhere offers a kind of McLuhanesque fascination. But you conveniently forget that the artist, however hermetic his life-style, is still in effect an autocratic figure. He's still, however benevolently, a social dictator. And his public, however generously enfranchised by gadgetry, however richly endowed with electronic options, is still on the receiving end of the experience, as of this late date at least, and all of your neomedieval anonymity quest on behalf of the artist as zero, and all of your vertical panculturalism on behalf of his "public," isn't going to change that—or at least it hasn't done so thus far.

G.G.: May I speak now?

g.g.: Of course. I didn't mean to get carried away, but I do feel strongly about the—

G.G.: —about the artist as superman?

g.g.: That's not quite fair, Mr. Gould.

G.G.: —or about the interlocutor as controller of conversations, perhaps?

g.g.: There's certainly no need to be rude. I didn't really expect a conciliatory response from you—I realize that you've staked out certain philosophical claims in regard to these issues—but I did at least hope that just once you'd confess to a personal experience of the one-to-one, artist-to-listener relationship. I had hoped that you might confess to having personally been witness to the magnetic attraction of a great artist visibly at work before his public.

G.G.: Oh, I have had that experience.

g.g.: Really?

G.G.: Certainly, and I don't mind confessing to it. Many years ago, I happened to be in Berlin while Herbert von Karajan led the Philharmonic in their first-ever performance of Sibelius's Fifth. As you know, Karajan tends—in late romantic repertoire particularly—to conduct with eyes closed and to endow his stick wielding with enormously persuasive choreographic contours, and the effect, quite frankly, contributed to one of the truly indelible musical-dramatic experiences of my life.

g.g.: You're supporting my contention very effectively indeed, Mr. Gould. I know, of course, that that performance, or at any rate one of its subsequent recorded incarnations, played a rather important role in your life.

G.G.: You mean because of its utilization in the epilogue of my radio documentary "The Idea of North"?

g.g.: Exactly, and you've just admitted that this "indelible" experience derived from a face-to-face confrontation, shared with an audience, and not simply from the disembodied predictability purveyed by even the best of phonograph records.

G.G.: Well, I suppose you could say that, but I wasn't actually a member of the audience. As a matter of fact, I took refuge in a glassed-in broadcast booth over the stage, and although I was in a position to see Karajan's face and to relate every ecstatic grimace to the emerging musical experience, the audience—except for the occasional profile shot as he might cue left or right—was not.

g.g.: I'm afraid you're splitting subdivided beats there, Mr. Gould.

G.G.: I'm not so sure. You see, the broadcast booth, in effect, represented a state of isolation, not only for me vis-à-vis my fellow auditors but vis-à-vis the Berlin Philharmonic and its conductor as well.

g.g.: And now you're simply clutching at symbolic straws.

G.G.: Maybe so, but I must point out—entre nous, of course—that when it came time to incorporate Karajan's Sibelius Fifth into "The Idea of North," I revised the dynamics of the recording to suit the mood of the text it accompanied, and that liberty, surely, is the product of—what shall I call it?—the enthusiastic irreverence of a zero-to-one relationship, wouldn't you say?

g.g.: I should rather think it's the product of unmitigated gall. I realize, of course, that "The Idea of North" was an experimental radio venture—as I recall, you treated the human voice in that work almost as one might a musical instrument—

G.G.: That's right.

g.g.: —and permitted two, three, or four individuals to speak at once on occasion.

G.G.: True.

g.g.: But whereas those experiments with your own raw material, so to speak, seem perfectly legitimate to me, your use—or misuse—of Herr von Karajan's material is another matter altogether. After all, you've confessed that your original experience of that performance was "indelible." And yet you blithely confess as well to tampering with what were, presumably, carefully controlled dynamic relationships—

G.G.: We did some equalizing, too.

g.g.: —and all in the interest of—

G.G.: —of my needs of the moment.

g.g.: —which, however, were at least unique to the project at hand.

G.G.: All right, I'll give you that, but every listener has a "project at hand," simply in terms of making his experience of music relate to his life-style.

g.g.: And you're prepared to have similar unauthorized permutations practiced on your own recorded output by listener or listeners unknown?

G.G.: I should have failed in my purpose otherwise.

g.g.: Then you're obviously reconciled to the fact that no real aesthetic yardstick relates your performances as originally conceived to the manner in which they will be subsequently audited?

G.G.: Come to that, I have absolutely no idea as to the "aesthetic" merits of Karajan's Sibelius Fifth when I encountered it on that memorable occasion. In fact the beauty of the occasion was that, although I was aware of being witness to an intensely moving experience, I had no idea as to whether it was or was not a "good" performance. My aesthetic judgments were simply placed in cold storage—which is where I should like them to remain, at least when assessing the works of others. Perhaps, necessarily, and for entirely practical reasons, I apply a different set of criteria on my own behalf, but—

g.g.: Mr. Gould, are you saying that you do not make aesthetic judgments?

G.G.: No, I'm not saying that—though I wish I were able to make that statement, because it would attest to a degree of spiritual perfection that I have not attained. However, to rephrase the fashionable cliché, I do try as best I can to make only moral judgments and not aesthetic ones—except, as I said, in the case of my own work.

g.g.: I suppose, Mr. Gould, I'm compelled to give you the benefit of the doubt—

G.G.: That's very good of you.

g.g.: —and to assume that you are assessing your own motivations responsibly and accurately.

G.G.: One can only try.

g.g.: And given that, what you have just confessed adds so many forks to the route of this interview, I simply don't know which trail to pursue.

G.G.: Why not pick the most likely signpost, and I'll just tag along.

g.g.: Well, I suppose the obvious question is: If you don't make aesthetic judgments on behalf of others, what about those who make aesthetic judgments in regard to your own work?

G.G.: Oh, some of my best friends are critics, although I'm not sure I'd want my piano to be played by one.

g.g.: But some minutes ago, you related the term "spiritual perfection" to a state in which aesthetic judgment is suspended.

G.G.: I didn't mean to give the impression that such a suspension would constitute the only criterion for such a state.

g.g.: I understand that. But would it be fair to say that in your view the critical mentality would necessarily lead to an imperiled state of grace?

G.G.: Well now, I think that would call for a very presumptuous judgment on my part. As I said, some of my best friends are—

g.g.: —are critics, I know, but you're evading the question.

G.G.: Not intentionally. I just don't feel that one should generalize in matters where such distinguished reputations are at stake, and—

g.g.: Mr. Gould, I think you owe us both, as well as our readers, an answer to that question.

G.G.: I do?

g.g.: That's my conviction; perhaps I should repeat the question.

G.G.: No, it's not necessary.

g.g.: So you do feel, in effect, that the critic represents a morally endangered species?

G.G.: Well now, the word "endangered" implies that—

g.g.: Please, Mr. Gould, answer the question—you do feel that, don't you?

G.G.: Well, as I've said, I—

g.g.: You do, don't you?

G.G.: [*pause*] Yes.

g.g.: Of course you do, and now I'm sure you also feel the better for confession.

G.G.: Hmm . . . not at the moment.

g.g.: But you will in due course.

G.G.: You really think so?

g.g.: No question of it. But now that you've stated your position so frankly, I do have to make mention of the fact that you yourself have bylined critical dispatches from time to time. I even recall a piece on Petula Clark which you contributed some years back to these columns and which—

G.G.: —and which contained more aesthetic judgment per square page than I would presume to render nowadays. But it was essentially a moral critique, you know. It was a piece in which I used Miss Clark, so to speak, in order to comment on a social milieu.

g.g.: So you feel that you can successfully distinguish between an aesthetic critique of the individual—which you reject out of hand—and a setting down of moral imperatives for society as a whole.

G.G.: I think I can. Mind you, there are obviously areas in which overlaps are inevitable. Let's say, for example, that I had been privileged to reside in a town in which all the houses were painted battleship gray.

g.g.: Why battleship gray?

G.G.: It's my favorite color.

g.g.: It's a rather negative color, isn't it?

G.G.: That's why it's my favorite. Now then, let's suppose for the sake of argument that without warning one individual elected to paint his house fire-engine red—

g.g.: —thereby challenging the symmetry of the town planning.

G.G.: Yes, it would probably do that too, but you're approaching the question from an aesthetic point of view. The real consequence of his action would be to foreshadow an outbreak of manic activity in the town and

almost inevitably—since other houses would be painted in similarly garish hues—to encourage a climate of competition and, as a corollary, of
violence.

g.g.: I gather, then, that red in your color lexicon represents aggressive behavior.

G.G.: I should have thought there'd be general agreement on that. But as I
said, there would be an aesthetic/moral overlap at this point. The man
who painted the first house may have done so purely from an aesthetic
preference, and it would, to use an old-fashioned word, be "sinful" if
I were to take him to account in respect of his taste. Such an accounting
would conceivably inhibit all subsequent judgments on his part. But
if I were able to persuade him that his particular aesthetic indulgence
represented a moral danger to the community as a whole, and providing
I could muster a vocabulary appropriate to the task—which would not
be, obviously, a vocabulary of aesthetic standards—then that would, I
think, be my responsibility.

g.g.: You do realize, of course, that you're beginning to talk like a character
out of Orwell?

G.G.: Oh, the Orwellian world holds no particular terrors for me.

g.g.: And you also realize that you're defining and defending a type of censorship that contradicts the whole post-Renaissance tradition of Western thought?

G.G.: Certainly. It's the post-Renaissance tradition that has brought the Western world to the brink of destruction. You know, this odd attachment
to freedom of movement, freedom of speech, and so on is a peculiarly
Occidental phenomenon. It's all part of the Occidental notion that one
can successfully separate word and deed.

g.g.: The sticks-and-stones syndrome, you mean?

G.G.: Precisely. There's some evidence for the fact that—well, as a matter
of fact, McLuhan talks about just that in the *Gutenberg Galaxy*—that
preliterate peoples or minimally literate peoples are much less willing
to permit that distinction.

g.g.: I suppose there's also the biblical injunction that to will evil is to accom-
plish evil.

G.G.: Exactly. It's only cultures that, by accident or good management, bypassed the Renaissance which see art for the menace it really is.

g.g.: May I assume the U.S.S.R. would qualify?

G.G.: Absolutely. The Soviets are a bit roughhewn as to method, I'll admit,
but their concerns are absolutely justified.

g.g.: What about your own concerns? Have any of your activities violated
these personal strictures and, in your terms, "menaced" society?

G.G.: Yes.

g.g.: Want to talk about it?

G.G.: Not particularly.

g.g.: Not even a quick for-instance? What about the fact that you supplied music for *Slaughterhouse Five*?

G.G.: What about it?

g.g.: Well, at least by Soviet standards, the film of Mr. Vonnegut's opus would probably qualify as a socially destructive piece of work, wouldn't you say?

G.G.: I'm afraid you're right. I even remember a young lady in Leningrad telling me once that Dostoevsky, "though a very great writer, was unfortunately pessimistic."

g.g.: And pessimism, combined with a hedonistic cop-out, was the hallmark of *Slaughterhouse*, was it not?

G.G.: Yes, but it was the hedonistic properties rather than the pessimistic ones that gave me a lot of sleepless nights.

g.g.: So you didn't approve of the film?

G.G.: I admired its craftsmanship extravagantly.

g.g.: That's not the same as liking it.

G.G.: No, it isn't.

g.g.: Can we assume, then, that even an idealist has his price?

G.G.: I'd much prefer it said that even an idealist can misread the intentions of a shooting script.

g.g.: You would have preferred an uncompromised Billy Pilgrim, I assume?

G.G.: I would have preferred some redemptive element added to his persona, yes.

g.g.: So you wouldn't vouch for the art-as-technique-pure-and-simple theories of Stravinsky, for instance?

G.G.: Certainly not. That's quite literally the last thing art is.

g.g.: Then what about the art-as-violence-surrogate theory?

G.G.: I don't believe in surrogates; they're simply the playthings of minds resistant to the perfectability of man. Besides, if you're looking for violence surrogates, genetic engineering is a better bet.

g.g.: How about the art-as-transcendental-experience theory?

G.G.: Of the three you've cited, that's the only one that attracts.

g.g.: Do you have a theory of your own, then?

G.G.: Yes, but you're not going to like it.

g.g.: I'm braced.

G.G.: Well, I feel that art should be given the chance to phase itself out. I think that we must accept the fact that art is not inevitably benign, that it is potentially destructive. We should analyze the areas where it tends to do least harm, use them as a guideline, and build into art a component that will enable it to preside over its own obsolescence—

g.g.: Hmm.

G.G.: —because, you know, the present position, or positions, of art—some of which you've enumerated—are not without analogy to the ban-the-bomb movement of hallowed memory.

g.g.: You surely don't reject protest of that kind?

G.G.: No, but since I haven't noticed a single ban-the-child-who-pulls-wings-from-dragonflies movement, I can't join it, either. You see, the Western world is consumed with notions of qualification; the threat of nuclear extinction fulfills those notions, and the loss of a dragonfly's wing does not. And until the two phenomena are recognized as one, indivisible, until physical and verbal aggression are seen as simply a flip of the competitive coin, until every aesthetic decision can be equated with a moral correlative, I'll continue to listen to the Berlin Philharmonic from behind a glass partition.

g.g.: So you don't expect to see your death wish for art fulfilled in your lifetime.

G.G.: No, I couldn't live without the Sibelius Fifth.

g.g.: But you are nevertheless talking like a sixteenth-century reformer.

G.G.: Actually, I feel very close to that tradition. In fact, in one of my better lines I remarked that—

g.g.: That's an aesthetic judgment if ever I heard one!

G.G.: A thousand pardons—let me try a second take on that. On a previous occasion, I remarked that I, rather than Mr. Santayana's hero, am "the last puritan."

g.g.: And you don't find any problem in reconciling the individual-conscience aspect of the Reformation and the collective censorship of the puritan tradition? Both motifs, it would seem to me, are curiously intermingled in your thesis and, from what I know of it, in your documentary work as well.

G.G.: Well, no, I don't think there's an inevitable inconsistency there, because at its best—which is to say at its purest—that tradition involved perpetual schismatic division. The best and purest—or at any rate the most ostracized—of individuals ended up in Alpine valleys as symbols of their rejection of the world of the plains. As a matter of fact, there is to this day a Mennonite sect in Switzerland that equates separation from the world with altitude.

g.g.: Would it be fair to suggest that you, on the other hand, equate it with latitude? After all, you did create "The Idea of North" as a metaphoric comment and not as a factual documentary.

G.G.: That's quite true. Of course, most of the documentaries have dealt with isolated situations—Arctic outposts, Newfoundland outposts, Mennonite enclaves, and so on.

g.g.: Yes, but they've dealt with a community in isolation.

G.G.: That's because my magnum opus is still several drawing boards away.

g.g.: So they are autobiographical drafts?

G.G.: That, sir, is not for me to say.

g.g.: Mr. Gould, there's a sort of grim, I might even say gray, consistency to what you've said, but it does seem to me that we have come a rather long way from the concert-versus-record theme with which we began.

G.G.: On the contrary, I think we've performed a set of variations on that theme and that, indeed, we've virtually come full circle.

g.g.: In any event, I have only a few more questions to put to you, of which, I guess, the most pertinent would now be: Apart from being a frustrated member of the board of censors, is any other career of interest to you?

G.G.: I've often thought that I'd like to try my hand at being a prisoner.

g.g.: You regard *that* as a career?

G.G.: Oh, certainly—on the understanding, of course, that I would be entirely innocent of all charges brought against me.

g.g.: Mr. Gould, has anyone suggested that you could be suffering from a Myshkin complex?

G.G.: No, and I can't accept the compliment. It's simply that, as I indicated, I've never understood the preoccupation with freedom as it's reckoned in the Western world. So far as I can see, freedom of movement usually has to do only with mobility, and freedom of speech most frequently with socially sanctioned verbal aggression, and to be incarcerated would be the perfect test of one's inner mobility and of the strength which would enable one to opt creatively out of the human situation.

g.g.: Mr. Gould, weary as I am, that feels like a contradiction in terms.

G.G.: I don't really think it is. I also think that there's a younger generation than ours—you are about my age, are you not?

g.g.: I should assume so.

G.G.: —a younger generation that doesn't have to struggle with that concept, to whom the competitive fact is not an inevitable component of life, and who do program their lives without making allowances for it.

g.g.: Are you trying to sell me on the neotribalism kick?

G.G.: Not really, no. I suspect that competitive tribes got us into this mess in the first place, but, as I said, I don't deserve the Myshkin-complex title.

g.g.: Well, your modesty is legendary, of course, Mr. Gould, but what brings you to that conclusion?

G.G.: The fact that I would inevitably impose demands upon my keepers—demands that a genuinely free spirit could afford to overlook.

g.g.: Such as?

G.G.: The cell would have to be prepared in a battleship-gray decor.

g.g.: I shouldn't think that would pose a problem.

G.G.: Well, I've heard that the new look in penal reform involves primary colors.

g.g.: Oh, I see.

G.G.: And of course there would have to be some sort of understanding about the air-conditioning control. Overhead vents would be out—as I may have mentioned, I'm subject to tracheitis—and, assuming that a forced-air system was employed, the humidity regulator would have to be—

g.g.: Mr. Gould, excuse the interruption, but it just occurs to me that since you have attempted to point out on several occasions that you did suffer a traumatic experience in the Salzburg Festspielhaus—

G.G.: Oh, I didn't meant to leave the impression of a traumatic experience. On the contrary, my tracheitis was of such severity that I was able to cancel a month of concerts, withdraw into the Alps, and lead the most idyllic and isolated existence.

g.g.: I see. Well now, may I make a suggestion?

G.G.: Of course.

g.g.: As you know, the old Festspielhaus was originally a riding academy.

G.G.: Oh, quite; I'd forgotten.

g.g.: And of course, the rear of the building is set against a mountainside.

G.G.: Yes, that's quite true.

g.g.: And since you're obviously a man addicted to symbols—I'm sure this prisoner fantasy of yours is precisely that—it would seem to me that the Festspielhaus—the Felsenreitschule—with its Kafka-like setting at the base of a cliff, with the memory of equestrian mobility haunting its past, and located, moreover, in the birthplace of a composer whose works you have frequently criticized, thereby compromising your own judgmental criteria—

G.G.: Ah, but I've criticized them primarily as evidence of a hedonistic life.

g.g.: Be that as it may. The Festspielhaus, Mr. Gould, is a place to which a man like yourself, a man in search of martyrdom, should return.

G.G.: Martyrdom? What ever gave you that impression? I couldn't possibly go back!

g.g.: Please, Mr. Gould, try to understand. There could be no more meaningful manner in which to scourge the flesh, in which to proclaim the ascendance of the spirit, and certainly no more meaningful metaphoric mise en scène against which to offset your own hermetic life-style, through which to define your quest for martyrdom autobiographically, as I'm sure you will try to do, eventually.

G.G.: But you must believe me—I have no such quest in mind!

g.g.: Yes, I think you must go back, Mr. Gould. You must once again tread the boards of the Festspielhaus; you must willingly, even gleefully, subject yourself to the gales which rage upon that stage. For then and only then will you achieve the martyr's end you so obviously desire.

G.G.: Please don't misunderstand; I'm touched by your concern. It's just that, in the immortal words of Mr. Vonnegut's Billy Pilgrim, "I'm not ready yet."

g.g.: In that case, Mr. Gould, in the immortal words of Mr. Vonnegut himself, "So it goes."

PART THREE
Media

THE PROSPECTS OF RECORDING

In an unguarded moment some months ago, I predicted that the public concert as we know it today would no longer exist a century hence, that its functions would have been entirely taken over by electronic media. It had not
occurred to me that this statement represented a particularly radical pronouncement. Indeed, I regarded it almost as self-evident truth and, in any
case, as defining only one of the peripheral effects occasioned by developments in the electronic age. But never has a statement of mine been so widely
quoted—or so hotly disputed.

The furor it occasioned is, I think, indicative of an endearing, if sometimes frustrating, human characteristic—a reluctance to accept the consequences of a new technology. I have no idea whether this trait is, on balance,
an advantage or a liability, incurable or correctable. Perhaps the escalation
of invention must always be disciplined by some sort of emotional
short-selling. Perhaps skepticism is the necessary obverse of progress. Perhaps, for that reason, the *idea* of progress is, as at no time in the past, today
in question.

Certainly, this emotional short-selling has its good side. The afterthought of Alamogordo—the willingness to kill off a monster of their own
creation—does more credit to the pioneers of the atomic age than all the
blessings this generation can expect that breakthrough to give birth to. And
if protest against the ramifications of man's ingenuity is inevitable, and even
essential to the function of his genius, then perhaps there really is no *bad*
side—just amusement at and, ultimately, acceptance of that indecisiveness
which proclaims the frailty of man's continuing humanity.

In any event, I can think of few areas of contemporary endeavor that
better display the confusion with which technological man evaluates the
implications of his own achievements than the great debate about music
and its recorded future. As is true for most of those areas in which the
effect of a new technology has yet to be evaluated, an examination of the
influence of recording must pertain not only to speculations about the future but to an accommodation of the past as well. Recordings deal with
concepts through which the past is re-evaluated, and they concern notions about the future which will ultimately question even the validity of
evaluation.

From *High Fidelity*, April 1966.

The preservative aspects of recording are, of course, by no means exclusively in the service of music. "The first thing we require of a machine is to have a memory," said a somnolently pontifical character in Jean-Luc Godard's recent film *A Married Woman.* In the electronic age a caretaking comprehension of those encompassing chronicles of universal knowledge which were tended by the medieval scholastics—an encumbrance as well as an impossibility since the early Middle Ages—can be consigned to computer repositories that file away the memories of mankind and leave us free to be inventive in spite of them. But in limiting our investigation to the effect of recordings upon music, we isolate an art inhibited by the hierarchical specialization of its immediate past, an art which has no clear recollection of its origins, and therefore an art much in need of both the preservative and translative aspects of recording. As a recent brief prepared by the University of Toronto's department of musicology proposing a computer-controlled phonographic information system succinctly noted, "Whether we recognize it or not, the long-playing record has come to embody the very reality of music."

As concerns its relations to the immediate past, the recording debate centers upon whether or not electronic media can present music in so viable a way as to threaten the survival of the public concert. Notwithstanding the imposing array of statistics which testify to the contrary ("Ladies' Lyric League Boasts Box-Office Boost Third Successive Year"), I herewith reaffirm my prediction that the habit of concertgoing and concert giving, both as a social institution and as chief symbol of musical mercantilism, will be as dormant in the twenty-first century as, with luck, will Tristan da Cunha's Volcano; and that because of its extinction, music will be able to provide a more cogent experience than is now possible. The generation currently being subjected to the humiliation of public school solfège will be the last to attain their majority persuaded that the concert is the axis upon which the world of music revolves.

It is not. And considering for what a brief span the public concert has seemed predominant, the wonder is that pundits allowed it ever would be. To its perpetuation, however, a substantial managerial investment is currently committed ("For Rent: Complex of Six Acoustically Charming Auditoria. Apply J. Rockefeller."), and we must realize that to reckon with its obsolescence is to defy the very body of the musical establishment. It cannot be overemphasized, however, that the fate of the public event is incidental to the future of music—a future deserving of far greater concern than is the fiscal stability of the concert hall. The influence of recordings upon that future will affect not only the performer and concert impresario but composer and technical engineer, critic and historian as well. Most important, it will affect the listener to whom all of this activity is ultimately directed.

If we were to take an inventory of those musical predilections most characteristic of our generation, we would discover that almost every item on such a list could be attributed directly to the influence of the recording. First of all, today's listeners have come to associate musical performance with sounds possessed of characteristics which two generations ago were neither available to the profession nor wanted by the public—characteristics such as analytic clarity, immediacy, and indeed almost tactile proximity. Within the last few decades the performance of music has ceased to be an occasion, requiring an excuse and a tuxedo, and accorded, when encountered, an almost religious devotion; music has become a pervasive influence in our lives, and as our dependence upon it has increased, our reverence for it has, in a certain sense, declined. Two generations ago, concertgoers preferred that their occasional experience of music be fitted with an acoustic splendor, cavernously reverberant if possible, and pioneer recording ventures attempted to simulate the cathedrallike sound which the architects of that day tried to capture for the concert hall—the cathedral of the symphony. The more intimate terms of our experience with recordings have since suggested to us an acoustic with a direct and impartial presence, one with which we can live in our homes on rather casual terms.

Apparently, we are also expected to live with it in the concert hall. Some of the much-heralded links in that prodigious chain of postwar auditorium catastrophes (Philharmonic Hall of Lincoln Center, Royal Festival Hall, etc.) have simply appropriated characteristics of the recording studio intended to enhance microphone pickup, the special virtue of which becomes a detriment in the concert hall. Proof of this is that when the audience is sent home and the microphones moved in close and tight around the band, Philharmonic Hall—like many of these acoustical puzzles—can accommodate surprisingly successful recording sessions.

Just how great a change has come about can be seen in a comparison between recordings made in North America and Western Europe and those originating in Central and Eastern Europe, where—for reasons both economic and geographic—the traditions of public concertgoing retain a social cachet which for North America's split-level suburbia has long since been transferred to twelve-tone doorbells, nursery intercom, and steam room stereo. One need only compare a typical Continental reverberation such as that present in the Konwitschny recordings from Leipzig or (though it somewhat contradicts the geographical assumptions of my argument) in van Beinum's from the Concertgebouw with the Studio 8H sound of Toscanini's discs of the late thirties and forties or with the Severance Hall balances for George Szell's recent Epic recordings to appreciate the modifications that the North American attitude to recording can impose on even the most resolute martinet.

A more precise comparison can be found between the discs made by Herbert von Karajan with the Philharmonia Orchestra in London for EMI-Angel and the same maestro's recordings for DGG in Berlin. Any number of the latter (I am thinking now of such releases as the 1959 performance of *Ein Heldenleben* with a distant brass and all but inaudible timpani) suggest a production crew determined to provide for the listener the evocation of a concert experience. The EMI recordings, on the other hand, provide Karajan with an acoustic which, while hardly chamberlike, at least subscribes to that philosophy of recording which admits the futility of emulating concert hall sonorities by a deliberate limitation of studio techniques.

Further evidence of this curious anachronism can be found in some of the recitals recorded by Sviatoslav Richter in Eastern Europe, of which the magnificent performance of Mussorgsky's *Pictures at an Exhibition,* taped in Sofia, Bulgaria, is a good example. Here is a great artist with an incomparable interpretation transcribed by technicians who are determined that their microphones will in no way amplify, dissect, or intrude upon the occasion being preserved. Richter's superbly lucid playing is sabotaged by some obsequious miking which permits us, at best, a top-of-the-gods half-earful. Unlike their colleagues in North America, who are aware of serving a public which to a considerable extent has discovered music through records and who evaluate their own presence in the booth as crucial to the success of the end product, the production crew in Sofia, offstage in the wings of some palace of municipal amusement, made no such claims for the autonomy of their craft. They sought only to pursue it as an inconspicuous complement of Richter's performance.

The North American and Western European sound strives for an analytic detail which eludes the Central European displacement. By virtue of this Westernized sound, recording has developed its own conventions, which do not always conform to those traditions that derive from the acoustical limitations of the concert hall. We have, for instance, come to expect a Brünnhilde, blessed with amplification as well as amplitude, who can surmount without struggle the velvet diapason of the Wagnerian orchestra, to insist that a searching spotlight trace the filigreed path of a solo cello in concerto playing—demands which contravene the acoustical possibilities of the concert hall or opera house. For the analytical capacity of the microphones has exploited psychological circumstances implicit in the concerto dialogue, if not within the ability of the solo instrument itself, and the "Ring" cycle as produced by a master like John Culshaw for Decca/London attains a more effective unity between intensity of action and displacement of sound than could be afforded by the best of all seasons at Bayreuth.

Another item to be added to our catalogue of contemporary enthusiasms is the astonishing revival in recent years of music from preclassical times. Since the recording techniques of North America and Western Europe are designed for an audience which does most of its listening at home, it is not surprising that the creation of a recording archive has emphasized those areas which historically relate to a *Hausmusik* tradition and has been responsible for the triumphant restoration of baroque forms in the years since World War II. This repertoire—with its contrapuntal extravaganzas, its antiphonal balances, its espousal of instruments that chuff and wheeze and speak directly to a microphone—was made for stereo. That prodigious catalogue of cantatas and concerto grossos, fugues and partitas, has endowed the neobaroque enthusiasm of our day with a hard core of musical experience. A certain amount of this music has then found its way back into the concert hall and re-engaged the attention of the public audience—sometimes, indeed, through considerable musicological enterprise. New York's Jay Hoffman, perhaps the last concert impresario truly deserving of that once-proud title, offered his audience on consecutive evenings during Christmas week 1964 comparative versions of *Messiah* according to G. F. Handel and other editors. But this scholarly exactitude has come about by virtue of a recorded library which enables such works to be studied in great number, in great privacy, and in an acoustic that fits them to the proverbial T.

From a musicological point of view, the effort of the recording industry in behalf of Renaissance and pre-Renaissance music is of even greater value. For the first time, the musicologist rather than the performer has become the key figure in the realization of this untapped repertoire; and in place of sporadic and, often as not, historically inaccurate concert performances of a Palestrina mass or a Josquin chanson, or whichever isolated items were heretofore considered approachable and not too offensively pretonal, the record archivists have documented a new perspective for the history of music.

The performer is inevitably challenged by the stimulus of this unexplored repertoire. He is also encouraged by the nature of studio techniques to appropriate characteristics that have tended for a century or two to be outside his private preserve. His contact with the repertoire he records is often the result of an intense analysis from which he prepares an interpretation of the composition. Conceivably, for the rest of his life he will never again take up or come in contact with that particular work. In the course of a lifetime spent in the recording studio he will necessarily encounter a wider range of repertoire than could possibly be his lot in the concert hall. The current archival approach of many recording companies demands a complete survey of the works of a given composer, and performers are expected to undertake productions of enormous scope which they would be inclined to avoid in the concert hall, and in many cases to investigate repertoire economically or acoustically unsuitable for public audition—the complete piano works of Mozart which Walter Gieseking undertook for Angel, for instance.

But most important, this archival responsibility enables the performer to establish a contact with a work which is very much like that of the composer's own relation to it. It permits him to encounter a particular piece of music and to analyze and dissect it in a most thorough way, to make it a vital part of his life for a relatively brief period, and then to pass on to some other challenge and to the satisfaction of some other curiosity. Such a work will no longer confront him with a daily challenge. His analysis of the composition will not become distorted by overexposure, and his performance top-heavy with interpretative "niceties" intended to woo the upper balcony, as is almost inevitably the case with the overplayed piece of concert repertoire.

It may be that these archival pursuits, especially where the cultivation of earlier literature is involved, recommend themselves to both the performer and his audience as a means of avoiding some of the problems inherent in the music of our own time. One is sometimes inclined to suspect that such phenomena as the baroque revival provide refuge for those who find themselves displaced persons in the frantically metamorphosing world of modern music. Certainly, the performance traditions indigenous to those areas of repertoire revived by the microphone have had an enormous influence upon the way in which certain kinds of contemporary repertoire are performed and have, indeed, bred a generation of performers whose interpretative inclinations respond to the microphone's special demands.

The recordings of Robert Craft, those prodigious undertakings in behalf of the Viennese trinity Schoenberg, Berg, and Webern—not to mention Don Carlo Gesualdo—tell us a good deal about the way in which performances prepared with the microphone in mind can be influenced by technological considerations. For Craft, the stopwatch and the tape splice are tools of his trade as well as objects of that inspiration for which an earlier generation of stick wielders found an outlet in the opera cape and temper tantrums. A comparison between Craft's readings of the large-scale orchestral studies of Schoenberg, especially the early postromantic essays such as *Verklärte Nacht* or *Pelleas und Melisande,* with the interpretations of more venerable maestros—Winfried Zillig's glowingly romantic *Pelleas* of 1949, for instance—is instructive.

Craft applies a sculptor's chisel to these vast orchestral complexes of the youthful Schoenberg and gives them a determined series of plateaus on which to operate—a very baroque thing to do. He seems to feel that his audience—sitting at home, close up to the speaker—is prepared to allow him to dissect this music and to present it to them from a strongly biased conceptual viewpoint, which the private and concentrated circumstances of their listening make feasible. Craft's interpretation, then, is all power steering and air brakes. By comparison, in Zillig's reading of *Pelleas* (on a now withdrawn Capitol-Telefunken disc) the leisurely application of rubatos, the sensual haze with which he gilds the performance as though concerned that clarity could be an enemy of mystery, point clearly to the fact that his interpretation derived from a concert experience where such performance characteristics were intuitive compensations for an acoustic dilemma.

The example is productive of a larger issue with which the techniques of the recording studio confront us, and I have deliberately chosen to illustrate it with an example from that area of twentieth-century repertoire least indigenous to the medium. Whether Craft's analytic dissection of such repertoire is appropriate, whether there remain positive virtues to the presentation of late romantic fare in the concert hall, is not really the point. We must be prepared to accept the fact that, for better or worse, recording will forever alter our notions about what is appropriate to the performance of music.

Of all the techniques peculiar to the studio recording, none has been the subject of such controversy as the tape splice. With due regard to the not-so-unusual phenomenon of a recording consisting of single-take sonata or symphony movements, the great majority of present-day recordings consist of a collection of tape segments varying in duration upward from one twentieth of a second. Superficially, the purpose of the splice is to rectify performance mishaps. Through its use, the wayward phrase, the insecure quaver, can, except when prohibited by "overhang" or similar circumstances of acoustical imbalance, be remedied by minute retakes of the offending moment or of a splice segment of which it forms a part. The antirecord lobby proclaims splicing a dishonest and dehumanizing technique that purportedly eliminates those conditions of chance and accident upon which, it can safely be conceded, certain of the more unsavory traditions of Western music are founded. The lobbyists also claim that the common splice sabotages some unified architectural conception which they assume the performer possesses.

It seems to me that two facts challenge these objections. The first is that many of the supposed virtues of the performer's "unified conception" relate to nothing more inherently musical than the "running scared" and "go-for-broke" psychology built up through decades of exposure to the *loggione* of Parma and their like. Claudio Arrau was recently quoted by the English journal *Records and Recordings* to the effect that he would not authorize the release of records derived from a live performance since, in his opinion, public auditions provoke stratagems which, having been designed to fill acoustical and psychological requirements of the concert situation, are irritating and antiarchitectural when subjected to repeated playbacks. The second fact is that one cannot ever splice style—one can only splice segments which relate to a conviction about style. And whether one arrives at such a conviction pretaping or posttaping (another of the time-transcending luxuries of recording: the posttaping reconsideration of performance), its existence is what matters, not the means by which it is effected.

A recent personal experience will perhaps illustrate an interpretative conviction obtained posttaping. A year or so ago, while recording the concluding fugues from volume 1 of *The Well-Tempered Clavier,* I arrived at one of Bach's celebrated contrapuntal obstacle courses, the fugue in A minor. This is a structure even more difficult to realize on the piano than are most of Bach's fugues, because it consists of four intense voices that determinedly occupy a register in the center octaves of the keyboard—the area of the instrument in which truly independent voice leading is most difficult to establish. In the process of recording this fugue we attempted eight takes. Two of these at the time were regarded, according to the producer's notes, as satisfactory. Both of them, number 6 and number 8, were complete takes requiring no inserted splice—by no means a special achievement, since the fugue's duration is only a bit over two minutes. Some weeks later, however, when the results of this session were surveyed in an editing cubicle and when takes 6 and 8 were played several times in rapid alternation, it became apparent that both had a defect of which we had been quite unaware in the studio: both were monotonous.

Each take had used a different style of phrase delineation in dealing with the thirty-one-note subject of this fugue—a license entirely consistent with the improvisatory liberties of baroque style. Take 6 had treated it in a solemn, legato, rather pompous fashion, while in take 8 the fugue subject was shaped in a prevailingly staccato manner which led to a general impression of skittishness. Now, the fugue in A minor is given to concentrations of strettos and other devices for imitation at close quarters, so that the treatment of the subject determines the atmosphere of the entire fugue. Upon most sober reflection, it was agreed that neither the Teutonic severity of take 6 nor the unwarranted jubilation of take 8 could be permitted to represent our best thoughts on this fugue. At this point someone noted that, despite the vast differences in character between the two takes, they were performed at an almost identical tempo (a rather unusual circumstance, to be sure, since the prevailing tempo is almost always the result of phrase delineation), and it was decided to turn this to advantage by creating one performance to consist alternately of takes 6 and 8.

Once this decision had been made, it was a simple matter to expedite it. It was obvious that the somewhat overbearing posture of take 6 was entirely suitable for the opening exposition as well as for the concluding statements of the fugue, while the more effervescent character of take 8 was a welcome relief in the episodic modulations with which the center portion of the fugue is concerned. And so two rudimentary splices were made, one which jumps from take 6 to take 8 in bar 14 and another which at the return to A minor (I forget in which measure, but you are invited to look for it) returns as well to take 6. What had been achieved was a performance of this particular fugue far superior to anything that we could at the time have done in the studio. There is, of course, no reason why such a diversity of bowing styles could not have been applied to this fugue subject as part of a regulated a priori conception. But the necessity of such diversity is unlikely to become apparent during the studio session, just as it is unlikely to occur to a performer operating under concert conditions. By taking advantage of the post-taping afterthought, however, one can very often transcend the limitations that performance imposes upon the imagination.

When the performer makes use of this postperformance editorial decision, his role is no longer compartmentalized. In a quest for perfection, he sets aside the hazards and compromises of his trade. As an interpreter, as a go-between serving both audience and composer, the performer has always been, after all, someone with a specialist's knowledge about the realization or actualization of notated sound symbols. It is, then, perfectly consistent with such experience that he should assume something of an editorial role. Inevitably, however, the functions of the performer and of the tape editor begin to overlap. Indeed, in regard to decisions such as that taken in the case of the abovementioned A-minor fugue, it would be impossible for the listener to establish at which point the authority of the performer gave way to that of the producer and the tape editor, just as even the most observant cinema-goer cannot ever be sure whether a particular sequence of shots derives from circumstances occasioned by the actor's performance, the exigencies of the cutting room, or the director's a priori scheme. That the judgment of the performer no longer solely determines the musical result is inevitable. It is, however, more than compensated by the overwhelming sense of power which editorial control makes available to him.

The characteristics enumerated on our inventory represent the past rendered in terms that seem appropriate to the electronic age. Although they compile, by themselves, an impressive list of present-day convictions about the way in which music should be performed, they do not, except by implication, suggest a direction for recording to pursue. It is quite likely that these preferences engendered by phonographic reproduction—clarity of definition, analytic dissection by microphones, catholicity of repertoire, etc.—will determine to a considerable extent the kind of sound with which we shall want our musical experiences to be endowed. It is less likely that the recording industry will always concern itself primarily with an archival representation of the past, no matter how painstakingly embalmed, but for a long time to come some portion of the industry's activity will be devoted to merchandising the celebrated masterworks which form our musical tradition. Before examining the larger ramifications for the future of recording, I should like to consider here some hardy strains of argument that perennially decry the influence of recording upon standard items of the repertoire and upon the hierarchy of the musical profession.

These arguments sometimes overlap each other, and it can become rather difficult to detect the area of protest with which each is concerned. However, under a general heading of "humanitarian idealism" one might list three distinguishable subspecies, which can be summarized as follows: (1) An argument for aesthetic morality: Elisabeth Schwarzkopf appends a missing high C to a tape of *Tristan* otherwise featuring Kirsten Flagstad, and indignant purists, for whom music is the last blood sport, howl her down, furious at being deprived a kill. (2) Eye versus ear orientation: a doctrine that celebrates the existence of a mystical communication between concert performer and public audience (the composer being seldom mentioned). There is a vaguely scientific pretension to this argument, and its proponents are given to pronouncements on "natural" acoustics and related phenomena. (3) Automation: a crusade which musicians' union leaders currently share with typesetters and which they affirm with the fine disdain of featherbedding firemen for the diesel locomotive. In the midst of a proliferation of recorded sound which virtually erases earlier listening patterns, the American Federation of Musicians promotes that challenging motto "Live Music Is Best"—a judgment with the validity of a "Win with Willkie" sticker on the windshield of a well-preserved '39 LaSalle.

As noted, these arguments tend to overlap and are often joined together in celebration of occasions that afford opportunity for a rearguard holding action. Among such occasions, none has proved more useful than the recent spate of recorded "live" performances—events which straddle two worlds and are at home in neither. These events affirm the humanistic ideal of performance; they eschew (so we are told!) splices and other mechanical adventures, and hence are decidedly "moral"; they usually manage to suppress a sufficient number of pianissimo chords by an outbreak of bronchitis from the floor to advertise their "live"-ness and confirm the faith of the heroically unautomated.

They have yet another function, which is, in fact, the essence of their appeal for the short-sellers: they provide documentation pertaining to a specific date. They are forever represented as occasions indisputably of and for their time. They spurn that elusive time-transcending objective which is always within the realization of recorded music. For all time, they can be examined, criticized, or praised as documents securely located in time, and about which, because of that assurance, a great deal of information and, in a certain sense, an emotional relation, is immediately available. With regard to the late Dutch craftsman who, having hankered to take upon himself the mantle of Vermeer, was martyred for a reluctance to live by the hypocrisy of this argument, I think of this fourth circumstance—this question of historical date—as the van Meegeren syndrome.

Hans van Meegeren was a forger and an artisan who for a long time has been high on my list of private heroes. Indeed, I would go so far as to say that the magnificent morality play which was his trial perfectly epitomizes the confrontation between those values of identity and of personal-responsibility-for-authorship which post-Renaissance art has until recently accepted and those pluralistic values which electronic forms assert. In the 1930s van Meegeren decided to apply himself to a study of Vermeer's techniques and—for reasons undoubtedly having more to do with an enhancement of his ego than with greed for guilders—distributed the works thus achieved as genuine, if long lost, masterpieces. His prewar success was so encouraging that during the German occupation he continued apace with sales destined for private collectors in the Third Reich. With the coming of VE Day, he was charged with collaboration as well as with responsibility for the liquidation of national treasures. In his defense van Meegeren confessed that these treasures were but his own invention and, by the values this world applies, quite worthless—an admission which so enraged the critics and historians who had authenticated his collection in the first place that he was rearraigned on charges of forgery and some while later passed away in prison.

The determination of the value of a work of art according to the information available about it is a most delinquent form of aesthetic appraisal. Indeed, it strives to avoid appraisal on any ground other than that which has been prepared by previous appraisals. The moment this tyranny of appraisal-dom is confronted by confused chronological evidence, the moment it is denied a predetermined historical niche in which to lock the object of its analysis, it becomes unserviceable and its proponents hysterical. The furor that greeted van Meegeren's conflicting testimony, his alternate roles of hero and villain, scholar and fraud, decisively demonstrated the degree to which an aesthetic response was genuinely involved.

Some months ago, in an article in the *Saturday Review*, * I ventured that the delinquency manifest by this sort of evaluation might be demonstrated

*See p. 92.

if one were to imagine the critical response to an improvisation which, through its style and texture, suggested that it might have been composed by Joseph Haydn. (Let's assume it to be brilliantly done and most admirably Haydnesque.) I suggested that if one were to concoct such a piece, its value would remain at par—that is to say, at Haydn's value—only so long as some chicanery were involved in its presentation, enough at least to convince the listener that it was indeed by Haydn. If, however, one were to suggest that although it much resembled Haydn it was, rather, a youthful work of Mendelssohn, its value would decline; and if one chose to attribute it to a succession of authors, each of them closer to the present day, then—regardless of their talents or historical significance—the merits of this same little piece would diminish with each new identification. If, on the other hand, one were to suggest that this work of chance, of accident, of the here and now, was not by Haydn but by a master living some generation or two before his time (Vivaldi, perhaps), then this work would become—on the strength of that daring, that foresight, that futuristic anticipation—a landmark in musical composition.

And all of this would come to pass for no other reason than that we have never really become equipped to adjudicate music per se. Our sense of history is captive of an analytical method which seeks out isolated moments of stylistic upheaval—pivot points of idiomatic evolution—and our value judgments are largely based upon the degree to which we can assure ourselves that a particular artist participated in or, better yet, anticipated the nearest upheaval. Confusing evolution with accomplishment, we become blind to those values not explicit in an analogy with stylistic metamorphosis.

The van Meegeren syndrome is entirely apropos of our subject, because the arguments contra the prospects of recording are constructed upon identical criteria. They rely, most of all, upon a similar confirmation of historical data. Deprived of this confirmation, their system of evaluation is unable to function; it is at sea, derelict amidst an unsalvageable debris of evidence, and it casts about in search of a point by which to take a bearing. When recordings are at issue, such a point cannot readily be found. The inclination of electronic media is to extract their content from historic date. The moment we can force a work of art to conform to our notion of what was appropriate to its chronology, we can attribute to it, arbitrarily if necessary, background against which in our analysis it can be portrayed. Most aesthetic analysis confines itself to background description and avoids the foreground manipulation of the object being analyzed. And this fact alone, discarding the idle propaganda of the public relations machines, accounts for the endorsement of the recorded public event. Indirectly, the real object of this endorsement is a hopelessly outmoded system of aesthetic analysis—a system incapable of a contribution in the electronic age but the only system for which most spokesmen of the arts are trained.

Recordings produced in a studio resist a confirmation of such criteria. Here date is an elusive factor. Though a few companies solemnly inscribe the date of the studio sessions with each recorded package, and though the material released by most large companies can, except perhaps in the case of reissues, be related to a release number that will suggest an approximate date to the aficionado, it is possible that the music heard on that recording will have been obtained from sessions held weeks, months, or indeed years apart. Those sessions may easily have been held in different cities, different countries, taped with different equipment and different technical personnel, and they may feature performers whose attitudes to the repertoire under consideration have metamorphosed dramatically between the taping of the first note and the last. Such a recording might currently pose insuperable contractual problems, but its complicated gestation would be entirely consistent with the nature of the recording process.

It would also be consistent with that evolution of the performing musician which recording necessitates. As the performer's once-sacrosanct privileges are merged with the responsibilities of the tape editor and the composer, the van Meegeren syndrome can no longer be cited as an indictment but becomes rather an entirely appropriate description of the aesthetic condition in our time. The role of the forger, of the unknown maker of unauthenticated goods, is emblematic of electronic culture. And when the forger is done honor for his craft and no longer reviled for his acquisitiveness, the arts will have become a truly integral part of our civilization.

All creative artists claim, when challenged, that they have nothing but disdain for the limited vision of their present audience, that posterity will be their judge. For composers, recording makes this threat a fact, and if they have some executant skill, ensures that posterity will judge them not only for their works but for their interpretations of those works. Since the advent of the phonograph, its impresarios have been intrigued by the idea of letting composers make their notations permanent. In the early days, such efforts ran to the dilettantish noodlings of Gustav Mahler's keyboard transcription of excerpts from his *Des Knaben Wunderhorn*. A decade or two later, full-length works were needed for the catalogue, and Richard Strauss, for instance, was represented by a performance of his own glorious *Bourgeois Gentilhomme* Suite—rendered with so contemptuously indolent a spirit that no conductor concerned about the renewal of his contract would dare to follow.

In recent years the archival policies of several of the larger record companies have prompted them to put on tape the works of some of today's most

distinguished composers in performances which are in every sense competitive with those previously in the catalogue. One thinks of Benjamin Britten's
superb realizations of his own major scores for Decca/London, interpretations which show no trace whatever of that understatement so often associated with the composer-executant. In this country, Columbia Records has,
for the past decade or two, been transcribing the complete works of Stravinsky with the composer at the helm. (Aaron Copland is even now embarking
on a similar project.)

Stravinsky's merits as a conductor have long been a subject of debate;
but as he proceeds each year with this monumental task, it becomes increasingly apparent that his rhythmic propulsiveness, melodic cynicism, and shy-
ness about rubatos are all performance characteristics which go to the heart
of Stravinsky the composer. The question, however, is to what extent these
authentic documents will inhibit future conductors from indulging that revelatory aspect of interpretation wherein they attempt to uncover new facets,
or new combinations of old facets, in the work of such a composer as Stravinsky. (Would our curiosity be more than academic were Beethoven's piano
sonatas listed by Schwann in performances featuring the composer?) If one
can judge by the efforts of such disparate Stravinskyans as Bernstein and Karajan (the latter rather uncharitably berated in the press by the composer for
a recent release of what is surely the most imaginative and, in a purely compartmentalized sense, "inspired" realization of *Le Sacre*), the influence of
these recordings cannot as yet really be considered decisive. On the other
hand, it may be that Stravinsky's Stravinsky will afford a scaffolding upon
which future conductors will feel compelled to erect their interpretations
of his works.

I should think the composer-recorded testaments are the thin edge of
a rather different sort of wedge. Their influence may have less to do with
inspiring or inhibiting future generations of interpreters than with discour-
aging the independent performance tradition itself. There is, after all, no reason why the performer must be exclusively involved with revisitations of
the past, and the re-emergence of the performer-composer could be the beginning of the end for that post-Renaissance specialization with which tonal
music has been conspicuously involved.

Even as one examines those works of the present day designed for conventional instrumental forces, it is apparent that electronic reproduction has had
an enormous (though perhaps for certain composers indirect, if not subliminal) influence. Paul Hindemith, for instance, with his Bauhaus modernism
and his joyous linear style, which sometimes suggests nothing so much as
a pre-Renaissance contrapuntal jubilee, was a composer whose works were,
and are, a "natural" for the microphone. Many other composers of compara-

bly conservative bent have been treated to recordings of their works which have made apparent balances that are virtually unobtainable in a concert hall. (An obvious example: Frank Martin's Petite Symphonie concertante, which—with its solo forces of harp, harpsichord, and piano against a tutti of strings—offers sonorities that having once been heard in a recording so splendidly engineered as the DGG performance conducted by Ferenc Fricsay will be forever unsatisfactory as offered in a public concert.)

With those works that utilize electronic equipment not only for their reproduction but to facilitate the process of their composition as well, one senses the fulfillment of certain dominant ideas manifest in the composing procedures of the twentieth century. Electronic music is an infant craft still toddling uncertainly between the comfort and security extended by those of its parent procedures that mimic the sonorities of conventional instruments and the intriguing challenge afforded by possibilities indigenous to electronic means from which new compositional premises will eventually be elaborated. Professor Marshall McLuhan, communication theory's man of the hour, has observed: "The meaning of experience is typically one generation behind the experience—the content of new situations, both private and corporate, is typically the preceding situation—the first stage of mechanical culture became aware of agrarian values and pursuits—the first age of the planter glorified the hunt—and the first age of electronic culture (the day of the telegraph and the telephone) glorified the machine as an art form." Perhaps for this reason, the most accessible electronic scores are those that superimpose conventional instrumental or vocal textures upon electronically produced sound sources—such works as Henri Pousseur's superb ballet score *Electre.* The one temporary disadvantage of these compromise works is that they create a climate of public acceptance which encourages the proliferation of recital evenings executed by stereophonically marshaled speaker platoons—exhibitions organized by diehard impresarios convinced that each auditorium is potentially St. Mark's, with or without a resident Gabrieli. The new audience at these events is as remote from a genuine electronic participation as were those skeptical window-shoppers who in the late 1940s queued up for an appliance-store demonstration of a ten-inch Milton Berle in glorious black and white.

Whatever the present limitations of electronic music, whatever the stimulus of that "feedback" through which it has inspired more conventional forms of music making, many of the constructive methods peculiar to it have transferred with remarkable ease to conventional instrumental and vocal idioms. The reiterated note pattern, with measured crescendo and diminuendo; the dynamic comparison between close-up and far-distant statements of the same configuration; the quasimechanical ritard or accelerando; above all, the possibility of a controlled release and attack of sound—all of these motives have been borrowed by the post-Webern idioms which so decisively influence our compositional experience at present. Indeed, the influence of these electronically derived manifestations is so widespread that they appear in any number of works by composers avowedly hostile to tape music. Consciously or not, they are employed because of the fascination that such gestures, symbolic of an autocratic composing process, hold for the creative musician.

One must be careful, however, to assert that "autocracy" in this sense does not necessarily suggest singleminded authority. The composer, indeed, may not long retain that splendid isolation which early electronic experiments indicated would be his. It may well be that the effect of editorial afterthought upon performance will breed a type of technician-cum-performer whose realizations of the diagrammatic intention will be just as essential to the reputation of a composer as was the devotion of the itinerant virtuoso in earlier times. "Autocracy," then, as a description of the composing process in the electronic age, may simply suggest the possibility that the composer will become involved in some portion of each procedure through which his intention is made explicit in sound.

One of the first musicians to grasp the significance of recording to the composing process was Arnold Schoenberg, who, in a dialogue with Erwin Stein transcribed in 1928, remarked: "In radio broadcasting, a small number of sonic entities suffice for the expression of all artistic thoughts; the gramophone and the various mechanical instruments are evolving such clear sonorities that one will be able to write much less heavily instrumented pieces for them." Intentionally or not, the development of Schoenberg's own style demonstrates his understanding of the medium and its implications, and it is hard to think of certain of his works, perhaps especially those from the earlier years of his experiments with twelve-tone technique (the Serenade, Op. 24, or the septet, Op. 29, for instance), without realizing how indigenous are their gloriously eccentric instrumental combinations to the mobile microphonic dissection. And the theories espoused by Schoenberg, as the leading radical of music in the twentieth century, have become so influential, so much a part of the contemporary musical gesture, that, approved or spurned, they have affected the music of the last two generations as profoundly by their intense molecular analysis as drugstore paperback psychology has been affected by Sigmund Freud. Schoenberg's theories, to simplify outrageously, have to do with attributing significance to minute musical connections, and they deal with relationships that are on the whole subsurface and can be projected with an appropriate definition only through the intercession of electronic media.

Even as Schoenberg strove for choice regulation, other composers have elected to delegate selection privileges. Both procedures, however divergent their sponsors' intentions, have in common a denial of that condition of compositorial ambiguity which was the essence of late-nineteenth-century romanticism. At the present time, in such excursions as aleatoric music—that triumph of quasi-improvisatory buck passing—these decision-making privileges have been relinquished ostensibly in favor of the performer. But it seems reasonable to suggest that such privileges will not need to remain the exclusive preserve of a tape editor-interpreter. They could quite possibly be delegated directly to the listener. It would indeed be foolhardy to dismiss out of hand the idea that the listener can ultimately become his own composer.

At the center of the technological debate, then, is a new kind of listener—a listener more participant in the musical experience. The emergence of this mid-twentieth-century phenomenon is the greatest achievement of the record industry. For this listener is no longer passively analytical; he is an associate whose tastes, preferences, and inclinations even now alter peripherally the experiences to which he gives his attention, and upon whose fuller participation the future of the art of music waits.

He is also, of course, a threat, a potential usurper of power, an uninvited guest at the banquet of the arts, one whose presence threatens the familiar hierarchical setting of the musical establishment. Is it not, then, inopportune to venture that this participant public could emerge untutored from that servile posture with which it paid homage to the status structure of the concert world and, overnight, assume decision-making capacities which were specialists' concerns heretofore?

The keyword here is "public." Those experiences through which the listener encounters music electronically transmitted are not within the public domain. One serviceable axiom applicable to every experience in which electronic transmission is involved can be expressed in that paradox wherein the ability to obtain in theory an audience of unprecedented numbers obtains in fact a limitless number of private auditions. Because of the circumstances this paradox defines, the listener is able to indulge preferences and, through the electronic modifications with which he endows the listening experience, impose his own personality upon the work. As he does so, he transforms that work, and his relation to it, from an artistic to an environmental experience.

Dial twiddling is in its limited way an interpretative act. Forty years ago the listener had the option of flicking a switch inscribed "on" and "off" and, with an up-to-date machine, perhaps modulating the volume just a bit. Today, the variety of controls made available to him requires analytical judgment. And these controls are but primitive, regulatory devices compared to those participational possibilities which the listener will enjoy once current laboratory techniques have been appropriated by home playback devices.

It would be a relatively simple matter, for instance, to grant the listener tape-edit options which he could exercise at his discretion. Indeed, a significant step in this direction might well result from that process by which it is now possible to disassociate the ratio of speed to pitch and in so doing (albeit with some deterioration in the quality of sound as a current liability) truncate splice-segments of interpretations of the same work performed by different artists and recorded at different tempos. Let us say, for example, that you enjoy Bruno Walter's performance of the exposition and recapitulation from the first movement of Beethoven's Fifth Symphony but incline toward Klemperer's handling of the development section, which employs a notably divergent tempo. (I happen to like both performances all the way through, but there's no accounting for taste.) With the pitch-speed correlation held in abeyance, you could snip out these measures from the Klemperer edition and splice them into the Walter performance without having the splice procedure either an alteration of tempo or a fluctuation of pitch. This process could, in theory, be applied without restriction to the reconstruction of musical performance. There is, in fact, nothing to prevent a dedicated connoisseur from acting as his own tape editor and, with these devices, exercising such interpretative predilections as will permit him to create his own ideal performance.

It's tempting to speculate upon the innovations which this splice-conscious listener will demand in the editorial practice of magazines such as *High Fidelity,* where the reviewing staff is already strictly segregated along chronological lines and where, for example, Nathan Broder is automatically restricted in his assignments to material deriving from the year 1756 (May to November). Clearly, this horizontal specification will need to be superseded by a more progressive—and perhaps, in the light of multichannel possibilities, more vertical—review policy, in which, at least for longer works, the staff might choose to spell each other relay-fashion, with Alfred Frankenstein handling splices in chromatic textures, Harris Goldsmith specializing in percussive overhang problems, and Denis Stevens dealing with choral climax adjacencies.

The listener's splice prerogative is but one aspect of that editorial mix which recorded music encourages. In terms of its unselfconscious juxtaposition of a miscellany of idioms, it will have an effect similar to that which André Malraux—in his *Voices of Silence*—attributes to art reproductions. One result of this stylistic permissiveness will be a more tolerant regard for the artistic by-products of those cultures which are, from our Western point of view, chronologically "out of sync." The transmission of events and sounds around our planet has forced us to concede that there is not just one musical tradition but, rather, many musics, not all of which are concerned—by our definition of the word—with tradition.

One thinks, for instance, of Russia, a country which—with its belated awakening to Western European tradition—offered as recently as the later years of the nineteenth century a splendid Shangri-La for the most extraordinary artistic experiments. By no means part of the mainstream of Western European thought, these were experiments of a culture which, because it had for centuries operated from a quasinationalistic limbo wherein it sought immunity to the modes and mores of the West, was oriented toward an altogether different chronological sequence. Having missed the adventure of the Renaissance, the empire of the Russias found a substitute Renaissance in the importations of that eighteenth-century "entente de culture"; and ever since, it has vacillated between an assignation with the traditions of Western thought and the fond hope of fidelity to the memory of its past. Surely, those contemptuously original masterpieces of Mussorgsky—with their deliberately awkward harmony, their ruthless simplicity cloaking a high complexity, their disdain for the worldly temptations of salon success—are implicit confirmation of the message of that extraordinary exhortation from Father Zossima in *The Brothers Karamazov,* itself an astonishing preview of electronic culture: "There are those who maintain that the world is getting more and more united, more and more bound together in brotherly community as it overcomes distance and sets thoughts flying through the air. Alas, put no faith in such a bond of union."

Through simultaneous transmissions, through radio and television particularly, the art of such a country becomes for those of us on the outside rather too easily accessible. Such media encourage us to invoke comparisons between the by-products of such a culture and those to which our own very different orientation gives rise. When we find that the expression of that culture represents what seems to us archaic ideologies, we condemn it as old-fashioned or sterile, or puritanical, or as possessed of any other limitation from which we consider ourselves emancipated. With simultaneous transmission we set aside our touristlike fascination with distant and exotic places and give vent to impatience at the chronological tardiness the natives display. To this extent, Professor McLuhan's concept of the "global village"—the simultaneity of response from McMurdo Sound to Murmansk, from Taiwan to Tacoma—is alarming. There just could be some fellow at McMurdo, "out of sync" and out of touch, revivifying C major as Mozart never dreamed of!

But these intrusions pertain only to those media developments that reproduce images or sounds instantaneously. Recordings arouse very different psychological reactions and should always be considered with this proviso in mind. Whereas simultaneous reception reveals differences on a current, comparative, indeed competitive basis, the preservation of sound and image makes possible the archival view, the unimpassioned reflection upon the condition of a society, the acceptance of a multifaceted chronological concept. Indeed, the two utilizations of electronic transmission—for clarification of present circumstances occasioned by radio and television and for indefinite future re-examination of the past permitted by recording—are antidotal. The recording process, with its encouragement of a sympathetic "after-the-fact" historical view, is the indispensable replenishment of that deteriorating tolerance occasioned by simultaneous transmission. Just as simultaneous reception tends to provoke unproductive comparisons and encourages conformity, preservation and archival replay encourage detachment and nonconformist historical premises.

In my opinion, the most important of the missing links in the evolution of the listener-consumer-participant, as well as the most persuasive argument for the stylistic mix, is to be found in that most abused of electronic manifestations—background sound. This much-criticized and often misunderstood phenomenon is the most productive method through which contemporary music can confide its objectives to a listening, consuming, Muzak-absorbing society. Cunningly disguised within the bland formulae from which background sounds are seemingly concocted is an encyclopedia of experience, an exhaustive compilation of the clichés of post-Renaissance music. Moreover, this catalogue provides a cross-referenced index which permits connections between stylistic manifestations with fine disregard for chronological distinction. Within ten minutes of restaurant Muzak one can encounter a residue of Rachmaninoff or a blast of Berlioz proceeding without embarrassment from the dregs of Debussy. Indeed, all the music that has ever been can now become a background against which the impulse to make listener-supplied connections is the new foreground.

The stylistic range of most background music at present offers an appreciably greater variety of idiomatic citation than can be found among all the disparate ideologies to which "serious" musicians of recent times have subscribed. For commercial images on television or for restaurant Muzak, the background may be confined to idioms which at their most advanced draw upon the clichés of impressionism. On the other hand, the musical backgrounds of many grade-B horror thrillers coming out of Hollywood exploit advanced idioms (Leonard Rosenman's score for *Cobweb* was a typical offshoot of late-Schoenbergian twelve-tone). As background material, some significant scores find their way into the listening experience of an audience that would almost certainly avoid them as concert music.

These scores achieve this, of course, under the cover of neutrality. It is axiomatic in the composition of background material that its success relates in inverse proportion to the listener's awareness of it. It attempts to harmonize with as many environmental situations as possible and to minimize our awareness of its own intrusion and character. Indeed, it can succeed only through a suspension of conventional aesthetic values.

There is an interesting correlation between the neutrality of this background vocabulary—the unobtrusiveness of its contribution—and the fact that most background music is conveyed through recordings. These are in fact two complementary facets of the same phenomenon. For since the recording does not depend, as does the concert, upon the mood of a special occasion, and relies instead upon relating to a general set of circumstances, it exploits in background music those abilities through which that phenomenon is able to draw, without embarrassment, upon an incredible range of stylistic reference—summoning to the contemporary world idiomatic references from earlier times, placing them in a context in which, by being accorded a subdivided participation, they achieve a new validity.

Background music has been attacked from many quarters—by Europeans as a symptom of the decadence of North American society, by North Americans as a product of megalopolitan conformity. Indeed, it is perhaps accepted at face value only in those societies where no continuing tradition of Occidental music is to be found.

Background music, of course, confirms all the argumentative criteria by which the opponents of musical technology determine their judgments. It has no sense of historic date—the fact that it is studio produced and the stylistic compote of its musical substance prevent this; the personnel involved are almost always anonymous; a great deal of overtracking and other electronic wizardry is involved in its making—hence such arguments as those of automation, aesthetic morality, and the van Meegeren syndrome find in background music a tempting target. This target, however, protected at present by commercial rather than aesthetic considerations, is immune to attack.

Those who see in background music a sinister fulfillment of the Orwellian environment control assume that it is capable of enlisting all who are exposed to it as proponents of its own vast cliché. But this is precisely the point! Because it can infiltrate our lives from so many different angles, the cliché residue of all the idioms employed in background becomes an intuitive part of our musical vocabulary. Consequently, in order to gain our attention any *musical* experience must be of a quite exceptional nature. And meanwhile, through this ingenious glossary, the listener achieves a direct associative experience of the post-Renaissance vocabulary, something that not even the most inventive music appreciation course would be able to afford him.

As this medium evolves, as it becomes available for situations in which the quite properly self-indulgent participation of the listener will be encouraged, those venerable distinctions about the class structure within the musical hierarchy—distinctions that separated composer and performer and listener—will become outmoded. Does this, then, contradict the fact that since the Renaissance the separation of function (specialization) has been the professional lot and that the medieval status of the musician, one who created and performed for the sake of his own enjoyment, has long since been supplanted by our post-Renaissance orgy of musical sophistication? I should say that these two concepts are not necessarily contradictory.

This overlapping of professional and lay responsibility in the creative process does tend to produce a set of circumstances that superficially suggests the largely unilateral participation of the pre-Renaissance world. In fact, it is deceptively easy to draw such parallels, to assume that the entire adventure of the Renaissance and of the world which it created was a gigantic historical error. But we are not returning to a medieval culture. It is a dangerous oversimplification to suggest that under the influence of electronic media we could retrograde to some condition reminiscent of the pre-Renaissance cultural monolith. The technology of electronic forms makes it highly improbable that we will move in any direction but one of even greater intensity and complexity; and the fact that a participational overlapping becomes unashamedly involved with the creative process should not suggest a waning of the necessity for specialized techniques.

What will happen, rather, is that new participation areas will proliferate and that many more hands will be required to achieve the execution of a particular environmental experience. Because of this complexity, because so many different levels of participation will, in fact, be merged in the final result, the individualized information concepts which define the nature of identity and authorship will become very much less imposing. Not that this identity reduction will be achieved without some harassment from those who resent its implications. After all, what are the batteries of public relations men, advertising executives, and press agents doing if not attempting to provide an identification for artist and producer in a society where duplication is everywhere and where identity in the sense of information about the authors means less and less?

The most hopeful thing about this process—about the inevitable disregard for the identity factor in the creative situation—is that it will permit a climate in which biographical data and chronological assumption can no longer be the cornerstone for judgments about art as it relates to environment. In fact, this whole question of individuality in the creative situation—the process through which the creative act results from, absorbs, and re-forms individual opinion—will be subjected to a radical reconsideration.

I believe the fact that music plays so extensive a part in the regulation of our environment suggests its eventual assumption of a role as immediate, as utilitarian, as colloquial as that which language now plays in the conduct of our daily lives. For music to achieve a comparable familiarity, the implications of its styles, its habits, its mannerisms, its tricks, its customary devices, its statistically most frequent occurrences—in other words, its clichés—must be familiar and recognized by everyone. A mass recognition of the cliché quotient of a vocabulary need not suggest our becoming saturated with the mundanities of those clichés. We do not value great works of literature less because we, as men in the street, speak the language in which they happen to be written. The fact that so much of our daily conversation is concerned with the tedious familiarities of common courtesy, the mandatory conversation openers about the weather and so on, does not for a moment dull our appreciation of the potential glories of the language we use. To the contrary, it sharpens it. It gives us background against which the foreground that is the habitat of the imaginative artist may stand in greater relief. It is my view that in the electronic age the art of music will become much more viably a part of our lives, much less an ornament to them, and that it will consequently change them much more profoundly.

If these changes are profound enough, we may eventually be compelled to redefine the terminology with which we express our thoughts about art. Indeed, it may become increasingly inappropriate to apply to a description of environmental situations the word "art" itself—a word that, however venerable and honored, is necessarily replete with imprecise, if not in fact obsolete, connotations.

In the best of all possible worlds, art would be unnecessary. Its offer of restorative, placative therapy would go begging a patient. The professional specialization involved in its making would be presumption. The generalities of its applicability would be an affront. The audience would be the artist and their life would be art.

MUSIC AND TECHNOLOGY

One Sunday morning in December 1950, I wandered into a living-room-sized radio studio, placed my services at the disposal of a single microphone belonging to the Canadian Broadcasting Corporation, and proceeded to broadcast "live" (tape was already a fact of life in the recording industry, but in those days radio broadcasting still observed the first-note-to-last-and-damn-the-consequences syndrome of the concert hall) two sonatas: one

From *Piano Quarterly*, Winter 1974–75.

by Mozart, one by Hindemith. It was my first network broadcast, but it was not my first contact with the microphone; for several years I'd been indulging in experiments at home with primitive tape recorders—strapping the mikes to the sounding board of my piano, the better to emasculate Scarlatti sonatas, for example, and generally subjecting both instruments to whichever imaginative indignities came to mind.

But the CBC occasion, as I've hinted already, was a memorable one: not simply because it enabled me to communicate without the immediate presence of a gallery of witnesses (though the fact that in most forms of broadcasting a microphone six feet away stands as surrogate for an audience has always been, for me, prominent among the attractions of the medium) but rather because later the same day I was presented with a soft-cut "acetate," a disc which dimly reproduced the felicities of the broadcast in question and which, even today, a quarter-century after the fact, I still take down from the shelf on occasion in order to celebrate that moment in my life when I first caught a vague impression of the direction it would take, when I realized that the collected wisdom of my peers and elders to the effect that technology represented a compromising, dehumanizing intrusion into art was nonsense, when my love affair with the microphone began.

I suspect, indeed, that if I were to assign an absolute time to the moment of recognition, that time would relate to the occasion when, later in the day, rehearing the acetate for the third or fourth time, I discovered that if I gave it a bass cut at a hundred cycles or thereabouts and a treble boost at approximately five thousand, the murky, unwieldy, bass-oriented studio piano with which I had had to deal earlier in the day could be magically transformed on playback into an instrument seemingly capable of the same sonic perversions to which I had already introduced Maestro Scarlatti.

"A plausible approach qua Mozart," you say, "but entirely inappropriate for Hindemith!" Perhaps; perhaps not. I'm reluctant to argue the case on musical grounds, for my intentions, of course, were only secondarily musical; they were primarily theatrical and illusory. I had prevailed upon the most primitive technology to sponsor a suggestion of that which was not; my own contribution as artist was no longer the be-all and end-all of the project at hand, no longer a fait accompli. Technology had positioned itself between the attempt and the realization; the "charity of the machine," to quote the theologian Jean Le Moyne, had interposed itself between "the frailty of nature and the vision of the idealized accomplishment." "Remarkable clarity—must have been an incredible piano," friends would say. "Believe me, you simply can't imagine," I would respond. I had learned the first lesson of technology; I had learned to be creatively dishonest.

Let me say straight off that I admit to no inherent contradiction in those terms. Technology, in my view, is not primarily a conveyor belt for the dissemination of information; it is not primarily an instantaneous relay system; it is not primarily a memory bank in whose vaults are deposited the achievements and shortcomings, the creative credits and documented deficits, of man. It is, of course, or can be, any of those things, if required, and perhaps you will remind me that "the camera does not lie," to which I can only respond, "Then the camera must be taught to forthwith." For technology should not, in my view, be treated as a noncommittal, noncommitted voyeur; its capacity for dissection, for analysis—above all, perhaps, for the idealization of an impression—must be exploited, and no area with which it is currently occupied better demonstrates the philosophical conflicts with which its practitioners and theorists have been too long preoccupied than the aims and techniques of recording.

I believe in "the intrusion" of technology because, essentially, that intrusion imposes upon art a notion of morality which transcends the idea of art itself. And before, as in the case of "morality," I use some other old-fashioned words, let me explain what I mean by that one. Morality, it seems to me, has never been on the side of the carnivore—at least not when alternative life-styles are available. And evolution, which is really the biological rejection of inadequate moral systems—and particularly the evolution of man in response to his technology—has been anticarnivorous to the extent that, step by step, it has enabled him to operate at increasing distances from, to be increasingly out of touch with, his animal response to confrontation.

A war, for instance, engaged in by computer-aimed missiles is a slightly better, slightly less objectionable war than one fought by clubs or spears. Not much better, and unquestionably more destructive, statistically, but better to the extent, at least, that, all things being equal, the adrenal response of the participants (we had better forget about the bystanders or the argument collapses) is less engaged by it. Well, Margaret Mead, if I read her rightly, disapproves of that distancing factor, of that sense of disengagement from biological limitation. But I do believe in it, and recordings, though they're rarely understood as such, are one of the very best metaphors we have for it.

A few months back, for instance, I was listening to the broadcast memoirs of the very distinguished and very venerable British conductor Sir Adrian Boult. At one point Sir Adrian was asked what he thought of recording, and he said, predictably enough, something to the effect that "Well, of course, it's fair game to make them, especially for those who can't get out to the concert hall, but they're never going to take the place of the concert, are they? I always say to my producer at the outset of the session, 'Look here, old man, it's my job to get the very best I can out of the band, and I shall strive to do that even if we need two or three takes. But I don't want any of this patching! That's all you young chaps seem to think of these days—patching. Should the horn fluff his part—well, bad luck, I say, and if time permits, we'll let him have another go at it. But I don't want you to repair the warts by patching, d'you see, because at all costs I must have the long line intact.' " (I hasten to add that I do not have Sir Adrian's transcript at hand, but the paraphrase is as accurate as memory can make it.)

In any case, Sir Adrian's attitude toward "patching"—which we call "editing" or "splicing" on this side of the water—and toward recording technology in general represents one of the more unbreachable sectors of the generation gap. He's wrong, of course—splicing doesn't damage lines. Good splices build good lines, and it shouldn't much matter if one uses a splice every two seconds or none for an hour so long as the result *appears* to be a coherent whole. After all, if one buys a new car, it doesn't really matter how many assembly-line hands are involved in its production. The more the better, really, insofar as they can help to ensure the security of its operation.

But what really bothers Sir Adrian, I suspect, is that since the splice divides the elements of a particular problem, it transcends the physical anxieties, the coordinative challenges, represented by that problem. It seems to preclude the possibility that man unaided is his own best advocate—the most unwarranted assumption of the post-Renaissance era—and for that reason to be, in some way, antihuman.

Of course, we very often tend to confuse a sense of humanity with the way in which human concerns are traditionally resolved. Traditionally, they're resolved by individual moments of enlightenment, of vision, and it's that almost mystical faith in the omnipotence of the enlightened moment, in the challenge honorably overcome, which makes people of Sir Adrian's generation distrust recording technology.

I mentioned already the generation gap, but there's also a geographical gap involved. The farther east you go, the more likely you are to find recordings which are in effect taped concerts. Of course, if you go far enough east, you get to Japan, and in that country, which has no inhibiting Westernized concert-hall tradition to reckon with, recordings are understood as indigenous experiences. But in general, as one heads east from the Rhine, the perspective becomes more distant, as in a concert hall, usually more reverberant, and less precise, for that reason, and the whole operation functions mainly as an exercise in memory.

Of course, there is nothing really wrong with making records for that purpose. Fifty years ago, most people thought that recording was essentially an archival operation, the better to remember Grandpapa's generation by. And, as I've said, that's part of what it does, but not at all what the process is about.

I do quite a bit of fancy editorial footwork with the voices of characters that I interview for radio documentaries, and if I do it well, I defy anyone to find in my editorial "patching" something other than a tauter, more coherent character synthesis. It is of course true that the amount of work one does is often relative to the value of what's being said by the character in question, and that if virtually nothing is being said, the sense of portraiture could conceivably be enhanced by leaving the material uncut. If, for instance, one stumbled into an interview with a character who said, "Well, like, man, I sorta don't wanna go out on a limb to, like, answer da question, you know, because, like, well, it takes all kinds, you know, and, well, either you dig it or maybe not, am I right? But, like, man, if I were to give a real conclusive answer, I'd say that—well, could be, you know." If he said that, it might be tempting not to cut it, to keep it intact as a portrait. If, however, one happened to deduce that what he was really saying was "To be or—like, uh—not to be," and those words were bound within that quote, then I really think that "like, uh" should go.

THE GRASS IS ALWAYS GREENER IN THE OUTTAKES: AN EXPERIMENT IN LISTENING

I can't help wishing that all recordings were live performances. . . . If this is totally unfeasible, then at least I'd like to know that there was no splicing within movements. . . . The whole intimidating idea of having all those guys around while you have to stop and ask for a retake . . . can be pretty terrible, especially if you have to start again and again. It can get you very uptight.
—André Watts, *High Fidelity,* June 1974

A recital will of necessity have flaws, but it will often have an in-built continuity, a spanning intellectual arch, that most recordings do not capture. The complexity of recording-studio conditions and the necessity that the score be rendered note-perfect . . . usually dictate doing more than one take for a movement or work, and the sense of a long line stretching across the whole piece can rarely be achieved unless the playing continues from beginning to end without stopping.
—Stephen Bishop, *High Fidelity,* February 1975

From *High Fidelity,* August 1975.

Strange notions, these. I wonder how often Hiroshi Teshigahai has been advised that intercuts with cover takes, scenes shot out of sequence, postproduction sound relays should be banned from the vocabulary of film because they fail to observe the limitations of stagecraft. I wonder how often Vladimir Nabokov's publisher has pondered a third and not-yet-final draft and declared, "Volodya baby, I've told you already, let it all hang out. So you dropped a comma, so you split an infinitive, that's truth, man."

There's a place for verismo techniques, to be sure. One wouldn't want to give the Kerouacian roadrunners writer's cramp; one wouldn't want to formalize the camera style of an Allan King or the production methods of a Craig Gilbert; I, for one, certainly wouldn't want to have missed that ultimate exercise in planned spontaneity, *An American Family,* but I bet if one could round up the Louds from the cutting-room floor, one would gain some insight into the ratio of cinema to vérité.

Stravinsky claimed that the business of art is technique; I do not agree. Nor do I believe that the business of technology is the rule of science—and, with all respect, I wish the good Professor McLuhan, who doesn't believe it either, would say so more often. But I do believe that once introduced into the circuitry of art, the technological presence must be encoded and decoded (no Dolby salesmen need apply) in such a way that its presence is, in every respect, at the service of that spiritual good that ultimately will serve to banish art itself.

So strange views, then, those of Watts and Bishop, but not without echo in the generation that they represent—a generation that, if no longer in swaddling clothes, was scarcely more than vertical when tape technology came of age, and a generation that, though young enough to know better, would now seem to be entering upon a period of technological neoromanticism.

Daniel Barenboim, for example, is, or was—the British monthlies are always behind schedule in the colonies—fond of the conceit that recording technique should involve two takes per work, take them or leave them. If nothing else, this view bespeaks an awesome metronomic consistency on Barenboim's part, always assuming that he permits his editors the occasional luxury of an intercut. Indeed, one thinks back almost fondly to such celebrated controversies of the early LP era as the Schwarzkopf-Flagstad high C episode (Mme S. extended the range of Mme F. by a semitone), which, however inefficient as a delivery system for the issues involved, could at least be charged to the account of music's senior citizens. But like Bishop, Watts, and Barenboim, other younger artists have begun to assert the artificiality of the recording, to insist that it be placed within precisely the sort of snapshot context that immunizes the music at hand against the benefactions of technology.

Now, of course, one can look for motives; one can be uncharitable; one can summon up scenes in a manager's office: "Listen, kid, you damn well better leave two clinkers a page in that platter or the live act just ain't gonna play in El Paso." In a way, it reminds me of those PR treks that Hollywood's brightest take, ostensibly in order to hype their current flick. Inevitably, in the process of covering the Griffin-Carson-Douglas circuit they're called upon to "set up" a two-minute clip from the film in question and, almost inevitably, having established that the heart resides on Broadway though the bank is in Bel Air, use the occasion to witness to their ignorance of the plot and names of their costars and, if possible, to get across the idea that they wouldn't be caught dead at one of their own films. "Yeah, well, Merv, I'm not just sure what the studio sent you here. Could be it's the place where I get shot up pretty bad. . . . Eh? . . . How's that? . . . Oh yeah, well, like, I don't really know if I pull through or not, tell you the truth, 'cause there was nothin' for me in the last scene, y'know, so I never finished the script."

But let us not be uncharitable; let us accept the statements at face value. Let us assume that, like Watts, Bishop, and Barenboim, some artists really do underestimate their own editorial potential, really do believe that art must always be the result of some inexorable forward thrust, some sustained animus, some ecstatic high, and cannot conceive that the function of the artist could also entail the ability to summon, on command, the emotional tenor of any moment, in any score, at any time—that one should be free to "shoot" a Beethoven sonata or a Bach fugue in or out of sequence, intercut almost without restriction, apply postproduction techniques as required, and that the composer, the performer, and above all the listener will be better served thereby.

Now, I have addressed myself to these questions on many occasions (most elaborately in the April 1966 issue of *High Fidelity* *), but in so doing I have always tried to elevate the argument to the level of abstract speculation. Indeed, I still think that a reasoned exegesis is the proper gentleman's response. But with the proliferation of statements like those of Watts and Bishop, it appeared to me that the time had come to set philosophic considerations aside and dig for statistics that would make or break the case.

Let me confess at once that I have no expertise as a poll taker, no credentials in the field of demographic studies. Let me further confess that, for professional purposes, my statistical sampling—eighteen auditionees—was undoubtedly too small and that it could unquestionably have been enhanced by any number of subtleties that did not occur to me until the test period was nearly at an end. I could, for example, have rotated the works in question, starting perhaps for some auditionees in the middle of the test and proceeding cyclically or, alternately, starting with the last work and presenting

---

*See p. 331.

The Program

BYRD: The Sixth Galliard
BACH I: Sonata for Viola da Gamba No. 1, third movement
BACH II: Sonata for Viola da Gamba No. 2, second movement
MOZART: Piano Sonata K. 311, third movement
BEETHOVEN I: "Emperor" Concerto, second movement, bars 1–59
BEETHOVEN II: Fifth Symphony, third movement
SCRIABIN: Piano Sonata No. 3, first movement, bars 1–94
SCHOENBERG: "Dank," Op. 1, No. 1

The eight items on the bill of fare (playing time: 34 minutes, 35 seconds) were dubbed from discs onto tape and arranged chronologically. Seven were drawn from my own catalogue; the exception is George Szell's performance with the Cleveland Orchestra of the Beethoven excerpt.

---

the program in reverse order. This would have provided some measurement of the fatigue factor involved, for, given the fact that each interview consumed at least two hours (not counting coffee breaks), the test was unquestionably too long and inconsiderately structured vis-à-vis the participants. Other faults come to mind as well: the predominance of piano music was undesirable but unavoidable (the problem was that I knew where the dirty linen lay); most of the eighteen auditionees were personal friends (the one purely orchestral insert was included as a loyalty control). But, overall, the study has confirmed some of my suspicions about the listening process, about the interaction of knowledge and attention, and it will, I hope, serve as a basis for more detailed interrogations to come.

The object was to test the degree to which my guinea pigs were able to detect the "in" point of any splice, whether carelessly or craftily constructed (*pace* CBS—there weren't too many of the former!). I was not interested in their reactions to the quality of the performances on the test tape (though there were some unexpected dividends in that regard); I simply wanted to know to what extent a splice can be detected, given optimum listening conditions (the laws of probability suggest that in any control sample the audio technician's motto, "A well-made splice is an inaudible splice," will *appear* to be invalid), and I was not interested in the views of my guests as to whether the splices that they heard—or, more commonly, thought they heard—compromised the musical experience. If, indeed, a significant percentage of splices were readily and consistently detectable, there would be something wrong with the product under consideration; if that were the case, the views of Messrs Watts and Bishop would be substantiated, and I would long since have fled for the hills.

The rules were as simple as I could make them, given the complexity of the information I sought:

1. Each auditionee was allowed to listen to each selection three times. All were encouraged to take advantage of this option and, of their own volition, heard each excerpt at least twice, the majority exercising the three-times-through provision.

2. Each auditionee was tested separately.

3. With the exception of the participants in category C (none of the laymen had more than rudimentary training in score reading), unmarked scores were available for optional use. During listening sessions, the auditionees' initials were entered over each splice guess in a score, which I retained; during replays of the same material, they had the right to withdraw the guess in question.

4. No information other than the title of the selection was provided in

---

The Participants

CATEGORY A—PROFESSIONAL MUSICIANS

Males:	*Females:*
Composer	Pianist
Cellist	Musicologist
Pianist	Singer

CATEGORY B—AUDIO EXPERTS

Radio executive	Radio producer
Radio technician	Radio producer
Radio technician	Announcer/editor

CATEGORY C—LAYMEN

Lawyer	Librarian
General practitioner	Journalist
Record reviewer	Insurance underwriter

In regard to the auditionees in category A, I opted to double up on pianists, given the heavy concentration of piano repertoire involved. In category B, all of the participants are committed to the "serious music" side of broadcasting, the executive and two producers being exclusively concerned with classical repertoire, both technicians having wide experience with symphonic recording, and the announcer/editor specializing in classical programming.

Glossary

TAKE: A recorded performance, or attempt thereat, usually commencing at the opening of a work, movement, or other major point of demarcation.

INSERT: A recorded performance usually designed to supplement a take; frequently of brief duration but on occasion extending throughout the major portion of a work and defined by the fact that it does not include the opening of said work. (In certain European studios, all recorded material is designated by the term "take," and "insert" has fallen into disuse.)

SPLICE: An edit point representing the confluence of two takes, two inserts, or one take and one insert.

REGENERATION: The dubbing from one tape machine to another of material that appears with identical note values at two or more spots in a work; usually of brief duration but occasionally, if ill-advisedly, used for da capos, double-bar repeats, etc.

INTERNAL CLOSE-UP: A splice or edit, without benefit of control-room announcement, made possible by the fact that the performer(s) doubled back prior to a convenient edit point and repeated on one or more occasions the material in question.

---

advance, except in the cases of the Byrd and the Schoenberg, where the auditionees were told how many splices were involved in each selection (one and five, respectively) and were consequently requested to restrain their sleuthing to a maximum of one and five guesses for the respective selections, though in these as in other examples no guesses were required.

5. Prior to the test, each participant was requested to place an X opposite the appropriate completion of the sentence "My attitude toward splicing is best summed up as follows. . . ."

(a) Strongly disapprove: Postproduction techniques inevitably disrupt the continuity of a performance.

(b) Disapprove in general: Postproduction techniques can disrupt the continuity of a performance.

(c) Have never given the matter much thought and/or couldn't care less what those weirdo Commie technocrats think up next.

(d) Approve in principle: Recording need not duplicate a concert experience.

(e) Approve without reservation: Recording should not duplicate a concert experience.

Options (a) and (b) were, not unexpectedly, bypassed by all hands; option (c) was tolerated as an exercise in whimsy. But the reactions to options (d) and (e) caught me off guard. Although I had anticipated (indeed, prayed for) several of the inverse correlations that the test was to disclose, I had not anticipated that four of the six auditionees who declared for option (e) would be laymen (a technician and a pianist supported the proposition as well). The remaining candidates, who opted for letter (d), supplied a list of elaborations in support of their choice that would have done credit to the essays of Watts and Bishop: "Couldn't give up my live-in-concert Nana Mouskouri discs" (radio technician); "Wouldn't want to rule out broadcast recordings" (radio executive); "Shouldn't make somebody look good who isn't" (pianist—that one caused me to blow my scientific cool and launch a lecture on the "monkey theorem"). The conclusion, however, was obvious: professional musicians have a vested interest in the status quo; producers, in the main, and to a lesser extent technicians, have a vested interest in professional musicians; neither group has come to terms with the degree to which the layman is prepared to accept recording technology as an indigenous phenomenon, distinct from the concert experience.

The test overall involved 66 splices. I prefer to think, in fact, that it involved 66.66 splices, and I trust the reader will indulge me in this arithmetical conceit later on. Since, as mentioned above, those 66 splice points were inserted within 34 minutes and 35 seconds of music, the splice density was one per 31.4 seconds. The density varied from zero (Bach I and Beethoven II) to one every 9.2 seconds (the Mozart Rondo).

And this brings us to the second inverse correlation: the ratio between splice density and guess density. Each example was selected in order to demonstrate, either by itself or in conjunction with a neighbor, some specific control feature, and the two Bach examples and the two Beethoven examples were selected with this density correlation in mind. Bach I, unimpeded by splices, was the object of 36 guesses overall (one participant abstaining), while Bach II, with 12 splices (density one per 12.5 seconds), elicited 22 guesses (three participants abstaining). The examples are of almost equal length—2 minutes, 25 seconds for Bach I, 2 minutes, 30 seconds for Bach II. And yet the guess-hazard rate in Bach I was 2.0 per participant, including abstentions, while in the densely populated splice thickets of Bach II the result was 1.2 per participant.

DENSITY TABLE I						
Composer	Splices	Density (in secs.)	Guesses	Correct Guesses	Guesses (per min.)	Correct Guesses (per min.)
Bach I	0		36		14.8	
Bach II	12	12.5	22	6	8.8	2.4

Similar, though less spectacular, results were forthcoming in the Beethoven items (nine and zero splices, respectively). Beethoven II, if adjusted chronometrically vis-à-vis its companion piece (6 minutes, 15 seconds for Beethoven I, 5 minutes, 30 seconds for Beethoven II), would have received 58 guesses instead of the actual count of 52, while Beethoven I drew a total of 64 votes.

		DENSITY TABLE 2				
Composer	*Splices*	*Density (in secs.)*	*Guesses*	*Correct Guesses*	*Guesses (per min.)*	*Correct Guesses (per min.)*
Beethoven I	9	41.6	64	15	9.9	2.4
Beethoven II	0		52		8.9	

This pair of examples served a more personal purpose as well. I begged CBS for access to one movement by one artist involving no splices so that what might be called the Kinsey, or "yes, but respectable people wouldn't answer those questions," syndrome could be discounted. Fifteen of the participants were personal friends, after all, and the reader might reasonably indulge a certain skepticism on the order of "Well, they probably limited their guesses so as not to hurt his feelings." Obviously, no such compunction would prevail in the case of Szell, and since in a movement devoid of splices (as rare a bird for him as for the rest of us, by the way) the guess pattern remained relatively consistent, no such collegial collusion could be laid to our account. An even more interesting correlation can be drawn in relation to the two unedited examples: if my unspliced Bach I excerpt had equaled Szell's Beethoven excerpt in length, it would have collected 81 votes instead of 36. Ergo, no quarter asked, no quarter given!

The Byrd galliard was chosen precisely because its long splice occurs at the most obvious and, consequently, most unlikely of places: it follows a double bar that demarcates the central section from the concluding paragraph. This test was devised in order to weed out the "sophisticates" from what one might call the "divine innocents"—i.e., no trick-conscious technician would be caught dead making so obvious a call, and indeed it was left to three laymen (the librarian, the journalist, and the record reviewer) to make a correct identification. Everyone else (there were three abstentions) looked for accented chords, sudden soft-pedal changes, or other coloristic effects that, in their minds, would indicate a splice. (More often than not, of course, such search-and-destroy missions are in vain; equivalence rather than its inverse is the editor's rule of thumb, and instead of a quest for problem areas one might profitably settle upon moments of particularly felicitous fluency.)

	GROUP ACCURACY TABLE—BYRD		
Category	*Correct*	*Incorrect*	*Abstentions*
Musicians	0	6	0
Technicians	0	4	2
Laymen	3	2	1

The Schoenberg was chosen for exactly the opposite reason: with one conspicuous exception—a G-minor chord with attendant fermata midway in the song—it is possessed of a seamless texture. Although the G-minor chord was selected by five participants (it is, after all, the postromantic equivalent of a double bar, the logical spot for a paragraphic splice, and is indeed the first of our five splices), only one other splice was correctly identified, and it involved a verbal rather than a musical alert. The word *"tief,"* bar 51, was slightly clipped due to a splice on the piano upbeat following, and one German-speaking auditionee identified the splice correctly. (Several others, also equipped with a modicum of German, sensed that we were indeed in *tief* trouble and placed their bets incorrectly on the word itself or on the preceding upbeat.)

The two remaining examples were a study in contrast. The Scriabin (five splices, or one for each 1.05 minutes) was chosen for three reasons: two of its splices are internal close-ups, and neither was identified; it represented a type of piano texture that, given its constant ebb and flow and always assuming a consistency in pedal overhang, is remarkably easy to splice; and it contains, nonetheless, the only splice in the test that is to my mind a giveaway. This splice was in no way the handiwork of an absentminded editor; I was the culprit, having miscalculated the ambient "in" vis-à-vis the less pedaled "out," but despite my qualms the spot in question collected no votes at all. Of the three conventional splices, one passed by unchallenged, one was identified by a pianist, and one, which coincides with an a tempo—poco scherzando, was identified by five participants. This was, indeed, the only example in which the musician's expertise proved of value.

	GROUP ACCURACY TABLE—SCRIABIN		
Category	*Correct*	*Incorrect*	*Abstentions*
Musicians	4	17	0
Technicians	1	6	2
Laymen	1	6	3

The Mozart was chosen because it contained more than half the splices in the test overall (thirty-four) and because the great majority of those were the result of either internal close-ups or regeneration. I confess that I use the technique of regeneration reluctantly, preferring instead to execute separate inserts for each problem area; in this case, however (we were running out the clock on the session in question, and I had to catch a train), I accepted the easy way out—after all, it is a rondo. Now, a regenerative splice is, on the whole, much more difficult to detect than its conventional counterpart. Its hallmark is consistency, especially if used within the immediate vicinity of its dub material, and such proximity was a feature of K. 311. Unlike conventional splices, however, where one may move from, let us say, take 1 to take 2 and stay with the latter for a considerable period of time, a regeneration—other than in a da capo situation—must, given the customary alterations in the harmonic order and, indeed, the overly consistent veneer that it encourages, be relieved of its duties as soon as possible. Hence the Mozart's density factor. The longest regenerative segment in K. 311, in fact, is six beats; the shortest, a single, solo eighth-note.

In its way, and not unlike the Byrd, K. 311 encouraged significant differences in the guess pattern of the three groups concerned; the professional musicians and the laymen, for the most part, opted for paragraphic, return-of-theme-style splice points, while the technicians, sensing regeneration in the air, went for broke and, in one spectacular case, for three correct guesses, including a very impressive call of "regeneration in/regeneration out" by one of their number. Yet, despite a splice-density factor 450 percent greater than, for example, its Beethoven concerto neighbor, the Mozart Rondo elicited only 8 percent more guesses (71 versus 66), only one more correct guess (16 versus 15), and only a 25 percent increase in correct guesses per minute (3.0 versus 2.4).

In general, the three groups revealed, through their guess pattern, quite different attitudes to and/or assumptions about the nature of the editorial process. The musicians, for the most part, opted for coloristic effects, sudden sforzandos, changes of pedal, unscheduled rubatos; the technicians were alert for "ambient dips," "overhang irregularities"; and the laymen tended to guess paragraphically and, wherever possible, to locate their guesses following a rest or other rhythmic interruption.

One might be inclined to discount the performance of the laymen group if that tendency were its only distinctive feature, but a probability study of the Mozart—the example most open to postrest, postfermata opportunities—did not reveal a particularly accurate guess pattern from the members of category C.

And now, as they say at Oscar time, the envelope, please:

ACCURACY RESULTS BY GROUP

Composer	*1*	*2*	*3*
BYRD	Laymen	Technicians	Musicians
BACH I	Laymen	Technicians	Musicians
BACH II	Laymen	Musicians	Technicians
MOZART	Laymen	Technicians	Musicians
BEETHOVEN I	Laymen	Technicians	Musicians
BEETHOVEN II	Technicians	Laymen	Musicians
SCRIABIN	Musicians	Technicians	Laymen
SCHOENBERG	Technicians	Laymen	Musicians

The largest number of accurate guesses (seven) was registered by two auditionees, the journalist and the singer. The singer, however, required more than two and a half times as many guesses to arrive at her total and was, consequently, penalized, as the error ratio was brought to bear upon her score. The highest correct-guess-to-error ratio was established by the librarian (two correct out of a very conservative total of three), the most impressive overall performance by the physician. The results, with their percentages adjusted for error pattern (after all, if allowed to play "Battleship" with the scores in question, somebody was bound to hit something), revealed that the highest group percentage (1.45) was attained by the laymen, the technicians scoring an average of .78 and the professional musicians .56. It was also worthy of note that the four highest scores (physician, technician, journalist, librarian) were all achieved by people with one thing in common—the inability to read music—and that two of the three lowest scores (0) were earned by radio producers.

INDIVIDUAL RESULTS—CORRECTED FOR ERROR RATIO

	Category	*Percentage*
1.	General practitioner	3.40
2.	Radio technician	2.70
3.	Journalist	2.62
4.	Librarian	2.00
5.	Radio technician	1.14
6.	Singer	0.94
7.	Pianist	0.92
8.	Cellist	0.70
9, 10	Radio executive, record reviewer	0.60
11.	Pianist	0.31
12.	Musicologist	0.25
13.	Composer	0.24
14.	Announcer/editor	0.22
15.	Lawyer	0.10
16–18	Insurance underwriter, radio producer, radio producer	0.00

Conclusions? Lots of them—homilies mostly. For example, the tape does lie and nearly always gets away with it; a little learning is a dangerous thing, and a lot of it is positively disastrous.

Favorite Moment Recollected? After two playthroughs, the cellist had contributed four splices to Szell's Beethoven and then, when about to hear it for the third time, asked: "Who's the conductor, by the way?" "George Szell." "Really! Is it okay if I take my splices out?" "That's your privilege. May I ask why?" "I've always heard that George Szell never used them." "Oh!" "By the way, do I get an extra point for knowing that there weren't any?" "No."

Future tests? Well, maybe. It would be fun to pursue one inverse correlation that was hinted at by the results from category A but that would need much more corroboration re the degree to which instrumental specialization, with all the tactile associations thereunto pertaining, handicaps a musician's judgment when listening to his own instrument. Our singer, for example, did not set any records in the Schoenberg, nor did the cellist in the Bach pieces. And the pianists—with the exception of the Scriabin sonata, where both admittedly did well—accumulated most of their points in the cello works, in the Schoenberg song, or in the Beethoven concerto's tuttis and made most of their errors by confusing moments of interpretative pianistic license ("Hey, you accented that F-sharp—I never do that—must be a splice") with edit points.

Preferred material for future tests? What else? The records of Stephen Bishop splice-guessed by André Watts, and the records of André Watts splice-guessed by Stephen Bishop.

"OH, FOR HEAVEN'S SAKE, CYNTHIA, THERE MUST BE SOMETHING ELSE ON!"

Do you remember the great television scandal of the late 1950s—the crisis over whether Charles Van Doren did or didn't on "Twenty-One"? And do you remember how when it finally leaked to the press that he wasn't just a walking encyclopedia of useless information—despite that classically furrowed brow and unique ability to sweat buckets while imprisoned in an air-conditioned isolation booth, he had, in fact, been fed the answers all along—corporate heads rolled and American television inaugurated a new era of "cleanse your soul and confess the tricks your show comprised"? Well, until the public outcry was assuaged, it was great fun, and some memorable credits rolled across the TelePrompTers of the nation: "Parts of the foregoing program were prerecorded, Miss Francis's gown was self-suspending, and Bennett Cerf wore braces."

But the real issues raised by the Van Doren caper had less to do with legal or even moral considerations than with purely aesthetic ones. And the commendable pragmatism with which Van Doren shed scholastic credibility in the interests of better program building afforded an object lesson for anyone concerned with the future of television and, in particular, for those of us perplexed by the less than cordial relations between musical performance and the camera. For just as television, despite the proliferation of closed-circuit teaching aids and "Twenty-One" 's ingenious approximation of a final semester's nervous prostration, cannot invalidate the classroom, neither can it simulate, for all its undoubted capacity to attract that substantial audience which no longer frequents the concert hall, the antiquarian charm of a public musical display. The concert is dying because it no longer adequately ministers to the needs of music in the twentieth century and not because television is waiting in the wings prepared to take up its burden and its repertoire.

Television, indeed, does not "replace" other outlets. It cannot be expected to take over the preoccupations of an outdated medium as a socialist government takes over steel. Necessarily and automatically it reinterprets by its own lights whichever experience engages its attention and disdains the criteria of those outlets through which the experience acquired altogether different connotations.

There are, of course, a few activities which adapt for television with but minimal redefinition of their structure or psychological emphasis. Hockey, for instance, works astonishingly well, not because of mass appeal or the expectation of a sharper look at rumbles behind the goal cage or even any disinclination on the part of its devotees to stir from their parlors, but because the structure of the game itself encourages split-screen techniques, replay insets, and a perpetuum mobile display by the camera. (Baseball, on the other hand, as a sort of animated chess, functions abysmally.) Drama can be brought off with astonishing élan on the small screen, especially if those cool, neodocumentary camera angles with which television reportage has influenced everyone from Bergman to Godard in the cinema are emphasized. But music, alas, and with very few exceptions, falls flat on its polyphonic face.

Polyphony, indeed, may be part of the problem. The laconic tenacity of plainchant works well in the flicks, since it compels the cameraman to devise props—torchlike parades, mocked-up ruins, and such—to sustain it. But confront a TV type with threats of diminution, augmentation, and canon at inversion and he'll freeze at the thought of showing the unshowable. Indeed, the real problems impeding music on TV can't be solved by berating those handy whipping-boys sponsor indifference (quite a few tycoons retain their institutional benevolence and distance simultaneously, and in countries other than the United States sustaining TV is the rule), acoustic deficiency (some television studios are adequate even to the loftier pursuits of radio), and camera immobility (when you've seen one bassoonist empty out the crook, you've seen them all).

The real problem is as simple and as complex as the inability of most musicians who get involved with the medium to disassociate themselves from the notion that music was represented by the concert in a manner that cannot be improved upon and must not be violated. ("I say, Mr. Severinson, do you mind if we avoid the recapitulation in the runthrough? These lights are a bother, and it's the same old material in the end, after all.") And these unrealistic demands are at least tacitly accepted by many obliging directors and producers who regard serious music as a wholesome activity to which they'll willingly consign a portion of their schedule in a lean year for drama or documentary assignments ("Let's try to hold the long shot on camera two, Ole baby. Sir Joshua's perspiring again").

And this unwitting alliance of musical reaction and executive disinclination inhibits most projects devised for television—or, perhaps more accurately, prevents them from *being* devised for television. For the trappings which attend the two most familiar approaches—the radio concert with cameras invited (open cyc, painted crescents on the studio floor—pop-art shades preferred, and the band displayed on risers like Benny Goodman's muscling in on Carnegie Hall, circa 1937) and the public-affairs-type inquiry (Danish modern coffee table, teacups mysteriously refilled after each station break, and ever-earnest host—"Tell us, Mr. Babbitt, just where do you find your inspiration?")—conspire to deny the medium's indigenous attributes.

In the United States, of course, the most determined exponent of music on television is Leonard Bernstein. In addition to all his other attainments Bernstein has that rare pedagogical gift—the ability to devise an analytic method which can simultaneously intrigue the pro and mesmerize the layman. He also has a McLuhanesque way of endowing dangerously familiar words with revealingly antithetical properties. He happens not to be hung up on the cool-hot dichotomy, but in his script words like "mode," "scale," "major," "minor," are at once personalized and illuminated.

Yet, perhaps because of these much-envied expository powers, Bernstein is content to use television as a means to an entirely worthy end—the musical enlightenment of the American public. And consequently the typical Bernstein television effort is a straightforward "This is your life, Ludwig Spohr" sort of show—taped before a live audience in Philharmonic Hall, Lincoln Center, with all the sound liabilities thereunto pertaining and with coy cutaways to some cute little kids in the balcony specially imported for the occasion from the Westchester Home for Insufferable Prodigies. The camera work isn't very elaborate, and if the director allows us a tight shot on the tuba, likely as not the tuba player will be holding up a banner reading "10 seconds to countdown for second theme." Bernstein's purpose is entirely didactic, and he simply isn't willing, or isn't asked, to compromise his podium-and-lectern stance to accommodate the demands of the camera. Yet, for all that, such is the force of his personality, the intensity of his performing style, and the constant insight of his analytic comment that Bernstein's innumerable television appearances have unquestionably, in the best and strictest sense of the phrase, "done a great deal of good"—even as the televised crusades of Billy Graham.

Otherwise, in America, the situation's rather bleak. The Bernstein success has produced a rash of imitators who clog educational television with music-appreciation-style monologues and round-table discussions which aspire to his tell-it-like-it-is directness but fall lamentably short of his style, lucidity, and wit. Then there's Sol Hurok with his annual tribute to the Columbia Artists roster, and usually a half-dozen or so pictorial essays on the state of American culture offered by that all-counts indictment of just what's wrong with it—"The Bell Telephone Hour."

This latter series has recently scuttled its time-honored policy of subsidizing the second team of the Met's Italian wing in favor of profiles which do homage to such solidly established American institutions as George Szell and the Berkshire Music Festival. In their attempt to capture the spirit of that summer orgy, the Bell's production staff allowed the Boston Symphony to play approximately one fifth of Elgar's *Enigma* Variations and almost two thirds of Smetana's *Bartered Bride* Overture while, in a series of capsule interviews, Erich Leinsdorf was encouraged to develop an analogy between an athlete's training and a sideman's schedule; Jules Eskin, the orchestra's first cellist, pursued the athletic simile by talking about "good days" versus "bad days"; and soprano Phyllis Curtin assured us that music is a "terrific means of communication." Yet one can't really blame these contributors, for all of their opinions were served up in response to some of the most naive off-camera interrogation I've ever heard, and the entire program was apparently designed to convince us that most musicians are just plain folks—the sort of persons you wouldn't mind having on your street, even if you'd rather that your daughter didn't marry one.

In Europe, where, as everyone knows, musicians aren't plain folk, Herbert von Karajan is as deeply engrossed in filmmaking for TV as Bernstein in America. In collaboration with such celebrated directors of the mainline cinema as Henri-Georges Clouzot, he's turned out a series of choral and orchestral concerts, deliberately and often ingeniously devised for the medium. The repertoire is conventional enough—Verdi Requiem, Tchaikovsky No. 1 (Weissenberg), Dvořák *New World*—but the directorial approach, while by no means uniform (the Verdi was distinctly, and surprisingly, square), has been contrived as an affront to the conventions of the concert hall.

In the Dvořák, at one moment we're confronted with a platoon of cellos arrayed in crescent formation, while in the next shot the same cello section is set out two by two with a single double-bass bringing up the rear. Karajan himself, attired in a turtleneck, is in most shots barely given elbow room amidst the strings, who, like their colleagues, are somewhat incongruously turned out in business suits. But even this sartorial discrepancy helps to refute proscenium psychology—a refutation further enhanced by Clouzot's habit of filling the upper edges of the screen with the jagged outlines of the contrabass, like some Max Ernst impression of the aftermath of war. The viewer is wholly engaged with the space allocated to the camera and oblivious of any area beyond. From the downbeat, this film develops an atmosphere of rehearsallike spontaneity—a rehearsal which might conceivably be brought to an end at any moment but which in this case apparently succeeded so well that it simply grew into a performance.

Not only are the visual constants of the concert hall scorned in this film but in a certain sense the audio expectations as well. Despite the ready rapture of the first clarinet, the determined resolution of the timpanist, and the zestful bowing of the second violins, almost every sound we hear, in the best post–Van Doren tradition, is faked. For anyone steeped in concert hall traditions, this film will be an infuriating experience—but I love it!

But even though every other attempt at orchestral shooting pales by comparison with the Karajan approach, it is by no means the final solution for music on TV. Indeed, one must seriously question whether the participating musicians need be shown in their working guise at all—whether television shouldn't perhaps be allowed to resolve that age-old hangup about the morality and desirability of watching while you listen, and resolve it, if need be, in favor of those of us who would claim that it never has been either moral or desirable.

Years ago, in the days when orchestral concerts went out "live," Canadian producer Franz Kraemer once cut out of a performance of Mendelssohn's *Italian* Symphony in order that the second movement could provide accompaniment for some stock footage of a mule train on a Sicilian hillside. It was pure *Fantasia* material, but it did get us out of that concert hall, the mules were a likable lot, and I've not been able to enjoy that second movement since unless taken at a tempo sufficiently brisk to accommodate on its subdivided downbeat the placement of one slow, sure mule hoof. In Paris recently, the cameras of Radiodiffusion Francaise panned for half an hour across the sculptures of the Cathedral of St. Denis while making their audio track—Messiaen's *Et expecto resurrectionem mortuorum*—sound better than it is.

After all, there's no need to assume that simply because you've got a screen you've therefore got to use it—and certainly not with routine coverage of sideman or soloist at work. Indeed, all aspects of the interplay between audio and video badly need reconsideration. There are musical moments of such grandeur that no screen can represent or interpret them adequately and for which the only appropriate visual response is abstraction, test pattern, or post-test-pattern snow. Similarly, a video component could surely go unaccompanied for significant stretches and the two forces be brought together even more significantly through a denial of that absurd unity which they've been forced to observe heretofore.

That audio and video should serve one another rather than simply come packaged together seems obvious enough. Yet up till now, no one active in the field has done more than pay lip service to the premise. And if McLuhan's right and it's a trend of our times to take an interest in the process of production, then surely that interest should do more than involve us with a notion of how, and why, and what happens when. It should free us from an expectation of a redundant coordination between production components. It should permit us to treat art as a source of greater mystery than symmetry and unity and all those analysis-imposed and analysis-limited conventions can define.

When that happens, a postprocess situation will exist. That shallow fidelity to an uncertain memory of an unsatisfactory past will no longer suffice, and the dream of Charles Van Doren will come true.

RADIO AS MUSIC:
GLENN GOULD IN CONVERSATION
WITH JOHN JESSOP

JOHN JESSOP: I think, for a start, we could explore some of the reasons for
your particular style of radio documentary—the roots where your concepts began.

GLENN GOULD: I suppose they began around 1945 or '46 when I used to listen
to the inevitable "Sunday Night Stage" something-or-others, for which,
in those days, Andrew Allan and Company were responsible. I was fascinated with radio. A lot of that kind of ostensibly theatrical radio was
also, in a very real sense, documentary making of a rather high order.
At any rate, the distinctions between drama and documentary were
quite often, it seemed to me, happily and successfully set aside. Then
again, living in a town—Toronto—in which there was relatively little
theatre—almost none of professional caliber—and being of sufficiently
puritan temperament to be disinclined to theatre even if there had been
much of it, I was fascinated with radio theatre because it seemed to me
somehow more pure, more abstract, and, in a certain sense, it had a reality for me that, later on, when I became familiar with conventional theatre, that kind of theatre always seemed to lack.

In the late fifties, I began to write scripts for documentaries occasionally, and I was always dissatisfied with the kind of documentaries
that radio seemed to decree. You know, they very often came out sounding—not square, because that's not necessarily a pejorative word in my
vocabulary, but they came out sounding—okay, I'll borrow Mr. McLuhan's term—linear. They came out sounding "Over to you, now back
to our host, and here for the wrap-up is"—in a word, predictable. I
wrote the script, for instance, for a program on Schoenberg in '62—a
two-hour program, and that's a fairly long documentary in anybody's
terms. I must admit that I am not sure whether I could sustain a program of that length on a subject like Schoenberg, using the techniques
that I later had to evolve for myself, but, in any case, it seemed that one
had to accept a linear mold in order to pursue any kind of career in

From *The Canadian Music Book,* Spring–Summer 1971.

radio at that time. So I was very dissatisfied with the available techniques, and in 1967, for the first time, I got a chance to try my hand at producing something on my own.

J.J.: This was "The Idea of North."

G.G.: Right. The north had always fascinated me, and it seemed logical that I should do a documentary about it.

J.J.: And this was where your experiments with radio technique began?

G.G.: Well, you know, it's a funny thing, but I had no idea what techniques were going to be involved when I started out. As a matter of fact, the early outlines of "North," to equate them in no other way, were intriguing in the way that Beethoven's sketchbooks are intriguing—rather naive and only distantly related to the eventual outcome. At one point, since I was dealing with five characters, I even envisioned five nightly episodes for the program.

J.J.: You're kidding!

G.G.: No, seriously, and if that wasn't harking back to the days of my youth and the patterns thereof, I don't know what was. I really thought in terms of five stories—one for each of our principal characters—with the other four members of the cast nodding in, providing supplemental ideas and counterthemes that related to what the chief character happened to be saying. So I foresaw a certain degree of counterpoint, if not character development, I suppose, but at the same time my mind was still geared toward linear separation—in this case, a separation of almost soap-opera-ish discontinuity; I still didn't see it as an integral structure.

And that remained true until something like six weeks prior to broadcast time, which is pretty frightening when you come to think of it. *Five* weeks prior to broadcast time, I suddenly decided that that wasn't at all what I wanted to do—that, obviously, it had to be an integrated unit of some kind in which the texture, the tapestry, of the words themselves would differentiate the characters and create dramalike conjunctions within the documentary. These, of course, would have to be achieved through some rather prodigious editing, and I spent something like two to three weeks occupied with fine editing, still all the while being unsure as to the eventual form that the piece was going to take.

The next step—I can only explain this sequence as a sin of apprenticeship, because I would be in complete panic if I had to approach the making of a documentary that haphazardly now, but I didn't know better in 1967—the next step, really, was to think in terms of the form. And at this point one crucial event transpired. I had laid out the program in terms of material that was appropriate to a certain number of scenes.

Well, it turned out that if we really wanted all of those scenes to be heard, we were going to need about one hour and twenty-five minutes airtime. We had, of course, one hour at our disposal. So I thought, "Well, obviously one scene has got to go." We had a scene on the Eskimo—couldn't lose that; we had a scene on isolation and its effects—that had to stay, obviously; we had our closing soliloquy, we had our opening trio and other indispensables—and I couldn't part with any of them. We had a scene on the media which somehow had seemed terribly relevant when I got going on it—the media in relation to northern experience, in relation to sensory deprivation—but it now seemed that that was the one scene that was not wholly communicative and which could be cut. That brought the time down to about one hour, twelve minutes—at least fourteen minutes too long, allowing for Harry Mannis's closing credits—and I thought to myself, "Look, we really could hear some of these people speaking simultaneously—there is no particular reason why not."

J.J.: That's a pretty inauspicious birth for "contrapuntal radio"!

G.G.: Well, perhaps I exaggerate ever so slightly, but far from being a carefully wrought plan, it came to pass, in terms of its form, almost that casually.

About a month ahead of time I decided that what I really wanted to do was to create a structure in which one could feel free to have different approaches and responses to the same problems emerge simultaneously, and I began to sketch out the scenes with that object in mind. At that point, the form—prologue, five scenes, and epilogue—became pretty well set in my mind and on paper and stayed that way, with minor alterations, to the end. But I took you through this chronology, John, with ever so slight exaggerations built in, simply because it shows the degree to which one sometimes has to stumble into these things in order to realize the way around a problem. I had been aware of the problem for a long time, but it seemed that one needed to establish a certain momentum in order to come by its solution.

J.J.: Well, one of the first things one notices in "North," which one doesn't usually find in documentaries, is the sense of drama. You seem to use your characters not only to give forth information and ideas but to create dramatic situations, and you allow for a good deal of give and take between them.

G.G.: Well, it's an inevitable correlation of the thought which most of us are pursuing these days, I suppose, that a work of art, as a specialized, stratified object, is nonexistent, or should be, anyway—that everything, in a sense, can be a work of art, or a documentary, or any other label you want to pin on it. The danger, however, lies in giving something a name and then expecting it to conform to that name.

There is a scene in my documentary about Newfoundland—"The Latecomers"—which would appear to be taking place between, I suppose, a man and wife, certainly a lady and gentleman who are engaged in rather intimate conversation. The scene is set very simply—the gentleman is slightly to the left of center ("The Latecomers," unlike "North," is in stereo, of course), the lady slightly to the right. There is an open space between them, as it appears, through which one hears water—the sea being the basso continuo for "The Latecomers" as the train was for "North." Anyway, we came to think of it as our *Virginia Woolf* scene—in Albee's sense—in that the relationship which appeared to exist between them developed some rather interesting overtones. Now, these were overtones, of course, which were manufactured by the razor blade. To the best of my knowledge these two people have never met—certainly, the dialogue represented in that scene never took place as dialogue, and yet I have a strange feeling that had they met, it would have.

In the course of my interviews with them, these two had very different reactions to me and to my questions, and it was precisely those divergent reactions which created the dramatic situation for that scene. The lady couldn't reconcile herself to the relative isolation of life in Newfoundland and offered comments such as "If I couldn't afford to leave when I want to leave, I'd never be able to stay in Newfoundland." The gentleman said, "Well, you know, Thoreau, who probably understood nineteenth-century America better than anyone, understood it from the perspective of a cabin in the woods, and I should like to use Newfoundland in order to live a Thoreauvian existence." This is a paraphrase, but substantially accurate, and naturally—I say "naturally" because I can't help hoping it shows—I found myself in sympathy with his Thoreauvian sentiments and not at all in sympathy with her rather mercantilistic ones. So when, in the course of the interview, this lady said, "You know, I have to get out of here once in a while," I kept saying, "But why?" and naive things of that kind. She kept repeating herself, essentially, though with infinite variations—she was a very articulate person—and finally turned on me with a fine fury, stopped short of insult, but indicated that my line of questioning was foolish, and naive, and lacking in any real experience of the outback, and that if I had such an experience I would turn my back on it and go home.

Now, of course, her irritation appears in "The Latecomers" not in relation to me but rather in apparent relation to our down-east

Thoreauvian cast opposite her. He constantly refuted her professed need for the amenities of civilization with such comments as "I believe that a person who is removed from the center of a society is always able to see that society more clearly." And eventually, since in the interview with her I had rather dopily kept saying, "But why? . . . Don't you think that . . . after all . . . what about Thoreau?," she got perhaps just a little bit snarky and said, "Well, you know, I go down to Portugal Cove sometimes and I see the women down there—well, they're turning up their hems now"—this was 1968; I take you back three years—"but that doesn't mean that they are with it," etc., etc.—or words to that effect.

Well, the scene, as I came to think about it, clarified itself in my mind to the extent whereby these two people obviously related to each other dramatically. At the same time, I had to at least infer a place called Portugal Cove, which is a very real place, a charming little village about six miles from St. John's. So I decided that this scene, which was located at the very center of the show, since it dealt most explicitly with the metaphor that preoccupied us in "The Latecomers," would have its own center as well. The scene would become an ABA structure—ternary form, as one would think of it in music—and since the two A segments would contain our primary characters, arguing at an increasingly frenetic pace with shorter and shorter responses, the B segment had to represent or infer Portugal Cove in some way. And so we found two old coots—quite extraordinary gentlemen, really, who did understand through experience the nature of solitude—moved the stereo perspective for the B segment over to extreme left, tried to convey the presence of a wharf of some kind with a lot of surf sounds slapping around (much louder water than was heard in the A sections of the scene), and that portion of the screen became, in effect, Portugal Cove. You hear these two rather touching soliloquies, and as the second of them fades, the water moves from left back to center and the lady is still talking about hemlines in Portugal Cove. We fade back up on her to find that nothing had changed—and with her perhaps nothing ever would.

So, anyway, it's a long way around the question, John, but yes, I agree—the characters in a documentary have to be part of a drama. At least, it's foolish not to try to locate them in one, if one can.

J.J.: Another form of influence, perhaps, would be your musical background. I notice when you are talking in terms of the structure of the documentary you use terms like ternary form, ABA. . . .

G.G.: That's perfectly true. In my mind, all of the scenes in "North," let's say, or "The Latecomers," have shapes which are at least conditioned by musical perceptions, with perhaps one exception: there was a scene in "North" which had a very unusual structure—none that exists in any music as far as I am aware. The center of it was a dialogue between two characters—BABABAB—a sort of inverted rondo without a center, perhaps—and the bookends for it were a C and D entry. I decided the only way in which we could project that kind of form was to forget about the idea of single sound chambers for the A and B people—in many other conversational situations, we had taken the residue of two interviews and put them into one sound chamber, very much in the way I described in the Newfoundland example—and to keep all of the characters apart at all times in this particular scene. They would appear in different sound chambers as though recounting the variety of insights they had had during this journey that they were metaphorically taking into the north. It was very cool, very detached; there was a deliberate lack of linear contact, though they were saying things which were related to one subject. And this detachment was abetted by the totally different sound perspectives for each speech.

So it's not just a question of dealing with musical forms. Sometimes one must try to invent a form which expresses the limitations of form, which takes as its point of departure the terror of formlessness. After all, there are a limited number of rondos you can exploit in the radio documentary; then you find you have to invent according to the criteria of the medium, which is essentially what we ended up doing.

J.J.: The opening segment of "North" would be a case in point, I imagine.

G.G.: Yes, the opening segment of "North" has a kind of trio sonata texture, but it really is an exercise in texture and not a conscious effort to regenerate a musical form. Three people speak more or less simultaneously. A girl enters first and speaks very quietly—we get logged for low-level start every time she's on the air—and after a time she says, "And the further north we went, the more monotonous it became." By this time we have become aware of a gentleman who has started to speak and who upon the word "further" says "farther"—"farther and farther north" is the context.

At that moment, his voice takes precedence over hers in terms of dynamic emphasis. Shortly after, he uses the words "thirty days," and by this point we have become aware of a third voice which immediately after "thirty days" says "eleven years"—and another crossover point has been effected.

The scene is built so that it has a kind of—I don't know if you have ever looked at the tone rows of Anton Webern as distinguished from those of Arnold Schoenberg, but it has a kind of Webern-like continuity-in-crossover in that motives which are similar but not identical are used for the exchange of instrumental ideas. So in that sense, textually, it was very musical; I think its form was free from the restrictions of form, which is a good way to be, you know, and the way in which one would like to be in all things, eventually. But that took time, and, as I said a while back, in the case of "North" it started with all kinds of forbidding memories of linearity. One had to gradually grow into a different sort of awareness.

J.J.: I recall that last summer, when I was working at CBC, we were doing overlays and multitrack mixes, and we found certain people who would say "This is great," "this is marvelous." But we also got people saying, "I thought I was listening to two radio stations."

G.G.: And you got logged for "crosstalk."

J.J.: We never got logged—we tried to get logged. We tried very hard to get logged on one particular collage.

G.G.: That's a pity.

J.J.: No, they've gotten wise to collages as far as logging is concerned, but as far as the audience is concerned some people would say that their first instinct was to go over and try to fine-tune the radio, and this sort of makes one wonder!

G.G.: It is a strange notion—this idea that the respect for the human voice in terms of broadcasting is such that one shuts down all other patterns to an appropriately reverential level. Very often in TV documentaries particularly I get very upset by the fact that the moment any character—the narrator, the subject, or someone talking about the subject—happens to open his mouth, all other activity has to grind to a halt or at any rate come down fifteen decibels to ensure respect. It's nonsense. The average person can take in and respond to far more information than we allot him on most occasions. Obviously, if you wish people to make distinct compartments for every piece of information you pass onto them, they will—that's the easy way out. If, on the other hand, you want them to be caught up, in the old Wagnerian sense, by a work of art, that's not the way to do it. The way to do it is to keep all of the elements in a state of constant flux, interplay, nervous agitation (using that term in a nonmedical sense, of course), so that one is buoyed aloft by the structure and never at any moment has time to sit back and say, "Oh, well, that's going to be the bridge to Act Two"—you know. Of course, that's the problem with Mozart opera, really—it just comes to a halt; one can predict its caesurae.

It seems to me terribly important to encourage a type of listener who will not think in terms of precedence, in terms of priority, and collage is one way in which to do it. I think, at the same time, it ought to be possible to play around with the time sense, the time scale in relation to an individual voice, to hear only one voice and yet receive separate and simultaneous messages, you know, from the statement it offers. That's something that, as far as I know, has not really been done in radio. I think it should be done. There have been some halfhearted attempts, perhaps. In "The Latecomers" we allowed one gentleman—a brilliant if compulsive talker—to waylay three different cronies with the same anecdote. It seemed consistent with his character (he—that is, we—changed the anecdote ever so slightly each time around), but still, in relation to what could be done with these techniques, it was a halfhearted attempt. Of course, I think that a lot of these things are going to straighten themselves out when we can have a real listening experience on the road to or beyond quadraphony.

J.J.: Four-channel sound?

G.G.: Yes, but I fear that people are going to misuse that frontier. They're already doing so, as a matter of fact. Some American companies are recording symphonic dates quadraphonically, and the quadraphony consists of having a lot of ambience for the rear speakers, a few coughs behind your left ear or something, which is utterly idiotic. Who ever said that that's what quadraphony was about? Who, for that matter, ever said that the radio documentary was about the subject to whom all others participating therein have to defer? It's the same kind of very limited thinking. But I think that by the time we have a really extensive experience of quadraphony a lot of this objection to collage—the sort of thing you were speaking about, where someone comes and tries to fine-tune it—will just sort itself out naturally. Because the sense of space, the sense of area, is something that is, I suspect, all too easily taken for granted when most people listen to sound.

  If—let's take a very simple example—if I'm playing a Mozart sonata on the piano, it's very important for me to maintain a sense of distance between motives which may accrue in one hand only, or both hands together, or cross over, or be in the lowest part of the left hand, or the highest of the right, etc.—to see those motives as a series of planes, not simple planes of legato versus nonlegato but planes of proximity. It's always seemed strange to me that we have never thought of recording the piano that way—in fact, I have already done this experimentally. It's not out yet, so maybe I shouldn't talk about it, but I have tried recording one piano on eight tracks, four ranks of three microphones per rank. But the tacit assumption in the record business has been that a piano is sitting more or less in front of you, and if you hear the first note in that position you are going to hear the last note accordingly. Nothing upsets a producer more than trying to mingle perspectives. For instance, if you carry over the recording of one particular movement of a work to the next day, the crew will measure off every inch of floor, make sure the instrument gets repositioned in exactly the same spot, count the number of dew drops per square inch, and just pray that the barometer is constant. Well, there may be a certain logic to it as regards Mozart, but I don't think there can be vis-à-vis Wagner or Scriabin. No one, for instance, has ever recorded an orchestra playing Wagner as they would automatically, in this age of John Culshaw, record a chorus singing Wagner. Well, why not, you know!

You see, the sense of area, the sense of space and proximity in the technology, is just not being used at all. But it is used the moment you say to someone, "But this has dramatic significance." Even in the earliest days of radio, back beyond those "Sunday Night Stages" we spoke of earlier, you would find very sophisticated mike placement, I'm sure. Because the moment you define characters as doing something—the moment you involve them in action—people assume that they ought to be more or less close, more or less distant from the auditor. The moment you give them only thoughts to express, the attitude is "Why don't they just sit there and tell you that?" And that's been the whole problem with documentary radio, you know. Thoughts have been disengaged from action and movement, and I think that that's one barrier which should be dissolved.

J.J.: I want to get into space and texture a little more. One finds it sometimes very difficult to use silence in the manner befitting its importance.

G.G.: This is very true.

J.J.: In radio, there is a certain hesitancy about it.

G.G.: Yes, I agree we have not thought about it very much. But, then, you know, the whole idea of the integral use of silence in music is a relatively new concept, really. It started with the Bauhaus, I suppose, with the idea of the total involvement of space, including the windows and the doors that make space meaningful, and musically it started, in that sense, with Anton Webern. With wonderful analytical hindsight, people began to say, "Ah, but Beethoven did it too! Op. 133, for instance—there are lots of silences in that. Very significant!" But with the best will in the world, you can't argue that he—Beethoven—weighted his silences with the same kind of arithmetic integrity—that's a bad combination—with the same kind of appropriate longevity in relation to sound that Webern employed. So, since it's basically a new concept in music, it doesn't surprise me that it hasn't been applied to the spoken word, documentarily. Well, of course, it has been in the theatre of Beckett, or of Pinter, for that matter. But, in a way, that's almost a by-product of sullenness rather than the integral use of cessation in a texture as a component of that texture.

J.J.: When you are envisioning the operations of a scene with perhaps two, three, four levels going, I sometimes sense in your work the operation of something very like a fugue.

G.G.: Yes, this is quite true, and I would again be hard-pressed to deny that that comes from a love of fugue playing and a lot of fugue playing, from childhood on. But I also think that it comes from an attachment to the organ, as opposed strictly to the piano, as a child, and of having a sense of what the feet can do. I don't think of myself as an organist in any professional sense, but anyone who has had experience of the organ feels that need for a bass foundation of some kind, you know. If you've played the organ for a certain period of time, it is always a very disillusioning experience not to have it. You desperately miss the hookup to a sixteen-foot or thirty-two-foot stop. It had never occurred to me until this moment that that may in fact be the reason that I've always felt the necessity of a continuum of some kind in everything that I've done in radio. In the case of "North" it was the train; in the case of the Newfoundland program it was sea sound; in the case of the program on Stokowski which I did most recently, it was a vast compote of music conducted by Stokowski—all of it running seamlessly, acting as a continuum. Maybe the experience of the organ does explain it. Certainly, I wouldn't be at all averse to trying something more monophonic sometime, but up to now I've felt the need of having some kind of backdrop against which I can pitch other things—other ideas which can find relief thereby.

There are two scenes in particular in the program on Newfoundland that relate to what we're talking about—the prologue and epilogue. They are the only segments of that program in which the entire cast, which was a formidable one—fourteen characters—appears, and they appear as a kind of Greek chorus. In fact, seven of these fourteen people had no occasion to make themselves familiar throughout the drama as such and appear only in these outer scenes as elements of texture. In these two segments, it seemed important to have everybody on deck, and consequently, the opening is a long, slow pull-in as though from a helicopter, into and through what would appear to be a fog bank. As you pass through the fog bank, voices begin to accumulate around you. They are, however, static—as though marooned, unable to move. For the listeners, however, the perspective seems to be moving, because one becomes more and more aware of a cliff against which surf is breaking.

The epilogue is quite different. Whereas in the prologue the water motion is left-to-right and the cliff seems to be someplace slightly right of center with each receding wave pulling back out across the screen, in the epilogue, on the other hand, we are clearly pulling away from the island, and as this transpires, the water motion changes and becomes left and right alternately. The effect is as though you are looking down from a considerable height and picking up surf sounds on both sides.

All of the characters that are there at the beginning are there again, with one great difference—they are all in motion. There is a trick to this because in the—I was going to say "score"—in the script, the chief character, the man who becomes the narrator of this program (and that was one of its weaknesses as opposed to what I would hope to be the strengths of quadraphony—that there had to be a narrator), the man who has told us the story, has been located in the right speaker throughout. He has been sitting right there talking at us, acting as a kind of *Our Town* host and a bridger of scenes. But at the onset of the epilogue he has a line in which he says, "I drive out across the country sometimes," and as he says this his voice for the first time begins to move—*he* begins to move. His journey takes him, ultimately, to the extreme left (though he stops for some time at center screen enroute), and during the three minutes, fifty-three seconds which constitute the epilogue, he encounters all of the other characters, who have at no time—even as the characters in "North" were held apart from the narrator in that program—have at no time directly confronted him. They are moving from left to right, and he is moving in the opposite direction. To what extent, then, his movement is an illusion, to what extent it is the old Hollywood trick of moving scenery past the stationary train, to what extent both movements are legitimate, is left unresolved.

They are, of course, moving past each other in another sense as well—most members of the cast are summing up their discontent ("We always damn our forebears, you know, saying, 'Why in the hell did they stay here in Newfoundland? Why were they foolish enough? Why would anyone settle on this foolish little rock?' ") while our narrator is finding a way of being optimistic in a very difficult world and a very harsh place ("People are ecstatic about getting into the mainstream, and I think it's a little bit stupid, since the mainstream is pretty muddy, or so it appears to me"). So, in a sense, they are moving past each other in terms of understanding as well, and the sequence seems to work on several levels—there seems to be a bit of a mystery in it.

As he passes them, he doesn't simply pass one at a time—not uncommonly, one voice has started up from the left, and several seconds later another follows suit (their closing speeches are very, very brief—I think the longest is something like eighteen seconds, and the average is about ten), and the words are chosen in such a way that words of his very often—just as "further" and "farther" are related in the prologue to "North"—clash with words of theirs. "Civilization," for instance, is exchanged between the narrator ("We invade Mars and we destroy the Martian civilization and we create our own pretty shoddy substitute for civilization in its place") and an elderly gentleman who is given the role of his grandfather ("Now, no reflection on civilization as it is, but I think we had a real civilization before they came in"). In "The Latecomers" the cast was distributed in such a way that all the principal characters were given inferred relationships of a family sort; but perhaps this is something that we should get into on another occasion.

J.J.: Okay, I'll take a raincheck on that. You mentioned isolating voices in different sound chambers—do you filter them at all to extend their differences, or to magnify their differences?

G.G.: Yes, I do. One of the best ways, in fact, to compensate for the lack of spread, if you happen to be working in mono, is via "traps" of that kind. In "North" we played around with filters on the voices in varying degrees to emphasize character differentiation. The anthropologist James Lotz, who recounts his early experiences of the north and who serves as a foil for the rather larger-than-human-scale explanations that are being offered by our host, Wally Maclean, was heavily filtered during his earlier exchanges with Maclean so as to suggest that a very distant experience was being recalled. The problem, however, was how to get him back into real time. This was a problem indeed, because at the end of what is nominally the first scene of "North" (discounting the trio sonata prologue for the moment) he directly confronts our Ottawa man, Bob Phillips, and begins a conversation with him. Well, obviously, this conversation, if remembered accurately, couldn't be all that distant—it had to be more or less present tense, so he had to come out of filter. But you can't just remove filter all at once—that tends to be, as you know, John, terribly obvious; you've got to do it plateau by plateau, in effect, like eliminating stops on an organ. So we decided to combine it with some other sort of dynamic activity, and consequently we began to accentuate his verbs by slight pulls on the "pot." Every time he used a verb that expressed his distaste for bureaucracy—and this was particularly meaningful at the end of the scene directly before his confrontation with the Ottawa man, because he was saying, "Of course, they *hate* Ottawa in the north, they just *loathe* Ottawa, they *despise* Ottawa"—we found it useful to underline such words as "hate," "despise," "loathe," and to reduce the filter, simultaneously, as we did so. When the final pull is given, he's out of filter, he's in his real voice, the Ottawa man says, "I was in the east block then," and their conversation proper begins.

The same problem arose in an altogether different dimension in the program on Stokowski. At one point, roughly two thirds of the way through the program, I wanted to get him talking about the old days, what it was like to make acoustic records, and so on. It was easy enough to get him into it—we simply projected, onto a symphonic backdrop, folk-song material which embellished or extended the harmonic effect of the backdrop—Shostakovich's Eleventh Symphony. At the end of the folk-song sequence a refrain of the Mormon hymn "Come, come ye saints" (he's talking about immigrant patterns in the settling of America) gets us to the key of G, and for its dominant—D—we included a few bars of "Ein feste Burg"—a performance that was recorded in Philadelphia in the early twenties. This reminds him of the old days, his early years in the recording studio (back to 1917, in fact), and he hears his earliest attempt at the *Rienzi* Overture—technologically pathetic but very funny—played for all its monaural worth exclusively in the right speaker. This, in turn, inaugurates a sequence of four or five monaural items culled from recordings of the Philadelphia in the tens, twenties, and thirties. The orchestra was clearly coming alive, getting better and better as an instrument with each succeeding example, and, of course, each successive 78 is technologically an improvement upon its predecessors.

But Stokowski left Philadelphia in 1938, and the problem was how to get him back into real time—into the present. Well, by sheer luck we found a recording which he made of the "Good Friday Spell" from *Parsifal*, in 1936, I think—in any case, it's one of the later discs from his Philadelphia years—and compared it with a recording that he made in Houston when he was conducting down there in the late fifties. We found, miraculously enough, that they ran almost note for note in tempo for forty-five seconds. Well, maybe there were a few places where some interesting suspensions resulted, but, at any rate, in the crucial seconds where we needed them, they ran together. So in the program, the Philadelphia version runs for about thirty seconds, and as it is swallowed up in the trough of a phrase, we overlay the Houston performance, moving it slowly from left to right and keeping it under compression so that it doesn't sound too good too suddenly. It sounds rather as though, indeed, the orchestra and the technicians were reaching out toward a new technological ideal and not quite making it. At this moment Stokowski says, "It is much better today, but I think it can still be much better than it is today"—and that's what gets him back to the present.

J.J.: That's fascinating. You mentioned a while back that narration was a "weakness," I think you said, and I must admit that I don't quite see what you mean by that.

G.G.: Well, it's a problem that I have only lately become aware of in terms of the radio documentary. One of the means to that awareness, as I mentioned, was the Newfoundland narrator. Indeed, I was unhappy about the fact that we had a narrator—not because of the gentleman himself, he was magnificent, but because of the fact that we felt compelled to have one. It seemed to me an advertisement of weakness, in the form of the program, in the present state of the medium, and I've been thinking about it a lot subsequently.

Just as certain limitations were imposed by the mono mode which were instantly bypassed the moment stereo came along, certain limitations are imposed by stereo as well. And in a funny, paradoxical sort of way, one of the things that is theoretically enhanced by stereo—separate voice placement—tends, unless you exercise a great deal of care, to bring about its own set of problems. I mean, it's marvelous that you can have two people running simultaneously as we did frequently in Newfoundland and not even feel it, you know—or, in other words, feel it so deeply, perceive it so integrally, that it doesn't bother you at all. But in a way, the dialogues and trios or whatever in "The Latecomers" are less dramatic by virtue of that separation than similar situations that existed in "North," despite the fact that in the case of "North" they're much less clearly defined by virtue of the mono mode.

The dissolve, for instance, to speak in cinematic terms, takes on a very different sort of role. In mono radio, the idea of the dissolve was terribly important, you know—it was one of the chief tools of narration. In stereo radio it is relatively less important. You can do left-right crossovers with such dexterity, you can run so many things simultaneously, you can hard-cut with such accuracy and deliberation, that there's really not so much need for the scene-change functions supplied by the dissolve. By extending the same problem, one begins to wonder whether if such separation exists, one shouldn't perhaps take advantage of it so that the elements which were normally part and parcel of the dissolve-making process—the element of narration, particularly—can be bypassed.

Maybe then one could find a way around the problem of narration. Because in the process of making "The Latecomers," it seemed more and more like that to me—it seemed to be a problem. It seemed to compel one to follow a specific pace in relation to the disposition of events, and I think that, way back, what you were implying when you said that there should be a way of making silence integral was to approach the same problem in another way—to suggest that there should be a way around the obvious explication of facts and series of facts.

As new possibilities for separation become available, one has to minimize these linear consequences—not in order to deny what was good in the past but in order to find a way in which to really take advantage of the new modality. One can't simply assume by going to stereo or, as we will now shortly do, to quadraphony, you can use the quadraphonic perceptions or the stereo perceptions in order to do a better job with the problems that grew out of mono techniques. You can't make a rationale for the new modality out of those solved problems—it's just not going to work, and that's precisely what I was trying to get at by saying we shouldn't have had a narrator. You know, it took me about six months after the show was completed to figure out why we shouldn't have had one. But I guess, in a way, the delay stemmed from the same slow, grudging acknowledgment of the medium that made me think that "North" was going to be a soap-serialized documentary.

The idea of silence, if I understand what you mean by it, is part and parcel of that acknowledgment. When one can separate characters—backward and forward, left and right, and in time from each other—this silence of yours becomes a very powerful stimulus. But the question is, how do you use it? Do you use it in the way in which Webern for instance, used silence? Do you measure off the duration of sound? Do you simply imitate what was done in a purely abstract medium forty years ago? Do you start by saying, "Well, I think we ought to serialize the silences in the documentary and for every fifteen seconds of sound have seven and half of silence, or some similar ratio"? Because the moment you do that, you are adopting the laws of Webernian polyphony and making the same mistake which every new medium encourages one to make initially. So I somehow don't think that's quite the answer.

Because the great joy of working with what we are pleased to call the radio documentary is that one is somehow freed from restrictions of that kind. The fact that the documentary is tied, supposedly, to hard information, the fact that there is presumably some kernel of news underlying your process, is an excuse. It's the most glorious of excuses, really—a passacaglia of fact—and it sets you free, first of all, to deal with art in the factual, assured way in which one customarily deals with pure information. At the same time, it permits you to transform that information into what in olden days one would have referred to as "works of art." One simply has to incorporate that information on its own terms—on terms which admit to no contradiction between the processes of "art" and of "documentation."

PROLOGUE FROM "THE IDEA OF NORTH"

MARIANNE SCHROEDER: *I was fascinated by the country as such. I flew north from Churchill to Coral Harbor on Southampton Island at the end of September. Snow had begun to fall, and the country was partially covered by it. Some of the lakes were frozen around the edges, but towards the center of the lakes you could still see the clear, clear water. And flying over this country, you could look down and see various shades of green in the water, and you could see the bottom of the lakes, and it was a most fascinating experience. I remember I was up in the cockpit with the pilot, and I was forever looking out, left and right, and I could see ice floes over the Hudson's Bay, and I was always looking for a polar bear or some seals that I could spot, but unfortunately there were none.*

M.S.: And as we flew along the east coast of Hudson's Bay, this flat, flat country

FRANK VALLEE: *I don't go—let me say*

M.S.: frightened me a little, because it just seemed endless.

F.V.: *this again—I don't go for this northmanship bit at all.*

M.S.: We seemed to be going into nowhere, and the further north we went

F.V.: *I don't knock those people who do claim that they want to go farther and*

M.S.: *the more monotonous it became. There was nothing but snow*

F.V.: farther north, but I see it as a game, this northmanship bit. People say, "Well,

M.S.: *and, to our right, the waters of Hudson's Bay.*

F.V.: were you ever up at the North Pole?"

M.S.: *Now, this was my impression*

F.V.: and "Hell, I did a dogsled trip of twenty-two days,"

M.S.: *during the winter, but I also flew over the country*

F.V.: and the other fellow says, "Well, I did one of thirty days"—

From the original transcript of Gould's radio play, 1967.

M.S.: *during the spring and the summer, and this I found intriguing,*

F.V.: *you know, it's pretty childish. Perhaps they would see themselves*

ROBERT PHILLIPS: And then, for another eleven years, I served the north in various capacities.

M.S.: *because then I could see the outlines*

F.V.: *as more skeptical . . .* [fade]

R.P.: Sure, the north has changed my life; I can't conceive

M.S.: *of the lakes and the rivers and, on the tundra,*

R.P.: of anyone being in close touch with the north, whether they lived there all the time

M.S.: *huge spots of moss or rock—*

R.P.: or simply traveled it month after month and year after year—

M.S.: *there is hardly any vegetation that one can spot from the air. . . .* [fade]

F.V.: *. . . more skeptical about the offerings of the mass media. . . .* [fade]

R.P.: I can't conceive of such a person as really being untouched by the north.

F.V.:   . . . And it goes on like this,

R.P.: When I left in 1965, at least left the job there, *it wasn't because of*

F.V.: as though there's some special merit, some virtue, in being in the north,

R.P.: *being tired of the north, the feeling that it had no more interest,*

F.V.: or some special virtue in having been

R.P.: *or anything of the sort; I was as keen as ever.*

F.V.: with primitive people—well, you know, what

R.P.: *I left because I'm a public servant* [begin fade].

M.S.:   . . . It is most difficult

F.V.: special virtue is there in that? [*begin fade*] *And so*

R.P.: *I was asked to do another job related to fighting*

M.S.: to describe. It was complete isolation, this is very true,

F.V.: *I think that I'd be more interested in Baker Lake right now,*

R.P.: *the war against poverty. . . .* [fade to loop]

M.S.: and I knew very well that I could not go anywhere

F.V.: *if indeed it is changing significantly. . . .* [fade to loop]

M.S.: except for a mile or two, walking. *I always think of the long summer nights when the snow had melted and the lakes were open and the geese and ducks had started to fly north. During that time, the sun would set, but when there was still the last shimmer in the sky, I would look out to one of those lakes and watch those ducks and geese just flying around peacefully or sitting on the water, and I thought I was almost part of that country, part of that peaceful surrounding, and I wished that it would never end.* [Fade to loop]

"THE IDEA OF NORTH": AN INTRODUCTION

The north has fascinated me since childhood. In my school days, I used to pore over whichever maps of that region I could get my hands on, though I found it exceedingly difficult to remember whether Great Bear or Great Slave was further north (and in case you've had the same problem, it's Great Bear). The idea of the country intrigued me, but my notion of what it looked like was pretty much restricted to the romanticized, art-nouveau-tinged, Group-of-Seven paintings which in my day adorned virtually every second schoolroom, and which probably served as a pictorial introduction to the north for a great many people of my generation.

A bit later on, I began to examine aerial photographs and to look through geological surveys and came to realize that the north was possessed of qualities more elusive than even a magician like A.Y. Jackson could define with oils. At about this time I made a few tentative forays into the north and began to make use of it, metaphorically, in my writing. There was a curious kind of literary fallout there, as a matter of fact. When I went to the north, I had no intention of writing about it or of referring to it even parenthetically in anything that I wrote. And yet, almost despite myself, I began to draw all sorts of metaphorical allusions based on what was really a very limited knowledge of the country and a very casual exposure to it. I found myself writing musical critiques, for instance, in which the north—the idea of the north—began to serve as a foil for other ideas and values that seemed to me depressingly urban oriented and spiritually limited thereby.

Now, of course, such metaphorical manipulation of the north is a bit suspect, not to say romantic, because there are very few places today which are out of reach by, and out of touch with, the style and pacesetting attitudes and techniques of Madison Avenue. *Time, Newsweek, Life, Look,* and the *Sat-*

Liner notes form CBC Learning Systems T-56997, 1967.

urday Review can be airlifted into Frobisher Bay or Inuvik just about as easily as a local contractor can deliver them to the neighborhood newsstand, and there are probably people living in the heart of Manhattan who can manage every bit as independent and hermitlike an existence as a prospector tramping the sort of lichen-covered tundra that A.Y. Jackson was so fond of painting north of Great Bear Lake.

Admittedly, it's a question of attitude, and I'm not at all sure that my own quasiallegorical attitude toward the north is the proper way to make use of it or even an accurate way in which to define it. Nevertheless, I'm by no means alone in this reaction to the north; there are very few people who make contact with it and emerge entirely unscathed. Something really does happen to most people who go into the north—they become at least aware of the creative opportunity which the physical fact of the country represents and—quite often, I think—come to measure their own work and life against that rather staggering creative possibility: they become, in effect, philosophers.

This should not suggest, however, that their philosophizing will achieve, in the end, a cohesive point of view. In the construction of "North"—which, though technically a documentary, is at the very least a documentary which thinks of itself as a drama—we relied, in fact, upon the interaction of our five characters; and just as one would want to plan a dramatis personae with care when setting out to compose a play, we were equally careful about the composition of our guest list for the program. We wanted an enthusiast, a cynic, a government budget-watcher, as well as someone who could represent that limitless expectation and limitless capacity for disillusionment which inevitably affects the questing spirit of those who go north seeking their future. I think that for each of these attitudes we found a notable and remarkably articulate exponent in the presence, respectively, of Marianne Schroeder, Frank Vallee, Robert Phillips, and James Lotz. All four of them have had a remarkable experience of the north—Marianne Schroeder served for several years as a nurse in a mission at Coral Harbor, Southampton Island, which, if you have your map handy, is more or less at the northwest corner of Hudson Bay; Frank Vallee's private preserve has been the Central Arctic, primarily, and he is the author of a book entitled *Kabloona and Eskimo in the Keewatin;* R. A. J. Phillips and James Lotz have both made substantial contributions to the bibliography of the north—Mr. Phillips's best-known work being his book *Canada's North,* while Mr. Lotz, who is both a geographer and an anthropologist, skillfully combines his two fields for innumerable appearances in print, including his recently published study *Northern Realities.* We felt, however, that we also needed someone whose experience of the north effectively encompassed all of these positions, who was at once a pragmatic idealist, a disillusioned enthusiast, and I think that in the presence of Wally Maclean, who becomes, in effect, the narrator of our story, we found him.

Our five guests were, of course, interviewed separately. They did not at any time during the making of "North" have occasion to meet, and whichever dramalike juxtapositions came about were achieved through some careful after-the-fact work with the razor blade on tape and not through any direct confrontation among our characters. Indeed, one of the five—Wally Maclean—was restrained by a caprice of editing from all confrontation except with his own poetic vision of the north and with the last movement of Sibelius's Fifth Symphony.

This work is the only conventional music employed in the program, but throughout the fifty-two minutes which precede it there are, in the prologue and the various scenes of which "North" consists, a number of techniques which I would be inclined to identify as musically derived. The prologue, indeed, is a sort of trio sonata (nurse Schroeder, sociologist Vallee, and government official Phillips engage in the first of several instances of a technique I've grown rather fond of dubbing "contrapuntal radio"). And there are other, perhaps more complex, occasions which simulate musical techniques as well. One such is the scene devoted to the subject of the Eskimo, which takes place, apparently, in a dining car aboard a train (the train being our basso continuo throughout most of the program) and in which Miss Schroeder, Mr. Vallee, Mr. Lotz, and Mr. Phillips are more or less simultaneously occupied in conversation—the resultant distractions making the listener's role not unlike that of a dining-car steward intent upon giving equal service to all.

The point about these scenes, I think, is that they test, in a sense, the degree to which one can listen simultaneously to more than one conversation or vocal impression. It's perfectly true that in that dining-car scene not every word is going to be audible, but then by no means every syllable in the final fugue from Verdi's *Falstaff* is, either, when it comes to that. Yet few opera composers have been deterred from utilizing trios, quartets, or quintets by the knowledge that only a portion of the words they set to music will be accessible to the listener—most composers being concerned primarily about the totality of the structure, the play of consonance and dissonance between the voices—and, quite apart from the fact that I do believe most of us are capable of a much more substantial information intake than we give ourselves credit for, I would like to think that these scenes can be listened to in very much the same way that you'd attend the *Falstaff* fugue.

In one sense, I suppose, the train's basso continuo is simply an excuse—a foundation for the vocal textures we wanted to concoct above it. But, then, "The Idea of North" is itself an excuse—an opportunity to examine that condition of solitude which is neither exclusive to the north nor the prerogative of those who go north but which does perhaps appear, with all its ramifica-tions, a bit more clearly to those who have made, if only in their imagination, the journey north.

"THE LATECOMERS": AN INTRODUCTION

In the summer of 1968 I paid my first visit to Newfoundland. I went there in search of characters for a documentary, the subject of which was by no means clear to me as I disembarked from the M.V. *Leif Ericson* late one Au-gust afternoon at Port aux Basques. In one sense, I suppose, the nominal sub-ject—Newfoundland itself—dictated the surface matter of the program. It was obviously to be about the province as island; about the sea, which keeps the mainland and the mainlanders at ferry-crossing's length; about the prob-lems of maintaining a minimally technologized style of life in a maximally technologized age. But it also had to have a point of view (or points of view; consensus didn't matter), and that could only emerge through dialogue with those who, defying the stereotypic trend to abandon ship and seek a living elsewhere—the ready source for anti-Maritime bias, sick Newfy jokes, down-east nostalgia—had chosen to remain aboard the "rock." I didn't know any stay-at-home Newfoundlanders at the time, but during the next four weeks or so I was to encounter, among others, the thirteen characters whose participation made this program possible and whose diverse notions about the role of Newfoundland in Canadian society gave to our documentary its subsurface raison d'être.

The Newfoundlander is first of all a poet. Spirits of Celtic bards linger on among these people; a sense of cadence, of rhythmic poise, makes their speech a tape editor's delight. Even when caught out with little to say—and that happens rarely—they say it in elegant metrics. But mingling with the urge to turn all observation into verse, a blunt, sagalike dispatch of detail gives point and purpose to their story. Perhaps the fact of life against the elements—as for the Iceland and Greenland peoples—disciplines their stan-zas, gives an underpinning of reality to their ever-ready impulse to fantasize.

In a certain sense, of course, Newfoundland itself is a fantasy—a disad-vantaged piece of real estate set adrift between two cultures, unable to forget

Liner notes from CBC Learning Systems T-57000, 1969.

its spiritual tie to one, unable wholly to accept its economic dependence on the other. But the reality of the Newfoundland experience cannot be found in per-capita debt tables, in great schemes to drain its central bogland, in fond hopes that some future transshipment need will arise like a new mid-Atlantic range, deflecting the trade winds which link both its foster cultures.

The reality is in its separateness. The very fact—the inconvenience—of distance is its great natural blessing. Through that fact, the Newfoundlander has received a few more years of grace—a few more years in which to calculate the odds for individuality in an increasingly coercive cultural milieu. And this topic, more than any other, is implicit in their conversation. They may not style it thus, but underlying their incessant talk about the island, its traditions, and its future, like a constantly embellished passacaglia theme, the cost of nonconformity is omnipresent.

Some would like to leave, or like their children to: "Fifteen years ago, I enjoyed life here so much that nothing would have induced me to leave. Now that I would probably like to leave, it's too late" (Ted Russell). Others who stay find nothing admirable in staying: "Well, put it this way—I would never be able to stay in Newfoundland if I couldn't afford to leave when I wanted to" (Penny Rowe). Still others, like the novelist Harold Horwood, who himself lives a modified Thoreauvian existence, maintain: "People who are removed from the center of a society are always able to see it more clearly."

Then there are those, like Eugene Young, who simply lament the passing of an age and the spirit of that age: "Old oaks can't live in flower pots and whales can't live like goldfish"; or like John Scott, who, when I talked to him, was pursuing doctoral studies at Edinburgh University but whose future is in Newfoundland, since "Newfoundland interests me; we can do anything here." Above all, there are those who, like our narrator, Leslie Harris, sense in the "rock" itself a metaphor for a way of life which while "in the mainstream" is not of it. "People are ecstatic about getting into the mainstream. I think its a little bit stupid, since the mainstream is pretty muddy, or so it appears to me."

When I had completed the interviews which provided raw material for this program, I set sail aboard the motor vessel *Ambrose Shea*—the long way home, Argentia to North Sydney, Nova Scotia. Gale warnings were hoisted, and after a few hundred yards the coastline disappeared. The gulf was turbulent that night; the coast of Cape Breton was a welcome sight next morning. But Newfoundland remained behind, secure.

PART FOUR
Miscellany

THREE ARTICLES PUBLISHED
UNDER THE PSEUDONYM
DR. HERBERT VON HOCHMEISTER

THE CBC, CAMERA-WISE

Editor's Note: With this issue we welcome to our columns the distinguished Canadian scholar and critic Dr. Herbert von Hochmeister. We know that Dr. von Hochmeister will need no introduction to those of our readers who have had occasion to observe the flourishing musical life of our good neighbor to the north, since for many years he has been the widely read fine-arts critic of The Great Slave Smelt, perhaps the most respected journal north of latitude 70°. His fine early essays, collected under the title Tundra-Kultur *(out of print) and published by I. Carp and Sons (out of business), first attracted for him an international following, while a later work in the same vein,* Fugue at Hay River, *proved of more specialized appeal. Having been granted an indefinite leave of absence by his home paper, Dr. von Hochmeister will explore the lower (latitudinally speaking) regions of Canadian music and will report to us intermittently.*

Not much happens in music in our country behind the corporate back of CBC. The very words "Canadian Broadcasting Corporation," wafted into the night air with the soporific white-noise comfort of a staff announcer confirming a station break, bring a catch to all loyal, and liberal, throats, a tremor to all tractionless spines, a welcome certainty that what we've just heard has been stamped culturally fit. From beneath the High Victorian turrets of a folksy house in downtown Toronto, known affectionately—and nationally—as the Kremlin, a shrewd covey of white-collar conciliators devote themselves with dedicated anonymity to governing our cultural life. And rare the artist, implausible the musical organization, able to remain in this country hermited against the trends they interpret for us. Fortunate it is, then, that—taken in the large view—the Corporation's efforts mightily deserve our commendation.

But perhaps one must be in, and of, the true north (as is your correspondent) to sense the miraculous chemistry between Canada and her Corpora-

---

From *Musical America*, March, August, and December 1965. The "Editor's Note" was apparently penned by Gould himself.

tion. We northerners have our complaints, of course. For those of us who elect to live beyond that populous ribbon of hamlets which the still rankling "Fifty-four–forty or fight" would separate from others of their bland provincial ilk south of the border, it seems bitterly unfair that seven nights a week, comes five minutes beyond the stroke of midnight and, the last news and weather having been pronounced, the studio compère mercilessly dispatches us to the pole-starred embrace of the night with that last emotionless plainchant: "We say good night now to those of you who listen on the low-power relay stations." "Does he indeed?" we fume—the set having meanwhile gone to crackling. "There'll come a night," we tell ourselves, "when some drunken sot of an operator will lie stupor-fallen over his switch in Toronto, or Montreal, or Winnipeg, or wherever it is they throw that wretched thing which disconnects us from our rightful, taxed pleasures. There'll come a night when we'll find out what it is they hear after midnight in Ottawa, and Edmonton, and the Lakehead. There'll come a night. . . ." A small complaint, perhaps, and one that makes us greedier for morning, so not without some purpose as it stands. Besides which, having come south this year, I know now that much of what goes through the night, most nights, is quite the same discreet mixture of Telemann, Respighi, Mendelssohn we guessed all along. No humor sophisticated beyond our territorial ken, no avant-gardism (not too much at any time) beyond our patience, no party chatter, through the night, to which our northernness could not relate.

Indeed, one could complain a bit about this balancing act of the CBC, this cover-it-all-but-don't-take-sides approach. And one might be tempted to do so were it not for the fact that the policy says so much so well about that compromise of peoples and faiths from which the confederacy of our country derives. There comes a time, though, when one must weigh the limitations of plain moderation. For instance, during the years following the Second Great Unpleasantness, the corporate moderateness elected Benjamin Britten the mainstream composer most worthy of our broadcast notice. It didn't matter whether our interest was left or right of center, whether turned toward Webern or toward Pfitzner—Britten was chosen, Britten we got, in most immoderate doses. In much the same measure, the corporate judgment of the early 1960s seems to have settled on Hans Werner Henze. We've lately had *Elegy for Young Lovers,* a wind quintet, a documentary on his Life and Neapolitan Times, not to mention numerous Canadian works turned out by authors as enviably prolific and disconcertingly eclectic as Henze himself.

It was not something on the crystal set, however, that prompted these thoughts on moderation. It was, rather, your correspondent's exposure to television, specifically to the first of a promised eight "specials" brought to us with the good wishes of "Your Telephone Company" (not "ours" in the north, I could assure them, just "theirs," the city-slicked direct-dialing softies, and they deserve it). It turned out to be a most extraordinarily purposeless squandering of great talent: that of two young westerners—Lynn Seymour, of British Columbia and now of the Royal Ballet, and Marilyn Horne, of Los Angeles and now (courtesy Sutherland-Bonynge) of London Records—and (sandwiched between them, believe it or not) that of the miracle called Sviatoslav Richter. What, I ask you, do Richter, Horne, and Seymour possibly have in common except talent and the telephone?

Not so many years ago, in a day of more flexible budgets, hungrier artists, and majority governments, CBC stoically spurned all sponsors' support, or, if allowing them access to the air at all, at least proclaimed the absolute autonomy of program content. In this case actual content may not have been dictated, though later listings—Rachmaninoff, Puccini on Program Two—read very much like every tired exec's cocktail-background preferred. But mood was dictated beyond a doubt. The whole operation was dressed in the same disconsolate, big-time-for-the-masses look that for so many years has helped the Stateside counterpart of this symposium to send its audience gratefully and swiftly long-distancing.

Of the program itself, Richter played Ravel, miraculously, as I never heard or imagined it could be. Miss Horne sang superbly—better than that even, if you like arpeggios, for she fastened herself to *Semiramide* with just a trace of that purely physical satisfaction one sometimes senses in Ysaÿe-struck fiddlers. Miss Seymour danced very well indeed, but was terribly handicapped by an incredible cotton-floss set that must have been left standing since the last Jenny Lind special.

This was all especially sad, because CBC has in the past been able to select indigenously videoistic musical material—a rare feat, the only purpose of televised concerts, and something that no U.S. network has thus far managed to do. But if CBC must go on deluding themselves with this sort of thing, the saving grace would be to turn the whole procedure—music, dance, sponsor's message—into what the neodadaists would call a "happening." Miss Horne could still sing, but why not into a bedside Princess phone (choice of colors)? And if Rossini didn't suit for that, Menotti would for sure. Miss Seymour could dance on (in this case her decor would be a must), but her accompaniment might be improvised by a 1907 Magneto Wall Set prepared for signaling by Morton Feldman. And since CBC has relaxed its import quota on Americans this year, why not Andy Warhol staging the whole as an "underground movie," barking orders authoritatively into a Call-Director Conference Intercom?

This leaves Sviatoslav Richter left over—but after all, camera-wise, what can you do with genius?

OF TIME AND TIME BEATERS

One of the more retarding conventions of our Western musical tradition is the habit of appointing "resident"—or, as they are sometimes erroneously called, "permanent"—orchestral conductors. The two terms are much confused, for they are not synonymous and indeed contain a certain mutual exclusivity. The situations where true "permanence" is involved (the life appointments of the Berlin Philharmonic would perhaps be the best example) render actual "residence" unthinkable. Karajan's coronation in 1955, for example, committed him to only eight series concerts, each rendered in triplicate in the old Hochschule für Musik, and left him free to schedule any number of state visits elsewhere. On the other hand, the conditions which make residence desirable—conditions which preserve something of the Kapellmeister's white-collar dignity—are, at least as realized in the North American provinces and with such happy exceptions as Vladimir Golschmann's twenty-six years of St. Louis notwithstanding, scarcely ever conducive to permanence. For conductorial permanence necessitates an autocratic regimen to which the real dictators of North America's symphony orchestras—the boards of directors, the women's committees, and the copy-hungry news scribes of the daily press—will seldom submit for more than a few seasons.

When the resident first takes up his post, it is reckoned an advantage that he be capable of essaying a vast repertoire, since in this way expensive specialty guests—Cluytens for French, Scherchen for baroque, Craft for contemporary, etc.—can be dispensed with and the conductor's salary amortized accordingly. The resident invariably stumbles into this trap (it is the first of many being baited for him), since from his point of view, what with getting the family settled and adding an indoor pool to the new split-level, the only tolerably safe guest conductors are Russian-speaking octogenarians with visa trouble. So the resident conductor takes upon himself a burden of repertoire not demanded by any other artist. No one would ask David Oistrakh to defy the comforting, if wrongheaded, ideologic convictions of a lifetime and tackle Schoenberg's Op. 36, any more than Artur Schnabel, the greatest pianist of his generation, was expected to discomfort himself playing Bach (he did play the C-minor Toccata once, rather unidiomatically, and that was that).

But were these men resident conductors, this is precisely what would be asked of them. And, truth to tell, most residents usually surmount these monstrous demands quite successfully for the first and perhaps the second seasons of their regime, during which time the occasional symphony-goer joins the subscription regulars to watch the new man being tried out. But invariably, along about the third season, the resident discovers that he is no longer pulling his weight at the box office and is therefore forced to counsel an immediate increase in the engagement of itinerant virtuosi whose exorbitant fees help to bring about the first budget crisis of his reign.

A vicious circle, quite enough to make men rage! Indeed, it does: the ability to rage convincingly has long been counted a prime asset in most conducting posts in North America, where it is tacitly understood that the resident will produce one temper tantrum for every $100,000 annual budget. In this way, the press is kept happy and alert, anticipating some good copy from the next podium blow-off, the ladies of the orchestra committee are provided with useful teatime gossip, and, most important of all, the rebellious sidemen of the orchestra are held in that state of awestruck snickering which, as is well known, augurs disciplined music making. It is, of course, most important to distinguish at this point between the genuine Central European podium pique, which in its invocation of Pan-Aryan deities displays an exquisite torment of soul for which the actual invective employed is largely incidental, and its poor relation, the verbally virtuosic but entirely external North American cuss-out, employed by conductors who are neither to the manor nor the region born.

For this and many equally valid reasons, the directorial boards of North America's orchestras have tended for many years to hire unemployed Kapellmeisters from abroad. Lately, however, a notable shift in geographic emphasis is apparent.

It all started several years ago with the appointment as director of Les Concerts Symphoniques de Montréal (the title has since been shortened, but the former euphony can scarcely be forgotten) of an extraordinarily gifted twenty-four-year-old, Zubin Mehta, who was born in India, academized in Vienna, summered in Tanglewood, and was, so the committee believed, a synthesis of three worlds. Mehta and Montreal were made for each other, and under his direction the orchestra prospered while offering such fare as a Beethoven Ninth of which the best part was a flowing, Weingartnerish slow movement, an appropriately egotistic *Ein Heldenleben* (type casting of a rather high order all around), and all the while doing its adventurous bit by the local and imported avant-garde. Such progress could not go unnoticed, and so the enterprising directorate of the Toronto Symphony, responding with what President Johnson is fond of calling "prompt and appropriate reply," accepted the resignation of Walter Susskind after a nine years' tenure made notable by a musical outlook at once sensitive and scholarly, an encyclopedic repertoire, and an inextinguishable fund of good humor tested to the full by the baying cubs of the local press.

Within a week it was announced that the post had gone to Seiji Ozawa, Leonard Bernstein's vice-president in charge of Far Eastern affairs.

Of Mr. Ozawa it is perhaps a bit early to form an opinion, though on the evidence of his guest conducting hereabouts, he would appear to possess a secure command of podium strategy, a somewhat academic turn of mind as regards programming, and an undisputed local record for family casting—he has managed to engage his wife as his first and third piano soloist (the second star, as they say in hockey, going to Emil Gilels).

Those of us who reside in the Arctic, having missed, through no fault of our own, the great age of the Central European Martinet, have ingenuously fused the older traditions with the exoticism characteristic of today's maestros in the personality of Jan Pieterzoon van Slump—our most celebrated musical figure and a man who has been portrayed picturesquely, if uncharitably, by the *Dawson Times* as "the tyrant of the tundra." As of this writing, van Slump reigns supreme over the Whitehorse Philharmonic, the Ketchikan Glee Club, the Sitka Musica Antiqua, and that jewel in the Crown of the Arctic, the Aklavic Orchestra (formerly known as L'Orchestre Philharmonique d'Aklavic but abbreviated last season at the insistence of Howard Grey Owl, the orchestra board's first vice-president and a fanatic admirer of George Szell). From our point of view van Slump's background is impeccable—his father having been an astronomically precise Dutch mariner and his mother an elegant Samoan socialite who, during the great storm of 1897, was carried screaming aboard the twin-masted clamscooper *Hook of Holland,* out of South Beveland and badly off course.

Van Slump would be first to admit, however, that the time-beating profession is undergoing a significant transformation—a transformation of rather greater momentum than can be contained by the commendably internationalist outlook which sponsored the recent Canadian appointments. The real issue concerns an audience growing bored with the conventions of the musical Establishment, among which civic podium appointments have for a very long while maintained a focal position. A none-too-educated guess suggests to me that the conducting of the future will be accomplished by a closed-circuit hypnotic-eye inspiration synthesizer, a democratically programmed compote of the interpretative ideas and ideals of all sidemen, managers, and critics everywhere. Its persuasive conception of the literature will be whammied to the sidemen in their acousti-tiled studios, in which all rehearsing and performing will, of course, be done—blend, as such, being achieved at the master control by programming another set of a priori specifications. Thus, the orchestral player will take several giant steps into the automated future. He can stay home to perform, forget about the car, keep an eye on the kids, save on the babysitter, and turn the wife out to work.

There will be wrinkles to iron out, of course. For sidemen of more conservative background, the automated conductor, no matter how expedient, may seem at first somewhat remote from the older traditions of stick waving. And here I should hope that we could call upon Mr. Hugh LeCaine, the ingenious inventor of the National Research Council's Touch-Amplitude Keyboard, which, with allied inspirations, has done so much to enrich the resources of the University of Toronto's Electronic Music Studio. With his unique awareness of the great Franco-Prussian traditions, it should be a simple matter to program the computer with a set of casual introductory remarks such as conductors traditionally use to inaugurate orchestral rehearsals, and which could be here set forth with such a *gemütlich* Bavarian accent as to afford the sidemen maximum environmental security: "Gut morning, tschentlemen!——Vot kann I zay!!!—ov ziss vourk . . . eggzept I @ % ¢—whrote itt $$$$$—meinzelf $**!!!"

L'ESPRIT DE JEUNESSE, ET DE CORPS, ET D'ART

If ever you come across an honest musician willing to recount for you his most memorable experiences of musical performance, be assured that he will cite among them an occasion when some green kid, still swaddled in conservatory blazer, stripped the clichés from a worn-out warhorse of the concert repertoire and revealed, as for the first time, its charms au naturel. Being human as well as being honest, our professional will most likely feel compelled to hedge his admiration by allowing that when Junior turned to other staples the affinity seemed somehow less pronounced. And being disposed to think this advocate uncommonly generous, you may perhaps elect to doubt his commendation of the first instant and help perpetuate the best-kept secret of the musical establishment.

At music schools across the land each week mere striplings confound their betters with such revelatory insights and cause some jaded masterpiece to come alive as it seldom does when rendered by even the most accomplished virtuoso. But lacking some assurance of tactical know-how or analytical know-why, these students do not attempt to distill from their achievement all-purpose formulae with which to speed the conquest of next semester's assignment. And their professors, lacking belief in an art subject to revelation, define their failure so to do—their failure to observe the example of the adult world and with a similar methodical expediency contaminate thereby both experiences—as a concomitant of immaturity.

The suppression of these unsettling prodigies has long since become instinctive, part and parcel of an educational system which has permitted music to remain, along with parliamentary politics, the last example of an art encouraged by the Renaissance that stubbornly retains a pre-Renaissance tutorial hierarchy. In music, as in politics, the ties that bind the pupil to the mentor are very seldom severed. And just as patronage and kickbacks and local postal contracts reward a faithful apprenticeship in the art of the possible, music, the art of the implausible, encourages its own method-mysteries—its own arcane cult credos, suitable for framing and the swift exclusion of the uninitiated. To get away with these chicaneries, musicians and politicians foster the belief that they operate at a level of abstraction which it would be in the interests of neither the listener's enjoyment nor the national security to define.

Insofar as these abstractions are meaningful at all and represent the ambiguity of the human situation, they elude no group more consistently than the musicians and the politicians—who are much too busy concocting campaign slogans which fragment and thus advertise their professional status to sit back and synopsize the mysteries of art. These slogans are designed to stress the solemn continuity of some special methodology, and so inevitably they fasten to the image of the mentor who is either very old or, better still, long gone. So, just as each quadrennial United States election reaps a new crop of modified Midwestern isolationists directing solemn tribute to the memory of the Tafts, the ill-tempered-clavier fraternity uncovers with each season's debuts aspirants the twitchings of whose triceps can be traced directly to the doorstep of Carl Czerny.

This curious attitude of affection for the errors of the past secures for the teaching of music more quack educators per square faculty than are the lot of any other major discipline. And it's an attitude, moreover, which was already regarded as passé by painters in the eighteenth century and by literary craftsmen with the advent of the printing press. But, of course, most everyone can read and write and even manage to draw a straight line, and for that reason painters and writers are judged by an audience which considers itself "on terms" with the artist—Nikita Khrushchev's problem in a nutshell. But not everyone who listens to music can decipher a stave or even carry a tune, and this gloriously exploitable situation is the source of all excess in the composing and performing of music, the source of that archaic preference for oral explication in the teaching of it, and the source as well for those pathetic classifieds which expose the confidence game for which so much musical instruction fronts: "Maestro Eruditto Assai, sole teacher and repetiteur of Madame Tessie Tura and exponent of the celebrated 'Throbbing Cavity Method,' is willing to accept a limited number of advanced beginners: by appointment." It is my view that this situation, though desperate, is not beyond reclaiming, and my belief that in music the hope of the future—to coin a phrase—rests with the young and that in the equally troubled preserves of politics (Canadian style, anyway) it rests with the northerner. As a northerner somewhat fond of music, I was gratified to find both auguries given credence this past summer.

For six years now, the month of July has been set aside by one-hundred-plus young musicians from across the country who converge on Toronto to form the National Youth Orchestra of Canada. Founded by Walter Susskind, whose encouraging baton elicited from them in past seasons some staggeringly authoritative interpretative essays, they were called to order this year by a guest conductor, Franz-Paul Decker, who chose the occasion as his Canadian debut. Decker, who appears from the podium very like Karajan in his Aachen days, but whose stick wielding eschews the choreographic involvements of that maestro for an explicit directional system more akin to Eugen Jochum's, arrived with a gathering Continental reputation to assuage the doubts of those who fretted that the slightly unkempt enthusiasm which had been the trademark and the glory of the NYO might not survive too stiff a dose of Central European pedagogy.

Unable to resist a preview of this head-on clash, your correspondent attended the season's first rehearsal, at which the orchestra read at sight the Tchaikovsky Fourth Symphony. This was distinctly the "pops" offering of their curriculum, which otherwise included the *Eroica*, the *Mathis* Symphony of Hindemith, Bloch's *Schelomo* (with Leonard Rose), and Symphonic Ode by the Canadian semiserialist John Weinzweig.

But I was most curious about the Tchaikovsky, because it seemed to me that of all the works programmed it would most closely identify with those environmental musical stimuli to which this younger generation is exposed. Just as in earlier, simpler times, young ladies of good breeding found the gentle airs of Mr. Sullivan's operettas a demurely secular embroidering of the neo-Mendelssohnian chorale, which codified Methodist music making in the home, so, it seemed to me, Tchaikovsky's Fourth would be indigenous material to a teen-age set for which chromaticism is a pseudonym for what André Previn adds to Frederick Loewe's show tunes, orchestration what Phil Spector tries when twiddling dials, and for which the produce of such diversions forms a diet round the clock, transistor portable, and parent proof.

And so it was! At the readthrough, the orchestra led Herr Decker through an occasion of the most jubilantly improvisatory do-it-yourselfness. The appropriate "Previnisms" served them well—especially in the finale, where only measures 101 and 102 gave them pause. But that's no fair—that's not chromaticism à la Previn: that's a neat sequential trick which not even "The Girl from Ipanema" has picked up yet.

Given a break to celebrate having arrived at the final cadence more or less intact, they adjourned and, under the discreet watch of their chaperones, stretched out upon the steps of the Faculty of Music Building. There, adding wraparound sun visors to the approved rehearsal garb of jeans, stretch pants, and sandals, and affecting that air of concentrated disinterestedness young people find supportive when choosing to make strange, they divided themselves into a consignment of apprentice Beatles warily assessing the potential of half a gross of Joan-Baez-as-muse. To break the spell, their concertmaster, who doubles as their steward, clapped his hands and announced recess was over, and with that admirably unprofessional commitment to the job of making music, which is not least among the attractions of this orchestra, the sun visors were snapped back into their holsters and the musicians went back indoors to start again with measure 101.

Another of the orchestra's attractions spent the summer at the last desk of the first violins. Miss Marie Lamontagne, an endearingly candid ("Chaikovsky, I not like listen him much, I like better play him") visitor from Chicoutimi, Province de Québec, was spotted in a vigorous tutti by a sharp-eyed snoop from the *Toronto Telegram* ("LAMONTAGNE'S VIOLIN-IST-SISTER PLANS MUSIC AS CAREER") and accorded for the balance of the season a prominence a divisi. This celebrity was due to the involvement—very much on the side of the angels and the Mounties, as it developed—of Miss Lamontagne's lawyer-brother, Pierre, in a political-judicial-criminal entanglement the ramifications of which make the wheelings and dealings of Mr. Robert Baker of Washington, D.C., seem no more serious a misreading of the letter of the law than a kiddie's lemonade stand's being run without a vendor's permit.

At the center of the fuss was the fate of one Lucien Rivard, an accused narcotics smuggler whose extradition the citizens of Texas much desired (and have since achieved, though in the interim the resourceful M. Rivard managed to surmount the walls at Bordeaux Gaol in Montreal and attain some four months' grace). As the U.S. Government's counsel in the case, Mr. Lamontagne had informed the RCMP in July 1964 (long before M. Rivard had opted for an unofficial exit) that the sum of $20,000 had been proposed to him as compensation for relinquishing his objections and allowing M. Rivard out on bail. Tales of other sums were entered in evidence before a Royal Commission appointed to investigate the case, with the opposition parties charging that the Liberals' campaign coffers were being replenished by special interest groups whose special interest at the moment was M. Rivard.

It is a source of pride to those of us who hail from the Arctic that the public's awareness of L'Affaire Rivard began with the disclosures of that adroit parliamentary tactician the Conservative Member for the Yukon Territories, Mr. Eric Neilsen. An inconspicuous back-bencher as recently as one year ago, Mr. Neilsen has gained perhaps more headline inches these past months than any other parliamentarian save the Prime Minister himself, and as a consequence of his virtuosic sleuthing has brought about the tactical demotion of the Minister of Justice, a compensatory reshuffling of the Liberal Cabinet, the expulsion from the Party of a former parliamentary assistant of the Prime Minister, and brought himself to a prominence vis-à-vis the flagging fortunes of Her Majesty's Loyal Canadian Opposition very like that of Representative John Lindsay for the Goldwater-devastated Republicans of the "Eastern Establishment." Neilsen, who has the inestimable advantage of representing a riding so sparsely populated that most every elector therein possesses for him a definable identity, brings with him to Parliament Hill a disdain for the expediential politics of block-interest consensus from which most backroom blunders grow. And while a further disentangling of these events must be expected so long as politicians' breaths and memories last, it is already clear that in this case a northerner, blessed with the integrity, forthrightness, idealism, and easy access to the Mounties' files that such a background assures, retained uncompromised his vision of the honor of the House.

Your correspondent, curious as to whether the NYO could manage with equal success to resist the encroachment of adult pragmatism and retain something of their own spontaneous vision of Tchaikovsky, returned for their dress rehearsal in the last week of July. With a Toronto concert scheduled for the next evening and a cross-country tour for the weeks to follow, the orchestra seemed keyed to a corporate intensity quite different from the reckless joie de vivre of three weeks earlier. Even Miss Lamontagne seemed rather pale and tense ("Such an excitement, such a feeling, I am shaking"), though she managed to provide a judiciously framed synopsis of the month's confrontation ("Monsieur Déckère is such nice man, but also most determined, yes? He is . . . how you say? . . . quite German").

Before the rehearsal could advance beyond a rather shaky statement of the opening measures' fanfare, a member of the brass choir had collapsed ("out of breath," the orchestra's nanny, who was summoned from the balcony, diagnosed), and the few minutes' respite allotted his recovery seemed to infuse all hands with fresh determination. For when the intermission terminated, the NYO produced a reading of this too familiar work which, if I may exclude that incomparably fluid improvisation Karajan made of it in his EMI recording, was, with all its gleaming, tactical precision, as faithful to the spirit of Tchaikovsky's zany, slightly vulgar devilments as any you could possibly imagine.

To be sure, some "niceties of expression"—the inevitable certifications of adult experience—had been appended in the intervening weeks: the whispered intonations of the violin and cello octaves at measure 27 (first movement) had been pointedly secured; the hairpin-shaped dynamic fluctuations of the Pizzicato ostinato (third movement) must surely have been accorded their own separate rehearsal; and even measures 101 and 102 had fallen into place. But these methodical intrusions were neither so numerous nor so predictable as to compromise the joy and wonder of that first encounter's spontaneity. Indeed, Decker's real achievement was to minimize the imposition of such expressive overdubbings and to retain as much of that premier occasion's star-struck inevitability as was consistent with the assertion of his directorial authority.

And this time, when the final cadence dissolved, the orchestra, their instructors, and the members of their board of financial recuperation gathered in mutually congratulatory knots about the auditorium. Decker moved among them offering the appropriate compliments and restraints, and they, it appeared, were returning them in kind. And, after all, why not? The bridge that spans the generations was built for two-way traffic.

TORONTO

I was born in Toronto, and it's been home base all my life. I'm not quite sure why; it's primarily a matter of convenience, I suppose. I'm not really cut out for city living, and given my druthers, I would avoid all cities and simply live in the country.

Toronto does belong on a very short list of cities I've visited that seem to offer—to me, at any rate—peace of mind—cities which, for want of a better definition, do not impose their "cityness" upon you. Leningrad is probably the best example of the truly peaceful city. I think that if I could come to grips with the language and the political system, I could live a very productive life in Leningrad. On the other hand, I'd have a crackup for sure if I were compelled to live in Rome or New York—and, of course, any Torontonian worthy of the name feels that way about Montreal, on principle.

The point is that, by design, I have very little contact with this city. In some respects, indeed, I think that the only Toronto I really know well is the one I carry about with me in memory. And most of the images in my memory bank have to do with the Toronto of the forties and early fifties, when I was a teen-ager.

Toronto's had a remarkably good press in recent years. It has been called "the new great city" or "a model of the alternative future"—and not by Torontonians; these delightful epithets have come from American and European magazines and city planners. But then Toronto has traditionally garnered very favorable comments from visitors: Charles Dickens dropped by

Adapted by Gould from his filmscript for a late-1970s documentary. Originally published in *Cities*, edited by John McGreevy (New York: Clarkson N. Potter, 1981, and Toronto: Lester & Orpen Dennys, 1981).

in 1842 and remarked that "the town is full of life, and motion, bustle, business, and improvement." Canadians by and large are less complimentary; until very recently "Hogtown" was the preferred description of Toronto by Canadians from other parts of the country, and it has been said that one of the few unifying factors in this very divided land is that all Canadians share a dislike—however perverse and irrational it may be—for Toronto.

When the St. Lawrence Seaway was completed in 1959, Toronto—though seven hundred miles uplake and upriver from the Atlantic Ocean—became in effect a deep-sea port. I've always been an incorrigible boat watcher, and I can still remember, when the Seaway had been completed, how exciting it was to prowl the Toronto waterfront and encounter ships that had brought Volkswagens from Germany or TV sets from Japan and had names like *Wolfgang Russ* or *Munishima Maru.*

But well before the Seaway was completed, Toronto had already become international in another way. At the end of the Second World War, there was a great migration to Canada from all over the world, particularly from Europe and Asia, and a good percentage of those immigrants opted for Toronto. As a result of that the population of the city, which had been predominantly Anglo-Saxon, underwent a profound sea-change. The Anglo-Saxons were reduced to a minority, though still the largest minority, to be sure, and the city began to reflect the cultural diversity of its new residents.

In 1793 Toronto's founder, Lieutenant-Governor John Graves Simcoe, predicted that the settlement would become a "palladium of British loyalty." And of his plans for the town Simcoe wrote: "There was to be one church, one university to guard the Constitution, at every street corner a sentry, the very stones were to sing 'God Save the King.' "

In Canadian political life, there's a saying, now almost cliché, that Canada is a "political mosaic." The point of this expression is to enable us to distinguish ourselves from the Americans, who are fond of describing their society as a "melting pot," and the implication is that in Canada (and nowhere better exemplified than in Toronto), however intense the heat, we do not melt.

Toronto is situated on the north shore of Lake Ontario, the most easterly and also the smallest of the Great Lakes. But it's a sizable pond, nonetheless. As a matter of fact, a Dutch friend of mine never tires of telling his relatives back home that you could drop all of Holland into this lake and still have room for enough windmills to keep Don Quixote busy for a lifetime. Actually, he's wrong: I looked it up, and Holland is almost twice as large as Lake Ontario. So you could drop it into Lake Superior or Lake Michigan or Lake Huron and it would disappear without a trace, but if you tried it here there would be very serious flooding.

A series of small islands overlap with one another like a crossword puzzle and protect Toronto Bay. The islands are primarily a recreational area, and during the summer ferryboats shuttle visitors and picnicking Torontonians back and forth across the harbor. But some hardy folks actually live on the islands all year round; in fact, there's been an island community of some sort for a century and a half.

Toronto's rationale as a city, indeed, is linked inevitably with its strategic location on Lake Ontario and, specifically, with its very fine harbor. After the American Revolution, the British were shopping around for likely spots to defend against the newly liberated colonists across the lake, and they elected to build a fort here. As an outpost of Empire, however, Fort York was by no means an unqualified success; the Americans sacked the town during the War of 1812.

Toronto's relationship with the American cities to the south, such as Buffalo, which is forty miles across the lake, has often been the butt of local jokes. In my youth it was said that for a really lively weekend, what you had to do was drive to Buffalo. Nowadays Torontonians do not seem to feel that that migration serves any useful purpose, but we still seem to have some deep-seated psychological need to *look* at Buffalo every now and then. So in 1976 we built a tower which, according to the tourist guides, is the tallest free-standing structure in the world. And they tell me that from up there, on a clear day, you can see, if not forever, at least to Buffalo.

There is no better example of the old Toronto versus the new than that shown by our two city halls, which stand on adjacent properties. The Old City Hall, which was finished in 1899, was built by a Canadian by the name of E. J. Lennox; he spent twelve years on the project and, by way of preliminary research, took a busman's holiday in Pennsylvania, where he was apparently inspired by the then new jail in Pittsburgh. When I was in that city once on a concert tour (which is the musical equivalent of a penitentiary sentence), I happened to take a walk past that jail, and, I must say, it looks not unlike our Old City Hall. Lennox maintained a remarkably consistent view of the appropriate enclosures for sinners and civil servants.

New City Hall was built in the early 1960s by the Finnish architect Viljo Revell. He died, very prematurely, just after his building was completed, and it was said at the time that his death might well have been hastened by the howls of outrage with which some of Toronto's elected officials greeted his remarkably imaginative design.

Toronto, at that time, was not exactly a hospitable place for contemporary art of any sort, and the decision to situate a large sculpture by Henry Moore in front of the New City Hall was the straw that broke the political camel's back. In fact, it was largely responsible for the electoral defeat of the mayor who supported its purchase. His chief opponent proclaimed that "Torontonians do not want abstract art shoved down their throats" and, of course, won the subsequent election handily.

Perhaps one indication of the remarkable change in Toronto's outlook during the last decade is that we now possess the largest collection of sculptures by Henry Moore in the Western Hemisphere; oddly enough, in view of all the earlier fuss, the collection was initiated by a gift from the sculptor himself. We Torontonians do have a way of ingratiating ourselves, I must say.

Beneath Toronto's towering bank buildings can be found underground shopping malls that one can follow throughout the better part of downtown, and it is similarly possible to walk through the city, out of doors, by following a network of ravines and river valleys, without once setting foot on concrete. Down the largest of these ravines runs the River Don, locally known as "the Muddy Don." It empties into Toronto Harbor, and if I were in marathon training, it would be possible for me to walk seventeen miles to its source without making direct contact with the city—although it would, of course, be all around me.

Another route to follow is Yonge Street, Toronto's original north-south artery, which demarcates east side from west side in much the same way that Fifth Avenue divides Manhattan. It was the trail by which settlers went north in the early years of the nineteenth century to homestead, and a favorite boast of local press agents is that it is, in fact, the longest street in the world. They arrive at this particular bit of propaganda by virtue of the fact that Yonge Street doesn't exactly end; it just sort of dissolves into the Ontario highway system, and it is possible to follow this road, north and west, for about twelve hundred miles (almost two thousand kilometers). Most of those miles traverse country that is absolutely haunting in its emptiness and bleakness and starkly magnificent beauty.

But the garish beginning of Yonge Street is not one of those miles. It's a bit of the street known as "the Strip"; I'm not sure who coined the name or whether he was aware of the double entendre involved. On a smaller scale, these few blocks pose for Toronto the same problems that Forty-second Street and Broadway create in New York. Civil libertarians find "the Strip" an irresistible cause; most of us simply find it an embarrassment.

Perhaps the single most important influence on Toronto during the sixties was, in fact, something that took place over three hundred miles away, in Montreal. That city played host in 1967 to the World's Fair, which was called Expo '67. The two towns, Montreal and Toronto, have always had a sort of anything-you-can-build-I-can-build-better rivalry, and Toronto subsequently became determined to create its own Expo—if necessary, block by block. Perhaps our most Expo-like construction is a recreational area on the lakeshore which is called Ontario Place.

Montreal's Expo was, of course, anything but an exercise in architectural consistency—it was actually a very eclectic assembly of buildings—and Toronto's substitute Expo has employed similar contrasts.

Toronto, by general consensus, is the financial capital of Canada. The contending office towers that dominate the downtown district house major banking institutions, and most of them are located on or near Bay Street, which is the Canadian equivalent of America's Wall Street. People who are not particularly fond of Toronto insist that we go about the making of money with a religious devotion. I don't think that that's more true of this city than of most others, but if it is, then I suppose that other cliché—the one about such buildings being cathedrals of finance—would have to be given its due as well. In any case, most of us do our banking at very modest branch offices, which, if the analogy must be pursued, are obviously parish churches.

A peculiar and important aspect of the Toronto mentality is a tendency to retain, even during times of radical change, a certain perspective, a certain detachment, a healthy skepticism about change for change's sake. I think it was probably that tendency which enabled Toronto to survive the sixties, when comparable cities south of the border were, quite literally, falling apart in both architectural and human terms. Toronto emerged from that turbulent decade as, arguably, one of the great cities of the world, certainly as an extraordinarily clean, safe, quiet, considerate sort of place in which to live.

Toronto's largest shopping concourse is called the Eaton Centre, and some people say it is Toronto's answer to the Galleria in Milan; but whether that's true or not, it certainly is not your average Ma and Pa Kettle corner store. It is in fact the flagship of a vast retail empire which despite its monumentality has remained a family concern. The family concerned are the Eatons, and they have been the leading lights of Toronto's, and indeed Canada's, merchandising for the better part of a century.

Timothy Eaton, founder of the business—who sits in bronze at the entrance to the vast new store—was always willing to gamble on somewhat off-the-beaten-track locations; sometimes a move of only a few blocks was involved, but Timothy always had the feeling that if he located his stores where shoppers were, by the time he had finished building them (usually an expansive as well as expensive operation) that's where the shoppers wouldn't be. Well, perhaps the descendants who run his empire now know something we don't: the new Eaton Centre is located, improbably enough, kitty-corner from the Yonge Street "Strip." Having cost almost a quarter of a billion dollars, it could be that it will revitalize this rather seedy quarter of Toronto. We can only hope so.

When I was a child, and indeed until very recently, this city was referred to as "Toronto the Good." The reference was to the city's puritan traditions: one could not, for example, attend concerts on Sunday until the 1960s; it was not permissible to serve alcohol in any public place on the Sabbath until very recently; and now a furor has developed at City Hall over the issue of whether Torontonians should be permitted to drink beer at baseball games.

But you have to understand that, as an antiathletic, non-concertgoing teetotaler, I approve all such restrictions. I, perhaps, rather than the hero of George Santayana's famous novel, am "the last puritan." So I always felt that "Toronto the Good" was a very nice nickname. On the other hand, a lot of my fellow citizens became very upset about it and tried to prove that we could be just as bad as any other place.

Toronto incorporates five boroughs which form a sort of satellite network around the original city. North York, which recently incorporated itself as a city, is the largest of these and houses about half a million people. It is my favorite area of the city by far, and although I live downtown, I keep a studio in North York. I think what attracts me to it is the fact that it offers a certain anonymity; it has a sort of improbable, Brasilia-like quality. In fact, it has much of the tensionless atmosphere of one of those capital cities where the only business is the business of government and which are deliberately located away from the geographical mainstream—Ottawa, say, or Canberra.

During the fifties and sixties, North York seemed to spring spontaneously from the soil; I can remember when the area was all farmland. And what developed was a community so carefully planned, so controlled in its density, in the structural and rhythmical regularity with which its homes, offices, shops, and public buildings come together, that it doesn't seem like a city at all—which, needless to say, is the highest compliment I can pay it. To me it seems, as I have said, like a seat of government, or perhaps, rather better, like a vast company town, presided over by an autocratic but benevolent chairman of the board, whose only order of the day, every day, is—Tranquility. It is fashionable to downgrade suburbia these days, of course. The march back to city center, with all its zooty renovated row houses, is all the rage, I know; but this part of Toronto, I think, represents the North American suburban dream at its best. And I love it!

In my youth, Toronto was also called "the City of Churches," and, indeed, the most vivid of my childhood memories in connection with Toronto have to do with churches. They have to do with Sunday-evening services, with evening light filtered through stained-glass windows, and with ministers who concluded their benediction with the phrase "Lord, give us the peace that the earth cannot give." Monday mornings, you see, meant that one had to go back to school and encounter all sorts of terrifying situations out *there* in the city. So those moments of Sunday-evening sanctuary became very special to me; they meant that one could find a certain tranquility even in the city, but only if one opted not to be part of it.

Well, I don't go to church these days, I must confess, but I do repeat that phrase to myself very often—the one about the peace that the earth cannot give—and find it a great comfort. What I've done, I think, while living here, is to concoct some sort of metaphoric stained-glass window, which allows me to survive what appear to me to be the perils of the city—much as I survived Monday mornings in the schoolroom. And the best thing I can say about Toronto is that it doesn't seem to intrude upon this hermitlike process.

It's been fascinating to get to know Toronto after all these years, but not even this filmic exploration of it has made me a city convert, I'm afraid. I am more than ever convinced, though, that, like Leningrad, Toronto is essentially a truly peaceful city.

But perhaps I see it through rose-colored glasses; perhaps what I see is still so controlled by my memory that it's nothing more than a mirage. I hope not, though, because if that mirage were ever to evaporate, I should have no alternative but to leave town.

CONFERENCE AT PORT CHILLKOOT

Author's Note: "Conference at Port Chillkoot" was originally conceived as a fictionalized documentary for radio and first performed on the Canadian Broadcasting Corporation in January 1967. Its appearance in print means, inevitably, that certain audio conceits available to the original version have undergone a sea-change in the process of transcription.

Certainly, words alone cannot convey the elegiac eloquence of Sir Norman Bullock-Carver, the hard-nosed practicality of Homer Sibelius, the avant-garde idealism of Alain Pauvre, or the political expediency of Councilman Stafford Byers. Indeed, one can do no more than hint at the hypnotic beat of the Skagway Princess's *diesels, the acoustic decay at the Loyal Coyote Lodge, or that unique combination of youthful exuberance and cavalier voice leading which was the hallmark of the Chillkoot Continuation School Choir and Silver Band's dockside serenade.*

The author would encourage the reader to invest the printed record of the

From *Piano Quarterly*, Summer 1974.

"Conference at Port Chillkoot" with some semblance of those aural properties in-
digenous to its conception, and to accept all appropriate assurances that any resem-
blance to any music critic, alert or inert, is purely coincidental.

The announcement that the North American Music Critics' Alliance was
to hold its annual conference-seminar in Port Chillkoot, Alaska, was the occasion for factional dissent within the ranks of that august body, casual surprise in the entertainment sections of the New York dailies, and utter disbelief in the forty-ninth state's fourth estate.

"AISLERS PIC PANHANDLE PORT" was Variety's headline, but the show-biz
weekly was hard-pressed to develop the item, since "no info on Chillkoot
draw power or seat cap available since '98." No such reticence prevailed in
Alaska, however, where the mainland dailies played the story front-page and
the Anchorage *Whaler and Spooner* got off a biting editorial under the title
"What Price Gratitude?" denouncing the Port Chillkoot Chamber of Com-
merce.

> In our opinion, no useful (not to say honorable) purpose can be served
> by the shortsighted opportunism of our fellow citizens of the Inside Pas-
> sageway in their ill-concealed attempt to siphon off the tourist flow
> upon which the economic growth of our great State depends. We would
> remind them that the S.S. *Skagway Princess* from which these learned
> gentlemen will disembark is a vessel subsidized by all the citizens of our
> State and an important lifeline for the oceanside communities therein.
> It is, moreover, patently foolish for a community of four hundred souls
> to covet and promote a convention trade for which they have neither
> the appropriate facilities nor, we respectfully submit, the "savoir faire."
> We would ask that His Honor Mayor Sven Wenner-Gren soberly and
> earnestly reconsider his position in this matter and, in so doing, reflect
> for a moment upon the fate of Brighton, or Ostend, or Scheveningen,
> were the intellectual luster and aesthetic glories of London, Bruxelles,
> or Amsterdam to tarnish and decline.

Curiously enough, the good citizens of Port Chillkoot were at this time
entirely unaware of the furor in which their community had become entangled and were to remain so until the sunrise edition of the *Whaler and Spooner*
arrived aboard the *Skagway Princess* at dusk the following day. Mayor Wenner-Gren, glancing over the editorial page on his way to the comics, elected
to bypass "What Price Gratitude?," assuming it to be yet another reappraisal
of the Franco-American Alliance, but was aroused from his contemplation
of "Brenda Starr, Girl Reporter" by an urgent call from Magdalena Murphy—copy editor and fine-arts critic of the *Port Chillkoot Packet*.

When His Honor's blood pressure had crested, he and Magdalena descended upon Harry Southam—owner and prop. of Southam's Sanitary Snacks, and participant, as Magdalena had discovered at the Western Union Office, in an unusually brisk telegraphic exchange in recent days. Sure enough, Harry Southam was able to produce from over the Kool-Aid counter a complete file of his negotiations with one Alain Pauvre, chairman of the Critics' Alliance accommodations committee and, in his own right, music critic of the *New York Witness-Centurion*. The exchange had begun when Mr. Pauvre, settling upon Port Chillkoot for reasons which were far from clear to Harry, inquired about the possibility of assembly space and lodgings (twelve singles, four doubles, six cots). Harry, after a consultation with his wife, Christobel, in which they agreed that fate was indeed knocking at the door and that this, perhaps, was the year for them to knock out the kitchen wall and add the east wing they'd talked of so often—"Bayside exposure," their ad in the *Alaska Auto Advertiser* could read next year—replied in the affirmative and assured Mr. Pauvre that meeting facilities were readily at hand (he was sure he could swing it with the Loyal Coyote Brotherhood for use of the lodge hall).

A subsequent wire from New York inquired whether "artist's rates" were available for the group—to which Christobel and Harry readily assented since, although no such precedent existed in the annals of Port Chillkoot tourism, they felt it would be best to give the critics the benefit of the doubt rather than risk losing the trade. Yet another wire was forthcoming—this time from Montreal, P.Q., where Kerry McQuaig, music critic of *L'Estralita de Montreal*, inquired as to whether the premises were licensed. Harry, by this time possessed of a cavalier telegraphic style, responded: "PLENTY BOOZE AVAILABLE STOP CAN ALSO ARRANGE GUEST MEMBERSHIP AFTER HOURS CLUB CALLED OILERS' ROOST REGARDS."

Back in New York, the conference plans were gathering something less than unanimous approval from within the Alliance. Alain Pauvre, as accommodations chairman (a compensatory post traditionally awarded the preceding year's runner-up for the presidency), used his considerable influence to bring off the Port Chillkoot decision, since, as nominal leader of the pro-composing faction within the Alliance, he was determined to seek out a place where the discussion of ideas would take precedence over their representation in performance. This, of course, was wholly antagonistic to the pro-performing faction headed by his archrival, Homer Sibelius, the chief critic of the *New York Square,* and as the Port Chillkoot decision drew nearer, both of them courted the votes of such middle-of-the-roaders as Waldorf Major, critic of the influential weekly *Old Gothamer,* and H. B. Haggle of the *Housatonic Review.*

A crisis loomed when the entire English-Canadian delegation withdrew, claiming, justifiably, that Whitehorse, Yukon Territories, a town of far greater historical interest, was the logical site for the convention. Only Kerry McQuaig of *L'Estralita de Montreal* decided not to boycott, since he felt that his sole presence, in addition to providing eloquent testimony on behalf of that brittle, biracial detente of modern Canada, would enable him to get in some research for his forthcoming Skira book, *The Klondike, Its Women and Saloons.* The decision, however, rested with Alain Pauvre, and he held fast to Port Chillkoot even when, a fortnight before the convention, Homer Sibelius threw a public tantrum, courtesy of his Sunday column in the *Square,* in which, for this occasion only, he abandoned his to-be-continued reminiscence of those glorious days of yore when giants walked the stages of the world and marshaled his celebrated literary style, forever made secure and immune to change during his interminable apprenticeship on the sports desk, in a public denunciation of Alain Pauvre:

"A strong criticism provides a strong musical environment. Unsportsmanlike though it may be, I am at last about to take off the kid gloves and to cease pulling my punches with my opponent Alain Pauvre. It is time my readers knew that this man, this 'critic,' has tried to kayo a strong criticism in this country."

And on he went, solidly building his attack, and for two or three days thereafter its substance was much debated in the Russian Tea Room.

Upon their arrival in the lovely harbor which serves the twin towns of Port Chillkoot–Haines (or Haines–Port Chillkoot, as they are known on the other side of the bay), the gentlemen of the press were greeted dockside by the members of the Chillkoot Continuation School Choir and Silver Band and favored with the inaugural rendition of a civic anthem specially composed by fourteen-year-old Graham W. Clarkson, Jr., whose father, Graham W. Clarkson, Sr., is vocational guidance instructor and vice-principal at Chillkoot C.S. Sung to a tune reminiscent of "Pomp and Circumstance" No. 1, it has, as Homer Sibelius was later to jot down while trying to fit it into the free-lance holiday travel piece he was determined to get out of the trip, "the hard, clear truth of northern light"—make that "the hard, clear light of northern truth," or perhaps "the clear, hard"—well, these things take time, you know.

> From Chillkoot's icy glacier,
> O'er Chillkoot's lowering fjord,
> A crack was heard, a rumble caught,
> A gathering roar, full danger fraught,
> And down the slope it poured.

From Chillkoot's icy glacier,
O'er Chillkoot's new-made plains,
A foot was seen, and then an arm,
Thank God, our town is safe from harm,
Tonight, it buried Haines.

Upon the conclusion of the anthem, to which, at the artful suggestion of Magdalena Murphy, the choir appended the Dresden Amen, the critics were greeted unofficially by Magdalena and Harry Southam and presented by Harry with mimeographed copies of their convention schedule, thoughtfully enclosed within a sample menu of Southam's Sanitary Snacks, which bore on the outside the legend "Lord, give us the grace to accept those things we cannot reject, and to reject those things we cannot accept"—at once a credo peculiarly befitting the critical profession and, as they were shortly to discover, singularly pertinent to Christobel Southam's cuisine.

Convention Schedule

FIRST DAY—SATURDAY

1:00 p.m.	Arrival via S.S. *Skagway Princess*
2:30 p.m.	Official Greetings—His Honor Mayor Sven Wenner-Gren (or deputy)
8:00 p.m.	Opening Forum: The Changing World of the Reviewer—Homer Sibelius

SECOND DAY—SUNDAY

8:45 a.m.	The Crotchet in Krenek (from a paper in progress)—Alain Pauvre
10:30 a.m.	Sightseeing Tour (including town dock; sewage disposal plant; pipeline maintenance workshop)—Hostess: Magdalena Murphy
2:00 p.m.	Leitmotiv in Carlisle Floyd—Waldorf Major
3:30 p.m.	Stravinsky as Dancer—H. B. Haggle
5:00 p.m.	Speculations on the Chemical Composition of *Tristan*'s Love Potion—Kerry McQuaig
8:00 p.m.	Closing Forum and Keynote Address: "The Future as Tradition"—Sir Norman Bullock-Carver (Guest Speaker)
10:00 p.m.	Departure via S.S. *Skagway Princess*

Luncheon over, the critics repaired to the Loyal Coyote Hall, where they were given official greetings by Councilman Stafford Byers, filling in for Mayor Wenner-Gren, who was called upstate on "family business" shortly after it occurred to him that another editorial like the one in the *Whaler and Spooner* would not appreciably enhance his prospects for the state assembly. In His Honor's absence, Councilman Byers spoke of those eternal truths in the relations of man and soil which he held appropriate for any audience, at any time, in any place:

"There are those of you, who—who will choose—to remain, and—become one—one with this land. To those, I would say to those—the land—the land is good—and—and will endure—and—and will bring—bring great reward—to those—who—who live—in harmony—harmony with its laws—and so I————(How's that? Critics?—I declare!)—I—I thank you."

For the most part, the conference sessions were well attended—the notable exception being Alain Pauvre's presentation "The Crotchet in Krenek," which Homer Sibelius, heading up the times and places committee, had scheduled for the prebreakfast slot on Sunday. However, Pauvre's paper was delivered to an appreciative audience consisting of Jessie Doolittle, the Loyal Coyote Brotherhood's cleaning lady, and Kerry McQuaig, who was picking his way home from the Oilers' Roost and who permitted himself a rather tiresome amount of heckling.

Primary interest, of course, was centered on the evening forums, and in the first of these Homer Sibelius, chairing the discussion "The Changing World of the Reviewer," suggested that in the absence of anything else worth reviewing in Port Chillkoot, he would not be averse to offering a brief piano recital. This he proceeded to do and, to the intense annoyance of Alain Pauvre, rendered in one sitting the complete keyboard works of Thalberg and Moszkowski. The interpretations partook of that same forceful athleticism for which his journalistic style is justly noted and, but for the three occasions when Albert Tanner, the handyman, was summoned from the wings to replace a bass string on the Loyal Coyote Lodge's upright, he continued, neither pausing for applause nor revealing the slightest indication of fatigue. "It was," stated Kerry McQuaig, who sensed his own imminent elevation to the presidency, "a direct, straightforward, yet strangely human exposition of this neglected literature." Less cordial was the review of H. B. Haggle, who, having long since resigned political ambition, remarked that it was, after all, "direct and straightforward music, and what do you expect?"

So it went throughout the convention, and all the members were much relieved when at last Sunday evening was at hand and factional differences could be set aside in anticipation of the keynote address. This was to be delivered by Sir Norman Bullock-Carver, critic emeritus of the Manchester *Spiritus et Angelus* and, by appointment, adviser-in-reviewing to Her Majesty Elizabeth II and instructor in counterpoint (first species) to the Lady Sarah

Armstrong-Jones (or at least he will be when the Lady Sarah attains her twelfth birthday).

Sir Norman, it must be admitted, was very much a compromise choice as guest speaker. Alain Pauvre was willing to settle for Knud Jeppeson, Henri Pousseur, or Hans Keller, but Homer Sibelius went out on a limb for Ruggiero Ricci and stayed there. For both factions, however, the title of Sir Norman's address, "The Future as Tradition," seemed promising, and all the delegates settled down that warm August evening to enjoy the venerable gentleman's remarks.

"I should like to say straight off that there are in our midst—anarchists—whose scheme it is—to jeopardize—the framework of our musical society."

(For Waldorf Major, this phrase alone justified the trip, and he gave a perfunctory sneeze in the direction of Alain Pauvre.)

"I have in mind—young Elgar, Holst, and others of their ilk."

(It was the address that Sir Norman had composed in the spring of 1902 upon the occasion of his being made don of King's College, Cambridge, and which he redelivered some eighteen years later at the time of his election to the Halle Society.)

"It is up to those of us—blessed with a reverence for the past—to enshrine that lofty sentiment forever in our breasts."

(Kerry McQuaig released an irreverent guffaw but hurriedly converted it to a spell of asthma when he noticed that Waldorf Major, whose vote he would surely need next year, appeared displeased.)

"As I look into the youthful faces assembled here today—I am compelled to urge you—to bear—that torch—brightly."

(A sudden and imperious toot from the S.S. *Skagway Princess* brought Homer Sibelius hurriedly to the rostrum to deliver the vote of thanks and summoned as well the Chillkoot Continuation School Choir and Silver Band, who were determined to bid the critics bon voyage with a reprise of Master Clarkson's anthem. Sir Norman, whose hearing had been in decline since the heroic holding action in October '99 when, serving at Mafeking under Baden-Powell, he directed for thirty-six harrowing hours the Percussion Ensemble of the Royal Winchester Fusiliers, was quite unaware of the convention's precipitous termination.)

SIR NORMAN: Into whichever distant lands . . .
HOMER SIBELIUS: Sir Norman, I know that I . . .
CCSC and SB: From Chillkoot's icy glacier . . .

SIR N.: your work may call you . . .
H.S.: . . . express on behalf of all present . . .
CCSC and SB: O'er Chillkoot's lowering fjord . . .

SIR N.: hold high your hopes and dreams!
H.S.: . . . our gratitude for your stimulating . . .
CCSC and SB: A crack was heard, a rumble caught,
  A gathering roar, full danger fraught.

SIR N.: . . . Remember always that the trust . . .
H.S.: . . . and truly memorable address. . . .
CCSC and SB: And down the slope it came.

SIR N.: . . . and faith of the Academy goes with you . . .
H.S.: May I remind the members . . .
CCSC and SB: From Chillkoot's icy glacier.

SIR N.: . . . and, need I say, the prayers . . .
H.S.: that they should pick up all their belongings . . .
CCSC and SB: O'er Chillkoot's new-made plains.

SIR N.: . . . of that England which we all do love . . .
H.S.: at Harry Southam's before proceeding to the dock.
CCSC and SB: A foot was seen, and then an arm,
  Thank God, our town is safe from harm.

SIR. N: . . . and now, Goodbye and Farewell.
H.S.: I hereby declare the convention adjourned.
CCSC and SB: Tonight, it buried Haines.

Once safely aboard, the critics quietly drifted apart. Kerry McQuaig, intent upon toasting his own incoming presidency, invited the navigator, Ole Olafson, to join him for a quick one, an invitation which caused the *Skagway Princess* to circle three times around Haines Island before setting course for Yokohama. The course was straightened out when Alain Pauvre, fascinated by the navigational possibilities of the hexachord, prepared a serialized compass system which he presented with his compliments to Captain Kurt Blitzleben. H. B. Haggle and Waldorf Major decided to bury ancient hatchets in the interests of expediting a palace revolution.

As for Homer Sibelius—the conference had not been a happy one for him, and on coming aboard he withdrew to his stateroom, informed the steward that he would be taking all meals in, and, after securely locking the door and covering the porthole which gave onto B deck, he produced from his luggage a carefully wrapped silver baton, which had been presented to him by George Szell on the occasion of his one hundredth consecutive bad review of Leonard Bernstein; and, tuning his transistor to CBC Vancouver, which comes in loud and clear in the twilit midnight of the Arctic summer, and hearing for the first time in his life the Symphony No. 14 by the Canadian transcendentalist Zoltán Mostányi, he raised the baton and, with firm, mascu-

line beats, vigorous, no-nonsense cutoffs, and withal maintaining an impeccable and confident posture, gave it a virile and thoroughly professional rendition.

At Port Chillkoot, life resumed its familiar pace. Magdalena Murphy
decided against a follow-up feature on the convention and on the following
Saturday carried in the *Packet*, without comment, a Reuters dispatch date-
lined Tutuila, Samoa, which noted that Sir Norman Bullock-Carver, the distinguished British critic, had spoken to the island's Historical Society on the
subject "The Future as Tradition" and had given warning of alarming and
revolutionary developments in the world of music.

FACT, FANCY, OR PSYCHOHISTORY: NOTES FROM THE P.D.Q. UNDERGROUND

On the night of April 26, 1965, New York's Town Hall played host to one
of the most striking events inspired by the so-called baroque revival. An audience grown weary of the bland cadential formulae of Vivaldi, the obligatory
coda-strettos of Handel, the "when in doubt, sequence" fugal style of Buxte-
hude, was confronted with a musical syntax in which ambiguity was all, in
which a priori determination played no discernible role. The occasion, of
course, was the first concert in North America devoted exclusively to the
works of P. D. Q. Bach, and the impresario responsible for that event—the
author of the present volume, Peter Schickele—had with one stroke lifted
the veil of obscurity with which history had sought to conceal the achievement of this last and, in Schickele's own words, "by all means least," of Johann Sebastian's twenty-odd children. In so doing, Schickele achieved for
himself a niche in musical archaeology comparable with that attained one
hundred and thirty-six years before by Felix Mendelssohn when, deleted
choruses and truncated recitatives notwithstanding, that master revived the
senior Bach's St. Matthew Passion and set the stage for the original "baroque
revival."

Strictly speaking, of course, P.D.Q. (the initials stand for nothing,
which, as Professor Schickele points out, "could be said of the composer him-

From *Piano Quarterly*, Summer 1976.

self later in life") was not a baroque figure at all. Born just eight years before his celebrated father's demise, he attained his musical majority at a time when the knotty contrapuntal complexities espoused by Johann Sebastian were dismissed, even by P.D.Q.'s own influential siblings, as an indulgent anachronism. By no means a prodigy, he wrote his first semiserious compositions in about 1777 (when their author was already in his mid-thirties), so they are thus roughly contemporary with Haydn's Op. 20 String Quartets, Gluck's *Iphigenie en Tauride,* and Mozart's "Parisian" piano sonatas. Understandably, perhaps, such early works as the Echo Sonata for Two Unfriendly Groups of Instruments or the Gross Concerto for Divers Flutes, Two Trumpets, and Strings pay little heed to the genteel conventions of the rococo; rather, they provide a shrewd, if not altogether affectionate, commentary upon those more vigorous musical styles which P.D.Q.'s good ear had assimilated during a childhood spent in Leipzig's most celebrated musical manse.

With his other ear, however, the lad intuitively rejected the structural properties of baroque architecture and wholeheartedly embraced the need to expand the limited instrumental resources normally associated with music of the eighteenth century. It may be that this consuming passion for instrumental esoterica which was to influence all of his major work and to create for P.D.Q. a role in eighteenth-century musical society analogous to that of Harry Partch in our own time was, however inadvertently, a tacit rebuff to his family in general and the memory of his father in particular. Certainly, P.D.Q. was the first Bach in five generations to be denied a musical grounding at home; only his eldest brother, the richly talented but riotously intemperate Wilhelm Friedemann, demonstrated a measure of filial concern for the lad, and if one wishes to go the psychohistory route, it is possible to speculate that the composer's adolescent identity crisis, shaped as it was by the perception of his father's benign indifference, could be resolved only with his identification of, and immersion in, an area where even Johann Sebastian's multifaceted musical endeavors would offer no competitive challenge. (An "Any instrument that has the range will do" motto might best sum up the notoriously casual attitude of Bach père in regard to matters of orchestration.) Professor Schickele, who seems rather to enjoy playing Erik Erikson to P.D.Q.'s Luther, posits the theory with enthusiasm, but in the absence of more detailed documentation one should, I think, withhold judgment.

In any event, it comes as no surprise that upon leaving home in his early teens P.D.Q. was apprenticed to one Ludwig Zahnstocker, a carpenter, instrument maker, and jigsaw virtuoso, and that under Zahnstocker's guidance the lad participated in inventions which literally shook the European musical community. Their last collaborative effort, indeed—the Pandemonium, or, as Zahnstocker preferred to call it, "Thor's Music Box"—was directly responsible, on the day of its debut, for the demolition of the famous Glaslusthaus (the Alpine glass palace for which it was intended as the conversation piece par excellence) and on the following day (though seismology was a primitive science at the time) for the largest recorded avalanche in European history. It was also responsible, thanks to that instinctive survival mechanism with which nature provides for those of her children cast prematurely adrift in a cold and hostile world, for the sudden departure from his homeland of P.D.Q. Bach and for the inauguration of an odyssey of Dickensian pathos of twenty-one years' duration. Professor Schickele is particularly effective in dealing with this period, and through his eyes we follow P.D.Q. from Salzburg (and a meeting with the infant Mozart) to Dublin (a visit with cousin Schweinhard, or "Piggy," as he came to be called) to London (where the renowned "English Bach"—his brother Johann Christian—provided room and board, for a price, and a letter of recommendation to the elders of a distant country parish, free of charge) to St. Petersburg (where, during a visit with his cousin Leonhardt Sigismund Dietrich, P.D.Q. encounters the great love of his life, L.S.D. Bach's only daughter, Betty-Sue). But Professor Schickele is never less than eloquent, and his identification with his subject permeates every facet of the story he recounts.

There are, to be sure, drawbacks to so intense a biographical involvement. As with Max Brod's passionate propaganda in behalf of Franz Kafka, Faubion Bowers's mystical hallucinations about Alexander Scriabin, or Paul Hiebert's earthy evocation of "the Sweet Songstress of Saskatchewan," Sarah Binks, it is sometimes difficult to spot the precise point at which fact and fancy merge. For example, Professor Schickele's not unfounded conviction that he alone is responsible for P.D.Q.'s current reputation encourages him to ignore the considerable evidence for what one might call the "P.D.Q. underground." This was a mid-nineteenth-century movement which, with guerrillalike tenacity, strove to defy injunctions from both the musical and theological establishments (P.D.Q., a convert to Catholicism, was excommunicated even before the premiere of the Missa Hilarious) and to keep alive the memory of this unique artistic figure. Schickele, in discussing the celebrated "demolition incident" of 1842 in which, with the complicity of the last legitimate Bach, Wilhelm Friedrich Ernst, a wrecking crew under the direction of Felix Mendelssohn overturned the mausoleum erected at Baden-Baden-Baden by Betty-Sue thirty-five years before, merely quotes the uninspired doggerel originally inscribed on the tomb:

> Hier liegt ein Mann ganz ohne gleich;
> Im Leibe dick, an Sünden reich.
> Wir haben ihn in das Grab gesteckt,
> Weil es uns dünkt er sei verreckt.

All well and good—except for the fact that the story, as Schickele must surely know, does not end there. Within a scant five years, Mendelssohn himself had gone to his reward, and in Liverpool, where Betty-Sue retired after P.D.Q.'s death, the local quarterly *Field and Theme—the Country Gentleman's Guide to Music and the Garden* carried in its winter issue of 1848 what appeared to be a four-part commemorative tribute to the great German romanticist. This consisted of an accurate but remarkably detached résumé of the composer's life and work (astonishing for its adjectiveless objectivity in view of the national-hero status which Mendelssohn had enjoyed in England for twenty years), a reprint of Queen Victoria's letter of sympathy to the composer's widow, Cecile, and a distinctly unenthusiastic review of the oratorio *St. Paul,* which had been given in London by the Sacred Harmonic Society as a memorial the preceding November. Running opposite these commemorative items was an indulgent, though unsigned, sixty-five-verse epic titled "Ode to a Lost Chord-Changer," for which space permits inclusion of only the penultimate stanza:

> Poor death, thou quiet pauper, didst thou query thy
>   posterity,
> Didst that quickening perception doom thy quest?
> 'Tis pity, desperate quantifier, peace doth quell thy
>   territ'ry
> Be flattered that the Antichrist honours thy behest.

One wonders how many *Field and Theme* subscribers could have looked beyond the apparent tie to Mendelssohn, beyond the fulsome Byronisms of the poetic manner, beyond the obvious thematic indebtedness to Donne, beyond even the curious correspondence between the number of stanzas involved (sixty-five) and the years granted to another "chord-changer" who had died four decades earlier, and noticed that, separated only by words beginning with the letter T—the symbol of the cross and the Trinity—an unbroken series of the initials P, D, and Q occupied 259 of the 260 lines involved. But that remaining line—actually, the 256th of the ode itself and the conclusion of the stanza cited above—provides several clues as to the type of personnel recruited by the P.D.Q. cells. The reader no doubt will already have spotted the B-A-C-H motif derived from the first, fifth and sixth words ("Be," "Antichrist," "honours") as well as the summative compression of the motive implied by the two syllables of the final word, "behest."

Less obvious, perhaps, is the raison d'être for the seemingly obtrusive presence of "flattered"—the only word in 260 lines which does not begin with the letters P, D, Q, B, A, C, H, or T. But the explanation is simplicity itself: in German musical notation the note B describes the scale position referred to in English as B-flat, while, again according to the German convention, the letter H defines the note described in English as B-natural. From Sebastian Bach's time to the present, innumerable fugues, canons, and passacaglia themes have been based primarily or exclusively on the notes B-flat, A, C, and B-natural and intended as tribute to the cantor of the Thomaskirche. The ode, consequently, was clearly the work of a German musical émigré (which goes some distance toward an explanation of the rather stilted poetry involved), but, cautious and cabalistic though it may at first have seemed, the message of the P.D.Q. underground, as of the early Christian church, was about to break loose from the confines of the Continent.

Finally, to matters musical: Professor Schickele devotes the fourth segment of his book (a handsome pictorial essay on the life of P.D.Q. and a somewhat self-serving photographic study of Schickele's own researches absorb the second and third portions, respectively) to a description of each of the composer's major works. Despite, or perhaps because of, his impeccable academic credentials (he's dean of fine arts at the University of Southern North Dakota at Hoople), Schickele seems unable to divorce these extraordinary pieces from their historical context and frequently overlooks the real import of P.D.Q.'s revolutionary message. In his discussion of the familiar (though, admittedly, overrated) Concerto for Horn and Hardart, Schickele dismisses the first movement, with the "truncated recapitulation one has come to expect from history's laziest composer," as though unaware of the influence of this fascinating, if ultimately unsatisfying, structure upon the cyclical idée-fixe sonata forms of Liszt, Strauss, and early Schoenberg. Similarly, in his analysis of the D-major Sinfonia Concertante, Schickele mentions that the "incompatibility" of the solo group (lute, balalaika, ocarina, and bagpipes) was used "as a structural element in the composition" but neglects to mention that this concept of "incompatibility" leads inevitably, if circuitously, to Elliott Carter's theory of metrical modulation.

Schickele's most astonishing lapse, however, is his inclusion, as a frontispiece and without comment, of a fragment from a work previously unknown to me, the *Songs Without Points*. Precisely why this example is of such particular fascination requires some explanation: seventy-seven years ago, Edward Elgar published his *Enigma* Variations—an opus that was instantly, and justifiably, acclaimed as the finest English orchestral work of its time. As regards the title, Sir Edward later volunteered that it had two applications—each variation, excluding those which profiled the composer and his wife, was a portrait in sound of one of their friends, and, in addition, the theme itself could function as counterpoint to yet another theme of great significance. The first part of the riddle—the variation portraiture—provided a diverting parlor game for the musical equivalent of the Bloomsbury set. But that second challenge—the thematic countertheme puzzle—intrigues British musicians, at least, to this day. Everything from Handel choruses to Gilbert and Sullivan patter songs to "Rule Britannia" has been tried and found wanting; one theme will be rejected for an un-Elgarian plague of parallel fifths, another for a patch of polytonal dissonance, and to this day the columns of several of the more conservative English journals offer sanctuary, from time to time, to new countertheme proposals by the leading Elgar scholars and, of course, in hot pursuit, nitpicking rebuttals in the form of letters to the editor from an erudite, if perhaps rather insular, readership.

Well, the puzzle is solved. Elgar's theme, without benefit of transposition or metrical alterations, can be supered upon, or rather applied as a cantus firmus to, the *Songs Without Points,* and the result, vertically and horizontally, is ravishing. Elgar's four beats to the bar and the crotchet rest which constitutes his theme's most expressive rhythmic feature merge with P.D.Q.'s three-quarter-time tune without incident; the anticipated clash of tonality (Elgar's G minor versus P.D.Q.'s C major) results only in a heightened harmonic consciousness, and the chromatic altercations (with the possible exception of a glancing semiquaver's worth of C-natural versus C-sharp, which both P.D.Q. and Sir Edward would surely have relished) actually serve to modify the occasional absentmindedness inherent in P.D.Q.'s voice leading.

So there it is, if my theory is correct: incontrovertible evidence that the "P.D.Q. underground" had triumphed, that the greatest English composer of his day paid tacit tribute to the most imaginative of his German predecessors, that ninety-two years after his death P.D.Q. Bach's presence lived on, as a spiritual continuo, for one of the most exquisite structures of the late romantic era, that the message of his life and work would not die but would, rather, rise again six decades later in Town Hall. Of course, I could be wrong.

THE RECORD OF THE DECADE

As any subscriber to *Billboard* magazine can tell you, the record business these days is a haven for the specialty interpreter and novelty producer. What with twenty-eight versions of the Beethoven Fifth threatening to remainder each other, it's just about impossible to coax an item of that kind up the charts unless you play it on the piano (as one indefatigable opportunist did quite recently) or rerelease at paperback prices a historic interpretation like that

From *Saturday Night,* December 1968.

of Toscanini for the perusal of a generation which missed being reared on B. H. Haggin and Marcia Davenport. It's a cultist market, sad to say, propelled by a particularly virulent strain of antiacademic sentiment. That admirable Yankee eccentric Charles Ives, with his Waldenesque clinkers, was unbeatable last year, but that was before *Time* mag discovered Harry Partch, and the trend just now is toward the fringe characters of Grandpa's generation, with Erik Satie, the patron saint of dada, being very big with the Electric Circus set at the moment. Even there, however, the sober archival approach which has determined the psychology of record buying since the advent of the LP is in operation, and Angel Records blithely releases the assured inanities of Satie's keyboard works with the same *gesamtkunstwerkisch* solemnity with which Deutsche Grammophon Gesellschaft will turn out the complete Frescobaldi. The days when anthologies culled from everybody's top twenty tunes and artists were surefire box office came to a halt about the time lighter tone arms made band jumping hazardous and development sections were first heard in the land.

It's a bit surprising, then, that the record of the year (no, let's go all the way—the decade!) is an unembarrassed compote of Bach's greatest hits—"Air on the G String," "Sleepers Wake," "Jesu, Joy of Man's Desiring," F-major and B-flat-major Two-Part Inventions, C-minor and E-flat-major preludes and fugues, and, as pièce de resistance, the Third Brandenburg Concerto—an assemblage that not even the *Reader's Digest,* in the days when they tired of abridging George Orwell and turned their attention to an evaluation of Tchaikovsky's better tunes, could have topped. (Have you ever given any thought to what might have happened if the *Reader's Digest* had served us expurgated Bruckner? Instant Dukas, maybe!)

In addition, the record of the year shuns that musicologically inspired instrumental authenticity which serves as a built-in component of most baroque collections. The inventions are not performed by a scholarly clavecinist diligently practicing *Nachschlagen* as the red light signals take i; the monumental prelude in E-flat major begins with appropriate modesty but, upon the arrival of its self-contained fugue, gathers within its diatonic sobriety a marginal spread and registrational flamboyance like that with which Arnold Schoenberg sacrilegiously suffered Bach's "St. Anne" Fugue; and the Third Brandenburg, though as a realization of this masterpiece for nine solo strings it's at least the equal of the near-legendary performance by the Stuttgart Chamber Orchestra, allows brass bleats to break in upon the triadic equilibrium of the fiddle sonorities. The whole record, in fact, is one of the most startling achievements of the recording industry in this generation, certainly one of the great feats in the history of "keyboard" performance, and, though it's bad news for Petrillo-land tonite, the surest evidence, if evidence be needed, that live music never was best. For this hit-parade-courting miscellany *is* rendered on a keyboard—the three-octave, electric-action, one-note-at-a-time keyboard of the Moog synthesizer.

With its spaghetti twist of patch cords compactly housed within three upended open suitcases and fronted by a two-foot-by-three-foot-by-(approximately)-three-inch-deep keyboard unit, this instrument is the brainchild of Dr. Robert Moog of Trumansberg, New York, and is designed to expedite the problem of turning white noise, sine, square, and sawtooth waves into recognizable musical constituents. Through its envelope controls governing attack, decay, and shape of the wave, and an ingenious filter system which can extract from the Niagara-like white noise or the overtone-rich sawtooth and square waves any combination of fundamental tone or overtone sources, the Moog represents a miniature laboratory, but it does not altogether substitute for the vastly more complicated and often computer-assisted systems in operation at many university workshops.

Purists, consequently, incline to sniff at its keyboard orientation, especially when, as on this disc, the instrument is specifically designed for touch and depth sensitivity, enabling its performer to give a vastly more musical account of himself than that tentative effort with which the RCA punch-tape synthesizer proved fifteen years ago that, if anyone was interested, it could make a good stab at sounding like, among other things, the human voice. Theoretically, the Moog can be encouraged to imitate virtually any instrumental sound known to man and, with the help of the touch-sensitive keyboard, manage it with a persuasively human rhythmic fallibility; but, although there are moments in this disc which sound very like an organ, a double bass, or a clavichord, its most conspicuous felicity is that, except when casting gentle aspersions on more familiar baroque instrumental archetypes, the performer shuns this kind of electronic exhibitionism.

And the "performer" for "Switched-On Bach"—yes, that's the title, and Columbia Records, whose December release it is but whose production it is not, should be ashamed of themselves—is no professional virtuoso taking time out from the winter tour for a visit to the recording studio but a young American physicist and audio engineer named Walter Carlos, who has no recording contract, whose most esoteric musical endeavor heretofore was the supervision of soundtrack material for a Schaefer beer commercial on TV, and who, over a period of many months, produced, performed, and, with the aid of a friend and musicologist, Benjamin Folkman, conceived the extraordinary revelations afforded by this disc in his living room. Indeed, it's difficult to guess how Carlos would stack up on the winter concert circuit—intraoffice scuttlebutt in New York has him musing upon the box-office potential of massed Moog synthesizer concerts—though insofar as one can judge from unaccompanied scale flourishes in spots such as the C-minor prelude, which appear to have been rendered without benefit of splice, he's possessed of commendable dexterity. But he does not, and should not, have to compete, for the real revelation of this disc is its total acceptance of the recording ethic—the belief in an end so incontrovertibly convincing that any means, no matter how foreign to the adjudicative process of the concert hall, and even if the master is white with splicing tape, as this one surely must have been, is justified.

Carlos, indeed, has discovered, in the acrostic of splices of which his disc with its not infrequent eight-track overdub consists, one solution to the stereo quandary posed by chamber music. Separate-channel pickup for each member of a string quartet is no surprise these days, but when was the last time you heard keyboard fugues realized with that contrapuntal autonomy which only electronic segregation can provide? Admittedly, it's easier to exploit the stereo potential in a score taped one note—or, at any rate, one part—at a time, as all items on a Moog must be, the directional implication of stereo quandary posed by chamber music often amounting to little more than the sort of antiphonal curtsies for which old Giovanni Gabrielli used St. Mark's as a lab. On this disc, however, contrapuntal give-and-take is enlivened by figures which cheerfully forsake their deskmates and wander purposefully across the wall to sit in with a neighboring combo—an inclination which would induce an apoplectic seizure in any conscientious union steward. Yet the real feat of "Switched-On Bach" is its unflagging musicality, if not necessarily in relation to our previous encounters with baroque performance practice, then at least through the way in which, citing certain of the more exuberant excesses in the history of interpretative transgression, Carlos locates our reaction to his own translative gaffs within the mainstream of the contemporary auditory experience.

There are nevertheless moments of rather questionable taste—the predictable and Mantovani-ish siren sound with which the main tune in "Jesu, Joy of Man's Desiring" salutes those commuter serenades your favorite Good Music Station spins to bring Dad safely down the freeway at 5:15 p.m., certainly; and I daresay, for many people, the electronic cadenza which Carlos interpolates between the two allegro movements of the Brandenburg concerto. Personally, I can't share this latter cavil—mind you, it hasn't been registered yet, but just wait till the *New York Times* reviews the disc—for in my view this extravaganza is alone worth the price of admission. The two tentative chords which Bach set down between the outer movements of the score, either as an inducement for harpsichord extemporization or cover-up for the tight schedule which kept him from getting round to an andante, have been subjected in the past to every conceivable combination of arpeggiated clichés with which the musicologically induced timidity of twentieth-century improvisers can in good conscience permit them to be decorated. Carlos simply tacks on a new vocabulary of cliché and, simultaneously taking a sharp jab at the unrealistic performance practice of "baroque specialists" and getting off the best inside joke in the music business '68, superimposes upon these eighteenth-century inanities a glossary of equally ludicrous electronic ready-mades, such as Vladimir Ussachevsky would have drummed out of the Columbia lab a decade back.

There are other moments of mirth as well. By controlling and reversing the attack-decay relationship in the first movement of the Brandenburg, Carlos simulates the frustration of all pooped trumpeters who ever peaked above unsympathetic and unretarding tutti forces. Similarly, at the end of that movement, after squiring a sequence of diminished chord arpeggios through a series of increasingly impure, if characterful, quasimetallic registrations toward the sort of Orientalized sheet-metal clatter that if discovered in time would have kept Charlie Chan a staple on the late show, Carlos gathers up his tutti forces and in one last fortissimo invites them to a boisterous backwoods shivaree.

But it's the sounds which recall no particular experience that underline what I take to be Carlos's prime motivation—a utilization of the available technology to actualize previously idealized aspects of the world of Bach. Now this may well be just the sort of argument Stokowski would use to justify his orchestral inflation of the organ works, and even Anton Webern would probably have claimed he was seeking a contemporary look for Bach as he set about pointillistically dissembling *A Musical Offering*'s last fugue. But Stokowski's indulgences simply celebrate the English vesper-service postlude circa 1910, while Webern's Viennese pontifications evoke all the hair-splitting, beard-stroking Freudian analysis that ever led to a faulty diagnosis.

Most of us, after all, tend to gauge our contributions in terms of an adjacent experience and, if we're musicians, to welcome the limitations of a defined system of performance capabilities. Even the most imaginative of these intrafraternal substitutions can do little more than evoke other performances of related material while remaining bound by their simulated liabilities.

But I don't think any such eminently datable contemporaneity is what Walter Carlos is about. Even though many of his registrational conceits seem conventional enough, he is really looking for an out from all the instrumental hangups which have demarcated intention and reality in performance. For him the scores of Bach are just what they should be for all of us, in fact—an excuse to build an infinite variety of pertinent performance systems. He has managed to tap sound sources which in their—literally—incomparable variety are perfectly mated to the sublime instrumental indifference of the composer. He has offered us not just, as everyone from Harold Samuel to the Swingle Singers is reputed to have done, a Bach for Our Time but a start toward an infinitely expanded re-creative capability and—even if this disc doesn't manage to nudge Satie from the *Billboard* charts—an inkling of the future as well.*

ROSEMARY'S BABIES

Much as I hate to admit it, this disc is a bit of a letdown. Years before the sari set mobilized a conviction about extrasensory perception as yet another weapon in its continuing skirmish with the linear persuasion of the "straight" world, I was already a more or less convinced parapsychology buff. Indeed, back in the days when the "Aquarian" generation was still being dubbed a "subculture" by its wishful-thought-prone elders, when Philips Records would scarcely have endowed an undertaking of this kind with two lavishly produced promotional brochures (forty-odd pages of essays and photos, most of them hokey, included), when even the farsighted editors of this publication would surely have consigned it for review purposes to the relative obscurity of "Recitals and Miscellany," I would have been willing, even eager, to defend Rosemary Brown's right to commune with the musical departed of her choice and to issue the more promising results of that communion as a commercial release.

As far as I'm concerned, then, and despite the condescension displayed by certain members of the critical fraternity in Britain toward this disc, there's simply no hint of fraud about Mrs. Brown's undertaking. But neither, on the other hand, with one conspicuous exception, do any of the seventeen *pièces de salon* listed below demand or encourage second hearings. In my view, the disc is clearly a labor of love for a sensitive, sincere, and in one way or another "gifted" lady. As one who would like to believe that such visions and fantasies as haunt Mrs. Brown could be rendered explicit and meaningful to others, I regretfully report that the musical results are rather less persuasive than the descriptions and implications of the methodology involved.

Rosemary Brown, in case you haven't guessed, is a medium. For four or five years now she's been keeping close tabs on a black-caped apparition named Franz Liszt and, using his calling card, has also made contact with such considerable talents as Chopin, Debussy, Grieg, Rachmaninoff, and

---

*In fact, "Switched-On Bach" became the best-selling classical album of its time.—T.P.
Review of Rosemary Brown's "A Musical Séance" (Philips PHS 900256, 1970); from *High Fidelity*, December 1970.

Schubert. Other distinguished visitors have graced her suburban-London living room as well, but in certain cases, notably that of J. S. Bach, the results, however socially diverting, have been less than felicitous musically. Mrs. Brown candidly confesses in one of the many jacket notes that since (prior to the intercession of the aforementioned Mr. Liszt) she had no professional experience of music, Bach's works are, to her at least, rather heavy going, and it's to his credit, I think, that thus far Johann Sebastian has taken this disclosure in good grace. Beethoven, similarly, is represented in this disc only by a bagatelle—well, for that matter, most of the compositions included in the package are bagatellelike in their brevity and ternary persuasion; but we're assured that the master is presently at work on a Symphony No. 10, which—shades of Rimsky-Korsakov—is expected to materialize in the key of C-sharp minor, and, to this end, Mrs. Brown is currently swotting over orchestration.

Just how such academic disciplines are expected to assist—transposable horns and Beethovenian deafness notwithstanding—is never made quite clear and it is, I think, one of the weaker links in the armor of argument with which Mrs. Brown's proponents cloak her efforts. Yet a good deal of space in both elaborate brochures, when not engaged in that substantiation of musical illiteracy upon which, inevitably, her case must rest, is, ironically, given over to her current and future tutorial plans. At the present time, for instance—presumably as a response to Mrs. Brown's keyboard efforts on one side of the disc, which are confined to the less demanding of the works represented (Peter Katin is the expert pianist who tackles the more problematic pieces on the flip side)—Rachmaninoff is attempting to pass on some tricks of the pianistic trade to Mrs. Brown, and if all goes well, we can assume that Mr. Katin will be banished from the sequel, if there is one.

A good deal of the evidence cited on behalf of Mrs. Brown's blissful ignorance is supported by the testimony of artists with impeccable credentials. Richard Rodney Bennett, Humphrey Searle, and Hephzibah Menuhin have, at one time or another, taken an interest in the case and, like many of their colleagues, are convinced by both Mrs. Brown's prescience and her integrity. The most revealing comment on her extramusical ability, however, is offered not by any of these contemporary spokesmen but, rather, by a gentleman who departed from this vale of tears some thirty years ago. In a jacket note dictated on New Year's Day 1970, the incomparable musicologist Sir Donald Francis Tovey reaches out from the beyond to assure us that "the possibility that composers of the past are still alive in different dimensions from yours, and endeavoring to communicate, should not be dismissed too perfunctorily."

Needless to say, Sir Donald's essay is subjected to almost as much analytic scrutiny as the phenomenon of Mrs. Brown herself. Philips's literary editor, A. David Hogarth, who suggested to Mrs. Brown that Sir Donald's approbation might be extremely helpful and who is himself a former Tovey student, has compared and contrasted the ratio of Greek versus Roman derivations, adverbial positionings, conceits of punctuation with a similar selection from Sir Donald's nontechnical prose. Even more remarkable than the statistical evidence of Mr. Hogarth's literary nose count, however, is the presence in this program note of that quality of gentle humor disciplined by charity for which, among its many other virtues, Sir Donald's prose was justly renowned.

Musically, the exception to that rule of improvisatory sobriety which appears to govern most of Mrs. Brown's intuitions is an item called *Grübelei*, attributed to Liszt, which, as Humphrey Searle points out, is, on its own merits and by any criterion, an altogether remarkable piece. It was dictated to Mrs. Brown at an audition attended by officials of the BBC, and in a spoken preface (band one, side 2) she recalls her consternation when, instead of the expected virtuosic rabble rouser, her resident muse offered a strange, rhythmically eccentric (5/4 against 3/2 is the prevailing superposition) mood piece. "I think," said Liszt, who obviously has BBC officialdom psyched out, "the music I am giving you will be far more impressive to them than a Hungarian Rhapsody."

Impressive as it is, *Grübelei* suffers, in common with its companion pieces, from one lapse which, though it fails to compromise my faith in Mrs. Brown's veracity, does minimize the effectiveness of much of her work. Many of the compositions display an inordinate inclination to settle most roulades and all real linear invention within the territory appropriated by the right hand—the left, even when coordinated by the proficient Mr. Katin, is rarely accorded its due share of the action. It is, of course, by no means surprising that on her side of the disc, Mrs. Brown's keyboard address, like that of most nonprofessionals, displays precisely that problem of digital unanimity which benefits from such preferential status, but it is disconcerting to discover that this purely physical impediment is permitted to compromise the quality of her intermediation.

I'm not suggesting that Mrs. Brown's receptivity is unworthy of her sponsors' claims—*Grübelei* and the Tovey paragraphs, however they may have been arrived at, are genuine achievements—but simply that a gift of ESP is, like faith, constantly in jeopardy from the accumulation of physical impressions to which all of us are heir. And while I wouldn't for a moment question the value of Rachmaninoff's instruction or even, for that matter, of orchestration lessons, I suspect that the success of Mrs. Brown's future efforts will depend on her ability to segregate those spiritual perceptions which brought *Grübelei* alive from the tactile and physical memories that made it less than a total success.

A DESERT ISLAND DISCOGRAPHY

In Canada, a nation where government radio is still alive, well, and subject to parliamentary questions, one venerable institution of the airwaves was recently disbanded. The program, "Hermit's Choice," afforded an opportunity for the selection of four books and an equal number of records which weekly guest/exiles pledged to take with them to some hypothetical desert isle (like many productions in the colonies, "Hermit's Choice" was a straight steal from the British Broadcasting Corporation, where an identical format had been exploited with great success for many years). In the Canadian version, would-be castaways frequently settled for some remarkably revealing inclusions—I remember with particular delight one edition which featured the selections of a psychoanalyst of Austrian extraction, who spoke incessantly not of his own favorite discs but of his *mother's!* Through some dreadful oversight of casting, and despite a peerless reputation as the country's most experienced hermit, I was never invited to contribute to the series. A year or so ago, on a program of my own, I took time out to remedy this oversight.

The inclusions I proposed on that occasion still seem valid enough, though I suppose one should draw some sort of fine line between discs which would fill the bill as companions-in-exile and those which at any given time one might count as favorites per se. Quite apart from the fact that the desert-island format can encourage unlikely choices—there's always the chap who, under cross-examination, will confess undying affection for *The Art of the Fugue* or the Elliott Carter string quartets but, when left to his own devices and with microphone removed, would in fact select *The Pines of Rome* and "Starlight Favorites from the Hollywood Bowl"—there are records that simply would not minister to one's island needs and would thus have to be rejected on therapeutic grounds alone. Karajan's *Walküre,* for instance, is perhaps my favorite album of the last few years; but I suspect that any work dependent upon the mechanics of a plot, no matter how metaphorically interpreted, would more closely approximate an absolute of human interaction than one could comfortably afford to contemplate if desert-island peace of mind is the goal.

In any case, my first three choices were all, in their way, therapeutic: the hymns and anthems of Orlando Gibbons as recorded for Archiv by the Deller Consort (ARC 3053, deleted), Schoenberg's Serenade, Op. 24, in the luminous realization by Bruno Maderna on Oiseau-Lyre (SOL 250), and Ka-

From *High Fidelity,* June 1970.

rajan's Berlin Philharmonic version of Sibelius's Fifth Symphony (Deutsche Grammophon 138973). The Karajan is a must because, even though some Sibelius discographers quibble about the quasi-impressionist textural refinements favored by that maestro, it strikes me as the ideal realization of Sibelius as a passionate but antisensual composer—precisely the dichotomy that endears the great Finn to me and that makes his scores, with their unique ability to ride out the more mundane ramifications of their material without embarrassment, the ideal backdrop for the transcendent regularity of isolation. (Besides, since I am an Arctic buff, my own notion of isolation involves, at the very least, a Helsinki-like latitude; the Aleutians, for example, would be quite acceptable, but if consigned to Devil's Island, I'd be the first prisoner to try an escape, swimming north.)

The Schoenberg, on the other hand, would be a bit of a risk, since the obvious advantage of life in exile would be the opportunity to re-create in one's own image whichever corner of the world caught one's attention and since, consequently, any conflicting, contemporary evidence should undoubtedly be screened with care. The Serenade, however, is one of my all-time favorites for reasons other than its germinal influence on the twelve-tone movement; it's surely one of the few works of its period which offset the idiomatic rigors of their discipline with a genuine out-of-doors delight in the act of making music.

The Gibbons, however, would be number-one choice on any list of mine, not only because, as a hermit, one would probably be grateful for a reminder of those antecedents of the modern world which one could endeavor to extenuate in quite a different fashion than post-Renaissance traditions decreed but, more subjectively, because ever since my teen-age years this music (and for close to fifteen years this particular record by the Deller Consort) has moved me more deeply than any other sound experience I can think of. In fact, this is the only disc in my collection three copies of which I have literally worn out. There would, however, be a fourth recording which I should take, not because it's a record to which I listen with great frequency any longer but because of the unique role it played during a particularly impressionable period of my adolescence.

When I was a tad of thirteen a misguided pedagogue at my alma mater, the then Toronto (now Royal) Conservatory of Music, suggested that I might prepare for my debut with orchestra, which was to coincide with the annual year-end blowout of the school band, and play Beethoven's Fourth Concerto. The suggestion, of course, was enthusiastically adopted, but, as I saw it, very little preparation was required: for two years I had been in possession of an RCA album—acquired with funds painstakingly set aside from my allowance—featuring Artur Schnabel, Frederick Stock, the Chicago Symphony, and, on the cover, surely the earliest example of pop-album art extant.

The illustration in question (an uncanny anticipation of Motown art nouveau) showed Schnabel—sleeveless, I believe—at the keyboard surrounded by a discreet platoon of sidemen all huddled beneath some lush vegetation of the sort that would be hard to come by in Upper Illinois (pitch pine, perhaps, or pecan trees, maybe—the memory plays tricks after a quarter-century) and which suggested to me that the date was probably scheduled while orchestra and soloist were touring the Carolinas. But though I was much attracted to the pictorial revelations afforded by the jacket, it was, of course, the Schnabel/Stock collaboration itself that was indelibly impressed upon my memory. Almost every day during the two years I owned it prior to the abovementioned invitation, some or all eight 78-rpm sides served as accompaniment for practice sessions in which I faithfully traced every inflective nuance of the Schnabelian rhetoric, surged dramatically ahead whenever he thought it wise—that is to say, in most reiteratively inclined and/or motivically awkward situations—and glided to a graceful cadential halt every four minutes and twenty-five seconds or so while the automatic changer went to work on the turntable.

These changeover points proved an especially significant formative influence; without them the D-major second theme, the ambivalent F-natural inauguration of the development section, the E-minor stretto at bar 235, and, of course, the cadenza—to mention only landmarks pertaining to the first movement—lost emphasis and pertinence and Beethovenian point. Indeed, to this day I am unable to tolerate any performance of this mellow opus that ignores these obvious points of demarcation, that does not pay at least token homage to that phenomenon of flip-side overlap—which those of us reared in the 78 era came to cherish and anticipate—but strides blithely, uncaringly, onward to the finish. And as the years have passed, the new lot—chaps like Casadesus and Serkin, Fleisher and Moravec—have simply not lived up to my Schnabelian expectations and have fallen by the wayside accordingly.

Anyway, as the concert date approached, my own Schnabel impersonation had acquired such awesome authenticity that my teacher, a scholar scarcely noted for his indulgence of student power, compelled me to hand over my album with the sort of pedagogical highhandedness that propelled S. I. Hayakawa into political prominence. Nevertheless, giving first evidence of the wily concert strategist I was shortly to become, I adopted a brisk, Serkinesque dispatch—I'd heard him play it with Toscanini in '45 or '46—somewhat tempered by a cultivated Casadesusish élan, and my good professor pronounced himself entirely satisfied with my progress, my tractability, and his own expertise in the field of tutorial psychology.

On the day of my debut it rained, and that evening—it was early May, the first week of daylight saving, and the sun set at eight—the low-pressure area moved eastward, the ceiling lifted, and the skyline of Toronto took on that misty, orange-shaded cyclorama effect that Walt Kelly would soon celebrate in the color installments of "Pogo" at Okefenokee. Surely this was no night for Marlborovian objectivity, or even for the worldly ironies of Fontainebleau. This was an occasion from which great cover art could draw inspiration. This was a time for personal statement—a moment to grasp and to make one's own.

Considering the fact that the subsequent performance was somewhat at variance with rehearsal procedures, the orchestra followed superbly. There was a moment of stress, perhaps, at the D-major entry, and the oboes and flutes didn't quite get the point at the E-minor stretto, but I left in high spirits, my teacher was shattered, and the press, on the whole, was quite kind. There was, to be sure, one dissenting report from a stringer attached to the morning paper—the Toronto *Globe and Mail:* "Beethoven's elusive Fourth Piano Concerto was left in the hands of a child last night," he noted. "Who does the kid think he is, Schnabel?"

THE FILM *SLAUGHTERHOUSE FIVE*

Kurt Vonnegut's *Slaughterhouse-Five* has been brought to the screen with such fidelity that if you happen to be one of that black-humored author's legion of fans, an outing at your neighborhood cinema will probably provide one of the cinematic highlights of the season. If, however, you happen to have a rather more ambivalent reaction to Vonnegut's work, as I do, the sheer virtuosity of the transcription may prove the greatest stumbling block for this undeniably virtuosic piece of cinema.

Vonnegut, of course, is to the current crop of college frosh as J. D. Salinger was to the youth of my day—a dispenser of those too-easily accessible home truths that one somehow never does get at home. And precisely because he quite ruthlessly exploits certain aspects of the generation gap—especially those widened by an inability to agree on forms of humor appropriate to the articulation of the human situation—I suspect that much of his work will date quickly and reveal the supposed profundities of an opus

From a CBC radio broadcast, August 1972. Gould served as musical director for the film.

like *Slaughterhouse-Five* as the inevitable clichés of an overgeneralized, under-particularized view of humanity.

Slaughterhouse is about the life—and death, though since Vonnegut's favorite message is that we must concentrate on the good moments and ignore the bad ones, there's rather less about the latter—of the novel's hero, or, in more fashionable parlance, antihero, Billy Pilgrim, a chaplain's assistant (as opposed to an assistant chaplain) in World War II. Billy becomes detached from his unit during that last great brushfire on the Western Front—the battle of the Ardennes Forest in December 1944—is taken prisoner and subsequently removed to a German POW camp in Dresden. Now, I know it's carping of the cheapest sort, and a demand for a form of logic to which the Vonnegut cult remains immune, but since the German elite tank corps lost that battle precisely because they ran out of gas, it's always struck me as a tactical oddity that so valuable a commodity as fuel would be expended on so incidental a maneuver as the transport of prisoners across the remaining, if diminishing, breadth of the Reich.

In any case, Billy does arrive in Dresden, and is housed in a converted meat locker beneath a slaughterhouse—hence the title, and the excuse for his survival of the forthcoming fire storm. But in encountering at first hand, the morning after, the vividly depicted desolation of the ruined city, he becomes, as Vonnegut puts it, "unstuck in time" and thereafter meanders back and forth across the expanse of his quite unexceptional life and finally uncovers an ability to project himself fourth-dimensionally as well. When the going on earth gets tough, Billy simply fantasizes an extraterrestrial existence, shacks up in a geodesic dome with the woman of his dreams—a *Playboy* centerfolder named Montana Wildhack—and surrounds himself with a cyanide environment which effectively keeps all worldly wolves at bay.

Billy Pilgrim, then, is the all-American dropout, 1940s style. Not for him the communal convictions, vegeterarian restraints, and pacifist pursuits of his present-day counterpart. Material success, in fact, attends his postwar experience of America. Billy marries a wealthy girl, runs a profitable optometry clinic, and eventually achieves that ultimate accolade of Middle America, a Lions Club presidency. For Billy, there simply is no respectable alternative life-style, but his commitment to a quarter-century of postwar America is constantly compromised by, and intercut with, the one decisive moral issue of his life: Dresden.

The gist of the novel, of Stephen Geller's enormously effective and entirely supportive screenplay, and of George Roy Hill's deliberately detached but supremely dexterous direction, is that no such contact is possible; but in the course of their proving the point we're offered a succession of times present, past, and future the sequences of which tend to be linked by the sort of last-line–first-line overlaps that Aldous Huxley used to bind *Point Counterpoint* together. For example, as Billy, circa 1970 and newly a widower, drags himself up a flight of stairs in his upstate New York home, his steps are intercut with a similar climb in 1945, out of the slaughterhouse and into the gutted streets of Dresden; when Montana tries on a dress specially rocket-mailed to the planet Tralfamadore from Sears Roebuck, her twirling motion reminds Billy of a Dresden figurine the possession of which brought about the summary execution of his only close POW friend, Edgar Derby. And in an earlier scene, the same Edgar Derby's acceptance speech as leader of the POWs is intercut with Billy's response at his Lions Club inaugural.

Well, this sort of staccato editing (magnificently executed by Dede Allen, whose other notable achievements include *Little Big Man* and *Bonnie and Clyde*) is cinematically a natural. In fact, in very many ways, beginning with Vonnegut's literary pointillism, the script falls almost effortlessly into the structural conceits of cinema. As a result, *Slaughterhouse Five* is a crew picture rather than a cast picture. There are, to be sure, some superb cameo performances: the great German actor Friedrich Ledebur as an elderly prison commandant; the American Ron Leibman as a psychotic GI who swears vengeance upon Billy for an imagined offense and who, in one of Billy's time trips circa 1990, does indeed bring about his demise. (It's worth pointing out, by the way, that vengeance in the Vonnegutian canon is leitmotivically linked to fourth-dimensional precepts.) But the abrupt transitions, the jagged, neoclassical rhythms, and sustained lack of interest in character development all rule out *Slaughterhouse Five* as an actor's showcase. Ultimately, it's a showcase for the editor, Miss Allen, for the cinematographer, Miroslav Andricek, and above all for the director, George Roy Hill.

And it's at this point that I find it difficult to comment objectively about this picture. Since I worked on it with many of these remarkable craftsmen, and tailored my own contribution to match a concept of cinema with which I cannot really agree, my admiration for it as a technical achievement remains undiminished, but my concern about it as a fairly representative product of contemporary American filmmaking grows apace.

Slaughterhouse, I think, belongs to that genre of American film which attempts to graft European avant-garde concepts onto a superstructure held together by good old U.S. knowhow. At the latter level, it's an unabashedly commercial film, fulfilling the obligatory quotas of sex and violence so as to earn for itself that irresistible lure of the collegiate set, an "R" rating. And it also offers with a vengeance the rapid-fire, antiromantic directorial approach which, like a latter-day Bauhaus manifestation, is intended to convey the essential divorce between professional engagement and structural objectivity.

I wonder whether anyone has thought about the fact that these hard-edged directorial techniques have certain features in common with music of the late rococo and, again, of the neoclassic decades—the twenties and thirties—of this century. There is the same allegro-adagio-allegro (or fast-slow-fast) concept of pace, the same loud-soft-loud (even sforzando) concept of structural dynamics, and, above all, the same attempt to court an intellectual coterie which finds the plight of less sophisticated souls a subject of merriment, if not, in fact, a theme beneath contempt.

In the music of Mozart, for instance, we're often treated to a gratuitous fortissimo or a sudden pianissimo, for no more convincing structural reason than that we haven't had one lately. In *Slaughterhouse Five*, as but one example, Billy Pilgrim's wife, Valencia, is, from the moment we first catch sight of her on their wedding night, an intended figure of fun simply because the lady happens to be, as the British might say, a stone or two overweight—and that, as the Pepsi generation will affirm, is proof positive of peer-group alienation in diet-cola America.

Consequently, whenever we do see her, which isn't often, some remarkably unfunny dialogue about dieting is foisted upon the unfortunate Valencia. Even after her death, indeed, Montana asks Billy, "What did you love most about your wife?" and, following a long pause, Billy replies, "Her pancakes." It's one of the very few lines in which screenwriter Geller fails to do justice even to Vonnegut's limited view of Billy Pilgrim. For Billy, however anesthetized his spiritual life, is essentially a good human being, and because of his essential goodness the line rings utterly false. I should add that as the inevitable concomitant of the prevailing lack of sympathy with which Valencia's appearances are greeted, her death is achieved via a car-crash sequence which combines the now celebrated *French Connection* chase with the animated irrelevance of Mack Sennett.

Billy Pilgrim himself is not to quite the same extent so unidimensionally a figure of fun. Indeed, I cannot recall any funny lines either dispensed by him or to which he is willing witness. Billy is so resolutely passive a character that, puppetlike, he witnesses everything and, on the surface, reacts to almost nothing. There's a touching relationship with his dog, Spot, newly acquired circa 1946 at the time of his marriage, who by picture's end, with Billy approaching the upper reaches of middle age, is a candidate for the *Guinness Book of Records* as most elderly canine in filmdom; there's a genuine attachment to Edgar Derby, the Colonel Hogan of the prison camp—and that's about it for emotional involvement.

And yet the pivot of this strange tale, after all, is that Billy Pilgrim has witnessed the cataclysm that was Dresden, February 13, 1945. And notwithstanding his subsequent nervous breakdown, his virtually catatonic later life, and his hallucinatory excursions to Tralfamadore, the employment of the cinematic equivalent of the *style galant* effectively prevents the depiction of any genuine emotional reaction sufficient unto the purpose. If you want yet another musical parallel for the relationship between *Slaughterhouse Five* and such European avant-garde antecedents as *Last Year at Marienbad* (which also displayed a precocious, if pretentious, interest in Einsteinian time retrieval), try imagining what *Tristan und Isolde* would sound like if reset by Aaron Copland.

Slaughterhouse Five, then, is a film about the banalities of Middle America which have impeded the moral and cultural evolution of that country. But it's a film produced for, and by, an elitist America, which, instead of turning sympathetically to its past in the hope of achieving some synthesis that might represent its true heritage, diminishes its present and jeopardizes its future by a total lack of faith in the incomparable virtue of charity. It's a film that was challenging and stimulating to work on, superbly crafted within the limits of its genre, deserving of (and, as its Cannes Festival award would suggest, already endowed with) the respect of its peers. But it's not a work of art that one can love.

A BIOGRAPHY OF GLENN GOULD

Geoffrey Payzant has written a book like no other about a performing musician. He has done this by de-emphasizing those aspects of his subject's life and work which relate primarily to the experience of performance and by concentrating instead on an analysis of Gould's substantial output as an essayist, broadcaster, and documentary maker. This is not to suggest that Payzant's study is lacking in musical insight; on the contrary, the author combines his experience as an aesthetician with his training as a practical musician to produce some of the shrewdest analyses of the psychology of performance I have yet encountered. He does not, however, aspire to an opus-by-opus survey of Gould's notoriously controversial interpretations, and when a musical work is cited, it is almost inevitably discussed in order to illuminate a moral or philosophical issue which has been developed previously. As but one example, Gould's celebrated skirmish with Leonard Bernstein in regard to appropriate tempo choices for the Brahms D-minor Piano Concerto is brought into play as the culmination of a chapter which otherwise examines the nature of the competitive experience; Payzant analyzes

Gould's review of *Glenn Gould: Music and Mind* by Geoffrey Payzant (New York: Van Nostrand Reinhold, 1978); from *Piano Quarterly*, Fall 1978.

the many essays, broadcasts, and interview statements in which Gould has expressed his unrelenting opposition to competition in all forms and simply employs the Brahms-Bernstein incident as practical evidence of the pianist's aversion to a peculiarly musical form of competition: the virtuoso concerto.

In his preface, Professor Payzant makes clear that he did not set out to write a book about a pianist but rather about a process of musical thought which from time to time is realized as keyboard activity. He also points out that he has not attempted a biographical study, that Gould's private life is, in fact, "austere and unremarkable," and that "a book on his life and times would be brief and boring." (Payzant, in fact, provides ample evidence for this contention with his own first chapter, a quick-and-dirty sketch of Gould's early years—which is indeed rather boring and by no means as brief as it should be.)

With chapter 2, however, Payzant hits his stride and for the first half of his study skillfully controls a gradually intensifying texture of themes and counterthemes—Gould's rejection of the public concert, his wholehearted acceptance of broadcast media in general and the recording process in partic-ular, his almost mystical belief that technology possesses a mediative power which can minimize or even eliminate the competitive follies which absorb so large a share of human activity. "Gould suggests one way of opting out creatively from our competitive society: accept the alternatives offered to us by technology. Technology introduces a protective shield around humanity which removes the necessity for humans to measure themselves against one another, on either a bodily or a psychical scale."

Payzant explains that in Gould's lexicon the ultimate achievement for "creative opter-outers" is the cultivation of a state of ecstasy. "He uses 'ecsta-sy' indiscriminately for a quality of the music, a quality of the performance, an attitude of the performer, and an attitude of the listener. But this lack of discrimination is intentional, and is the essence of Gould's meaning: that 'ec-stasy' is a delicate thread binding together music, performance, performer and listener in a web of shared awareness of *innerness.*"

As stated above, Payzant does not attempt a biographical study but from time to time pays his respects to the psychobiographical process and, on one such occasion, seeks support from Anthony Storr's *The Dynamics of Creation.* "Since most creative activity is solitary, choosing such an occupation means that the schizoid person can avoid the problems of direct relationships with others. If he writes, paints, or composes, he is, of course, communicating. But it is a communication entirely on his own terms. . . . He cannot be be-trayed into confidences which he might later regret. . . . He can choose (or so he often believes) how much of himself to reveal and how much to keep secret." This citation seems indicative of Payzant's own attitude in regard to his subject and adroitly summarizes Gould's abhorrence of city life, his distaste for public appearances, his predilection for telephonic communication, his belief that solitude nourishes creativity and that colleagual fraternity tends to dissipate it.

Throughout the chapters in which these themes are explored, Professor Payzant sets a brisk developmental pace and achieves an intensity which one encounters all too rarely in a work of scholarship. There are, to be sure, a few statistical thickets which might profitably have been trimmed—a set of figures and facts on graded examinations and local music festivals, for example, betrays a momentary lapse of editorial concentration. And there are also a few occasions on which Payzant appears determined to uncover inconsistencies in Gould's attitude and takes time out to play devil's advocate accordingly. "There is a competitive streak in everyone, including Glenn Gould himself. Friends of his family remember croquet games on the lawn in front of the cottage in which it was desperately important to young Glenn that he should win; in later years he drove powerful cars at high speeds. And sometimes his piano playing on television seems competitive, or at least a tour de force." As an example of this latter shortcoming, Payzant cites Gould's transcription of Ravel's *La Valse*, in which, he suggests, Gould "seemed bent upon surpassing those virtuosi who dust off the more spectacular transcriptions of Liszt—to dazzle us with the sheer physical improbability of their display." This is, I should think, a singularly inappropriate example, since Gould is known to dislike the music of the French impressionists and on his rare forays into such repertoire invariably imposes elements of Teutonic severity and formal sobriety.

In the last three chapters of his study—there are ten in all—Payzant concentrates on the "creative cheating" employed in Gould's recordings (his conviction that the musical end justifies the editorial means), on a discussion of his subject's radio-documentary techniques (like many listeners, Payzant appears to have problems unraveling the contrapuntal textures of Gould's multivoice production methods), and, particularly, on an analysis of Gould's literary output. He points out that "a recurrent philosophical theme in his writings is the relation between art and morality. . . . According to Gould, artists have a moral mission and art has an unrealized potential for the betterment of humankind. Human improvement can occur only as the result of modification in our attitudes as solitary, private individuals, and not as some kind of collective modification of our species, voluntary or not."

Payzant then perceptively analyzes Gould's growing antiart stance: "At around this same time [1974] Gould seemed to be developing a new theme. It is hinted at [when] he says that technology 'imposes upon art a notion of morality which transcends the idea of art itself.' . . . He expresses it more strongly and much more pessimistically in an article published earlier in the same year: 'I feel that art should be given the chance to phase itself out. I think that we must accept the fact that art is not inevitably benign, that it is potentially destructive.' " The author further suggests that "a hint of where Gould is going with this new line of thought is found in an article published in 1975: . . . 'I do believe that, once introduced into the circuitry of art, the technological presence must be encoded and decoded—in such a way that its presence is, in every respect, at the service of that spiritual good that ultimately will serve to banish art itself.' "

It's obvious, especially in these latter chapters, that for Payzant his subject's true "biography" began in 1964, when, with his rejection of the concert hall, he was free to develop the literary and technological experience necessary to deal with the "recurrent themes" which Payzant discusses so persuasively. And it is also interesting to note that Payzant is least at home in the central chapters of his study, which focus on the relationship between the mind and the tactile experience of instrumental playing. An organist himself, he devotes a disproportionate amount of space to Gould's one recording on that instrument (the first nine fugues from Bach's *The Art of the Fugue*) and, in discussing piano technique and tone-quality production, is inclined to issue pronouncements that only a "kist o' whistles" player could love: "It does not matter whether a key is depressed by the finger of Arthur Rubinstein or by the tip of his umbrella. . . . For any given level of loudness there can be only one tone quality, and any particular tone quality can only be delivered at its precisely corresponding level of loudness." Payzant is, of course, addressing himself to the question: Can the pianist, by altering his manner of pressing down the key, produce two or more notes of equal loudness but different tone quality? He concedes that "people will go to the stake in support of their answers"—and indeed they will, especially if such people happen to be pianists. Professor Payzant could check out his theory by inviting Claudio Arrau, Paul Badura-Skoda, Clifford Curzon, and Jörg Demus (choosing randomly but alphabetically) to settle in before the same instrument, agree upon a VU meter objective, and tape the same note or series of notes. Moreover, the mental imagery involved with pianistic tactilia is *not* related to the striking of individual keys but rather to the rites of passage *between* notes.

Throughout his study, Professor Payzant maintains an impeccable academic objectivity, and there does not appear to have been any interviewlike contact between subject and author. In chapter 5, for example, Payzant devotes three pages to a discussion of the various ways in which Gould has employed psychoanalytic terminology in his writing, presents evidence for and against Gould's having been psychoanalyzed, and, in the end, leaves the question up for grabs. Given that Payzant and Gould are both residents of Toronto and that this sort of speculation could presumably have been settled with a simple "yes" or "no," such inconclusive testimony—verging, indeed, on idle musing—can produce a rather comical effect. But its obverse is that quality which lends to Payzant's book its greatest strength—the author's obvious determination to prepare his portrait without being interfered with, or influenced by, the conversational connivance and media manipulation at which Gould is allegedly a master.

Payzant's *Gould* is drawn sympathetically but with clear-eyed detachment. Its thematic strands are leitmotivically controlled, integrally interwoven, and balanced with great editorial skill. One could, of course, as Payzant concedes in his preface, reach other conclusions about his subject, and there will doubtless be many readers who will prefer to exercise that option and maintain the conventional image of Gould as an eccentric and erratic pianist-pundit. Payzant, however, has chosen a different course and has harmonized Gould's musical predilections, moral persuasions, and behavioral extravagances, creating in the process a texture as structurally secure and chromatically complex as the baroque fugues which first awakened Glenn Gould to the wonder of the art of music.

CODA

Glenn Gould in Conversation
with Tim Page

TIM PAGE: Glenn, it's now about seventeen years since you left the concert stage. I'm not going to ask you why you left or whether you will return, both questions that you have answered eloquently on a number of occasions. But when you quit the stage, you stated rather unequivocally that the live concert was dead, period, and that recordings were the future of music. Since 1964, however, we have seen a tremendous resurgence of interest in the concert hall—the success of such endeavors as New York's Mostly Mozart Festival is a good example—while the recording industry is in serious trouble. Any second thoughts on this subject?

GLENN GOULD: Well, I did give myself the hedge of saying that concerts would die out by the year 2000, didn't I? We still have nineteen years to go, and by that time I will be too old to be bothered giving interviews [*laughs*], and I won't have to be responsible for my bad prognosis! As to the recording industry being in trouble, I remain optimistic. I suspect this is a cyclical thing; recording is not really in trouble in those countries where classical music means a great deal—in Germany, for example. This trouble is, to a large extent, North American; it's been coming on quite gradually for a number of years now, and it may or may not reverse itself. If it does not, it simply means that Americans are not terribly interested in classical music.

On the other hand, it doesn't seem as though the concert is going away as fast as I rather hoped it would . . . for the good of all mankind. It has, however, changed. I haven't been to a concert since 1967, when, under considerable pressure, I attended a friend's recital. But I get the impression that a great many contemporary concerts are like reincarnated versions of the kinds of shows that Hans von Bülow did in Toronto a hundred years ago, when he played Beethoven's "Appassionata" Sonata immediately following a trained-horse act!

T.P.: A sort of contemporary vaudeville?

G.G.: Exactly! There is a return to that "trained-horse act" type of concert where a bit of this is followed with a bit of that and then a bit of something else—which I think is actually very nice. Twenty years ago there were very few flexible chamber concerts; you had a string quartet playing Beethoven or whatever, but there was no intermingling of interchangeable modules as now exists. That's all changed; I don't know if

From *Piano Quarterly,* Fall 1981.

this is a sign of desperation—that the solo act can't sustain an entire evening anymore—or simply a more imaginative way of thinking, or possibly even a complete return to the musical thought of the 1880s. I'm not sure what significance this all has.

T.P.: I know you have a dim view of concerts in general. You once told the *New York Times* that you found all the live arts "immoral" because "one should not voyeuristically watch one's fellow human beings in testing situations that do not pragmatically need to be tested."

G.G.: Yes, I confess that I have always had grave misgivings about the motives of people who go to concerts, live theatre, whatever. I don't want to be unfair about this; in the past, I have sometimes made rather sweeping generalizations to the effect that anybody who attends a concert is a voyeur at the very best, and maybe a sadist to boot! I'm sure that this is not altogether true; there may even be people who prefer the acoustics in Avery Fisher Hall to those in their living room. So I don't want to be uncharitable. But I do think that the whole business about asking people to test themselves in situations which have no need of their particular exertions is wrong—as well as pointless and cruel.

I'm afraid that the "Let's climb Everest just because it is there" syndrome cuts very little ice with me . . . there's a pun in there someplace. It makes no sense to do things that are difficult just to prove they can be done. Why climb mountains, or ski back down, or dive out of airplanes or race motor cars, unless there is a manifest need for such behavior?

The concert has been *replaced,* you know. I don't want to bore you with all the reasons why I think technology has superseded the concert—I've enumerated them on many other occasions, and I don't want to do that act again. But there is one reason which I think bears on this question: technology has the capability to create a climate of anonymity and to allow the artist the time and the freedom to prepare his conception of a work to the best of his ability, to perfect a statement without having to worry about trivia like nerves and finger slips. It has the capability of replacing those awful and degrading and humanly damaging uncertainties which the concert brings with it; it takes the specific personal performance information out of the musical experience. Whether the performer is going to climb the musical Everest on this particular occasion no longer matters. And it's for that reason that the word "immoral" comes into the picture. It's a difficult area—one where aesthetics touch upon theology, really—but I think that to have technology's capability and not to take advantage of it and create a contemplative climate if you can—*that* is immoral!

T.P.: When I said the recording industry was in trouble, I was perhaps thinking too much of economics, for in a strictly artistic sense it is certainly alive and well. In recent days there have been recordings of much formerly obscure material—early Haydn symphonies, Schubert operas, lesser-known Bach cantatas—which went unheard for many years. And a lot of new works have been recorded. Let's talk about your repertoire. While you have recorded a fair amount of the standard literature—Bach, Beethoven, Mozart, etc.—you have avoided recording some of the standard piano composers. For instance, do you think you will ever make a Chopin record?

G.G.: No. I don't think he is a very good composer. I played Op. 58 when I was younger, just to see how it would feel. It didn't feel very good, so I've never bothered to play any more Chopin.

I have always felt that the whole center core of the piano recital repertoire is a *colossal* waste of time. The whole first half of the nineteenth century—excluding Beethoven to some degree—is pretty much of a washout as far as solo instrumental music is concerned. This generalization includes Chopin, Liszt, Schumann—I'm tempted not to say Mendelssohn, because I have a tremendous affection for his choral and chamber works, but most of his piano writing is pretty bad. You see, I don't think any of the early romantic composers knew how to write for the piano. Oh, they knew how to use the pedal, and how to make dramatic effects, splashing notes in every direction, but there's very little real *composing* going on. The music of that era is full of empty theatrical gestures, full of exhibitionism, and it has a worldly, hedonistic quality that simply turns me off.

Another problem as I see it is that Chopin, Schumann, and company labored under the delusion that the piano is a homophonic instrument. I don't think that's true; I think the piano is a contrapuntal instrument and only becomes interesting when it is treated in a manner in which the vertical and horizontal dimensions are mated. This does not happen in most of the material written for it in the first half of the nineteenth century.

In the late romantic period lies the big tragedy, for the composers in that period—Wagner, Richard Strauss, possibly Mahler—those composers who could have written with a tremendous penetration of the intermingling of harmonic and thematic language just basically chose not to write for the piano at all. Wagner wrote an early sonata, but it makes Weber look like one of the great masters of all time by comparison. I suspect that Wagner had no real understanding of the piano, for the accompaniments to the *Wesendonk Lieder,* which are fine in their orchestral arrangement, don't work well on the piano at all. I transcribed and recorded a few of Wagner's large orchestral pieces some

years back. It was a real labor of love; I simply wanted to have something of Wagner's I could play.

On the other hand, I have been recording the early Richard Strauss
piano works—Op. 3, Op. 5, pieces Strauss wrote when he was sixteen—and they are minor miracles: as refined, as polished, as anything
Mendelssohn did in his teen-age years. And with the exception of Mendelssohn, no sixteen-year-old has *ever* written with such craft and assurance—I am *not* forgetting Mozart. Strauss could write superbly for the
piano—in the *Burleske,* in *Le Bourgeois Gentilhomme,* and particularly
in the later songs, such as the *Ophelia Lieder,* which I recorded with
Elisabeth Schwarzkopf. His piano writing is devoid of any ostentation,
any exhibitionism or fake virtuosity. But he didn't choose to do much
work in that genre.

That is the great pity—this gap in the piano repertoire. It was an
orchestral period, and the piano was little more than a backup, a poor
man's orchestra, a substitute, "first draft" kind of instrument.

T.P.: The only piano piece by Strauss that comes easily to my mind is that
little "Träumerei" that used to be included in those Theodore Press-
er–type "Great Musical Masterpieces for Piano" collections that were
so prevalent at the turn of the century.

G.G.: I'll bet that's from Op. 9, which I haven't played yet. I've played Op.
3, which consists of sturdy little pieces in the intermezzo style. None
of the Op. 3 pieces have names, but all those in Op. 9 do. They're generally weaker pieces than those in Op. 3.

T.P.: My vision of Strauss is an unconventional one. Although he is often
thought of as the late romantic par excellence, my favorite Strauss pieces
are those from his old age, from his last period. I love the serene, nostalgic, and ultimately classical purity of such works as *Daphne, Capriccio,*
and *Metamorphosen.*

G.G.: Do you know the writer Jonathan Cott? A very interesting man, and
a friend of mine. We've actually never met; our relationship is . . . terribly telephonic. Jonathan is a devoted, *fanatic* Straussian of the most lyrical order, and he speaks with the same reverence and enthusiasm that
you do for works like *Metamorphosen, Capriccio,* and the Oboe Concerto.

It's interesting: when I made a documentary about Strauss last
year, I got a strong response for the last pieces from a number of the
younger people I talked with . . . Jonathan Cott and the composer Stanley Silverman, for example. Silverman has considerable reservations
about Strauss as an opera man but, again, loves the late works. It's the
elder statesmen—like Norman Del Mar, who wrote the three-volume
study of Strauss—who don't think so highly of the last pieces; but then

you have a young man like Jonathan going on in an ecstatic way. Extraordinary—quite the reverse of the generation gap one would expect.

T.P.: There *is* a decline in Strauss's middle period.

G.G.: Oh, no question. I've never been able to take a work like *Ariadne* seriously—in fact, I'm not fond of *Der Rosenkavalier*. But even a work like the *Alpine* Symphony . . . now this is a work which has had a very bad press all its life, but there are *moments* in that piece—even though, yes, the coda *does* go on forever, and no, he doesn't seem to know how to get off that pedal point at the end [*laughs*]—but there are those moments—indeed, great long swathes—that put to shame even the best of the early tone poems. It doesn't hold together structurally in the way that something like *Till Eulenspiegel* does, but there is a seriousness of intent that simply wasn't there in the early years. And then pieces like *Capriccio!* I don't know *Daphne* that well; now that you mention it, I will have to study it.

T.P.: It's gorgeous. You can pass up the opera *Friedenstag,* however.

G.G.: Yes, I have a score of *that* one! [*laughs*] You know, Strauss was a much more abstract thinker than most people give him credit for, and the only romantic composer after Mendelssohn who never violated the integrity of what I might call the *inferential* bass of the voice-leading components in the structure of the music. (Some people would put in a claim for Brahms on that score, but he does slip up occasionally, and the rest of the time he's so *bloody* self-righteous about *not* slipping up.) *Metamorphosen* is my favorite Strauss piece, because in it he has finally come to terms with the abstract nature of his own gift. In a way, it's Strauss's *Art of the Fugue.* It's an *asexual* work, if you like, a work that has no gender. It could belong to the organ, or to the human voice, just as easily as to the twenty-three solo strings for which it was written. But, anyway, I wandered off the point, because I started out to say that it was a great shame that Richard Strauss did not write more for the piano. But I can tell you right now that I'm not going to help him out by transcribing *Metamorphosen*, because I haven't got that many fingers!

T.P.: Sibelius is also considered a late romantic, but once you get past the first couple of symphonies, there are few more austere and classical composers. You have recorded some of the piano music, which is all but unknown today.

G.G.: Yes, if you count little pieces within opus numbers—titles like "Träumerei" or "To a Fir Tree" [*laughs*] or whatever—Sibelius wrote something like a hundred and seventeen pieces for the piano. Most of them are completely insignificant, but I am fascinated by the three sonatines I recorded. They have the same spartan concision, bordering on the stingy, that is found in his symphonies, but their idiom is almost neoclassical. Quite extraordinary, considering these sonatines predate World War I, yet they contain an anticipation of the postwar zeitgeist. But of course they are not masterpieces; nothing Sibelius wrote for the piano really was. He was mainly interested in the orchestra. I *do* admire the fact that when he does write for the piano, he doesn't attempt to make it into a surrogate orchestra. It is always definitely piano writing.

T.P.: I can understand how the Nordic music of Sibelius must appeal to you, for your interest in the far north is well known. You have made a radio docudrama entitled "The Idea of North," and I seem to remember that you once said something to the effect that it was difficult to go far north without becoming a philosopher.

G.G.: What I actually said was that most people I have met who actually did immerse themselves in the north seemed to end up, in whatever disorganized fashion, *being* philosophers. These people I met were government officials, university professors, and so on—people who had been very much exposed to a kind of unifying atmosphere. None of them were born in the north; they all *chose* to live there, for one reason or another. Whatever their motive in moving north may have been—and it varied from person to person—each individual seemed to go through a particular process which greatly altered his life.

At first, most of these people resisted the change; they reached out, contacted friends, made sure their subscription to *The New Yorker* was intact, and so on. But after a while they usually reached a point when they said to themselves: "No, that's *not* what I came up here to do."

In general, I found that the characters who had stuck it out long enough and removed themselves from the sense of curiosity about what their colleagues were thinking, or how the world reacted to what they had done, developed in an extraordinary way and underwent an extreme metamorphosis.

But I think that this can be true of anybody who chooses to live in an isolated way—even in the heart of Manhattan. I don't think the actual latitudinal factor is important at all. I chose "north" as a handy metaphor. It may be that the north is sometimes capable of providing a helping hand in getting people out of a situation they couldn't pry themselves loose from otherwise; it may be that looking at endless flowers on the tundra during the two procreative weeks in July is inspiring, but I don't think that the latitude is what made these people philosophers—if indeed that is what they became. No, it was this sense of saying, "I don't really *care* what my colleagues back at the University of Fill-in-the-Blank or at the department of external affairs think about this solitude, for *I* am going to do it, and *I* am going to discover something!"

T.P.: A purification process.

G.G.: Yes. This process could have occurred even had these people simply locked themselves in their closets . . . although that might have been rather less attractive visually.

T.P.: So you really mean the disembodied "idea" of north.

G.G.: Precisely.

T.P.: In your docudramas you often use a technique where three or more voices are all talking at the same time, making it very difficult to zero in on any single sentence or idea. You have referred to this as "contrapuntal radio."

G.G.: Yes. I don't honestly believe that it is essential in radio that every word is heard. One emphasizes just enough key words in the . . . countersubject sentences, if you will, so that the audience knows that voice is still happening, but it still allows them to zero in on the primary voice or voices and to treat the others as a sort of basso continuo.

We come from a long and splendid tradition of radio, but it has always been a tradition that was very, very linear. One person spoke, then the next person spoke, and occasionally they interrupted one another with an "and" or a "but." Two people never spoke together; that made no sense. I grew up in that particular tradition and enjoyed its products hugely. Nevertheless, I always felt that there was a musical dimension in the spoken word which was being totally ignored.

I coined the term "contrapuntal radio" to respond to certain criticism. When "The Idea of North" first came out in 1967, the fashionable word was "aleatory," and some critics were quick to apply this term to my work. *Nothing* could have been further from the truth, and to counter this impression, I began to speak of "contrapuntal radio," implying a highly organized discipline—not necessarily leading to a fugue in every incident, but in which every voice leads its own rather splendid life and adheres to certain parameters of harmonic discipline. I kept a very close ear as to how the voices came together and in what manner they splashed off each other, both in the actual sound and in the meaning of what was being said.

Now I am drafting an idea that I don't really expect to get to work on for a year or so, but at that point I intend to do a radio equivalent of Tallis's sixty-four-voice motet [*laughs*]—but I don't intend to say anything more about that, as it will probably jinx the whole project if I do!

T.P.: You have also worked with some of the same ideas in television.

G.G.: Yes, I've written a television script on the fugue, part of a series of five programs on Bach that I am doing for a German company. I've been having a really hard time with this project, because the rough guidelines are for forty minutes of music and only twenty minutes of talk. It is an absolutely impossible task to try to deliver any important thoughts on the nature of a fugue in twenty minutes.

There is nothing aleatoric about my television work, either. In the film, there is a discussion between myself and the director which will appear to be spontaneous. In reality, it will be the product of months of hard work, concise scripting, and rehearsal.

T.P.: Turning back to your piano recordings, I'd like to talk about your oft-quoted statement to the effect that the only excuse for recording a work is to do it differently.

G.G.: That's true, but I've always meant to immediately interject that *if*, however, that difference has nothing of validity to recommend it musically or organically, then better not record the work at all.

I am not without stain in this regard, because there are works that I have recorded simply for the sake of completeness that I had no convictions about whatsoever.

T.P.: Would this include some of Mozart's piano music? Your performances of some of the sonatas strike me as possibly your least successful records.

G.G.: Yes, a couple of the later Mozart sonatas. The early works I love, the middle one I love, the later sonatas I do *not* like; I find them intolerable, loaded with quasitheatrical conceit, and I can certainly say that I went about recording a piece like the Sonata in B-flat major, K. 570, with no conviction whatsoever. The honest thing to do would have been to skip those works entirely, but the cycle had to be completed.

T.P.: You're not very enthusiastic about much of Beethoven's work, either.

G.G.: I have very ambivalent feelings about Beethoven. I'm absolutely at a loss for any reasonable explanation as to why his best-known works—the Fifth Symphony, the Violin Concerto, the "Emperor," the "Waldstein"—ever became popular, much less as to why they have retained their appeal. Almost every criterion that I expect to encounter in great music—harmonic and rhythmic variety, contrapuntal invention—is almost entirely absent in these pieces. In his middle period—the period which produced those works—Beethoven offered us the supreme historical example of a composer on an ego trip, a composer absolutely confident that whatever he did was justified simply because he did it! I don't know any other way to explain the predominance of those empty, banal, belligerent gestures that serve as his themes in that middle period. The later years are another story—my favorite Beethoven symphony is the Eighth, my favorite movement in all of his sonatas the opening of Op. 101, and, for me, the "Grosse Fuge" is not only the greatest work Beethoven ever wrote but just about the most astonishing piece in musical literature. But even the late works are remarkably inconsistent—for instance, I don't think that the remainder of Op. 101 has much to do with the extraordinary first movement, except for that quotation right before the finale.

All in all, I'd have to say that Beethoven's most consistently excellent works are those from his early period, before his hearing started to go—let's face it, that *did* affect his later work—and before his ego took complete command. Almost all of those early piano works are immaculately balanced—top to bottom, register to register. In these pieces, Beethoven's senses of structure, fantasy, variety, thematic continuity, harmonic propulsion, and contrapuntal discipline were absolutely, *miraculously* in alignment. I'm talking about the Sonatas Op. 26 and 28, and the variations like that marvelous set in Op. 34. These works have such a sense of peace, such a wonderful, pastoral radiance, and every texture is as carefully worked out as it would be in a string quartet. What I'm going to say now may surprise you—musicians are supposed to have more sophisticated tastes than this—but I think that one of Beethoven's real masterpieces is the "Moonlight" Sonata.

But even in these early years, I have to tell you that Mr. Beethoven and I do not see eye to eye on what constitutes good music. About 1801, Beethoven wrote a letter in which he stated that his best piano sonata to date was Op. 22. And much as I love the early sonatas—and I really *do* love them—there is one dud in the batch . . . and that is Op. 22.

T.P.: Do you think it is time for a return to epic forms? Many artists seem to believe this is what will be occurring in the next decade.

G.G.: I try to avoid thinking in such generalizations about musical/artistic trends. If I said, "Yes, it is time for the return of the epic," that would imply that there was some point in the past when it was *not* right to produce one. And I don't think that that is necessarily so.

Let's look at the year 1913—no, no, 1912, even better. You have Arnold Schoenberg writing *Pierrot Lunaire;* Webern is working on the short pieces that immediately follow his string quartet miniatures, and Berg is composing the *Altenberg Lieder.* If the world stopped at this point, a historian would have to say, "The Age of the Epic is over; we are now in an age of fragmentation and the breakdown of the idea of the great long-breathed line of continuity in music." I simply *cannot* believe that this would be an adequate summation of the year 1912—even though many music historians would describe its prevailing tendencies in this way. But at the same time Jan Sibelius was working on the first draft of his Fifth Symphony, which is certainly closer to epic than fragment! I don't think I need go any further than to point out the complete underlying absurdity of such generalizations.

I find it very disturbing to contemplate the lemminglike tendencies that artists in general assume—you know: the *anti*hero is in this year, the hero will be back next year. It shouldn't matter; one should be free of all that.

T.P.: Along the same lines, what would you say are the important issues confronting a composer in 1980?

G.G.: *Well* . . . I don't really know. I am unable to react to a situation in which a zeitgeist-compelled tendency suggests that a particular motivation is adequate or appropriate for more than one individual at a time. I would like to see a world where nobody cared what anybody else was doing—in which the entire group-think "You hold a C-major chord for thirty minutes, I'll hold it for thirty-one" syndrome utterly disappeared. This is not entirely a contemporary problem—twenty years ago, it merely manifested itself in a different way.

For this reason, I don't have an axe to grind. I can't say, "I would like to see the reaffirmation of the tonal system in all its original glory," or "I would like to see a return to pure Babbitt serialism, circa 1959." What I *would* like to see is a situation in which the particular pressures and polarizations that those systems have engendered among their adherents and their opponents just didn't exist.

I would think that the New York music scene would be a terribly difficult thing to be involved with unless one simply lived there and was quite specifically *not* a part of it. I find it very depressing to hear about situations in which this very competitive/imitative notion of what is au courant rules creativity. I can't think of anything *less* important.

One of the things I find most moving about the final Contrapunctus in *The Art of the Fugue* is that Bach was writing this music against *every possible tendency* of the time. He had renounced the kinds of modulatory patterns that he himself had used successfully six or seven years earlier in the "Goldberg" Variations and in book 2 of *The Well-Tempered Clavier* and was writing in a lighter, less clearly defined early-baroque/late-Renaissance manner. It was as though he was saying to the world, "I don't *care* anymore; there are no more Italian Concertos in me; *this* is what I'm about!

T.P.: One final question, Glenn. If a record store flew off the planet into space, and our music was picked up by alien creatures who knew nothing of the circumstances of its composition, or what the pieces were meant to represent, or what the composer's reputation was, what pieces would be taken to heart by this alien community? In this context-free situation, what would make their top ten?

G.G.: [*laughs*] Once again, I don't know quite how to answer that! But I will say that one composer who wouldn't make it—except for the last pieces and a few of the first ones—is Beethoven. He is one composer whose reputation is based entirely on gossip. The "Grosse Fuge" would make it, the early piano sonatas, maybe the Op. 18 quartets, but I don't think that there is room in space for the Fifth Symphony. Not at all.

INDEX

Some of the essays have been previously published by *Canadian Magazine, HiFi/ Stereo Review, Music Canada, The New Republic, Saturday Night,* and the University of Cincinnati.

Grateful acknowledgment is made to the following for permission to reprint previously published material:

ABC Leisure Magazines, Inc. The following articles by Glenn Gould are reprinted from *High Fidelity:* "The Search for Petula Clark," November 1967; "An Argument for Richard Strauss," March 1962; "We Who Are About to Be Disqualified Salute You," December 1966; "Streisand as Schwarzkopf," May 1967; "Glenn Gould Interviews Glenn Gould About Glenn Gould," February 1974; "The Prospects of Recording," April 1966; "The Grass Is Always Greener in the Outtakes," August 1975; "Liszt's Lament? Beethoven's Bagatelle? Or Rosemary's Babies?," December 1970; "His Country's 'Most Experienced Hermit' Chooses a Desert Island Discography," June 1970. The following articles by Glenn Gould are reprinted from *Musical America:* "Let's Ban Applause," February 1962; "Yehudi Menuhin," December 1966; "Oh, for Heaven's Sake, Cynthia," April 1969; "The CBC, Camera-wise," March 1965; "Of Time and Time Beaters," August 1965; "L'Esprit de jeunesse, et de corps, et d'art," December 1965; "The Ives Fourth," July 1965. Used by permission of the publisher. All rights reserved.

Associated Music Publishers, Inc. Excerpts from Sonatina No. 2 by Sibelius, copyright 1912 by Associated Music Publishers; Sonatina No. 3 by Sibelius, copyright 1912 by Associated Music Publishers; Piano Sonata No. 3 by Krenek, copyright 1945 by Associated Music Publishers. Used by permission.

Barger and Barclay. Excerpts from String Quartet by Glenn Gould. Published by Barger and Barclay. Reprinted by permission of the publishers.

Belmont Music Publishers. Excerpts from works by Schoenberg: Chamber Symphony, Op. 9, copyright 1922 by Universal Edition, copyright renewed 1950; Three Piano Pieces, Op. 11, copyright 1910 by Universal Edition, copyright renewed 1938 by Arnold Schoenberg; Six Piano Pieces, Op. 19, copyright 1913 by Universal Edition, copyright renewed 1940 by Belmont Music Publishers; *The Book of the Hanging Garden,* copyright 1914 by Universal Edition, copyright renewed 1941 by Arnold Schoenberg; Five Piano Pieces, Op. 23, copyright 1923, copyright renewed 1951 by Wilhelm Hansen, rights in U.K. administered by Edition Wilhelm Hansen; Chamber Symphony No. 2, Op. 38, copyright 1952 by G. Schirmer, Inc.; *Ode to Napoleon Bonaparte,* copyright 1945 by G. Schirmer, Inc., copyright renewed 1973 by Belmont Music Publishers, rights in U.K. administered by G. Schirmer, Inc.; Piano Concerto, Op. 42, copyright 1944 by G. Schirmer, Inc., copyright renewed 1972 by Belmont Music Publishers, rights in U.K. administered by G. Schirmer, Inc.; Fantasy, Op. 47, copyright 1952 by Henmar Press, Inc., rights in U.K. administered by C.F. Peters Corp.

CBC Enterprises. The publishers wish to express their appreciation to the Canadian Broadcasting Corporation for its cooperation and assistance in the development of this project.

CBS Masterworks. The publishers wish to thank CBS Masterworks for its cooperation.

European American Music. Excerpts from *Das Marienleben* (1924 version) by Hindemith. © B. Schott's Soehne, Mainz, 1924. © renewed 1951. All rights reserved. Used